THE LOST JOURNALISM OF **RING LARDNER**

THE LOST
JOURNALISM
OF **RING**
LARDNER

Ring Lardner

Edited by Ron Rapoport

Foreword by James Lardner

University of Nebraska Press

Lincoln and London

Library of Congress Cataloging-in-Publication Data
Names: Lardner, Ring, 1885–1933 author. |
Rapoport, Ron, editor.
Title: The lost journalism of Ring Lardner / edited
by Ron Rapoport; foreword by James Lardner.
Description: Lincoln: University of Nebraska Press,
2017. | Includes bibliographical references.
Identifiers: LCCN 2016031018
ISBN 9780803269736 (hardback: alk. paper)
ISBN 9780803299412 (mobi)
ISBN 9780803299429 (pdf)
Subjects: LCSH: Sports—United States. |
Newspapers—Sections, columns, etc.—Sports. |
Sports journalism—United States. | BISAC: SPORTS
& RECREATION / Essays.
Classification: LCC GV707 .L365 2017 |
DDC 796.0973—dc23 LC record available at
https://lccn.loc.gov/2016031018

Set in Ehrhardt by Rachel Gould.

"A considerable body of first-rate Lardner is entombed in back-number magazines and disintegrating newspapers."

—MATTHEW J. BRUCCOLI
and RICHARD LAYMAN

Contents

5 POLITICS

Foreword

James Lardner

My father was the third of Ring Lardner's four sons and got named after him over his publicly stated objections:

> "When you are christened Ringworm by the humorists and wits;
> When people pun about you till they drive you into fits;
> When funny folks say "Ring, ring off," until they make you ill,
> Remember that your poor old dad tried hard to name you Bill."

A songwriter on the side, my grandfather could sit down at the piano and play from memory long stretches of a Broadway show he had seen. He could work similar and greater wonders with the talk of ballplayers and other unschooled Americans. Many writers "tried to write the speech of the streets as adeptly and amusingly as he wrote it, and they all fell short of him," H. L. Mencken said. "The next best was miles and miles behind."

Mencken based this assessment of Ring Lardner largely on Lardner's short stories. It was the body of work that also led Edmund Wilson to compare him to Mark Twain, Virginia Woolf to hold him up as the best prose stylist in America even though he had a habit of writing "in language which is not English," and Ian Frazier to judge him "the literary equivalent of a once-in-a-generation athlete, like Ty Cobb or Mariano Rivera." But it was in his newspaper and magazine pieces where he honed and originally deployed his skills.

The *Chicago Tribune* set him loose by giving him a daily column in 1913. He filled it at first with inside dope about the Cubs and the White Sox, as expected; then, when the season ended and there were no more real games to cover, he told the story of a made-up game in the voice of an unashamedly self-important slugger (not unlike Jack Keefe of the *You Know Me Al* stories that would start appearing in the *Saturday Evening Post* a year later). This slugger is fixated on a miscalled third strike that was "a mile outside," he says, "but if I'd knew he was goin' to call it on me, I coulda hit it 'way out o' the park." The story ends with an aside about a female spectator: "Ja see that doll in the box back o' our bench? She couldn't keep her eye off o' me. We'll get 'em tomorrow, the yellow, quittin' dogs."

Three years later came a short sketch that foreshadowed the darker and more elaborate "Haircut," about a barbershop patron held captive to a monologue that begins with the senselessness of the conflict raging in France ("Most o' them don't even know what they're fightin' about. Nobody knows except the kaiser and the king and the fella that started it, and they don't know themselves."), moves on to praise for the president who had kept America out of the war ("All as I hope is that we don't get mixed up in it. But I guess they's no danger o' that with Wilson at the hellum. We'd been mixed up long ago if Rusefelt was president."), takes a poke at Wilson's leadership chops ("Every time they sink a boat and kill a few hundred people he writes them another note and they say it was a mistake and they was aimin' at a fish or somethin'"), and concludes with nostalgia for T.R. ("You wouldn't never see them monkeying with old Teddy that way").

The *You Know Me Al* stories made Ring Lardner's byline so precious that his editors started sending him to the same places they sent their serious reporters. At the 1924 Democratic convention he had instructions to seek an interview with William Jennings Bryan. "So I went to his room and rapped," he relates, "and a voice says, who is it, and I told him the truth, and the voice says no, they's nobody home. It was the same voice," he adds, "that said we shouldn't ought to crucifix mankind upon a cross of gold in 1896 or any other year." That may have been as close as Ring Lardner came, in his many political assignments, to a scoop.

Once in a while a sense of historical duty caused him to tell a story straight. This impulse took hold of him when, for example, he was writing about Babe Ruth, or the Dempsey-Firpo fight, or the seventh game of the 1912 World Series, tragically lost by the New York Giants and the great Christy Mathewson, who is described by Lardner at game's end sitting "on the New York players' bench with bowed head and drooping shoulders, with the tears streaming from his eyes, a man on whom his team's fortune had been staked and lost and a man who would have proven his clear title to trust reposed in him if his mates had stood by him in the supreme test." Students of baseball, football, and boxing history can learn much from these columns and from the excellent notes and introductions supplied by Ron Rapoport, an editor superbly well-matched to the task.

By contrast, the stories Ring Lardner filed from political conventions and other heavy-news venues often have the flavor of those *Daily Show* standups in front of a green screen; and there is something quite Stephen Colbert–like about his mock candidacies for mayor of Chicago in 1919 (promising "a bone-dry United States, but a ringing-wet Chicago") and for U.S. president in 1920 (on a platform of having the "prettiest middle name in the democrat party.")

His highbrow admirers—Edmund Wilson, F. Scott Fitzgerald, and others—tried to guilt-trip him into writing longer works about loftier subjects. But he knew his comfort zone and I, for one, am glad he never decided he was too much of a bigshot to spend time on, say, a contemporary retelling of the Snow White story in which she marries a "wealthy bond thief who liked them young," or a gossip column parody in which we learn that "George Gershwin is Sullivan-Gilberting with his own brother, Ira," and "Aleck Hamilton and Aaron Burr have phfft," or a gangster-movie riff on Verdi's "Rigoletto" in which the assassin "Frank Sparafucile" bemoans a spell of underemployment, singing:

"Since Christmas I have killed only one man.
  This war is sure hell on a poor honest gunman.
  My funds are so low it's beginning to scare me.
  Have you a few lires on your clothing to spare me?"

And Rigoletto ("Rig") replies:

"I have a few lires on my clothing, but really
  I haven't so much I could Sparafucile."

In 2013 the Library of America came out with a Ring Lardner anthology containing all the great short stories—"The Golden Honeymoon," "I Can't Breathe," "Alibi Ike," and the rest—along with much of his previously published fiction and some nonfiction. Thanks to Ron Rapoport and the University of Nebraska Press, we now have this rich collection of Ring's journalism—work that was widely read in its day (his columns ran in as many as 150 newspapers) but then sat mostly undisturbed in archives for the better part of a century.

The British comic novelist David Lodge has identified two good reasons for reading Ring Lardner, and they both apply to this rediscovered journalism as much as to Ring's short stories. One is his trailblazing place in modern American literature; the other, which Lodge has properly put first, is the fact that he was "a wonderfully entertaining writer" and one of "that select company of writers who can make posterity lift its head from the page and laugh aloud."

Introduction

Ring Lardner was a journalist his entire working life. From his first articles as a sports reporter for the *South Bend Times*, where he covered Notre Dame football, minor league baseball, and local events, to the columns of radio criticism he wrote for the *New Yorker* just a few months before he died, Lardner never abandoned his roots.

Writers of fiction often begin their careers as reporters for newspapers or magazines, only to leave journalism behind when their novels or stories become successful. Not Ring Lardner. For all intents and purposes, Lardner pursued parallel careers, turning out the short stories that secured his place in American literature while carrying on as a journalist all the while.

His output was astonishing. Between 1913 and 1919 Lardner wrote more than sixteen hundred "In the Wake of the News" columns and other articles for the *Chicago Tribune*—which is to say he wrote virtually every day—even as he was publishing *You Know Me Al*, *Alibi Ike*, *Gullible's Travels*, and *Champion*, among other stories. The fact that the overall quality of his columns remained so high, says Jonathan Yardley, one of Lardner's biographers, "must be counted among the extraordinary accomplishments of American journalism."

After leaving the *Tribune* and moving to Long Island, Lardner continued writing fiction and began writing for the theater as well. His primary outlet, though, was a weekly column for the Bell Syndicate that ran in more than 150 newspapers and reached some eight million readers. For three years he also wrote the continuity for a comic strip based on "You Know Me Al" that ran in many newspapers around the country. By then he was one of the most famous men in the United States and bigger than many of the stories he covered.

"Lardner Gives Real Dope on N.Y. Fans" read one newspaper headline over a column he wrote about the 1921 World Series. "Ring Lardner Will

Run If Coolidge Withdraws" appeared over a political column in 1924. And in 1922 there was this: "Lardner Balks at Knickers for Women." He was consistently afforded this name-in-lights treatment, and since the Bell columns were accompanied by sketches drawn by Dick Dorgan, in which he was prominently featured, Lardner's face was just as familiar to the public. When the *Indianapolis Star* wanted to tell its readers it would be publishing Lardner's coverage of the 1925 World Series, it simply ran his picture under the headline "No Need to Introduce This Guy."

Between 1919 and 1927 Lardner wrote more than five hundred columns for the Bell Syndicate, most of them as a weekly Letter to the Editor. He wrote about politics, war, prohibition, social conventions, family life on Long Island, sports, and any other topic that came into his mind. Occasionally he wrote extra pieces for the syndicate on the major events of the day. He covered the World Series, heavyweight championship fights, political conventions, the inauguration of Warren G. Harding, a disarmament conference held in Washington DC, an America's Cup in New York, and more.

Lardner also wrote about the theater, which was a particular passion, as well as spoofs of opera plots and fairy tales, and he often included poems in his work. At the same time he wrote a number of nonfiction pieces for magazines, such as the *Saturday Evening Post, Cosmopolitan,* and *Colliers,* which also published his short stories.

In assessing the sheer volume of this output, one question arises: where did he find the time? Lardner was not a recluse working undisturbed in a lonely garret. He had a wide circle of friends, was an avid golfer and bridge player, a regular theater-goer, a frequent traveler, a prolific letter-writer, an occasional visitor to the Algonquin Round Table, a loving husband, and a devoted father of four sons. For a number of years he was the bemused lord of a manor house in Great Neck, Long Island, where titans of business and show-business celebrities lived in close proximity and where the party scene was so relentless that his neighbor and drinking companion F. Scott Fitzgerald moved to France in order to get some work done. Lardner was also a drinker of legendary proportions—he and another neighbor, a silent movie actor named Tom Meighan, called themselves "two-bottle men"—which may have contributed to his death from tuberculosis at the age of forty-eight.

Because he was so busy, and because his Bell contract paid so well, Lardner abandoned writing fiction for three years after moving to Long Island. But when, at Fitzgerald's urging, a compilation of his early stories was published, and it was well received by both the public and critics, his editor, the legendary Maxwell Perkins, insisted that Lardner return to fiction. Lardner gave up the comic strip and within three months wrote "Haircut," his most anthologized short story. Over the last eight years of his life Lardner wrote fifty more short stories, two plays that appeared on Broadway, and three unproduced musicals—practicing journalism all the while.

The one constant in Lardner's fiction and journalism is his use of the vernacular, which depends on such literary aberrations as ungrammatical dialogue, misspellings, haphazard punctuation, and odd abbreviations. He must have driven his copy editors crazy. Indeed, a comparison of his Bell columns as they appeared in various newspapers shows that some editors "corrected" what he wrote. Thus, "instants" became "instance," "happly marred men" became "happily married men," and so forth. Hugh Fullerton, the Chicago baseball writer who helped Lardner get several jobs early in his career, tells of a spring training trip they took with the Cubs to a small southern town where a telegraph operator had some trouble transmitting their copy. When Fullerton asked if it had finally been sent, the operator said, "Yours went all right, but that other fellow's was awful. It took me an hour or more to correct his spelling." To the extent Lardner learned of these and other outrages, they must have driven *him* crazy.

When Lardner took over the "In the Wake of the News" column at the *Tribune,* he inherited what had previously been little more than a collection of notes about sports. But almost from the beginning he indicated that he wasn't interested in simply stretching boundaries. He meant to break them altogether. Buried near the bottom of a column barely a week after his "Wake" debut in 1913 was an item bearing the title, "The Pennant Pursuit. A Novel. [By the Copy Boy.]":

As Vern Dalton strod passed the jymnaseium one day in April, bound for the college ofice, where he was going to make arrangmunts for entring the college next fall, the ball nine composed of 20 (twenty) or more members came out on its way to the athletic feild. O said Verne I wonder if Ill ever have a posichion on that team and figth for the glory of my ama mather, but he did not have much hope because his parents had said he must devoat all his time to study. (To be continued.)

This was Lardner's first shaky attempt at using the vernacular in print and would soon be followed by others. Lardner also expanded the boundaries of the column's subject matter. He wrote numerous poems and song lyrics and told of his growing family. (To a reader who complained these columns had nothing to do with sports, he answered, "If kids ain't sport, what is?") He regularly ran letters from readers and answered them. He turned comments on pressing baseball issues—the inability of the White Sox to score runs, the spitball, the upstart Federal League that was posing a threat to the American and National Leagues, and more—into "Cubist Baseball," a brilliant parody of literary modernism. And he wrote about himself in a comical way, as when he declared his candidacy for mayor of Chicago:

Me for Mayor:

The formal petition which will place the Wake's editor in the running as a nonpartisan dependent candidate for mayor was filed yesterday with a window washer in the office of Judge Scully and Denny Egan. The petition was written on the back of the carte du jour of a well known dive on Dearborn street . . .

A *Tribune* editor was the first to suggest that Lardner write a baseball story to be printed in the feature section. When Lardner submitted one in the form of letters from a vain and clueless but somehow endearing pitcher named Jack Keefe to a friend back home, the editor thought misspelled words, shaky grammar, and use of the vernacular were out of place in the paper. So Lardner sent "A Busher's Letters Home" to the *Saturday Evening Post,* where it was printed in June 1914 and created a sensation.

The public and the magazine demanded more "busher" stories, and by the end of the year he had written another five. They were collected two years later in the book *You Know Me Al,* one of Lardner's crowning achievements. In all he wrote ten magazine pieces in 1914 and twenty-nine more over the next three years. This allowed him to double his *Tribune* salary of $100 a week and put him well on the way to stardom.

While it is clear that Lardner used "In the Wake of the News" as a laboratory where he could practice the techniques of his fiction, the reverse was also true. Suddenly finding himself acclaimed for his stories, and becoming more comfortable and proficient in writing them, he brought his new craft to the pages of the *Tribune.* At about the time the Jack Keefe stories were being published, the "Wake" column began running letters from a ballplayer named Bill to his friend Steve that are similar to the original, if not always as well crafted. Beyond that, Lardner moved into territory no sports columnist before or since has ever occupied on a regular basis. He left not only the events of the day behind, but sports as well.

He gave his readers an inside look at the newspaper business and, in the "Friend Harvey" letters to his editor, Harvey Woodruff, he complained about his working conditions. He sent up the plots of "Carmen," "Rigoletto," and "Madam Butterfly." He made sport with Arthur Conan Doyle, lyrics of war songs, and love letters. He wrote a parody of golf instruction manuals purporting to show how to use a spoon while eating. He chastised a *Tribune* editor for fussing over the misspelling of the name of a character in *Oliver Twist,* and wrote a column titled "Fifteen Cents Worth" that directly prefigured "Haircut." Weeks would go by without any reference to sports.

No matter how far Lardner strayed from writing about athletes and the games they played, however, "In the Wake of the News" never left the *Tribune* sports section, where it appeared alongside reports of baseball and football games, horse races and golf tournaments. It doesn't seem to have occurred to the paper that the column might have been more appropriate in the news or feature sections. Lardner had established himself as a sports humorist and, in the eyes of his editors and readers, that is what he would remain for six years.

"All I ask from Lardner," Woodruff once said, "is copy."

Lardner's commitment to journalism has led to an ongoing debate over what might have been. Did it distract him from concentrating on writing fiction? Did it keep him from writing the Great American Novel? Did it ultimately consign him to a lower place in the pantheon of American writers than he otherwise might have earned? Edmund Wilson, one of the leading critics of the era, expressed these concerns after some of Lardner's early work was republished in a book. Wilson admired the stories, but wanted more. "Will Ring Lardner, then, go on to his *Huckleberry Finn* or has he already told all he knows?" he asked. "Here is a man who has had the freedom of the modern West no less than Mark Twain did of the old one. . . . If Ring Lardner has anything more to give us, the time has now come to deliver it."

Fitzgerald also weighed in after Lardner died in an otherwise affectionate tribute to the man with whom he had spent so many companionable hours in Gatsby country. Lardner's achievements fell short of his capabilities, Fitzgerald wrote, because, "During those years, when most men of promise achieve an adult education, if only in the school of war, Ring moved in the company of a few dozen illiterates playing a boy's game. A boy's game, with no more possibilities in it than a boy could master, a game bounded by walls which kept out novelty or danger, change or adventure. . . . However deeply Ring might cut into it, his cake had the diameter of Frank Chance's diamond."

But Lardner knew himself better than any critic. Ring Lardner Jr. wrote that "when I asked my father if he would ever write a novel, he said that after one chapter he would be even more bored than the reader." And in a letter to Theodore Dreiser, Lardner spoke of "novelists, whose patience and energy are far beyond any good traits I can claim."

So Lardner spent his life writing what he wanted to write: the short stories that are held in such high critical esteem, the theater pieces and song lyrics he enjoyed beyond measure, and the journalism that has been neglected, and uncollected for too long.

A Note to Readers

Ring Lardner's fiction has been reprinted and anthologized many times over the years, but the only two books devoted solely to his journalism—*What of It?* (published in 1925) and *First and Last* (1934)—all but ignored his work in Chicago and are now long out of print. Other anthologies have included some examples of his nonfiction, but these are always as an appendage to his short stories. The time seems right then for a fresh look at Lardner's journalism, most of which has never been republished in any form.

In disinterring the archival tombs that are the only places where much of Lardner's journalism can be found, I encountered a few problems. Occasionally Lardner would drop a word or compose a sentence that made no sense, hazards that every journalist working on a deadline confronts. He was also inconsistent in his usage. He variously rendered the New York Giants' ballpark, for instance, as Polo Grounds, Polo grounds, polo grounds, Polo's grounds, and pologrounds. And his haphazard use of commas could lead to consecutive sentences like these: "If you are in the Monday Opera 500 club, you belong. If you ain't you don't."

As noted above, Lardner was also the occasional victim of indifferent copy editing and linotype operators working on deadline presented another hazard. The result was that a column could vary significantly from newspaper to newspaper and contain numerous typographical errors.

I have used my best judgment to try to determine what Lardner actually wrote and I apologize for any mistakes I may have made. The same is true for any errors that may have crept in during the sometimes fraught process of converting blurred and darkened copies of microfilm into a digital format.

Lardner often made reference to people and events in the news at the time, and since the time was close to, and in some cases more than, a century ago, a number of those references are now obscure. I have supplied context in footnotes for some of them, which I hope will offer useful perspective, as well as explanatory notes for some of the pieces.

Finally, it should be noted that nearly all the articles and columns in this book are presented as they were written. A few of Lardner's accounts of baseball games have been made shorter by leaving out his lengthy description of the play-by-play. This was a convention of baseball coverage before radio and television revolutionized sports reporting but makes for tedious reading today, a fact that Lardner acknowledged in a parody of the form that appears in this book. I have indicated these and a few other cuts with ellipses. Also, I have changed some of the headlines—and written a few for the "In the Wake of the News" columns that didn't have them to begin with—to make them correspond more closely to the subject matter.

THE LOST JOURNALISM OF **RING LARDNER**

Ring Lardner Tells His Sad,
Sad Story to the World

OMAHA WORLD-HERALD, BELL SYNDICATE, JUNE 8, 1924

The best of men will break into verse at times. It now becomes Ring Lardner's hour. Ring, you must know, is striding toward Cleveland right now in order to help "cover" the republican national convention for the *World-Herald*. On the eve of the big conclave he steps to the front of the stage with the following, which he entities, "An Autobiography":

Hardly a man is now alive
Who cares that in March, 1885,
I was born in the city of Niles,
Michigan, which is 94 miles
From Chicago, a city in Illinois.
Sixteen years later, still only a boy,
I graduated from the Niles High School
With a general knowledge of rotation pool.
After my schooling, I thought it best
To give my soul and body a rest.
In 1905 this came to an end,
When I went to work on The Times in Souse Bend,
Thence to Chi, where I labored first
On the Inter-Ocean and then for Hearst,
Then for the Tribune and then to St. Lews,
Where I was editor of Sporting News.
And thence to Boston, where later a can
Was tied to me by the manager man.
1919 was the year
When, in Chicago, I finished my daily newspaper career.
In those 14 years—just a horse's age—

My stuff was all on the sporting page.
In the last five years (since it became illegal to drink),
I've been connected with The Bell Syndicate, Inc.
I have four children as well as one Missus,
None of whom can write a poem as good as this is.

1

Getting Started

Ring Lardner got his first newspaper job, so the story goes, when the editor of the *South Bend Times* came to his home in Niles, Michigan, in 1905, looking for his brother. Rex Lardner, who was four years older than Ring, had established himself at the *Niles Daily Sun* and Edgar Stoll, the *Times'* editor, wanted to hire him. But Rex was out of town and Stoll asked Ring whether Rex had a contract with the Niles paper.

"I said yes, which was the truth," Lardner wrote years later. "I asked how much salary he was willing to offer. He said twelve dollars a week. Why? 'Oh,' I said, 'I thought I might tackle the job myself.'" When Stoll asked if he had any writing experience, Lardner said he often helped Rex, which was, he admitted, "far from the truth."

Lardner, who had failed at a number of jobs, and not enjoyed any of them, was then working as a meter reader and collector of bad debts for the Niles Gas Company. ("I never heard of any good ones," he wrote.) He was ready for something more interesting and was not about to let the truth get in his way. The following week, he reported for work at the *Times*, where, for twelve dollars a week, he covered everything from high school sports to Notre Dame football, with some general news, court reporting, and society and theater news thrown in. He never received a byline but it was the best on-the-job training a twenty-year-old reporter could have had.

Though his writing for the *Times* was competent enough for a beginner, it seldom gave any indication of the imagination he would apply in the future. One exception was a roundup of the previous year's sports news that appeared on New Year's Day, 1907. The first sentence showed he meant to have fun and he kept his tongue firmly in cheek throughout.

Lardner would summon up the memory of his days in South Bend a few years later in articles he wrote for the *Chicago Tribune*—his first "Memoirs of a Baseball Scribe" is one example—just as he wrote a number of pieces about leaving South Bend for Chicago, as shown in the second "Memoirs of a Baseball Scribe." And he would summarize the origins of his career in a nutshell in the poem preceding this section that appears to have run only in the *Omaha World-Herald*, which ran nearly all of his Bell Syndicate columns.

Lardner's first job in the big city was with the *Chicago Inter-Ocean*, where he wrote his first article on major-league baseball in 1908: "Twenty-Six Cubs Will Be Taken On Southern Journey." He does not appear to have met any of these Cubs, nor would he write about them again until the following year when he was at the *Tribune*. But the article is noteworthy on two accounts. First, it adopts the jocular tone he would seldom abandon in the future when writing about baseball—Vicksburgers and Vicksburgerines, indeed—and second, a look at the Cubs' roster in the closing paragraphs gives an indication of what Lardner and his readers were in for.

These were the Cubs of Tinker to Evers to Chance. They had played in the last three World Series, and won the last two, and were the reigning lords of the game. But beyond that, the team contained some great characters who soon came to enjoy Lardner's dry wit as much as he enjoyed them. Players like Frank Schulte, Jim Schekard, Heine Zimmerman, Mordecai Brown, and others were story-tellers, practical jokers, poker players, drinkers, and all-around good companions who made numerous appearances in Lardner's work. The players and reporters mixed freely on their long train rides together and Lardner took copious mental notes.

Nor did the players seems to object when Lardner made them figures of fun in print. They enjoyed his satirical parodies of popular songs, which he sang while accompanying himself on the piano, and regarded him as one of them. It may have been for the best, however, that the St. Louis Browns had left the Cubs' spring-training site in West Baden, Indiana, before Lardner wrote of their best pitcher: "Rube Waddell left in his wake various broken hearts and bottles." Lardner's description of the first game ever played at Forbes Field in Pittsburgh shows he could also write a sweetly evocative piece when called upon, while his story on the Cubs winning the 1910 National League pennant demonstrated the creativity that would always be one of his hallmarks.

Looking for more money—and, as he was about to be married, a less itinerant life-style—Lardner left Chicago late in 1910 to work for *The Sporting News* in St. Louis. He lasted there only three months before leaving in a dispute with his bosses, but he made the most of them, turning out 10 "Pullman Pastimes," which gave his first extended look at the lives of ballplayers and reporters on the road. As such, they provided the template for the short stories that would make him famous. He then moved to the *Boston American* where he covered the Boston Rustlers—they would become the Braves the following season—who had yet another colorful bunch of players.

Another disagreement with management led to Lardner's resignation during the 1911 World Series and he returned to Chicago. He was twenty-six years old and had worked at five different newspapers. It had been a remarkable apprenticeship, one that pointed him in the direction of bigger and better things.

South Bend Has Cause to Be Proud of Athletic Record the Past Year

SOUTH BEND TIMES, JANUARY 1, 1907

Looking back over the past year local followers of sport have three things to be thankful for. There were no fake fights pulled off in our midst, the High school football team went through the season with no deaths and only one defeat and the South Bend ball club did not run absolutely last. For the first of these sources of gratefulness, let us extend a vote of heartfelt thanks to the local promoters of pugilism, who have booked very few matches; for the second to the High school football team itself for its great and successful fight for the sectional championship; and, for the last, to the Terre Haute club, which absolutely refused to give up its hold on the cellar door.

There are also manifold matters of deep regret to the heart of the true sport lover, but these we will pass over in brief, since it is not good for the heart to be sorrowful at the opening of the new year. For one thing the tennis championship of Navarre Place was never satisfactorily settled. There were innumerable claimants of the honor, as there are of every championship title, but on the showing of all the wielders of the racket north of the bridge, it would be unfair to single out anyone as being superior to his neighbors. The bait casting club has not held its regular meetings for some time and there is really no telling whether or not it has breathed its last. The tournament arranged with Kalamazoo which was to have taken place last summer has been postponed until the 22nd of August 1952 and the locals are already hard at work in preparation.

The career of the 1906 South Bend baseball team is as a sad tragedy, which we will call "The Broken Elevator." For some reason or other, the promoters of the play lost sight of the plot and allowed several villains to make their entrance at the wrong time and break up the action. These same villains were originally slated to appear in the role of heroes and their sudden change of heart was thus rendered all the more grievous. One of them was found guilty and sent to the reformatory at Grand Rapids, while another waived arraignment, pled guilty and is now serving a life sentence in the Three I league. The Grand Rapids prisoner has visited here twice on parole since his conviction and on both occasions, proved that he had entirely reformed and was leading a model life.

When the villains got in their cruel work, the play was running most smoothly, having only the production led by Actor Ganzet to cope with. The climax did not come all at once, but in chunks of a little at a time, until the damage was done and the stage too hot to hold the offenders. However, the chance for revenge has not passed forever and we all take comfort in the time-worn adage "He who laughs at the finish, laughs like——.

Begging your pardon for switching figures, the South Bend ship sank gradually until it struck what it thought was bottom. This afterwards proved to be merely the hull of another ship which had suffered a like fate and was covering the whole bed of the sea. For some time after the first sinking, those on shore daily cast anxious glances at the surface of the water and hoped against hope that the masts would be seen to rise again.

But there was nothing doing in the rescue line and the life saving crew was powerless to give sufficient aid.

However, to the cheerful among the owners of the South Bend ship there is ground for consolation in the fact that some parts of the vessel were not hurt by the wreck at all . . .

The high school football team of 1906 will be looked back to for many seasons by the members of elevens to come, with reverence and pride. The boys, under the skillful coaching of Donald DeShane and the captaincy of Otis Romine, swept everything before them with the exception of the teams representing Winona and the High school of a hamlet known as Niles. The only defeat of the season was suffered at the hands of the Winona aggregation, which is recognized as being in a higher class than the average high school team. The locals did not have their full strength in the contest with Niles, although the last named team was not one to be sneezed at by any means.

The Notre Dame football eleven was one of the best in the history of the college and this after a discouraging outlook at the opening of the season. The success of the gold and blue is due to the clever drilling of Coach Barry and the presence on the team of three or four stars of the first water. A victory over Purdue and a great fight against the Indiana team[1] are among the team's achievements. Judging by the comparative scores, Notre Dame ranked well in Western football and the students are looking forward to a state champion eleven next fall.

The lack of snow last winter was fatal to the racing game in this city, as there is no track where summer racing can be held. If the plans of many of South Bend's leading citizens do not go amiss, there will soon be a driving park in this city and the regular summer meetings will become a feature of local sport.

Rowing races in South Bend are mostly indulged in by teams of opposite sexes, which makes the sport doubly interesting, but precludes the possibility of making public the records. Boat races are numerous on the old St. Joe in the warm summer evenings and slow races have become quite a fad among the rowers.

Bowling has made rapid strides during the past twelvemonth and is now at its zenith in this city. The formation of the Elks' and Antlers' leagues has done much to bring the sport to its present place of popularity and there has not been any flagging of interest in these organizations since the season opened. The bowling stars of former years have maintained their reputations and others, unknown previously to the sport, have come forward to take their places in the front ranks. Among the latter class are Chief of Police James McWeeny, for whom an average of 115 is now a mere bagatelle, and F.E. Hering, who rolls 233 in one game and, then, feeling sorry for his less fortunate competitors, drops to 98 in the next.

Golf has taken its regular place among the summer sports and its advance must be attributed partly to the efforts of Harry S. Turple, who instructs the members of the St. Joseph Valley Country club in the Scotch game. His able tutelage has aided many of the golfers to play a greatly improved game and as a result, to take much more interest in the sport.

That chess and checker records are not available is to be regretted. Playing the slot machines was very popular at an earlier season of the year, but has fallen off a trifle in the last two or three weeks. Curling is confined mostly to daintily scented boudoirs, although we have heard some curlers on the street.

Memoirs of a Baseball Scribe (Part 1)

CHICAGO TRIBUNE, JULY 15, 1915

Grand Rapids had a third baseman who thought that water was created for chasing purposes only. But for his insatiable thirst for something stronger this man would have been in a big league—a star in it, too. He might even have "gone up" if he could have got enough liquid refreshment at night. But no; he had to have it in the morning, which, as every ball player is supposed to know, is unethical.

He had a whip of steel and a fast ball as smoky as most pitchers'. He preferred warming up with some catcher to practicing in his regular position.

South Bend, where I first reported the pastime for gain, had two press tables. They were in front of the grandstand, on the field. Mine was a few feet from the visitors' bench and the rival sheet's close to the home dugout.

John Ganzel's Grand Rapids team came down for a series and the third baseman proceeded to light himself up the minute the club got in town.

By game time he was so bad that Ganzel wouldn't allow him to play. Being near the Grand Rapids bench, I heard the torrid dialogue between manager and man. Ganzel came over to me at length and asked that I print nothing about the matter. Being agreeable in those days, I promised to pass the story up.

The rival sheet's reporter, however, had no such request from Ganzel and ran half a column of the stuff, with pictures. It was in his paper the next afternoon.

The afternoon after the next afternoon I took my place as usual and proceeded to write down the batting order in my massive score book. I was interrupted by a sharp pain in the shin. A ball had struck me, and the ball had been thrown by the steel whip of the Grand Rapids third baseman. He was doing his customary warmup stunt and one of his shots had escaped his catcher.

The catcher, Dan Howley, was standing directly in front of me, not ten feet distant.

"Move over a little, will you?" I said. "I don't want to get killed."

Dan moved to a position which made mine safe except from a ball thrown deliberately at me.

And right away there was a ball thrown deliberately at me.

I ducked and the ball whistled past my ear.

"What are you trying to do?" I yelled at the third sacker.

"You'll find out if you set there long enough," he said.

The ball had bounded back off the screen and he had recovered it. Taking careful aim, he shot at me again. Howley was quick enough to get his glove in front of the ball and divert its course.

"Cut it out,—!" said Howley. "You'll get in trouble."

"I don't care if I hang," said——. "I'm goin' to get that bird."

Howley picked up the ball and held it. The third baseman went to the bench to secure another ball. Failing to find one, he grabbed a bat and let fly. The missile fell short.

"Give me that ball," I said to Howley.

Howley gave me the ball and, standing up, I threw it as hard as I could at my friend. If it had hit him in a vulnerable spot it might have hurt him. But he caught it in his bare hand and it came back several times as fast as it had gone. It missed target by inches.

Ganzel and the other Grand Rapids players were returning to the bench from their practice. I summoned Ganzel.

"——is pegging at me," I said. "You'd better make him cut it out."

—— came over to the table.

"This is the guy [he didn't say guy] that knocked me in the paper," he said.

Howley interposed.

"No, it ain't," he said. "It was the other fella."

"It don't make no difference," said——. "They're all alike."

"You lay off'n my ball players!" said Mr. Ganzel.

"It was the other fella," repeated Howley.

"Whoever it was," said, Mr. Ganzel, "you lay off'n my ball players or you'll get killed. I'll do it myself."

Grand Rapids had lost two straight.

"The next time you tell me not to print a story I'll run it on the first page," I said.

"You do and see what happens to you," said Mr. Ganzel. "I got a notion to fix you now."

The arrival of Chief McWeeny (Jim) and a short speech by him saved my young life.

I shed few tears when —— guzzled himself out of baseball and when Manager Ganzel suffered worse than death—the management at Cincinnati.

Lardner told this story somewhat differently for a 1931 article in the *Saturday Evening Post*. In that version the aggrieved player became angry when Lardner, the game's official scorer, called an error on what he insisted was a hit.

Memoirs of a Baseball Scribe (Part 2)

CHICAGO TRIBUNE, JULY 28, 1915

There came a day in the late summer of 1907 when I was taken violently ill with big league fever.

"I'm going to Chicago for Labor day," I told my boss.

"You have fine taste," said he.

But it was not for pleasure that I was going.

I went, or came, and on my arrival called up a friend who had the honor of knowing Hughey Fullerton personally to speak to. On Labor day morning my friend escorted me to the newspaper office where Hughey was working. If we'd known anything about the metropolitan newspaper business we never would have sought Hughey at his office in the morning. Our ignorance took us there, and there, for some queer reason, was Hughey.

"Glad to know you," 'I said.

"Glad to know YOU," replied Hughey, with no regard for the truth.

"This fella," said my friend, "wants a job on one of the papers."

"What line?" asked Hughey.

"Sporting," said I.

"Well," said Hughey, "I don't know of any openings just now, but if you'll go out to the game with me, we'll talk it over."

That day was one of the most enjoyable in my existence and doubtless the most boresome in Hughey's.[2] He wasn't writing baseball at that particular time and he put in an off-day at the Sox park purely as an accommodation to a busher whose dissertation on the national pastime must have been as entertaining as brown pop.

A canvass of the representatives of the various papers developed nothing in the way of a job and Hughey could have been forgiven if he had dismissed me permanently from his mind. But at the parting he said:

"Try to get up for the world's series, and maybe we'll have better luck."

And it was at the fourth game of the series in Detroit. that he introduced me to Duke Hutchinson, sporting editor of the I.O., and Duke, in an unguarded moment, engaged me.[3]

A week later I reported at the I.O. sport desk for duty.

"Sit over there," said Duke. "You'll find shears and paste in that drawer."

So I sat over there and opened that drawer. A large rat jumped out.

"Eighteen-fifty a week isn't a bit too much for this," I thought.

"That's Ben," said Duke. "You'll like him when you get better acquainted." . . .

Twenty-Six Cubs Will Be Taken on Southern Journey

CHICAGO INTER-OCEAN, FEBRUARY 2, 1908

The world's champion Cublets went so far last summer and fall that the training trip laid out for them seems short by comparison. The West Side bugs are rather glad than otherwise that their favorites will not stray a long way off. It will be an easy matter to secure daily tidings of the world beaters' doings when they are as close to civilization as Mississippi.

Mr. Chance will load his likely stable on an Indiana bound rattler March 3. The car will first hesitate at West Baden, where the champs will bask in the baths for ten more or less sunshiny days. Very little actual work will be done at the Hoosier resort, the stop there being almost solely for the purpose of dragging the kinks from twenty-six frozen backs.

On the 14th, the band will ramble southward toward Vicksburg, Miss., where it will be loudly welcomed by all the Vicksburgers and Vicksburgerines. The inhabitants of this sedate city have been saving up all winter to make a big noise when the Cub flyer toots its station toot. Vicksburg is said to be the ideal spot for training, particularly at times when snow, sleet, and chill blasts kindly remain absent.

The champs will sojourn in Vicksburg until the 24th, playing exhibition games with the natives daily, or at convenient periods. On the 24th the Chicagoans will again take to the road and will play in Meridian on the 25th. The monotony of the saunter homeward will be broken by the following stops.

Montgomery, Ala., March 26 and 27.
Atlanta, Ga., March 28 and 30.
Chattanooga, Tenn., March 31 (with Toledo).
Birmingham, Ala., April 1, 2, and 3.
Memphis, Tenn., April 4 and 5.
Nashville, Tenn., April 6 and 7.
Evansville, Ind., April 8.
Terre Haute, Ind., April 9.

Fort Wayne, Ind., April 10.
Indianapolis, Ind., April 11.
Dayton, Ohio, April 12 and 13.

From Dayton the team will go to Cincinnati, where the opening game of the real fight is slated.

Manager Chance will not be burdened by a large assemblage of hopefuls on the trip South. The team which swallowed the Tigers whole will be re-enforced by only five youngsters. These will be Catcher Evans, Outfielder Elston, and Pitchers Walsh, Merker, and Donahue.

Of this quintet Evans is a recruit from the Lynchburg Virginia league club. He was some slugger with the Southerners and was also considered one of the best receivers in the organization. Outfielder Curt Elston hails from Lancaster, of the Ohio and Pennsylvania circuit. He is touted as cute on the bases, a skillful trapper of flies, and a trusty batsman. There are a few other good qualities which this youth is said to possess, but no one seems to know what they are.

Martin Walsh has been heard of before. He is a brother to the famous Edward[4] of the same name and about the same size. He was seized from the Danville team, where he made an enviable record and was the source of many misgivings amount the batsmen.

The two other young pitchers are Chicagoans by choice. John L. Donahue is a former member of the stout Spaulding semipro team and Albert Merker heaved for the Swing aggregation of the Commercial league. They have both been the object of several major league scouts' admiration for some time past and are said to ripe for fleeter company.

Twenty-six Cubs will be in the party when the start is made for West Baden. They are as follows:

Pitchers—Brown, Ruelbach, Lundgren, Frazer, Overall, Pfiester, Walsh, Donahue, Merker, and Durbin.
Catchers—Olis, Kling, Moran, and Evans.
Infielders—Chance, Evers, Zimmerman, Howard, Tinker and Steinfeldt.
Outfielders—Schulte, Sheckard, Slagle, Hofman and Elston.

The Peerless Leader Takes Charge

CHICAGO TRIBUNE, MARCH 4, 1909

West Baden, Ind.—Jack Pfiester and a miniature blizzard were almost simultaneous arrivals at this treacherous place today and their coming was about the only instance worthy of note. Jack was greeted with a smile by Manager Chance. The snow was not.

It appeared in time to dispell all thought of gamboling on the green, so gambling of less strenuous, but more costly nature was indulged. Southpaw Floyd Kroh, who called with four kings[5] in a battle last summer, proved conclusively he had been putting in a hard winter of practice at the indoor national pastime and has added to his deposits of the Bolivar bank.

Mr. Pfiester was "called" by the peerless leader for not coming earlier to training quarters. As he is three ounces overweight, he will have to work night and day to get in shape for the first brush with the Giants. He says his arm has felt good all winter and that he has tried it out a trifle, not curving them, however. He came up from Cincinnati, a three hour and a half ride, which always takes five hours.

The athletes were hustled out of bed at seven bells and taken out to a covered promenade, bundled in heavy sweaters. They were hustled three miles around the track and then sent to breakfast. In the afternoon most of them varied the monotony by a hike to French Lick and a bath in the rejuvenating waters.

Jimmy McAleer and his fat Browns had stolen away in the night, bound for permanent training quarters in Texas. Rube Waddell left in his wake various broken hearts and bottles. He also left a note saying he would pitch all the games in the next world's series against the Cubs and would call in all the fielders. This had a discouraging effect on Chance, and he does not know whether or not it is worth while to continue training.

Orvall Overall[6] was the hardest worker of the day and he took off four pounds, leaving only a paltry 220 to carry around with him. Frank Schulte did not put in an appearance, nor did Jimmy Sheckard. In the latter's case, Chance received a letter telling him that James had started for Hot Springs and would join the crowd there on Sunday.

The manager has to watch Jimmy Archer continually, because the latter has discovered an outlaw cave which sometimes is called the Archer cave, and the P. L.[7] is afraid he will jump to the outlaws. Overall and Brown wish he would, as there is no chance of their winning a pool game or bowling match as long as he is in the camp.

If there is a cessation of snow, uniforms will be donned tomorrow. The 7 o'clock Marathon race has been ordered again, but Chance is not satisfied to let his youngsters and "oldsters" get away with nothing but that. If the blizzard continues and keeps the men off the playing field, a long dash over the hills will be added to the program. And there are some hills in these parts. A. Bert Semmens, standing on the top of one of them, looked down and saw Overall and thought it was Jimmy Slagle.

The Badger fight for the benefit of Catcher Malone is scheduled for tomorrow or Friday night. This squad has little time to stay in Indiana, and whatever is due to be pulled off must happen soon. The bunch will leave these parts Saturday for Hot Springs, and West Baden will be left without excitement until Tuesday, when the rest of the Cubs and Pittsburgh batteries will blow in.

There is no telling whether Acting Manager Tommy Leach will consent to let his pitchers work with the Chicagoans, as the latter thus would be given an opportunity of learning in advance what new deceivers Maddox, Willis, and the rest have in stock.

F. Chance has admitted he would not stay among the oranges. "I wouldn't miss our fun this season for all the fruit in California," said the P. L. "Of course, there is sure to be something beside fun, for I think the Giants, Phillies, Reds, and Pirates will be hard to beat. But our reception the first time we appear at the Polo grounds will be worth sticking around for. If you want to add any pet names to your vocabulary just open your ears and listen to what these 'bugs' call me and the rest of the boys when we make our entrance. We'll be about as popular there as a distillery in West Baden."

Floyd Kroh is sure to be as well received as Chance or any of them, for there are two Polo grounds fanatics who did ground and lofty tumbling stunts when he swung his long left arm in a mixup that followed Merkle's generous act,[8] but Kroh will meet the onslaught cheerfully if he is but given an opportunity to work against the tribe of McGraw.

First blood was reported today. Jimmy Archer showed up late in the afternoon with a dislocated cheek, caused by a disagreeable tooth. The jaw is to be lanced tomorrow, and in the meantime Jimmy is forgetting the pain with a long succession of strikes and spares.

Record Crowd Opens Forbes Field

CHICAGO TRIBUNE, JULY 1, 1909

Pittsburg,[9] Pa.—Before the biggest crowd that ever saw a ball game the world's champion Cubs beat Fred Clarke's Pirates on Pittsburg's beautiful new field this afternoon, 3 to 2. A throng of 30,338, or ninety one more than the former record, paid their good money to Messrs. Dreyfuss and Murphy, and there were at least 5,000 more who came in on invitations from the president of the Pittsburg club.

If there had been no ball game at all the masses of sweltering humanity would have paid for their coming, for the stands on Forbes field look out on some of the prettiest scenery to be found in Pennsylvania. And the stands themselves are pretty enough to draw sightseers even if there were nothing else for them to see.

A sight of the crowd was worth a journey to the park, although said journey is anything but comfortable. From early in the forenoon until the game started the masses of people crowded their way into the beautiful suburb, Bellefield, and fought for points of vantage.

The women came dressed as if for the greatest society event of the year, and perhaps it was for Pittsburg's year. Gorgeous gowns, topped by still more gorgeous hats, were in evidence everywhere. Most of the gowns were white and formed a pretty combination with the prevalent green of the stands.

Beyond the outfield fences Schenley Park and some of the handsomest buildings of the Carnegie Institute were visible. The stands, themselves constructed almost entirely of Pittsburg steel and concrete, completely surrounded the field and yet were not big enough to hold the mammoth crowd.

There was an overflow from first base all the way around the outskirts of the yard to the home of Jap Barbeau and Harry Steinfeldt.[10]

Policemen were scarce, but the throng, disappointed though it was by general appearance and the final outcome of the game, was a peaceable assemblage and was just as polite as it looked. When most of Pittsburg's inhabitants and excursionists from the surrounding cities and villages had found seats either in the boxes or stands or on mother earth, Prof. Nerillos' military band began attracting much attention to itself by parading toward the home bench. There the usual line of athletes was formed and the procession started for home plate.

At that point the Cubs themselves, officers and magnates of the two big leagues, including President Pulliam and Acting President Heydler of the National league, President Dreyfuss of the Pittsburg club, and President Ben Shibe of the Philadelphia Athletics, who came over to see whether or not Barney had anything on him in the way of a ballyard, joined the crowd and started for the flag pole. Then, without any of the usual accidents, the stars and stripes were hoisted with a pennant bearing the words "Forbes Field," trailing a little below.

When the ceremonies at the flag pole had been completed the procession came back to the playing field and the two teams took their fielding practice amid more noise than ever has been heard in Pittsburg or the adjacent locality. When the gong rang for the beginning of the game, John Morin, director of public safety, which in English means chief of police, appeared in the middle of the diamond and looked bashfully up at the third deck of the box seats. There was seated Mayor Magee, and he threw the first ball on to the field. Director Morin caught it neatly and journeyed to the pitchers' mound. From the slab the strong arm of the law hurled it almost over the plate and into the waiting hands of catcher Hackenschmidt[11] Gibson. After that all human obstacles disappeared from view and the battle was on.

P.L.'s Team Leads Arabella to the Altar

CHICAGO TRIBUNE, OCTOBER 3, 1910

Cincinnati, Ohio—The wedding of Miss Arabella Cinch to Mr. Chicago Cub occurred this afternoon at the first Cincinnati Pastime church, Mr.

Garry Herrmann officiating. Ed Reulbach was best man and Harry Gasper bridemaid.

For some reason or other, several pews were vacant. But the guests who were present were charmed by the beauty of the ceremony. One of them was so charmed that he gave vent to his enthusiasm in loud conversation with Usher Brennan, and was led down the aisle and out of church by a policeman. The simple bat ceremony was to have been used, but it was decided at the last moment that it was too simple. So a bunch of Cincinnati friends of the bride and groom enlivened things by throwing some old and new boots at the happy pair right while the service was going on. Seven red boots were collected by the janitor after it was all over.

The marriage was the culmination of a long and romantic engagement. Mr. Cub met Miss Cinch down south last spring and it was a case of love at first sight on both sides. Miss Cinch's parents were agreeable, but rivals for the fair lady's hand tried to break off the match several times after the engagement was announced.

In July last, Mr. Pittsburg Pirate became a dangerous suitor and it was predicted freely that he would come between the engaged pair, for Mr. Cub was losing some of his good looks by a series of accidents and illnesses. However, Miss Cinch finally made up her mind that she would rather marry Mr. Cub disfigured than Mr. Pirate handsome. Mr. New York Giant hung around until the last moment hoping she would prove untrue to her first love, for he, too, was enamored of her, though he really was not in her class. But he knows tonight that it is all over with him and he may as well join with the rest in congratulating the newly weds.

A wedding breakfast at the Havlin hotel followed the ceremony. The parents of the groom, Mr. and Mrs. Chance Cub, signed for all the refreshments, which certainly were some refreshments, believe them. The young couple will remain in Cincinnati until Tuesday night. Then they will go on a honeymoon trip to Chicago and will pass one day at the end of the week in Pittsburg before finally settling down to light housekeeping. They will be at home at Polk, Lincoln, Taylor, and Wood streets.

In other words, the score this afternoon was 8 to 4 in favor of the Cubs. The latter gave Harry Gasper an awful trimming and did some mean things to Bill Burns after Harry had been chased. Furthermore, the Reds did all the awful fielding of which they are capable, and they are capable of a great deal. Ed Ruelbach had everything he ever had in his life, and it's remarkable that the Reds hit him as hard as they did.

The P.L., seated on the bench, thought they must be getting the signs, not in any illegitimate way, however, so he had Kling and the big pitcher switch their signals two or three times, but the switching didn't seem to do any good. However, it didn't make any particular difference whether Edward was hit hard or not, for Gasper, Burns, and the Cincinnati defense were a strong enough combination to offset any heavy batting on the part of the home folks.

The Cubs were not shy with the stick themselves. They grabbed off thirteen base knocks, of which three were made by Henry Zimmerman, successor to John Evers. Steinfeldt really hit the ball harder than any one else on either club. He drove runs in with two singles and was the victim of two swell catches by Paskert and Miller of long, vicious swipes.

The victory gave the pennant to Chicago beyond peradventure. The Giants can win all the rest of their games and the Cubs can lose everything else on the schedule and it won't make a bit of difference, so far as real results are concerned.

This is Mr. Chance's fourth pennant in the five years that he has been the Peerless Leader. He is proud of the accomplishment and proud of the team. Also, he is looking forward to a night of sweet sleep, something he hasn't enjoyed in a month.

This is a true statement. The P. L. has been worrying his head off because of the condition, or lack of condition, of his men especially his pitchers, and he was the most tickled gent in Cincinnati when this game was over and the flag was cinched.

In 1907 and 1908, after nailing the bunting Chance and his wife divided between them a bottle of wine. Subsequently, the Cubs copped the world's championship. So you can bet that Mr. and Mrs. P. L. had a cold bottle tonight, and it was the same brand they had consumed in other years.

No, he isn't superstitious. He said after the game that the number thirteen had made it possible for him to lead his club to the championship. It was his thirteenth year with the Cubs and he had berth No. 13 and locker 13 all through the season. When there was a twelve section sleeper he took the drawing room and numbered it 13. Once more, no, he isn't superstitious.

Now that the strain is over, the Chicago players will have to go on working pretty hard They will be asked to practice every morning here, at home, and in Pittsburg. Some of the regulars, Kling, Steinfeldt, and Sheckard, for instance, may be allowed to sit on the bench and watch some of the games, but the pitchers will keep on working in turn unless the P. L gets a hunch that some of them would do better resting. Hank Weaver will have a chance to butt in, and so will Frank Pfeffer and Tom Needham.

But we mustn't forget the feature of the afternoon's doings, which was the champion long distance triple play of the age. It helped Ed Reulbach out of a deep hole and Jimmy Sheckard was the hero of it, because he started it with one of the prettiest throws he ever made.

In the third inning, Egan singled to center. Corcoran was hit by a pitched ball. Gaspcr laid down a bunt. Zimmerman was slow to cover first and Reulbach's throw was bad. so the bases were full with none out. Miller lifted a fly to Sheckard and it was a pretty long one, too. The fleet Egan started for home as the ball was caught. Sheckard's peg hit bottom just at the edge of the infield grass. It skipped straight into Kling's hands without wasting any time and Egan was tagged out. Corcoran was afraid to go to third on the play and Gasper, who had started for second, was forced to turn around and hike back to first. Kling's relay beat him there and Archer did the rest of it.

Pullman Pastimes: Frank Schulte Is His Own Entertainer

THE SPORTING NEWS, JANUARY 12, 1911

Never an ardent devotee of poker, never much of a reader or magazines nor novels and never a singer with enough confidence in himself to give the entire public the pleasure of hearing his voice, Frank M. Schulte, alias "Schlitz," alias "Bud," alias, "Wildfire," alias "Schultz," is thrown on his own resources when the Chicago Cubs are journeying hither and thither. And they certainly are some resources. Mr. Schulte careth not whether he has an audience. When he is in the mood to talk, he will talk and talk loud, and he isn't particular whom he criticizes nor who is listening to his monologue. Mr. Schulte is at his best after the Cubs have lost a hard game. He likes to win, all right, but he doesn't see why defeats should be the cause of tears or post-mortems.

Aboard the sleeper after one of these defeats, for which two or three slips were responsible, there are gathered various little knots of athletes telling each other how it happened, how the beating could have been averted, and mourning and wailing over the unkindness of fate. In his seat all alone, or with a willing listener, sits Mr. Schulte.

"The boys seem to forget there'll be a game tomorrow to play. They act as if this was the last one they ever were going to get into. The pennant is lost now, and there isn't a chance for us to cop that World's Series money. Let's hope the White Sox don't finish first. A city series[12] with them will net the boys enough to worry through the winter on. They didn't trim us today because they played better ball. Oh, no! There never was a day when any team played better ball than these ten-time champion Cublets. Rigler called everything wrong and the luck was dead against us from the start.

"You saw Jack Murray hit that one out of the ball yard? Well, that's no credit to Murray. He had his eyes shut or was talking to someone back in the grandstand when he let that one loose. He didn't meet the ball square. Oh, no! The ball hit his little fingernail and bounded off over the fence. Besides, Edward (that's Reulbach) intended to get him to bite on his fall-away. Edward didn't want to get the ball over the plate. No, Edward was blinded by the dust and he pitched within Murray's reach when he really thought he was throwing to catch Doyle off second.

"Yes, and Schulte played that ball wrong, too. He ought to have left the park and stood on the approach to the elevated station. Then, you know there was a high wind blowing. Otherwise, that would have been a foul fly that Archer could have eaten up. But the pennant's gone now and we might as well arrange a barnstorming tour of some kind."

Then, if feeling particularly good, Mr. Schulte breaks into song, so softly that he can't be heard more than two seats away.

"Kidney stew and fried pig's feet—

"That's the grub I love to eat.

"I guess there's no use of our going to Boston at all, the way luck's breaking against us and with all the umpires in the league ordered to give us the worst of it, we haven't a chance to take a game, even from the Doves.

"Heard a lot of talk about the champagne wine,

"But a great big stein of beer for mine.

"Here, boy, bring up that pair of cobs. Born and bred in the Rockies, sound as a dollar, catch him around the collar, hit him with a bootjack and—sold for 40 dollars to that gentleman right over there.

"Fancy foods I leave alone.

"For they ain't the kind of grub I'm used to gettin' down home.

"Never mind, boys. There'll be another ball game tomorrow and Schulte will play right field and bat third. Three cheers for the national pastime!"

This is followed by a few moments of staring out the window into the dark night. Then, if he is one of his rare poetic moods:

"This baseball season soon will end,
Or else I'm a liar;
Then I'll go back to Syracuse
And drive my old Wildfire.
Against the fastest horse there
My old Wildfire will go
And show his heels to all of them
Upon the pure, white snow.
How glad I am the time is nigh
When reins and whip I'll wield;
'Tis easier to drive a horse
Than run around right field."

Another five minutes of staring out into the gloom. Then: "Kind of looks as if the Athletics would cop that other piece of bunting. Well, if we can recover from today's hard luck and disaster and win a few more ball games on the field and forget the ones in front of the hotels, we may still climb up to that old pennant pole.

"Just let Edward get that fall-away perfect and teach Leonard (King Cole) that the plate is only a couple of yards wide, and the swatters are not all eight-feet-two like himself, and let Harry McIntire slip that old spitter across a couple of times and John Pfeister ease a few hooks over with that left soupbone of his and patch the bones of big Orvie's arm together and have Mordecai warming up back of the clubhouse all the time and Rich rolling a ball around in the palm of his hand, and maybe we'll get there yet.

"Course, there's not much chance for us against all that hard luck and with all the umpires leagued on the other side, but those old Cublets never quit.

"Say, if we should happen to win out against the umpires and score-keepers and the president of the league and the President of the United States and all the governors, that World's Series would be pretty soft for us, wouldn't it? The Athletics would probably forfeit the games when they knew we were going to play.

"I've heard a lot about this Eddie Collins. I've never seen him, but I wouldn't be surprised to find out that both his legs were cut off just below the waist and that he didn't have any arms and was stone blind. Harry's spitter will make him look sick. He's never seen any good spitball pitching. He's only been up against Ed Walsh. And those Philadelphia catchers can't be much account, either. Why, Detroit runs wild on them. Yes, it does. The Tigers never get less than 46 runs against the Athletics. I guess they must just waltz around those bases.

"Talk about Coombs and Bender. What would they do with Artis or Joe or the P. L. or Frank Schulte up there?

"They've never seen any good batters except guys like Cobb, Crawford, Speaker and Lajoie. No, I guess we'll probably scare them so that they'll refuse to play."

More looking out the window.

"Put on your own gray bonnet
With the big 'C' upon it
And we'll board the Pennsylvan-i-ay.
In the town of Philly
We will knock them silly
On that first World's Series day."

"What's the matter, Joe? Some one have a pat hand? Must have grabbed 'em off the bottom, sure. Don't let them get the best of you."

"But, just to argue, suppose we did get into that World's Series, and the Athletics refused to run out of the park and Bender and Coombs didn't make any attempt to faint, and Thomas and Livingston didn't tell Mack their arms were broken, and suppose Harry's spitter wouldn't break and Orvie's arm was as badly broke as I am, and Collins should happen to catch hold by accident, of course, of one of Leonard's fast ones and we should lose a game or two or three or four. I guess we'd go off and die then. There wouldn't be anything left in life. Of course, they'd offer us the losers' end of the money, but we wouldn't accept that. No, it would be much better to starve to death. What do you think about it, Mr. Kling?"

Mr. Kling is Mr. Schulte's roommate and each is so doubtful about the sincerity of any of the other's remarks that their conversation is a guarded affair.

"Lay off me," returns John. "Your job is to get out there in right field, catch 'em when you can reach 'em, chase 'em when they go past you, throw 'em when you get 'em and hit 'em when they're over. You don't belong in the real mechanism of the team and you talk a lot too much for an outsider. You and Hofman and Sheckard ought to pay to get into the ballpark."

"Yes," is Mr. Schulte's comeback, "and I guess you can lay off the rest of the season. You won't have anything to do if we should happen to get into that World's Series. Just as soon as O'Day says, 'Brown and Kling for Chicago,' the Athletics will tie their legs together for fear they might forget and try to steal a base or two. You can play pool with your right hand during the games, because it will be easy for you to do all that catching and throwing with that big mitt.

"Sing, sing. What shall I sing?
I'll sing you a song about Johnny G. Kling.
When Collins starts stealing the bases on him, he
Will holler to Archer, 'Help, Jimmy! Help, Jimmy!'
"I wish it would hurry up and be midnight, so I could go to bed."

Pullman Pastimes: Dawson's Reform
Credited to Two Cubs

THE SPORTING NEWS, FEBRUARY 2, 1911

Last year the Cubs had some mighty good-looking youngsters on their training trip: "good-looking" referring more to their athletic ability than their facial beauty, although some of them might have classed as comely. They showed so much of merit in the practice down at New Orleans that Manager Chance had to do a lot of thinking before letting them out; in consequence, they stayed longer than is usual. Some of these recruits were not "city broke" and it became the duty of the veterans to teach them things about street, parlor and table manners.

One pitcher in particular—we will call him Dawson because it's such a pretty name—was new to the habits and customs of the great world. It's a safe bet that he never saw a hotel before he went to West Baden. We're too tired to look it up but we firmly believe he must have stayed at home while his bush league team was traveling and his home must have been a cave. At any rate, he didn't know how to start putting on any clothes but his baseball uniform and his use of table weapons was original, to say the least. The man who made seven million dollars on that combination necktie and mop invention would have been able to sell this recruit any amount of these goods, provided the ties were flaming scarlet and pale pink with heliotrope stripes.

Now ball players are not a mean lot at all. When something like this breaks in, they carefully refrain from hurting its feelings by unkind remarks. Rather, they go about the work of reform in the most gentle manner possible. Among themselves they will ask "Where did this circus get the new clown?" or "Where is the sword swallower from?" but they don't fling their superiority in his face. However, it generally becomes necessary to take action to make the poor object human, especially when he demonstrates at the outset that he and a bath tub are only casual acquaintances.

To return to Mr. Dawson, Schulte and Sheckard appointed themselves a committee of two to make a man of him. They got along so well that he was able to consume a meal of victuals without adding anything to the color scheme of his trousers before he was sent back for "more season-ing." Which reminds us that Charley Dryden originated this one on him: "Why did Dawson get this pepper and salt suit?" ("I'm sure I don't know, Mr. Dryden. Why DID Mr. Dawson get that pepper and salt suit?") "So he could wear it two seasons."

There was a quick jump out of Montgomery one afternoon and dinner had to be eaten on the way to Birmingham. Sheckard, Schulte and Daw-son sat down at the same table; design on the part of Schulte and Sheck-ard and accident on Dawson's, for he didn't care what celebrities dined with him. The two celebrities ordered large steaks; so did Dawson.

Sheckard came right down to the point while the meat was on the fire: "Frank," he said to Schulte, "I've been watching you eat for three years and I haven't been able to catch onto the way you do it. Why, you can fin-ish in ten minutes a meal it would take me an hour to eat. And it's all because you have the knack of getting your food all in a bunch and then getting it all in your mouth in a hurry. You could really leave the dining room after the first mouthful and then go back in the other car and finish your supper at leisure."

"Yes," admitted Schulte, "I know I don't waste any time at table. I learned a long time ago that it doesn't pay. I attribute my speed to the ease with which I can use a knife and I'll bet there isn't another man on the ball club who can get a plate full of food from the table to his mouth as fast as I can without spilling a lot of it."

This dialogue was continued until the waiter returned. Then the lec-ture became an illustrated one. Before he had eaten anything, Schulte ordered some wheat cakes and when they came he started a wonderful exhibition of the conservation of time. Three wheat cakes, a quarter "chunk" of a large steak and four or five French fried potatoes were rolled up together by the aid of a knife and fork and delicately conveyed to the mouth, the knife alone being used for cartage. There wasn't room for all of it between the right fielder's lips, but most of it made an entrance and the balance was suspended on the knife until available apace within the mouth was found.

Mr. Sheckard expressed his admiration of the feat. But Dawson just looked. It's one cinch he that he was disgusted, for he didn't wait to fin-ish what was before him. At breakfast in Birmingham next morning, he sat with the manager and Joe Tinker and Archer and it was noted and reported that he had become acquainted with a fork and was getting more friendly with it every moment. Ever and anon, he looked at Schulte's table, then then turned away with an expression of horror. Frank of Syracuse and James of Columbia got no credit for their labor, but they had started Dawson on the road to "recovery."

"We saved his life," remarked Sheck. "If he had kept up that clip he surely would have cut his face open from ear to ear before the real season started. And he never would have made a good pitcher with only half a head."

"Oh, I wouldn't make it as strong as that," replied Frank. "There are two or three good pitchers right on our club who get along with no heads at all."

Mr. Dawson was now a friend of the fork, but he was a stranger to the barber. He shaved himself, but he hadn't endured a hair cut since Methuselah was a messenger boy.

At this time, the real Cubs were playing the exhibition games, the young team having done its heavy work during the New Orleans stay. But the young pitchers were still being used.

"Dawson," said Sheckard one night, on the way from Birmingham to Memphis, "the chances are you'll work part of the game tomorrow. Chance told me that he was going to play first base. Now, two pitchers have been let out on this club for a peculiar reason: Their hair was so long and thick that P. L couldn't see across the diamond to Steinfeldt. You know, he gives Steiny all the signs—what hop to take a ground ball on and all of that kind of thing. If his vision is obscured, it makes him so sore that he not only releases the man responsible for his anger, but usually scalps him. If I were you I'd sell about 75 cents worth of that lettuce."

This drew a smile from the ordinarily glum countenance of Dawson, but he was relieved of half his hair the next morning and much improved in appearance.

A discussion of the cost of Pullmans came up on the way from Memphis to Nashville. Harry Steinfeldt said they were built at an approximate cost of $30,000 apiece and Ed Reulbach said they were worth at least three times that sum. Inasmuch as neither athlete had the faintest idea of what he was talking about, this debate proved very interesting, The youngsters, including Dawson, listened to it breathlessly at first, but even their interest waned when the debaters got down to such prosaic arguments as the cost of the soap used. Seeing that enthusiasm was lagging, Mr. Hofman felt it his duty to revive it.

"Boys," he said, "you ought to see the sleeping cars over in Persia where I used to live. They cost 8,000,000 pesos each; that's about three billion dollars in our money. The climate is much warmer there and there are no roofs on the cars. Every berth is built out in the open air and each one is 200 miles from its nearest neighbor. The space between is filled with beautiful beechnut groves, gardens of underground moose plants and lakes of hair tonic. The porters always travel around the cars in electric runabouts and it takes the slow ones two years to make up all the berths. Wire screens are built over the berths, but at that, the occupants would die of suffocation it they didn't carry strychnine guns with which to shoot the elephants that try to make their beds on top of these screens."

"Yes," added Mr. Sheckard, "and the dining cars they use over there are nothing short of miraculous. You could put three Deserts of Sahara into one of them and still have room for the forests with which they are decorated. The waiter rides in on a camel to take your order and he can't serve you inside of eight years, even if both he and the camel get humps on them."

To all of which the kids listened intently; and they probably wondered if insanity was the keynote of success in the big leagues.

The Rustlers Go Marching Through Georgia

BOSTON AMERICAN, MARCH 15, 1911

Augusta, Ga.—Just a week ago to-day the Rustlers arrived at Augusta and it is the opinion of every man on the squad that the week has been well spent. Up to yesterday the weather was ideal, and there is no reason to believe that yesterday's chilly unpleasantness will be repeated. But the cold air and slight mist failed to stop the Regular rehearsals and it will take a lot of worse weather than that to break up Manager Tenney's plans. The men were up early this morning ready for another hard day's labor.

The usual morning batting and fielding practice was on the card with a game between the Regulars and Yanigans[13] booked for the afternoon.

Manager Stouch of the Augusta team informed Tenney that it would not be probable for his club to meet his team before Saturday, but this did not bother Fred much, as the present system is rapidly rounding the athletes into form.

The news that Pitcher Cecil Ferguson would not be with the Rustlers was heard with sorrow in camp for Fergy is a great favorite with the other players. Also, he is recognized as a good pitcher and the Rustlers realize that they can't probably be as strong without him as with him. Ferguson thinks his services are worth more than his contract calls for and he is reluctant to give up his job as salesman for a Boston plumber's supply house.

It must be a pretty good job he has if it can keep him away from the pastime which pays salaries that are not to be sneered at. The bunch is still hoping he will change his mind and it is probable he will be unable to resist the call of the game when the real season opens.

Poet Collins,[14] being informed that President Russell[15] was tired to death with the showing so far of his recruits, thought it proper to express William Hepburn's sentiments in verse. So he took his pencil in hand and dashed off the following masterpiece:

"Hurrah, hurrah," the magnate said, said he,

"Hurrah, hurrah," they all look good to me,

"Right now I'd like to bet we will finish one or two or three,

"While we are marching through Georgia."

Mr. Collins said the word "Marching" should be capitalized, explaining that it meant spending the month of March, just as Wintering means—"Oh, well, you know what it means."

The five athletes, Clark, Burke, Perdue, Collins and Rariden, who had their heads shaved,[16] have been dubbed the "convicts," and they certainly do look the part. Mr. Burke is sorry he fell for it now, but his sorrow won't hasten the return of his hair, which was one of his chief beauties. Wilbur Goode desires to inform the public that his name is pronounced just plain "good," to rhyme with "would, if he could," "stood," "hood," etc. He has been called "Goodey," "Gooda," and lots of other things and has stood for the mispronunciations long enough. He says he can't see why it is so hard to get it right, for no one ever thinks of saying "Josh Clarkee," or "Bill Burkey." The "e" in all those names is silent, as in hippopotamus. Speaking of a hippopotamus, Hub Perdue announces that he is good enough to pitch in the National League or the American, and that it will take some hard luck to keep him away from a regular berth on the staff.

Hub hasn't had a chance to exhibit any real pitching powers to date, but he surely possesses confidence, ginger and a sense of humor three times very valuable to a big league slabman.

Yesterday's game, which went to the Yanigans in six innings, 4 to 2, was marked by the fact that one pitcher worked the full route for the defeated Regulars. The pitcher was Buster Brown. He didn't exert himself a great deal, but was glad to learn that he felt no ill effects from his trial gallop. Hub Perdue pitched the first two innings for the Yanigans and Chick Evans finished it up. Hub was in a tight place in the first inning and a double play saved him a lot of trouble.

Two weeks later, in a dispatch from Roanoke, Va., Lardner described the after-effects of a 34-0 victory by the Rustlers over Greensboro.

. . . Sunday at Greensboro was necessarily quiet. It would have been quiet anyhow from choice, for the players were so weary from Saturday's chase around the bases that they had no pepper to do anything but just sit around.

Peaches Graham remained in his apartments and conversed with the rats. One of them, a big fellow, told Peaches that he was a catcher on the Rodent team that plays a bunch of field mice every Saturday for a pound of cheese. His name is Trap, probably because he is a rat catcher. The manager on the team is the Pied Piper of Hamlin and he and Trap are having a disagreement over salary. So Peaches and the Rat had much in common to discuss.

Hub Perdue stood up all day because he had slept on what he called a tombstone and his feet having extended several feet over the end of it, were not as badly bruised as the rest of his body. However, there was one nice thing about that hotel. It gave you plenty to eat and the plenty was good, too, but as Hub said, you couldn't sleep in the dining room. There must have been a private eating place for the rats, for they didn't disturb the athletes at their meals.

Bill Sweeney took advantage of the holiday to catch up with his business correspondence. You know Bill is the company in the J.M. Sweeney Company, of Newport, Kentucky, which makes and sells various patent medicines. Among its productions are pills that cure colds, grippe, charley horse, mumps, measles, croup, rheumatism, gout, diphtheria, whooping cough, toothache and warts.

2

Baseball

Baseball was good to Lardner and he was good to it. When his "busher" stories were published in the *Saturday Evening Post*, and later collected as *You Know Me Al*, they became enormously popular with readers everywhere. In Oak Park, Illinois, a young Ernest Hemingway began signing articles for his high school paper "Ring Larder, Jr.," while in England, Virginia Woolf, whose knowledge of baseball was nil, pronounced herself a fan of Jack Keefe.

But the stories had a larger effect, one that is felt to this day. They established baseball as a fit subject for literary fiction. In the decades that followed Lardner's work, important American novelists such as Bernard Malamud, Philip Roth, Robert Coover, Mark Harris, Don Delillo, Chad Harbach, and others would follow Lardner into ballparks and locker rooms and emerge with stories of their own.

This all began with Lardner's baseball reporting and particularly his fascination with the men who played the game. He wrote about the great stars of the era—Babe Ruth, Ty Cobb, Christy Mathewson, Casey Stengel—but also about the game's "characters," the players whose company he most enjoyed. Frank Schulte, Rollie Zeider, John Kling, Ping Bodie, Peaches Graham, Jim Schekard, and others made repeated appearances in his articles.

Lardner attended many World Series games while working in Chicago and later for the Bell Syndicate in New York, and his coverage of the series over the years shows his development as a writer. Early on he proved his mastery of the straightforward game story. His accounts of key games in the 1909 and 1912 World Series, for instance, are expertly constructed, full of keenly observed detail, and, in the description of Mathewson's loss in the latter, heartbreaking.

Once Lardner took over the "In the Wake of the News" column at the *Tribune* in 1913, his approach to the game quickly changed. His "A Athlete" column, which leads off this section, was written shortly before the World Series that year and was a forerunner of the "busher" stories, as well as an indication of things to come. Nothing was off-limits, even if it meant he would often leave the games themselves entirely behind.

At later series he would write "Friend Harvey" letters about his travel plans, make fun of play-by-play accounts, send up wartime propaganda, talk about his golf game, comment on what the umpires were wearing, and more. Of all these, his articles during the 1922 series must be counted as his masterpiece. He wrote five columns about his quest for a fur coat for his wife, and I could not resist including them all.

Lardner's coverage of the 1919 World Series deserves special attention. The legend is that he quickly became aware that his beloved White Sox were throwing games to the Cincinnati Reds. He is said to have called Ed Cicotte, one of his favorite players, to his hotel room after a game in which the star Chicago pitcher had been badly beaten, and demanded to know what was going on. He also collaborated with his *Tribune* colleague James Crusinberry on the lyrics to a song that began "I'm Forever Throwing Ballgames."

Yet none of Lardner's suspicions appeared in his coverage of the series. While Crusinberry wrote several articles in which White Sox manager Kid Gleason, sensing that something was amiss, agonized over his team's poor play, Lardner wrote one lighthearted story after another. The closest he came to mentioning the scandal, which did not come to light until the following year, was a cryptic reference in a column that appeared October 9, in which he said he was examining a baseball used in a game and that "it looks soiled on the northwest side and I will worry my life away wondering who put a dirty finger on that ball which I have got and my children will still have it after me."

In the years that followed Lardner sometimes said that the Black Sox scandal destroyed his interest in baseball, but this is an exaggeration. He well knew that gambling had long been a part of the game—he refers to it several times in pieces here—and that there had been suspicious occurrences in previous years. Lardner himself often bet substantial amounts on the events he covered and, wrote Ring Jr., "the way he spoke about the event later gave me the feeling he was at least as concerned about losing a substantial bet . . . as he was about the moral turpitude of the players."

What did decrease his interest in the game was the arrival of Babe Ruth and the lively ball, a subject he discussed at length in "Br'er Rabbit Ball" and "Why Ring No Longer Covers Baseball." (It should be noted that he covered four more World Series after writing the latter.) In a letter to the legendary New York Giants' manager John McGraw, when both men were nearing the end of their lives, Lardner did not sound like a man who had turned his back on the game that had defined his life in so many ways. "Often I have wondered whether you ever enjoyed the feeling of security and comfort that must be a manager's when the reporters assigned to his club are 'safe' and not pestiferous," Lardner wrote, "a gang such as Chance and Jones and Jim Callahan were surrounded with for a few years in Chicago, and I don't say that just because I happen to be one of the gang. . . . The managers referred didn't wince when they saw one of us approaching. They were our friends and we were theirs." He did have to admit, though, that "Baseball hasn't meant much to me since the introduction of the TNT ball that has robbed the game of the features I used to like best."

The First Game

CHICAGO TRIBUNE, SEPTEMBER 28, 1913

By A Athlete* [*Unassisted]

We ought to of trimmed 'em. When Egan, the big slob, said I was out at second he musta been full o' hops, the big boob. I like t'know where he was at las' night, the big bum. Some o' them umps oughta be on the chain gang, the big boobs.

Matty pitched wrong to Collins. That little bum couldn't hit a curve ball with a mattress. Matty's been pitchin' long enough to know how to pitch, but sometimes he pitches like a damfool. I wisht he'd let me tell him somethin'. But d'ya think he'd listen to me? He knows it all. He oughta knew he didn't have speed enough no more to get one past that guy.

Wisht Mac had let me wallop when I had the big Indian three and nothin' that time. 'Member? Merkle was on third base. I looked 'round and Mac gives me the sign to take one. That's rotten baseball, I think. I took one that I could of hit out o' the park. Then the big Indian hooks one on me and I missed. Then I'm lookin' for another hook and he comes with a fast one. And the Catfish calls me out. That last one was a foot outside. If I'd a known he was goin' to call it on me, I'da hit that one out o' the park. The big rum.

Then there was that third innin' decision, when Egan calls me out at second, the big slob. Barry missed me that far. I wouldn't lie about it. He missed me that far. If I'da been out, I'd never opened my clam. But Barry missed me that far. The big slob. He was lookin' out in right field some-wheres. Barry missed me that far. Bet if you was to go to Barry now and ast him, he'd come through and say he missed me that far. The big rummy. I'm glad we don't have them umpires in our league. No wonder Milan steals bases. He's probably out all the time, but the umps is lookin' out the window. Why Barry missed me that far.

I ain't no pitcher, but I bet I know as much about pitchin' as some of them pitchers. Ja see what Matty handed Collins? He slips him a fast one right over the heart when all he had to do was hook one and Collins woulda fell dead. Matty's been pitchin' fifty years and he don't know no more'n a baby. McGraw'd oughta tell some of them guys somethin'. But no, he sits on the bench and don't say nothin' till the inning's over. And then it's too late.

'Member when Merkle was on third base? I'da busted 'er up right there if Mac had let me alone. But he makes me take one when I had the big Indian three and nothin'. That first one came right over and I coulda hit it out o' the park. But, no, I had to stan' there and take it. Then he comes across with a hook and I missed it. And then I'm lookin' for another hook and he comes with a fast one and Klem calls it on me. The big rum. It was a mile outside. But if I'd knew he was goin' to call it on me, I coulda hit it 'way out o' the park. Some o' them umps oughta be on the chain gang.

How long's this Egan been umpirin'? I thought Finneran was the worst I ever see, but this Egan's got him skun.[1] Didja see what he pulled on me?

Mac tells me to steal and down I goes. Schang makes a perfect peg, but I give 'im the hook and Barry missed me. Egan says: "Yer out" I says: "What fer, you big rum?" He walked away. He knew damwell what I'da said to him if he'd stuck around. He walked away and didn't give me no chance to say nothin'. Barry missed me that far. The big, no-good slob.

Matty's been pitchin' a hundred years, but he don't know no more about pitching 'n some kid. He goes and hands Collins a fast one when the old hook woulda knocked him dead. His fast one ain't what it was. It's straight as a string and it don't hop. But he goes and slips it to Collins and that's jes' what Collins was layin' for. At that, it was a wild pitch. It was six feet over Collins' head, but he was jes' lucky enough to meet it. No wonder them Athletics wins the pennant every year. I never seen a team have the luck break for 'em like it does for them big slobs.

We'da got 'em. though, if Mac'd left me alone when Merkle was on third base. The big Indian had me three and nothin', and I wanted to take my wallop. I knowed he wouldn't have nerve enough to hand up three hooks, and I knowed the first one was a-goin' to be a fas' one. But I looked at Mac and he shook his head no. He makes me take the first one and it's a straight one, right over the heart. Then the big Indian hands me a hook and I swung at it 'cause it'd been a strike anyway. Klem was callin' 'em all strikes anyway. So I swung and missed, and then he comes back with a fast one when I'm lookin' for another hook, and the stuff's off. I took it and Klem says it's a strike. Mighta knew he'd call 'em all strikes. It was that far outside.

Bender pulled a boner at that. He oughta walked me and took a chance on Larry. But he got away with it, the big lucky slob. But he never woulda got away with it if it hadn't a-been for Mac and then Klem callin' that third strike on me.

An' didja see what Egan done to me? Where'd they get them umpires. They oughta be peddlin' eggs, the big boobs. Barry missed me that far.

We'll get 'em tomorrow. Big Rube'll make 'em quit like dogs, the big, lucky rums. They was ready to quit today, only Egan and Klem wouldn't give 'em no chancet.

Watch me tomorrow. Plank's pie for me. I'm liable to knock a couple men dead in them bleachers. We'll fix 'em. the big, lucky slobs. Rube'll make 'em look sick.

Ja see that doll in the box back o' our bench? She couldn't keep her eye off o' me.

We'll get 'em tomorrow, the yellow, quittin' dogs.

Peaches Graham: Nine Men in One

BOSTON AMERICAN, MAY 28, 1911

"You know," remarked the Sporting Editor, "we get out a Sunday paper once a week, so you needn't sit there doing nothing just because there's nothing in sight to do. There's a certain amount of space to fill and you're supposed to be one of the fillers. How about interviewing a catcher?"

With that, he turned away without giving the reporter a chance to reply. So the poor slave knew that it was up to him to make the perilous journey to the Rustlers' clubhouse again and run the risk of arousing the displeasure of one or more of the idols of the town. The necessary nickel was borrowed with no little difficulty, but the journey to Walpole street was made without mishap.

As luck would have it, the only occupants of Mr. Neary's hotel, aside from the proprietor, were Messrs. Rariden and Graham, whom the reporter recognized as catchers by their receptive attitude. The Rariden party looked far less formidable, so it was to him that the reporter spoke first. But the result showed clearly the truth of the old saw "Appearances are deceiving."

"What do you want, boy?" came from the lips of G. Graham, whose countenance now looked kindly by contrast with that of his brother artist. "Perhaps I can do something for you if it isn't too hard, and if you refrain from asking foolish questions. If you have come to find out how to catch, you're wasting your time. I'm a baseball team—do you get me? A Baseball Team."

"There he goes," remarked Mr. Rariden, as he started out the door, while the reporter wondered how anyone ever got sufficiently familiar with him to call him "Bill."

"That's what I am—a baseball team," screamed Mr. Graham, and the reporter, anxious to humor him, smiled and nodded sympathetically.

"I won't be interviewed on how to catch," the famous athlete continued. "That's just like trying to tell how to enjoy a sirloin steak—one's as simple as the other. But if you'll give me all your attention and not misquote me. I'll tell you how I became a baseball team and some of the things I did when I was one."

The reporter was cute enough to know that it was too late to stop now, so he produced a cigarette paper and prepared to take notes, and the nine ballplayers in one got the following out of his system:

"First and foremost, even you must have noticed that I am called 'Peaches,' not merely 'Peach.' Why? Because I'm plural. Ty Cobb is sometimes spoken of as the 'Georgia Peach,' but never as the 'Georgia Peaches.' That's because he's just a fielder and only one peach. I'm a catcher, a pitcher, four infielders, three outfielders, one utility man and one pinch batter. That's why I'm Peaches, a whole crop of them.

"I ought to speak of myself as 'we' and 'us,' but if I did, folks probably would call me conceited. I started playing professional ball when I was four years old. You know I was born in Persia and came to this country in one of the old fashioned balloons when I was a little over two. For the next year and a half I worked as a drummer on a street car, selling transfers, but the pay was small, a little over $140 a week, and that was just about enough to keep me in collars.

"Our trolley line passed a ball park in Spring Valley, Ill., and it was there that I first saw the national pastime. The Spring Valley team used to play the Kewanee club once every Saturday and two or three times on Sunday. There was great rivalry between the two towns and sometimes pools of as much as eighteen cents were up on the games.

"My entrance into the sport was the old story—one of the stars hurt and no one to take his place. I volunteered and played shortstop one day so much better than the star that they sent the latter to jail for thirty years.

"Well, it happened that there was a contagion of croup in Spring Valley that year and every ball player on the local team was taken with it except me. I had my throat removed before I came across the ocean.

"The manager was in an awful fix, or thought he was till I came to the rescue. He had all those games scheduled with Kewanee and had posted a forfeit of $2,300,456 to insure his playing them.

"That night the epidemic hit the town, he came to me and said:

"'Peach'—I was only one, then—'I'm up against it right. I've got some ball games booked and no players.'

"'Manager,' I answered, 'why do you say you have no players when I'm still here?'

"'But you can't play the whole game,' said he.

"'Try me and see,' said I. For in those days I had more confidence than money.

"So the posters advertising the next day's game were left up, and when the hour for the battle arrived the park was crowded. Every fan present was a doctor, for all the rest of the people had croup. The Kewanee team came on the field joyously for the players thought the series would be forfeited. You can imagine their astonishment when they saw me in uniform. Their astonishment turned to alarm when they witnessed the spectacle of one man going through fielding and batting practice and warming up to pitch besides.

"Perhaps batting practice was hardest for me to master because it came first. I hadn't yet worked up the full speed of my legs by running, so I had to pitch slow ones from the box so I could get to the plate in time to pick up a bat and hit at them. It didn't do to miss any swings or foul off any for that meant I had to run back to the grandstand and tire myself out.

"I was so fast on my feet by the time the bell rang for my fielding practice that it was simple for me to hit a ground ball or a fly and then run to one position or another and field it. I completed my preparations by acting as catcher to warm up to the pitcher, and as pitcher to do the warming up.

"The game being played on the Spring Valley grounds, the Kewaunee team was first to bat. I cut loose two fast ones at the first hitter. He missed them both. The effort of getting from the box to the catcher's position was proving terribly wearing and I knew I couldn't stand it long. So then and there, I invented a new delivery, which I called the Round Trip. It was thrown with a caressing, beckoning motion. When the ball wasn't hit, it came right back into my hands.

"You can imagine that this delivery was a great saving of energy. I couldn't use it continually, else it would lose its power to deceive, but I signed myself for it six or seven times an inning.

"The Kewanee hitters were helpless before me for eight innings. Meanwhile, I had been unable to score a run myself. The hit-and-run play was my favorite, but you must know it was hard to pull off. To accomplish it I had to start from first toward second, or second toward third, while the pitcher was winding up and at the same time dash for the batter's box so I would be on hand when the ball came up to the plate.

"The result was I couldn't get set to swing. Several times I missed connections at the plate and the catcher would throw me out at some base or other because I had been obliged to stop short on my journey on the base lines to return to bat.

"So the count was 0 to 0 when the ninth inning came. In Kewanee's half my real troubles started, for the opponent began to bunt. It took me by surprise and eight runs were scored before I thought out a way to spoil the play. I finally did it by mastering the pop-up delivery, which forces batsmen to hit little flies.

"I wasn't feeling exactly gay when I finally got the side retired and went in to try to overcome that lead of eight runs. But the owner of the team had bet a pound of chocolates on the result, and I knew I was as good as dead if I failed him in this crisis.

"Did I get the nine tallies? Yes, I did and not by hitting them over the fence, either, although I could tell you I did that and get away with it. I beat Kewanee at its own game—I began to bunt.

"First I laid down a perfect one and easily beat it out. Then I bunted another one and sped for first, yelling at the top of my voice, 'Second base, second base.'

"The pitcher, who picked up the ball turned to throw to second but no runner was trying for that bag. Then he started to throw to first. I immediately changed my course and started for second. He did finally throw to first, and the first baseman made the catch just as I landed at second.

"A big argument followed. Kewanee claimed it had one out.

"'But who's out?' I boldly asked.

"'You are,' was the reply.

"'Where and why am I out?' said I.

"'At first base because the ball got there before you did,' said they.

'How do you figure that?' said I. 'I left first base as soon as the succeeding batter bunted, and here I am safe at second. Nobody tried to get to first, so there was no play there.'

"Well, the umpire and the Kewanee players finally had to admit the force of my argument. The game went on and on the next bunt the pitcher unhesitatingly threw to third. I dashed to first and no effort was made to stop me. Thus the bases were full and the rest was simple, so long as I could keep the bunts on the ground.

"I succeeded beyond my wildest dreams. All I had to do then was lay down nine straight bunts and just touch the plate with my foot after each one, thus scoring one tally at a time until I had nine.

"The Kewanee boys were a pretty sick looking lot when it was all over. But the Spring Valley owner was tickled to death and that night, on the way home, he took a crisp dollar bill out of his pocket and handed it to me. 'This is a loan,' he said, 'but there'll be no interest.'

"There isn't much left to tell. I beat them three more games and then they quit coming. Finally it got so bad that no team would play at Spring Valley unless I left town. So I left and since then I have been forced to play only one position at a time, which, as you may imagine, is pretty tame sport."

"A posse of cops is on the way here," remarked Jimmy Neary.

Mr. Graham paid no heed.

"Yes, sir, I have played first, second, third, fourth and fifth and all the outfield positions, and I have pitched and caught."

"And what do you like best to do, Mr. Graham?" asked the reporter.

"Smoke a pipe," said they.

Always a better talker than player, Graham was in the twilight of his career when Lardner caught up with him. He was traded to the Cubs midway through the 1911 season and his career ended the following year. He finished with a .265 lifetime batting average and one home run.

Ty Cobb's Inside Baseball

BOSTON AMERICAN, JUNE 18, 1911

He's Always Quarreling, but His Craze to
Win Does That, and He's Popular.

He was here last week, not long enough to get very well acquainted with the general public of Boston, but plenty long enough to convince said public that he is not yet prepared to yield the baseball crown to Joe Jackson or any other "upstart from the minors."

It is not strictly accurate to say there is only one Cobb, for he has a brother, also a ball player, and a son, who may be one. But there is only one Ty Cobb, and, as Charles Comiskey says, you have to hand it to him. This same Charles Comiskey had seen "King" Kelly, Bill Lange, Hugh Duffy and all the other great ones perform in their palmy days and he hesitated not a moment when the question was put to him: "Who is the greatest ball player of all time?"

Cobb had beaten Comiskey's team time after time, had taken the pennant from the White Sox in the final game of the 1908 season, and yet the Chicago owner gave him his full meed of praise, instead of calling him "lucky," or "fresh," or "dirty," as many another has done.

Cobb's various accomplishments are ancient history. There is nothing to be said of his mechanical ball playing that the "fans" have not seen for themselves and appreciated. But there is a great deal to Cobb's work that does not appear on the surface or that is overlooked by the public because it is busy watching something else.

The general impression prevails that Cobb is not popular with his teammates and that he has hardly any friends on rival teams. Nothing could be farther from the truth. Ty has an argument with one of the other Tigers almost every time the Detroit club engages in a close game. Other great ball players have their "spats" under similar conditions, but that does not mean that they are disliked. Cobb quarrels more often with his mates simply because victory means more to him than it does to the majority of athletes. He is crazy to win, and he sometimes forgets his manners in the heat of battle.

For the benefit of the "fans" who have been led to believe that Cobb has few friends on his own team or on others, it might be well to call attention to the scene that takes place before every Detroit game. Cobb will usually be found "warming up" with some of the members of the "other" club. He is "kidding" them and they are handing it back to him, but there is no real hostility between him and the men with whom he happens to be conversing. And the same is true when he is with the rest of the Detroit players. Ty is something or a "kidder" and he likes word battles next to the actual conflicts of the diamond.

In the Spring of 1908, Cobb had a real fight with Catcher Charley Schmidt. It took place in the Southern training camp.[2] It was caused by a disagreement between the two over Ty's treatment of colored people; rather, one colored person. Schmidt and Cobb went behind the stand at the ball park and had it out, and the catcher, who has taken up the fight game professionally, had all the better of it. Cobb admitted that he was licked and then he and Schmidt became fast friends. As for the other Tigers, they were divided about evenly in their partisanship, but none of them held anything against Cobb for his share in the proceedings.

The recent coldness between Cobb and Sam Crawford was brought about by an argument between Ty and Donie Bush over signs. Bush was, and still is, just ahead of Cobb in the batting order. Now Ty has a complicated set of signals for the man on base when he is at bat. He claims that he must use at least five hit and run signs to deceive the opposing battery. Most players have only one. Bush got mixed up two or three times and failed to read Cobb's signs aright.

In the middle of one game, in the 1910 season, one of these mix-ups occurred and it resulted disastrously for the Tigers. Whereupon Cobb gave Bush a sharp "call" and Donie, who is some conversationalist himself, came back. But be seemed to be getting the worst of it and Sam Crawford went to his rescue.

It was then that Sam and Tyrus got into a rapid-fire duel of epithets that could scarcely be called complimentary. They said everything they had to say and then didn't speak to each other for a long time. Manager Jennings insisted on a patching up of the quarrel this Spring, and now the two are good friends.

Crawford, who, by the way, is faster this season than he has been for years, seldom gets mixed on signs. Cobb is ahead of him, and Ty does whatever he is told to do by Sam when the latter is at bat. And the plays that the two pull off through their silent understanding are good samples of the real value of "inside baseball."

In the first inning of last Monday's game here two were out and the bases were empty when Cobb came up and beat out a slow hit to Purcell. It was natural to suppose that he would either attempt to steal on the first or second ball, or that Crawford and he would work the hit and run. Two balls were pitched out, but Ty failed to go.

On the next one he started at full speed and Crawford, instead of swinging or letting the strike go over, laid down a bunt and beat it to first. It didn't have to be a perfect bunt, for the Red Sox were taken entirely by surprise.

Purcell came in to field the bunt and third base was left unguarded for the moment. Of course, Cobb kept right on going, and, of course, he reached it in safety. The play was a dandy, but it was wasted, for the usually reliable Delehanty fell a victim to Hall and struck out.

If it had been in the latter part of the game and if the Tigers had needed a run to win or tie, you can bet that Cobb would have attempted a theft of home, and he would have come close to getting away with it. As it was, he had to play safe and conserve his best efforts for later on.

The public gains its impression that Cobb is unpopular through his evidently harsh verbal altercations on the field, with members of his own and rival teams. He does argue with the rest of the Tigers and he does quarrel with his opponents, but it is all in the day's work, and is usually forgotten the moment the game is over. It is Cobb's overwhelming desire to win that is at the root of all his squabbling.

Cobb appears unable to get through a battle at Philadelphia without some sort of unpleasantness. He has quarrels with Frank Baker and Cy Morgan, which appear to be fixtures. Boston "fans" will remember the birth of the Morgan-Cobb disagreement.[3] The controversy with Baker arose over the latter's assertion that Ty had spiked him purposely. There was a great of fuss about this case, and the two players have been at each other ever since.

The Tigers say that Baker deliberately kicked Cobb when the latter was sliding back to third base in one of the games of Detroit's recent series at Shibe Park. Cobb then attempted to tread on Frank's foot. It is hard to get at the truth of these complaints and cross-complaints because each club backs its own man. But Cobb has friends among the Athletics and that was proved last Fall, when he took part in the All-Star series that helped the American League champions in their preparation for their brush with the Cubs.

Cobb doesn't care whom he "bawls out." Hughey Jennings has been scolded fiercely by the "Georgia Peach." To be sure, Hughey has been there with the back talk but it never served to frighten Cobb into silence.

Cobb stands out there in center field and tells his mates about all the mistakes they make. Then he tells them again on the bench. He informs the pitchers that they worked like high school kids against certain batters, charges the infielders with ignorance and negligence and even "calls" his fellow outfielders when he thinks they have pulled a "bone."

Some of them shoot hot language back at him and swear they will never associate with again, but they are all his friends after the game, or after they have had two or three days in which to think things over.

Tyrus isn't immune from criticism. When he makes a mistake it never goes unnoticed. But he doesn't make many and so his critics don't have much chance to get back at him.

If Cobb were born to be unpopular, his sharp tongue would surely make him very much so with his fellow players. But to prove to your own satisfaction that the other Tigers are his friends, you have only to "knock" him in their presence, or assert that Jackson, Wagner, Lajoie, Speaker, or someone else is his superior as a ball player. If they don't just laugh at you they will show temper and express themselves after the manner following: "If you'd travel around with us and see him every day you wouldn't talk about other ball players in the same breath. And if you claim that Wagner or Jackson or anyone else is in a class with him you'd better go to the nearest alienist and have your bean examined. We'll pay the fee."

Ping Bodie's Monologue

CHICAGO TRIBUNE, OCTOBER 3, 1913

If you live on the south side you undoubtedly have gathered from the billboards the info that Frank Bodie has sold his soul—i.e., decided to go on the stage. If the city series is over before Oct. 10 which we earnestly hope and pray will be the case, Ping will open a four days' engagement at the Alhambra on that date. If the city series is not over by Oct. 16, which heaven forbid, Ping will appear the first three days of the following week. So reads his contract, which also provides that his stunt be a monologue, duration not set, subject matter, baseball.

The management assures us that Ping will not be the only thing on the program. The subject, baseball, is a broad one, as is the monologuist. But the chances are that Ping will confine himself to those details or phases of the sport with which he is most familiar. He might talk interestingly on "Pilfering the Pillows" or "Sliding into the Sacks." However, without having seen him for some weeks—not since he accepted the theater's generous offer—we guess that his real theme will be "Inside Ball" and that he will handle it about as follows:

"I can sure hit that old pill.

"Some of you smart guys say I'm solid ivory. Do I look like solid ivory? Or solid anything?

"I don't pull no more boners than some of you smart guys. But Ping's to blame for everything. If Buck misses a fly ball Ping had oughta run in and caught it. It wasn't Buck's fault. It was Ping's. If I'm on first base and they give me the hit and run and I go down, and Larry misses his swing and I get throwed out twenty feet, it's 'Whadd'ya think o' that big bonehead trying to steal?'

"I don't have to play ball in this league. If they don't want me, why don't they can me? I know where I can go and play ball, in the bushes where they pay the money. Couldn't hurt my feelings by canning me. I wish they would let me out. I should worry.

"I can sure hit that old pill.

"I guess I'm a bonehead. I don't know anything. But the guys that talk that way about me are sitting on the bench while I'm out there working and winning ball games. How many games would we have won from Philly if Bonehead Bodie had been on the bench?

"I don't have to play ball. I can go out there to San Fran any time I want to and get a job. But I'll be playing ball long after some of those smart guys have got the can.

"If I'm so rotten, why do the play me? They've got a lot of fellers sitting on the bench, doing nothing. They don't have to use me. Let 'em put me on the bench. Iskabibble.

"I can sure hit that old pill."

One of the most feared sluggers of the 1910s, Frank Stephen Bodie was nicknamed Ping for the sound of his fifty-two ounce bat hitting the era's dead ball. When he played with the Yankees, Bodie was Babe Ruth's first roommate and delivered a classic response when asked about it. "That isn't so. I room with his suitcase."

Matty

THE AMERICAN MAGAZINE, AUGUST 1915

What kind of a pitcher *was* he? Where do you get that "was" stuff? When he's through it'll be time enough to talk about him like he was a dead corpse.

Oh, yes, I've heard all that junk they been pullin', but wait till he comes acrost with four or five good games in a row! Then you won't be able to find nobody that even suspected he was done. The boys that's been writin' subscriptions on his tombstone will pretend as if they was just jokin' and really knowed all the time that he was the same Matty, only a little bit slow about gettin' started.

He's been all in a whole lot o' times before this, if you b'lieved what you read. They was namin' his pallbearers as far back as 1909, and they been layin' him to rest every year since, but when they've drove back downtown from the cemetery they've always found him standin' on Main Street, big as life and wonderin' whose funeral it was. You've heard the old sayin' that a cat's got nine lives? Well, boy, Matty makes a cat look like a sucker.

They called in a special doctor to look him over last time their club was West. He couldn't sleep and they was a pain in his left arm, and his neck kept stiffenin' up on him. The special doctor says it was some kind o' nervous trouble. Great stuff! If Matty was goin' to be bothered with nervousness I guess it would of happened before this. If he was nervous every time he had a chanct to be, he'd of broke both legs ten years ago, knockin' his knees together.

Besides, do you think a stiff neck and a pain in the left arm and unsomnia is goin' to stop him from pitchin'? His brain ain't diseased and he's still got the same right hand he always used. And as for the not sleepin', I never noticed him out there on the field with his eyes shut.

So give him a chanct. The year's still young yet. Leave him get warmed up and then give him a good look. This spring was hard on old soupers. You can't expect a bird that's been hurlin' the pill in the big show fifteen years to set the league afire in June when May mistook itself for Feb'uary. Don't talk like he was gone and ask me what kind of a pitcher *was* he. If you want to know what kind he *is,* I'll try and tell you.

You're just bustin' in, kid, and I don't know if you're there or not. But if you don't want to be huntin' a job as floorwalker or night watchman somewhere in a few years, the best thing you can do is find out all the bad habits Matty's got and then get 'em yourself.

It must be a awful strain on McGraw, handlin' this bird. Unless he keeps his eye right on him, he's li'ble to sneak up to his room some night and play a game o' checkers. That ain't all, neither. If McGraw is ast out to somebody's house or to go to the theayter, he don't enjoy himself on account o' worryin'. How does he know that Matty ain't smokin' a see-gar or lappin' up a dish of ice cream? Mac can't never leave the hotel without bein' a-scared that Matty'll buy a magazine and read it. And I s'pose that oncet or twicet a season he goes all to pieces and chews a stick o' gum.

I don't know if the job o' managing him is worse off the field or on. When he's out there in the box he seems to lose his head entirely. With the bases loaded, they's always a chance that Matty'll make a guy pop out instead o' whiffin' him. Then, with a man on first base and nobody down and the batter sent up to bunt, he's li'ble to forget he's a pitcher and try to do a little fieldin'. You can't never tell. Maybe he'll run in and grab the bunt and force a man at second base, instead o' standin' still like a see-gar sign and hopin' somebody else'll do somethin'. Yes, sir, I bet McGraw don't sleep a wink on the road, or to home neither, from frettin' over this guy and wonderin' how he can learn him somethin'.

They's a flock o' pitchers that knows a batter's weakness and works accordin'. But they ain't nobody else in the world that can stick a ball as near where they want to stick it as he can. I bet he could shave you if he wanted to and if he had a razor blade to throw instead of a ball. If you can't hit a fast one a inch and a quarter inside and he knows it, you'll get three fast ones a inch and a quarter inside and then, if you've swang at 'em, you can go and get a drink o' water. He plays a lot o' this here golf, and I bet if they'd let him throw at the hole instead o' shootin' with a club, he'd stick 'em in there just as often as he wanted to from sixty foot away.

I ain't tryin' to make you believe that he don't never fail to pitch where he's aimin' at. If he done that, he wouldn't be here; he'd be workin' agin the angels in St. Peter's League. But he's got ten to one better control than any guy I ever seen, and I've saw all the best o' them. If one o' these here Af'can dodgers[4] seen him comin', he'd either quit his job or fix it up for a A.D.T. boy[5] to notify his widow, 'cause even iv'ry'll crack if it's hammered steady enough.

I s'pose when he broke in he didn't have no more control than the rest o' these here colleges. But the diff'rence between they and him was that he seen what a good thing it was to have, and went out and got it, while they, that is, the most o' them, thought they could go along all right with what they had. Well, you don't see many o' Matty's schoolmates pitchin' in the league now, do you?

Matty didn't never take the trouble to tell me nothin' about himself and how he got wise. Maybe he seen in the Bible where it says about you should not ought to ride a good horse to death. That's it, ain't it? He's just like one o' these here misers. They get a-hold of a lot of money and then they don't let none of it go, except just enough to keep 'em from starvin'. Instead o' money, Matty got a-hold of a curve ball and there here fadeaway and a pretty fair fast one and a slow one and a bunch o' control, and then he locked it all up and took a little bit of it out to spend when nec'sary, only most o' what he's been spendin' is control, which he's got the most of, and which it don't hurt him none to spend it.

Take him in a common ordinary ball game, agin a average club, and every day pitchin', and what he's tryin' to do is stick the first one over so's he won't have to waste no more'n one ball on one batter. He don't stick it over right in the groove, but he puts it just about so's you'll get a piece of it and give the Giants a little easy fieldin' practice. If the Giants gets a flock o' runs and goes way out in front, he'll keep right on stickin' that first one over, and maybe he'll allow a little scorin'.

But if the guy workin' agin him is airtight, and the game's close, and you get a couple o' men on and a base hit'll do some damage, he unlocks his safe and pulls out some o' the real stuff he's got and lets go of it. Maybe the curve he'll show you ain't as good as some you've saw, but it'll come where you can't get a good hold of it. Or if it's a fast one you don't like, that's what you'll get, and even if it ain't as fast as Johnson's, you'll find that it comes past you a couple of inches higher or lower or this side or that side of where you could wallop it good. Or maybe you'll see this fadeaway that he got up himself, and it's about as easy to hit as this here Freddie Welsh.[6]

That's the way he works in a reg'lar game, when they ain't much dependin' on it. He don't really pitch till he's got to, and then he sure does pitch. The rest o' the time, he's puttin' that first one where they either got to hit at it or have a strike called on 'em, and leavin' it to the guys back of him to take care o' what's hit. That's why he's been good so long and that's why he's goin' to be good a whole lot longer. And McGraw's smart enough to help him save himself. You don't see Matty pitch one day and warm up the next. When he's pitched his game, he's through till everybody else has tooken their turn, except oncet in a while, when the race gets hot, and then maybe he works a innin' or two and pulls out one o' the other guy's games, besides winnin' his own. But that ain't often. He ain't never tried to make no Walsh[7] out of himself, and if he had tried, the Giants might maybe of win one more pennant, but they wouldn't have no Matty round to keep 'em in the race for another.

McGraw treats him just right to keep him a-goin'. But I don't give Mac no credit for that. He'd be a sucker if he didn't. It's pretty soft for a manager to be able to set down by the fire in January and say to himself: "Well, we got to win ninety-five games next season to cop. That means that Marquard, Tesh-er-eau and my young fellas must grab seventy between 'em. Matty's twenty-five is already in."

When it comes to a World's Serious, that's diff'rent. If the Giants wins it, it means more dough, not only for the players but for the owners o' the club. And as soon as it's over, Matty's got five months to rest up.

So he's in there about every other day, and he ain't savin' himself neither. He's still tryin' to get that first one over, but they's a lot more stuff on it than when he's pitchin' a reg'lar season game. He ain't so willin' to let guys get on the bases and he's ready to do more work himself and leave less to his club. Well, the Giants hasn't set the world afire beatin' the clubs in our league, but where'd they of been in any one o' them Serious's if 'twasn't for Matty? And if you want to make them Ath-a-letics or the Boston Red Sox either one give you the horse laugh, tell 'em Matty's easy to beat.

He's been beat in every big Serious he's been in, except in 1905, when he was still a kid. You know what he done then, don't you? He worked three o' the five games and if goose eggs had of been worth a dollar a dozen, the Ath-a-letics could of quit playin' ball and toured the world in a taxi. As I say, he's been beat in all the other big Seriouses, but I seen the most o' them and I'm tellin' you that most o' the games he lost was a crime.

You know, kid, I'm with our league all the while and pullin' for 'em whatever they're up agin. But they's been times when I felt like as if we should ought to be ashamed to take the money, when I couldn't holler none over winnin' because I was feelin' so sorry for this big guy we'd beat and didn't have no business to beat. A man can't have no real time celebratin' when he knows that if the luck had of broke even, he'd be payin' off. At least, I can't.

I wisht you could of saw him tryin' to hold a jubilee that night in Boston a couple o' years ago. The Red Sox winnin' give me a even two hundred bucks, but all the while I was spendin' it, I felt like as if it didn't belong to me. Honest, I'd of almost gave it back and seen the Boston club licked rather than to of saw 'em win me the dough the way they did. If I'd of stayed in Chi and just read about it in the papers, it wouldn't of been so bad. But to be right there and see him get robbed o' that decidin' game, and the honors that should ought to of been his'n, was enough to upset my stomach and take all the joy out o' the two hundred.

You remember how it was: They'd win three apiece, and the Giants was full o' the old con-feed-i-ence, while the Boston club's dauber was way down in their shoe. They'd had the Serious all but won, three games to one, and then New York had came along and evened it up. McGraw has Matty ready and Stahl[8] uses this young Bedient, who'd pitched a whale of a game a few days before, but was nothin' but a kid and up agin a tougher proposition than a kid should ought to be ast to face.

Well, I'll have to slip it to young Bedient. He was about as nervous as if he was pitchin' to the batters in practice. You'd of thought, to watch him, that it was a exhibition game and that the only crowd there was a few hundred rubes from Jones's Crossing. He wasn't a bit scared, and he give 'em a awful battle. The Giants got a run off'n him; I don't remember when or how they done it. Anyway, they done well to get a run and the bugs should ought to of throwed their money at him when he was tooken out.

I think it was the eighth innin' when Bedient got through. The run scored off'n him was the only one o' the game, 'cause Matty was workin' like they ain't nobody else can work. With that "1" up on the score board, it looked all over. I didn't think they'd tie it up in a thousand years. Well, in Boston's half o' the eighth, or seventh, maybe it was, Stahl or Wagner happened to get a hold of one and cracked it for two bases. They was down to the tail-end o' the battin' order and I think one was out before the ball was hit.

Whoever the guy was, he was left there till they was two out and it come Bedient's turn to hit. Stahl took him out and sent up this Henriksen. He was a new one on Matty, and it's a good thing for him he was. The count come to two and two on him and then he reached outside the plate and cracked one down the third base line. It was a two-bagger and the score was tied up. Hooper went out and the innin' was over. The crowd went crazy, but, honest, I figured that was the last run the Boston club would ever get and that it was just a question o' time till the Giants grabbed another and settled it.

Stahl sticks Woodie in to pitch and they was no scorin' did on neither side in the ninth. But in the tenth, Murray catched one o' Woodie's fast ones on the nose and drove it a mile into center field. It come near clearin' the whole works and bein' a home run. It didn't make no diff'rence, 'cause Merkle was there with a base hit and Murray scored. They was two down when Meyers come up, and he hit one just as hard as he ever did in his life. The ball come right at Woodie and hit him in the side. He was game enough to pick it up and throw it to first base, but I bet he couldn't of pitched another ball if his life had of depended on it.

They helped him off'n the field and they was a pretty sad lookin' gang. They figured just like me: That they'd been lucky to tie up the score in the seventh or eighth, or whenever it was, and that they had about as much chance as a rabbit o' doin' it again.

Then come the mess that spoiled my meals for a week, and me pullin' my head off for Jake and the boys. Jake sends Engel up in Woodie's place for two reasons: because he's a better hitter, though Woodie ain't no bum at that, and because Woodie prob'ly couldn't of walked that far. Well, Engel sends a fly ball to center field and it should ought to have been the one out. But it wasn't. Snodgrass drops it and Engel pulls up at second base. Now they're playin' for one run and Hooper goes up to sacrifice. I never seen no better pitchin' than Matty done to him, and they was no more chance of him buntin' the first two fair than they was o' hittin' 'em out o' the park. I think he missed one entirely and fouled the other one. Then Matty gives him one that he couldn't meet right and he flies out to center. Snodgrass held onto this one. Well, I guess Matty must of gave Hooper everything he had, 'cause when Yerkes came up, the old control was gone. He walked him, and everybody went completely nuts, 'cause it was Speaker's turn.

The Giants crowded round Matty to give him a chance to rest up, and when he begin pitchin' to Speaker, he wasn't wild no more. He slips Spoke one that he had to take a wallop at, but all he done to it was pop it up in the air. The ball was foul and I guess I could of jumped out o' the stand and ran out and catched it. But Merkle thought Meyers was goin' to get it, and Meyers thought Merkle was goin' to get it and finally Matty seen they wasn't neither one going' to get it, so he started after it, but he was too late. The ball fell about fifteen feet this side o' the coaches' box, and when it come down they wasn't nobody under it.

I could hear Spoke yellin': "Pretty lucky that time, Matty! But I'll crack the next one." Speaker's all right, but he should not ought to of called Matty lucky; not that day. If he was lucky that day, I'd hate to see him when things was breakin' agin him.

This foul ball o' Spoke's was the third out by rights. The game should ought to of been over, and me settlin' with the guy I made the bet with. But the way things had came off, they was one out, and men on second and first and Speaker up, and I don't care who the pitcher is, he can't fool this here Speaker all the time. Spoke done just what he said. He cracked one and before Devore could get it back to the infield, Engel was acrost with the tyin' run, and another base hit would finish it.

I'd like to of knew what Matty was thinkin' about. He could be excused if he said "Golly," even if he don't pitch on Sundays. But if he was sore, he kept it to himself, and he went out there and give Lewis what he had left. He was just as wild as when he was pitchin' to Yerkes; that is, he wasn't exactly wild, but he wasn't given' 'em no good balls to hit and he couldn't bunk 'em into swingin' at bad ones. Lewis stood up there just as patient as Yerkes, and Matty walked him, too.

That's about all they was to it. The bases was choked and Gardner wound it up with a fly ball to Devore, which should ought to of been four out. Yerkes come in with the winnin' run and I guess Devore's throw is just about gettin' to the plate now.[9]

That's how lucky Matty was in that last game in Boston, and that's a fair sample o' the luck he's had in all these World's Seriouses except the first one. If a rotten pitcher got a dose like that, I wouldn't slip him no sympathy. But it sure does give me the colic to have them things happen to a guy that don't have to take off his hat to nobody, and then see the bugs run round hollerin', "Well, I guess we can beat the great Mathewson!" Yeh, they can beat him with a whole blacksmith's shop full o' horseshoes.

What makes him the pitcher he is? I been tellin' you he's got a lot o' stuff, but so has other pitchers. They's others that's got pretty near as good control, but they ain't nobody that's got the combination like him and knows how to use it like he does, he's a tight-wad with his stuff, and they're spendthrifts. Some pitchers can't see Wagner come up without wantin' to whiff him and hear the crowd cheer. Matty don't want to whiff him. He'd a lot rather have him hit the first ball and pop it up in the air. Cheers won't do them others no good when their souper's gone. They can't live on what the crowd thought about 'em that time they made the big Dutchman take a drink o' water. Then, he's got this fadeaway that none o' the rest has got; not like he's got it.

His curve is somethin' like Joe Wood's, only now he ain't as fast as Woodie; that is, not all the time. Maybe he's got enough real speed left to cut loose a little of it two or three times a day, and he don't never cut it loose till he's got to. But goin' along that way, he'll have his fader and his curve and his speed when I and you is thinkin' about who we'll call on for pallbearers.

But his fadeaway and his curve and his fast one and his control wouldn't none of 'em be worth near what they is worth if he didn't know all they is to know about pitchin'. It's the old bean that makes him what he is. When somebody cracks one off'n him, it ain't because he guessed wrong; it's because the ball come about a inch away from where he was goin' to put it; maybe it slipped or somethin'. When this young Saier has pulled one over the fence on Matty, McGraw don't say:

"Why didn't you keep it outside?" or "Why didn't you do this or that?" He knows Matty was tryin' to do the right thing and knowed what was the right thing to do. He don't have to sit up nights with him, learnin' him. And it ain't nec'sary for Matty to buy one o' these here books on "The Art o' Pitchin'." He could write a whole sacklapedia on that, and then not tell half he knows.

He's just a little ahead o' the rest o' the gang in them things—stuff, when he wants to use it, and control and noodle. And besides that, he's a ball player. They ain't no danger of him hittin' .400, but at that they's a whole lot worse hitters right on his club. When he goes up there with a bat, it ain't just to kill time or because it's his turn. His intention is to get on, or to push somebody else round, or drive in a run, and he don't swing at everything that's pitched or keep his bat on his shoulder neither, like some o' them pitchers. He's been known to crack one when it counted, and you don't often look in the papers and see "So-and-So batted for Mathewson in the ninth."

He ain't no speed marvel on the bases, yet I've saw him steal a base and slide into it, too, where most pitchers would be a-scared they might soil their pants. As for fieldin' his position, he's just as good as anybody, and to have him in there is just like havin' five men on the infield. He can grab the bunts, and after he's grabbed 'em he knows where to peg 'em. He don't never fail to cover first base when he should ought to, and you'll always find him backin' up plays where some pitchers would be takin' a afternoon nap. Yes, sir, he's a ball player, and that's a whole lot more'n you can say for a lot o' guys that's gettin' by with a pitchin'job.

They tell me Matty is some golf player. I didn't never have no golf bat in my hands, and I don't know nothin' about the game, but I bet all I got that if he plays it at all, he plays it good. Yes, sir, I bet he's a whale of a golf player, and they tell me they ain't no ball player can touch him in a checker game. Well, I've did some checker playin' myself, and I know they ain't no thick skull can get away with it. It's a game that takes brains, and Matty's the boy that's got 'em. But if he was to tackle blind man's buff instead o' checkers or golf, he'd make a go of it. That's the kind o' guy he is. They's nothin' he's tried that he didn't keep tryin' till he could do it and do it good.

It didn't surprise me none when he turned down that trip round the world. I guess none o' the boys that made the trip is any the worse off for it, but it wouldn't of been in line with Matty's dope to go along. It would just of meant spendin' some o' the stuff he's savin' up to keep him in the league. Every game he pitched would of been just one less game he'd of had left in him, and the games wouldn't of got him nothin' neither. And still, he'd of had to let himself out and do some real pitchin', or else the crowds would of got sore on him. At that, I guess he'd of went if he hadn't of made the first part o' the trip with 'em, the trip from Cincinnati out to the Coast. They tell me that he had to shake hands with two thirds o' the population of every burg they stopped at. The bugs flocked round the train, and the hotels, all yelpin' for Matty, and it was up to him to let 'em see him, or they'd of been a riot. Well, they all had to shake hands with him, and by the time a couple o' million hicks has shooken your hand, you feel like as if your old souper was beginnin' to go back on you. I s'pose that's the way you'd feel; I don't know, 'cause I wasn't never pestered much with people tryin' to slip me the glad hand. Matty prob'ly says to himself: "London and Paris and Egypt and Rome and them other towns on the schedule is all big towns with big populations. If half them populations shakes hands with me, I won't have no more arm left than a angle-worm." So he scratched his entry, and you can't blame him. And I bet McGraw didn't coax him much.

When the Giants don't want Matty no longer, he can make a world trip of his own, and go acrost the ocean in his own yackt. But I guess by that time they'll be runnin' trains acrost or maybe the oceans will of went dry.

College man, war hero, Christian Gentleman (one of his actual nicknames), Christy Mathewson may have been the most beloved baseball player of his time. Whereas players like Ty Cobb, Honus Wagner, and Walter Johnson were admired—Lardner did a similarly appreciative long article on Cobb for *The American Magazine* in 1915—they were not adored in the manner of Mathewson.

Lardner's hopes that Mathewson's poor start in 1915 was nothing to worry about were not realized. He won only eight games and lost fourteen, a great comedown from his 24-13 record the year before. The following year he was traded to the last-place Cincinnati Reds, which inspired Lardner to write the following poem, which is sometimes mistaken for an obituary. Mathewson died in 1925 of tuberculosis, which he developed after a chemical gas attack during a World War I training exercise in France.

My eyes are very misty
As I pen these lines to Christy;
Oh, my heart is full of heaviness today.
May the flowers ne'er wither, Matty
On your grave in Cincinnati,
Which you've chosen for your final fadeaway.

Mordecai Brown: The Reporter's Friend

CHICAGO TRIBUNE, DECEMBER 6, 1916

So far as the big leagues are concerned, Mordecai Brown, they say, is through. If the gentleman from Indiana needs consolation he may perhaps find a bit in the knowledge, hereby imparted to him, that there is more genuine regret among the baseball writers of our beautiful city over his departure than over the passing of any other athlete whose work has redounded to the honor and glory of Chicago, etc.

Brownie was not only the most popular ball player among the ball players, but also far and away the most general favorite among the scribes.

That he was liked and respected by fellow members of the Cub pitching staff, speaks volumes for his personality. Pitchers, most of them, are human, and being human, not apt to harbor the tenderest feelings toward those indubitably their superiors in skill. Brownie was, in his top form, the best of a great pitching corps. Yet every other member of that corps was sincerely fond of him.

However, we are dealing here with his standing with the newspaper men. He was not a live source of news, owing to his reticence. His modesty prevented his giving us valuable columns about himself for use on rainy days.

But he could tell, by looking at you, when you were broke. While you were still wondering from whom to borrow five, he would come up and, without a word, hand you ten.

As present day salaries go, he was drawing far less than he was worth. But he was drawing far more than were we reporters, and knowing this, it hurt him to see us spend. So he did most of the spending for us, against our protest, of course.

We (editorially, this time) never fully appreciated Brownie, though he had done us innumerable favors, until one day in the season of 1909. It was the last day in Philadelphia and the next stop was in New York. We had a tentative engagement in New York at eight-thirty that evening, an engagement we wanted to keep. In the forenoon, we sought out Charlie Williams, the walking time-table.

"Is there a train out of here for New York round six o'clock?" we asked.

"Why?"

"I want to get there early this evening."

"So does everybody else," said Charley.

(Everybody was young then.)

"There's a train on the Reading at six," continued Charley, "and we can get it at the station near the park if the game's over in time. I asked Shettsline[10] if he'd start early, but he wouldn't. So we'll just have to take chances."

The P. L. tried to help by selecting as pitcher, Orval Overall, one of the fastest workers in the pastime. Big Orrie proved fast, and effective, too, but no more effective than Sparks of the enemy. At the end of the eleventh, we had given up hope of an extra evening on Broadway, for it was a quarter after five and everything pointed to a long tie.

But in their twelfth, the desperate Cubs fell on the Philly pitcher and drove home two runs, the first of the game.

"Now, if he can just hold 'em!" we said, and started making up the box score.

But the Phillies weren't quite through. The top of their batting order was up, and whoever was lead-off man singled. Otto Knabe walked and the next gentleman sacrificed. A base hit would tie it again, and two such wretched hitters as Magee and Bransfield were in line.

Out went Orrie and in came Brown; the tying run on second base; the crowd barking at him; one out, and Philadelphia's best batsmen to face.

Six balls Brownie pitched, six curve balls, the curvin'est balls we ever saw. And three times apiece Magee and Bransfield swung, and missed threes time apiece.

While the Cubs hurriedly changed their clothes, we as hurriedly wrote our story; a story about one per cent as good as the game warranted.

On the train we shook the three-fingered hand.

"Much obliged, Brownie. I've got a date in New York this evening."

"So Charley said," replied Mr. Brown. "Come on in the next car and I'll buy you dinner."

Mordecai Brown, nicknamed "Three Finger" because of a childhood farm-machinery accident, won 239 Major League games, and his 2.06 lifetime earned-run average was third lowest in history. Lardner's affection for him was returned, as shown in a letter Brown wrote to *The Sporting News* when his "Pullman Pastimes" articles were reprinted in 1941. "That series should bring back many happy memories for us old-timers," wrote Brown, who was then sixty-five and operating a gas station in Terre Haute, Indiana. "Ring is dead, but all of us old Cubs remember his rich humor and the youngsters of today should get a kick out of his yarns, too."

Noisy John Kling

CHICAGO TRIBUNE, MAY 16, 1917

The Cubs nicknamed him Noisy because they thought he didn't say anything. But the gentlemen who hit against the Cubs when he was catching, especially the very young gentlemen, will tell you there was never a catcher who could tie him for garrulity.

"His line of chatter was effective, too," says Larry Doyle.[11] "McGraw warned me, when I broke in, that Kling would try to get my goat, but the warning led me to expect that he'd be rough, the way the catchers had been in the Three Eye, when I was a recruit there. They'd called me a busher and criticized my appearance and found fault with my swing. They had me so mad for a while that I couldn't do myself justice, but when I got up nerve enough to give them as good as they sent, I had them stopped.

"Kling was different. His stuff kept my mind off what I was trying to do, and a kid facing pitchers like Brown, Pfiester, Overall, and Reulbach didn't have much chance unless he concentrated.

"First time I met him was at the Polo Grounds. I came up in the first inning.

"'Well, Boyle,' he said, 'I bet you're glad to get away from Davenport.'

"I told him my name was Doyle and that I came from Springfield.

"'Did you always hit left-handed out there?' he asked me, and while I was saying yes, Brownie slipped over a fast ball for a strike.

"'You stand up like a veteran,' said Kling. 'From the way you hold your bat and stand, I'd say a curve ball wouldn't bother you any more than a fast one.'

"I told him I didn't know which I'd rather hit.

"'Well,' he said, 'we'll have to try you on both and find out. This next one's going to be a curve.'

"Then I thought to myself that it would surely be a fast one and I got all set to crack it. It was a curve and I guess I pretty near broke my bat swinging.

"'You thought I was stringing you,' said Kling. 'You don't know me. But you took a mighty nice cut at that ball and now I know you're stuck on the fast ones. So I guess we'll have to slip you another curve.'

"So Brownie pitched another curve and again I was looking for a fast one and I was out on strikes.

"'Don't blame that on me,' said Kling. 'It's your own fault if you don't take a fella's advice.'

"When I got back to the bench, McGraw asked me whether Kling had been riding me. I told him no; that he'd talked all right.

"'You forget that!' said Mac. 'Don't pay any attention to anything he says. He's John Bull.'

"But I made a nice play on the infield before it was my next turn to hit, and when I went up there again he wasn't talking curves and fast balls. It was all about what a beautiful stop that was, and how I looked as if I'd make good whether I could hit or not. And he made me foul out on a bad ball in the pinch.

"I'll bet it was two or three series before I learned not to listen to Kling and I don't know how many base hits I lost by my innocence. But I have one consolation. I know of other players in the National league who didn't get wise to him for years, and they weren't bushers either."

An exceptional defensive catcher, Kling played a key role on the Cubs' world championship teams in the first decade of the Twentieth Century. He was also an excellent pool player and several times threatened to stay home and play the game professionally if the Cubs didn't pay him more. In 1909, he actually did so and won the world's championship of pool while the Cubs finished second in the National League. He returned the following season and the Cubs won the pennant.

Casting Stones with Rollie Zeider

CHICAGO TRIBUNE, MAY 23, 1917

The editor has just received a letter which begins, "Dear Owl-eyes." A person who remarks on or calls attention to the physical defects of others is perhaps unworthy of notice, but in this case the writer is so manifestly unfair that we cannot resist brief comment in defense of ourself and in justice to humanity.

In the first place, any one who has seen us will testify that our eyes are probably our most elegant feature. They are large and lustrous, expressive to a remarkable degree and practically irresistible. They compare very favorably with Anna Held's.[12]

In the second place, the person who wrote the letter is not what you could call a Venus D. Milo. If we look like an owl, he certainly is twins with a parrot.

The person who wrote the letter is said to be a ball player, but has never succeeded in proving it. At different times he has occupied every position on the infield, but has failed to make good in any. He cannot field, he cannot run bases, he cannot think; in fact, he cannot do nothing except ridicule the personal appearance of others.

This person was at third base for a time, but the occupants of the third base seats objected to the management, claiming their view of the shortstop was shut off by his profile. He was shifted to second base, but his nose prevented the center fielder from seeing the first baseman. He moved to first base, but the other infielders were so affected by his appearance that they could not throw straight. This person is now trying to play shortstop and making a mess of it.

This person once batted .300 and stole over 100 bases in the Pacific Coast league. It must have been a fine league.

Some enemy of Mr. Comiskey's recommended him to the White Sox and he tried to play the different infield positions on the south side. He made a mess of it. He is now with the Cubs.

His limbs look like a wishbone.

He came from Auburn, Ind.

Many believe he is a German spy.

A utility infielder who played all four positions, Zeider is one of a handful of players who played for three Chicago teams—the Cubs, White Sox, and Whales of the short-lived Federal League. One of the fastest players in the game, Zeider's 49 stolen bases for the White Sox in 1910 remained the club record until 1986.

Casey in the Field

CHICAGO TRIBUNE, MAY 13, 1919

Characters.

Casey Stengel, Pittsburgh's right fielder.
Bugs, occupants of the right field stand.

Time—Sunday P.M.
Place—Cubs' park.

Act 1.

[Pittsburgh's first inning is over. Casey, who has flied out, dons glove and sun glasses and takes his position.]

A Bug—Well, Casey, back to Pittsburgh for you.
Casey—O, I get three more raps today yet.
Second Bug—You ought to be wrappin' bundles somewheres.
Casey—That's what you do week days, I guess.
Second Bug—Do you want me to git you a job?
Casey—Not in a cheap dump like where you work at.
Second Bug—Well, we wouldn't have you there.
Casey—Well, don't worry. I ain't lookin' for a job.
Second Bug—Well, you will be lookin' for one if you don't wake up.
Casey—You should worry.
Third Bug—What do you wear them glasses fur, Casey? Can't you see without them glasses?
Fourth Bug—He's gittin' old. His eyes is failin' him.
Casey—You should worry.

Act 2.

[Pittsburgh's fourth inning is over. Casey has been called out on strikes and is pretty mad about it]

A Bug—Never mind, Casey. You can't hit 'em if you can't see 'em.
Second Bug—Was the sun in your eyes, Casey? You ought to wore them glasses up to the bat.
Casey—Some of them umpires ought to wear them, I guess.
Third Bug—Why, what's the matter with them umpires, Casey?
Casey—O, they's nothin' the matter with them umpires. They're the best in the league except when I'm up there.
Third Bug—You better shet up or they'll tie a can to you.
Casey—You better shut up yourself.

Act 3.

[Pittsburgh's sixth inning is over. Casey has been left on second base, which he reached on an error by Pick.]

A Bug—Well, Casey, you didn't git fur.

Second Bug—That was some hit, Casey. It pretty near got past the second baseman.

Casey—I should worry as long as I get on there.

Third Bug—Douglas is makin' a monkey out of you.

Casey—Well, you're makin' a monkey out of yourself.

Third Bug—And you're makin' a monkey out of yourself, too.

Casey—Well, I get paid for makin' a monkey out of myself. But you pay to get in here and make a monkey out of yourself. That's the difference between you and I.

Third Bug—You won't be gittin' paid very long if you keep this up.

Casey—You should worry.

Act 4.

[Pittsburgh's eighth inning is over. Casey has flied out again.]

A Bug—Well, Casey, you've had your four raps. You're some rapper.

Casey—Well, I either get out or I don't get out, so I should worry.

Third Bug—Your team's licked, Casey.

Casey—Yes, we never win when I don't hit.

Third Bug—You must be in last place, then.

Fourth Bug—How'd you like to play on a good team, Casey?

Third Bug—It wouldn't be a good team no more with him on it.

Fifth Bug—Well, good-by, Casey. Don't forgit to write.

Fourth Bug—He can't write.

Casey—Neither can you.

How to Pitch to Babe Ruth

BELL SYNDICATE, AUGUST 8, 1920

To the Editor:

This is just a few items of information about a ball player that maybe you haven't never heard of him so I will tell his name in the first paragraph and his name is George Ruth but they call him Babe on acct. of him being over 6 ft. tall and pretty near as wide and he is a great left hand pitcher that don't pitch.

Well 1 day in May I had seen a whole lot of different sporting events that bores you to death and the White Sox from old Chi was playing in New York City so I thought I needed a little more boreing and I went out to Polo's grounds and went down on the bench and Mgr. Gleason was setting there and he says hello to me, but I just made a face at him, but he asked me to set down a minute and a boy name Wilkinson was going to pitch and he was out there warming up and finely he got warm and come into the bench and Mgr. Gleason said:

"Come here and set down a minute Wilkie, as I want to talk to you."

So Wilkie set down and Mgr. Gleason said to him:

"Say listen Wilkie. They's a man on this New York club name Ruth and he isn't Cobb and he isn't Speaker or Sisler or Jackson. He's a bird that if you ever throw a ball where he can reach it, that ball won't be available for tomorrow's game and baseballs cost as much money as other commodities now days, so if you don't mind, why when this guy comes up there don't pitch him nothing that he can lay his bat against it, but roll the ball up there on the ground and I will take the consequences." So Wilkie said yes sir.

Well they started this game in the first inning and the White Sox didn't do nothing and it comes the N.Y. club's turns to get their innings and they was 2 out and Pipp got on 1st. base and along come Ruth. The next I seen of that two dollar ball was when it was floating over the right field bleachers. So when Wilkie come in to the bench Mgr. Gleason says what did I tell you and Wilkie said I didn't mean to pitch it where it went.

So the next time Babe come up all as he got was a 3 base hit cause they were pitching more careful to him. Well after a wile it come necessary to put in a pinch hitter for Wilkie and little Dickie Kerr was sent in to finish the game. Mgr. Gleason didn't tell Dickie where to pitch to Babe because Dickie's what you might call a old timer, so Dickie pitched one at this bird's Adam apple and he hit it into the right field stand for another homer, as I have nicknamed them.

Now this isn't no reflection on neither of these pitchers which I hope is both friends of mine, but, if I was managing a ball club in the American League, I would tell them how to pitch to this bird. I would stand on the mound and throw the first ball to first base and the second ball to second base and the third ball to third base, and then I would turn around and heave the fourth one out in right field, because he couldn't be in all those places at once, and further and more they's a rule that makes a batter stand in the batter's box and if a person pitches in that direction with this guy up why all you can say about them is that they're a sucker.

For inst. the last time the White Sox was here, a certain prominent Chicago baseball writer was setting next to Col. Huston that owns a chunk of the Yanks and this George Ruth comes up and the Col. says to him how much will you bet that he don't crack one out of the park on this occasion. So the baseball writer says what's the proper odds. So the Col. says well I don't want to cheat you and I will bet a pt. to qt. that he murders one. So the sucker took it and the first ball was a foul that went into Mr. Schalk's ft. and the next was a ball and then the old boy took one right over the middle for another strike and the next one hasn't yet been located, but when last seen was soreing over a cigarette sign in right center.

The most useless thing in the world when this guy's up there to bat is the opposeing catcher, because if you can throw a ball past Mr. Ruth why it don't make no difference if it's catched or not, whereas if you try and throw one over the plate, it won't never get as far as the catcher.

A couple wks. ago a guy come here with the St. Louis Brown and struck the Babe out 5 times in 1 afternoon and if he is smart he will let that go down into posterity and the next time they tell him its his turn to pitch vs the N.Y. Club he will say he has got a sore arm.

Baseball Poems

Lardner began including poems in his baseball coverage as early as 1910, his second season covering the Cubs. They usually appeared in notes at the end of his game stories and were often "written" by Frank Schulte, the Cubs' right fielder. Schulte was an excellent ballplayer who twice led the National League in home runs and won two World Series with the Cubs. Beyond his ability as a player, Schulte was a kindred spirit and Lardner was lucky to find him. A clubhouse entertainer who specialized in satire, poetry, and comic depictions of his teammates, Schulte was clearly an influence on Lardner's early depictions of baseball players, in both his journalism and fiction. At first Lardner adopted Schulte's verses; later, with the player's acquiescence, he simply took over his voice. Lardner became so protective of Schulte's work, in fact, that he complained about how it was treated by his editors. "They are making such awful mistakes with Mr. Schulte's poetry up in The Tribune office," he wrote Ellis Abbott, the woman he would marry, "that I am almost discouraged by it, or with it, and will pass it up entirely unless they leave it alone. It is bad enough to start with, without their ruining it."

On March 6, 1910, after injuring a finger in a spring-training game in New Orleans, Schulte wrote:

> Right field it is not play,
> I proved that very fact today;
> Yes, yes, I showed them how today.
> The first fly ball that came my way,
> I caught it on my finger's end.
> It made my finger break or bend.
> So just remember this one thing,
> Get out there early in the spring.
> And stick your finger through the ball,
> And then lay off till next fall.

On April 12, after a game was rained out, Schulte wrote:

Rain, rain, go away.
Save yourself for some sad day,
When Schulte doesn't want to play.
Now I don't mind a little storm
Quite early in the day.
But when I've donned my uniform
I'd sooner, rather play.

Though Schulte would remain Lardner's go-to poet, other players were also given a chance to exhibit their literary style. Heine Zimmerman, the Cubs' third baseman, led the league in batting and home runs in 1912 and when he put together a 23-game hitting streak early in the season, Lardner wrote the following on May 23:

Heine Zimmerman's exuberant spirits, resulting from his tremendous batting streak, have overflowed in the form of poetry. "If Schulte can write it, why can't I?" remarked Heine last night, and slipped us this child of his brain:

There is an outfielder named Frankie,
He's homely and ugly and lanky.
A good hitter once,
But now he just bunts,
And daily grows more and more cranky.

There is a third baseman called Heine,
A better third baseman than Steiny;
When, he meets one square,
Each lady bug fair
Says: "Golly, I wish he was meine."

By the time Lardner returned to Chicago after his year in St. Louis and Boston, he was confident enough to use rhymes in his game coverage—or, rather, in his off-day and rainout coverage—as in the following lead from the *Chicago Examiner* on April 13, 1912:

It didn't rain so awful hard, it didn't rain so much; there wasn't any blizzard that could really be called such; we asked most everybody that we met upon the street and couldn't find a single soul who'd swear that there was sleet; we asked some information from the man who gathered mail, and he said that nowhere on his route had he encountered hail; we ran across a pioneer who'd lived here since a boy, and he vowed he'd seen a stronger wind sometimes in Illinois; but the awful combination of the wind and rain and all, it rendered quite impossible the scheduled game of ball.

And so the Cubs, who play (at times) with so much skill and science, were forced to wait until today to get back at the Giants . . .

When Lardner noted another rainout in the same fashion on July 12, the *Examiner* copy desk responded with a headline that neatly captured the spirit of the story:

Sox and Athletics Have to Fly
For When One Inning Has Gone By
Water Issues From the Sky

Philadelphia, Pa.—The lightning flashed, the thunder roared, and then suddenly there leaked and poured the wettest rain that ever caused a postponement of a game. Now, just one inning had gone by when water issued from the sky. One inning of a game you know will never in the records go. But still, if you would like to hear what happened, listen, reader, dear.

The pitcher for the Sox was Benz, who in the Winter butchers hens. Chief Bender was Mack's pitcher bold. He's pretty good, but pretty old. Well, Rath could find no ball he liked, and, sad to say, right out he striked. But Captain Lord, sometimes called Harry, beat out an infield hit to Barry. Jack Collins, who does lots of things, on this occasion took three swings. Ping Bodie's name was quickly Dennis; he died from Barry to McInnis.

And when he accompanied the White Sox to Boston, the following appeared on August 26, 1912:

Boston, Mass.—Dear Reader: Here we are once more in Boston by the ocean's shore, in Massachusetts' famous town, the fish is fresh and bread is brown, where it is sure a royal treat to eat and eat and eat and eat.

Three men are missing from the fold, the rest are lonesome, young and old. Ed Walsh, he stopped in Meridian to see his two kids once again. He'll be here in the morning mail to beat the Red Sox without fail. Jack Collins went to Pittsfield, Mass., to call upon his fair young lass. At least, that's what the boys all said; when we asked Jack, he turned real red.

Well, there's another absentee, the holder of the captaincy. Way amid the pines of Maine to see his family again went our smart captain Harry Lord, for virtue is its own reward. He's going to remain up there till we have had our first affair with Boston's Red Sox, then return, his well known salary to earn . . .

There were also were times when Lardner would write a poetic sidebar to his main story, as in this one from the *Examiner* of July 22, 1912:

New York—We interviewed the latest addition to the pitching corps [Eddie Cicotte] on the proper pronunciation of his name. Here, is what he has to say:

This pretty name of mine is not,
As some folks claim, just plain Si-cot;
Nor is it, as some would have it, Sic-ot,
Although I'm sure I don't know why not.
And furthermore, take this from me,
I don't pronounce it Sick-o-tee;
And you can also make a note
That it is surely not Si-cote.
You stand to win some easy cash
By betting it's not succotash,
Nor is it sassafras so cute,
Nor any other kind of fruit.
I do not call it Kokomo,
Though many folks pronounce it so.
I guess you're wise enough to know
That this sweet name's not Cicero.

And now you've learned it's none of those
Why I will just jump back to prose
And tell you plainly, truthfully,
The way you should refer to me

Having muttered all this, he went on to inform us that the proper way is See-cot, with the accent on the first syllable, as in Fogarty, McIntyre, Lord or Rath.

Lardner's use of poems in what were, after all, reports of games, might have seemed out of place to some readers, but once he returned to the *Tribune* in 1913 to write "In the Wake of the News," there could be no complaints. He had a columnist's latitude now and he meant to use it. His very first "Wake" column, which appeared on June 3, gave a sample of what was in store as he celebrated the fact that he would no longer be a traveling baseball writer:

Opening Chorus

Good-by, everybody; good-by, Jimmy Cal;
Good-by, William Gleason; good-by, Doc, old pal;
Sully, Matty, Harry, and Morrie, good-by, good-by.
Sure hope you all will feel sorry the same as I.
Good-by, good old Edward; good-by, little Ray;
Good-by, all you White Sox—I quit gadding today.
[Encore]

Good-by, Johnny Evers; good-by, Lurid Lew;
Good-by, Charley Williams; good-by, Lower Two;
Schulte, Heine, Jimmy, and Larry, good-by, good-by.
P'rhaps you'll look me up when you tarry awhile in Chi.
Good-by, clams and swordfish; good-by, Gay White Way;
Good-by, joys of Brooklyn—I quit gadding today.

A few weeks later, he took his poetic relationship with Schulte to another level, throwing in Zimmerman for good measure, and then inventing a feud between them. It began with a story in the *Tribune* on June 19, where he claimed that a Cubs fan was offering Zimmerman, a notorious baiter of umpires, $100 if he could control his temper and avoid being thrown out of a game for the next two weeks. Half a $100 gold certificate would be presented to Zimmerman before that day's game and the other half if he stayed on his best behavior.

The Cubs and Major League Baseball went along with the gag and, in a ceremony at home plate, umpire Bill Klem gave Zimmerman one half of the bill. The *Tribune* commemorated the event with a picture of Zimmerman in uniform examining his prize; the following day, Lardner enlisted the aid of Tennyson to sum up the situation in a poem:

A Split Century

Half a C, half a C,
Half a C, sundered,
Cut from the other half,
Half a big hundred.
Forward the Cub Brigade!
"Charge at the umps!" they said,
But Zim in silence stood.
O you big hundred!

Past the Great Zim the pill
Whistled. "Strike three," said Bill,
And the Great Heine knew
William had blundered;
His not to make reply,
His not to query why,
'Though 'twas outside and high.
Silence is golden, Zim.
O you big hundred!

Players to right of him,
Players to left of him,
Players in front of him
Hollered and thundered,
Bellowing like a calf
At the whole umpire staff,

But Heine's jaws are locked,
Earning the other half
Of the big hundred.

The *Tribune* milked the story for the next two weeks, noting every time Zimmerman's patience was tested and on July 2, a day before the two weeks were up, Lardner wrote another poem, this time enlisting Shakespeare as his muse:

Heine's Soliloquy

The C or not the C, that is the question—
Whether 'tis nobler for the dough to suffer
Mistakes and errors of outrageous umpires,
Or to cut loose against a band of robbers,
And, by protesting, lose it? To kick—to beef—
To beef!—perchance to scream: "Ah, there, you dub,
You———!!!"
But that sharp flow of breath, what would it cost,
A sloughing off of these one hundred bucks,
Must give me pause—there's the respect
That makes dumb agony of two long weeks;
For who would bear the crazy work of Klem,
Cy Rigler's slips, the raw mistakes of Quigley,
The guesses wild of Orth and Hank O'Day.
When he himself might his quietus make
With a few cuss words! Who would Brennan bear,
Or shut up under Eason's worst offense,
But for the dread of dropping all that dough,
Of losing all those togs, deprived of which
No guy is really swell!—Yes, I'll keep still.
Thus money does make cowards of us all;
And thus the native Bronx disposition
Is stifled by a bunch of filthy luc;
And ravings of my own fantastic sort
Are all unheard, though my long silence does
Disgrace the name of Heine.

The following day, Zimmerman at last won the other half of the bill. To the surprise of no one, the *Tribune* revealed that the anonymous "fan" who had put up the money was the newspaper itself. And Lardner, who knew a good thing when he saw one, was not about to let the story end and enlisted Schulte to keep it alive. First, though, he had to be sure of Schulte's bona-fides.

"In recent interviews," he wrote on July 6, "Luke McGluke, owner of the Dublin club in the Japanese League, has made vicious attacks on the Wake . . . asserting that the Wake was trying to deceive the public by signing Schulte's name to stuff he did not write and charging that the Schulte poems, than which there is none other, were direct and uncalled for knocks at the Dublin club.

"The Wake stands for clean sport and clean sport reporting and desires to assure the public that it has been deceived if Mr. Schulte is not the author of the things he writes." He would print Schulte's reply, he said, and let his readers decide for themselves.

"In answer to the vicious charge made by President McGluke," Schulte wrote, "I will say that, to all intents and purposes, I write the verses over which my name appears. By this I mean that I read them the day after they are written, or rotten . . . I nearly write them; that is, I sit near the person who do. I will admit that (Cubs infielder) Red Corriden writes some of them, but I give him the inspiration and always approve what is rotten before it appears in print. Hoping I have convinced you that I write what I write. I am, etc."

That was good enough for Lardner, who wrote, "Mr. Schulte's gentlemanly note convinced the Wake that in regard to this here now controversy, to which there is nothing to it. Mr. Schulte does not draw his enormous salary from the Wake for the mere use of his name." But on July 18 the plot thickened when Schulte expressed some petulance over the attention, and the money, Zimmerman had received in a poem titled "Life."

For two whole weeks, I've wrote this poem;
But not a cent for mine,
'Though Heine got a hundred bucks
For not saying nothing the same length of time.

I need some money to buy fudge
And lemonade and clothes,
But I'm not getting any,
So I guess I'll have to close.

Note—Nevertheless, Mr Schulte has promised us another poem entitled "A Epick," the first installment of which will appear in an early
issue.—Ed.

"A Epick," turned out to be a series of poems that Lardner purported
to believe wasn't up to Schulte's usual standard and he responded on
July 28 with a parody of the battles between managers and players that
are a regular occurrence in baseball under the headline "Schulte Suspended; Wake's Great Poet Bawled Out and Punished for Loafing."

"Frank Milton Schulte, considered by many the most reliable and consistent hitter on the Wake team, was last night severely reprimanded and
then indefinitely suspended for alleged soldiering on the job. The suspension followed a war of words between Schulte and the manager of the
Wake, during which Schulte sassed his boss. Regarding the trouble, Manager Lardner gave out the following statement:

"Ever since the start of the Epick series, I have been convinced that
Schulte was not trying. I have been in the game long enough to know
that he is one of the greatest poets of modern times, but I must say that
his work on the Epick has been awful. I knew he was capable and naturally reached the conclusion that he was loafing. I won't stand for anything like that among my men. Hence his suspension. He will be reinstated only when he apologizes to me and promises to try to give me his
best services."

"A few details of the quarrel between the manager and his star were
gleaned from some of the other players. After Saturday's Epick, Schulte
was called on the club house carpet. "You've been laying down on me,"
the boss is reported to have told him. "You've got to brace up or stand
for a fine." "If you don't like my stuff," Schulte retorted, "get somebody
else." This made the manager mad and he said: "That remark means a
vacation for you."

It is said that Schulte has long been dissatisfied with his berth on the Wake and wants to be traded to Breakfast Food or Day Dreams.[13] But the Wake manager has no intention of letting go a man who is capable of filling so much space."

Two days later, after two Cub players "substituted" for Schulte, Lardner relented and the story came to a merciful end. "Schulte reinstated," the headline read. "Wake's Great Poet Will Be Back in Game Tomorrow."

"It was formally announced at Wake headquarters last night that the differences between Frank Marvelous Schulte and the management had been patched up, and that Schulte would have his regular position in tomorrow's lineup. While Manager Lardner would not admit it, it is said that he was far from satisfied with the work of substitutes, Art Phelan and Red Corriden. Schulte has promised to work harder . . ."

Lardner's baseball poems could be terse, as in one that ran on June 20, 1913:

Short Story
Shotten-walk:
Stovall-bang;
Pratt-Biff, blooie;
Good-by, Lange.

Or sardonic, as in one that ran on August 2, 1913:

Just Now—
Their game is
Famous
For its
Witless
Blunders;
Those runless,
Wonless,
Catchless,
Matchless,

Stopless,
Copless,
Useless,
Mooseless,
Spitless,
Hitless Wonders[14]

Or mocking as in one that ran on December 15, 1914:

Baseball—A Sport
Players who jump for the dough,
Bandits and crooks, ev'ry one.
Baseball's a pleasure, you know.
Players should play for the fun.

Magnates don't care for the mon'.
They can't be tempted with gold.
They're in the game for the fun—
That's why Collins was sold.[15]

Or, Lardner's speciality, a play on words, as in one that ran on December 10, 1918:

The New Cub Boss
Some folks undoubtedly will speak
Of William Veeck[16] as William Veeek,
But those who wish to be correc'
Will speak of him as William Veeck.

As for those readers who preferred sports coverage of a more traditional bent, Lardner had this answer: "A Sioux City reader says there is too much poetry in the Wake. We haven't noticed any."

1909

Exhausted Tigers Extend Series

CHICAGO TRIBUNE, OCTOBER 15, 1909

Detroit, Mich.—The Detroit Tigers won the sixth game of the world's series this afternoon, 5 to 4, and thus made necessary a seventh contest to decide the title.

But that doesn't tell half of it. Without a doubt it was the most exciting world's series game ever perpetrated. There may have been just as close battles in world's championship wars in the past, but there never was such a nerve racking one when so much depended on the result. Whatever the reputation of the Tigers in the past, it must be admitted that they showed their gameness today and came out on top in a combat which many clubs would have given up as lost at the end of the first half of the first inning.

It cost Detroit something to win the game, but no one is counting the cost, and Tom Jones and Charley Schmidt, both of whom were hurt badly in the tense ninth inning, would take the same wounds a thousand times provided they could be received in such a good cause.

The Tigers didn't dash gleefully off the field at the finish. One of their number, Tom Jones, was carried away to the clubhouse by his teammates unconscious. Another one, Charley Schmidt, hobbled painfully to the dressing room, and all but fainted when he reached it. And still another, George Moriarity, dragged his spiked limbs at a snail's pace while the rest of his pals gave him and the other two injured their expressions of sympathy.

While George Mullin will be hailed universally as the real star of the contest, one must not lose sight of the fact that the work of Charley Schmidt had as much to do with the result as anything else. Never before today did Schmidt catch a world's series game that earned him so much as honorable mention. But he was there this time and no backstopper in the country could have worked more consistently and brilliantly than the stocky Tiger. He didn't figure much in the hitting, but he did catch wonderfully, and he was the chief engineer in two double plays that did much to bring victory Detroitward.

Gathering a bunch of three runs before a soul was out in the opening round, the Pirates looked like winners all over until the home part of the fourth. In this round the Tigers tied up the score and then proceeded to get a little lead for themselves. They reached the ninth inning two runs to the good, and because the weak end of the Pittsburg batting order was coming, the game looked as good as won for the American leaguers.

But the Pirates had not quit. Jocko Miller, who had been doing better hitting than at any time in his world's series career, led off with a clean single to right. Bill Abstein, who looked like a joke before Mullin in his previous attempts, followed with a safe wallop to center, and there were men on first and second no one out, and only two tallies needed.

Of course, it was up to Wilson to bunt. He did so, and laid down the ball so perfectly that he probably would have beaten it to first base even if Tom Jones had not dropped Schmidt's throw. Tom made a nice try for Schmidt's peg, but he had to get in front of the runner to do it. Wilson crashed into him with no thought of hurting anybody. The ball sailed out of Jones' hands and the Tiger first sacker toppled over as if shot. Before Delehanty could recover the ball Miller had scored, making the Tigers' margin only one. Abstein raced to third, while the Detroit players rushed to the side of the injured athlete. Wilson stopped at first.

Jones was unconscious. He lay there, dead to the world, until Trainer Tuthill and four other Detroiters lifted him to carry him to the clubhouse. He was awake for a second during his trip, but he relapsed into the Land of Nod and didn't know a thing until it was all over. In the meantime the crowd had forgotten the injured hero and was looking with all its eyes at the two Georges—Gibson and Mullin—on whom everything depended.

Manager Jennings was out in the middle of diamond giving words of encouragement to Mullin and readjusting his team. Matty McIntyre was called to left field and Davy Jones moved to center. Sam Crawford, whose reputation as a first sacker is not to be sneezed at, came in to take up the task of the wounded member of the Jones family. Sam had a chance to show his skill immediately.

Mullin, cool and slow, shot a curve over for Hackenschmidt. Gibby leaned against it and sent it bounding to Wahoo Sam. The latter picked it up cleanly and shot it home, whither Abstein was hastening to register the run that would tie it and give the Pirates a chance to go home tonight with the title. But Schmidt took Sam's peg, blocked the runner off the plate, and tagged him out while the crowd yelled madly. It was not known at the time that Schmidt was even badly hurt. But the contact with Abstein's spikes tore a huge chunk out of the catcher's thigh and he suffered intense pain when he tried to stoop and sign for the next pitch.

Mullin's troubles were not over by any means. There was only one out, Wilson was on second and Gibson on first and the Pirates still needed one to make it a draw. Of course, Phillippe[17] was not given a chance to bat. In his place came Eddie Abbattichio. The Italian fouled off two and then waited for three balls. It was up to Mullin to retire him on his next swing or hand back the advantage for which the Tigers had worked so hard to their rivals. Mullin put all his stuff on what he offered Abby in the pinch. As he raised his arm Wilson started running for third and Gibson for second. Abby missed the ball entirely and Schmidt's hurried but perfect throw to third caught Wilson and wound up the game.

It was in this last play that Moriarity was hurt. He couldn't get out of the way of Wilson's spikes without risking defeat for his team. He stood the gaff and did the tagging part so plainly that there wasn't a murmur about Klem's correct decision.

The noise made by the Detroit bugs at the conclusion of the game surpassed in volume anything that has been heard since the proceedings began last Friday. There was a rush to congratulate the Detroit headliners, but the crowd, seeing the plight of Schmidt and Moriarity, gave up the plan of carrying the athletes off the field by cheering the limping pair all the way to the clubhouse. . . .

Perhaps because the Tigers had no more to give, the final game of the series two days later an anticlimax. Pittsburgh won 8–0.

The Tears of Christy Mathewson

CHICAGO EXAMINER, OCTOBER 17, 1912

Boston—When Steve Yerkes crossed the home plate yesterday it made the Boston Red Sox the world's champions in the tenth inning of the deciding game of the greatest series ever played for the big title. While the thousands, made temporarily crazy by a triumph unexcelled, yelled, stamped their feet, smashed hats and hugged one another, there was seen one of the saddest spectacles in the history of a sport that is a strange and wonderful mixture of joy and gloom. It was the spectacle of an old man, as baseball players are called, on the New York players' bench with bowed head and drooping shoulders, with the tears streaming from his eyes, a man on whom his team's fortune had been staked and lost and a man who would have proven his clear title to trust reposed in him if his mates had stood by him in the supreme test. The man was Christy Mathewson.

Beaten 3 to 2 by a club he would have conquered if he had been given the support deserved by his wonderful pitching, Matty is greater in the eyes of New York's public than ever before. Even the joy-mad population of Boston confesses that his should have been the victory and his the praise. The game was over, the title that probably will be the last one fought for by that king of pitchers was lost, and Mathewson, cool and usually unaffected by adverse fortunes of war, was a broken man. The majority of the thousands present were too busy with their wild celebration to notice him, but there were a few who watched his slow and sad progress to the bench and later to the club house.

Charley Herzog, who certainly cannot be blamed for New York's failure to win, rushed up to Matty as he staggered off the field, threw his arm around the big pitcher's neck and poured forth words of comfort and sympathy. Mathewson did not seem to hear them. He shook Herzy off and had no answer to the condolences offered by Doyle and McGraw, who were eager to impress on him that he was in no way to blame for the defeat.

Matty picked up his sweater and moved on in silence. Soon he had disappeared under the stand to join the other Giants in their dressing room, to hear their bitter arraignment of each other and to be told, time and again, that he deserved better, a truth that none knew more positively than himself. The Red Sox, fearful that they would be hurt in the rioting of the crowd if they loitered on the field, had hastened to their own club house, and the scene there was vastly different from that a couple of doors away.

Boston had come from behind twice, had tied New York's early lead in a brilliant seventh inning rally, had almost despaired when the Giants scored again in the tenth, and then, to cap it all, had not only caught up once more but had counted a third run, just enough to settle the question of supremacy beyond all doubt. What difference did it make to the Red Sox that they had been blanked in their part of the tenth and that the world's title would have belonged in New York, if Matty's backing hadn't crumbled to pieces?

The palm was theirs and they remembered nothing else. They had been accused of quitting and they had seen some of their opponents give up more bare-facedly than they had ever done. The score was down in black and white, 3 to 2, in favor of Boston, and that was enough to drive sympathy for Mathewson from their thoughts.

Well, to begin with, the score was tied up at one to one when the Giants came into their end. The party Snodgrass, more famous than he ever was before, was thrown out on a ground ball to Smoky Joe Wood. Red Murray, who had driven in New York's only previous tally and who was still engaged in the task of making the country forget his falldown against the Athletics, smashed a fierce double into the temporary bleachers between Speaker and Lewis. Merkle immediately came through with what most people considered a title winning hit. It was a sharp single to center, and Murray had no trouble.

Speaker made a hurried play on the ball, for it was his duty to try for a peg to the plate, but he fumbled in his haste and Merkle ran to second. One of the most surprising things in the series followed. Herzog, who has played in the series as if he were super-human, struck out. There was no question about it. He just naturally whiffed and went back to the bench without audible comment. The next occurrence was lucky for Wood in two respects. Chief Meyers' blow might have gone through to center and scored Merkle. Furthermore, it might have killed Smokey Joe. As it was, it hit him in the right side and dropped lifeless in front of him. He had sense enough left to pick it up and toss it to Stahl in plenty of time to get the chief for the last out. Wood was badly hurt by this clout and he had to be assisted to the bench. Fortunately, there was no more work for him to do.

Down in the right field corner Ray Collins had been warming up constantly and it would have been up to Ray to get busy if the Sox had tallied only one run instead of two.

Wood is a pretty fair hitter, but in his helpless condition there was no chance to send him up to bat. So Clyde Engle was the party chosen. It will be remembered that Clyde, in one of the other battles, had delivered a double in a pinch. This time he hit as hard as he could, but he struck slightly under the ball. Snodgrass raced over toward left, waved Murray away and camped under the falling pill. It struck his hands squarely and kept right on to the ground, moved by the law of gravity.[18]

Engle had not run as fast as he could from the plate, but he speeded up enough to get to second before Fred could recover the sphere and hurl it to the infield. The Sox were now playing for one run, so Hooper was sent up to sacrifice. His two attempts went foul. When he had to hit, he sent a long fly to center, and it must be confessed that Snodgrass made a good catch of it. At this juncture, Matty made his only mistake of the inning. He passed Yerkes. We are not saying that the cool youngster wouldn't have hit safely, but it was bad business to walk him and Mathewson didn't mean to.

Then came Merkle's contribution to the cause. Speaker lifted the first pitch for a foul and it struck bottom, although it ought to have been caught easily. As was mentioned before, Merkle, Meyers and Matty started for it, and all of them stopped. It isn't safe to trifle this way with the Speaker person. He picked up his bat, which he had thrown in disgust toward the bench. The next thing Matty served him he cracked on the nose. It traveled to right field a mile a minute and Engle sped home with the tying run. Yerkes hustled to third. Tris waited to see what became of Devore's throw, and when he observed that Meyers fumbled it he chased to second. Duffy Lewis came up with the chance of a lifetime staring him in the face. Matty tried to make him swing at two bad ones. He refused. Then Meyers and Mathewson consulted and decided it was better to walk Duff and try for a double play rather than put one over. So Lewis strolled and choked the bases. Matty pitched all he knew to Gardner and was rewarded by getting two strikes on the Boston third sacker. Two balls followed, and then Larry pulled a long fly to right, a fly that Devore had to go back after.

He caught it all right and aimed a throw toward Meyers, for that was his duty. But the throw reached the Indian long after Yerkes had touched the plate . . .

1915

A Plea for Help

CHICAGO TRIBUNE, SEPTEMBER 29, 1915

Frend Harvey. I recd. yours of the 27 int. and would say in a reply that I would jest as leaf go to the worlds serious under certun conditions. In the 1st. place please make Mr. Sanborn[19] keep the score of the diffrunt ball games because I have forgot how to keep the score. All so in the 2d. place have Mr. Sanborn write in his stuff how the games come out who wins and who looses and so 4th. because I would probly over look miner detales.

In the 3d. place I would expect the paper to pay my expences to and fro Boston and Phila or where ever it is there going to play the game at. All so my bord bill at the diffrunt hotels and on the bord of the trains accept when I am invited to meals by some sucker. And I will try to fill my self up good when some sucker is paying for the meal so as the paper wont be stuck so hard when I hafe to pay for them my self.

In the 4th. place I wisht you would ask Mr. Sanborn to get a hold of a ticket to all the games for me and see that I get in to the press box and dont half to set on some bodys lap behind the club house or over in the next block. If it was here in Chi I wouldnent have no trubble because people knows me here but its diffrunt in the east and not even the pollicemans knows who I am because when I was trying to get some wheres near the ring side at the Mcfarland Gibbons dance I ast a policeman to help me and I told him my name and where I come from and he says What the (he used a bad word) do I care who you are or where you come from. And he wouldent act like my escort.

It might be a good idear to leave me set between Mr. Sanborn and 1 of the boys from the other Chi papers and I would pertend like I was busy writeing my own stuff but all the wile I would be lissening to what the man from the other paper was dictateing to his operator and then I would leen over and tell Mr. Sanborn and he could use it like he made it up his self.

I supose you will want me to pick the winner of the serious like I picked the winner of the brutal prize fight down to Brixton beech. I can pick the winner O .K. if you give me time to think over it. But may be it wouldent be a bad idear if I and Mr. Sanborn was to both of us pick the winner and him pick 1 club and I pick the other and then witch ever club come out on the top you could put a peace in the paper that our man picked the winner.

I want it under stood that I been in both Phila and Boston many a time in fact I lived in Boston for a while so its not no treat for me to vissit ether place and I will expect my expences pade and I dont consider it no vacation.

I wonder if you could give me a little information a bout what should a man ought to take a long on a trip like that in the way of close. I got 1 sute case and I know where I could borry an other 1 but I dont know will it be necessary to take a long 2 peaces of baggage but still I want to be drest jest as good of the rest of the repporters. I was thinking I would take a long my buster Brown sute and my sailor sute and ware my velvet sute on the train going and comeing. And then of course I will need a change of linens and a extra hankercheif and a extra pare of hoses and a night gown and I wont only need 1 night gown because I will spend most of the nights on a train going back and 4th. bet. Boston and Phila if they deside to play the serious in them 2 towns. But you know best a bout these things and give me what ever information you can. And of coarse I will get all cleaned up and shaved beffore I start.

And 1 more thing Harvey do you want my storys sent in by telegram or male? I hope you will find time to give me all this information and all so agree to the conditions named in the above and Im sure you will find them fare to both sides.

Respy. R.

A Rainy Day in Philadelphia

CHICAGO TRIBUNE, OCTOBER 8, 1915

Philadephia, Pa—Frend Harvey: Unlest it rains like its been doing all day today there going to start the world serious here tomorrow. I and Mr. Sanborn is stoping in the same hotel that the Boston Americans is stoping at and the Boston Americans is 1 of the 2 clubs thats in the serious so if they call off the game tomorrow we will know a bout it right away and will send you word so you wont think there playing a game when they aint playing a game because we will be right here in the hotel and will see for our self weather the boston players gos out to the park or stays here in the hotel and if they stay in the hotel that will mean its raining out doors. But I want to tell you something funny about us picking out this hotel to stop at.

1 dident pick it out myself but Mr. Sanborn did. I says to him the other day in Chi where are we going to stop in Phila. he says we will stop at the Aldine. I says fine its a good hotel. He says well the reason I picked it out was because it will be quiet and not crowded and they wont be no ball club stoping there so we will have plenty of room and be a way from the bugs.

So we come here to the Aldine club and come to fine out the hole Boston eleven is stoping here and all so the Boston news paper men witch is even worse. Of coarse the Boston clubs not here today because they been playing a important game over to NY city but they will be here before I get threw writeing this junk and the hotel will be jammed with people that knows the diffrunt players by there 1st names to speak to. So when we found this out I says to Mr. Sanborn your a fine guy and the next time I and you comes to cover the world serious I will do the picking of hotels and I will pick a hotel thats so good that the ballplayers wont never think of it.

And he says he got mixxed up because he had been stoping here all summer and evry time he come here they wasent no ball players here accept the Chi white sox and he figgured the Chi white sox wouldent be here this time because they was playing some practise games with the Cubs out in Chi. And he figgured the Boston Americans wouldent be here because they hadent never been here when he was. Fine figgureing hay Harvey because of coarse evry time he was here with the white sox the

Boston Americans was on there home grounds playing some other western club and not on in Phila a tall.

Well anyway as a result of his figgureing wear in the same hotel where the Boston Americans is comeing and if we half to sleep 4 or 5 in a bed its mr. Sanborns falt. If it doesnt rain tomorrow they will be a big crowd that ever seen a game in Phila on the National league grounds. Every body will be there accept the people that lives in Phila. The latter cant get no tickets. There the people thats supported the Phila ball club ever since 1876 so the owners figgure they saw enough baseball and don't need to see the world serious.

People that lives right here has been a round the hotel all day begging we fellows from out of town to get them some tickets so they can see the ball games. But we havent got no tickets to give them because all the tickets had all ready been gave out to people from Seattle Washn and New Orleans, St. Lose and Boston.

The owners of the Phila club has been very carefull to suply tickets to these royal rooters from Boston that never done nothing for no body includeing there wifes. They had to be fixxed up with tickets because 1 of them is the mare of Boston and would make a big holler if he and his friends dident get in to the ball pk. In order to be elected mare of Boston you got to be a base ball bug and all so a royal rooter and a man that will stand up for Boston rights and can sing the river shannon. When a mans running for mare of Boston the only pledge hes got to make is that he will go to all the ball games and act crazy. He don't half to sine no promuss to keep the salloons open on Sunday.

They isent much to write a bout here today. Mr. Sanborn went down to press head quarters this pm and got us both fixed up with a ticket to the games. Besides the ticket we was both gave a red badge to ware on our sutes to show that we was news paper men and entitled to get in and not peeple from Phila. When I seen the color of the badge I was glad I bought a gray sute for fall instead of a pink 1.

Theys a lot of roomers going a round but you cant tell what to beleive and what not to beleive. 1 of the roomers is that Alexander will pitch tommorows game. I wouldent bet a nickle on it because the papers says that Pat Moran told them so and of coarse Pat Morans is to smart to tell the news papers what pitcher hes realy going to use. If he says its going to be Alexander its safe to bet that it will be Baumgardener or some body may be Kiliifer.

Theys an other roomer that the Phillys isent going to play there 1st inning because they dont think theys any use because Hughey Fullerton says in his dope that there going out in 1 2 3 order, so instead of playing and waisting the time they will just tell the repporters to mark them out in there score books and then they will start-in with the 2d inning and cravath at bat because hughey says that Cravath will get to 1st base. It would simplefy matters a hole lot if Hughey would tell what was going to happen evry inning threw the hole serious and then the clubs wouldent half to play and the people and the reporters wouldent have to watch them but just let Hughey tell how it was comeing out and save all the ware and tare. Of coarse they wouldent be no money tooken in at the gate that way but the club owners could fine there own home town fans so much a peace to pay expenses of the serious and the home town fans would be just as well off because they cant get tickets to the games any way.

They was a big parade on Broad st today and I and Mr. Sanborn and some bum repporters from other towns was watching it and we dident know what it was so finely Mr. Sanborn ast 1 of the by standers what was it and he says it was the Phila firemans celebration. So Mr. Sanborn says what is the Phila firemans celebrateing and the man didnt answer so I horned in and says there celebrating because they put out a fire. Pretty good hay Harvey.

And 1 more thing. I dont want to give no free advertising to no body but Ive got 1 of these here watchs that cost a dollar. Well when I left Chi yest the watch was on Chi time. And when I got to Pittsburgh last night it jumped a head a hour to eastern time with out no body touching it. Hows that Harvey?

Your Correspondent Sizes Up the Series

CHICAGO TRIBUNE, OCTOBER 6, 1916

New York—Mr. Bud Fisher, who draws the petey and Gaston cartoons, called up today and asked: "How are you going to Boston?"

"In good shape," was my apt answer.

"But listen," was his startling rejoinder, "I am going to drive up there friday and I will have room for you in my car."

"That sounds fine," says I, and I immediately went out and bought a seat on the train that leaves here at one P.M. and gets to Boston at six oclock. That's what I think of Bud Fisher and his cat and his cartoons. Bud Fisher may be a nice guy and everything, but the day I ride anywhere with him and his car will be the day Brooklyn wins the World's series from Boston.

And speaking of that, the World's Greatest Newspaper has probably been informed by its New York correspondents that there is a great deal of betting and that the odds favor Boston, 8 to 5. Well, listen, as Bud Fisher says, I was up in John Doyles billiard parlors today and John Doyles billiard parlors knows all about the betting on everything, and the betting on the World's series is nothing to nothing. For some reason or other, everybody seems to know that Boston is going to walk in and while the people who live in Brooklyn are, ipsofacto, or whatever it is, crazy, they have not reached the stage where they will back their so-called ball club at odds of anything less than twenty eight to one.

Now, mind you, I am not saying that the Robins will lose, but if they dont lose, I will work the rest of the winter for nothing.

Walter Trumbull, who writes baseball on the New York World, or something, says I ought not to use the capital "I" so much.

"What ought I to say," I asked him, "when I am talking about myself?"

"Use we, or the writer, or your correspondent," he says.

So your correspondent will try to remember that for the rest of this remarkable story.

Your correspondent arose at ten o'clock and answered the telephone and the man at the other end was Jerome Kern, who wrote most of the music to the Follies, and I cant say that fearlessly, but if we said he wrote the libretto, he would sue the paper for a million dollars libel.

"Will you come to lunch?" he said.

So the writer said he would, and at lunch your correspondent met Pelham Grenville Wodehouse, the Britisher, and he acted just as glad to see the writer as if we had been Wilhelm Tell, the Kaiser of Germany.

So they talked and your correspondent tried to listen and finally got bored and thought we had better hustle around and get some baseball news. So your correspondent sought out Harry Hempstead, the owner of the Giants, and asked him whether it was true that John McGraw would be fired for saying that his team laid down to Brooklyn.

"Yes," said Mr. Hempstead. "I am going to fire McGraw and here are some other things I am going to do: I am going to make the price of box seats ten cents a piece, and I am going to play Schupp at third base on account of his left handedness, and I am going to trade Zimmerman back to Chicago for Al Campion, and I am going to take the club to Medicine Hat to train next Spring."

In other words, the stories to the effect that McGraw is going to lose his job are nearly as true as the ones about Brooklyn backing its ball club at odds of eight to five.

John K. Tener[20], Garry Herrmann,[21] and Ban Johnson[22] were interviewed today on the big scandal, meaning the game New York is said to have thrown to Brooklyn.

"What are you going to do about it?" the Commissioners were asked by your correspondent.

Ban answered first. "I have been asked to take charge of the United States army commissary department," he said.

Garry Herrmann said: "Sweet Adeline. Sweet Adeline, at night, dear heart for you I pine."

Mr. Tener said: "May Old Glory long wave over the National pastime and the home of the free."

Some Brooklyn writer said today that the Robins would probably win because they are not afraid of anything and that just about hits the nail on the head, because if the Robins had been cowards they would have faded in front of the fierce opposition of the Giants tuesday and on the other hand, the Red Sox with the exception of Heine Wagner and Bill

Carrigan, will probably be scared to death of catching in-fantile paralysis during the two games here.

The latest dope on the series itself is that Rube Marquard will pitch the first inning for Brooklyn and Babe Ruth will pitch the first nine for Boston.

Lardner Story Starts as Verse, Turns to Prose as Fattens Purse

CHICAGO TRIBUNE, OCTOBER 7, 1916

Boston, Mass.—I thought that this was just the time to write my story all in rhyme. I rose this morn at half past 8 and wondered how it got so late. I shaved and dressed and packed my grip and got all ready for the trip and went downstairs and paid my bill and said "I'm from Chicago Ill."

The cashier said: "Why, I dont care if you're from there or anywhere, so long as you have got the dough; just say good-by and off you go." So off I went and with elation rode to the new Grand Central station and paid the driver forty cents for taking me from there to thence.

In fifteen minutes there I found a train that was Massachusetts bound and got aboard and took a seat and ordered something nice to eat and then the Cleveland boys came in and wanted money for to win and asked me for to play some poker with nothing wild but the joker, Hugh Fullerton, he just came in and ordered both of us some gin so then I whispered: "I suppose I'd better write the rest in prose."

So the details are that I won $7 in the poker game with the Cleveland boys and they play the funniest game you ever saw. Six cards are dealt to you on the draw and the joker is wild and then you draw down to five cards. So I won seven and a quarter in their crazy game and then we were in Boston.

So then I went to the hotel and the first person I saw was Hank O'Day and I said to myself "Here's a story." So I bot him a cigar. And I did not get any story that you could print.

"Hank," I said to him, "will you try not to make any mistakes in this series?"

"I never made a mistake in my life," was his reply.

"No," I says, "but it is a matter of record that you signed to manage Cincinnati."

So he did not have any answer to that, so then I left the hotel and went down to where the Brooklyns were stopping. Now you know and I know that I only know five men on the Brooklyn club, namely Larry Cheney and Jimmy Johnston and Jack Coombs and Chief Meyers and Rube Marquard.

So I was going to interview one of them but could not because they were all out at a show. So all the news that I got was that Marquard is going to pitch the first inning for Brooklyn as I told you yesterday and Coombs will pitch the second inning and Pfeffer the third inning and so on and I know a whole lot more of inside stuff, but if I wrote it I might be interfering with Mr. Sanborn and besides the cost of white paper is high. I will try to write a good story tomorrow.

Inning by Inning with the Red Sox and Robins

BELL SYNDICATE, OCTOBER 8, 1916

Boston, Mass.—Mr. Sanborn is supposed to be writing the game in detail, but I will send it that way, too, and try to get it different. So here is what happened:

First Inning.

We came out in a taxi, and somebody else paid for it. The umpires pointed around for a quarter of an hour and as there wasn't anybody on the field except the ball players and the Brooklyn club, one could not help from wondering, as they say, what they were pointing about. The announcer said that Mr. Shore and Mr. Marquard would pitch. As regards Mr. Shore, we believed it.

So the first inning started and Mr. Shore pitched a fast ball over the plate and a man named Myers hit it and broke the altitude record, and Mr. Cady caught it and Mr. Myers was mighty glad, because he thought all the time he was going to strike out. So then Jacob Daubert struck out, and there was no question about it, because Jacob had three healthy swings.

Then Jake Stengel, or whatever his first name is, rolled out, and then the Bostons came to bat according to the rules, and Hooper and Janvrin struck out and everybody said what a great pitcher Marquard is. But Tillie Walker hit one on the beak for 3 bases and then Marquard was not such a great pitcher. But Richard Hoblitzell grounded out.

Second Inning.

For the life of me I can't remember what the Brooklyns did, but it wasn't worth mentioning. Duffy Lewis came up for Boston and walked or something. It was Gardner's intention to sacrifice, but he did not figure on who was catching for the Dodgers. He bunted and Chief Meyers gummed it all up. Scott did sacrifice and Cady was passed a-purpose and Shore struck out and Hooper hit one in the eye, but Myers caught it.

Third Inning.

In Brooklyn's half, Daubert struck out only once because they would not let him bat twice. In Boston's half, two guys struck out, and then Hoblitzel, who cannot possibly hit a left-handed pitcher, tripled to right, and George E. Lewis. who cannot hit anything except in the regular season and during the world's series, doubled to left and scored a run, and then they caught him off second base and nothing else happened until the.

Fourth Inning.

Believe me, Shore looked almost good enough to pitch for the Niles high school team in this round. Stengel hit one somewhere and Wheat kissed one in the eye and it went over Hooper's bean, and Stengel scored and Wheat was on third, and then this here George Cutshaw hit a single to right field, only it wasn't a single, because Hooper catched it prone on his back and Wheat tried to take an unfair advantage and score while an outfielder was sitting down with the ball, but Hooper, remaining seated, threw him out as far as from here to the city hall. The Bostons done nothing.

Fifth Inning.

I was out getting a sandwich.

Sixth Inning.

From where we are sitting we could see the Charles river and a man went by in a rowboat and Mr. Sanborn said: "Do you see that man?" and I said "Yes," so he said, "That man is a sculler." "Yes," was my reply. "What is the difference between he and a world's series ball player?" asked Mr. Sanborn. "I don't know," was my reply. "What is the difference between a sculler and a ball player? " " "Well," said Mr. Sanborn, "a ball player has only one skull." No runs.

Seventh Inning.

Olson and Cutshaw played up to form and Boston scored three runs.

Eighth Inning.

Pfeffer pitched for Brooklyn and held Boston to one run.

Ninth Inning.

Shore left his fast ball on the bench and Brooklyn was just about to tie the score when Carrigan cheated and changed pitchers. Boston refused to play the last half.

Nothing Happened

CHICAGO TRIBUNE, OCTOBER 10, 1916

Boston, Mass—Friend Harvey, this is just a few lines to leave you know how we are getting along. We are getting along good now Harvey and it looks like we would be all through Wednesday night and back home some time Friday.

A man named Hi Myers came pretty close to being killed today and this was how it happened. He hit a ball in the first inning and touched all the bases and the Brooklyns had one run. Then the Bostons tied it up and acted like they were through for the day till a man named Del Gainer hit one in the fourteenth inning and then it was all over. But if the home run

Myers made had of win the game for Brooklyn and prolonged the series to five games instead of four or if it had of wound up in a tie, I would of borrowed a gun and shot Hi Myers. That is how I feel about the series.

Well Harvey I got up at nine o'clock in the morning and dressed in an hour and a half like usual and had some breakfast and a man from St. Paul paid for it. Then I packed up my typewriter and Bozeman Bulger had a taxicab hired and took us out to Braves Field and I forget who paid for it, but I know who did not. So pretty soon we wended on our way up to the press stand and the royal rooters band was playing "Tessie" and I did not have no gun on my person and besides I could not see them but could only hear them and that is bad enough.

So somebody asked me who I thought was going to pitch, so I picked up a copy of the Boston paper that I used to work on till they threw me out and the paper said the pitchers would be Leonard and Cheney, so then I knew it would be Ruth and Smith.

Well nothing happened till the first inning and then they was two out and this here Hi Myers kissed one in the eye and it was a home run and I dont know why they call him Hi because the ball he hit never went more than three feet above terra and firma and everything.

So then nothing happened till the third and it was Scotts turn to bat first for the Red Sox and it is a notorious fact that he never hit a ball in his life. So he hit for three bases and then he staid on third base while Thomas was getting himself threw out and then Ruth hit to Cutshaw and you could not expect a Brooklyn infielder to make two perfect plays in succession so Cutshaw fumbled long enough to let Scott romp in from third and the game was tied up.

So then nothing happened till the fifth and then they was two out and Thomas cracked one down the third base line and Wheat played it like an old washer-woman and instead of it being a single like it ought to been it got through Wheat and Thomas was going to make three bases. But Ivan Olson conceived the brilliant idea of tripping him up and he did so and nobody was looking except all the umpires, so after Thomas picked his self off of the ground they told him to romp along to third base. Then Mr. Olson and Heine Wagner, who was coaching at third, had some bitter words and it looked like one of them would kill the other and make a good story, but no such luck and when I say that I dont mean that either one of them deserves to die because they are both nice fellows, but it would of made a good story.

So then nothing happened till the seventh inning, when Myers hit a ball to Janvrin and the young dancing master kicked it round awhile and finally picked it up and threw it to first base and Mr. Quigley said Mr. Myers was out though nobody knew why until somebody explained that Mr. Quigley was graduated from the University of Kansas.

So nothing happened until the last half of the ninth until Janvrin hit a left ball to left field and Wheat could not reach it so Janvrin was safe at second base. So then Tillie Walker was sent up to bunt and Mr. Carrigan knew he could not bunt and never could bunt but gave him one more chance to prove it so Tillie staid up there till he fouled one and then Jimmy Walsh came up instead of him and bunted one straight at Smith and Smith threw it to Mowrey and Janvrin ought to of been out as far as from here to Amsterdam, but Mowrey dropped the ball. This looked like the end of a perfect day, but Hobby sent a short fly to Myers and Janvrin was a dead baby at the plate. So somebody told Smith about Duffy Lewis and they walked him a purpose and Gardner fouled out and we had to sit there awhile longer.

So then nothing happened till the tenth this here Hitless Scott hit another single and Thomas sacrificed and Ruth came up and if he had of hit as far as he wanted to the horsehide as they call it would of died an early death in the Charles River, but Babe did not touch it so far as the naked eyeball could judge and William Dinneen said he was out.

So then Hooper hit one about as hard as last summers ice cream and it was a single and Mowrey picked it up and made a smart play, whether you believe it or not. He seen he had no chance to get Hooper at first, so he bluffed to throw there and Scott overran third and set out for home, but Mowrey still had the pill and tagged him.

So then nothing: really happened till the fourteenth and the Robins done nothing, so Bill Carrigan decided this would be the last inning and if nobody scored they would call it a tie and it took smart management to figure that out because nobody could of possibly known it without look-ing at the atmospherical conditions. So Hobby walked and Lewis sacri-ficed and Carrigan told Lawrence Gardner to seek the shower bath, so Gainer went up to hit and got one strike and then Hobby was invited to share Gardners bath and McNally went on to run for Hobby and the next thing you knew, Gainer hit one to left field and McNally kept on going till he got home and Wheat made a throw that might of caught Larry McLean or Larry Lajoie but it did not catch McNally, who all he can do is run. So the game was over, but the official scorers said Gainer made a two base hit and insisted on it till we all booed at them. Nothing happened after that and nothing will happen.

1917

Lardner returned from Paris, where he had been writing columns about World War I, which American forces had recently entered, just in time to see his hometown White Sox play the New York Giants in the World Series. (More about his trip home appears in the following section.) His experiences in France were reflected in several of those World Series columns.

Report from Behind Enemy Lines

CHICAGO TRIBUNE, OCTOBER 5, 1917

To Commander in Chief Rowland, General Headquarters,
White Sox Armies, Comiskey Park.

I have the honor to report that I have just completed a trip here from Philadelphia with the enemy's expeditionary forces. Disguised as a neutral observer, I was able to gather much information which I trust will be of value.

The army is made up of about twenty active units and is charge of Major General McGraw, or some such name. Accompanying it are nine or ten enemy correspondents, some of them apparently intelligent. I talked with them and with several of the soldiers, including one commissioned officer, Captain Herzog. The latter advised me that he had never tried to raise honey dew melons in Maryland, but might plant some next year.

I had a highly unprofitable session with one Zimmerman, said to be a brother of the man who wrote the famous Mexican note.[23] He is from the Bronx and claims to be one of the heavy artillery.

"Hello, Heine," I said to him. "Why, hello, Lahdi," was his reply. "Gimme a cigarette."

And a moment later——

"Gimme a match."

Some of his comrades called him Zimme, but Gimme would be more appropriate.

I got a rise from one Private Rariden by asserting that only one railroad went through Bedford, Indiana. He flared up and retorted that there were actually two regular passenger and freight lines and two coal roads. This was exactly the information I was after and I have no doubt you will find it useful. I feel quite proud of the strategy that brought it out.

Private Holke showed me a letter he had received from a friend in Texas, asking for three tickets to each game played in New York.

"I hear the tickets are three dollars apiece per game," said the writer, "but I feel that we cannot afford to pay more than two-fifty. See whether it is possible to get them at this price."

Mr. Holke is unable to figure out why people who can pay their expenses from Texas to New York and back for the sake of a few ball games should feel it beyond their means to come through with the regular price for seats.

By careful questioning, I learned that in the initial battle, the enemy's defense against our possible counter attacks would be hand grenades thrown by one of four experts—Schupp, Sallee, Porritt or Anderson. Schupp and Sallee throw their bombs with the left hand, which should be contrary to international law. Sallee, in addition to being a left-hander, is thin to the point of invisibility, another violation of the spirit of the rules of warfare. His camouflage is very effective, as he is frequently mistaken for one of the pickets on the fence. This is also true of Porritt, but he has sufficient sense of honor to bomb right-handed.

Enemy correspondents are evidently convinced that the eastern invaders are stronger and better prepared than your own men and a few express the opinion that you will surrender in five days. I have pretended to agree with them in their arrogant views, so as to foster in them, and indirectly in their army, a chestiness which may result in disaster.

On our transport train was a heavy set genial young man whom I instantly recognized as another spy, Germany Schaefer.

"Hello, Germany," I whispered to him when no one was looking.

"S-s-s-h," he shushed. "Call me Schaef. I got through with that other name the sixth of April."

Well, sir, I trust that your armies will fight with that indomitable courage and aggressiveness which has made them conquerors in Autumn wars of the past, wars forced on them by barbarous West and North Siders moved to hatred through jealousy of the South Side's superiority in culture and invention, and that with Gott's help, you may gain an early and decisive military victory so that our people may return to their homes and live in the peace and comfort to which they are accustomed and of which these eastern vandals would rob us.

Respectfully

L.

The Modern Voltaire

CHICAGO TRIBUNE, OCTOBER 8, 1917

At the French Front—[Special to Le Petit Journal, Paris.]—Les Bas Blanc made it deux out of deux from Les Géants hier après midi, winning the second game of the serie, sept to deux. Le jeu was un battle royale up to the fourth inning, when the Sox lit into Monsieur Anderson all spraddled out.

M. Anderson was taken hors de combat before the inning was over and M. Perritt got his. The round netted the Sox cinq runs et settled le jeu.

Directeur McGraw crossed everybody by starting another lefthander, Herr Ferdinand Schupp. This Boche was a world beater for un inning, but in the deuxiéme he looked like un franc cinquante.

Opposed to the Hun at the start was M. Rouge Faber of Cascade, Iowa. Rouge was hit hard in the deuxiéme inning, then settled down et pitched très bien. Rouge also gave un grande exhibition of base running, stealing third in the cinquiéme inning avec that base already occupé. Plays like that make the enemy look like a sucker.

M. Burns, avec trois ball et deux strikes, singled to droit. Herr Herzog forced him at deuxième, M. Gandil to M. Weaver. Herr Kauff lifted une mouche to right et Jacques Collins dropped it, but recovered in temps to force Herr Herzog at deuxiéme. Foreign Secretaire Zimmerman was hors at first, Eduoard Collins to M. Gandil.

Herr Schupp fanned M. McMullin et M.E. Collins in the Bas demi.

Le deuxiéme inning was plein of excitation. Avec une out, M, Robertson beat out an infield coup. Herr Holke singled à concentrer. M. McCarty singled to gauche, scoring M. Robertson, Herr Holke following him in when Herr Schalk messed M. Jackson's throw to lieu natal. Herr Schupp et M. Burns wore très facile outs.

In le Chicago demi, M. Jackson led off avec un single. Herr Felsch singled à droit et M. Jackson took troisiéme. M. Gandil hit sauf over Herr Schupp's kopf, scoring M. Jackson. Herr Schalk tried to sacrifice, but bunted into Herr Schupp's mains et forced Herr Felsch at troisiéme. Then Herr Schupp gave M. Faber une basse on balle, filling la bases. That was bien suffisant pour M. McGraw et he yanked Herr Schupp et substituted Anderson. Directeur Rowland took M. Jacques Collins out and substituted Herr Leibold, un gauche-handed hitter. Herr Leibold whiffed et M. McMullin forced Rouge Faber at deuxiéme. La taille was now un tie.

Anderson went très bien until the quatre. M. Weaver opened le Chicago demi of that round by beating out a balancoire bunt. Schalk singled à droit. Rouge Faber popped hors trying to sacrifice. Mais Herr Leibold et M. McMullin both hit sauf, scoring deau runs. Anderson was taken hors and in came Poll Perroquet. M. E. Collins et M. Generale Jackson greeted this oiseau with hits et le totale pour le round was cinq runs before Herr Felsch lined into un double play.

Le feature of the troisiéme inning was Rouge Faber's base-running. Avec un hors, M. Weaver reached premier on une botte par M. Fletcher. He advanced to deuxiéme on Herr Schalk's hors et to troisiéme on un single par Faber. Le dernier took second on M. Robertson's useless throw a lieu natal. M. Rouge then stole third and was très surprendre to find M. Weaver there. Le New York catcher threw a troisiéme et Herr Zimmerman, exhibiting grande presence de la intelligence, tagged Rouge. Il est un wonder Herr Heine didn't throw the ball à le champ droit.

Les scorers officieles went noix in the sixiéme et gave M.E. Collins un hit on a play un M. Collins was called hors par le umpire until le dernier saw that M. Perroquct had dropped Herr Holke's throw at first base.

Otherwise, there was not beaucoup more to le jeu. Directeur McGraw proved his generosity of spirit by letting us see quatre of his pitchers. M. Tesreau butting in pour le final Chicago inning and retiring le coté runless.

Le New York neuvieme brought up Herren Kauff et Zimmerman and M. Fletcher. Le first two named kept their records pure et M. Fletcher grounded out to the world's greatest series player, M. Weaver.

Il est the unanimous verdict autour de here that les Giants are the most consistent world's series team in le monde.

The following day, under the headline "The Modern Balzac," Lardner wrote another column in fractured French. We can only wonder if he recalled his jovial suggestion to Eddie Cicotte after the World Series two years later.

New York—Je came East today avec les bas blanc et we had un unremarkable trip. You know there is a difference between the White Sox et les Giants. The ball players on the former don't speak to the reporters, but the manager is friendly. On the Giants team, le Managere don't speak to reporters, but the ball players are cordial.

This is what I was told. But je saw some of the Chicago ball players I know and I couldn't resist talking to them. The first was Eddie Cicotte, who happened to be setting at the same petit dejeuner table. No sooner had we got settled when a telegraph guy came in and said:

"The next stop is Syracuse. You can file there."

So we said, "we have nothing to file there." So the telegraph guy says "haven't you nothing to file?" So I and Mr. Crusinberry said, "No." But Eddie Cicotte said, "wait a minute. I'll get off and file my spikes." That a right-handed pitcher's idea of wit.

Mr. Crusinberry and I made all kinds of offers to Mr. Cicotte to throw the next game he pitches, but the poor boob would give us no respectable answer . . . .

Lardner missed the conclusion of the 1917 World Series, perhaps because he had been away from home so long and didn't want to go back to New York. Of course, he couldn't pass up the chance to make light of his defection.

"The boss has just informed me that I won't have to go back to New York with the other Rats," he wrote.

"'Why not?'" I asked him. "'Don't you like my stuff?'"

"'Yes, indeed,'" he replied. "'But you can write it just as well from here.'"

So he wrote about the game, which clinched the Series for the White Sox, from home, noting that "You get all the thrills of writing, if any, without enduring the pains of looking at the so-called athletes on the field of play."

1918

18 Holes

CHICAGO TRIBUNE, SEPTEMBER 7, 1918

Friend Harvey:

Well, Harvey, it was the first time Geo. Tyler ever pitched at Comiskey Pk. and of course he hadn't no idear where they kept home plate, though it was right in plain sight, but anyway he couldn't seem to see it, and when he borrowed a handkerchief off Umpire Hildebrand in the 2d. innings to get something out of Bill Killifer's eye, I felt like hollering at him to pluck the bean out of his own eye before he went after the molt in his catcher's, but they was all ready enough hollering in the press coop with Bill Phelon and Rube Cook and Sam Hall in full bloom, and Sam's the bird that was tipped off in advance that the govt. was going to make all the seniles either work or fight and he's a sporting editor, so he fell down and broke a leg and I only wished it had of been his larnyx.

But when it come the Cubs' second innings, Tyler had a turn at bat and found out where the plate was and after that his control kept getting better and it got so good in the 9th. innings that he hit Strunk's and Whiteman's bats right in the middle and all that saved us was Jean Dubuc striking out in the pinch and Jean was with Detroit long enough so as the ballyhoo boy ought to know the way to pronounce him which is the same as in Iowa, but instead of that, the boy called him Debuck like he was a cartoonist, but he couldn't even draw a base on balls. Jean hit .340 or something out in the Coast League this yr., but it seems Tyler was pitching in the National League all summer.

Well, everybody was crabbing about the 1st. game and how dull and stupid it was, but they couldn't nobody fall asleep watching this one, not even the Deans that had been out on one of Tiny Maxwell's personally conducted slumming tours to the public library. I suppose you heard about the two Irishmen, Otto Knabe and Heinie Wagner, and all of a sudden Col. Barrow looked over the top and seen Heinie inside the Cubs' barbed wire and he shouted "Boys, who will volunteer to bring back my star lieutenant?"[24] and several responded, but by the time they was half way across nobody's land, Otto and Heinie was yelling kamerad at each other. It seems Otto called Heinie something that got him mad and Heinie is one of the best tempered birds in baseball and it takes a mean lexicon to rile him, so Otto was the logical choice.

Well, Sam Agnew caught Bush for 7 innings, but he caught cold when the band played the S.S.B. and made him take off his cap, so Schang went up to hit for him in the 8th. and he hit all right, but they nailed him trying to romp to third base on a single by Hooper and I couldn't see where he wouldn't of been as well off on 2d. base with his club 3 behind, but I can't manage the Boston club very good from the press coop, though Bill Phelon directed the Cubs O.K. from up there, because I heard him yelling "pitiful fools" and I thought at first he was referring to those who had paid to get in, but it was the Cubs he meant and he hadn't said it more than five or six times when they went out and grabbed themself a three run lead. But as I say, I couldn't stop Schang at second base and he probably cost Boston a tally and when he was throwed out, poor Joe Bush was so desperate that he took off his shoe to see if they was any runs in his stocking.

Well, Harvey, in regards to the morning game, we played out to Jim Cruisinberry's club, Lincoln Pk., and I and him beat the eastern cracks, Nick Matley of Boston and Harry Cross of the Times Square A.C. and at that I didn't play my best game because it says on the score cards out there that players must start from the first tee and besides when you live in a loop hotel and step out of the elevator in the A.M. with your suitcase and bat bag, you half to fight 3 or 4 bellhops that wants to caddy for you over to the desk and the management thinks you're trying to jump your bill and make you wait till somebody has run up to your rm. and seen that you left your toothbrush and all and all it kind of throws a man off, and besides the dressing room out there is a bench back of the first tee and it's a co-ed club so I played in my civies, but I did change a tire on Shields Ave. right after the afternoon battle.

Just as we was going to tee off, a young man that Nick said was the managing editor of the course come up and asked me if I had a button and I said no I hadn't been home for a week, so he said if I didn't have a button I must pay a quarter and he charged all of us a quarter apiece, but we played the match for the lunches and I and Jim didn't mind the quarter when we seen we had them beat, but where do you think they took us to lunch, Harvey? Out to the bards room at the ball pk., where it's free.

Well, Harvey, they won't be no morning game tomorrow though Chas. Weeghman invited us out to Edgewater, but I have got to hustle around all morning and find out how I am going to register here when I'm not, and besides the Dr. says he wants to take a look at my throat and he's been so good to me that I can't hardly refuse him a good time once in a wile.

But they's another ball game tomorrow and I hope those aviators[25] stays away so as I won't half to carry a stiff neck on my vacation, and they call them aces, Harvey, but I would say they was deuces wild, but if they must see the game, why can't they loosen up and pay to get in instead of wanting everything free like a reporter.

R. W. L.

1919

A Hot Tip from the Umpire

BELL SYNDICATE, OCTOBER 1, 1919

Cincinnati, O—Gents: The world serious starts today with a big surprise. A great many people figured that the White Sox would be scared out, and would never appear. But sure enough when we woke up this morning and come down to breakfast, here was the White Sox as big as life and willing to play. The first bird I seen amist them was Ray Schalk, the second catcher.

"Well, Cracker," I said, "I never expected to see you down here as I had been told that you would quit and would never appear." "Well, Biscuit," was his reply, "here we are and that's the best answer."

So after all that is said and done the White Sox is down here and trying to win the first 2 games on their merits so it looks like the serious would not be forfeited after all.

Most of the experts went to the 2 different managers to try and learn who was going to pitch the opening game. So to be different from the rest of them as usual, I passed up the two managers and went to the umpires. The first one I seen was Cy Rigler and I have known him all my life.

"Who is going to win, Cy?" I asked. "I don't know," was his ample reply. You can take that tip or leave it. Personally I am betting on his word. He will give them the best of it if possible.

The next umpire I seen was Quigley. "My system," he said, "is to call everybody out."

The two American league umpires could not be seen as they was both up writing their stuff, but you can be sure that neither of them will give anybody the best of it. So all and all, it looks like a even break in the umpiring.

That brings us to the hotel accommodations. A large Chicago newspaper has got the prize rm. of the lot, namely, the smoking rm. off the ball rm. in the Gibson. This means that if any body wakes up at 3 in the morning and wants to smoke why they can do so without moving out of their rm. And if they want to dance why all as they have to do is go in the next rm. and look for a partner.

A great many people has written in to this hotel to ask how I am going to bet so they can do the opposite and make big money.

Well, Gents, I might as well tell you where I stand. I dont believe either club can win as neither 1 of them has got a manager. But I do know both of the so-called managers personally and I have asked them who is going to pitch the opening game and they both say everybody on the staff so it looks like a free hitting game with Gerner and Mayer in there at the start and Mitchell and Lowdermilk to relieve them, but neither has made any provisions in regards to who is going to relieve us newspapers guys.

The other day as you may remember, I tried to make a comparison of the 2 clubs man for man and when I come to the shortstops why I said the logical thing, which is that no shortstops can win the serious as nobody ever hits to the shortstops in a big event like this. But thousands of birds wrote in personal letters to know what I thought of the 2 shortstops any way so I suppose I have got to tell them.

Well of the two shortstops mentioned Risberg and Kopf will be in there at the start of the serious but they will both be took out before the serious is nine games old. Comparing the both of them, Risberg is a Swede, but on the other hand Kopf hits from both sides of the plate. Both of them is tricky and is libel to throw a ball to a different base than expected.

Kopf is the better looking but Risberg is the tallest and if they ever try to drive a high line drive over his head they will get fooled.

The two stars of the coming serious has both been overlooked by the experts and I refer to Sherwood Magee and John Collins whom a lot of you think won't be in there. Even if they are not they are both good fellows.

Another question the public keeps asking we experts is who gets the advantage of having the serious go nine games in the stead of seven. Well, Gents, all as I can say is it isn't the newspaper men. Further and more I wouldn't be surprised if neither ball club liked the new regime as I have nicknamed it as it looks to me like both mgrs. would use up all the pitchers they have got tomorrow and wouldn't know what to do next.

All together it looks like a long serious, and whoever made it nine games had it in for us.

Kid's Strategy Goes Amuck as Jake Doesn't Die

BELL SYNDICATE, OCTOBER 2, 1919

Cincinnati, Ohio—Gents: Up to the eighth inning this pm, we was all setting there wondering what to write about and I happened to be looking at Jake Daubert's picture on the souvenir program and all of a sudden Jake fell over and I thought he was dead so I said to the boys: "Here is your story:

"Jacob E. Daubert was born in Shamokin, Pa., on the 17 of April, 1886, and lives in Schuykill, Pa. and began playing with the Kane, Pa., club in

1907. With Cleveland in 1908 and Toledo for two years. Joined the Brooklyn club in 1910 and remained there until this season. Then joined the Cincinnati Reds and fell dead in the 8th inning of the 1st. game of the world serious."

So everybody got up and cheered me and said that was a very funny story but all of a sudden again Jake stood up and looked at the different pts. of the compass and walked to 1st. base and wasn't dead at all and everybody turned around and hissed me for not giving them a good story.

Well gents, I am not to blame because when a man has got a fast ball like Grover Lowdermilk and hits a man like Jake in the temple, I generally always figure they are dead and the fact that Jake got up and walked to 1st. base is certainly not my fault and I hope nobody will hold it vs me.

That was only one case where Mr. Gleason's strategy went amuck. His idear there was to kill the regular 1st. baseman and then all Mr. Moran would have left to do would be to either stick Dutch Reuther on 1st. base where he couldn't pitch or else stick Sherwood Magee over there where he couldn't coach at third base. But Jake gummed all up by not dying.

Well another part of Mr. Gleason's strategy was dressing the White Sox in their home uniforms so as they would think they was playing on the home grounds in front of a friendly crowd but the trouble with that was that the Reds was all dressed in their home uniforms so as you couldn't tell which club was at home and which wasn't and it made both of them nervous.

Then to cap off the climax Mr. Gleason goes and starts a pitcher that everybody thought he was going to start which took away the element of surprise and made a joker out of the ball game. If he had of only started Erskine Mayer or Bill James or any of the other boys that I recommended why the Reds breath would have been took away and even if they had of hit they couldn't of ran out their hits.

The trouble with the White Sox today was that they was in there trying to back up a nervous young pitcher that never faced a big crowd in a crux before and when he got scared and blowed why it was natural for the rest of them to also blow up. But just give these young Chicago boys a chance to get use to playing before a big crowd with money depending on it and you will be surprised at how they get on their ft. and come back at them.

Nobody should ought to find fault with Mr. Gleason, however, for what happened today. As soon as it was decided that they would have 9 games in this serious why the Kid set down and figured that the rules called for 9 men on a side and if 1 Red was killed per day and the serious run the full 9 games why they would only be 1 man left to play the final game and 1 man cant very well win a ball game even vs. the White Sox the way they looked. But Daubert didn't die as expected and they will know better next time then to hit a left handed 1st. baseman in the egg.

As for the game itself they has probably never been a thriller game in a big serious. The big thrill come in the 4th. innings when everybody was wondering if the Sox would ever get the 3rd. man out. They finely did and several occupants of the press box was overcome. The White Sox only chance at that pt. was to keep the Reds in there hitting till darkness fell and make it a illegal game but Heinie Groh finely hit a ball that Felsch could not help from catching and gummed up another piece of stratagem.

Before the game a band led by John Philip Sousa played a catchy air called the Stars and Stripes Forever and it looks to me like everybody would be whistling it before the serious runs a dozen more games.

It now looks like the present serious would be 1 big surprise after another and tomorrow's shock will occur when the batterys is announced which will be Rube Bressler for the Reds and Lefty Sullivan for the Sox. This will be the biggest upset of the entire fiasco.

I seen both managers right after today's holy cost and Moran said hello old pal, and Gleason said hello you big bum so I am picking the Reds from now on.

A Dirty Finger on the Ball

BELL SYNDICATE, OCTOBER 9, 1919

Cincinnati—Gents: This is the most scandalous and death dealing story ever wrote about a world serious ball game. They have been a whole lot of talk in this serious about one thing and another and it finely remained for me to get at the facts.

Well, those of you who was out at todays game don't have to be explained to that in the fifth inning Eddie Cicotte pitched a baseball to Larry Kopf and Larry missed it and turned around to Mr. Quigley who was supposed to be umpiring behind the plate and asked this bird to let him (Kopf) see the ball.

Well, Mr. Quigley give Mr. Kopf the ball and he looked at it and Mr. Quigley said "Larry do you want the ball," and Larry said "No I don't want it." So Mr. Quigley said "All right throw the ball back to the pitcher. I can't stop this ball game all day to let an infielder look at a ball." Then I stepped in and said "Give me the ball" so they did.

Well, they give me the ball and here it is laying in front of me and I want to say to all infielders who of course never keep a ball long enough to look at it just what a baseball looks like and if I was an infielder I would catch a ball some time and hold on to it till after the game was lost and then I would study the ball.

Well, here is the ball right in front of me as I try to write. I will describe to you guys as I see it. Well, this ball looks to me like a National League ball. That is what probably deceived them.

Well you see the reason that an infielder don't know what a baseball looks like is because the minute he gets it he has to throw it somewhere. Well as I said before here is what the baseball looks like.

The National League baseball is nearly round. This baseball which I am going to keep and give to my oldest child is a baseball that needs further description. It is the same baseball that Larry Kopf looked at and I only wished I was as nice looking as him and I wouldn't be writing this horrible stuff or working at baseball.

Well, then, here is about that baseball. It is nearly round and looks nearly like an American League baseball except it has more seams and to be exact it has got 126 seams and if you take an American League ball why it has got 140 seams so why shouldn't you hit them. But at that you take any ball and start counting seams on it and you can count all night and get innumerable seams.

Well, to distinguish this ball from its brothers it says John A. Heydler on it which makes it a cinch that it is a National League ball as it is a certainty that John wouldn't sign a ball that belonged to the other league.

Well as for the rest of the ball it looks soiled on the northwest side and I will worry my life away wondering who put a dirty finger on that ball which I have got and my children will still have it after me. Now, we have wrote almost a whole story about a ball.

Now, let us take a different angle about the game and start in on Morris Rath. At one stage of the game Morris hit a ball and broke his bat and the man setting next to me said that is the only time Morris ever broke a bat in a world serious.

Another funny thing I heard was as follows. A man named Wingo come up to the bat and the bird setting next to me said come on Wingo get a bingo.

1920

No Need to Bribe Brooklyn

BELL SYNDICATE, OCTOBER 4, 1920

Long Island—Well, Brooklyn winning the Natl. League penance gives the comeing world serious a international odor, but it is hoped the flavor don't last as long as the sweet perfume witch is still exhaleing out of the 1919 classic. In the early days of the world serious they was a theory that the boys on the winning eleven made more jack than the loosers, but last yr. the Reds only drug down $5,200.00 apiece, witch some people inclusive of the Cook County grand jury say was just pin money along side of what a few of the victims grabbed off.

All joking to 1 side, I wouldn't be surprised if this serious was win and lose on its merits. I will promise the fans that if either club is boughten off it won't be the Robins. The gamblers seen them perform in the serious of 1916, and feel like it would be a waist of money to bribe them to not play their best. They can do that without no bonus. Besides witch the boys on the Brooklyn nine is as nice a bunch as you would want to meet, and I would trust them with anything I got at 6 per cent though several of them has often double-crossed the men they was working for. For inst., they led Stallings and Chance and McGraw and etc. to believe that they wasn't no good so as they could get to Brooklyn, and as soon as they got there—look at them.

Experts is divided amongst themself as to who should ought to cop this setto. The Robins is doped to win by some of them. Others say they would half to be. The latter point to what happened in 1916, but they want to remember that Brooklyn 4 yrs. ago and Brooklyn now is two different boroughs. Some of the Robins witch was in their early forties when they played the Red Sox has had time to mellow without getting over ripe or rancid, as Robbie has kept them in a cool place near the cellar most of the while. And, with a few exceptions, they are mostly all birds that has had too much experience to get scared in a pinch

To Rube Marquard, for inst., a world serious is just like a bathtub. He has been in more of them than anybody in the Natl League outside of Bill Klem. World serious, I mean.

Personally I don't like neither club's chances, and won't recommend neither of them because even a man like myself can't know everything. Last yr., for example. I told my friends that the White Sox was a cinch and go bet on them, but that was because I didn't have no idear how many good ball players was playing for the Reds that never had their names in a Cincinnati box score. I wish I had my money back. My advice to the fan this time is to watch the umpires close, and if one of them pulls a close one that looks raw write him a abusive letter.

The genl. custom for a expert at this stage, is to take the 2 opposing teams and compare them man for man and in that way the readers will get a pretty good idear of nothing. Look at last fall for inst. All the nuts that writes base ball agreed before the serious that when it comes to the rival 2d basemans, why Morris Rath wouldn't never be on speaking terms with Eddie Collins. But in the games themself Morris was on the bases so much that he got to be a pest, while Columbia's favorite alumnae never found out where 1st base was only by hearsay.

So I am under the delusion that they's other ways of waisting the readers' time and my way is to write a few vital statistics in regards to Robbie's boys witch is not so well known to base ball dumb in genl. as their great American league oppts.

Well then, Konetchy, Kilduff and Kreuger all starts their last name with K. Mamauz, McCabe, can outsing anybody in the American league and the Robins boasts of the best quartet that has been in agonized base ball since the Red Sox left go of Buck O'Brien, Hugh Bradley, Marty

McHale and who ever was the 4th thrust in that bird's nest. Robbie's pitching aces is expected to be Smith, Grimes, and Cadoro and we defys any American league mgr. to produce 3 good pitchers with as pretty a 1st name as Sherrod, Burleigh and Leon. The Olson that plays shortstop is the only Olson that his 1st name ain't Ole and the Griffith that plays the outfield is a great grandson of Clark Griffith of the Washington club.

In 1916 President Ebbets of the Brooklyn club was so pleased with his boys winning the penance that he treated them with a ride to Boston in a day coach for the 1st game of the serious. So this yr. the Robins was kind of pulling for the Yankees to win in the other league as they wanted to experience the delights of a trip from Brooklyn to the Polo Grounds in a wheel barrow. However the fates ruled otherwise and it is announced that when the National league champs leaves for the west it will be in a smoker equipped with seats that you can turn over and park your dogs on the top seat and plenty of floor space to throw ashes and get rid of used up eating tobacco.

Two days later, Lardner again referred to the previous year's World Series:

Brooklyn, N.Y.—Just befor I left the heavily mortgaged this a.m. to go to Brooklyn, a bird that said he represented a cootie that represented a former champion prize fighter that represented a master mind, called me up on the phone and says they was prepared to make it worth my while if I would agree to not write my best about this world serious. For a minute I thought about the wife and kiddies and then I thought about the money and I say something to the bird on the other end of the wire and hung up on him and I will leave it to the public to judge whether I listened to reason or no . . .

Ring Splits Double-Header

BELL SYNDICATE, OCTOBER 12, 1920

Cleveland, Ohio—They was a double header in Cleveland today. The 1st game was played this morning at the Mayfield Country club between the Bell Syndicate vs. Nick Flatley of Boston and Rube Goldberg of Brooklyn. It came out a tie. I and Rube played for a dollar a hole on the side and I got two dollars of the poor hick's money and he can't afford to loose that kind of money either. The medal score refused to give out for the fear of incriminating itself. Leave me tell the world that Mayfield coarse makes the engineers club on long island look like a billiard table and Alexa Stirling[26] must be a pretty good female golfer to make it an eighty even if one of the Clevelanders does call her Alex A. Stirling.

The other game was what I have nicknamed a duel between two rival south paws or left handers. The Robbins has now had sixteen innings of "Duster" Mails[27] and they hope they won't get any more of him. They will probably get what they hope. Sherry Smith and the rest of the Robbins acted kind of grouchy towards Tommy Connolly all afternoon. They has a little matter of $1,600.00 a piece involved in some of Tommy's decisions and as the Brooklyn players is both older and there are more of them than the Cleveland players why naturally they have got more wives and kiddies and more mortgages on the heavily mortgaged farm. So they thought maybe Tommy would give them a little the best of it on ball and strike.

To an impartial and very ignorant observer like the handsome writer it looked like Tommy was as fair to one side as the other and that aint saying much. His right arm seemed to have suffered a stroke of paresis during the night and he didnt like to call strikes unless the ball was either somewhere near the plate or the batter swang at it either one but all and all I have watched the work of the umpires pretty close during this series and none of them has been any better than the rest of them and most of them not one half as good as the other three.

Bill Dineen is the only one who you might say has disgraced himself so far. Bill was due to umpire behind the plate in Saturday's game and his colleagues is very particular about their personal appearances on account of umpires being unpopular enough without looking like a rummy, so they noticed that Bills umpiring pants had run out of creases and they was no chance to get them pressed as it is still Yom Kippur in Ohio, so they signed a petition asking him to wear another pair. So Bill happened to have a pair of street pants which is same cerulean blue that agonized baseball requires the umpires to wear when they are pretending to work, so he decided to put them on but when Bill walks around the street in his trousers he dont wear shin guards under them, as never in his whole life has man or beast came up and deliberately kicked him in the shins wile he was merely walking up and down the st. so the seamstress that made Bill's trousers didnt allow for shin guards and the result was that when the shin guards was stuck under them, the trousers all worked up.

During the last ½ of the Saturday game Bill was wearing involuntary knickerbockers and the fans and fanettes was so busy admiring his charms that they could not look at the ball game.

Amongst those seen today's pastime was Denton Cy Young, the old pitcher that Hughey Fullerton claims to of discovered and Secretary of War Baker. Newt set up in the upper deck and said it was one of the best battles he ever saw closer than from 3,000 miles away. Willie Wambsganss and Elmer Smith was called up to the plate before the game and presented with a couple of watches for what they done in Sunday's game.[28] Elmer's alleged timepiece had his name engraved on it but when the generous jeweler wanted the same thing done for Wamby, the engraver busted him in the jaw and quit.

A kite flew over the field during the battle with Harding and Davis wrote on. It didn't say what business they was in. That is about all that happened today except George Burns' double in the 6th, witch isn't the same Geo. Burns that plays left field for the Giants and lives in a funny town named Little Falls in the off seasons.

Tomorrow is the last day of our enjoyable stay in the 5th city of the grand old U.S. and president Jim Dunn of the Indians better git a hump on himself or Charlie Ebbets of Brooklyn will finish one up on him. It will be remembered by those that was still able to see the last day in Brooklyn, that Charley not only showed us a ball game but also throwed in a vaudeville skitch for one and the same admission. This skitch was a race around the bases between Brooklyn ball players and a heel-and-toe pedestrian almost in the nude. The man in the nether garments was supposed to walk around once before the other bird run around twice. He done it and it looked to him like somebody had put something under the ball player's pillow, but the crowd would of went nuts over the exciting event if they hadnt already been that way before they come in the park.

Anyway, it looks like it was up Jim to put on a skitch before tomorrow's game, and may I not suggest that he got hold of the gal that plays "Aphrodite," witch is in Cleveland this week and have her come out and practice sliding to bases in her stage costume, witch is put on with a brush. The boys from Brooklyn is feeling pretty chipper as we go to press because although the Indians has now won 4 games to the Robbins 2, why it looks like Mgr. Speaker with his inferior pitching staff, is now up against a tough proposition and may be forced tomorrow to depend on an unreliable young cuckoo named Coveleskie.

1921

Lardner Hitting 1.000, Peeved at Weatherman

BELL SYNDICATE, OCTOBER 9, 1921

New York—This was one of the stormy days exclusively predicted by the undersigned and now all I need to make my world series prophecy 1000 per cent perfect is another p.m. of rain and a couple of tie games. The boys will still be playing this series a week from today and by that time some of the visiting firemen will be asking their nurse how the game came out. The spirits is plentiful but the flesh is weak.

When news come that it was raining many out of town fans who had been asleep under the grand stand got up and sought vantage points from which to enjoy the novelty as it was their first glimpse of water since reaching New York.

The opinion amongst the experts seemed to be that the postponement helped the Yankees. It gives Huggins pitchers a chance to rest up, though I wouldn't be surprised if some of them had from now till spring to do that. It also was good for Babe Ruth's arm which is said to be infected so that he can't hardly write,[29] but who ever it benefitted the most, I know who it didn't benefit the most and that is the visiting Elks and scribes. It means ruin and the breaking up of homes for some of we boys, thats what it means. The storm caused a rush of brains to Harry Stevens cafe under the stand, down there I run into Judge Landis to say nothing about George B. Christian, secretary to President Harding, and Bill Pipp, who is Wally Pipps old man. Mr. Pipp introduced us all to Mrs. Pipp and a couple of pippins. Mr. Christian wouldn't say what was the object of his visit to New York, but he made the remark that the President would like another golf game with I and Grantland Rice, so that may of been it.

They was a large policeman in the runway between the press box and the lunch room and he challenged everybody that tried to go to and fro, including not only Judge Landis but his secretary Mr. O'Connor. As these two gents is really the two who are running the series, its a wonder the officer didn't bean them with his billie. A policemans place is on the third base coaching line.

Well, friends, that is all I am going to write about a game that wasn't played, this is going to be a long series and us experts will need all the words we got without wasting none on a rainy day.

Scribes Saved from Overflow of Brains

BELL SYNDICATE, OCTOBER 10, 1921

The fans maybe don't realize how close we was to having a holocaust at this passtime. In the second innings, Shufflin' Phil[30] pitched a sour one that just missed cracking Ward[31] square on the egg. An inch lower and the athlete's brains would of come hurtling into the press coop which was already overcrowded with same. You can imagine what the congestion would of did to the scribes in their weakened condition.

As it was, the only casualty of the day was Carl Mays, who the Giants finally got to in the eighth innings and when they got to him they done a man size job of it. Before the game Carl was a good bet to shut them out again like he done the other day as the first 100 times you bat against him is supposed to be the hardest and this was only the Giants' second chance.

And for seven innings today he held them to two clean hits and a scratch single by Snyder which I call a scratch because the official scorers scratched it off the records.

But before they was a man out in the eighth the tail-end of McGraw's batting order had earned the run that tied the count and had two men in position to score on George Burns' double. Carl was socked for three hard wallops and a safe bunt in this frame and in the ninth his defeat was turned into a disgrace. For three more guys plastered him and one of these three was George Kelly.

Instead of taking his place in the world's series hall of fame along with Ed Walsh, Christy Mathewson, Chief Bender and Red Faber, Carl's name will now go down in history as the pitcher who Bill Lange's grandson got a base hit off of in the series of 5862, New York time. Saturday's rain was supposed to be soup for Carl as it give him an unexpected day of rest. He looks now like he ought to of took another one.

The real heroes of this battle was Emil Meusel, who the Yankee nuts speak of as that brother of Bob Meusel's, and Johnny Rawlings, the weak sister of the series, according to the boys that play the games a few days ahead of the athletes. An explanation of Emil's conduct may be found in the fact that he was with the Phillies up to two months ago and never knew they was one big league, let alone that Carl Mays was the star pitcher of the other one. Rawlings has been a busher, too, but you'd think he had been around long enough to hear of Carl. Rawlings' work so far can't be explained in no legitimate way and it seems to me like they ought to keep men like he out of an important series. All he does is make a sucker out of the law and prophets.

People that thronged the Polo grounds this time went there without no expectations of seeing Babe Ruth as the Babe was alleged to be out of it for this game at least and maybe for the whole series on account of a poisoned arm. But the Babe fooled everybody and got in the game after telling his Dr. to go to a place which is said to be already overcrowded with the medical profession.

Babe played with his souper all bound round and it seemed to bother him in throwing. But he grabbed himself off another single and made a new world's record by hitting the most useless home run in the history of organized baseball.

The Giant infield played for Ruth pretty near the same way that National league infields play for Cy Williams of the Phillies. Bancroft moved over to the right field side of second base. Rawlings camped in short right field and Kelly hugged the foul line. The whole left side of the infield was left to Frankie Frisch. Babe's first effort was a roller that went right where Kelly was. playing. His second was a single to right field which, by the way, George Burns, the centerfield, was set just right to stop. When he came up the third time he whiffed and as luck would have it, Snyder was playing right where he could catch the third strike. And if Ross Young had only been setting up in the right field seats he could of catched the one Babe hit in the ninth, and took it home to the wife and kiddies, if any.

In this infield arrangement Bancroft is the one that is taking the chance, as he stands right where Babe pickles his line drives. One of these days George Burns will see two balls coming at him at once and one of them will be Bancroft's head. For some reason or another, the Yankees has quit stealing home. Two of them made efforts to steal second today, but they will go down in history as efforts. Roger Peckinpaugh's attempt was a delayed steal in the sixth inning, They was so much delay that Roger ain't there yet.

One thing I would like to call attention to and have Judge Landis do something about it before the next series is, namely, the practice of having the band play the "Star Spangled Banner" just before every game. Gents like myself and George Moriarty and Fred Toney is as patriotic as everybody else, but the exposure is terrible. If we have got to keep doing it, at least make the women do it, too. They ought not to be barred when they have already win the right to smoke cigarets, drink gin and pick their teeth.

That is about all I have got to say except that I was woke up this morning to receive seventy-six telegrams from Nick Altrock, the main idear of which was that I hadn't mentioned him and his partner, Al Schacht,[32] in none of these articles. So here is your name, Nick, and don't send me no more telegrams and I would of give you a write-up, only if a man starts mentioning the names of different comedians in this series they's no place to draw the line. I might even half to include the box score.

The Most Important World Series in History

BELL SYNDICATE, OCTOBER 3, 1922

New York—All though they have been world serious practally every yr. for the last 20 yrs. this next world serious which is supposed to open up Wed. P.M. at the Polo grounds is the most important world serious in history as far as I and my family are conserned and even more important to us than the famous world serious of 1919 which was win by the Cincinnati Reds greatly to their surprise.

Maybe I would better exclaim myself before going any further. Well a few days previous to the serious of 1919 I was approached by a young lady who I soon recognized as my wife and any way this woman says would I buy her a fur coat as the winter was comeing on and we was going to spend it in Connecticut which is not genally considered one of the tropics.

"But don't do it," she says, "unless you have got the money to spare because of course I can get along without it." "In fact," she added bursting into tears, "I am so used to getting along without this, that and the other thing that maybe it would be best for you not to buy me that coat after all as the sight of a luxury of any kind might prove my undoing."

"Listen," was my reply, "as far as I am concerned you don't half to prove your undoing. But listen you are in a position to know that I can't spare the money to buy you one stoat leave alone enough of the little codgers skins to make a coat for a growed up girl like you. But if I can get a hold of any body that is sucker enough to bet on Cincinnati in this world serious, why I will borrow from some good pal and cover their bet and will try and make the bet big enough so as the winnings will buy you the handsomest muleskin coat in New England."

Well friends I found the sucker and got a hold of enough money to cover his bet and not only that but give him odds of 6 to 5 and that is why we did not go out much in Greenwich that winter and not for lack of invitations as certain smart Alex has let fall.

I might also mention at this junction that they was a similar agreement at that serious between Eddie Collins the capt. of the White Sox and his

Mrs. only of course Eddie did not make no bet, but if his team win, why he would buy the madam a personal sedan whereas if his team lost, why she would half to walk all winter. Luckily the Collinses live in Lansdowne, Pa., where you can't walk far.

Well friends I do not know what is the automobile situation in the Collins family at the present writeing as have not saw them of late but the fur coat situation in my family is practically the same like it was in 1919 only as I hinted in the opening paragraph of this intimate article, it is a d–am sight worse.

Because this yr. they won't be no chance for the little woman to offset her paucity of outdoor raps by spending the winter in the house. She is going to need furs even there.

Therefore as I say this comeing serious is the most important of all as far as we are conserned for Mother ain't the same gal when she is cold and after all is said and done what is home without Mother in her tantrums?

So I and my little ones is hopeing and praying that the boys on who I have staked my winters happiness this yr. will not have no meetings in no hotel rooms between now and Wednesday but will go into this serious determined to do their best which I once said was the best anybody could do and the man who heard me say it said "You are dead right Lardner" and if these boys do their best, why it looks to me like as if the serious should ought to be well over by Sunday night and the little woman's new fur coat delivered to our little home some time Monday and maybe we will get invited out somewheres that night and they will be a blizzard.

The Fur Coat Is Already Bought

BELL SYNDICATE, OCTOBER 4, 1922

New York—In the last 24 hrs. the telegraph office at Great Neck has been swamped you might say with telegrams from baseball fans all over the country wanting to know who I have bet on in the world serious in order to win the little woman the price of a costly fur coat.

Well friends as I have not got no broad casting station in our little home, why I guess the easiest way to satisfy the nation wide curiosity in regards to my choice is to make my announcement through the press and I realize that this announcement is going to come like a big surprise as a great many people thinks I am crazy.

Well friends I have bet on the Yankees.

Further and more I would not be throwed into fever of excitement was the Yankees to win in 4 straight games though I have not bet no fur coat on that kind of a proposition.

I hope they won't be no National league fans in N.Y. or elsewhere who will take offense at these here statements and I want to assure one and all that my attitude ain't been influenced in no way by personal animals as some of my best friends is in the National league and my favorite athlete from a stand point of good cheer is young Mr. Stengel.

Not only that but I win a very small wager on the Giants last fall and therefore feel sympathetic towards same. But a man can't let their sentiments run away with them when their Mrs. is hollering for a flee skin coat.

Now I suppose my readers who is reading this article will no sooner read which team I have picked when they will want to know the reason why. Well friends I will exclaim in a nutshell.

The serious last yr. was a triumph of mind over matter but this yr. they ain't nothing the matter.

The Yankees went into the serious last yr. with the Babe crippled and only 2 guys that could pitch. Bob Shawkey who is one of the best pitchers in the league looked like the game of baseball was to him a new toy. Well at this writeing they aint nothing the matter with the Babe and Shawkey is his old self and for the rest of the pitching corpse, you can realize the difference between last fall's and this fall's if you stop to think that Carl Mays, who everything depended on him last year, may not even half to warm up.

Further and more the weak spot of the 1921 defense which was the left side of the infield is now being took care of by the best pair since Weaver and Risberg on the other side. Pipp and Ward are at least as good as ever and Whitey Witt is a pillow of strength to the outfield as Lou Ritchie used to say and all and all you can't find no weakness outside of the lack of a good left hand pitcher which of course is Harry Frazee's fault not mine.

Now then how does this season's Giants compare with the champs of 1921? Well, they have got Heine Groh who is good enough to help anybody's ball club, and they don't miss Geo. Burns on acct. of the way young Stengel is going.

But when old Shufflin Phil wrote that mash note to his dear friend Les, he not only wrote goodbye to his own big league career but also a fond farewell to the Giants' hopes of repeating. Under good management you can stagger along and win a pennant without pitchers a specially if the competition is weak. But a world serious is something else.

These is some of the things which has caused me to rely on the Yanks for the madam's eel skin coat and while I am predicting will also state:

That the Babe will hit at least 3 out of the park.
That Joe Bush will pitch at least one shut out.
That people who never seen Shawkey pitch except last fall will be surprised.

This is how I feel about it brother and of course I may be wrong which won't be the 1st. time. But if I am wrong it won't be necessary for Giant fans to write and call my attention to same. The Mrs. will let me know in her own way.

Mr. Lardner Corrects a Wrong Impression

BELL SYNDICATE, OCTOBER 5, 1922

New York—Well friends you can imagine my surprise and horror when I found out tonight that the impression had got around some way another that as soon as this serious was over I was planning to buy a expensive fur coat for my Mrs. and put a lot of money into same and buy a coat that would probably run up into hundreds and hundreds of dollars. Well I did not mean to give no such kind of a impression and I certainly hope that my little article was not read that way by everybody a specially around my little home because in the first place I am not a sucker enough to invest hundreds and hundreds of dollars in a garment which the chances are that the Mrs. will not wear it more than a couple times all winter as the way it looks now we are libel to have the most openest winter in history and if women folks should walk along the st. in expensive fur coats in the kind of weather which it looks like we are going to have why they would only be laughed at and any way I believe a couple can have a whole lot better time in winter staying home and reading a good book or maybe have a few friends in to play bridge.

Further and more I met a man at supper last night that has been in the fur business all his life and ain't did nothing you might say only deal in furs and this man says that they are a great many furs in this world which is reasonable priced that has got as much warmth in them as high price furs and looks a great deal better. For inst. he says that a man is a sucker to invest thousands and thousands of dollars in expensive furs like ermine, muleskin, squirrel skin and Kerensky when for a hundred dollars or not even that much, why a man can buy a owl skin or horse skin or weasel skin garment that looks like big dough and practically prostrates people with the heat when they wear them.

So I hope my readers will put a quietus on the silly rumor that I am planning to plunge in the fur market. I will see that my Mrs. is dressed in as warm a style as she has been accustomed to but neither her or I is the kind that likes to make a big show and go up and down 5th avenue sweltering in a $700 hog skin garment in order so as people will turn around and gap at us. Live and let live is my slocum.

So much for the fur coat episode and let us hear no more about it and will now go on with my article, which I must apologize for it not being very good and the reason is on account of being very nervous after our little ride from the Polo Grounds to Park Row. It was my intentions to make this trip in the subway, but while walking across the field after the game I run into Izzy Kaplan, the photographer, and he says would I like to ride down in a car which him and his friends had hired, so I and Grantland Rice got in and we hadn't no sooner than started when one of our fellow passengers says that we ought to been with them coming up. "We made the trip from Park Row in 24 minutes," he says, "and our driver said he was going to beat that record on the return trip."

So we asked what had held them back comeing up and one of them said that the driver had kept peeling and eating bananas all the way and that he did not drive so good when both hands was off the wheel. Besides that, they had ran into a guy and had to wait till the ambulance came and picked him up.

Well friends I will not try and describe our flight only to say that we did not beat the record but tied it and the lack of bananas didn't prevent our hero from driving with his hands of the wheel as he used the last named to shake his fists at pedestrians and other riff raff that don't know enough to keep off the public highways during the rush hour.

Most of the things I was going to mention in this article was scared out of me during our little jaunt. One of them however was the man from Toronto that stood in line with his wife from 8 p.m. Tuesday night till the gates opened Wednesday morning so as to be sure of good seats. According to officials of the club, they could of got the same seats if they had not showed up till a couple hours before the game, but if they had of done that, why the lady would not of had no chance to brag when she got back home. The way it is, why she can say to her friends, "Charley may not be much for looks, but he certainly showed me the night life of New York."

Dividing interest with this couple was a couple of heel and toe pedestrians that done their base circling stunt just before the start of the game. One of them was the same guy that done it before the first game last fall, but this time he was accompanied by a lady hoofer and it is not too much to say that the lady was dressed practically as though for her bath. Casey Stengel expressed the general sentiment in the following words, "If that is just her walking costume I would hate to see her made up for tennis."

The following day, after the second game of the series was called because of darkness and recorded as a tie, Lardner wrote, "the only thing I liked about the day was the weather, and it goes to show what a sucker a man would be to squander thousands and thousands of dollars in a fur garment and then maybe have a whole winter of just such days like today. Personally, I seen a girlie on the St. last night wearing a linen duster and you have no idear how good they look on some people and keep you plenty warm too if you move around and don't stand still."

It Looks Bad for the Three
Little Lardner Kittens

BELL SYNDICATE, OCTOBER 7, 1922

New York—Amongst the inmates of our heavily mortgaged home in Great Neck is 3 members of what is sometimes referred to as the feline tribe born the 11th day of last April and christened respectully Barney, Blackie and Ringer. These 3 little ones is motherless, as the lady cat who bore them, aptly named Robin Hood took sick one June day and was give away by Fred to a friend to whom he kindly refrained from mentioning her illness.

These 3 little members of the feline tribe is the cutest and best behaved kitties in all catdom. Their conduct having always been above reproaches outside of a tendency on the part of Ringer to bite strangers' knuckles. Nowhere on Long Island is a more loveable trio of grimalkins, and it pierces my old heart to think that some day next week these 3 little fellows must be shot down like a dog so as their fur can be fashioned into a warm Winter coat for she who their antics has so often caused to screek with laughter. Yes boys the 3 little kittens is practically doomed you might say and all because today's game at the Polo grounds was not called on account of darkness long before it started though they was no time during the afternoon when the Yanks could see.

I probably never would of heard of a cat skin coat was it not for an accidental introduction last night to a man who has did nothing all his life but sell and wear fur coats and who told me that no finer or more warmer garment can be fashioned than is made from the skin of a milkfed kitty.

"Listen," was the way he put it, "you would be a even worse sucker than you are if you was to squander thousands on thousands of dollars on the fur of a muskrat or a mule when you have right in your own asylum the makings of the most satisfactory and handsome coat that money can buy."

"Yes," was my reply, "but the fur of 3 kittens would make a mighty small coat."

"Small coats is the rage," was his reply, "and I personally seen some of the best dressed women in New York strolling up and down 10th avenue during the last cold snap with cat skin garments no bigger than a guest towel."

So while I said a few paragraphs back that the result of this ball game spelled the doom of our little kitties, why as a matter of fact I have just about made up my mind to not buy no costly furs even if the Yanks does come through and bring me out on the right side of the public ledger. Whatever I win in bets on this serious I will freely give to charity.

I would try and describe the game to you in intimate detail was it not played in such darkness that I was only able to see a few incidences. One of these occurred in the 3rd inning and consisted of Whitey Witt getting caught asleep off of first base by a snap throw from one of the Smith brothers. Henry Edwards, the dean of Cleveland baseball experts, explained this incidence by saying that Whitey thought he was still with the Athletics. It is more likely however that Whitey was deceived by the darkness into believing it was his bed time.

The next incidence come in the 4th inning when the Babe tried to go from first to third on a wallop by Bob Meusel that got away from Frisch. Frankie pegged the ball to Heine Groh who stood in Babe's path to third but it was so dark that Babe crashed right smack into him and secured a rolling fall. For a minute it looked like they would be fisticuffs between the 2 famous athletes but Heine suddenly remembered the advice given him by his first school teacher, "Never be a bully," and the fight was over before it begun.

Fifteen minutes before the start of the game the official announcer come up to the press box and said that McQuillan was going to pitch for the Giants. A minute later he come around again and said to make it Scott instead of McQuillan. McQuillan thus broke Fred Toney's record for the length of time spent in a world series ball game.

I will close this article by making a apology to the boys to who I have give tickets for games no 1 and 3 and whose seats is in section 24 which is as far north as you can get without falling out of the grandstand. The gents who sold me these seats thought I was a close friend of the Meusel boys and might want to set out there myself and kid with them.

Yanks Lose, But Lardner Kittens Spared

BELL SYNDICATE, OCTOBER 9, 1922

New York—Well boys it looks like it was all over and the only complaint I have got to make is that the traffic regulations was not handled right. The next time the Yankees takes part in a World Serious they should ought to have a traffic policeman stationed between 1st and 2nd base and another traffic policeman stationed between home and 1st. The former should tell the boys when it is o.k. to run to 2nd. And the latter must inform them that when a ground ball is hit to the infield in a world serious the general theory which has never been disapproved is to run on high speed to 1st base which is the base towards the right field from the home plate. The lack of a adequate stop and go system is what lost this serious on the part of the Yanks. The final game of the serious was marked by the only incedence of brains exhibited by the Yanks during the whole serious. In the 2nd innings with two boys on the bases and one out Joe Bush passed Arthur Nehf to 1st base so as to get the head of the batting order up and not confuse the official scorers. This bit of thinking probably was responsible for nothing.

I will not try and dilate on the rest of the serious only to say that Charles A. Hughes and Eddie Batchelor of Detroit spent this a.m. at the Bronx Zoo to try and see more animals. It is hard to satisfy the boys from Detroit.

All as I know what to write about on a occasion like this kind is little incedence that come off. The 1st incedence that calls to mine is in regards to Tommy Rice of the Brooklyn Eagle. Tommy wrote 7000 words in regards to the 1st game of the serious and page by page it blew out of the window in the costly apartment building in which Brooklyn experts lives. There is no telling what the loss to the world is on account of not being able to read Tommy's story to say nothing about the readers of the Eagle.

Now boys I suppose they is a few interested in whether the little woman is going to get a costly fur coat. The other day I wrote a story to the general effects that we was going to kill our cats and use their fur to make the costly garment. This story was not apreciated in the heavily mortgaged home. After a long argument the master of the house compromised and decided to not doom the little members of the finny tribe to death. Instead of that we are going to use a idear furnished by the same Eddie Batchelor of Detroit mentioned a few thousand words ago. Eddie's idears is to start a chain letter to all our friends and readers asking them to look around the old homestead and find their family albums and take the plush off of the covers and send it to the undersigned and make a plush coat which everybody tells me is the most fashionable fur on the green footstool. The little woman can wear plush and a specially the red pigment but black and tan plush covers will be welcomed and this man tells me theys nothing more attractive than a black and red and tan blocked coat made out of plush albums.

I was going to say further in regards to the plush albums but Harry Frazee has just butted in with the story of his life. It seems like when Harry was a young man in Peoria his father said to him if you don't be wild and go into the theatrical business and stay around Peoria you will be as big a man as your uncle. So Harry looked at his uncle who was getting $125 per month staring at books. "Well," says Harry, "I can get more than that catching runaway horses." So he is now catching runaway horses and selling them to the New York baseball club.

As I now sit here and write I am surrounded by a corpse of experts just as ignorant as me and they don't seem to be none of them able to tell who is going to pitch tomorrow. Personally I think it will be Col. Ruppert and Huston.

1923

Fans Agrog as Series Opens

BELL SYNDICATE, OCTOBER 10, 1923

New York—Nationwide baseball fans is all a grog tonight over the threatened opening tomorrow of a world serious which after a careful study of who is to be the two opening teams, I have no hesitants in nicknaming it a novelty,

It is possible that the same two clubs has met a couple of times previous in the last few yrs. for baseball's highest horrors, but according to

Sam Crane, a veteran expert, this will be their first clash at the Yankee Stadium. This in itself enough to give a person the creeps but to add to the confusion, the opening game will be preceded by a interesting program of track and field events as follows:

1 P.M.—Base-running contest between Casey Stengel and Papyrus.[33] The pair will start from the home plate at the same time and circle the bases in opposite directions. Papyrus going to third base first as horses always run backwards in England. In this connection it may be news to horse lovers, if any, that the big match race at Belmont a wk. from next Saturday will be ran under the same auspices, namely Papyrus will go the wrong way of the track, and those intending to bet on the contest should be warned that the other way round is longer. Conditions will be just the reverse in the brush between Mr. Stengel and Mr. Horse, as first base at the Yankee park is easier to get to than third. The winner will be the one that meets each other and the contest will be judged incognito by the man that refereed the Dempsy-Firpo fight. Donoghue will ride Papyrus and the crowd will ride Casey.

1:12 P.M.—Long distance throwing contest between Geo. Kelly of the Giants, Bob Meusel of the Yanks and Bud Fisher's recent race horse, Hyperion. Geo. and Bob will throw baseballs and Hyperion will throw a jockey.

1:26 P.M.—Radio lecture on "Thrift" by prominent bankers from Shelby, Montana.

1:35 P.M.—Optical test for the umpires to see if they can tell dark from light.

1:55 P.M.—Rendition of the "Star Spangled Banner" by Brooklyn Tree Surgeons military band to allow I and Judge Landis to show our hair.

Before the serious last yr. I come right out in print and told who I was betting on and a good many people took advantage of same. This yr. who I am backing will remain a secret till the 15th of November, when you can find out by inquiring at some of the dept. stores. My winnings last yr. was to of been spent on a fur coat for the Mrs. and it may be of interest to fans that I bought her the coat irregardless rather than see both of us freeze. No matter which way I come out this yr. I am at liberty to spend the winnings on something for myself as I have got the little woman so browbeaten by this time that she will wear the same coat two winters. Personly I ain't made up my mind what to buy, but it will either be a ½ dozen new blades or a hot dog depending on results.

Jokes to the side for a moment, it seems to me like the first inning of this first game will give us all a hunch one way or the other in regards to what to expect. If the Babe busts one, the Yankees still has a chance to lose. If he don't do nothing, the Giants may win.

The umpires for the serious was closeted for ½ hour last night with Judge Landis and instructed that daylights savings went out of operation in New York ten days ago. These instructions is hoped to prevent a reputation of last fall's special extra surprise when the umpires saved so much daylight one day that a fan living in East Orange, N.J., got off his train 2 hours after the game was called and died of sunstroke.

Fans who may be a bit timid about attending these games may rest assured that they will be able to enter both parks and showed to their proper seats without no danger of getting hit over the head by a group of bold policemen as baseball is not ran under the influence of the N.Y. state boxing commission.

As the two teams is straining at the leash, all eagerness to get out there on the field and count the house, a old time baseball expert can't resist calling attention to the sad plight of Ernie Johnson, utility infielder on the Yankee team. Ernie started the season as shortstop with the Chicago White Sox, but along in June or some time Chicago ast for wafers and the Yankees refused to wafe. Manager Huggins figured that if they was one thing he needed it was a substitute shortstop, as at that time the regular shortstop, Everett Scott, had only been able to play 1000 consecutive games and might get sick again any day. So Ernie is now a full fledge member of the Yanks, who, according to Hughie Fullerton, finished in first place. And he can't prevent a slight cough when he thinks of the White Sox, who finished in Cleveland.

Only One Team Could Lose that Game

BELL SYNDICATE, OCTOBER 11, 1923

New York—Well, boys, they have started again, and it looks maybe we would be out of the trenches by Saturday night. At the conclusion of this battle the general concensus of opinion among us half-witted newspaper men was that it was a game that could of been lost by only one team in the world, namely, the Yankees.

It takes real genius to get beat in a ball game like this one, and it don't seem hardly possible that the Giants can lose any of the rest of them no matter how hard they try.

The only thing that might save the American league champs would be to have last year's umpires re-engaged so that some game might be called wile it is still a tie. However, it might help a little if Manager Huggins would change his tactics and every time one of his boys get a base, send in somebody to run for him. The Yankees made a whole lot of runs this season and in order to make runs they must of visited different bases but today they acted like it was their first trip away from home. This aint knocking the Giants, who played their regular world serious ball and deserved to win. And personally I am glad it was Casey, mighty Casey, that busted it up though I don't suppose he cares whether I like him or not. Well, to begin with the beginning,

On the way to the subway to the press gate the writer must of passed 50 policemens but was neither recognized nor hit over the head. Outside the gate I run into the high commissioner of baseball who asked the newspaper boys the other day to kindly keep his name out of the paper on the grounds that the people was not interested. The judge helped me get away with a couple of Harry Stevens hot roast beef sandwiches which was so good that I took some of the juice home on my coat to show the wife and kiddies,

At 1 o'clock Judge L—s went out on the field and decided it was light enough to play. The clients was then entertained by a novelty in the way of batting and fielding practice, which is usually held in secret before a big game. Messrs, Altrock and Schacht staged their imitation of the misunderstanding between our champion and the wild bull[34] and it was voted the best stunt baseball's star comic has over put on.

The gent that announced the batteries in the press box said that Hurt would pitch for the Yankees. This is what they call him in Brooklyn. Amongst the prominent experts present was Jack Hendricks and Clarence Rowland. Jack is covering the series for Jim Jam Jems and Clarence for the Enclopedia. When Mr. Watson was named as the Giant pitcher, Nick Flatley of Boston said that McGraw was probably sending him in as punishment for not obeying the training rules. He was released on parole after two nervous innings. Mr. Hurt got bumped off in the next innings and I practically decided to nickname the game a airtight pitchers battle. It took one hour and five minutes to get the first three innings over and Judge L—s gave the gathering gloom couple of dirty looks.

During the long and tedious progress of the third innings I sought an interview with Mrs. Caroline Dorsey, of Traverse City, Mich. Mrs. Dorsey is the lady who had stood in line in front of the general admission ticket window since the 14th of May hoping against hope that she would get a ticket. At ten o'clock this morning she received the coveted pasteboard and picked out a choice seat under the scoreboard.

"Mrs. Dorsey," I said to her, "What do you think of the game?" She did not hear me the first time on account of being so far away so I had to put the query once more.

"Mrs. Dorsey," I said, "what do you think of the game?"

She did not hear me this time either, and when the game was over I talked to several people who had sat near her if they had heard her say what she had thought of the game, but I could get no information that sounded reliable.

The pastime speeded up after Bush and Ryan took what is called the helm. With the sun under cover the Giants was unable to see Mr. Bush's fast ball until he got in the hole to Mr. Stengel in the ninth when Casey ran an exhibition circuit of the bases.[35] He had been scheduled to run this race against Papyrus before the game but the horse failed to leave his stall. Plenty of Yanks planks got on base but once there, they seemed to be overcome by Nausea.

The disease was contagious and Yankee fans all had it leaving the park.

Blizzards and Politics Hit Pirate Punch

BELL SYNDICATE, OCTOBER 11, 1925

Washington, D.C.—They had better get this over quick or there won't be space enough in the District of Columbia asylums to hold all those who are going to apply for a room without bath.

In the first place the people who came to the ball park without being obliged to can be voted a little off color as it was no place to be for a person with any regard for health.

The cold seemed to go to everybody's head in the eighth inning. It was in this wild session that Sam Rice fell into the right field seats after a terrific smack by Earl Smith and, sooner or later, came up with the ball.

Whether or not Sam caught the ball will always be between him and his Maker. I am not his maker.[36]

Several of those setting in those seats were in position to tell the truth, but it is kind of hard to reach people by phone in Washington this week especially when you don't know their name and don't want to.

A moment later, Washington sent Marberry to bat in somebody else's turn. At least that was what we thought in the iceberg they have nicknamed the press box. I mean those of us who weren't too congealed to think. Nobody in the playing field seemed to agree with us and maybe we were all wrong. It wouldn't be the first time or yet the last time.

Anyway, it didn't make a difference in the result and neutral element is tickeled to death that the pastime didn't go into extra innings, in which event they would have had to chip one and all out of the ball park with ice picks.

Washington is supposed to be far enough south to get out of October blizzards, but if that is the case it is just as well for our widows and kiddies that the American league pennant was not won by Philadelphia.

If any of the ball players or umpires are accused of having cold feet at this game they can justly retort, "Who didn't?"

Oswald Bluege may consider himself unlucky, left at home in a warm bed, waiting for somebody to come and replace the chunks Vic Aldridge had sliced out of his head.[37] But, Oswald, there are hundreds who would gladly have changed places with you, including the undersigned.

The leader of the greatest band we have ever heard at a serious seen president Coolidge approaching down the aisle and ordered his men to play "I'll See You in My Dreams." They say it is very difficult for lots of people to see him any other way.

No sooner had the president got seated when they played the "Star Spangled Banner" and he had to stand again. He seemed to be singing under his breath and it is said that he was making up a parody line dedicated to the Washington players who failed to get some very important hits in Pittsburgh Thursday.

The line was as follows:

"The bums popping in air gave proof through the afternoon that Vic Aldridge was still there."

Judge Landis went and set in the president's box for a moment. The president was decked out in a beautiful new salmon colored hat, while, with all due respect to the judge, it must be admitted that his own Fedora looked like it had spent two or three days in Pittsburgh.

The visiting boys scored a run in the second because J. Harris tried to make a catch of Pie Traynor's short Texas leaguer to right. Pie dashed around to third and came in on Wright's long fly to J. Harris whose throw home might have caught somebody who was in no special hurry.

The Senators lost a slim chance to score in their half when Max Carey dropped Peck's fly with two out. Max should not be found fault with for this little slip. He has been smacked three times with pitched balls in his throwing arm and was beginning to wonder whether a world serious is worth while after all.

Oswald Bluege was wondering the same thing with what Vic Aldridge left of his wondering apparatus.

Max stopped wondering in the fifth long enough to take two bases on a single which is against rules in polite leagues.

When the score was 3 to 1 in favor of Pittsburgh in the sixth, Goslin smacked a home run into the right field seats. Anybody but a goose would have waited till there was a man on base, in which case the wallop would have tied the score.

However, his mighty blow gave the Pirates such a crop of goose flesh that they stood flat footed and watched him beat out a bunt when he came up in the seventh inning calamity. Those of us up in the exposed press box were enjoying the same ailment for another reason.

A good many of the experts were expressing mystification in regards to the manner in which Peck and other star members of both clubs had shown a tendency to juggle ground balls and to nearly throw them away after once picking them up. Also why some of the big hitters had been accumulating batting averages that won't never cause their wife and kiddies to shout with joy and sing look what my red hot papa done.

It seems to me like the solution is to be found in the boys' literary efforts. A bat feels awful big and awkward in your hands after you have set up half the night juggling a pen. And it is a difficult matter to pick up a ball clean and throw it straight when suffering with writer's cramp.

Never in my experience of world's series have I seen or heard of so many athletes devoting themselves to authorship. If there is any member of either team who ain't dashing off literature during the present brawl, why it must be the nephew of the 3d assistant bat boy.

As a result of this situation a movement has been started amongst the regular baseball writers to have the players set in the press coop next year while us boys take their place on the field. This would insure the serious being indefinitely postponed during the first game to permit of the removal and disposal of the bodies.

One of the sensations of today's pre-game episodes was the big cheer that went up when the writer of these lines entered Mr. Griffith's stadium. It was learned later that I had been mistaken for President Coolidge's father.

As we struggle out of the park there is a report that Bill McKechnie has protested the game. My reply to Bill is, "So do I."

Ring Hears the Game He Is Seeing

BELL SYNDICATE, OCTOBER 5, 1927

Pittsburgh—Well, friends, you can see for yourselves that I am back in the city where I lost my shirt[38] just two years ago and swore at the time that I would never come here again, but it is the inalienable right of every free born partly white American citizen to change his mind, if any, especially when one's dear public demands it.

Furthermore, this is one world's series which I am interested in personally and my nerves has been so shattered during the last couple weeks that I can't risk the lives of my wife and kiddies by listening with them to the play by play account over the radio, even though same be recited by the always engaging and generally accurate Graham MacNamee. On Friday, the 23rd of September, I set in front of the loud speaker while somebody at WNYC reported the third battle between the Giants and Pittsburgh and when Freddy Lindstrom broke up the game with a hit that hopped over three or four of the Waner boys' heads, I kicked our darling dog Peter through a costly plate glass window and called the parrot everything but Polly. If any of my little ones had been in the room I would have knocked them for a Chicago count, and the madam herself would not have escaped without her quota of contusions.

No doubt you are in a fever to know the reasons for this renewal of the baseball rabies in a torpid old stiff like the undersigned. Well, last spring, before the season opened, I wagered a pretty penny at odds of 3 to 1 that Pittsburgh would win the pennant and another pretty penny that Pittsburgh would beat out the Giants. But that ain't nowheres near the half of it. Pittsburgh's present manager and I broke into the national pastime in the same league, the same year, and I have always felt toward him the way you feel toward whoever shared with you the griefs and mortifications of harassed saphood. Veteran ball players in that league, the Central, used to take inhuman advantage of Donie Bush's unsophistication and mine and kid us to such an extent that we almost wept together, evenings, into steins of South Bend's best beer. That was 22 years ago, when the hick shortstop was 19 years old and the hick reporter 20. Which would make him 41 at the present writing and me 42; that is if we hadn't aged 10 years apiece since last April. Jack Hendricks, whose Cincinnati Reds scrunched St. Louis Thursday, had the best ball club in that Central league and Bush would have been a member of it if Jack hadn't been blessed with Champ Osteen, one of the greatest of minor league shortstops.

Just the same I claim credit for first calling a big league scout's attention to Donie. The scout was George Huff, athletic director at the University of Illinois and ivory hunter for the Boston Red Sox. George had an engagement one afternoon at Notre Dame, but I persuaded him to come out to the South Bend ball park and take a look at Bush. It was Donie's bad day. Hitting three times left-handed and threetimes right-handed, he amassed one home run, two triples and three singles. George wired that night to John I. Taylor, who owned the Boston club. John I. wired back that be was perfectly satisfied with the shortstop he had. Which was reasonable enough, his shortstop being Heinie Wagner.

(Editor's note: Why don't you talk about yourself a little?)

(Author's note: All right. I will)

Donie was drafted by Detroit, sent to Indianapolis for a year's seasoning and then recalled by Hughey Jennings. He had several run-ins with Ty Cobb. I met him in Chicago one time and asked him what the trouble was.

"Nobody in the world," said Donie, "can get along with that so-and-so. He's driving me crazy. He's handed me 26 signs to remember, and if I miss one, he rides me. He's a so-and-so."

"I'm supposed to be writing a story about him for the American Magazine," I said.

"Well, then," said Donie, "you're writing about the greatest ball player that ever lived or ever will live."

And he proceeded to give me 15,000 words of instances of Ty's superiority over all other ball players, past, present and to come.

Donie hasn't had what you would call a perfect year. In April, with an eye to economy, Barney Dreyfuss took a long-term lease on a stretcher to carry his stars to and from the hospital. It was what the railroads call a two-way haul. The athlete who was pretty near all right again would ride from the hospital to Forbes Field, where the stretcher would pick up the one who had just got hurt and take him to the hospital. The club went along without a left-handed pitcher, and Ray Kremer, one of the best right-handers in the league, was injured most of the season. Johnnie Morrison dropped out of sight. Earl Smith was set down 30 days for smacking Dave Bancroft, and there was an argument with Kiki Cuyler which resulted in the latter's enjoying the cool shade of the bench all through August and September. On the other hand, Bush hasn't been obliged to do the managing single-handed. A great many baseball writers have helped, and without his even having to ask them to. If he is half the guy I think he is, he'll repay us all next year by telling us how to write our stuff.

Well, it's over now and I can forget recent nightmares about Giants chasing me all over the room, nightmares from which I awoke to behold a white-sheeted figure at my bedside moaning, "I am the Spirit of St. Louis." I will admit that the New York bunch had me scared when (if they were quoted correctly) they began talking like Jack Sharkey, to the effect that they would "blow Pittsburgh right out of the league." They came close to doing it, too, but the trouble with them was that they contracted the blowing habit and blew in Philadelphia, against a club that hardly ever beats anybody on purpose.

There is a good deal of talk always about this club being game and that club being yellow, but the club that wins is usually the club which, on a given day, gets the best hitting, the best pitching, the best fielding and the best luck. The Giants are a good, game ball club, handicapped by erratic battery work. Their gameness didn't get them anywhere when they couldn't hit Petty and Ulrich, and when the Phillies could and did hit Grimes.

(Editor's note: Have you forgotten yourself entirely?)

That reminds me. I telephoned John Heydler last Thursday morning and asked him what would happen if the Thursday game between St. Louis and Cincinnati had to be called off on account of wet grounds.

"I'm glad you brought that up," said John. "I suppose you didn't think I had enough to worry me already. Well, if the game is called off, St. Louis, which has no game scheduled for Friday, will insist on playing Cincinnati Friday morning. Pittsburgh will protest and it will be up to the board of directors. And while you are looking for trouble, I may as well tell you that this pennant race is likely to end with three clubs tied for first place. In that event, there will be a series of three-game series before the world's series and the next time you want to play golf, you can tee up on snow drifts."

For the benefit of those who have just tuned in, the club that is going to oppose Pittsburgh in this world's series is the New York American League club. I am going to bet on them, a very small percentage of my winnings. And I hope I lose, but please don't repeat that to the Babe or Mr. Huggins. It's a tough series to guess. You can't tell how the Yankees will act in a regular ball game after playing exhibition games all season. Anyway I have decided that the only way to keep a shirt in a World Series is to keep it on, and this shirt is going to remain right where it is till the series is over. So may the best club win quick.

After a day of reflection on listening to Graham MacNamee's radio broadcast of the game, Lardner wrote, "Here I was watching a World Series ballgame and listening to the broadcast of it at one and the same time. You might almost say I attended a doubleheader, the game Mac was describing and the one I was watching."

SOME FINAL THOUGHTS ON THE GAME

Oddities of Bleacher Bugs

BOSTON AMERICAN, JULY 23, 1911

If reporters of baseball didn't have to sit up in the press box they would probably like their jobs better. Not that said box is such a dull place, with all the repartee of the scribes, operators and "critics." But it would be much more fun to listen to, and take part in, the conversations in the bleachers, where the real "bugs" sit.

Time was when we liked nothing better than to pay our two bits, rush for a point of vantage back of first or third base or out in the neighborhood of right or left field, invest a nickel in a sack of peanuts, another nickel in a score card, and then settle down to try to prove, by our comments and shouts, that we knew more about baseball than anyone around us.

That was when we spoke of "inshoots" and "outs" and "drops" and "outdrops"; wondered who that was hitting in place of So-and-So and thought ball players were just a little bit better than other people, because they wouldn't pay any attention to us if we drummed up nerve enough to speak to them outside the park.

It was before we knew that there's no such thing as an inshoot, that "outs," "drops" and "outdrops" are merely "curve balls"; before we could identify a substitute batter or a new pitcher by just glancing for an instant at his left ear, or his walk, or noting the way his hair was brushed in the back; before we were absolutely positive that the players are just common human beings and that some of them are really no better than ourselves.

But it was lots more joy in those days. There may be a certain kind of pleasure in brushing majestically past the pass-gate man, strutting along the rear aisle of the stand in the hope that some one will know you arc a baseball writer, speaking to a player or two and getting answered, finding your own particular seat in the press box and proceeding to enlighten the absent public regarding the important events on the field, in your own, bright, breezy style. But what fun is all that compared with scraping up the necessary quarter, or half dollar, and knowing you are going to SEE a game, not report it?

The man who is on intimate terms with the ball players, who calls at their hotel and takes them out in his machine, goes to the station with them to see them off, gets letters from them occasionally, and knows they are just people, isn't the real "fan" or "bug," even if he does have to pay to get into the park.

The real article is the man who knows most of the players by sight, as they appear on the field, but wouldn't know more than one or two of them if he saw them on the street, struggles hard to keep an accurate score and makes a mistake on every other play, or doesn't attempt to score at all, disputes every statement made by his neighbors in the bleachers whether he knows anything about said statement or not, heaps imprecations on the umpire and the manager, thinks something is a bonehead play when it really is good, clever baseball, talks fluently about Mathewson's "inshoot," believes that Hank O'Day has it in for the home team and is purposely making bad decisions, and says, "Bransfield is going to bat for Moore" when Walsh is sent in to hit for Chalmers.

He doesn't know it all, but he's happy. He is perfectly satisfied when the folks around him believe what he says, and sometimes he almost gets to believing it himself. He's having a thoroughly enjoyable afternoon, if his team wins. If it doesn't, he knows just why and can tell his wife, his brother or his pal, that evening, how the tables could have been turned if only Manager Tenney had used a little judgment.

His imagination is a wonderful thing. Without it he would be unable to make any sort of an impression on his fellows. He must talk unhesitantly, as if he had all the facts, and never stammer or back up when his assertions are questioned.

Pat Moran is catching for the Phillies. Everybody knows Pat. He is getting a chance to work because President Lynch has set down Charley Dooin for a "bad ride." A tall foul is hit. Pat gets under it but makes a square muff.

"He's a rotten catcher," says a nearby fan.

"He's a mighty good catcher when he's right," replies our friend.

"Why isn't he right?" queries the nearby one, sarcastically. "He's had time enough to get in shape, hasn't he?"

"No ball player can keep in shape and drink the way Pat does," is the come-back. "I was down town last night and I saw the whole Philadelphia bunch. Pat was certainly pouring in the strong stuff. He's a regular reservoir."

This remark is greeted with silence because no one has nerve enough to come out with a positive denial of the tale. As a matter of fact, Pat never touches the "strong stuff," and if he bunched all his annual drinking into one night, he'd still be thirsty. But that doesn't make any difference with our friend. He has scored a point by seeming to know why Pat dropped the foul ball.

Charley Herzog is on first base. He starts for second with the pitch. Kaiser, at bat, takes a healthy swing and fouls one over the third base seats. Charley crosses second, but is called back.

Our friend is in a rage.

"He had it stole," he roars, "and that bonehead Kaiser went and spoiled it by fouling off that ball. It was a bad ball, too. They must have chloroformed Tenney when they handed him that guy."

If you'd tell the angered one that Kaiser and Herzog were trying to work the hit and run, and that Kaiser would have been "called" if he hadn't swung, you would be laughed at or treated with contemptuous silence. It never happens, on a hit-and-run play, where the pitch is fouled, that some one doesn't say "He had it stole," and storm at the batter.

The Rustlers are at bat in the last half of the ninth. The score is 5 to 3 against them. Jones singles, and Spratt, batting for Mattern, sends a double to right. "Buster" Brown, coaching at third, makes Jones stop there. There is a pretty good chance for him to beat Schulte's throw to the plate. There is also a small chance that Schulte's throw will beat him. Coacher Brown's act raises a storm of protest.

"You BONEHEAD. He could have walked in. Get somebody out there that knows something."

And just because Brown DOES know something, he has held Jones at third. What he knows is that a 5 to 4 defeat is just as bad as a 5 to 3 beating, that Jones's run isn't worth six cents if Spratt doesn't score, too, and that Jones's run is almost sure to be scored if Spratt's, the needed one, is.

Sweeney fans, Tenney fouls out and Hoffman takes Herzog's long fly. The fan goes home convinced that "Buster" Brown has an ivory dome. If he stopped to think, he would realize that Jones's record of runs scored was the only thing that possibly could be affected by the act of Mr. Brown, and that there was just a chance that Schulte's throw would have hastened the end.

The argument that Schulte might have thrown wild and thus allowed Spratt also to score doesn't hold water, for good outfielders aren't taking any chances of overthrowing in cases like that. They are just getting the ball back into the diamond, so that some one can prevent liberties on the bases.

Here's one that actually did happen. It was at the Detroit game on the Huntington Avenue grounds on the twelfth day of June. With one out, Nunamaker singled through Bush. Hall sent a grounder to O'Leary, who tried to nail the catcher at second, but was too late. Hooper popped a fly which Bush gathered in.

Gardner hit a slow one over second. O'Leary picked up the ball, but saw that he had no chance to throw out Gardner. He bluffed a peg to Delehanty, who was playing first, and then uncorked a throw to Moriarty. Nunamaker had reached third and wandered a few feet toward home. He tried desperately to get back, but it was too late, and Moriarty tagged him for the third out.

Almost simultaneously the following storms broke from two real fans:

"Well, what do you think of that stone-covered, blankety-blank Irish Donovan letting him get caught like that?"

"Well, that fat-headed bum of a Dutch Engle. Who told him he could coach?"

Bill Carrigan was the coacher, and Bill has no strings attached to Mr. Nunamaker's feet. Nor had he done anything to deserve being called a stone-covered Irish Donovan or a bum of a Dutch Engle.

However, Bill and "Buster" Brown and Pat Moran and all of them are still alive and happy, and the fans are even happier. They go out there to have a good time and they have it. Things are often done which don't please them at all—things that would be done differently if they were in charge. But, believe us, they wouldn't have half as much fun if they were in charge, or if they got in through the pass gate.

Kill the Umpire

BELL SYNDICATE, JULY 23, 1922

Sport columns in our daily newspapers is beginning to read like the official communiques that use to be printed on page 2 dureing the late war except that the papers used to publish the communiques from both sides so that which ever side you was pulling for, why you could read that side's communique and feel like your favorite team had got the best of it, whereas amongst all the stories you see about the battles between the umpires vs. the ball players and bugs, you don't never find a case where the umps claims near as good as a draw and in most cases the said umps don't claim nothing because he is either still unconscious or hideing in a hollow tree when the report is sent out.

Maybe my readers have overlooked the quaint little coincidence that has been comeing off lately in different leagues around the U S and our neighbors to the north. Well to begin with they was a couple of cuties staged in the Eastern Canada League and the scene of action was Three Rivers which lays about ½ way between Montreal and Quebec.

This little city couldn't use to support a ball club, but a franchise was recently boughten by public spirited citizens who became wealthy during the Stillman spat. Well they was a umpire named Burneau who made the rash remark that one of the Three Rivers players was out and the crowd amused themselves by tearing off pieces of the grand stand and throwing them at the umps.

After the game they waited for him outside the park and was going to present him with a necktie made entirely of rope, but the police got him and his Adam's apple out of town and nothing happened till later in the same week, when another ump named Mahoney said in a jokeing way that a certain player on the visiting Montreal club had reached the base ahead of the throw.

Catcher Bailey of Three Rivers knocked Mr. Mahoney for an afternoon nap, but when he woke up he fined Bailey $50.00 and canned him out of the game whereupon the bugs took up a collection amounting to $65.00 which they give to Bailey, netting him a profit of $15.00. The bugs left the park before the game was over and adjourned to the hotel where Mahoney was stopping at and they went right up to his room and waited for him and gave his a house warming that is said to of been very carefully thought out.

Mr. Mahoney afterwards sent a telegram to Eddie Guest the poet asking him to please not to forget Three Rivers wile he is writeing hymns of praise in regards to different cities.

Well about a wk. after the Three Rivers incidence, they was a ball game played in Crisfield, Md., in the Eastern Shore League and the bugs let the game go three full innings before one of them jumped out of the grand stand and cracked Umpire Knowlton on the chin. The umps was a game bird and umpired the last six innings from the hospital.

Down in Durham, N.C., where you would think there would be plenty of bulls, the crowd lit into a couple of policemens that was trying to escort Umpire O'Keefe from the ball yard to his hostelry. The policemens was allowed to escape with a few bruises, but the gang toyed with O'Keefe till they had broke his leg. Boys will be boys.

And in that same wk. Catcher Allen of St. Paul got mad at Umpire Shannon in Milwaukee and tore off the ump's mask and smacked him but the umps managed to stay on his ft. and continue to render perilous decisions.

This is the gen. lay of the land in the north, south, east and middle west with several California precincts still missing.

Well, Judge aint it about time you done something a specially with dog days coming and conditions libel to go from bad to worst. Next thing you know some of these fans and ballplayers will loose their temper and make trouble for some umpire.

The 1st thing that has got to be realized is that the present system of umpireing is all wrong. Men in charge of our national pastime has made the mistake of insisting on the umpires studying the baseball guide and mastering the laws of the game with the result that they have finely became monomaniacs on the subject of haveing games played according to the rules.

Practically all the fans and a big majority of the players ain't read the rule book since pitchers wore a mustache and therefore they can tell a umpire what is what without being hampered by no printed code.

Another mistake is for the umpires to try and umpire from right down there on the field where they are too close to the game to see it good. The place to umpire a ball game is either up in the grand stand or on the players' bench and the umps should either be made to set in one of them 2 places or else give up their job entirely and leave the fans and bench warmers take turns giveing decisions.

A good many experts is in favor of the umpireing being done by who ever is catching as the catchers generally always seems to know when a decision is wrong, but this scheme would result in practically everybody strikeing out which the fans don't like to see.

Whatever is decided on it is to be hoped that they will be some radical change, but if the moguls is stubborn and hanks on to the present system, why the lease they can do is fix it so as when a umpire makes a decision vs. Three Rivers or Durham it won't be necessary for either athletes or bugs to soil their hands on same.

Every ball park should ought to be equipped with a expert sniper that could pick off the umps the minute he went wrong and then the ground keeper's staff could rush out and roll him out of the way like a canvas infield cover.

Why Ring Stopped Covering Baseball

BELL SYNDICATE, JULY 17, 1921

To the Editor:

I got a letter the other day asking why didn't I write about baseball no more as I usen't to write about nothing else, you might say. Well friends, I may as well admit that I have kind of lose interest in the old game, or rather it ain't the old game which I have lose interest in it, but it is the game which the magnates has fixed up to please the public with their usual good judgement.

A couple yrs. ago a ball player named Baby Ruth that was a pitcher by birth was made into an outfielder on acct. of how he could bust them and he begin breaking records for long distants hits and etc. and he become a big drawing card and the master minds that controls baseball says to themselfs that if it is home runs that the public wants to see, why leave us give them home runs so they fixed up a ball that if you don't miss it entirely it will clear the fence and the result is that ball players which use to specialize in hump back liners to the pitcher is now amongst our leading sluggers when by rights they couldn't take a ball in their hands and knock it past the base umpire.

Another result is that I stay home and read a book.

But statistics shows that about 7 people out of every 100 is ½ cuckoo so they's still some that is still interested in the national pastime so for their benefit I will write a little about it as long as I don't half to set through a game of it to get the material.

Well, I was in a certain town a little while ago and run acrost a friend of mine that is a big league ball player which I won't say which club he is on, but he made the remark that now days when his club comes to the Polo Grounds, N.Y., he don't never see me setting in the press coop no more, and I says I was working pretty hard and he says:

"You would be surprised the number of people that is too busy to come and watch us play ball."

So I said it wasn't only his club that I didn't have no time for but it was all the clubs and I couldn't get steamed up over them no more and maybe it was because I was getting old.

"Well," he says, "they's a lot of others getting old, too, and if they keep on ageing like they have so far this season, why pretty soon we will be haveing secret practice at 3:30 P.M."

Well, I finely got up nerve to ask him where his club stood in the race.

"We are a good eighth," he says, "and we are proud of it. A club that is out in front in this race hasn't got nothing to brag about as you can't see how they can help it. But when you look at the 8 clubs in this league, you will half to own up that it takes genius to be worse than the other 7, and believe me we got genius."

"Listen," he says, "why don't you come out and set on our bench some day and get an education? They's 2 of the new boys that was overseas together in the war and after they got back to America they didn't see each other till this spring when they both joined our club. So one of them asked the other where he played last season and he says he didn't play only a couple months. He says he was laid up with a long sledge of sickness.

"Then one day one of the boys was talking about a pitcher on another club and we hadn't seen this pitcher yet, but this boy had been in the same league with him last season. So we asked this boy what this here pitcher had and he says he has got a great curve ball that ain't fast or it ain't slow, its just mediokum."

"Listen," says my friend, "they use to say that Connie Mack had intricate signs that it took smart ball players to learn them. Well, you ought to try and learn the signs we are useing. For inst. say the other club has got men on second and third base and it's a close game and their best hitter is up and we don't want to take a chance on him.

"Well, Bill sets there on the bench and yells at the pitcher and finely the pitcher looks and Bill holds up four fingers. This means he wants the pitcher to give the man four balls. Then Bill points to first base. That is to show the pitcher that it is first base and not third base that he wants the man passed to. Then the pitcher is as libel as not to stick one right in the groove and the star batter knocks it cock eyed and we lose the ball game and Bill asks the pitcher what was the matter and the pitcher is libel to say he thought Bill only held up three fingers, meaning to try and strike the guy out."

"Listen," says my friend, "you think Schalk and Killefer and them babies is brainy catchers and they are supposed to outguess the batter and etc. Well, our catchers has to outguess the pitchers, too. Like for inst. take Schalk. If he signs for a curve ball, why he can get ready to catch a curve ball. But if one of our catchers signs for a curve ball and the pitcher says all right, why he is just as libel as not to be kidding and the catcher has got to guess what he is going to throw and most of the time, when it comes it is a big surprise.

"A little uncertainty like that is what keeps us from going to sleep out there, as they's never no uncertainly in regards to who is going to win the game.

"But we have other excitement, like for inst. they's a big thrill every time we are in the field and somebody on the other club hits a fly ball. We know 2 or 3 of the boys is going to have a collision but we don't know which ones or whether they are going to get hurt or killed. So far they ain't none of them been killed, but the season ain't only about ½ over and this is no time to give up hope."

Br'er Rabbit Ball

NEW YORKER, SEPTEMBER 13, 1930

In spite of the fact that some of my friends in the baseball industry are kind enough to send me passes every spring, my average attendance at ball parks for the last three seasons has been two times per season (aside from World's Series) and I probably wouldn't have gone that often but for the alleged necessity of getting my innumerable grandchildren out in the fresh air once in a while. During the games, I answer what questions they ask me to the best of my knowledge and belief, but most of the afternoon I devote to a handy pocket edition of one of Edgar Wallace's sex stories because the events of the field make me yearn for a bottle of Mothersill's Remedy.[39]

Manufacturers of what they are using for a ball, and high officials of the big leagues, claim that the sphere contains the same ingredients, mixed in the same way, as in days of old. Those who believe them should visit their neighborhood psychiatrist at the earliest possible moment.

When I was chasing around the circuit as chronicler of the important deeds of Cubs or White Sox, it was my custom and that of my colleagues to start making up our box scores along about the seventh inning in cases where one club was leading its opponent by ten runs. Nowadays the baseball reporters don't dare try to guess the answer even if there are two out in the last half of the ninth inning and the score is 21 to 14.

I have always been a fellow who liked to see efficiency rewarded. If a pitcher pitched a swell game, I wanted him to win it. So it kind of sickens me to watch a typical pastime of today in which a good pitcher, after an hour and fifty minutes of deserved mastery of his opponents, can suddenly be made to look like a bum by four or five great sluggers who couldn't have held a job as bat boy on the Niles High School scrubs.

Let us say that the Cubs have a series in Brooklyn. They get over there at eleven in the morning so they can find the park by the time the game begins. The game develops into a pitchers' battle between Charlie Root, Bud Teachout, Guy Bush, and Pat Malone for the Cubs and Dazzy Vance, Jim Elliott, and Adolfo Luque for the Robins. The last half of the ninth inning arrives with the score 12 to 8 in Chicago's favor—practically a no-hit game in these days. Somebody tries to strike out, but Malone hits his bat and the ball travels lightly along the ground toward third base. Woody English courageously gets in front of it and has two fingers broken. This is a superficial injury for an infielder of the present, so Woody stays in the game. The Brooklyn man is safe at first. The next Brooklyn man, left-handed and a born perpendicular swatsman, takes a toehold and crashes a pop fly toward Charlie Grimm. The pellet goes over the right-field fence like a shot and breaks a window in a synagogue four blocks away.

Manager McCarthy removes Malone and substitutes Blake, hoping the latter will give a few bases on balls and slow up the scoring. But Blake gives only two bases on balls and then loses control. He pitches one over the plate and the batsman, another left-hander who, with the old ball, would have been considered too feeble to hit fungoes on one of these here miniature golf courses, pops it over the fence to the beach at Far Rockaway, where it just misses a young married couple called Rosenwald. The victory is Brooklyn's and the official puts the names of a lot of pitchers, including Rucker and Grimes, into a hat and the first name drawn out gets the credit.

I mean it kind of upsets me to see good pitchers shot to piece by boys who, in my time, would have been ushers. It gnaws at my vitals to see a club with three regular outfielders who are smacked on top of the head by every fly ball that miraculously stays inside the park—who ought to pay their way in, but who draw large salaries and are known as stars because of the lofty heights to which they can hoist a leather-covered sphere stuffed with dynamite.

Those who are cognizant of my great age ask me sometimes what Larry Lajoie would do in this "game." Well, he wouldn't do anything after one day. Larry wasn't a fly-ball hitter. When he got a hold of one, it usually hit the fence on the first bounce, travelling about five feet three inches above the ground most of the way and removing the ears of all infielders who didn't throw themselves flat on their stomachs the instant they saw him swing. They wouldn't have time to duck this ball, and after the battle there would be a meeting of earless infielders, threatening a general walkout if that big French gunman were allowed in the park again, even with a toothpick in his hand.

But without consulting my archives I can recall a dozen left-handed batsmen who hit fly balls or high line drives and who hit them so far that opposing right and centre-fielders moved back and rested their spinal columns against the fence when it was these guys' turn to bat.

I need mention only four of this bunch—two from each league—to give my contemporaries a talking point when their grandchildren boast of the prowess of the O'Douls, Kleins, and Hermans of today. The four I will select offhand are Elmer Flick and Sam Crawford of the American League and Harry Lumley and Frank Schulte of the National.

In the year 1911 (I think it was) Mr. Schulte led the National league in homers with a total of twenty-one. Such a number would be disgraceful in these days, when a pitcher gets almost that many. Just the same, I am willing to make a bet, which never can be decided, that Frank, with the present ball in play, would just about treble that total and finish so close to the Babe himself that it would take until December to count the ballots. I have frequently seen, in the dim, dead past, the figures of Fielder Jones and Eddie Hahn backing up against the haywire when Flick or Crawford came to bat, and on one occasion, when we travelled east on the same train as the Detroit club, I overheard a bit of repartee between Jones and Samuel. That afternoon Jones had caught three fly balls off Sam without moving more than a yard out of his position, which was a comfortable one, with the fence for a back rest.

"Why," said Sam grumblingly, "were you playing pretty near out of the park for me?"

"Why," said Jones, "do you always hit to the same place?"

Right-fielders were constantly robbing Lumley and Flick of two-base hits or worse by lolling against the bleacher wall—and it must be remembered that in those ancient times bleachers were far enough from the playing field so that the first and third-base coachers couldn't sit in them.

Speaking of Mr. Lumley (if you've heard this before, don't stop me), we (the Cubs) came east one season and we had a pitcher named Edward Reulbach, who was great when he had control and terrible when he lacked it. On this trip he lacked it to such an extent that Manager Chance ordered him to pay forenoon visits to each hostile battlefield and pitch to the rival batsmen in their practice. The latter had no objection—it just meant somebody to hit against without wearing out one of their own men.

Well, we got to Brooklyn and after a certain game the same idea entered the minds of Mr. Schulte, Mr. Lumley, and your reporter, namely: that we should see the Borough by night. The next morning, Lumley had to report for practice and, so far as he was concerned, the visibility was very bad. Reulbach struck him out three times on low curve balls inside.

"I have got Lumley's weakness!" said Ed to Chance that afternoon.

"All right," said the manager. "When they come to Chicago, you can try it against him."

Brooklyn eventually came to Chicago and Reulbach pitched Lumley a low curve ball on the inside. Lumley had enjoyed a good night's sleep, and if it had been a 1930 vintage ball, it would have landed in Des Moines, Iowa. As it was, it cleared the fence by ten feet and Schulte, playing right field and watching its flight, shouted: "There goes Lumley's weakness!"

Well, the other day a great ballplayer whom I won't name (he holds the home-run record and gets eighty thousand dollars a year) told a friend of mine in confidence (so you must keep this under your hat) that there are at least fifteen outfielders now playing regular positions in his own league who would not have been allowed bench-room the year he broke in. Myself, I just can't stomach it, but Brooklyn recently played to one hundred and ten thousand people in four games at Chicago, so I don't believe we'll ever get even light wines and beer.

3

Ring Goes to War

Lardner was writing "In the Wake of the News" during World War I, and his columns on the subject of war were, for the most part, written in his familiar jocular style. He sent up martial war songs, wrote several times about his attempts to avoid the draft, mocked Kaiser Wilhelm, and ridiculed the notion of "do-without clubs" to raise money for the war effort.

One exception was a rare column in which he showed real anger. It resulted from a trip to Springfield, Illinois, in 1916, where members of the Illinois National Guard were training to join the fight against Pancho Villa in Mexico. Appalled at the lack of equipment the soldiers had been provided, Lardner imagined how the Mexican Army "would fade away and quit when confronted by anything like the First and Second regiments of infants which know everything they is to know about fighting except that they havent never seen a battle and never shot off a gun and all they done was play horse tennis in the armory."

Along with other prominent American writers, Lardner was asked to support the government's liberty bond campaign. He responded with two columns in 1917, one of them a letter from Jack Keefe to Friend Al. (Later he sent Keefe off to war, with predictable results, in stories that first ran in the *Saturday Evening Post* and were later collected in *Treat 'em Rough* and *The Real Dope*.)

In 1917 Lardner went to France to write some articles about the war for *Collier's*. The pieces were later collected in the book *My Four Weeks in France*, a comical reference to a best-selling book written by the former U.S. ambassador to Germany, James W. Gerard, titled *My Four Years in Germany*. While he was in France Lardner also filed stories to the *Tribune*, some of which appeared under the heading "In the Wake of the War." He never got near the front, writing instead about such things as Paris traffic, attending a pickup baseball game, and trying to find a uniform that fit.

The closest he came to any actual fighting was at an army hospital in Paris, where Americans wounded in a German bomb attack were recovering. Confronted with an actual news story—and a wounded doctor from Neenah, Wisconsin, which was in the *Tribune's* circulation area—he wrote a straightforward piece describing what had happened and quoting some of the doctors involved.

But he could not resist taking a shot at wartime censorship—"They took us the other day to a certain place where certain hospitals were bombed on a certain night last week by certain Germans"—and puckishly referring to the enemy attack as having been "in the hope of killing somebody or of destroying property or perhaps it was for some other laudable motive." The identity of the doctor injured in the attack, Thaddeus D. Smith, was revealed a few days later, and many years later Smith's wife told the *Tribune* that her husband and Lardner had conspired to have the article contain just enough information to assure her that he had suffered only minor injuries.

Lardner seemed oddly indifferent to the ending of the war, writing how unfair it was that he had to work while everybody else was celebrating. He was cheered up by an editor who said everybody would be too hung over the next day to read him anyway.

A War Ballad

CHICAGO TRIBUNE, AUGUST 1, 1914

Irving Berlin must be sick. War has been on nearly a week and we have heard nothing from him. Pro bono publico, as the fella says, we will step into his breeches and tackle the job for him:

> Honey, don't you hear it?
> Honey, don't you fear it?
> Don't you tremble at the cannon's roar?

Isn't it excitin'?
Ev'rybody's fightin'
In the European ragtime roar.
Serbia was naughty.
Austria was haughty.
Germany and Russia, England, too,
Waited for a minute,
Then they jumped right in it.
'Cause there wasn't nothin' else to do.

Chorus:
Austria's hat is in the ring;
Servia's servin' Servia's king;
France and Italy,
Dolled up prettily
In their war togs, fightin' bitterly;
Russians rushin' ev'rywhere;
Prussians brushin' back their hair;
Pushin' and a-shovin'
In that ever-lovin'
European ragtime war.
The second verse is left out by order of the board of health.

Why I Can't Fight

CHICAGO TRIBUNE, MAY 11, 1915

Chicago—Frend Harvey.

Well Harvey I hope they aint going to be no war bet. europe and this country and if they is I feel sorry for the peopl that has to go and leave there famly and still in all I wouldent blame them for going because they aint no able boded man with red blood in there vanes that would feel like stain at home when there country was in apparel.

I certunly hope they wont be no war not only because I hate to see the

wommen and childern suffer by there husband going a way but I would
be jellus of the men that could go and fight for there country when Im so
tide up I couldent get a way. I guess you know harvey that I would be the
1st. 1 to in list my service if I could get a way but you know why it would
be unpossable for me to join the army.

In the 1 place I limp badly when I walk and theys some thing the matter with 1 of my ft. so as they wouldent be no chanst of me passing by a
sergical exxamination and the minut they seen me walk they would say
nothing doing and in the 2 place I got 1 of these here computation tickets
on the R.R. back and 4th from where I live at and the tickets only good
for 1 mo. the mo. of May and if they wanted the violent tears to leave for
the front right a way in a hurry I probily couldent find no body to buy my
ticket off of me and it wouldent be fare to the R.R to go a way some wheres
and not use up them rides when there all reddy payed for. And then I got
a contrack with the paper I work for it that I got to turn in some thing
every day and if I was over there at the front how would I know weather
they was geting my stuff evry day or not and if they dident get it 1 day
that would be violeting my contrack and that wouldent be fare to no body.

And I ordered some new close from the taylor and how would he feel
if I run a way some wheres and left him with the sute on his hands and
he would probily think I was a crook and chase after me and I would probily get arested beffore I ever got out of the U.S. so all to gether they dont
look like they was much use of me trying to get a way and be a solder and
I will certunly envy them fellow thats at liberty to go and fight for there
country and wisht I was 1 of them but it dont look like I would be able to
leave Chi for a wile.

Well Harvey I hope you will be able to go provide it some thing comes
up where they call for violent tears and I know how you would feell if you
couldent get a way so for that reason Im going to tell you that they wouldent nothing prevent me from doing your work supose you want it to get
a way for a wile and go to war and if you feel like youd ought to go just
call me up and I will take care of your work O.K. and you know where to
reach me by the tellephone but if theys a call for violent tears and they
ast you where Im at you tell them Im on vacation or just moved to crown
Pt. or some wheres and leave them look for me because I would hate to
have them find me because its bad enough to be dissapoint it like I am a

bout not bean able to go and I would feel all the worst a bout it if they ast me and I had to tell them I couldent go and theys no use makeing me feel any worst a bout it than I feel now and I been afrade all this wile that probily war would brake out at a time when I was so tide up I couldent get a way and it looks like as if thats whats going to happen now. But dont for get I will try and do your work if nessary and that will be some thing because this country would look pretty sick with war and no sporting page at the same time.

You know where to find me Harvey but kind of keep it quite. I would give my right eye to go to the front but you can see where its unpossable and I only wisht I was in your shoes and could get a way.

Respy, R

A Free Trip to Europe

May 13, 1915

. . . In the 1 place supose they should be war they aint no chanct of it comeing off a round Chicago because the europes cant spair no men to send over here but even if 3 or 4 of them could get a way and cross acrost the Ocean they would half to stop off in N.Y. city 1st. and probibly wile they was waiting for a trane to come on out here they would drop in to the brooklyn ball Pk. and get a look at the dodgers and good night. But as I say if wear going to war we would half to go over there in the sted of them comeing over here and they aint no other way of geting a free grant us trip to europe unlest you win 1 of them contests in the american. A chanct to go over there free for nothing and see West Mr. abbey and the Tour of london and all the sites of Paris 22nd. St. and Napolleons tum and so 4th. and the diffrunt kings and queens aint nothing to be snezed at and a mans a sucker to pass up a chanct like that and I only wisht I could spair the time to get a way myself . . .

A Message to Sec. Baker

July 25, 1918

Dear Newt:[1] I noticed in our paper this A.M., where Art Henning[2] says you was thinking about raising up the draft age to 45 and while you probably wouldn't send none of we spavins that have dependables to France to fight, you would make everybody that's included in the new draft limits get themself an essential job unless they all ready had one. Well, Sec, I don't suppose you have time to read our sporting pages and maybe you don't know much about this column I run, so I guess I better wise you up to the facts so as you won't pull off a boner.

Well, the paper gets out two sporting pages on week days and the lord knows how many of them on his day and that means that the boss is kept on the key of E to find good live stuff to fill up all that space with it. Well, I generally always manage to occupy about ¾ of a column and that's a big load off of their mind, but if one of you birds without thinking was to take me off of the job, they would either half to go to press with ¾ of a column of white space, which would make it look ridiculous, either that or they would half to print something like the complete results of a roque tournament, or increase the dose of Gumps to a quantity that would prove fatal . . . .

And speaking about space again, if they isn't no more baseball news to write up, why its going to be all the tougher to fill these pages and maybe you don't realize it, but you take a few names like Laudermilk and Wambsganss and Peckinpaugh off a page and its going to leave some No Man's Land . . . .

Daddy's Alibi

July 3, 1916

> Children, Bill, and Jim, and John
> While this war is going on,
> Earnestly, I beg you to
> Be more careful what you do.

Bill, don't tumble out of bed
On your little neck or head.
Jimmy, don't run out and play
In the flivvers' right of way,

John, you demon climber, please
Don't fall from the tops of trees.
You're my three excuses for
Not competing in this war.

Ring Hears Government Plans to Scare Mexico

CHICAGO TRIBUNE, JUNE 29, 1916

Springfield, Ill—There is a rumor going the rounds tonight that the First and Second regiments of infants are to be sent to the border and Springfield is all agog.

Because it is perfectly apparent that the arrival of any portion of the Illinois national guard at the border will scare all the Mexicans to death and probably mean the end of the war.

Because any army, even though it be as fierce and warlike as the Mexicans, would fade away and quit when confronted by anything like the First and Second regiments of infants which know everything they is to know about fighting except that they havent never seen a battle and never shot off a gun and all they done was play horse tennis in the armory.

But if the First and Second infants fail to scare the Greasers we still got left the cavalry and artillery and they will certainly make Mexico look like a sucker. The cavalry hasn't got even a flivver to ride in and wouldn't know what to do with it if they had one and cavalry is supposed to have something to do with horses but these poor boobs haven't no horses and wouldn't know whether to say, Gee or Haw if they seen one.

And I found out all those facts by going round through Camp Dunne and Camp Lincoln and before I visited them two camps I didn't know nothing about war and after I got through visiting them and talked to all the soldiers, I didn't know no more about war than before I seen them.

Today I went out to the camps to investigate what there like and try and find out what I was down here for and the first camp I visited was Camp Lincoln and I ast for Ash Guthrie, a private from Riverside and somebody says, Oh, yes, he is in the machine gun corpse. So I says where can I find him and they says just go over and look for the machine guns and he will be there, so I went over and looked for the machine guns and they was just as easy to find as bell hops in the Leland hotel.

But while I was looking round I run into Mr. Guthrie and I says:

"Hello, Ash," and he says, "Hello, Ring," because I and him are just like that.

So he says, "How did you find me?" and I say I had made inquiries and found out he was in the machine gun troop and it was easy to find a man in the machine gun troop because all you had to do was look round till you found a place where they wasn't no machine guns and that would be the machine gun troop.

So I and Ash talked together a long while and when I got through talking to him I knowed even less about machine guns than before and he never seen a machine gun and no one else in the troop ever seen one and if they should see one they wouldn't know if it was a machine gun or a bath towel.

I don't want to encourage the Mexicans. but they should certainly ought to come down here and see the Illinois National Guard and see how good its prepared and they would certainly be scared to death for fear they would get arrested for murder and mayhem the first time they fired a shot against these poor, defenseless, unarmed Henry Ford soldiers.

And the thing that scares me is this: about the time all these here national guards is all dead on account of not having nothing to fight with and wouldn't know how to use it if they had, the war will get serious and us poor married guys with a flock of children will have to go down there and make a target out of ourself and get killed and everything, and our posterity about forty years from now will read about us getting killed and will get angry and mad and go down there and clean up them belligerent suckers because by that time they would probably have something to fight with besides there fist.

Serve Your Country with a Minimum of Effort

CHICAGO TRIBUNE, JUNE 2, 1917

[This is one of a series of articles by western writers of national note in support of the $2,000,000,000 Liberty loan.]

The population of the world is 1,675,000,000, including the Bronx, and it is estimated that all but one of this number dislike William Hohenzollern and wish he would resign. He has been told this, but he doesn't believe it.

Just because 79,000.000 Germans, 50,000,000 Austrians and Hungarians, and 27,000,000 Bulgarians and Turks, of whom more than 23,000,000 are wrestlers, break down and cry when he scolds who he thinks is Grand Exalted Ruler of the Ancient Order of Humans and first cousin to the Lord.

He won't quit of his own accord, but he will if 1,519,000,000 of us insist on it.

The most effective way of insisting is to get into the trenches. A great many have done it and a great many more intend to. A vastly greater many can't or won't.

The next most effective way, and the easiest way, is to buy a Liberty bond.

You may be too young or too old or too ill or too timid or too poor to fight. None of these alibis applies to the Liberty loan. The age limit for purchasers is one minute to 147 years old. If you are sick, send Kenneth or Dorothy.

Timidity and poverty don't enter into the case. The bonds are as safe as buttermilk and as cheap as you want to make them. You can buy one for $50 and pay for it as you would an encyclopedia, and no taxes can touch you.

Your neighbor who is killed at the front gives his life for his country and his country gives him credit. You who buy a Liberty bond give your country nothing but your support and confidence and your country gives you $3\frac{1}{2}$ per cent.

When you take three people to lunch and it costs you $5 you may be doing good to four people, your guests and the proprietor.

When you deposit $5 for a Liberty bond you are doing good to 1,674,999,999 people, including the 7,915,101 Norwegians and Swedes, all but five of whom are blondes.

The White Sox' victory in the 1917 World Series played into Lardner's hands a few months later, when he was asked to write another column promoting the sale of Liberty Bonds.

A Good Tip to Friend Al

CHICAGO TRIBUNE, OCTOBER 22, 1917

Washington, D.C.—Ring W. Lardner, "The Chicago Tribune" humorist, has been enlisted by the treasury department to aid the flotation of the second Liberty loan. This is the way he responded to the call:

Chicago—Friend Al:—"Well, old pal, I guess you seen by this time what we done to the New York City Giants in the big serious and McGraw got just what was comeing to him and I should think he ought to know better by this time than try and win a big serious with left hand pitchers that are just about as relible as a baseball reporter or something.

I suppose you and the rest of the boys have been wondering why didn't Rowland stick me in there and I will tell you why, Al. The 1st two games my arm was so sore I couldn't even raze it up to leather my face let alone shave and of coarse I couldn't pitch in that condition and then we got down to New York and I ast Rowland would he pitch me and he says No, we got them 2 games to 0 now and I want to show them up and win 4 strate without useing my best men.

But our club played like a high-school those two games and Benton and Shup win the 2 games, the lucky left hand stiffs. So then Rowland was afraid we was going to have to play all 7 games and the 7th game would decide the serious so he was saveing his ace for the 7th game and of coarse we didn't have to play it so I got no chance to work.

That's how it was Al, and I guess Herzog and Zimmerman and Kaff and them was tickled to death I wasn't in there though the rottenest pitcher in the world could make them look like a rummy because they strike at a ball if you throw it to lst base.

Well Al I would be home by this time only we haven't split up the money yet but we are going to do it today and tomorrow I'm going to put my share where they can't take it away from me but I can get it back whenever I want it and draw 4 per cent interest all the while. At 1st I was going to invest in some kind of business and stay right here in old Chi but I spoke to Kid Gleason and he says "what and the hell do you know about business you big busher and the 1st thing you know you won't have enough money left to buy a hair cut for a billiard ball." So I ast him where would he invest it if he was I so he says "put it the same place I am going to put mine, in Liberty bonds."

So that is what I am going to do with the $3,600 I got comeing, Al and I will buy 3 $1,000 bonds and 6 $100 bonds and that will give me something on the side for a rainey day besides $144 dollars per annum int and no chance to lose out.

And besides Al I kind of feel like as if I ought to loan my money to the govt on acct of not being able to go over there and fight myself on acct of haveing 2 dependibles Florrie and the kid.

They isn't nothing I would like better than get right in to the trenchs but as long as I can't do that I feel like it is up to me to leave them have some of my money especially when it ain't really giveing it to them but just loneing it and they go to give me int and Kid Gleason is 1 of the smartest men I ever seen even if he does call me a busher but of coarse he is jokeing when he says that but he wouldn't tell me to buy Liberty bonds if they wasn't the right thing to buy.

If I was you Al and had a little dough saved up I would buy 1 or 2 for myself and of coarse I know you can't plunge into them like I but youre a sucker if you don't take advantage of this chance and be helping your country at 1 and the same time especially when you might of enlisted in the army and been over there yourself because Bertha could support herself makeing dresses or something and you got no kids tying you down like I and Florrie.

Think this over Al and tell the boys I will be home Saturday night and if they want to give me a little feed all O.K. but not speeches.

Your pal,

Jack.

E'en War So Grim Refuses to
Dim Humor of Him

CHICAGO TRIBUNE, AUGUST 22, 1917

Paris, Aug, 21

> *Grave Doubts*
>
> Although preliminary dope
> Had driven me tres frantic,
> I didn't see no periscope,
> While crossing the Atlantic.
> Although my friends—if any—
> Had told me we would have to cope
> With one and maybe many,
> I didn't see no periscope,
> I never hope to see one.
>
> I'd doubt it even if the Pope
> Should tell me that there be one.
> I didn't see no periscope.
> And I believe, be gorry,
> That Gibbons's Laconia dope[3]
> Was just a fairy story.

In Darkest Paris. Your correspondent arrived at 9 o'clock Saturday night. He first hired himself a room avec bain and then then went in search of The Tribune office. He finally found it, but the proprietor had locked up and gone home.

It was darker than pitch when I started back to ye beanerie, and although I have established a reputation as a regular bloodhound of direction, the abiding gloom threw me off the scent. Summoning all my courage and a majority of my Francais, I stopped a stranger.

"Pardonnez moi, monsieur, ou est l'Hotel Ritz (adv.), s'il vous plait"," I stuttered.

"Hell," replied the perfect stranger, "go right ahead to that monument and then chasse to the left."

The Double Intent

Besides attempting to save the world from militarism, France also is trying to cure it of the tobacco habit.

Lines inspired by the traffic laws:

> Keep on buzzing, airship man,
> Buzz as long as e'er you can,
> Up above the streets so high,
> You are safer far than I.
> Watching these taxis in motion,
> I've just got a sneaking idee,
> That it's safer to cross any ocean
> Than to cross any street in Paree.

A Ball Game in France

CHICAGO TRIBUNE, AUGUST 28, 1917

Paris—Friend Harvey: Well, Harvey, they picked on me today to cover a baseball game between the American field service nine and the Canada field service nine and they said that the game would start out by St. Cloud at 2 p.m.

St. Cloud is pronounced with all the vowels and consonants silent. So I asked them how should I get there, and they says, "take the Metro," which is French for subway but they says it keeps going in circles. So I hinted to a guy that I knew he had money, and he finally fell and road us out there in a taxicab.

The place we went to was some kind of a hospital and it was after two p.m. and they was no ball game rageing but a French general was pinning medals on a lot of guys and I thought at first they was some of the ball players but afterwards I seen the ball players in action and then I knew better. The ball game was across a race track. We started over but a officer told us we couldn't cross across the track for fear of spoiling it.

I wisht you could have seen it, Harvey, the grass was so long that Fred Falkenberg[4] could of hid himself in it standing up. The American boys was practicing when we got there and it was not like they did not need it.

The game started an hour and a half late and the America team scored in the first inning when they got the bases full up and the empire called a fourth ball on a guy that was standing as far out of the batter's box as from here to Petrograd.

In the second inning the Canada boys sort of lit into our pitcher, a boy named Crowhurst. They says he was from Philadelphia and judging from his control I would say that he was a refugee from the Philadelphia Athletics. He had a No. 3 on the back of his sweater but the Canada nine didn't pay no attention to that and made it four before the inning was over.

At the end of the fourth with the score five on each side I got up and left on account of illness. I found out later that the game was stopped by rain at the end of the first half of the eighth. The rain came about two hours too late.

The game was probably a record-breaker in one respect—none of the fielders stopped a ground ball.

Setting Out for the Front

CHICAGO TRIBUNE, SEPTEMBER 11, 1917

Paris—Friend Harvey: Well, Harvey I wish you could see me now and see what I look like in a khaki uniform and I wisht the girls could see me too only for their own sake it's better for them not to.

I have not become a soldier, Harvey, but the other day a gentleman from England and Great Britain asked me would I like to go to the British front and I was afraid to say no so he made a date for me to go there and when you go there and ride around you've got to wear a uniform because if you didn't look just like the rest of them you would be a regular target for the snipers. So I was wondering where I could dig up the price of a uniform on account of they being a big shortage of loose money in Paris and Floyd Gibbons came to my rescue and said he had uniforms and he would lone me one and he certainly ought to because I let him use my typewriter because his is at the bottom of the Atlantic ocean being needed by another fish.

So this a.m. I put on his uniform to get used to it and I must say Harvey that while Floyd Gibbons has some good qualities I wisht he was several inches taller and a few kilometres bigger around the knee joints. Well all Floyd had was the coat and trousers and shoes and puttees and of course they's more to the uniform than that and I had to go and buy a shirt and a tie and some socks and handkerchiefs and a cap and the store keepers in this burg are not what you could call modest when it comes to charging prices.

The shirt was only twenty five francs and the cap was 26 francs and the socks is 5 francs and the neckties and hand kerchiefs are something awful and I would go without a handkerchief only Floyd says it isn't done and you can't use a white one because the Heines might think it was a flag of truce.

But anyway I look simply grand so what's the difference how tight I feel? All I hope is that the Germans won't be in a angry mood the days Im there and that the people that are driving me around won't think I'm near sighted . . .

On Being Bombed

CHICAGO TRIBUNE, SEPTEMBER 12, 1917

Paris—They took us the other day to a certain place where certain hospitals were bombed on a certain night last week by certain Germans. We visited one of the hospitals and talked to a nurse from whom we learned that one of the doctors wounded by a bomb was Dr. Smith of Neenah, Wis.

You must call a man something, so why not Smith? I had heard of Neenah and I asked the nurse if I might see its wounded citizen. She was a nice nurse and she said yes. Dr. Smith proved to be a nice doctor and was glad to see me.

Dr. Smith has been over here a little over three weeks. The boat on which he crossed was the target for a sub, but the darn thing missed fire. The sub was sighted and all the passengers were warned to get busy. Dr. Smith was out on deck in time to see the torpedo's wake and he confessed that the narrow squeak kept him nervous for some time thereafter.

Well on a certain night last week a boche came over this certain place and began dropping bombs, probably in the hope of killing somebody or of destroying property or perhaps it was for some other laudable motive.

It happened that Dr. Smith of Neenah. Wis., was standing next to Dr. William M. FitzGibbons of Kansas City, Mo.

"We're in a pretty dangerous spot," Dr. Smith said.

"We might as well be here as anywhere else," said Dr. FitzGibbons, and an instant later the Kansas City man was blown to atoms and Dr. Smith was laid out with a cracked knee. Dr. Smith was still laid up as he told me about it.

"From now on," he said, "fear and I are strangers. The sub scared me and scared me good, but it missed me and the bomb took the poor fellow next to me and left me with a bad knee. I'm too lucky to be badly hurt and I don't believe I'll ever be scared again."

A piece of shrapnel had been removed from the Neenah man's knee and with it a piece of clothing he had worn at the time of the crash. I saw them both and I am glad that it wasn't my knee they entered so unceremoniously.

Dr. Smith is resting comfortably and he wants me to tell his partner, whom we will call by the grand old name of Dr. Donovan, that he has been having a grand time and he wishes you was he.

A Letter to Home

CHICAGO TRIBUNE, SEPTEMBER 12, 1917

Paris—Friend Harvey: I see by the papers that the White Sox are seven games ahead of the Red Sox with only about sixteen games left to play and it looks as if the world series would be between we and New York and I was thinking the fans would be sorry if I didn't write something about all the games but it takes a long time to cross across the Atlantic these days and maybe I will just be landing when the series opens up and I can't land in Chicago on account of the ocean stopping before it gets there so will you fix it up with Ban Johnson or somebody to have them start the series in New York instead of Chicago and then I can go straight from the dock to the Polo grounds and get there about the time Bill Klem and Schupp and Rariden and Cicotte and Schalk.

You ought not to have no objection to doing this for me Harvey because it will save The Tribune some money in railroad fares and that's what we all are always trying to do is to save money for The Tribune.

Speaking about baseball I and Floyd Gibbons was up to behind the British front the other day and some of the Canadians that was having a vacation played a ball game between each other and one side was shy of a first baseman so they asked Floyd to play and I don't know why they asked him unless its because he went to Georgetown university and ought to be a ball player, but Floyd didn't take a baseball course at Georgetown and I wish you could of seen the exhibition he put up. I think it was along about the seventh or eighth inning that he caught a ball that was throwed to him and the Canadians cheered him to the echo. Canadians are very fair minded and always give credit where credit is due.

Floyd played the whole nine innings in a brand new pair of army boots and of course a few other articles of clothing but its boots what he blames for his boots in the game and he says nobody could expect him to play his best with boots on so I guess nobody was disappointed. Some of the Canadians are pretty good ball players and they seem to like baseball a whole lot better than cricket or hockey or them things so there's some hope for the world after all.

R.W. Lardner

Two days later, a short item appeared on the *Tribune*'s sports page under the headline "From the Front":

Lardner will return from France in time for "Big Show"—i.e. World's Series. Beneath it, there was a Special Postcard to the Tribune:

Paris—Friend Harvey: I will be back for the big show if the subs don't get me.

R. W. L.

Back in Les Etats Unis

CHICAGO TRIBUNE, OCTOBER 3, 1917

New York—Mon Ami Harvey—Je arrived ici this matin on a ship whose nom je suis not supposed to mention. It seems tres bien to be back in les etats unis where nobody looks on vous with suspicion so long as you pay for what you order. The premier thing je ordered was a cup of cafe which vous can't got over there. The French have no cream to put in your cafe and the English don't know how to make cafe and that's why they drink tea.

Ah oui, je came back by way of England which may be you didn't know. Nous had a grand trip et saw no sign of submarines and je am more convinced than ever Floyd Gibbons' story was a doggone mensonge. Deux of mon follow voyageurs were Elisha Hanson and Mary Isabel Brush Williams, both of whom used to work on *Le Tribune* and they both acted like as though they were jaloux of me because je still work there and will keep on till je get fired or quit.

Another fellow passenger was Francis Bowes Sayre who married a Miss Wilson and he looks exactly like President Wilson must of looked when he was Mr. Sayre's age and that is a very good system, to marry a girl that you look just like her father because then everybody can tell who you married, especially if your picture has been in the paper tres beaucoup times like Mr. Wilson's has.

Je dont know whether you'll believe it or non but honest Harvey, until je got off of the boat and bought a New York paper, je wasn't sure that les White Sox had won the pennant and je had no idea ou the world's series was going to start, or where. But this paper said the premier jeu would be played in Chicago next Samedi and then I got busy and found out what train the Giants were going on and je suis going to take the same train. We are due at the Union station jeudi apres midi at two o'clock.

And please tell Percy Hammond[5] and whatever other male friends I have left not to be surprised if I kiss them on both cheeks.

What's the Matter with Kaiser Bill?

CHICAGO TRIBUNE, FEBRUARY 15, 1918

SPA, Belgium—Dr. Einmal Ueber, the eminent diagnostician, today completed his preliminary examination of Kaiser Wilhelm H., who arrived here Tuesday to take the cure. The Wake's spa correspondent visited the Doktor tonight and obtained a brief statement of the results of his investigation.

"What ails the old geezer?" Doktor Ueber was asked.

"I can't go into detail," he replied. "I have an engagement the first of July. A mere outline will have to suffice. Beginning at the top, our friend is suffering from cerebral malfitis. This condition occurs when one's bean is too large for its content, and is caused by a combination of dwarfiture of the brain and an exaggerated attack of Grosskopf. The brain, being loose, romps tomboyishly all round the interior of the skull and, in its childlike frolics, is constantly bumping into the bone-lined walls. This old goof's brain has received so many hard knocks in this way that it is incapable of functioning."

"What is the cure?"

"There is none," replied the Dok. "We can only hope to prevent further bruises. It is impossible to enlarge a brain that was born a dwarf; therefore, the size of the head must be decreased to provide less cerebral playroom."

"And will an operation be necessary to reduce the head's swelling?"

"Yes. We are planning a liberal application of Dr. Wilson's Documentary Liniment in conjunction with an operation by Dr. Pershing. Next," continued Dr. Ueber, "we come to his eyes. He is troubled with what is technically known as Hinterland-Stigmatism. He can see a foot in front of him, but he can't see the one behind him that's getting ready to kick."

"I should think," the interviewer ventured, "that that might be remedied by the application of a mirror."

"We tried a mirror," said the Dok, "but when he looked into it, all he said was 'Ach, Gott!' There is nothing to do but wait for him to discover that poised foot by his sense of touch. And now we come to his mouth and find chronic Ich-coughs. Besides 'Ach Gott!' the only sound he makes when he tries to talk is 'Ich-Ich-Ich-Eurrup.' The best way to deal with that is to cut off his tongue at the base."

"And what else."

"Hohenzollern of the vermiform heart," replied Dr. Ueber.

"The knife again?"

"No, it would be folly to make a large incision when the affected organ is so small as to be practically undiscoverable. An injection of shrapnel is the advisable procedure. Nether-abdomenally," continued the Dok, "Wilhelm is in fairly good shape save for a superabundance of gall, for the cure of which we must again depend on Dr. Pershing and his colleagues. And that's about all, save knockitis of the knees and an increasing indication of cold feet. The feet, I fancy, will have to be cut off and sent back to Berlin as Kalter Aufschnitt."[6]

"But do you think Wilhelm is in shape to survive all this?"

Doktor Ueber was optimistic.

"Not a chance," he said.

Wake Travel Guide (European Branch)

CHICAGO TRIBUNE, JUNE 21, 1918

Americans now in Europe are constantly writing the Wake Travel Bureau to ask advice on where to go after they have seen the principal points of interest in France. We believe they can do no better than visit that interesting old country, Germany, planning to spend considerable time in Berlin, but taking in Cologne, Wiesbaden, Leipzig, etc., en route. There is so much to see in the capital city that the stopovers at intermediate places must be brief.

A word or two of general information about Germany may not be amiss. The principal export is gas. The chief import at present is alibis, but it is predicted these will soon be second to U.S. marines. The standard of money is the mark, but a great deal of it seems to have mysteriously disappeared; at least, lots of Germans have recently been missing their marks.

America will always have a warm spot in its heart for Germany because it gave us German measles. American parents are so tickled to find out that what the kids have isn't regular measles that they just can't help loving the Germans for inventing the other kind.

Germany has always been strong for athletics, excelling in two sports—Lushing and Pushing Pedestrians off the Sidewalk. At the Olympic Games in Stockholm a German broke the world's record in the Guzzle, setting a mark of 98 steins in :49 1–5.

Berlin is distinguished by a large number of imposing public edifices and numerous monuments. The most notable building is the Royal Palace, which is soon to be converted into a pest house for the accommodation of native survivors of the war.

Tourists will find a source of great enjoyment in the numerous statues of heroes, of which the equestrian statue of Frederick the Great and the imposing monuments to William 1. and Prince Bismarck form ideal targets for hand grenades of ripe fruit and eggs.

Educationally, Berlin has a university, a military academy, and an artillery and engineering school, but needs a College of Good Behavior. It is understood one is soon to be established with a former Princeton University president at its head.

In 1912 the population of Berlin was 2,082,440. Based on the normal rate of increase, the present figure would be about 2,468,000, of whom 70 per cent are dead and the rest dangerously ill.

The Do-Without Club

CHICAGO TRIBUNE, JULY 23, 1918

Friend Harvey

Well, Harvey, I near forgot to tell you about another scheme they got up over there and when I say over there I mean on W. Adams St and this is what they call the Do Without Club and I suppose you will think its a scheme for doing without different clubs like a niblick or like I was to say I would do without the club I use on my kids or maybe you would think I referred to the club I have been doing without over on Mich. Ave. or you might even think it was a nickname for the White Sox.

But no, Harvey, its a scheme to help win the European war by people depriving themself of this and that and the way you join it is you go over and tell them you are willing to swear off on sugar one day a week or not eat no bread every Tuesday or Thursday and they give you one of the buttons with Do Without Club on them, and it shows you are making up some kind of a sacrifice to help the country, but you half to remember that when you declare yourself and they give you the button, it's like you had signed a pledge, and if you got a hold of a button by telling them you wouldn't buy no more cigarettes till the duration of the war, and then went ahead and bummed cigarettes off of everybody in the dept. and smoked your head off as usual, you would be a slicker, and of course I don't refer to you personly in regards to these cigarettes because I know you don't use them and even if you did I wouldn't call a tension to it on acct of you being over me.

But they tell me its another good scheme, Harvey, because it gets people into the notion of sacrificing themself and the button keeps reminding you about it and not only that but when somebody else sees the button they will probably say what and the he——ll is that button and you tell them and first thing you know, they frisk over on Adams St. if they are not there all ready and they promise to lay off of licorice gum on Sunday mornings and they get a button and somebody else sees it and etc.

So it looks to me, Harvey, like it would be a good idear to get the boys in the sptg. world to get busy and join up and for inst. Walter Johnson could promise to do without his fast ball vs. the White Sox and a whole lot of the wrestlers could do without suspenders and maybe you might even talk to the sptg. page itself and ask it to do without Mr. and Mrs. G.[7] a few days per wk.

As for me, Harvey, the buttons are so cute that I feel like I have got to have one and from now on I am going to do without my tonsils. Respy,
R. W. L.

Ring Can't Smile at War's End

CHICAGO TRIBUNE, NOVEMBER 12, 1918

Friend Harvey:

Well, Harvey, I come in the office this A.M. and everybody had a leer on their face and I was the only one that wasn't grinning and the day city editor ast me what the he—ll so I said everybody in the world only me is getting a day off but I have to write something just like any other day. So he says what have you got to write something for? So I said I have got to write my regular stuff for the sporting page. So he said and who and the he—ll is going to read the sporting page tomorrow morning and you certainly are flattering yourself. Because in the 1st. place the people that's still able to read yet tomorrow morning will be tray few and those that is will never get past Page 1 without falling asleep. Further and more if you think you have got a tough job how would you like to be a traffic policeman?

So after all, Harvey, it looks like I had a cinch and as long as they won't nobody only you read this what is the difference what I write but still and all I know you want the page filled up with something so I will write out a few verses that have come to me without no effort on my part.

> I suppose the crown prince feels miserable today,
> Both him and his pop,
> But how would you like to be
> A Chicago traffic cop?

> I am glad I am an American,
> But I wouldn't mind being a Frenchman or wop,
> But I certainly would feel miserable
> If I were a Chicago traffic cop.

> Usually when they blow two whistles
> The north and south traffic will stop,
> But on a day like this they can blow their heads off
> And nobody pays any attention to
> The Chicago traffic cop.

> R. W. L.

4

Football

Before becoming established as a baseball reporter in Chicago, Lardner covered many college football games and a few local boxing matches. In an early assignment for the *Inter-Ocean*, he also reported on a relatively new indoor game between Yale and the Chicago YMCA. He was not impressed. "My ignorance of, and disinterest in, basket ball, is something that could not be set down in one volume," he wrote years later. " I am proud to state that never since that evening have I consciously been within a block of an armory or gymnasium where basket ball was scheduled."

But college football was a different story. Lardner simply couldn't get enough of it. He reported on teams coached by Amos Alonzo Stagg at the University of Chicago, Fielding H. Yost at the University of Michigan, and Robert Zuppke at the University of Illinois. He got along famously with these well-known coaches—Yost was a particular favorite—though he occasionally teased Stagg for refusing to put numbers on his players' backs. (Stagg said this was to confuse scouts from opposing teams.)

Lardner's affection for the game didn't prevent him from writing up zealous coaches and "aluminum," who hounded reporters for their negativity, most notably in a column he wrote titled "The Perils of Being a Football Writer." By and large, though, football was the one sport that saw him check his natural skepticism at the door. Whether this was because he was charmed by what he saw of the college life he had missed, or because he felt the players were amateurs who should be exempt from mockery, or for whatever other reasons, Lardner's coverage of football was notable for its gentleness and rah-rah spirit. This approach began early in his coverage of Notre Dame football at the *South Bend Times*: "The varsity 11 is back from Lafayette after one of the victories that will be long remembered by the student body at Notre Dame," he wrote after a 2–0 win over Purdue in 1906. "There was a great ovation for the team when the bunch landed at the college yesterday, and cheers for Coach Barry. Captain Bracken and every member of the victorious eleven were given with a will by the students."

After the team lost to Indiana that season, Lardner's lead was, "Notre Dame rooters received the football players with hearty congratulations when they returned from Indianapolis last night. Despite the fact that Indiana fairly and squarely defeated the varsity, only words of praise were heard from the eleven." Teams were not exempt from Lardner's sense of humor, of course. After Cornell beat an underdog University of Chicago team in 1910, his lead in the *Chicago Tribune* was, "Far above Cayuga's waters/with its waves of blue / Those Maroons did just about / What people thought they'd do."

Even after he took over "In the Wake of the News," he would sometimes cover a game in addition to writing his Sunday column. He also used the column to choose his own All-America team, pick the winners in the upcoming weekend's games, and write poems about the sport. Such as the one that ran on November 18, 1916:

> This is another Saturday
> And many different teams will play.
> It is my duty to predict
> Which teams will win and which get licked;
> And also for to prophesy
> One single, solitary tie . . .
>
> And if the teams that I have picked
> To win do one and all get licked;
> If victories are scored by Penn,
> Purdue and Yale and so forth; then
> Be sure to pan me; do not fail,
> I love to get a lot of mail.

Lardner made fun of his devotion to college football in what might have been the longest running gag he ever attempted. In December of 1913 he began a column asking Harvey Woodruff, the *Tribune* editor, to be assigned to cover Michigan's game at Harvard the following November. The ensuing campaign went on for months and included a series of letters begging for the assignment.

These were followed by Woodruff's responses, as well as a guest appearance by Lardner's friend, the noted New York columnist Franklin P. Adams, in a breathtaking (and breathless) four-hundred-word sentence purporting to be a chastising letter from an illiterate fan, in a column on the trip to Massachusetts, in notes on the team's lost uniforms en route, and more. When the game was finally played, his story showed where his feelings lay: "Following the instructions of my boss," he wrote, "I will state here in the first paragraph that Harvard beat Michigan, 7–0, and then try to write an impartial story of the game, giving Michigan a little the better of it."

In contrast to his famous falling out with baseball, Lardner's love of college football never abated. While covering the all–New York World Series of 1923, he wrote a plea to baseball commissioner Kenesaw Mountain Landis to call off a Saturday game so he could watch his beloved Notre Dame football team play Army in Brooklyn.

The Perils of Being a Football Writer

BELL SYNDICATE, NOVEMBER 6, 1921

Well friends here it is the middle of the football season and maybe your favorite team looks like it will win the championship, and I don't want to be no kill joy but I can't resist from telling you what a treat you missed this fall namely I was going to write up some of the big games down east but at the last minute the boss said no. He didn't state no reasons but I wouldn't be surprised if I knew what they was and guess he is right for once. I don't know nothing about the game but that don't seem to stop a few of the other boys that is writeing it up and I doubt if my mgr. took that part of it into consideration but I guess he felt like my write ups would be kind of silly and I might get smart and introduce a spirit of levity into my write ups which would be out of keeping with a game which is almost sacred you might say and the coaches and aluminum of all the different colleges would be off of me for life. Then in the 2d place maybe he asked the different newspapers if they wanted the stuff and they all said no. If that is the case it may of had something to do with his decision as he is funny that way.

Well anyway I ain't going to write up on football games but wile we are on the subject I would like to say a few wds. in regards to this great autumn complaint and firstly I beg to assure my readers that when informed that my services as football reporter was neither required or desired I managed to not break down in public because I once had that job for several seasons and I wouldn't number it amongst the melons of journalism.

From the middle of Sept. till xmas a football reporter can't go in his office without they s a bunch of letters from students or old grads or the coaches themselfs and the letters always starts out by calling you some name and then the writer goes on to say why and the he—ll don't you give more space to the old Yellow and Pink. All we ask is a square deal, but we ain't getting it. By a square deal they mean 8 columns about the old Yellow and Pink and nothing about nobody else and the 8 columns has got to be 8 columns of glory hallelujah. Maybe it's necessary to mention that the Yellow and Pink was beat 98 to 0 last Saturday by the Old Mauve, but you are supposed to excuse this on the grounds that Buster Gifford the Yellow quarterback, was out of the game with a hangnail, but even at that the old Yellow would of rallied and tied the score in the 4th period only just as they were getting started, Jesse James, the head lineman, called an offside and the 5 yd penalty took the heart out of our boys. Coach Dunglebury says the penalty was a outrage as none of his men was ever offside in their life. He had learned them different.

Well friends when a man is a football reporter he gets acquainted with the different coaches and asst. coaches and theys a few of them that is as good fellows as you want to meet a specially some of the asst. coaches and some of my best friends is asst coaches and a few head coaches too. And if any of the last named is reading this article I want them to understand that they are not the ones I am talking mean about. It's the ones that ain't reading this article that I refer to when I say that they's no class of people that compares with head coaches when it comes to fair mindness unlest it's the boys that wrote the official communiques during the war.

Dureing my turn of service as a football expert they was numerous occasions when different head coaches spent the sabbath writing a letter to my sporting editor asking him to give me the air as a special favor to them. And they were also 2 occasions when coaches wrote to him and said that my write up of their game the day before was the best football report they had ever read and lest my readers should think I am bragging I will hasten to exclaim that in each of these 2 cases the teams who these gents coached had win a close game and my articles was nothing but hymns of praise for how well the teams were coached.

One of a football reporter's little chores is generally to look up both coaches after the game and see what they have got to say for themself. The coach of the winning team pretty near kisses you but you don't no sooner than lay eyes on the other guy when you realize for the first time that the result of the game was your fault. I won't repeat none of the alibis that these birds have thought up as you would think I was copying out of Joe Miller's joke book but instead of that I will tell you about the time I got the surprise of my young life and that was up to Ann Arbor, Mich. Cornell and Michigan had just had a alleged contest and the score was something like 35 to 10 in favor of Cornell. So afterwards I went in the Michigan dressing room to see Mr Yost and there he was smileing from ear to ear and I says

"Well what about it?"

"Well," he says, "I guess we was lucky to score."

The trainer worked on me for a hr.

I don't know how they are running it out west now days but here in the east the coaches has a meeting in the off season and picks out the officials for their next season's games and here is another place where fair play and sport for sport's sakes comes leaping to the surface like a ton of lead. I don't need to go into no details but it would be kind of fun to see the same system tried out in big league baseball, namely let the managers pick out their own umpires. As soon as a ball club lost a game, why the manager would say, "He can't never umpire no more games for me" and when 8 games was lost the manager would be out of umpires and congress would half to pass conscription.

And it would also be fun if the football coaches was allowed to tell the newspapers who they could send to report their games. A lot of the boys that is now writing up the games would have their Saturdays free for golf.

A Letter

CHICAGO TRIBUNE, DECEMBER 17, 1913

Dear Mr. Woodruff: I am a young man,—years old. I have had some experience in covering football games. I will be at liberty on Oct. 31, 1914, to cover the game at Cambridge between Harvard and Michigan. I hope Mr. Eckersall will have a refereeing engagement on that date and that Mr. Weller will be on a hunting trip. I would be willing to make the journey to Boston and back for just my expenses. Trusting to hear from you in regard to this matter, I am, dear Mr. Woodruff,

Respectfully yours.

R.W. Lardner

How I'll Get That Story

JANUARY 21, 1914

Dear Mr. Woodruff: I believe I could so arrange my autumn work as to be at New Haven on the 17th of October and at Cambridge two weeks later. Between those two dates I might visit various points east of Buffalo and perhaps secure data for some interesting articles on eastern habits and customs. Sincerely, R. W. L.

A Persunal Appeal

SEPTEMBER 8, 1914

Chicago, Ill.—Mister H. T. Woodruff. Dear sir. Sevrel months a go I applide to you for the job as reporter for your paper at the football game on the 31 of Oct. at Cambridge, Mass. between the Michigan and the Harvard but I have not heard nothing from you in regard to same neither yes or no. If you give me this job I will try and do a good job and if you dont think I am qualifide I will tell you a few things and you will see I am qualifide. I am a personal aquanetence of Yost and know him persunly to speak to and I have talked with him and he has told me all most all he knows a bout football and he knows a hole lot and he would be glad to tell me any thing he may of lerned since I seen him the last time so if they was some thing I dident happen to know but thats impossable I could go up to him and ask him and he would tell me.

An other qualificashon I got is I use to live in Boston and I lived there a bout a year just long enough for people to like me and not long enough so as they begin to not like me. So I am pretty strong a round Boston and any news they is a round loose I can get it where them other reporters could not get it. I have met 1 or 2 of the Harvard players includeing this here Brickley[1] but I never give him a chance to take a kick at me. So you see I am pretty strong a round Boston and most every body likes me but they is 1 or 2 people there that dont like me and if evry body had of liked me I would of been there yet and where would you of been at.

Besides what Yost has told me a bout football I have read a hole lot and have got a hole lot of dope from my neighbor that use to play with Dart Mouth and besides that I read the rules and know them throughly and if 1 side or the other is penalized 15 yds. for some thing and I dont know what is it for I dont write that it was for off side like some of these here reporters because I know they dont give 15 yds. for off side but I say it is something thing else like punching a man in the jaw or wearing a dirty uniform.

I seen a lot of football games and reported a lot for diffrunt papers and I all ways reported them pretty fare and dident favor l side or the other and I would be fare if I reported this here game though I am pulling for Michigan and I dident never go to there university but I come from Mich. and I pull for Mich. but I dident never go to no university not even Smith's college. The games I report I all ways go in to the jimnasium after the game and talk with the coachs of both teams and find out what really come off and whose fault was it and who scored the touchdowns so I am sure when I send in my write up that I dont have a man creddited with 3 or 4 touchdowns that is sick in bed & in a hospitle some wheres and wasent never in no game but his name was on the line up. Then I generally all most all ways try and see 1 or 2 of the officials and get a lot of dope from them and then I write it all up just as if I hadent saw no body but knowed the hole thing my self and it makes people think I am a expert and if they think that they aint so far from wrong as they might be.

All so I try to menshon the name of evry body that takes part in the game and I don't say that 1 man carrys the ball all the time but I pick diffrunt men and that tickels them all to death espesially those that dident never run with the ball in there lives but when they see in my account where they gained 5 or 10 yds. they buy a hole lot of papers and send them home to there mother and there girl. But I dont never say that the center rush scores a touchdown from the scrimidge like some reporters,

If you would give me this job I would do it for nothing just my bear expences includeing my R.R. fair both ways and back and my meals on the R.R. dinning car and in the hotel and my room in the hotel and taxi cabs and bagage transferred and tips and phone calls, but I would expect to pay for my own cigarretts even if they was a big item and amounted to a grate deal of money.

Well sir I hope you will give me this job and will let me know if you will give it to me pretty soon so as I can begin packing my suit case because I will take a lot of close with me when I go because I want to look my best when I go back to Boston but I guess they would all be tickeled to death down there if I wore old close just as long as I come.

Well sir I will expect to hear from you and will wait your anser till I get it but pleas dont keep me waiting to long because I got trouble with my nerves.

Yours respectively, R

A Friend Indeed

SEPTEMBER 11, 1914

Chicago, Ill—Dear sir—I notise in the paper where you applide to a man by the name of Mister H. T. Woodruff to get a job as a reporter for this paper at the football game on the 31 of Oct. at Camebridge, Mass., between the Michigan and the Harvard. But I do not know why no man that is in his wright sences shood want to do it. I have also reported a lot of football games and I know and if they is enny way which to spoil a perfeckly good football game it is to set in the pres stand where they is a lot of wise guys that think they know all about it but they dont know nothing and I was always the only reporter there that new annything and they kep asting me all the time, like who it was makeing that ten yards around Hod Ofstie and if it was Steffen but you know Ring, Steffen aint playing no more since Stag got wavers on him and mostly it was this guy Rusell.

On account of the above reeson I have got a lot of simpathy for you even if you do want to see youre own team the Michigans get kicked all to peaces by this here Brickley and a very big score agenst them when you mite as well stay here or maybe go to Madison, Wis. where the R. R. fair both ways and back and meals aint near as much as to Camebridge, Mass. and I mite get you speshul rates at the hotel up their, which a friend of mine that I know persunly to speak to is manager of.

But annyway if you are realy so sot on seeing this here Camebridge slaughter, and have Red Parker go up to Madison which he likes to do becaus he once belonged to one of these here Greek eating houses up their, why then I wood like to see you go to Camebridge, and if this here Woodruff shood be to meen to pay youre R. R. fair both ways and back and youre meals on the R.R. dinning cars ets. ets. why then I wood start a subscriptshun list for the peeple that read youre stuff and who wood pay to see you go away. So I am encloseing four (4) $.02 stamps to start this list and this ammount will pay youre R .R. fair for four (4) miles because the price is to (2) c for each mile or you can by cigarrets if you dont acsept my idea which I wont charge you nothing for.

So now you can go to this here Woodruff and tell him look how manny frends I have got that read youre paper just because I am writeing in it, and they buy it on account of me which in a year ammounts to a grate deal of money that they pay for there papers every day.

And you shood not forget that I am sending you this letter when I mite sell it to a magazine like some other reporters that I know of and make a grate deal of money, but I am sending it to you, and hoping that some day you will do the same for me I remane,

Yrs. respectively, Bogus

Perseverance Wins

SEPTEMBER 22, 1914

Mr. Ring W. Lardner

CHICAGO, ILL.

Dear Sir:

We received a letter from you several days ago asking for the assignment to cover the Michigan–Harvard football game at Cambridge Mass., on Oct, 31, and stating that you would not expect any salary but would be content with payment of your railroad fare and other expenses.

We have decided to accept your proposition. It is entirely satisfactory to us to pay you no salary. Your other expenses, outside of railroad fare, should not be very heavy because you admit you have many friends in Boston who surely would not want you to eat in public restaurants. On the train, Coach Yost, whom you say you know well, probably will ask you to dine with him. Anyway, please keep your expenses as light as possible for you know it costs a great deal of money to get war correspondents out of jail in Belgium.

You will please go to Ann Arbor in time to make the trip to Cambridge with the Michigan team. Better write to Phil Bartelme, who is a good fellow, to include you in the official football party, if possible—if not, to book you with the rooters.

Send a story every night by telegraph—if you mailed it, it would not arrive in time. In the story of the game, we always like to have the winner and the score given in the first paragraph instead of reserved for the climax in the last paragraph as perhaps you were taught in the rhetoric class at Niles High school. File your story of the game at the telegraph office before you go to the theater.

Please remember that it is the duty of a great newspaper like The Chicago Tribune to give a fair and unbiased report. We wish you success and if you do well on this assignment, we will have other work we can give you from time to time.

Yours very truly,
Harvey T. Woodruff, Sporting Editor.

Nor is it every one who can get his boss to write half his stuff.

He Has It All Planned Out

SEPTEMBER 26, 1914

Riverside, Ill.—Mr. Harvey T. Wood ruff. dear Sir, I would of wrote you a long time ago & thanked you for giveing me the job of reporting the Michigan harvard foot ball game only before I wrote you I wanted to write to mr. Bartelme like you sugjested & see was he wiling to leave me ride east to Camebridge with the foot ball players. So I wrote to mr. Barteleme & just like I thot he was tickled to death & says sure & he would leave me know when they was going & let me set in the same car with the foot ball players & probly before he answered my letter he went & seen Yost & Yost was even more tickeld then he was tickled & says to mr. Bartelme sure get him to go a long with us & all so try and get him to come back with us after the game because probly that is the time when we will need to be cheered up.

any way mr. Bartelme wrote me a nice letter & he says I wont even half to pay him for my r. r. ticket in addvance but he will let me know how much is it when I get There & then I can pay it & may be on acct. of the big party going the r. r. fair will be redused but may be I wont remmember that when I send in my expence acct. I will hang a round Yost when it comes near meal time like you sugjest & if he should happen to ask me to go in to the dinning car & eat with him I will say I just ett a little wile a go but I will go in & set with you & then he wont think wear trying to spung off of him but when we get in to the table he will say you better have a sandwitch or some thing & I will say well just to keep you Co. & then I will order what ever I want to & I will pay for my meals by telling him a bout the harvard who I saw play 3 yrs. a go & all the men that played then is gone but that dont make no diffrence because I will tell him what plays they used then & them plays dident work very good so they probly got diffrent plays now & if he knows what plays they had that dident work he should ought to be able to gues what plays they got in the place of them that dident work.

but I dont think I said to you that I wouldent expect no salery but what I says was that I wouldent expect no rase in salery for going to the game & would do that work for just the same as what you would give me if I stade here & done nothing like I usuly do. what you say a bout me having lots of friends in Boston is o k but I hope you wont expect me to eat many meals with them wile I am there because I get tired easy & most of the freinds I got in Boston eats standing up.

I will send you a tellegram every night like you say & I all ready got some of them framed up so as I wont half to take no time to write them on the trip & when we get to Boston I will send 1 that says Arrived safe evry one o k wisht you was here. Thats just even 10 wds. & wont cost only 50 c. & if you say so I will pay for it my self & then colleck off of the paper after words & the day of the game I will send you 1 that says Michigan & harvard awaits whistle. gridiron warriors ready for fray. & after the game I will send 1 of 3 or 4 that I got framed up like as following. Brickleys toe flays Michigan in growling Combat 40–0. or. Yosts 4 word passes down crimson 2 to l. or. Michigan & harvard fight fifteen feirce innings to a tie. & then when I get back to the hotel where ever wear stopping at I will write you a letter or may be a post card & tell you how was the scores made & who was the feature. It wont take me hardly no time to get the letter or post cards wrote & I will send them speshal dellivery so as you will get them 1st. thing monday a m & may be I better send them to your house so as you will know all a bout it before jake & louis & the other office boys cops your male.

I will try & be as fare as I can & not favor 1 side or the other & wont give Michigan to much the best of it but if Michigan gets beat I will come right out & say they got beat & give the score & how they happened to get beat & how if I was coaching there team I could of fixed it so as they wouldent of got beat. & I will be glad if you have other work for me after words only please remmember I live a long ways from evanston.

resp'y, R. W. L.

A Fresh Guy

SEPTEMBER 29, 1914

New York.—Friend Woodrough: Saw by your paper, The Chgo Tribune, where you are contemplating to send Mr. Lardners to the ft. ball game in Cambridge, Massa., on the 31st prox. Now Mr. Woodrough I am right here in N.Y. city which is a short trip to there and I would give you a write up of that game for just the r. r. fare the most it would cost being about $12 and no 100 Dollars.

Perhaps you never heard of me but you can ask Fielding H. Yost or Bill Edwards or pretty near anybody do I know a lot about ft. ball, Yes & Grantland Reiss will tell you I am the 1 who said about the Yales 2 yrs. ago that they were more Flynned against than Flynning. I could get off a couple like that for the game bet. the Harvards and the Michigans. Last yr. the 1 I got off was: the Harvard of the species is more deadly than the Yale. Also Mr. Woodrough in addition I use to go to the Univ. of Mich and would of been in right with a lot of the big players had I of went through and while I would like to see them smear the Harvards the lucky stiffs I would make my write up un-bioused as anything. If you would care to give me a chance I would appreciate same and would just as leave write up the world seres for my expenses and 60c an hour which you would have to pay for a ½ way decent billiards table.

Give my reg. to Mr. Lardners and I am glad he wont have to make that there long trip on the 31st prox.

And oblige

Franklin P. Adams

The above would have been thrown into the waste basket if we hadn't already had the trip clinched.

Where There's Real Sport

OCTOBER 2, 1914

Chi, Ill. Say Guy: Wereinhell do you get the idear that there is a hole lot of people in this town crazy to reed about that game bet. harvard & mich say jack it gets me nuts & theres more like me in this burg too I spend a ¢ for that w. g. n. to see wots going on in the world & wot do youse eggs report about why all about some thing that is happynig on the other side of the world wot does us fellers in this here burg care wot those blokes in harvard & mich do i dont know a 1 of them & wot do they kno notin same like any other umane person there old man sends them there so he dont have to see them every day but wot I want to get into you is this why dont your boss give you a dime and save that 100 bucks an send a copple of you free lunch inspecters out to see a reel game on the prairies like us guys do on sunday there are about 20 or 30 teems in this this joint playing good base ball every sunday if you ride on the cars you must see the posters in the saloon windoes I see a game every sun. but on Mond. am, when I go to work & I want to reed about how some oder teem came out yesterday kin I reed about it nix but I kin reed about some skirt champeen gulffer or some willie boy tenis player not 1 word about pinky gray or scudders & I tell you does guys kin play ball if you got any nerve at all come out by polomia pk. cor. of elston & blackhok sts some sunday youl see a game where dog eats dog but be car ful wot you say about the romeos or some goof might bust you on the nose insted of writing a colom youse guys cud writ six pages and insted of interesting 100 people you would plese 1000000 because every game draws about 5000 if its a close game & they always bet about $40 ea. that harvard mich game will look like a checker mtch in comparison any way it would do you good to stand up for a copple hrs. and get that kink out of your leg which serfers you rite for hanging it on the bar rail so much.

Yourn in haste

J. S. E.

PS Dont blame me if you kom out to that game & a rock hits you on the hade but iguess no one wood miss your stuff much bekause there lots left like you in harvard & mich.

Please Don't Go and Ruin It All

OCTOBER 24, 1914

Mr. Woodruff, dear Sir. I got a faver I want to ask & here it is. Im all packed up & made all my arrgts. to go on that trip to camebridge & report that game bet. the Michigans & the harvards & Im going Sun. a m to Anna arbor & may be I will stop off for a hour or 2 at Niles on my way to Anna arbor & I got my ticket all boughten & evry things all fixed up & I bought a new shirt. So you see where I would be pretty much dissapointed if some thing hapend & I couldent go & I wouldent be the only 1 dissapointed but they would be a lot of people dissapointed includeing the people at Niles & Anna arbor & camebridge not to say nothing a bout my own famly thats looking for'd to me going on acct. they like to get letters from me because I write better than I talk. Besides it wouldent be fare after you hireing me to go make the trip & puting me to all that trouble & expence & so many people being dissapointed for you to not send me after all & thats why Im writeing this letter.

Im afrade that may be if Syracuse beats the Michigans in that game tomorrow you will say to your self well the Michigans must be pretty rotten & not worth sending a man to report there games & you wont send me but will make me stay here & work & I know you havent made no thrett like that but Im afrade if Syracuse beats the Michigans you might may be change your mind & then I would be up against it propper & that's why Im writeing you this note. May be you havent herd nothing a bout the Syracuse nine & dont know is they week or strong but Im teling you some thing Mr. Woodruff I herd some thing a bout them the other day & I wouldent be a bit supprized if they was to be lucky enough to beat the Michigans but even if they do that wont be no sign that the Michigans is no good because from what I herd the Syracuse nine is a bunch of whales & are libel to do most any thing & they made Prince Town go some & they cleaned up some other team last wk. a bout 40 to nothing or some thing like that & they got a club of vetruns & look at poor Michigan that aint got no body left that ever seen a foot ball accept this here Lyons & the captain I forget his name but the Lyons isent the same 1 thats acrost the river from Riverside. But the only 2 others they got that ever seen a foot ball is both in the Hosspittl I refer to Hugit & Galt who both of them are badly hurt & wont neither 1 of them be able to play against Syracuse but may be Hugit will be able to play against the Harvards & for that reason the Michigans is libel to be better against the Harvards then against Syracuse so you see even if they get beat tomorow that aint no sign they wont do good against the Harvards 1 wk. latter.

Now I dont think Syracuse is sure to beat them but still in all it looks like they would & I read in a Boston paper where they would beat them sure & I wisht I hadent never seen the paper but it was gave to me & I read what it said & it says Syracuse have got a great club & should ought to be faverite to beat the Michigans on acct. they haveing so many more old men on there club & the Michigans havent got no body accept this captain & this here Lyons so you see it looks bad & Im afrade some people will think if the Michigans gets beat that there no good & may be you will think the same thing & thats why Im writeing this here letter to you & I hope you will see the matter in the right light & not fall for no story a bout the Michigans not being no good because Syracuse beats them because may be you would think you shoulent ought to send me on that trip & that would put me in bad all a round & not only on acct. of people being dissapointed but the mrs. has all ready ordered the stable & fancy groserys for Sunday thinking I wont be here & if I should be here for Sun. diner I would probly starve to death on acct. of she thinking I wouldent be here & not ordering nothing for me to eat because I a sure you they dont have much to eat a round the house when Im not to home & I guess you would feel pretty sore at your self if you was the cause of me not getting no big Sun. diner like I usuly get. So I hope you will not pay no a tension to what the Michigans do at Syracuse & may be they wont get beat down there after all but from what I herd & read they cant help it so please bare this in mind.

Resp'y R. W. L.

Blue Monday at Michigan

Ann Arbor, Mich—As soon as one becomes a war correspondent he is privileged to write of himself as "I" and "me." If you don't object I will work that privilege to the limit and state right off the reel that I arrived in Ann Arbor last night and nobody was down at the train to meet me. So I called a taxi, which will be duly charged on the expense account, and was driven up to the hotel.

The name of the hotel has been changed. It used to be the Cook house and now it's something else. Its new name is deleted by the censor under the rule which prohibits free advertising, but if mail is addressed to me at the Cook house I will get it.

I registered, engaged a room and had a good night's sleep. I arose early this morning, shaved, dressed and had breakfast, and then was steered up to the Athletic Association's office, where director Phil Bartelme and his assistants, and Asst. Coaches "Germany" Schultz and "King" Cole were mourning over the outcome of the Syracuse game. (Syracuse 20–Michigan 6)

Along came Yost, and the mourning stopped, partly because he didn't appear downhearted and partly because there was no time to do anything but listen with him around . . . .

Coach Yost finally asked us to take a ride in his car and four of us did so. The coach is a good driver, aside from the fact that he is likely to take his hands off the wheel and dive into his pocket for a paper and pencil with which to illustrate where the defensive half backs should play on a shift formation. However, he brought us safely back to headquarters after showing us the beauties of the town, and then I was agreeably surprised by being invited to have lunch at the training table. I hope this part of it will be forgotten before the expense account it turned in . . .

Wolverines Off for East Today;
Big Squad to Go

OCTOBER 28, 1914

Ann Arbor, Mich. The Tribune correspondent had to pay for his own breakfast this morning, because he got up too late for training table. To switch back to the first person, I landed at athletic headquarters about 9 o'clock, and found Coach Yost, Assistant Coaches Schultz and Cole, and Freshman Coach Douglas amusing themselves with a new game of indoor football, in which the spinning of a wheel plays a prominent part . . . .

From the time the train leaves Ann Arbor until it arrives at Auburndale there will be no practice for the Wolverines, owing to the Pullman company's failure to build cars anywhere near the size of football fields. But there may be more lectures and a rule quiz or two from Mr. Yost, who finds it an easy matter to make his voice heard above the well known noise and confusion of the journey on steam cars . . .

Yost's Squad Loses Outfit; Railroad Fails to
Drop Off Baggage, Handicapping Workout

OCTOBER 30, 1914

Auburndale, Mass—The Wolverines—so called because they represent the state of Michigan, where animals of that name are said to abound and run amuck, though I lived in Michigan for twenty-two years and never saw a wolverine nor a picture of one nor any human being who ever had seen one or expected to see one—probably will lose to Harvard on Saturday because they have contracted the losing habit in its most virulent form.

A fortnight ago the said Wolverines lost their best half back, Mister Galt. Then they went to Syracuse and lost a game and the services of their most aggressive end, Mister Whalen. Now they have went and lost their football suits and an afternoon of practice.

The Michigan squad arrived here today, but the suits did not. They were left in the capital city of New York and may get here tomorrow morning. On the other hand, they may not get here at all, for suits are funny that way, and you never can tell what they are going to do next.

If they get here tomorrow morning, as the railroad has promised, the team will don them twice in practice. If not the boys from the middle west will have to borrow suits from the Harvard squad, and I suspect that the Harvard squad hasn't many to spare, for it must take a whole storeful of suits to clothe such a crowd of athletes as P. Haughton is said to possess.

The loss of suits was a terrible blow to Yost, because they were about the only things connected with the Michigan team with which there was nothing the matter.

The suits were in a baggage coach when the train left Ann Arbor, but it seems that when that particular train reaches Albany it is like the Michigan team—all busted up. The coach containing the paraphernalia was mislaid, and during the general confusion the Boston part of the train came away without it. Student Manager Jack Leonard didn't learn the crushing truth until after the squad had lunched at the Woodland Park Inn.

Yost had ordered everybody out in football togs at 2:45 o'clock, but when the boys came to look for the specified togs there weren't none. Mr. Leonard spent a large sum of money in telegraph and telephone tolls and finally made the discovery that I have hinted at. Fortunately the athletes had brought their suitcases and handbags with them, and so were not bereft of clean collars and nightgowns . . .

The following day, buried deep in his story, Lardner noted simply, "Their lost suits arrived from Albany in the morning."

Yost's Cripples Meet Harvard in East Today

OCTOBER 31, 1914

Auburndale, Mass—Harvard and Michigan await the whistle. That, I believe, is the proper way to start a Saturday morning football story. Not only does it give the head writers a valuable hint, but it also describes the situation so clearly that no reader can go wrong; that is, no reader with an ounce of intelligence. A boob might gather that a factory whistle was what they were awaiting, but your normal man with a normal brain knows at once that the one referred to is Referee Langford's.

Twenty-five thousand people will have paid admission into the stadium before the whistle blows, if the Harvard Athletic association is a true prophet. Of the twenty-five thousand approximately 24,000 will be pulling for the Crimson. The other 1,000 will yell for the "best team ever developed in the west" (joke), and 270 of the 1,000 are in Boston tonight, making enough noise for five times that number.

Michigan rooters probably know that Michigan is up against it. If they know what I know (cries of "Impossible!") they are aware of the fact that the signs favor Harvard. The Crimson is present with bigger and better material and infinitely more experience. If the best man in the Harvard lineup is disabled it will be a trifling bit of hard luck. If the best man on the Michigan team is put out of it, good night.

I believe Coach Yost looks at the matter thus: The Michigan team is capable of playing three kinds of football—phenomenal, average, and punk. If Michigan plays phenomenally, that is, its very best game every minute, it has a chance to win. If Michigan plays its natural game, the game it has played most of a season of discouraging accidents and upsets, it will lose. And if it plays punkly, to use the adverb, it will be swamped—not really swamped, either, for if Harvard sees that it has a cinch it will undoubtedly save its best men and its best plays for Princeton. . . .

Luck Favors Harvard in Beating Michigan

NOVEMBER 1, 1914

Boston, Mass—After this when an easterner tells you that football teams in this neck of the woods outclass those of our middle west try not to laugh yourself to death. The second big intersectional game of the season was won today by an eastern team, but the eastern team came terribly near to being licked, 14 to 0. Following the instructions of my boss, I will state here in the first paragraph that Harvard beat Michigan, 7 to 0, and then try to write an impartial story of the game, giving Michigan a little the better of it.

Johnny Maulbetsch of Ann Arbor, a 155-pound sophomore, gained more ground through Harvard's line this afternoon than all eastern backs combined have been able to gain in the last three years. Moreover, the same Johnny Maulbetsch of Ann Arbor gained more ground against Harvard by rushing all the Harvard backs combined gained against Michigan . . .

A mixup in signals cost Michigan one touchdown. A bit of bad judgment was responsible for the loss of the other. Larry Splawn missed the signal and Tommy Hughitt displayed the bit of bad judgement. Splawn was playing his first big game and is just a kid. Hughitt was in the game game on his nerve, so it would be worse than folly to find fault with either of them. Besides, they played good football, great football in Hughitt's case, considering the condition he was in, and it was just their bad luck that their mistakes should be made when they did most harm. . . .

Harvard had just one chance to score and scored. Michigan had two wonderful chances and lost them both. Harvard is credited with the victory and Michigan was charged with the defeat. But no one who saw the game can look you in the eye and tell you that Harvard was better than Michigan. . . .

5

Politics

Lardner's natural cynicism and eye for foolishness all but assured his readers he would eventually turn his attention toward politics. He covered the conventions of the Democratic and Republican Parties in 1916, 1920, and 1924. He also attended Warren G. Harding's inauguration in 1921, at which he noted, "The idear of simplicity was carried out to the bitter end. Even when the new Congressmen were swore in they looked simple-minded." Such was Lardner's fame by then that a month later he and Grantland Rice were invited to Washington to play golf with the new president. One of his drives hit a tree branch, which fell and hit Harding. "I did all I could to make Coolidge President," he later wrote.

Lardner also covered the international disarmament convention of 1921. He summed up the event as an effort "to get all the different nations to quit building war ships and making ammunitions and etc. and it looks now like they would all agree to the proposition provided they's an understanding that it don't include they themselfs."

Occasionally he wrote about political issues—his column about the Ku Klux Klan ran in many newspapers around the country—but his own politics never surfaced in his writing, as he preferred to take the approach that all politicians were "simps" and no more worthy of respect than baseball players.

The Democrats' platform, he wrote in *Collier's Weekly* in 1928, stated that "The Democrat party is the party of Thos. Jefferson and Little Lord Fauntleroy while the Republican party is the party of Jesse James and Al Capone." The Republicans' platform, on the other hand, took the position that "Last year's Mississippi floods stopped after a severe reprimand by a Republican Administration, and it ain't likely they will try it again for a while," and "Negroes shouldn't be lynched."

He did write a humorous letter to the left-wing journal the *New Leader* in 1932, saying he would vote for Norman Thomas, the socialist candidate for president, but that was out of friendship for his colleague Heywood Broun, who was running on the socialist ticket for mayor of Hartford, Connecticut.

Political conventions were a perfect venue for Lardner because there was little real news to report but many reporters on hand to report it. Therefore he was free to make fun of William Jennings Bryan, Herbert Hoover, and Calvin Coolidge, cover the trials and tribulations of Abel Woose (a "neutral delegate from Gangrene, Texas"), and complain about the length of the speeches he was subjected to. As Harding went on and on at the 1916 Republican convention in Chicago, Lardner turned to the man next to him with a question:

"Is he pretty near through?" I ast him.

"Oh, no," he says, "he has only said 'Old Glory' once and hasn't mentioned Lincoln."

And just as he had declared his candidacy for mayor of Chicago at the *Tribune,* where his motto was "More Beer—Less Work," Lardner then set his sights on a higher office. Several times he made himself available as a presidential candidate, and at the 1920 Democratic Convention in San Francisco he and fellow humorist Irvin S. Cobb struck journalistic pay dirt. As the convention droned on through ballot after ballot, Lardner declared the race had come down to himself and Cobb, whom he called "one of the foothills of Kentucky," and added, "This bird is OK till he forgets himself and talks the native Paducah, which gives the alphabet 25 letters and denies suffrage to the letter R." Cobb responded in kind: "Lardner is ideally built to be a standard bearer. With his vest unbuttoned he looks like a flag at half mast. He has molting eyes, but there is nothing else about him that could melt. . . . I have suggested to him my ideal platform, which suits him, too. It consists of four planks, namely, wines, ales, liquors and cigars."

As the balloting continued, a few bored delegates responded to the long feud between the candidates with some nonsense of their own.

On the twenty-third ballot Lardner received half a vote, while Cobb got 1½. On the next ballot, when Lardner got the vote of Mrs. James J. Shepard of Kansas City, the *Kansas City Star* ran her picture along with Lardner's column, which made news around the country. Other papers commented on these antics, which they viewed as something new in political coverage.

"There was a marked air of cynicism in the press in all the articles about the conventions," the *San Jose Evening News* editorialized. "Ring Lardner, Irvin Cobb, and the other avowed and confessed humorists made no bones about making all kinds of fun of the delegates and their intentions and general infirmity of intention. And the supposedly serious writers were almost as bad. There was a time when national political conventions were not so regarded. It was then considered quite a solemn and important thing. At first glimpse, such an attitude seems preferable. But after all, this light easy cynicism of the press may do good, and may cause the mass of the voters not to take too seriously the pretensions of the mass of the politicians." Finally, on the forty-fourth ballot, the convention nominated James A. Cox and the fun came to an end.

In his second column from the 1916 Republican convention, "Ring Takes the 'Pomp' Out of Pompey," Lardner tells of taking a black delegate to a hotel bar in Chicago, where he is not welcome. It is a heartening story of thumbing his nose at racism that is somewhat marred by Lardner's references to the delegate as a "culled gemman."

In other pieces in this volume Lardner uses such words and phrases as Jap, greaser, wop, frog, ebony hue, descendants of sunny Africa, partly white American, and others that may make today's reader wince. They also made Ring Lardner Jr., Ring's son, who was a devout champion of social justice, ponder his father's contradictory attitudes toward blacks and Jews that he had witnessed while growing up.

On the one hand Lardner offered to resign from a Long Island country club that complained when he brought Ed Wynn, a Jewish comedian, to play golf. On the other hand Ring Jr. wrote in his memoir, *The Lardners: My Family Remembered*, "I can also remember him speak, in a burst of justified indignation, of 'that damn Jew Ziegfeld,'" who occasionally hired Lardner to write sketches for his famous follies. As for blacks, Lardner's son wrote, "He somehow kept on believing, as he had been brought up to believe, that blacks in general were inferior, even after he had come to admire individuals like [singer and comedian Bert] Williams, Paul Robeson, and the composer J. Rosamond Johnson."

But there is another element to consider, which is that Lardner's use of language of this sort was in accord with what often appeared in American newspapers in the early part of the twentieth century. Even those who have learned to heed the historian's warnings about "presentism"—observing events of the past in light of current practices and beliefs—will find themselves appalled at the gratuitous manner in which prejudice was expressed by writers and cartoonists in general circulation newspapers and magazines of the era. Minorities in general and blacks in particular were consistently ridiculed, marginalized, patronized, and caricatured in ways that would not be tolerated in the media today.

So while Lardner's biases may have been a part of his upbringing, those same biases were also prevalent in the journalistic atmosphere in which he worked. This is not to say, however, that he didn't understand and occasionally comment on the absurdity of some of the customs of his era.

The best baseball player in Chicago—and perhaps in all of baseball—in the first two decades of the twentieth century was John Henry "Pop" Lloyd, a hard-hitting shortstop who played for the Chicago American Giants of the Negro Leagues. In 1914, as the Cubs were meandering through a mediocre season, Lardner had some advice for the team's manager, Hank O'Day, in a poem titled "Then We'd Cop Sure":

If I were Hank I b'lieve that I
Would go out south some night,
And there corral a certain guy
Named Lloyd and paint him white.

If You Don't Know What He Writes About You Have Nothing on Him

CHICAGO TRIBUNE, JUNE 6, 1916

I usually write stuff on the sporting page, but along last May or April I received a letter from a newspaper in Quakertown, where there's a Quaker Girl, and this letter said they would slip me so-and-so if I would cover the Republican and Democrat conventions. So I took the letter in to the boss because the letter offered me a flat offer of some money and he says:

"What about it?" he says.

"Well," I says. "I would love to do the work on account of the money."

"Yes," he says, "but are you working for a Quakertown newspaper or are you working for us?"

"Either way, you flatter me," I says.

"Well," he says, "if you report this convention for anybody, we would rather have you do it for us that pays you your salary for doing nothing. If you finely made it up in your mind to work, it is only just and fair that you works for us."

"All right," I says, on account of loyalty.

But lately I got thinking about it and thought maybe this will be a whole lot of work and something I don't know nothing about, and if I can duck it and play golf every P.M. and just keep up the Wake of the News column on the sporting page that's easy as pie to write so much the better. So the day of the parade of the people that would a whole lot rather walk around the loop than fight I went to the managing editor and says:

"Say," I says, "this was a kind of a joke about me reporting the convention."

"Yes." he says. "I thought so, too, but the higher ups says you was to do it and that settles it."

"Yes," I says, "but I don't know absolutely nothing concerning politics."

"Listen," he says. "Don't you often write something about football?"

"Yes," I admitted.

"Do you know something about it?" he ast me.

"No," I admitted.

"Also," he continued, "you write about dancing and baseball and fighting and babies and poker games and auction bridge whist and so on. What do you know about them?" he ast me.

"Nothing"," I admitted.

"All right," he says. "Then your stuff about politics can't be no worse than anything else you do."

"All right," I admitted.

So he says I was to start Monday and stick to the politics till it was all over, meaning the convention here and the banquet in St. Louis.

So I found out by inquirys that the convention didn't start till Wednesday and I would find the news Monday and Tuesday at the Congress hotel, that was named after Congress, but not the Congress that's been down to Washington, D.C., recently because you would not name a hotel after that unless you was pretty sore at the rooms and board.

So I showed up at the Congress yesterday P.M. and the first thing that happened after I got in the lobby was a whole lot of musicians and saxophone players come in ahead of a parade and the parades was all yelling something and I could not make out what it was, but they all had Indiana banners and what they yelled sounded like Wabash, but I didn't believe they would be boasting about a thing like that, so I went up closer and listened and found out it was Fairbanks that they was yelling. They was just boosters for soap or scales one of the two.

But I forgot to say that before I went to the Congress hotel I got a shave and all cleaned up and when I got there and seen the delegates I realized where I had made a mistake and had become a conspicuous figure.

I knocked several delegates down and got across the lobby to the desk and ast them where was the newspaper men located at because I had not seen one soul that acted like he knew me or wanted to.

"Where is the newspaper men?" I ast the clerk.

After waiting on everybody else he says:

"Try Room 1606," he says.

So I tried four or five times to get in the nearest elevator and was told I was too big and finely one of the elevator men let me get in and we went up near the top and I says:

"Where is 1606?" I ast him.

"Not in this building." he answered. "It's in the other building," he replied.

I went in all the surrounding buildings and when I ast for 1606 I got laughed at, so I came back to the Congress and went in the Pompey room and ast them for a sandwich and while I was masticating it I noticed that they was boarding up the fountain in the middle of the room and I ast them why and they says because some of the delegates might walk into it by mistake and get bathed.

So then I went in the other room and met a man that was cordial and he says:

"Are you for Weeks?" he ast me.

"Yes," I says, "two of them. But it looks like I wouldn't last."

So he didn't laugh enough to suit me and the next guy I run into was Mr. Runkel that's got stock in the Cubs and Sen. Sherman.

"What do you think of our chances?" he ast me.

"You'll be all right when Saier[1] starts hitting," I replied.

"I mean, what do you think of Sherman's chances?" he ast me.

"What position does he play?" I ast him back.

"He is running for president," he says.

"Oh," says I, "you mean he is running for president of the United States. I am for Roosevelt," I says.

"Why?" he ast me.

"Because I wrote a song about him," I says and give him the name of the song and publisher.

"Why didn't you write about a live one?" he ast me.

And then we got in to a politics argument and I got the best of it. It follows.

"They call this a government by the people," I says. "But fifteen out of every twenty people wants to vote for Roosevelt, but they can't because the delegates probably won't nominate him."

"That's bunk," he says. "The delegates no matter how they're instructed must please the people that elected them delegates. It's the people that decides."

"Yes," I says. "I suppose that's how Mr. Taft got nominated in 1914 or whenever it was."

"This is different," he says, and walked away from me.

But I run into him later on and talked baseball and parted friends.

Then I made it up in my mind that they was no news to be got in the hotel and started out and run into some of the delegates from Maryland. We got up an informal quartet and sung brown skin where you been.

But I couldn't come back to the office without no politics and I hunted around till I found out what the convention was about to tell the readers.

You see they're here to nominate a president to succeed Mr. Wilson. It looks now like they would be a hot fight for the nomination, and the man that wins it will run for president. It looks like it's between several people. If I was ast to make a prophecy I would say that Wm. Hale Thompson or Jim Larkin would be nominated on the first ballad. They's been several other names mentioned, including Weeks, that played halfback for Columbia and Hoot that led the cheers at the football game, and Hughes that used to pitch for Washington and now he's out on the coast somewhere's and Lodge that must be an Elk or a Odd Fellow or something, and Ford and Bryan and Debs, and so on.

So when I got all this information I come back to the loop and run in to Charley White, the boxer, and he ast me would I have dinner with him, and I says when at, and he says right away, because he had to go home soon, and I had to turn it down on account of writing this stuff.

Tomorrow I will know the ropes and the stuff will be better.

The next day Lardner and some friends took a taxi to the Congress Hotel to see what kind of a story he could dig up.

Ring Takes the "Pomp" Out of Pompey

CHICAGO TRIBUNE, JUNE 7, 1916

. . . So we went in the hotel and I says, "Let's pick out a delegate and interview him," and they says all right and the man we happened to pick out was a culled gemman and we walked right to him like we knowed him all our life and says how do you do and he was cordial and we says, "Let's go in the Pompey room." He says:

"All right," he replied.

So we go in the Pompey room and I wish you had seen everybody look mad at us. You see this is supposed to be a free and equal country and everybody believes it except the cullud gemmen and the white men. And here is what happened:

We ast him what did he want to inhale and he says, "Beer," and that's a mild drink, and nobody should ought to have objected to he having it, but when they brought it to him they gave him a glass that was all busted up at the bottom because they was sore on we bringing him in there. That is, they was going to give him this busted glass, but instead of giving it to him they give it to one in our party that was white and always been that way by mistake they give it to him. So the one that got it made a holler and of course the waiters had to give him a regular glass and try to smile and say it was a mistake and it was. But our friend the cullud gemman had a glass without no leak in it so we all set around and laughed at the waiters.

Then we interviewed this here delegate and he was from New York city and we asked him who he was for.

"How about Roosevelt?" I ast him on account of me writing that song about Roosevelt.

"He is no good," the man said.

"Why not?" I ast him.

"He is against the cullud gemmen," he says.

"How is it then," I ast him, "how is it that he had Mr. B. T. Washington call on him at the White House?"[2]

So that made this here delegate keep still like all my arguments.

Well we kept interviewing him while the other people around kept getting madder all the time. We found out from him that he is for Weeks and Sherman and Fairbanks and Borah and Burton and Cummings and Hughes and Whitman and Mathewson and Brickley and almost everybody else you can think of except Roosevelt. So it looks like Roosevelt would be defeated on the first ballad . . .

Key-Noting with Lardner

CHICAGO TRIBUNE, JUNE 8, 1916

Arose yesterday morning at 10 'of the clock, and it was raining felines and canines. Far away from the Coliseum I found out that the convention was to start there at 11. I thought it had started several days ago.

"Well," I says "I guess I will get a taxicab and charge it to the paper."

The idea was grand, but the execution was ridiculous. Ast the man in the hotel whether he could get me a taxicab and he says sure and that shows that you can't never be sure because about forty minutes later he says he couldn't get me one and I and my straw hat and new suit went over to Wabash avenue several blocks away and I got a public street car that was full to the guards and rode out to the Coliseum.

I got off the car and pinned on my badge and walked in two or three wrong doors and then in the right door and ast a policeman where my badge took me and he sent me to the reporters box and it was then ten minutes past twelve and Mr. Harding from Ohio had only been talking an hour and was just about in the first paragraph of his speech. I crawled over Art Henning and Percy Hammond and set down next to Mr. Hyde. The seat was perfectly comfortable except that you couldn't lean back or put your feet anywhere and you couldn't smoke or drink or talk or dance or nothing but just set there and draw pictures.

Mr. Hammond says:

"Look who's over there," he says.

He pointed and I looked and it was Irving R. Cobb and William J. Bryan setting next to each other.

"They must keep all the humorists together," I says, and Percy laughed till I thought he would die and hoped so.

"I got a good idea for you," he says, when he had come out of it.

"You ought to have a good idea for somebody," I says.

"You're a baseball writer." he says. "Why don't you write up Harding's speech in baseball parlance? Call him a pitcher on account of his delivery. Then you could go on and say he made two base references to Bryan and Wilson. And instead of calling it the keystone speech you could say it was the keynote position."

"And," I says, "you could say he made a shortstop every once in a while for applause."

Again Percy laughed.

So I turned to Mr. Hyde, wishing to be fair and give everybody a good time.

"What do you think of the speech?" I ast him.

"Grand," he says, and turned over on his other side.

"Is he pretty near through?" I ast him.

"Oh, no," he says, "he has only said 'Old Glory,' once and hasn't mentioned Lincoln."

So I laughed at that on account of being appreciative, and if anybody else says something funny I laugh just as much as if like I said it myself.

I suppose somebody else will write up Mr. Harding's speech, so all I got to say about it is that it was the longest speech ever made and he committed it to his memory and by mistake he had the same sentence twice in it and the second time he said it he thought it was the first time, and he said what come after it the first time all over again, about 10,000 words, and thought he hadn't never said it before. I always wanted to be an orator so I studied this guy pretty close and I noticed that he bowed his knees every time he expected applause and always got it. I will have to practice with my knees out to the golf course.

Along about midnight he got through and then they made their motions about who was going to be temporary chair guy and so on, just like in the Berrien County convention in Niles, Mich. So I turned to Mr. Hyde and ast him if he thought he could cover it without no help from me and he says he could, so I walked out and not having had no breakfast I went to the restaurant and run into Mr. Kalver and he says:

"What are you going to do, eat?"

"What do you think I would do in a restaurant, sew buttons on a hook and ladder?" I says.

He give me the laugh I deserved and says he would pay for the lunch. So he took I and three other singers and bought us our lunch and we had a ham sandwich and it was the same ham sandwich I met in Boston in 1913 on a Sunday when you got to have a sandwich or you can't have nothing else. Also a cup of coffee is what they called it because they hadn't studied the matter over. And the bill was one dollar and forty-five cents.

The restaurant didn't serve no water or napkins with the meal because they had to get even some way.

I forgot to say that when Mr. Harding got through his speech the crowd got up and yelled for joy and I didn't blame them.

When Mr. Kalver had been revived I says good by to him and went back in the convention and found out it had been adjourned till this morning and everybody was down to the Congress hotel. So I went outside and it was still pouring rain and I know I should ride in a taxi, but didn't see nobody that I thought would pay for it and the street cars wouldn't stop so I become a walking delegate. I wish you could of seen my suit when I got to the Congress.

First thing I got in the hotel I run into the degredation from Kansas and you can't blame them for the way they're acting here because where they live at it's dry.

So I ducked away from them and went into the Pompey room and the head waiter must of recognized me as the guy that brought the cullud gemman in day before yesterday or else he thought I was he himself and any way he wouldn't give me no service. So I breezed out of there and into the lobby and a quartet was singing a Roosevelt song. This song they were singing was not the song I wrote but another song that was written and published by other people and the reason they wrote it and published it was on account of them hearing my song and thought it was so good they should have one like it. But honestly the song they've written isn't like it and the song they've written is no good and if I had written the song they've written and if anybody ast me did I ever write a song I would say no with a clear conscience.

They was six people from Riverside in the Congress at one time.

So finally we went out in the rain again and a man stopped us at the door and says,

"Will you have a button?"

"Will you sew it on where I tell you?" I ast him back.

But the button he had was a Root button and the button I lacked was off of my shirt.

So then we went to Rothschild's, and when I say that I don't mean the store, but where we went a man recognized us and says he would sing us a song.

"Did I write it?" I ast him.

"No, you couldn't," he says.

So he sung it with the Jaz band, and I owned up I couldn't of wrote it, because here are some of the words:

"Who're you for, Brown Skin?"

"I'm for you, white folks."

"Who're you for, Palm Beach?"

"I'm for you in the summer time."

"Who're you for, sweet mamma?"

"I'm for you, sweet papa."

"Give it back, take it hence.

Wrap it up and fetch it home."

The next person I seen was Barney Oldfield[3] of the California degredation.

"Who's you for, Brown Skin?" I ast him.

"I'm for Barney and I hope he'll win," he says. "Are you coming to the race Saturday?"

"It depends on this convention," I says. "If Harding makes another speech, I won't be at the races."

"I hope you'll be there," he says, flatteringly.

"If I come," I says, "I want a pit badge and set in somebody's pit and I would like somebody that's going to have lots of trouble and have to stop every few minutes."

"Come to my pit," says Barney.

Next week, St. Louis.

The United States of Old Glory

CHICAGO TRIBUNE, JUNE 14, 1916

St. Louis, Mo.—Found out a whole lot of political dope today, the most important of which is that Woodrow Wilson will be nominated for president between 12 and 1 o'clock Saturday morning, because if they nominated him on Friday it would be bad luck, just as if it wasn't the bad luck any time they nominated him. The nominating speech will be made by Mr. Wescott of

New Jersey, who done the same outrage at Baltimore four years ago.[4] Here is what Mr. Wescott will say and no other reporter has got it only me.

"Mr. Chairman and Gentlemen if any of the convention: I have been a Democrat all my life and when I say that it shows I am not given to boasting.

"The United States of Old Glory is facing a climax and the time for plucking the fragrant flowers of eloquence is past and done for. At present there is a big war raging in Europe, which possibly you didn't know anything about it. The United States of Old Glory has kept out of the war so far. Why? Because of the Democratic administration, if it had of been a Republican administration we would have kept out of the war just the same. Why? Because how is a country going to fight when it hasn't got nothing to fight with?

"I am a Democrat, and when I say that I refer to Thomas Jefferson (laughter) and Andrew Jackson (smiles) and Grover Cleveland (cheers) and Woodrow Wilson (unbridled giggles).

"What I say to you gentlemen is, why not leave well enough alone? Why not hold onto a president who has kept us all laughing for two years, or 50 per cent, of his administration? Why dispense with the complete letter-writer?

"We are always hearing of the American sense of humor. Then, why fall for Gov. Hughes, who we don't know if he is funny or not?

"The American nation is little different from a musical show. And the producers of a musical comedy always aim to engage a good comedian to head the cast. Gentlemen, the man I am about to name has made the biggest hit of the century, both at home and across the pond.

"The man whose name I will present to you is well qualified for the high office for which he is willing to run, heaven knows why.

"Aside from his availability, he has the assets that make the common people love him and foreign nations respect him. He has the barbers' vote sewed up. He shaves or gets shaved every day of his life, and he does not allow his back hair to run amuck. He is such a nice guy that Bryan, who he had in his chiffonier couldn't get along with him.[5] He is so strong for Americanism that any man who wears or exhibits the American flag is just as safe anywhere in the world as a cow in the stock yards.

"Gentlemen, I desire to present the name of Woodruff Wilson, or whatever it is, and you all got to like it."

Mr. Westcott's nominating speech will be followed by a much bigger demonstration than that accorded Hughes in Chicago, because the delegates and the gallery will be more demonstrative at 1 o'clock in the morning than they were at 12 noon.

After obtaining the above scoop, I was told to set round and notice things and interview whoever I could get a hold of and write something decent. The first thing I seen was Col. Fairman from Pennsylvania who wears a round straw hat that stops when it hits his ears and a collar that he hides behind when he walks and which was designed to protect his Adam's apple from the severe St. Louis winter, and a suit of clothes that would be loose for Frank Gotch.[6] I tried to find my roommate, Mr. King, to get a picture of this guy, but Mr. King had gone out to Forest Park to spear hazelnuts.

The next guy I seen was Secretary Daniels of the navy and I decided to not tell him I was from the South Bend News-Times, but to tell him the truth and see what comes of it.

I told him who I really was.

"Glad to meet you, Mr. Gardner," he says. "I'm going up to my room and take a nap."

"As far as I'm concerned, you can go up in your room and take cyanide of potassium." I says, but not till he was out of the earshot . . . .

. . . The conventions going to open up tomorrow, but the session will only be about ten minutes long because they're afraid they will get through too quick. And it still looks like Roger Sullivan O'Heels and Gov. Major of Missouri and the rest of the candidates for vice president has as much chance of getting nominated as Jim Larkin. Us reporters are wondering what would happen if Mr. Major would be nominated and elected and then have Wilson pass away and Major be president and what would happen?

Well, it couldn't be no worse and it might be better because they ain't but very few good dancers among the rulers of this lovely world.

Lardner began his second column from the convention at the ballpark with a lengthy description of a game between the Washington Senators and the St. Louis Browns, who were managed by Fielder Jones, his old friend from the White Sox.

Ring Is Through with Conventions
But Fielder Jones Is O.K.

CHICAGO TRIBUNE, JUNE 16, 1916

. . . I didn't ask the boss should I go out and write up this game, but I went out to the game without asking nobody, because I thought they would probably be something funny come off worth writing about when Washington and the Browns clashed. But a 1 to 0 game ain't never worth writing about, and especially when the club that loses it is managed by Fielder Jones, and I don't like to write about any game he lost because it makes me mad when he loses a game on account of how good he treated we newspaper men when he was with the White Sox.

I would write some convention stuff today except for two facts, and the first one is that I didn't have the heart to attend the convention this morning because they say Ollie James was going to speak and they says he was better than Gov. Willis of Ohio or Senator Harding of same state or former Gov. Glynn of New York and I knowed when they says he was better that they meant he could say more useless words and believe me if I heard Old Glory and Thomas Jefferson and Abraham Lincoln mentioned a couple more times, I wont have enough patriotism left to fill up a vanity box. And if I'm round anywhere in the next two weeks where they play America and the Star Spangled banner, I will shoot their horns full of cyanide and hope that the inhalations kill them. In other words I'm through with the two leading parties, and I'm for a party that will talk about what's going to come off instead of having their bands play songs that everybodys sick of them and make speeches that remind a guy of eighth grade.

But to get back to events in this chronological order.

I got up this morning in plenty of time to go to the convention, and picked up the morning paper and read where Ollie James was going to make a speech, and I says to myself that a man could not only stand so much and I would not go to the convention.

Then I read in the morning paper where the convention was going to be adjourned between 2 and 3 o'clock to attend the ball game, so I says to myself I would go to the ball game and meet them. But the guys I met out to the ball game was not Democrats, but Fielder and Alvah Williams and Ernie Johnson and Babe Borton and Clark Griffith and Nick Altrock and Silk O'Loughlin, and, believe me they're a whole lot more interesting than politicians, both Democrat and Republicans.

We stuck out there and watched the ball game except when it was raining and I want Mr. Phil Ball to know that I came in on a paid ticket, only I didn't pay for it. But the man that paid for it took us to the racquet club and the country club and showed us what's known as a good time, and his name's Dick Kennard and all O.K.

Then when we got back to the hotel, the boss says:

"When are you going home?"

"What do you mean?" I ast him, because I and he are just close as him and Percy Hammond.

"You're through," he says. "You can blow whenever you feel like it."

"Do you mean I aint done no good work?" I ast him, but he was too clubby to tell the truth. So I can go home whenever I feel like it, and, believe me, I feel like it right now, and the first train that's got a place to sleep on it, that's the train I will go home on and all I got to say about conventions, either Republican or Democratic, is that they're wrong, all wrong, and the gang that'd been down here reporting this convention is for prohibition heart and soul except one or two of them.

I hate 'em all.

Me for Mayor

CHICAGO TRIBUNE, MARCH 5, 1919

Responding to popular demand, the editor of this column has consented to enter the lists as a nonpartisan dependent candidate for mayor. A petition bearing dozens of signatures will be filed tomorrow or next day, and then the "people's candidate," as he aptly styles himself, will enter upon such a campaign as was never before known in this city.

Contrary to the general belief, this is not our candidate's first venture on the so-called political seas. He ran for, and was elected, class poet at the Niles High school in 1901. He ran for, and was elected, Grand Wazir of the Chu Chin Chow club in 1919. He ran for, and was elected, exalted ruler of the Pretty Name Lodge in 1919. He has never been defeated in a political campaign and if elected your mayor will be one of the thinnest mayors in the history of Chicago.

This candidate's stand on the prohibition question is a bone-dry United States, but a ringing-wet Chicago. His motto, in a word, is "More beer—Less work."

This candidate's record in this war is an open book. When it was announced that Papa Joffre[7] and Uncle Viviani[8] wished to visit Chicago, this candidate said, "Let them come." This candidate went to la belle France in the summer of 1917 when Americans were really needed over there, returned the same year with wounds received in the battle of Paris, and talked about his experiences only in response to point-blank questions. He was the only American visiting France that year whose ship was not hit or just missed by a torpedo.

This candidate was drafted last fall and was to take the physical examination on Friday, Nov. 15.

This candidate severed close connections with the gas interests in 1905 when he resigned as bookkeeper for the Niles Gas Company. He is now interested in the gas business only once a month, though occasionally indulging in the wish that they would come out and fix our oven door.

If elected your mayor this candidate agrees to move away from Chicago within six months after his inauguration, thus ameliorating congested conditions on the Broadway surface line.

Four days later, under the headline "To The Public," Lardner wrote:

The formal petition which will place the Wake's editor in the running as a nonpartisan dependent candidate for mayor was filed yesterday with a window washer in the office of Judge Scully and Denny Egan. The petition was written on the back of the carte du jour of a well known dive on Dearborn street.

On April 1, the day of the election, Lardner withdrew from the election, writing:

Parades are the criterion by which I judge a man's chances of election. After watching the Loop parades of the supporters of Hoyne, Sweitzer, Thompson, and Fitzpatrick, and contrasting them with mine, which consisted of one taxicab driver, circling the Loop in search of me because he alleged I had not paid the bill, I came to the conclusion the public does not want me for mayor at this time.

A Taxing Situation

CHICAGO TRIBUNE, APRIL 9, 1919

Dear Cong:

You know the name of my column means behind the news and once in awhile I get way behind it and I have a tough time catching up and it wasn't till yesterday that I found out that you had plastered a tax onto sporting goods and if I had known it before I would of congratulated you all the sooner.

It's a great move, Cong., and a step in the right direction as it will put a stop to a lot of brats playing ball in the park and tramping down the grass and it will keep them at home where they belong out of the open air. Children of all kinds is getting too much encouragement, Cong., and having too good a time and by slapping a tax onto baseball bats and gloves and etc. and make them too dear for the boys to buy them you have certainly gone a long ways towards checking such evils like outdoor exercise.

But I do think you have overlooked a lot of bets that would improve the situation still more yet and I am going to make a few suggestions for some more taxes and you can take them or leave them and no harm done. For one thing the children that's too young to play ball and etc. is still old enough to drink milk and some of them has actually got the habit so bad that they cry if they can't have their bottle. Well, Cong., if you would stick a tax of about ten to fifteen cents on a pt. of milk a bunch of kids that their parents hasn't much jack would just simply have to break themself of the habit and maybe they might cry a little for a few days but after that they wouldn't mind.

And another good one would be to levy a heavy vehicle tax on go carts as the way it is now a person can't hardly walk a block in the day time without he has to pretty near get off the walk to keep from being ran over.

And also it would be a great idear to plaster a stiff tax onto school books and school supplies of all kinds as they tell me the public schools is over-crowded but if you would fix it so as the books couldn't be boughten by nobody only the rich you would soon have plenty of room in all the schools.

Think this over, Cong., and if you like these idears why you are wel-come to them and if not why no harm done but anyway congratulations on the moves you have already made.

Respy,

R. W. L.

On Jan. 11, 1920, Lardner noted the large number of potential candidates for President in the upcoming elections and wrote that "unless a com-promised candidate comes to the 4 and relieves the congestion they will half to shut down on the last few 100 nominateing speechs so as the newspaper men can go to the worlds series." He proposed himself as that candidate.

He "would run on either ticket if nessary and from any state that seen fit to nominate me except Rhode Island witch they tell me is so little that the higher class of people like myself would half to stand up all the time they lived there."

Starve with Hoover or Feast with Lardner

BELL SYNDICATE, FEBRUARY 8, 1920

To the Editor:

Following on my announcement last month that I would sacrifice my per-sonal ambitions and run for president on ether party if they demanded it, several aspirants for the chair has realized what a fat chance they would have vs. a man like myself and has withdrew from the race witch narrows the field down to 146 candidates. When I consented to let my name be used in connections with this event I made the sullen promise to not indulge in no personalitys in regards to other candidates for instants like saying that Will Bryan genally looks like he was all ready dressed when he got up and etc. But I didn't make no promises to not say a word or 2 of warning in regards to the political beleifs of some of my oppts. and I consider it my duty today to pt. out what would happen to this great country was some of my rivals to win this high office witch not only pays pretty fair money but not only that but you get your rent for nothing in a city where rents is said to be he–ll.

In the 1st place let us have a look at this man Hoover's record, who has been give a lot of space as a compromised candidate on both tickets. Well gents what happened the last time this bird held a position of authority? No fats, no candy, no sugar for your mush melon, no meat except for Thursday night supper or something, and bread that tasted like a first baseman's mitt.[9] No statistics has as yet been published on how many pounds of flesh this modern Sherlock took off of American abdomens, but it must of been something prodious. And what man done once he will do again except get born or get dead. Well friends do you want 4 yrs. of fatless meatless sweetless wheatless eatless days like this guy is bound to give you if elected to this high salary office? Not only that but didn't this cuckoo knock decent beer for a goal by telling Pres. Wilson that all the hops should ought to be saved for the Chinamens or something?

Compare this bird's record with Lardner's. Was they ever a time when I swelled up and told people outside of my own family what they could eat and what they couldn't eat? On the contrary every morning that I am up for breakfast the wife leaves the table dureing the salad coarse with the remark that she has got to call up and order the groserys. Well I don't jump up and follow her to the telephone and boo every item she orders though heaven knows we sometimes have vegetables that I wouldn't no more think of putting in my mouth than a public mouth organ. One of the planks in my platform will be eat for tomorrow you may die, and I also plege myself to try and put the words drink and be merry back in that proverb witch has been all shot to pieces by the 18 amendment witch reminds me that another of my planks will be that its vs. the rules to have more than 17 amendments to the U.S. constitution and all the amendments upwards of 17 is null and void.

Yes friends and if you ever come to the White House dureing my reg-iment and it happens to be meal time you can stand in the next room and watch us tear into red meat and sweet sugar and greasy bacon and they will be a understanding through out the entire country that anybody can eat whatever they can pay for because I believe that wile the battle of Waterloo was win on the cricket feilds of the University of Iowa, the 2d battle of the Marne forest was win on the mission dinning room chairs of the sweetest of American institutions since the saloon was wiped out namely the home.

And just 1 more word about this bird Hoover. Was they ever a presi-dent of the U.S. that was worth a d—m that his 1st name was Herbert? Name me 1.

That brings us to the next candidate that has recently been egging him-self on namely Will Bryan who I can dismiss the subject in a few words. This bird styles his self the great commoner but show me where he is any commoner than anybody else or ½ as common like I am for instants. Is it common for a full growed man of 60 Novembers to like grape juice better than a drink? Is it common for a big man that the newspapers print his articles on acct. of his name to write his own stuff for them to print? What do common people do? They play rum and red dog and go to the races and get their suit pressed and drink what they can get in the hopes that its at lease 90 proof. and they go to girl shows and shoot African golf[10] and etc. Witch of these things does Will do that makes him common?

Also what is common? Well my $1.50 dictionary gives definitions under 4 different numbers and No. 2 is the only one witch comes near fitting Will. It says common means usual or frequent or customary witch he is certainly all of that but so is bad weather or a hole in your stocking or a baby named Jr.

No my friends Will isn't no commoner than anybody or as common and has not got no license to run under such colors and shouldn't be spoke of in the same breathe as myself though I have got a good deal of respect for him ever since he walked into the press box at the Republican conven-tion in old Chi 4 yrs. ago and the band played Rock of Ages.

That brings us back to a candidate who I have dismissed before namely Gen. Wood and only for my duty I wouldn't say no more about him on acct. of him being a soldier wile I stayed home on acct. of one flat ft. and one cold one. But I can't help from reminding the public that a little wile ago this gent visited New England, Mass., and about the same time they was a good many deaths in that neighborhood from alcohol that was named after the Gen. and there we will let the subject drop.

Suming it all up (1) vote for Hoover and you don't eat, (2) vote for Bryan and you drink grape juice, (3) vote for Wood you drink wood alcohol, (4) vote for Lucy Page Gaston[11] and you smoke cubebs,[12] (5) but not lease, vote for me and run wild.

In a latter article I will have something to say about Daniels and Sims the 2 recentest entrys in the race whose records I haven't had time to look up yet but in the mean wile keep your eye on the decentest entry namely

Ring W. Lardner

Ring May Run with Debs on Prison Ticket

BELL SYNDICATE, JUNE 7, 1920

Speaking about setting into old Chi, well how did the other candidates for the president's chair get into old Chi? Personally I came in on the next to the most expensive train that a candidate or anybody else could come in on. It looks to me like Hiram Johnson come on the Erie and probably General Wood on the Nickelplate and Admiral Hoover on the Wabash. As for myself I come on a train that you have to pay extra fare and not only that but I travelled with the real people like Irving R. Cobb and Bud Fisher that had all paid extra fare to say nothing about a lot of delegates from Pennsylvania and New York who got in on a pass.

But on the whole you might say most of the delegates come in on cheap trains and freights and etc., on account of giving all their jack to campaign funds which I didn't. Before this convention opens I want to make one more statement to my constituents, and that is, that if I am not nominated at the Republican convention and am not nominated at the Democratic convention I will run on Socialist ticket with Eugene Debbs[13] who is now in jail where most of the rest of the candidates ought to be.

Mr. Hays and Mr. Lodge gentlemen: if it does not make much difference to you, it would be very nice of me if you would nominate me at this convention instead of San Francisco or jail where Mr. Debbs is, because I am in a hurry to get back home and see my family and make arrangement to move to Washington next fourth of March. It will probably cost me $126.00 for myself and family to move from Long Island to Washington, and personally I don't like to talk about financial matters, but I have not yet had a contribution for my campaign. As a matter of fact, I think it would pay me not to accept the office, even if I get it.

I am taking this office, if I get it, solely as a matter of patriotism. I think I owe my country this much, and I will tell you how much I owe other people: Lord & Taylor, New York, $9.50; Marshall Field & Co, $36; A. Porter on this train 50 cents. I am not like William Jennings Bryan who according to Ed Wynn is closely related to Washington and Lincoln. He lives in Lincoln and once went to Washington.

I have been around the different hotels looking for my rival candidates and could not find a one of them. They are all staying in private houses, which shows what kind of cheap stiffs they are.

This candidate arrived in Chicago today two hours younger than his watch. My platform is as follows: There are two things I have never seen in my life—one is a republican convention and the other is a picture of Shakespeare with his hat on.

The town is full of delegates tonight. Did you ever look into the bear face of a delegate? I did it today. It is just something he wears on top of his collar. It breathes and eats and crosses the streets alone and Taxi-Cabs miss him. All delegates seem to be the same age, but why? You have got to give them credit. Most delegates are married unless otherwise employed.

Ring Says the Race Is Between Himself and Cobb

BELL SYNDICATE, JUNE 26, 1920

San Francisco, Cal—The race for the Democratic nomination for the president chair seems to of narrowed down to a 2-handed fight between I and Irvin S. Cobb, who is one of the foot-hills of Kentucky that we been reading so much about on stuff that you get out of drug stores these days.

But if you ever seen him you wouldn't say that the race had narrowed down but you would say it had widened up.

But what I wanted to say was that if this bird wants to make a mud slinging campaign out of this campaign why I will also make a mud slinging campaign and between you and I dear reader he is a whole lot better target.

Well to begin with do you want a man in the president chair that can't speak the American language? This bird is O.K. till he forgets himself and talks the native Paducah which gives the alphabet twenty-five letters and denies suffrage to the letter R which is why my name begins with it and shows how venomous this bird is.

Another point is that furniture is selling higher than it ever did in its life and if I am elected they wont half to be no new furniture boughten for the Whitehouse where as if he is elected, the president chair will half to be a davenport which costs like hades, or as I have nicknamed it, hell.

Now what about me personally? Mr. Cobb has broughten charges that I once had an operation for the removal of my brains.

Well that is true enough but I will say to you gentlemen and girls that the reason he didn't have the same operation was on account it not being necessary. In fact he has been brushing his hair all his life with a vacuum cleaner.

Another charge he has broughten is that I walk with a slight limp and drag one foot. Well friends I sprained my foot in a football game where feet was meant to be sprained and not standing on a Chatauqua platform and the reason he don't drag both ft. is because his momentum carries them along.

Well friends I will not do more mud slinging today as we are all out of mud but I better tell you something about the so-called convention. Well friends everybody in the world seems to be here and in other words they'r nobody home. Our party left Chicago last Monday night and the first man we met on the train was Mr. Gerard the author of "My Four Years in Germany" and he told us the story, so I will tell you the story of "My Three Days on the Train."

Well in the second place we overlooked the whole train and found that it didn't contain nobody but Democrats and their grandmothers and newspaper men. On the morning of the second day I eat breakfast with Mr. Gerard, and found out that his platform was to free Ireland which is directly opposition from my platform which is to keep each and every nationality and race in captivity like my principal opponent Eugene Debs.

In the evening of the same day the second section catched up with us the contents of which was some more Democrats and Detective Wm. J. Burns and J. Ham Lewis and his wiskers. Mr. Burns was sent along to keep an eye on the train barber and see that Mr. Lewis did'nt get robbed.

The next day was Irvin Cobb's 85th birthday and I bought him a shave and he promised to buy me a haircut on my birthday which is the 6th of next March or 2 days after my inauguration but you can't trust the promises and vows of a man like he. I also bought him a box of matches as he travels very light though you would'nt never believe it to look at him.

On the third day we clumb up 6 thousand ft. high which is probably this years record for the Democrats but while I was eating breakfast with a chicken of 60 summers from Pennsylvania the train started to slip back on its haunches and my gal got kind of scared and said did I suppose the brakes would hold and I said I didnt suppose they would, but what was the difference as the second section was behind us and would stop us at the foot of the hill. This cheered the little kid considerable.

The train finally got started ahead again and a cuckoo brakeman come in and told us that this was the Great Divide, but that don't affect the Democratic party this yr. So we slept the rest of the day and finally hit the Oakland Mole[14] and was stopped by a mole trap and come acrost the bay to where we are at and as I say everybody in the world is here and they's nobody home.

It Looks Like a Stampede to Lardner

BELL SYNDICATE, JUNE 27, 1920

San Francisco—Willie Bryan hit the old burg last night and took a load off the party's mind if any, as they thought he'd might probably not show up and that would make this convention illegal in addition to useless.

Jimmy Montague, the poet, who is also my boss on this trip asked me to go to the great uncommoner's room and get an interview, so I went to his room and rapped and a voice says, who is it, and I told him the truth, and the voice says no, they'se nobody home.

It was the same voice that said we shouldn't ought to crucifix mankind upon a cross of gold in 1896 or any other year. This year, he wants a dry plank in the platform which means that prohibition will keep on coming and crucify mankind upon a cross between ether and prune juice at twenty dollars a quart.

Any way I didn't get no interview out of him, but I did talk to a lot of the delegates, and the idea now seems to be the only chance the Democrats got to win this fall is to either nominate a lady or else get a man with as cute a middle name as Mr. Harding's, which as everybody knows is Gamaliel.

As soon as this idea was decided on the head guy went out and paged all the candidates to see whom had the cutest middle name. But the results wasn't all that could be expected. For instance, they found out that Irvin Cobb's is Shrewsberry and Senator Lewis' is Ham and Marshall's is Weasel and Gerard's is words or something, and Cox's is waffles or something, and Wilson's is Woodrow, and in fact pretty near all the leaders has middle names that begins with a W. including myself, but none of them as cute as Gamaliel. So me being a pretty fair politician by this time, to say nothing about quick thinker, why I told them why not pick on me as their candidate on this plank because my middle name also begins with a W.

But it's a whole lot cuter than the other birds and especially when you put it into combination with my first name, so they asked what was the combination and I told them Ringworm. Well that isn't the truth and I won't tell nobody what the real combination is but the delegates have fell for what I told them and it now looks like I will stampede the convention on this basis, that is provided I keep out of the taxicabs in San Francisco until it is time for the nominations or otherwise, there will half to be put up a corpse for their candidate and at that I suppose that they might just as well.

We thought the taxi drivers in old Chi was a little bit slaughterous till we seen the birds here, and they make the Chicago boys look different. Last night I and Mr. Montague and Mr. Cobb decided go out and call on Hiram W. Johnson[15] and congratulate him, and got in a taxi and the driver believed in saving tires by only running on one at a time and I was setting next to Mr. Cobb in the back seat and even Mr. Cobb can't help lurching sometimes and it looked like I would become a mess of debris and I knocked on the window and asked the driver if he had anything on me and he said no it was pedestrians he was after, so I felt a little more safer, but the more pedestrians we missed the madder he got and finely we got on a street where they wasn't no pedestrians, so he clumb up on the porch of a private home in the hopes he might catch a young couple sparking and knock them for a goal, but they wasn't nobody there either, so we finely come to Mr. Johnson's home which is 6000 feet above the street level or otherwise he would of ran up into the front parlor and demolished a few Johnsons.

Well, Mr. Johnson seen that I was kind of shaky and cured it, and if I had known what kind of a guy he was in Chicago I would of withdrew in his favor and stampeded the convention for him. Thats about all the news except that the fire that shook down a few houses in Los Angeles hasn't spread here yet.

Vice=Presidency

BELL SYNDICATE, JUNE 28, 1920

San Francisco—The race seems to be all over but the shooting and if I am not nominated on the first or second ballot I will do the shooting. The plank which I selected yesterday to run on, to wit, that I have got the prettiest middle name in the democrat party, seems to of made such a hit with the delegates that they looks to be no doubt that I will romp in on a stampede, and now all people wants to know is who will get second place on the ticket.

Well friends, if I am nominated and elected I don't expect to live long anyway so the vice president nomination this yr. is more important than ever before. I will be satisfied with anyone of 2 men for this office. The first of these is Riley Wilson of the Sixth Congressional Dist. of W. Va., who is now running for congress or something and is opposed by the wets and will willingly and gladly withdraw in order to run on the same ticket with a man like I.

Mr. Wilson's qualification is as following:

He can sing a song called the Oyster Cutter's Revenge, which nobody else can sing.

He can and does buy out of turn.

This man, gentlemen, is my first choice for the first lady of the land, but if he can't land I am in favor of William A. Lange of San Francisco.

Mr. Lange's qualifications is as following:

When he was a ball player he could go back farther after a fly ball and miss it than anybody but Tris Speaker.

He is the only ball player in the annuals of the National pest that ever had four home runs hit over his head the same day by one man named Ed Delahanty.

He can shimmy. Either one of these birds is satisfactory to me if they insist on nominating a vice president on the democratic ticket. This year it is a good deal like starting a brewery.

Theys very few news to write about what come off today as most of the delegates and newspaper boys was trying to get over a party that was given last night in honor of Damon Runyon. Two men was put out of the banquet hall and two others was licked and one was took to the best jail on the coast. It was a dandy party and I wished they was somebody that has still got words to describe it. Mr. Bryan was not there. Rumor had it today that he had give up hopes of getting a dry plank into the platform and was going to substitute a dry gin plank and get the country sobered up.

The convention is supposed to open tomorrow at noon Chinese time and like all conventions will be opened with a prayer and no convention ever needed one as much before, and after the prayer Sen, Robinson from Arkansas will stand up on his haunches and present my name and then as I say it will be all over but the shouting.

On July 6, the convention nominated James M. Cox for President and Franklin D. Roosevelt for vice president. Under the headline, "Ring to Sue Democrats for Libel," Lardner wrote:

The one day rest seemed to of cleared some of the fog in delegates heads if any, and when I woke up this am, James W. Gerard, the author, was in the room and told me that they had just took another ballot and I had half a vote and I. Cobb had 1 and ½. You may not believe this, and if you don't why please look at the official record. Having found that I am telling the truth I wish to explain the reason why Mr. Cobb leadeth me: Mr. Cobb, who I have nicknamed one of the foothills of Kentucky had a daughter, wile I have nothing but sons and therefore no chance to have a son-in-law to continue the dynasty.

Dressing for the Inauguration Is Some Job

BELL SYNDICATE, FEBRUARY 27, 1921

Well I don't suppose it is necssary to tell my readers what is going to come off in Washington D.C. next Friday but maybe some of them will be supprised to hear that I am going to be there though not in the capacity like it looked like at one time last summer during the Democrat convention held at Tait's in San Francisco.

I am going in the roll of a private citizen instead of what might of been if the salary inducements had of made it worthy my wile and they had agreed to fix the plumming in the White House, but all and all I like it this way a whole lot better and perhaps some of my readers feels the same way. Henry Ford once said:

"I would rather be right than be president," and I will go him one better and say:

"I would rather have a Ford than be Henry."

Jokeing a side, me going to Washington as a sight seer will give me a chance to pal around with my old pals and maybe get acquainted with you dear readers who I feel all ready like I know you personaly and I want you to feel that way about me as long as it don't go no further, but it might be a good idear to warn my admirers amongst the opp. sex that expects to be there that I expect to be accompanied by she who come so close to being the first lady of the land, and I thought she was or I wouldn't of married her.

We will leave N.Y. city Tuesday noon so as they won't be no chance of not getting there in time as the trains is obliged to run slow through the zone of Quiet where the declaration of independents was signed over 50 yrs. ago. The depot we are going to leave N.Y. out of is being kept a deep misery on acct. of the Mrs. being scared of flash lights but sufficient to say that we haven't no intentions of leaving from the Grand Central.

Arriveing in the capital as I sometimes refer to it, we will be wisked in a taxi to a hotel with a bath. Personaly I always prefer stopping at a hotel so as a person can get their pants pressed wile you sleep, but of coarse my readers will realize that we didn't have no lack of invitations to stay in a private house. For inst. as long ago as Jan. I told one of my Washington friends that I expected to be there at this time and he invited me to stay home.

I don't know yet what is going to be the program for the various ceremonys but we will take things as they come and if people finds out we are there and begins to rush us, why all right and if not, all wrong. I am all set in regards to wardrobe though I had to go to the shops myself to pick it out whereas when the next 1st. lady of the land was in N.Y. the different merchants didn't make her come to them but they took their stuff to her hotel and showed it to her, but I bet that after she bought her clothes they didn't send one of their men right to her house a couple times, like they done in my case.

For street wear I have boughten me a suit of Mrs. Harding blue with 15 pockets includeing the vest, ½ inch cuffs on the bottom of the pants and straps around the waist to run a belt through if necessary. With this suit I will wear high 11 shoes of Pumpkin yellow that laces up the middle and ties in a bow around the shapely ankle. The hosery will be plain and very little of it showing.

For the inauguration proper I have boughten me a pair of President suspenders and also a pair of Boston garters in honor of the vice president.

If they have a inaugural ball I will loom up in a shirt of Chinese white over white B.V.D's, a 15½ collar of the same hue, flowered white silk brassiere, and soup and fish of Sam Langford black with shoes and sox of some dark tint. I won't wear no ornaments except a place on my knee that somebody mistook for a ash tray New Yrs. eve and if you see it in a certain light it looks like the knee cap was Peeping Tom. The old nose will carry a shower bouquet of violet talcum powder.

Those of my readers that is going to be present and have never saw a inauguration will maybe want to know what it is like. Well the one next Friday is suppose to be very simple but they generally always have 3 big events that is opened to the public witch is the inaugural parade and takeing the oath of office and the inaugural address. The parade is in 2 divisions and in the 1st. section you will see Pres. Harding and the Senators and the foreign ambassadors and dips and their wifes. The Washington ball club will be in the second division.

These same readers has maybe never even been to Washington before, so I will tell them a little about the town. It was named after Geo. Washington who married Martha Curtis, but they say Geo. swore a good deal himself and had the Washington record till Chas. Dawes hit town.

Washington is often called the city of magnificent distants because if you go a block from the hotel you will go 9 blocks trying to find the way back. The town is divided into 4 sections witch is northwest, northeast, southwest and southeast and it was layed out that way to make it simple and I guess even Houdini could get from one place to another if they was a lot of policemens in route.

But don't buy no guide book as the streets is all named after the different states and letters of the alphabet and you can save money by just takeing along a atlas and a primer. They's been a lot of argument about who I street was named after but they say now that the honor lays between Pres. Wilson.

One of the first buildings you see when you get off of the train is the station. Then they's the govt. printing office where Sam Lloyd mapped out the income tax blanks. Up in the hotel dist. you will see the I.O.U. storage ware house, formally the treasury bldg., and a magnificent distants from there is the Washington monument witch become famous back in 1909 or 1910 when Gabby Street, the Washington catcher, catched a ball that was dropped off of the top of it. Everybody said he couldn't do it, but he done it on the 14th trial and people thought it was a great trick till along came Billy Sullivan of the Chicago White Sox and catched the second ball dropped off.

At that time Abe Attell was still sticking to the fight game.

Another bldg. you will want to see, especially if you are expecting any mail, is the dead letter office witch they say has tripled its receipts in the last 3 or 4 yrs.

Wile the inauguration ain't till Friday the city will begin to fill up tomorrow and the next day and most of the visitors will probably stay in Washington till Saturday night. Sunday March 6 is my birthday and everything will be closed up.

The last time I was in Washington was back in 1917, the first yr. we was at war with Germany. I never expected it would last this long.

Simplicity Reigns in Washington

BELL SYNDICATE, MARCH 3, 1921

Washington, D.C.—Well, the boys wanted this inauguration to be pulled off with Jeffersonian simplicity and it looks like they are going to get their wish. The old town is filling up with simps and by tomorrow night they ought to be as many of them here as during war time.

Amongst the young visitors expected tomorrow is Sammy Pass[16] of Chicago, the boy that showed up the 1919 world serious scandal. He is coming to see that the inauguration is on the square and that Mr. Harding is really toying when he makes his speech. But don't think I am including Mr. Pass in the list of simps. Sammy is unmarried and nobodys fool.

Plans for Friday's simple ceremonys is practically complete, the committee from congress will pick up Mr. Harding and Mr. Coolidge at the New Jess Willard at 10:30 a.m. and take them to the White house to get the rest of the party. They will be 6 or 7 automobiles in the parade from there to the capitol. Messrs. Wilson, Harding, Knox and Cannon will ride in the first, but Philander and Joe is still scrapping over which one will drive. Boys will be boys.

The 2d car will carry Mrs. Wilson and Mrs. Harding. Messrs. Marshall and Coolidge will be in no 3 and Mrs. Marshall and Mrs. Coolidge in no 4. Mr. and Mrs. Lardner, however, is still on such terms that they can ride together in the same car.

They will be still another machine for the secret service and a good many of the guys that hangs around Washington in officers' uniforms is fighting for places in this car on the grounds that if they ever seen service its a secret.

The parade will go from the White house to the capitol escorted by the US cavalry which hasnt had no outing since the civil war. Mr. Harding will be swore in on the east portico. The original idear was to have him take the oath inside the building, but Gen Dawes used all they had there.[17] Both Mr. Harding and Mr. Coolidge will both make speeches and I called up Mr. Burleson to find out what they was going to talk about, but he said he dident know nobodys address.

Pretty near all the members of the Harding cabinet is in town all ready.

Mr. Weeks called on Newt yesterday and asked him all about the war department and will go to work next Saturday with an open mind. It was generally supposed that Chas Hughes was going to be secretary of state till it come out in the papers this morning that he had moved here with his family and took a house, so it looks like he intended to go into some business in Washington.

Mr. Hayes was on the scene early and him and Mr. Burleson was showed through the PO department where they seen many different colored stamps. They laughed heartily at a blue one that says "special delivery" on it. Mr. Hays wouldnt take no chances and wore a big placard on which was wrote: "Return after five days to Will H. Hays, Shoreham Hotel." Which reminds me of a gag I just thought up. Suppose somebody was to phone the Shoreham and say, "Is Mr. Hays there?" "Why, yes," the clerk would reply. "He is amongst the registered males."

At this writing, all the cabinet jobs has been officially announced except secretary of labor which the favorite for the job is J. J. Davis, head of the Loyal Order of Moose. I heard they was 2 things delayed his appointment. One was that Mr. Harding dident want no lodge in his cabinet or he would of chose Henry or Sir Oliver and the other was that the salary is only $12,000 per annum which you cant expect a labor man to live on, let alone pay his loyal moose dues.

The new president has give it out that he won't tell us for 2 weeks who is going to be US ambassadors to different foreign countries. He would like to go to France himself as he used to play a French horn in the Marion band but congress wont stand for no more presidents monkeying around gay Paree. All the other diplomatic posts is a secret except ambassador to the court of St. James which they say W. R. Hearst will have first refusal of it.

Personally I and the Mrs. is putting up at the Wardman park hotel which admits its the most exclusive hotel in Washington and as far as we are concerned its telling the truth. If it was a couple of more miles from where its at, it would be the most exclusive hotel out of Washington. I rolled a cigarette in the dinning room this am and the waiter looked at me like he thought I was a hick so I left him a dime to learn him different.

Tonight we was hosts and guests at a theater party in Waydown East but we dont intend to do much socially until we get invited some place. I didnt let nobody know I was coming, but I noticed that several persons looked at me on the streets today. I seem to be the only guy in town thats wearing a winter overcoat.

They are planning a charity ball at the Willard Friday night to take the place of the inauguration ball, but when I and the madam had made a couple of taxi trips from the hotel to town and back we decided that charity begins on longisland.

Harding Inaugural Is Simps' Delight

BELL SYNDICATE, MARCH 5, 1921

Washington—Well, its all over and everybody was here but Judge Landis. Mrs. Harding is now the first lady of the land, and Mrs. Denby will soon be the first lady of the sea, while Mr. and Mrs. Wilson are the last couple out. The idear of simplicity was carried out to the bitter end. Even when the new congressmen was swore in they looked simpleminded.

When I entered the press gallery at 11:20 one of the first brother simps I seen was Hughie Fullerton, the dean of baseball mathematicians. Hughie come here under the impression that it was a sporting event. But, in an inauguration, you generally always know how it's coming out, where as in a sporting event theys an element of uncertainty, unlest its a wrestling match or a white sox world serious, or a football game at Yale.

When Ring entered the ring, the retiring senators was being treated to some sweet words of farewell by hang over senators with their fingers crossed. The democratic side of the chamber was vacant, which is as it should be. Senators of this party had given up their seats to cabinet members and the ambassadors from foreign lands.

When the foreign diplomats come in and I seen their costumes, I thought we was at the funeral of a prominent lodge man. The different dips wore the grave yard uniforms of the royal arcanum, the knights of pythias, the knight templars and the loyal order of moose. One of them had ten medals on his chest to show that he had broke all the commandments at one time or another, and one dip had on a dinner coat on acct of the difference in time between Washington and wherever he come from.

The next bunch to arrive after the dips was the justices of the supreme court. You cant keep the kiddies home on circus day.

Mr. Marshall, the retiring vice president, responded to a toast and got some applause, but nowhears near enough for an encore. Amongst other things, Mr. Marshall said: "Clothes do not make the gentleman," and Heywood Broun, that was standing next to me, said the remark was a direct insult to the foreign ambassadors. But the latter didn't act insulted and seemed to be having a good time, as they couldnt understand the speeches.

Pretty soon Mr. Harding come in and throwed his eyes all over the joint like he was looking for somebody, but by this time Mr. Broun was standing right in front of me. The president-elect wore the suit he bought the time they had that noon wedding in Marion.

One by one, the other celebritys was broughten in and introduced. Besides Gamaliel they was Gen. Pershing and the head of naval operations whoever he is, and the chief of staff of the army and the head of the marines, and vice president Coolidge. I was tickled to death every time they was a new celebrity, as all the people that had seats was expected to stand up and find out how my foot must feel standing up all the while. Mrs. Coolidge wasnt going to stand when her husband was showed in, but her two kids made her.

The administrations is supposed to change hands at 12 o'clock, but it was way past that before they was ready, so what did they do but set the senate clock back to where they wanted it. This idear ought to be tooken up in civil life, and maybe you could fool the baby with it.

Mr. Coolidge told a couple of anecdotes and wound up with the story about Pat and Mike. Then the new Senators and Representatives was called up the sawdust trail to be swore at and the meeting adjourned to the east porch. It was the original scheme to have Mr. Harding inaugurated in the Senate chamber, but he can't talk unless he's on a porch. I stood on stones instead of wood when we got outside. The day was just right for the players, but a little chilly for the spectators. I couldn't help wishing all through Mr. Harding's speech that I hadn't rushed away from the hotel without a handkerchief. When Gamaliel loomed up on the porch the band played the "Star-Spangled Banner," and the gents had to remove their hats, but it looks to me like if the ladies wants all the rest of our privileges, they should ought to enjoy this one, too.

For his porch specialty, Mr. Harding wore a Harding blue overcoat over his trick suit, so he wouldn't catch his death of cold as Mr. Coolidge feared. The papers is printing the monologues in full and you don't half to read it. He got it across pretty good, though some of the gags sounded familiar.

I had managed to get a hold of a ticket for the madam that said on it "Admit bearer to the grass plot north of the speaker's stand." She said afterwards that it wasn't a bad show, but she didn't think much of the plot.

That's all they is to write except that this a.m. I didn't want to lug my Corona typewriter all over the place, so I called up the Washington Star office and asked them if I could use one of their machines this evening. So the man said wait a minute and I waited 3 or 4 minutes and I was beginning to think he wasn't very hospitable when all of a sudden he come back to the phone and said that all they could let me have was a Ford. So I told him I couldn't use a Ford as I didn't expect to write an anti-Semetic story.

Presidential Golf

BELL SYNDICATE, MAY 1, 1921

To the Editor:

Everybody I seen lately has asked me to tell them about my golf match with the President and it looks like they was nation wide interest in same so I will repeat the story over again for the benefit of those which ain't been lucky enough to see me since the mammoth event came off.

Well, Grant Rice, the poet, called up one day and says he had made a date for he and I to go to Washington and play golf with the President so we got there early on a Thursday A.M. and went to the Willard and eat our breakfast at the next table to Mr. and Mrs. Coolidge who however remained in blissful ignorance of same. After a wile we visited a barber shop wile Grant was trying to get a hold of Mr. Christian[18] on the telephone and the manicure gal asked me where did I come from and I says N.Y. and she says she would hate to live in N.Y. but wouldn't mind working there if she could have a home at Newark or Brighton and she asked me when I got in and when I was going back and finely what was I doing in Washington and I says I come to get a manicure.

"You are a great kidder," she says, so all in all I come out of the barber shop feeling pretty good.

Well it seems Mr. Christian had asked I and Grant to lunch with the President and Mrs. Harding and Grant had said yes without even asking them what they was going to have, so we got our suitcases and golf bags and went out to where the taxi cabs are and the starter says:

"To the station?"

"No, to the White house," says Grant and I shoved the two bits back into my pocket figureing we had give him enough of a thrill.

Well we was wisked to the office entrance and showed right into the private office and shook hands with the President, but he also had a lot of other saps to shake hands with so we stood and talked with Mr. Christian to try and find out the attitude of the administration towards some of the big questions of the hour, and he as much as admitted that he didn't see how Cobb could get anywheres with them pitchers.

Finely the President was through holding hands with the brother Elks from Spring Valley and took us over to the White house, and we had to keep calling him Mr. President as Mr. Christian had kind of mumbled his name when we was introduced and we met the 1st. lady of the land and eat our lunch which was liver and bacon, new potatoes, asparagus, biscuits and some kind of a tart.

Mr. Rice had on a gray pin stripe suit without no vest wile the writer wore a Harding blue suit complete in 3 pieces. After I had drank 2 cups of coffee mine hostess asked me wouldn't I have some more, and I says yes and she made them get it for me without no argument. Up to this time I had felt right at home.

The President and Mr. Rice talked golf wile I and the 1st. lady indulged in the light chit-chat which makes the present writer so sought after by fashionable N.Y.

"I expected you would be a man 20 yrs. older." I just smiled and said banteringly:

"Did you?"

After lunch the President showed Grant and I over the cozy little home includeing the state bedrooms which he didn't say what the names of the different ones was but they all looked like Texas and finely he turned us over to a valet that took us to a room where we was to dress for the game. Dureing this incidents I and Grant realized that peopel that lives in the White house has got a servant problem like everybody else. The problem there is how to get the valet out of the room wile you dress and neither of us were able to solve it. Further and more, we had broughten white pants to match the house where we was visiting and mine had just came back from the cleaners and was dareing to say the lease.

So all and all I was blushing furiously when we joined the President again and was introduced to Mr. Fletcher the under secy. of state who was going to make the 4th. man though neither Mr. Rice or myself is use to playing with underlings. The 4 of us stood on the front porch wile a couple photographers took our picture which I am afraid mine will be very risque.

Well, we all got in a car and was wisked away and the President talked about this in that and says he supposes we had noticed in the White house that he had to get in the elevator ahead of the Mrs. and go through doors 1st. and etc. and it was a rule that the President always has to do everything 1st. and he wished it was different as it made him feel uncomfortable. Well, out on the golf course, they forgot this rule and go according to the golf rules, and I guess he generally always feels pretty comfortable out there.

"They's a nice course here in town now," he says. "But I guess we'll go over in Maryland and play Chevy Chase."

This was another thing that upset my game as I had expected to stay right in Washington and play capital golf.

Well we figured out that it would be a even game if I and Grant stood the president and Mr. Fletcher, as Grant was supposed to be very good, Mr. Fletcher good, Mr. President pretty good and me terrible. Without wishing to brag I was the only one in the party that lived up to expectations. We hadn't went more than 2 or 3 holes when I understood why the man they had broughten along to keep score was from the secret service.

In regards to the course we played on, why if Washington is the city of magnificent distances they's no words left to describe Chevy Chase. They had the yards wrote down on the score card like at all golf courses, but if the man that measured them had of counted Mr. Harding's votes we would have been playing vs. Gov. Cox. It's a pretty course though and I seen it all and when I got home I looked up in the atlas to see where was it located, but the only town I could find in Maryland that sounded like it might be it was Trappe.

Well when we had went 9 holes I asked our score keeper Mr. Jarvis how we stood and he read off the scores and Mr. Harding had 54 and Mr. Fletcher 50 and Mr. Rice 44.

"Well," I says, "I would rather be Rice than the president," but it's vs. the rules for Mr. Jarvis to laugh, a specially on the golf course.

I was asked to not say what the other birds got on the last nine, but personly I cut off 5 strokes and come in in 65. All this wile I thought we had been playing for the president's cup or something, but when it was over and Mr. Fletcher give me 10 golf balls which he said I had win

on the match, why you could of knocked me down with a girder. If that's the way things is going this yr. it looks like we'd have the whole world series in Philadelphia.

It was after 6 o'clock when we got through and Mr. Harding asked us to stay at the White house for supper but if the 1st lady is anything like the 2nd, she don't want the grand exalted ruler inviteing no surprise guests to supper on a Thursday, so we stopped just long enough to get our regular clothes and catched the 7 o'clock back home no worse for the trip except that it will take a long wile to get use to dressing ourselves.

Ring Organizes the Ku Klux Klan

BELL SYNDICATE, OCTOBER 9, 1921

Well friends it looks like all the advertising the Ku Klux Klan has been getting ain't going to get them much business and in fact is libel to put them on the blink as a good many of the boys that use to brag that they belonged to the invisible empire has now became invisible themselfs and the grand exalted Kleagles that use to get $6 apiece for every new member won't half to bother no more about the sir tax. Well I don't suppose it can be helped, but it seems kind of sad to see a organization like this kind break up and all the Kleagles and Goblins forced to go back to driveing a dray.

Wile the Klan was maybe too rough in their work still and all it seems to me like it is too bad to bust up a club that a good many people has became fond of without giveing them something in its place so for that reason I am going to suggest a new Klan that will be a substitute for the old Klan but will cut out all the rough stuff and still have enough mystical rights to satisfy the clients but won't offend nobody that can't take a joke.

For a name for this new organization I would adopt a suggestion from Bugs Baer and call it the Ku Ku Klan and in order to join it a man would half to prove that he was more or less Ku Ku. Anybody applying for members would half to answer a few leading questions which would be something like as follows:

Animal, mineral or vegetable?
Tonsils and adenoids?
Maiden name?
Demi tasse or large cup?
Ever eat chop suey?
Ever ride on a sleeping car that employed colored help?
Was your suit ever pressed by a Jewish tailor?
Ever go to a ball game where any of the players was Knights of
    Columbus?

A man that could answer all these questions yes or no would be eligible for members.

After that would come the initiation held out doors and conducted by a Klodd. The Klodd and members of the Klan would wear night gowns with a pillow case over their head to laugh in. As the klandidate for members come into their presence the Klansmen would all stand up and utter the mystical wd. kluck kluck. The klandidate would then take the sacred oath on a stack of wheat cakes promiseing that he won't never observe eastern time or western time or daylight saveings time but will always tell time by Ku Ku Klox. He won't never play golf with a foreign born kladdy. He won't never ride in a non union klab. He will always wear klassy klothes and look klean klut and will always sleep in a sacred night gown and never klajamas. He will kling to the Klan and carry out their objects regardless of klith or klin.

Now in regards to the objects of the Ku Ku. This order won't be out to get no particular race or kleed but will pick on individuals as they seem to need it. Like for inst. suppose they's somebody that one of the Klansmens don't like for some reason another, why he will tell the nearest Klodd about them and the Klodd will call out the Klan, and they will pick out a dark, dreary, rainy night and take the poor victim to a sacred refuse dump and give them a dose of white pine and tar, at the same time tickleing them with a feather to make them cough. In extreme cases, the victim could be took to a Klansmen's house and obliged to drink a glass of home made beer.

As soon as they's enough members for a klorum the Ku Kus will of course want a whole lot of victims to get busy on, and in case they can't think of nobody that needs vengeance I will name a few that it would please me personally if they was reeked on and the first one I name is a gal I played bridge partners with the other night and somebody bid a spade and I doubled a spade and the gal past. Another one is the man that got up the N.Y. traffic laws and another one is the man that grabs hold of your arm and tells you the one he just heard about the Englishman and another one is the man that says Carpentier could of won if he had fought different.

I suppose my admirers would expect me to accept the post as emperor of the new Klan but must decline that honor as I could not give all my time to it on acct. of golf and besides I believe that the man holding this office should ought to be 100 per cent Ku Ku, and I can't think of no one better qualified than the man who give the Klan its title, namely Mr. Bugs Baer.

Personally I would be willing to serve a wile as grant exalted Gobbon and for Klodds and Kleages I would nominate some of the boys that is only a few points shy of 100 per cent includeing the boys that draws the comical picture in the paper and the boys that buys ring side seats to a alleged wrestling match and the boys that pays to get in the ball pk. at Philadelphia.

The national headquarters of the Klan would be Mr. Baer's home on the Brooklyn Bridge and the Klan grip would be the hand on the emperor's neck with the thumb pressing the Adam's apple.

No Navy=No Fight

BELL SYNDICATE, NOVEMBER 13, 1921

Washington, D.C.—Well, I don't suppose it will surprise anybody to find out that I am in Washington for the disarmament conference as it is getting so that they can't put on no event of worldwide interest without they have me there and if you look it up you will find that I have been behind the scenes at every real big occasion that has came off in the world in the last five years, except the tennis match between Mrs. Mallory and Miss Lenglen—and what a flop that was.[19]

Anyway here I am a good five hours from Long's Island but no chance to get lonesome as this old town is full of celebritys and it seems like every time I turn around H. G. Wells or M. Briand or somebody hollers:

"Hay, Ring."

Wells and some of the other visiting firemen is stopping at private homes but personly I always prefer a hotel where a person can get their pants pressed nights and look like something in the morning and besides if you stay at somebody's house that don't know you very well you are libel to set down to meal after meal of cheese omelet and sliced bananas.

Of course, the paper Wells is working for done a smart thing when they stuck him in a private home. Hotel grub runs into real money even when you only put on the feed bag three times every twenty-four hours but imagine having an Englishman knocking over seven meals per day at your expense.

I am stopping at the Willard which is the same hotel where the French delegation is at but so far I ain't ran acrost many of them in the lobby and the bell captain says the most of them spends their time in their room looking curiously at the bath tub.

Another thing that got them puzzled is a concoction that the waiter sticks in front of them as soon as they set down in the dining room. This is a glass that has got a piece of ice floating in a liquid that ain't red or white or no color of at all but when you tip the glass a little the ice hits against the side of it and tinkles so maybe it is some kind of a musical instrument.

They may be some of my readers that is dumb enough to not know what this conference is all about. Well, friends, it has been called together to see if they ain't some way of stopping war and that is what the League of Nations was supposed to do but the league has been to bat five or six times and ain't even got a foul. So the idear is to find a substitute for the league and a lot of the boys figure that the disarmament scheme will do the business so the object of this meeting is to get all the different nations to quit building warships and making ammunitions, etc., and it looks now like they would all agree to the proposition provided they's an understanding that it don't include they themselfs.

They's no question but what the United States would be tickled to death to see all the ships sank and all the guns and bombs and brick bats throwed in the ash can. That would leave every nation in the same position, namely, without nothing to fight with except their fists. And we have got Dempsey.

Jokeing to one side, this country goes into the conference in dead earnest and fully prepared to cripple ourself from a fighting standpoint provided the other nations does the same and as a evidents of good faith President Harding is planning a public bonfire at which he will burn his niblick.

The main idear of course is to persuade everybody to quit having a big navy. Rifles can do a whole lot of damage in a neighborhood brawl but you can't hide behind a tree in Omaha and snipe guys on Main St., Tokio. So if war ships was done away with they wouldn't be no danger of another real war breaking out till the next time Germany and France gets mad at each other which ain't libel to happen for a long wile, say six months.

So all this conference has got to do is make everybody give up their navy and some nations is expected to agree wile others will take a lot of coaxing. Like for inst. Switzerland will probably make a big squawk wile on the other hand Spain is already counted in the yes column as they are really the pioneer in this enterprise. They quit having a navy in 1898.

However, we won't never know what the Swiss delegation has to say as the sessions of the conference is going to be held in secret and the public is barred. The American delegation would like to have everything open and above the boards but the foreigners won't stand for it. This same explanation is give out in England and France, only over there it's America that insists on secrecy.

Well, whoever it is that insists on it, they can have it, as I know a whole lot better ways of spending my time in Washington, but as far as I am concerned suppose they did let me in their old meeting wile the Japs or Swedes was airing their views. Why I could set right in their lap and hear it all and it would still be a secret from me unless they sell librettos.

Seriously speaking, I am for secret sessions if secret sessions is going to accomplish what the boys has set out to accomplish. They's nobody in this country or anywheres else that is pulling harder for war to be stopped than this native son of Berrien County, Mich. Because I have got a little male quartette in my home which in twenty years from now they will all be draft age at once and it ain't on the cards that the whole four of them will be lucky like their dear old dad and have falling arches.

War With Japan May Have to Be Fought with Postcards

BELL SYNDICATE, NOVEMBER 16, 1921

Washington—Another packed house seen the show at Continental Memorial Hall yesterday and while the performance lacked some of the zip that Mr. Hughes put into it opening night, still the audience acted like they was pleased and I wouldn't be surprised if the piece run all winter.

The boys finely gave me a pass this morning and I was amongst the first to arrive in the hall, but pretty soon the other newspaper men begin dropping in and several of them wore frock coats, which would never be tolerated in the press stand at the world's series. Personally, I was married at night, and have got just a gray business suit for day time wear.

The man setting next to me pointed out the delegates of the different Powers as they come in and took their place at the tables, which look like they had been borrowed for the occasion from the Hotel Commercial writing room. The delegate that took my eye was Mr. Schanzer from Italy, who looks like one of the apostles. I asked my informer how an Italian come to have the name Schanzer and he says it was because he come from Trieste. It seems reasonable explanation though personly I never was in Trieste and don't know the Schanzer boys. The delegate next to Mr. Schanzer was also quite a sight, as he was a Hindu named Sastri who had just been getting a shampoo and the barber forgot to take the towel off his head.

Chairman Hughes got up and asked if anybody wanted to reply to what he had to say at Saturday's meeting, and we was all in a sweat to hear from England and Japan but before they was allowed to talk a tenor leapt to his feet and sung a French translation of what Mr. Hughes had just said. Then Mr. Balfour made the longest speech of the day and he was followed by Messrs. Kato, Schanzer and Briand. Mr. Kato give his speech in Japanese and Mr. Schanzer spoke in what he thinks is English and of course M. Briand used French and he is the only man I ever heard talk that language that didn't seem to think it was a foot race. All the speakers was tenors except Messrs. Hughes and Briand.

Well, anyway, they still said they was agreeable to the idear of cutting down the navies and if we do have a war with Japan it begins to look like it would half to be fought with souvenir post cards. I thought Mr. Balfour made a very eloquent speech, but Mr. H. G. Wells, who I have now had the pleasure of meeting him, says that if you was to tell Mr. Balfour that he had made an eloquent speech he would feel very much hurt and promise to not forget himself next time.

After the five great Powers had been heard from, Mr. Hughes adjourned the meeting though the delegates from Portugal and Holland set there with their tongues hanging out ready for action. I am told that the rest of the sessions is libel to be held in secret and not even newspaper men will be admitted which suits me o.k. as they don't allow smoking.

In the meanwhile things is beginning to perk up in a social way around the nation's capital as I have been invited to attend the regular Wednesday luncheon of the Washington Rotary Club at which occasion the Chinese delegates will be the guests of honor and principal speakers and I would advice them to make their speeches long as theyre no telling when they will get another chance.

Last night President Harding and I attended the Merry Widow but not together. After the show I got introduced to H. G. Wells and during the course of the conversation it developed that one of us had never heard of the other.

Coolidge Awaits Word of Landslide

BELL SYNDICATE, JUNE 10, 1924

Cleveland, Ohio—Not since Man o' War quit horse racing and became a father has they been so much uncertainty over a contest of any kind as seems to exist in regards to the battle for the republican presidential nomination which opens here tomorrow with a prayer. High paid journalists of all sexes, seeking high and low for a suitable comparison, have agreed that the thing like which it will be most similar to is a scuffle between Dempsey and what he laughingly calls his sparring partners.

President Coolidge is said to be still hoping vs. hope that they will be a last minute landslide in his direction when it becomes evident that his opponents is permanently deadlocked. I forget their names. He won't be able to attend the convention in person as it is the nurse's day out, but he has had a private letter box nailed up on the porch of the house where he lives in Washington and as soon as a choice is made he will be notified by a souvenir postcard showing the proposed new union station in this city.

If Mr. Coolidge should happen to win out the next problem is who to have for vice-president. They used to call the vice-presidential nominee the running mate, but whoever it was that was on the ticket with Mr. Cox four years ago claims they's no truth in that rumor.

Experts say Mr. Coolidge is a kind of a flop as a stump speaker so if he runs, why they want somebody on the ticket with him that can talk. Looks to me like they might half to go outside of the party to find somebody that can help it.

Joking to one side or the other, the newspaper boys that writes politics all the year round and knows even more about it than I do have arranged a all-day golf tournament to take place at the Oakwood country club in Cleveland this here coming Friday. You can figure that out for yourself. Personly I have made a engagement to go eel shooting in the Chicago river Friday night.

But they don't nobody need to feel sorry for the Cleveland bonifaces as us visitors was give the choice of taking our rooms for the entire week or sleeping in the branches of a tree. Besides which if this convention is anything like some conventions I been to, why the big majority of the out of town guests will need their rooms all week.

The town where they hold the democrat convention don't half to worry about it being over too soon. Baltimore was practically permanent and in St. Louis eight years ago, where everything was set even before Bryan got there, the boys managed to hang around till Saturday midnight when the stores closed. But to mention San Francisco where they took 44 ballots and the nominee got more votes all told than he did that autumn. As for the gathering in New York two weeks from now, they tell me that some of the right minded lady democrats of what I once dubbed the Big Town have made the worst saloons promise to stay closed till June, 1925. Safety first is their slocum.

It may not be generally known, but I was in Washington in March and attended some of the oil hearings, to get material for a risque novel and while I was there a blond boy named Al Jennings said he heard that big oil interests had a whole lot to do with naming the ticket in 1920. His story was substantiated by a couple of anonymous telephone calls and we boys was talking about it last night and I said I hoped they wouldn't be no suspicions attached to this here session and we agreed they wouldn't be, still and all why are they holding it in the town where Mr. Rockefeller lives when he ain't gadding around the country with a bag of golf sticks?

Seeking enlightenment today on this grave question I made myself acquainted with a delegate who is stopping in this hotel. He is located in the lobby and has a suite consisting of two chairs and a cuspidor. He gave his name as Mr. Abel Woose. He hails from the natural state of Texas and is a roving delegate to both conventions. He is between 74 and 74½ years of age.

"I haven't missed a national convention in fifty years," said the lobbyist.

"What of it?" I asked him.

"I helped nominate Harrison in 1892, and then I voted for Cleveland," continued Mr. Woose.

"Yes," I said, "and speaking of Cleveland, did you ever stop to think that this is Mr. Rockefeller's town?"

"My home town is Gangrene, Texas," said Mr. Woose, who is also a little hard of hearing.

"I would like to get your views," said I.

"Tomorrow, tomorrow," replied Mr. Woose and stepped into his bath.

So tomorrow I may be able to give the readers some of the views of Mr. Woose, of Gangrene, Texas.

Lodge Nearly Achieves Acquaintance with Ring

BELL SYNDICATE, JUNE 11, 1924

Cleveland, Ohio—It begins to look like this show was going to be a decided flop. The boys ought to of tried it out for a week in Atlantic City or Stamford instead of opening cold in Cleveland. Opening cold is right. I been to many convention of one kind and another and never attended one where they was less laughs. Mr. Burton of Ohio got very few laughs, as the most of the boys and gals in the audience had heard his act in Chicago eight years ago and it sounded like he had not re-writ it only to change a few names.

Mr. Burton used to be a senator and now he is a representative. The way he is going ahead, why the next time we hear him speak he probably will of rose to the position of a page in congress. You can't keep a good man down. Mr. Burton was all-in a brand new pall bearers suit and Hendrik Von Loon asked William Allen White to try and find out who was his tailor so Mr. White made inquiries and found out that the costume was made by the American Tent and Awning Co.

The other Burton brother will do his stuff Thursday. He has been selected to nominate Calvin Coolidge who is nicknamed the dark horse of this convention. This other Burton used to be president of Smith's female college and was chosen to make the nominating speech out of due respect to the number of lady delegates, the most of whom looks like they was charter members of Smith and played guard on the football nine.

As exclusively predicted in these columns yesterday the convention opened up with a prayer in which the bishop told who ever he was talking to what we was all here for so they wouldn't be any misunderstanding in heaven. Everybody had to stand up during the prayer and had not no sooner sat down when John Phillip Sousa led the Star Spangled Banner. The band then played Mr. Sousa's "Stars and Stripes Forever" but forever was nothing compared to Mr. Burton's speech. Then we stood up again while they played "America" and after that a man who was so famous that I did not recognize him come to the front of the platform and said a few words in regard as to how the United States had growed. I can only remember his first sentence.

"It is now sixty years since Lincoln was president." This statement practically throwed the house into a panic, coming as it did like a bolt out of the blue. When quiet was restored the man went ahead and told the one about Pat and Mike and then came the Burton monologue which I noticed a good many people walking out on same including the undersigned.

A shorthand reporter stood right behind Mr. Burton and took down the speech word for word. As copies of it had been distributed last night to all the papers in the world including Snappy Stories, why the sight of the shorthand man taking it down was like as if you would see Umpire Clarence Rowland standing behind the plate in the 14th inning clad in his mask and protector when the game wound up in the 9th, with the score, 4 to 0, in favor of Harvard, and all the athletes had went home to tea. Girls will be girls.

The writer got up this morning at an unseemly hour and bathed and shaved which is more than you can say for some of the delegates and walked over to the convention and during the last block of the journey I was walking side by side with Henry Cabot Lodge but neither of us spoke to each other. He looked at me once like he wanted to strike up a friendship but I pretended I was a democrat as you can't be too careful and especially in Cleveland.

The boys still seem to be at a lost in regards to who will they nominate for vice-president. The vice-president of the United States is captain of the senate and it is his task to set all day and look at the senators and not laugh out of turn and they can't find nobody who will assume this chore. If I was running it I would nominate a democrat and get votes from both parties and I have suggested the names of Will Rogers and Joe Fogg. Mr. Fogg is now a Cleveland boy and used to play quarter back for the University of Wisconsin football nine, and married a Goshen girl and carries eight iron clubs in his golf bag and calls them by number. Mr. Fogg promises that if elected he will remain in Cleveland where he won't have to look at the senate.

"If elected, Mr. Fogg, will you remain in Cleveland?" asked an interviewer.

Mr. Fogg did not reply as he was at Cornell college, Iowa, receiving a Phi Beta Kappa key with which to open the cellar door. Your correspondent had another interview with Abel Woose, the neutral delegate from Gangrene, Texas.

"What do you think about this third party talk?" inquired the interviewer.

"Third party?" said, Mr. Woose, "Why I don't believe I could stand a third party, I been to two of them here in Cleveland. And felt like h— the next morning."

Double-Header in Cleveland
Finds Gaps in Bleachers

BELL SYNDICATE, JUNE 12, 1924

Cleveland, Ohio—This convention has been such a frost in regards to drawing crowds that the boys today borrowed a page out of the baseball book and played a double-header, but even at that the bleachers was full of seats with nobody to set in them.

In fact some of the seats that was occupied might as well of been vacant. At the morning session the boys done more stalling than a couple of umpires before a world's serious game. Finally when they couldn't stall no more a motion was put to adjourn till evening and when the vote was taken about twenty-two people said aye and the rest said no, but the chairman was hard of hearing and the session stood adjourned.

This was a terrible blow to some of the delegates from the outlying precincts as they had boughten tickets for tonight to a high brow drama entitled "the keep kool kuties, or putting pep in politics," but the delegates was not sent here to study the drama and a good many of them is trying to find out what they was sent here for. They have got about as much to say as the third assistant bus boy in a lunch wagon.

Mr. Sousa and his band was not on the job this time and the meeting opened with a organist playing the appropriate "Love's old sweet song."

Pretty near everybody cheered this number thinking it was Dixie or the Battle Hymn of the Republicans. The Wisconsin delegates did not cheer. They ain't cheering nothing.

Experts tells me that the stalling was done on act of a disagreement in regards to what is going into the platform. By the first of August if you ask somebody what was put into the platform they won't know what you are talking about, but it is something a party has got to have at a convention, like delegates.

Two or three hundred more guys was mentioned during the day as possible candidates for vice president. If you ain't been mentioned for vice president at this convention you are a pretty poor fish. The trouble seems to be that as they think of a new prospect they call him up and he says no. Mr. Coolidge looks too healthy. The question will be settled by nominating somebody that ain't been consulted and then adjourning the convention before he has had a chance to be notified. Proceeding on this theory the committee on vice presidents is now trying to think of some guy who is over in Siberia spearing hazelnuts and way out of the reach of a telephone so that by the time he finds out he is running, the election will be over and what and the hell can he do about it.

One of the sights of Cleveland this week is a male quintette from Mr. Coolidge's home town in Vermont. Four of them sing and the fifth one is Bruce Harper, a composer. They go around to the different hotels dressed up in street clothes with a night gown outside of same and sing Mr. Harper's composition which the composer fondly hopes will become the official campaign song. Here is the chorus and you had better commit to memory as it looks to me like it would be very difficult to obtain copies later on:

Keep Kool and keep Coolidge is the slogan of today.
Keep Kool and keep Coolidge for the good old USA.
A lot of politicians cannot do a thing but knock.
But Calvin Coolidge is a man of action and not talk.
So just keep kool and keep Coolidge in the white house four years more.
We have a chance to do it in this year of twenty four.
He's been tried, he's never wanting, he is giving of his best.
Keep Kool and keep Coolidge is our country's mighty test.

I did not want to encourage the gent so I refrained from telling him my experience in regards to writing a campaign song. This was away back in 1916 when they seemed to be a chance that Mr. Roosevelt would win over Mr. Hughes or if he did not win, why he was going to run independent.

Well anyway I turned out a master-piece entitled: "Teddy you're a bear"[20] and Lee Roberts wrote a beautiful tune to it and we went around with a quartette plugging it at the different Chicago hotels and finally Mr. Roosevelt said he would not run on any ticket and the song sold four copies and my royalties amounted to 2 cents in round numbers. Mr. Roberts afterwards wrote "Smiles" and cleaned up a fortune, but I am still reporting conventions.

I had another interview today with delegate Abel Woose of Gangrene, Tex., who is a delegate to both conventions. He was just climbing out of his bath in the lobby of the hotel Cleveland.

"Well, Mr. Woose," I said, "are you a wet or a dry?"

"I am always kind of wet when I first get out of the tub," said Mr. Woose.

"Would you take the nomination for vice-president?" I asked him.

But he had left the stopper out of the tub and went out through the pipes.

The 1924 Democratic convention, which was held in New York and ran from June 24 to July 9, remains the longest political convention in U.S. history. Longshot John W. Davis was nominated on the 103rd ballot.

Ring Will Run Under One Condition

BELL SYNDICATE, JUNE 24, 1924

New York—If I was a democrat and if it was me that was running this convention I would see to it that the thing did not drag out over the coming week-end. Judging from the eagerness with which the visiting firemen has started out to see New York, why if it lasts any more than five or six days the voting strength of the party will be decimated by he whom I sometimes refer to as the grim reaper, and even if the boys is obliged to keep up the pace past Friday it will be hard to get them out of bed in time to vote at the November election.

A delegate named Knute Casket from Willy Nilly, Vermont, whom I talked to today was very anxious to have it end up Friday so he could stay over in New York Saturday and try and find out where Madison Square Garden is located. Mr. Casket has to be back at Willy Nilly Sunday to milk the goat.

"I must be back at Willy Nilly Sunday," said Mr. Casket.

"Why is that, Mr. Casket?" the interviewer inquired.

"To milk the goat," replied Mr. Casket.

The interviewer then left him to his own thoughts if any.

Abel Woose, the neutral delegate from Gangrene, Texas, who was one of the leading spirits at the Cleveland convention, arrived in New York yesterday in a kiddy kar and at once went to his suite at the Aquarium which he is sharing with a salt macqerel.

"Well, Mr. Woose?" I inquired, "how do you like the Big Town?"

"Can a duck swim?" said Mr. Woose. "I had not no more than got off the train when the two girls smiled at me."

"Are you sure they was not laughing?" I inquired.

"You seem to feel pretty fresh," said Mr. Woose.

"Well," I says, "anybody that can feel fresh after the Cleveland convention is a hot sketch."

Mr. Woose intends to present his own name to the convention here while the other delegates is out.

Speaking about presenting names, I have been asked by some of the leaders to allow them to present my name as a dark horse.

"You are dark," said one of them, "and you look a good deal like a horse."

I laughed off this flattery, but seriously speaking I would not be surprised if they was another landslide towards me like out in San Francisco, when I developed unexpected strength along the 42nd ballot and got ½ a vote. Some folks said it was just a complimentary vote while others said it was insulting. Be that as it may, if conditions get to be the same here like they was in San Francisco, they's no telling what will happen, and from all appearances this is going to make San Francisco look like a meeting of the ladies guild.

A good many of the other dark horses that has been mentioned won't say whether or not they would accept the so called honor if nominated. Personally I don't think it is just or fair to keep your admirers in the dark in regards to your intentions and if you ain't got no intentions why come out and say so and give somebody else a chance. As far as I am concerned, while I never sought political honors, why if my friends wants to run me, I will accept on one condition, namely, that Mr. Coolidge withdraw.

Women Held to Blame for Long Session

BELL SYNDICATE, JUNE 30, 1924

The convention has now took a rest over Sunday and it aint like they didnt need it. If they was a doctor in the house his advice to the delegates would be to stay quietly in bed a few days and try and sip down a little clam juice.

Newspaper men was today recalling with terror a situation that came up in 1860 when the convention met in Charleston and took plenty of ballots and finally adjourned to Baltimore and took plenty of more ballots and then nominated Mr. Stephen A. Douglas and you know what happened to him. Well anyways please don't leave us adjourn to Baltimore this time and when I say that I dont mean that I have got anything vs Baltimore but leave us adjourn to Great Neck where a man can get a clean shirt and see their family.

The trouble with this convention seems to be that for the first time the women is practically running it, and when I say that I don't mean nothing vs the women, but you know how they are. They never stop to realize that anybody might be in a hurry to get home. And the queer of that is that when it gets late enough at night, they all want to get home when nobody else does.

Well anyways the most of the gals in this convention so far has all appeared in short hair but the most of we boys wished they would cut the convention short instead of their hair.

Well a few days ago Mrs. Izetta Brown from West Virginia got up in bobbed hair and seconded the nomination of John W. Davis. Her plea was that he was a handsome man and this country should ought to have a handsome president. I felt like getting up out of what I laughingly call my seat and asking her why didnt she second the nomination of Valentino or the younger of the Barrymore boys.

The next woman to get up was a Mrs. Barrett of Virginia who seconded the nomination of Senator Glass. Everybody applauded her and in response to same she blew kisses instead of continuing to blow glass. Women aint got no idear of time.

Anyways most of the women delegates and alternates is from out of town and they dont seem to be in no hurry to get home but some of the rest of us is and if the gals dont stop interrupting the proceedings why I for one will try and get the 19th amendment repealed so as women will half to remain in the home and men also.

This is supposed to be a day of rest and as far as I see it aint been no different than all the rest of the days we have been having since this convention started and my suggestion is that the next time we have a democrat convention, make all the delegates be men or women who have got some business to tend to as we can get home some time and go to work.

Ring Defends His Socks

BELL SYNDICATE, JULY 3, 1924

New York—I don't like to get personal at this stage of what I have nicknamed the game. but a good many people has been criticizing my appearance in the last two or three days. I don't mean my face, which is beyond criticism, but what I and they refer to as my clothing which I will admit is not beyond criticism. If the boys would hurry and nominate somebody or anybody I would go home and get myself dressed up decent and parade through the Garden and show the visiting Elks that I ain't always as deshabille as I may of seemed.

Now for one thing in regards to my hosiery. There is something about my ft. that makes everybody look at them and I want to exclaim that a brother-in-law of mine in a complimentary spirit give me a pair of size 10 sox for last Xmas and my usual size is No. 11, but somehow the two pairs got mixed up in the wash and that is why my two ft. don't act like they was on speaking terms. In regards to my shirt I won't defend myself only to say that a man can't afford buying a shirt every day of a Democratic convention and will go a step farther and state that the one that has been keeping company with me for the last four days ain't no more familiar looking than the shirts I have seen lately on certain delegates I could name, but I won't.

So much for the personal element. But I would like to say that if nominated and elected I will try and get better laundry service than you can by commuting between Great Neck and the Garden. Speaking about the Garden, after they have had numerable prize fights and a circus and then this convention in same, why a rose by any other name would smell as sweet . . . The wise boys was telling me along about supper time that it might yet wind up Wednesday night, but they said the same thing Monday and it don't look to me like they was any hope and I am sorry to be boring everybody with this kind of writin' but I have got to get even with somebody and my only suggestion is that they hold the next Democratic convention by souvenir post cards which would give everybody a chance to stay at home and change their shirts once in a while.

Ring Wants Bryan Lured Away

BELL SYNDICATE, JULY 4, 1924

New York—At a special meeting of the newspaper men tonight we all agreed to keep on trying to coax some of the visiting democratic leaders to go home or some wheres so as us boys can get some sleep. Each of us was assigned one special man to work on, and Mr. Bryan was the name I drawed out of the hat, but I don't hardly know him well enough to invite him out to the house and besides which we already got company and furthermore Great Neck where I live is too close to New York and he might hop on a train any minute and come back to town and start it all over, but if theys some public spirited men or ladies in Maine, or Oregon or somewheres far off and they happen to read this, why please send him an invitation to pay you a visit and I assure you he is a very interesting talker and just like one of the family and no trouble at all to entertain and if theys any expense connected with it, I will pay half.

This town made a great effort to get this convention and extended a warm welcome to the visiting firemen but they did not mean that the visit was to last all summer. In a little while we have got to be getting ready for the Wills-Firpo fight and then comes the World's serious, and after that the football season. And here we still are and nobody has said a word about going home. There is a persistent rumor around town that the reason the visitors keeps hanging around is that they can't pay their hotel bill let alone buy a railroad ticket. Another report is that they are trying to hold up the nomination till a couple of days before election so the public won't have time to forget the name of who is running. Be this as it may, the situation is desperate and several of the newspaper boys has took off their badges on which the words "Active press" is printed and have tore off the adjective. Personally I left everything flat long enough to get home and change shirts and one of my kids still knowed me by sight and he told me Washington was in first place in the American league and Hagen had won the golf championship in England or somewhere. He also reminded me that tomorrow was the 4th of July and said "surely Daddy (he calls me daddy) you don't have to work on the Fourth of July."

"Yes, John," I replied, recalling his first name, "the Fourth of July is just another day for your poor old dad."

Now I will not bother you with the rest of the conversation, but at the finish the both of us was in tears. . . .

Democrats Are Out to Set New World Record

BELL SYNDICATE, JULY 8, 1924

New York—It only took seven days to make the world, but that don't satisfy the democrats. These boys and gals are going out for a record. A musical show named Sally lasted something like three years and a plain comedy named Lightnin' run on Broadway about that long. Abie's Irish Rose begun three years ago and is still going strong. The civil war and what is known as the world's War, run about four years a piece. And then they was the seven years war. And the children Moses led out of Genesis into Exodus was fasting forty days in the Wilds. Those is some of the marks that the democrats seems to be shooting at. It looks like they want to get up a record that everybody will be shooting at for the next 20 years. According to the hotel proprietors they have already beat Moses' children's records as far as fasting is concerned and now all they have got to do is surpass Methuselah's record for longevity. . . .

It is recorded that last Friday a delegate from Iowa went home on acct. of it being the anniversary of what he called his wedding and it was late at night and he rapped at the door and Mrs. Gargle answered for that is their name, and he says I have come home on acct. of our anniversary.

"But who are you?" she said.

"I was married twelve years ago to a young clean cut looking boy who quite a while ago left for New York to attend what they call the democratic convention and he said he would be back in a week. I certainly was never married to a person like you that has got a beard as long as the Woolworth building and circles under his eyes that looks like the arctic circle and a collar that has become a part of his neck."

So Mr. Gargle was forced to leave his home and borrow $78.00 from the night police force in this town named What Cheer and he got back here Monday morning and in the meanwhile had forgot who he was suppose to be voting for but when they called the first roll it was found that it made no difference.

Another casualty of the convention turned out to be none other than Wilfred Leetle, of Parnesia, Arizona. This delegate come here with only one razor blade, expecting to stay two weeks at the outside. But although he has been staying at the outside he can't find nothing that his razor blade will cut except new potatoes in cream, so all as he can do is go from restaurant to restaurant with his razor blade, cutting new potatoes in cream. . . .

Ring Knew It All Along

BELL SYNDICATE, JULY 10, 1924

New York—If any of my readers is still living they will recall that two or three weeks ago or whenever the convention was in the throes of its infancy, I made the prediction that John W. Davis would be the nominee. I said at the time that the nomination would be made on the 41st ballot, but I must give you an exclamation of how that happened. In the first place I knowed that the nomination would be made on the 103rd ballot. But my telephone number is 103 and I did not want to mention that number as I was afraid some of the delegates would be calling up. In the second place I purposely underestimated the ballot by 62 ballots as 62 is my present age though I was only 39 when the convention started.

Now it can be told why I might state that at one time Mr. Glass was to of been the nominee but it was decided at a conference between I and Mr. Bryan that if he was put at the head of the ticket, the slogan couldn't of been nothing but "look out for Glass," that is why Mr. Glass was throwed into the receptacle kept for that purpose.

And now it can be noted the reason the nomination took place today was because the health board had been working on a problem of how to dispose of delegates and the last named was getting kind of scared. A man from the Kiwanis club in Madison, Georgia, wired me this morning to the effect to warn delegate-so-and-so, that he better come home as the cat had given berth to six kittens, the cellar was flooded with wine, the mortgage on the old home had not been paid, and she, the wife, was sewing for a divorce on conventional grounds.

Meanwhile the health board had made the following report:

"In the last few years, great progress has been made in the war against bugs and pests of all kinds. Three years ago a successful battle was waged in certain parts of Long Island against a bug known as the mosquito. It was found after careful investigation that the parents of mosquitoes lives to have their young born in stagnant water, probably so as to get out of giving them a bath for the first two or three days. Anyway it was discovered that young Mosquitoes did not like to be born in oil so the heard hearted humans around Long Island proceeded to spread oil on the troubled waters and the result was the elder mosquitoes got discouraged and practically quit having children.

"The children that was born and did survive could be kept away from their natural food, which is human bodies, by spreading citronella over the last named. So much for the war against mosquitoes."

Now in regards to the war against moths. Why all you have to do is keep the close closets well aired and fill the pockets with what is commonly known as moth balls and the moths will avoid your home like as if it was bone dry.

"They have found that roaches and other germs can be chased away by cleanliness and sunshine and there is several poisons that banishes rats from the house. Cold cream will dispel the effects of sunburn and there is a certain poison that can be spread at intervals around the room and you won't be troubled no more by those little fellows who we have dubbed bedbugs.

"Now we are working on a plan to rid New York of delegates and it won't be more than a day or two when same is perfected and in the meanwhile we would warn all delegates to leave the city before this exterminator is given its first trial."

That report is what brought the democratic national convention of 1924 to its premature end and all I can say further is that after this when you want to know how a convention is coming out, lay off the experts and read the undersigned.

In 1924, progressive farm-bloc senators, claiming "secrecy is the greatest aid to corruption," pushed a bill through Congress requiring the names and addresses of all those paying federal income tax be made available to the public, along with the total amount paid. "Though some newspapers refused to publish this information, coverage was extraordinarily comprehensive," wrote Mark H. Leff in *The Limits of Symbolic Reform: The New Deal and Taxation*. "Whole pages were devoted to lists of payments by local citizens. Feature stories reported on the biggest corporate assessments and the tax payments of prominent out-of-towners like Babe Ruth or Standard Oil. Teasers told of divorcees who were investigating their husbands' income and wealthy taxpayers who escaped with paltry tax payments." The measure ended in 1926 in response to a movement led by President Coolidge and Treasury Secretary Andrew Mellon.

Ring's New Tax Bill to Include Congressmen

BELL SYNDICATE, JUNE 29, 1924

By this time pretty near everybody has made their comments pro and con in regards to the tax bill passed by congress and I have heard some say that they shouldn't be no sessions of congress allowed between March and November or else move it away from Washington to some place where the boys ain't so libel to be affected by the heat. But with all the remarks that has been made I don't believe that the gen. public or our law makers themselfs realizes what a upheaval the new law is going to cause and a specially that part of it which provides for publicity in regards to income.

The bill says that as soon as everybody has filed their returns, why the collectors in their district must make out a complete list of same with the figures that has been swore to before a notary and the said list will be hung up in the nearest postoffice so as everybody and their neighbor will know just who is who and what is what.

After this when you ask a man how he is getting along, he will think twice before saying "Oh, pretty good, I am knocking out $12,000 per annum," because he knows that you can run down to the postoffice and find out if he has added on one cipher too many. Personly the law is going to cost me a lot of money as the most of the people who I am wild to know how much they are making lives in places like Florida and Texas and California and to visit their home postoffices means hundreds of dollars in R.R. fares alone.

While the bill provides for tax reduction amounting to a billion dollars or some such chicken's food, still and all the govt. can make some of that back if they take full advantages of the situation. For one thing they can save the salaries now paid the mail carriers who they won't be no use of same when everybody wants to go down to the postoffice themselfs to find out how much Doc Roberts cleaned up last year and by the same tokens you will see a big increase in the sale of stamps as a good many citizens is too much of a lady or gentleman to hang around a place all day without buying nothing. Further and more the govt. can add to their revenue by either selling the refreshment privileges, camp stool concessions and etc. to the highest bidder or running same itself.

Of course on the other hand it may be necessary to spend some money building bigger and better postoffices in the home towns of people like star ball players, movie actors and pugilists whose salary as reported in the public prints ain't always exactly equivalent to the figures on their pay check. Like for inst. we will say that they's a ball player named Gus Siegel that lives in Tetter, Ohio, and when the winter time comes around Gus gives out the news that he ain't going to sign up again with the Browns unless they come across with a $2,000 raise.

"I wasn't only getting $8,000 last season," said Mr. Siegel, "and I led the league in fouls so it seems to me like I am entitled to $10,000 and if I don't get it I will quit baseball and go into the owl trapping business."

Well, they's a lot of persiflage back and 4th between Mr. Siegel and the owner of the Browns and finely it is give out that Mr. Siegel has signed up and the league is saved at the expense of the owl trapping business, but neither side will give out any figures except to say that terms was amicable to both.

"I got what I was after," is what Mr. Siegel told some of his friends in strict confidence.

Well, a year from March they will half to build a new postoffice in Tetter to accommodate the crowd that have came from all parts of the country to see what Mr. Siegel really did get and it may surprise some to find out that his former salary of $3,500 and he was raised to $3,550 with the understanding that he lay off the home made beer.

Now it must be remembered that when congress put this publicity clause over they wasn't betraying no secrets in regards to themselfs. If you don't know what salary a congressman gets you can look it up in the World Almanac. Whatever else he gets wouldn't be on his return anyway as it is technically known as a gift or loan. So all in all it seems to me like it ain't quite fair to make we boys tell what we are getting without wheedling some kind of secrets out of the boys that passed the law and for that reason I suggest that wile we are prying into people's affairs, why let's go ahead and pass some more publicity measures to include congressmen and everybody alike and make them hang up in the postoffice or some other public place their sworn answers to the following questionaire:

How many baths do you take per week?

Did you ever flirt?

Do you ever get tired of your wife (husband)?

Was you ever stewed?

Why I Will Vote Socialist

NEW LEADER, NOVEMBER 5, 1932

On November the 8th my vote, as such, is liable to be cast for the Socialist candidates for president and vice-president. I have the impressive figure of Heywood Broun in mind when I say this. The big fellow, I am told, is very thick with your candidate for national honors, Norman Thomas, and it seems probable that if the latter is elected he will take Broun, the rail-splitter, to Washington with him to occupy some comfortable berth in the cabinet. As a citizen of New York I feel that Broun's place is in Washington, and I would be willing to cast three or four votes and any number of aspersions to get him there.

My friends reel back in amazement when I tell them, after a certain amount of preliminary fencing, that I am going to vote the Socialist ticket. Their comments are not printable, but the gist is as follows:

"You are just wasting your vote, kid. Who do you like in the fifth at Empire City?"

Throwing out the last sentence for reasons of policy, I am moved to ask in turn:

"What am I doing when I vote for Hoover or Roosevelt?"

This, you understand, is strictly between myself and the Socialist National Campaign committee. Under no circumstances would I care to have such old golfing buddies as John McCooey[21] and Everett Sanders[22] know that I am planning to knife them at the polls.

The other day my doctor, while strapping me to a bed, pointed out that if Mr. Thomas is elected Mr. Hoover and Mr. Roosevelt will be out of a job.

"Don't worry, doctor," I replied, recognising him without difficulty.

"There is a big demand for comedians, and both those boys will be able to land swell jobs on the radio."

He parried this threat with a gag from one of the Old Music Box Revues, and left me composing this campaign plea, which should stir up no little discussion around White's drug store in East Hampton. Until you are ready to hand me my piece of America, I remain.

Without rancor,

Ring Lardner

6

Boxing

Though Lardner didn't cover much boxing while working in Chicago, he did travel to Milwaukee in November 1914 to see Packey McFarland, a popular local lightweight, where he wrote: "Friend Harvey: Here I am, Harvey, up to the ringside in Milwaukee. Ring beside ringside. That's pretty good, eh, Harvey? I don't believe I will write anything funnier than that the rest of the evening, but when a man figures out a good gag like that he should ought to put it in the first paragraph and then people will say this is going to be pretty good and read it all the way threw." The *Tribune's* headline writer took the pun one step further with, "Ring Lardner Wrings Detail from Ringside."

This early dalliance with boxing turned into a full-fledged love affair when Lardner left the *Tribune*. His first columns for the Bell Syndicate were written in June of 1919 from Toledo, Ohio, where Jess Willard was defending the heavyweight championship against Jack Dempsey. The first paragraph of his first column, "Jess' Stomach Shouldn't Be Worried," was an indication of what the syndicate's readers were in for in the years ahead.

Like political conventions, heavyweight championship boxing was a perfect subject for Lardner. Following the custom of the day, he would begin writing about an upcoming title fight two or three weeks in advance, sometimes turning out as many as a dozen columns before the fight took place. He would visit the fighters' camps, talk to the trainers, promoters, and fans, play golf, and enjoy the company of his friends. Eventually there would be a fight and eventually he would write about it, but during the buildup he was free to go where his imagination led him.

And as he had with baseball, he came to a sport at just the right time. Dempsey knocked out Willard—Lardner would often write about his losing bet on the reigning champion—then went on to become one of the major figures in America's golden age of sport. Three of his fights in particular generated frenzied anticipation that was just right for Lardner's approach.

The first, against Georges Carpentier in 1921, captivated the nation and produced boxing's first million-dollar gate. Shrewdly promoted by Tex Rickard, the fight cast Carpentier, a French pilot in World War I, as the hero, and Dempsey, who had been accused of dodging the draft, as the villain. Lardner had interviewed Carpentier a year earlier and played golf with him before the fight. But those who covered the sport weren't the only ones fascinated by Carpentier. His good looks made him a curiosity among women who normally paid no attention to boxing, and his intelligence encouraged writers not associated with the sports pages to widen their horizons. George Bernard Shaw, who had been a recreational boxer in his youth, was particularly enamored of Carpentier. Upon meeting him for the first time, Shaw wrote, "I was startled by the most amazing apparition. Nothing less than Charles II, 'the madman of the North,' striding along in a Japanese dressing gown as gallantly as if he had not been killed exactly 201 years before."

In the days leading up to the fight Shaw wrote that Carpentier was the best boxer in the world, that the odds should favor him 50 to 1, and "I stake upon Carpentier's victory over Dempsey my reputation for knowing what I write about." After Carpentier was knocked out in the fourth round, Shaw wrote that Dempsey had been lucky. Lardner was so affected by the fight that after describing the frenzied scene at ringside he turned his narrative powers on a climactic sporting moment without adopting his usual comic pose.

Two years later Dempsey's fight against Luis Angel Firpo, the first Latin American to challenge for the heavyweight championship, was similarly ballyhooed. Billed as "the Wild Bull of the Pampas," Firpo was bigger than most heavyweights of the era and Lardner had fun speculating on how much he ate. He wrote some excellent pieces leading up to the fight—the opening of "Lardner in Great Shape for Wordy Battle" is a classic parody of prefight stories—and for once he witnessed a fight worthy of the hype.

Dempsey knocked Firpo down seven times in the first round before the challenger trapped him against the ropes, knocked him out of the ring, and, according to Lardner, into Grantland Rice's lap. Dempsey was helped back through the ropes and knocked Firpo out in the second round. The fight is considered among the most exciting in the history of the sport, and Lardner gave his approval when he wrote, "It was a FIGHT."

Lardner was also on hand when Dempsey lost the title to Gene Tunney in 1926, and therein lies another tale. Lardner revived the story of his wife's fur coat in his coverage of the fight, then offered to help Rice, who said he had been "fighting a cold all week with no sleep and too much Prohibition whiskey." After Rice dictated his deadline story, Lardner told him, "Take a slug of bourbon and lie down. I'll file your overnight."

"That story appearing the next day under my byline blistered the hide of both Tunney and Dempsey," Rice wrote years later in his memoirs. (Actually, the story generously praised Tunney.) "Neither spoke to me for several months. I couldn't blame either, but I couldn't open my mouth. I had a ghost."

Lardner had a personal reason for venting his anger on Dempsey. He had bet $500 on the champion at 2 to 1 odds and was more than a little suspicious of the outcome. "The thing was a very well done fake, which lots of us would like to say in print, but you know what newspapers are where possible libel suits are concerned," he wrote to Scott and Zelda Fitzgerald in France, a few weeks after the fight. "As usual, I did my heavy thinking too late; otherwise I would have bet the other way."

An Evening Accumulating Culture

BELL SYNDICATE, JANUARY 2, 1921

I read somewhere a wile ago that wile life in small towns and on the farm was in many ways desirable, still and all a person that lives in a big city, like N.Y. for inst., has many chances to improve their mind which is not enjoyed by the rural population in spite of the chautauquas and strolling players that visits the outlaying districts giveing performances of King Lear, Mutt and Jeff and etc., but it was also true that they was a whole lot of city dwellers that don't never take advantages of their opportunity and spend their time and money on Fatty Arbunkle and Marion Gish when they might be grabing off a little culture and refinements for themself at the Public Library or the museum of Fine Arts or the aquarium and etc.

Well at first I thought how lucky I was to live in a suburb of N.Y. city where they's nothing worth wile, you might say, that a person can't get there in a ½ hr. but on 2d. thoughts it come to me that I seldom never profitted by my location and as far as acquireing elegants and Polish and etc., I might as well be receiving teller on a garbage wagon in Rumford Corners. So I made a resolution to turn over a new leaf and went right to the phone and called up Tex Rickard and got 2 tickets to the Dempsey-Brennan fight, and as of coarse they was only a very few of my readers that was able to be there I may as well try and tell them a little about it so as they can be obtaining culture second hand, you might say.

These educational evenings is generally always held in Madison Square Garden where they also devote a whole wk. every yr. to the 6 day bicycle race between 10 or 12 teams of Belgium, Cuckoo and other birds, than which they's no more inspireing sight unlest it's the Philadelphia Athletics. Well on this night I and a friend of mine named Arthur reached the Garden a ¼ after 3 but they was all ready several 1000 other diletants there ahead of us. Our tickets said working press so we assumed a rakish expression and stuck a pencil behind our ear and was showed to a ring side seat with no questions asked.

Erudite N.Y. was out in mess includeing many fashionably drest members of the demi mondaine accompanied by their escorts in head waiters' regalia. All and all the scene was one that made a lasting impression on the eye and nostrils.

We hadn't hardly had time to locate the different aromas, however, when a man named Joe Humphreys clumb up in the ring and begin announceing where the St. Angus guild was going to meet and etc. and the gentlemen is kindly requested to refrain from smoking which seemed to be a signal for everybody to throw away their costly cigars and light a fresh one. They say Mr. Humphreys has been makeing announcements from the prize ring for 30 yrs. without the English language ever even getting a draw with him.

The first bout of the evening was between 2 representatives of sunny Finmark named Marty Farrell and Frank McGuire. Marty had his gloves perfumed and Frank couldn't keep his nose off them. The old snoot lasted the full 6 rds. but it looked like somebody would half to tell him if the dressing for his Xmas turkey was flavored with garlic or bay rum.

Mr. Humphreys next introduced Bartley Madden and Charley Weinert, the Adonis of Newark. I and Arthur decided that they couldn't be a safer place to trust a romantic young girl than Newark. But maybe Mr. Humphreys said that so as Charley wouldn't feel out of place alongside of Bartley whose natural charms was added to by the elegant handiwork of some old master amongst tattooists. The ornaments was confined to his arms before the bout started but after 10 rds. of it they wasn't hardly a part of his carcass that wasn't tattood. At that Bartley done pretty good for a fighter named Bartley, but the bout was slow and some of the birds in the $27.50 seats began wishing that they had put in another dollar and bought a ton of coal.

The 3d. event was a fight between 2 descendants of sunny Africa which I suppose you might call it a riot of color. One of them, Kid Norfolk, had a whole lot more color and done pretty near all the rioting. When he come in the ring he had on a night cap though they was no chance of his oppt. Big Bill Tate rocking anybody to sleep. Norfolk seemed to realize this when he set down in his corner, and he took the cap off and when you seen him bare headed you couldn't help from believing maybe after all Darwin was right. He had his monogram K. N. embroidered on his trunks though as far as I was conserned they was as safe as his tooth brush. Mr. Humphreys introduced him as Kid Norfolk from Baltimore which added a touch of mystery.

Big Bill Tate is Dempsey's sparring partner in every day life which I have often wondered whether I would rather have that job or a tumor. Big Bill fights on the side for rest and relief but he didn't get neither from Norfolk.

Big Bill stands about 6 ft. in his socked ft. and Norfolk ain't no bigger than a cutie but he's even more of a pest. He kept pokeing Bill in the eye though you couldn't see how he ever reached up there. They said before the Toledo fiasco that Dempsey couldn't reach Willard neither. Norfolk's favorite punch, however, was a straight left that lit anywheres below the belt and about the only way Bill could of protected himself from a licking was to wear shin guards.

Bill might of claimed a foul 8 or 9 times but when you got a all day job like Dempsey's sparring partner what is a kick in the shins more or less?

Bill didn't show nothing, and before the bout had went far the crowd was calling him Big Bum instead of Big Bill. Big Bum is a crowd's pet name for anybody over 6 ft. tall that tries to partake of athletics. Don't I know?

Referee Houkop which sounds like he had drank his ginger ale too fast refereed the main event of the evening which it won't be nessary for me to describe, as it has all ready been wrote up by better men than I am or Gungha Din either. Mr. Humphreys announced before the bout that the winner was to receive a diamond belt, the gift of Tex Rickard. So Arthur made the remark that he couldn't think of nothing handier to have around the house and he wished he was Dempsey.

Mr. Brennan got a belt in the 12th rd. but they wasn't no diamonds in it, only stars, and then Mr. Dempsey stood up in the middle of the ring to get his. Mr. Humphreys give it to him and he took it with a elegant bow a good deal like Willard's bow when he entered the ring at Toledo. That bow of Willard's was the 1st. inkling anybody had that they was something the matter with the big fellow.

Well, Mr. Dempsey made his bow but the presentations wasn't over yet. The crowd got up all of a sudden and give him a elegant shower boquet of raspberries.

All and all, I felt like it was an evening well spent and from now on I am going to try and go somewheres once a wk. and improve my mind, and if I feel like I can spare any of the culture I pick up I will pass it on.

DEMPSEY VS. WILLARD

Jess' Stomach Shouldn't Be Worried

BELL SYNDICATE, JUNE 21, 1919

Toledo, Ohio—Gents: Well gents I lit into Toledo tonight with a pocket full of raisins but no rye and I am supposed to write you something every day about how the fighters is coming along but I hope you will excuse me this time for not going out to either one of thems camps as the first thing a man has to do when you land in Toledo is look for a bed which is about as plentiful here as a beer garden. But I expect to get myself parked somewheres tonight and by tomorrow I will have time to go out and overlook the boys in their training and give you the real inside dope on how the big fiasco is coming out though I may not get into Willard's camp as they say he is charging everybody 25 cents apiece to see him work, hence the expression, training quarters.

But even if I can't afford to watch the big fellow as I have nicknamed him, I am all ready well acquainted with him and though I have never seen him fight I have seen him eat and it kind of makes me half smile when I hear people say that Dempsey will get him with stomach punches, as his stomach has stood up under more punishment than any little upstart like Dempsey can meat out, you might say.

Another thing that kind of spreads my risibles is this stuff about Jess being too old to put up a real fight. He says himself that he is 36 and Tom Jones says he is 40, but what of it. Look at Foch.[1]

And also they have got a hotel full of so-called fight experts here that claims that Jack the giant killer will wind it up with a knock out but they don't seem to figure that Bill Tate which has been standing up in front of Jack every day for a month and which is a couple sizes smaller than Jess hasn't been knocked out yet in a month so what is Jack going to do to Jess in one afternoon.

On the other hand certain birds claims that Jess is too big for Jack and a good little man can't never lick a good big man. Well we will have to grant that the both of them is good men or at least they will be good men after July 1 like everybody else, but still and all I don't know if you know it or not but I am bigger than Dempsey and if I was matched up with Benny Leonard, which isn't knee high to a grass hopper along side of me, I wouldn't bet the war tax on myself. So you can see what I think of a good little man vs. a good big man and if the little man is the best man why good night big man.

Well, I suppose a lot of gents will wonder how a bird that has wrote baseball all their life knows anything about fighting, but I done most of my baseball experting in old Chi, as I have nicknamed Chicago, and that is where they combine one with the other you might say, and it was less than a month ago when I was out to the White Sox pk. and just about dozing off when the next thing you know Speaker and Gandil was in a little misunderstanding that went one round to no decision but afterwards

I asked several fight critics who they thought win and they all thought the same like I did and I don't know if Gandil was betting on himself or not but any way he lost his shirt. And another thing I want to say about myself is that I will write fair and impartial and with no fears and favors and come right out and say what I think about the two beneficiarys because while I have met the both of them neither one ever asked for the check while I was amongst them and I am not afraid of neither one of them because I don't believe Jess or Jack would lay a hand on anybody for less than $100,000 or $27,500 respectively, and am certainly not going to offer them that and they's very few people that would pay $60 a seat to see it though several birds I know would give that amount to have it done.

Well, as I say I haven't had time yet to overlook either of the two matadors, but when I come into this hotel tonight I bumped into Ad Thacher of Toledo, that the papers said he had a $50,000 interest in the brawl and nobody denied it except Ad Thacher and Tex Richard and Frank Flournoy, but any way he is a wise bird and he's been on the ground and I had to talk to him about something, so I asked him if it looked like they would have a big house and he said, "Oh, yes, because they tell me that everybody that was picked for referee have got reservations."

Well, after I had gave up hopes of starting a flirtation with the room clerk I writhed over to the news stand to buy me something to read in the case I would have to park vs. a pillar all night and the book I got a hold of is called "Toledo" and it certainly grips a man's interest from cover to cover. As a lot of you gents probably hasn't seen this book or ever will see it, you wouldn't know unless I told you that Toledo is the lzargest cloverseed market in the world and the third largest roaster of coffees and excels all ports on the Great Lakes in tonnage of cargo coal and has got the fourth biggest zoo in the United States, which is located in this hotel, to judge by the eardrums. That's Toledo, gents, and the book says the town's motto is "I serve, I conquer," and I don't know if the last part of it is true or not, but so far the service is punk.

Ring's Funny Stories Make the Operators Sick

JUNE 24, 1919

Toledo, O—Gents: Well, gents, when I woke up this morning there was several hundred telegrams from different parts of the country and Scandinavia saying why didn't you write any stuff yesterday. Well, gents, I did write some stuff and my boss said it was pretty good stuff but when I gave it to the telegraph company most of their operators laughed themself sick and couldn't send it. Well I don't want to make any of you gents sick, but still and all if you didn't get yesterday's story, you won't know what made the operators sick so I guess I better repeat the two gags that nauseated them.

Well, the first one was like this: I said Rube Goldberg and Jack Wheeler came in from New York and came up to my room and Jack said I have got a present for you and he pulled out a bottle of Scotch and I wrote in the story that it was like bringing coals to Newcastle.

Well, the second was like this: I said that Bat Nelson would probably be referee of the fight only for a difference of opinion between he and the producers. He wanted to referee free and they wanted him to pay as you enter. There was also many another funny in my story which I can't recall.

Since I wrote that about Bat Nelson, however, there is a new story going the rounds that instead of having one referee they are going to have one referee in the ring and two judges outside the ring and if the fight goes twelve rounds, which heaven forefend, the three of them would get together and vote which man had won the fight and whoever two out of three voted for, he would be declared the champion. Well, I noticed by this morning's paper that the big fellow, as I have nicknamed Jess, insists on them only having one referee and Dempsey also only wants one referee and it looks to me like they are both making a mountain out of a mole trap and believe me, if I was going to get $127,500 for thirty-six minutes so-called work they could have the twelve apostles refereeing and I should worry.

But if the producers are open to suggestions I would suggest to them that they stick a good male quartet in the ring and let them sing and kind of try to distract attentions from the holocaust itself and I could suggest no better quartet for this purpose than myself and Hype Igoe and Sam Hall and Tad.

Well, this noon my boss came up to my room and said after this you will have to have your stuff written by 4 p.m. and I asked him what for and he said so that if any telegraph operators laugh themselves sick over it there will still be time to go out and hire some other ops and get it sent out in time. So I said I thought the best idea would be for me to cut out stuff that is funny enough to sicken them and not write it, but he said, "you know very well that you can't help from sickening them and I have thought it over and my orders is for you to have your stuff ready by 4 o'clock."

So that is the situation now gents and I can't see how a man is going to go out to the training quarters where they don't begin to perform before 3 o'clock and watch them and interview them and then get back here and write an intelligent story about what you've seen and heard and have it done at 4 o'clock when it takes an hour to get back here and another two minutes to write the stuff. So I guess I will have to try and write my stuff without going to see the two gladiators and anyway when you ask the big fellow if he is going to win he says yes and you ask Dempsey if he is going to win and he says yes and one of them must be a liar and I can't find out which one it is.

But the hotel has got signs pasted all around that all rooms are sold for July 2, 3 and 4, and so it looks like I would have to move out of here for those three days at least and I figure that if I walk the streets the second and third I will be pretty sleepy on the fourth and my boss has got a place for me to sit down by the ringside on that day and maybe I will catch a glimpse of the two warriors before I doze off and if I do I will try and write you my opinion of them.

Lardner Hears Peace Trio
Will Officiate at Bout

JUNE 27, 1919

Toledo, O—Gents: I was talking today to Mr. Runyon from New York who Tad[2] calls him the Benny Kauff[3] of journalism on account of every time you see him he is parked in a new suit of clothes.[4]

Well, anyway he told me that the referee business was all settled and there was going to be three of them, one of which is to stand in the ring and look out and the other two set outside the ring and look in. So I asked him who was they going to be and he said the announcement was due tomorrow morning, but he had heard it was going to be Wilson, Lloyd George and Clemenceau.

Well, a lot of us set around and figured out how the three of them should ought to operate, and it looked to some like the best scheme would be for them to fix up a set of signals, which would be announced out loud to the goofs just before the battle, and then the minute the twelfth round was over everybody would know who got the decision.

For instance, if Willard was their choice, they would all point up toward the sky with their forefinger, meaning the big fellow. If Dempsey was their choice they would point down, meaning the little fellow, and if it was a draw they would all point straight out.

There is nothing the matter with this idea except that the three of them might have three different opinions. For instance, suppose Wilson thought it was a draw and Clemenceau wanted to give it to Dempsey and Lloyd George strung with the big fellow. Well, in that case, the one that done the pointing first would be the one whose decision counted.

But there is also several other possibilities of a mix-up in case the spat goes the full route. Suppose Wilson and Lloyd George said it was a draw and Clemenceau gave it to Dempsey. Would the two draws offset each other and make Dempsey the winner, or vise versa?

Personally, I think that in a matter as important as this there shouldn't ought to be no undue haste in arriving at a decision and the three pleni-potentiaries ought to withdraw to some quiet spot like this hotel we are stopping in and lock their self up and think it over and in the meantime the newspaper men and geese could go home and the minute the gents made their decision Mr. Wilson could set down and write us each a note on a postcard just mentioning the name of the winner and whatever else he wanted to say.

All this I have been talking about only goes if the fight lasts 12 rounds. If there is a knockout one way or the other that means a whole lot more complications. Suppose, for instance, that one of the belligerents felled the other and the knockee was down for just 10 seconds and Mr. Wilson was the third man in the ring and counted the stricken man out.

Well, the outside referees would probably insist on counting also and they might not count him out on account of the difference in time between here and Europe. Altogether it looks like a mighty delicate situation, and when I come to think it over I am kind of glad that I refused to allow my name to be used in connection with the referee embroglio.

After Seeing Jess in the Movies, Ring Wonders How Jack Can Win

JUNE 28, 1919

Toledo, O—Gents: As it looked like as if it might rain yesterday p.m., three of us decided to not go out and visit the training camps, but in order to not cheat our readers, we thought we better see the Willard moving picture[5] and write about that.

Well, in this picture, the Big Fellow takes the part of a cowboy or something named Joe Bates and when we got in he was riding on a train somewhere in Texas and the train stopped right in front of a corral or whatever you call it and Joe Bates looked out the window and seen a man beating a horse and he couldn't stand that, so he jumped off the train and ran over and beat up the man that was beating the horse.

Well, if the man could beat a horse and Joe Bates could beat him, what chance has Dempsey got?

Well, in the next scene, Joe Bates had accepted a position as horse buyer in a livery stable and the "prop" of the "livery stable was the same bird Joe had beat up, only neither of them knew it till they seen each other. This bad guy was trying to get hold of a lot of horses and take them over to Juarez and deliver them to the Mexican insurrectos.

So after that there's a girl in it that Joe Bates kept from getting beat out of her horses and jack, and also there's some big scenes in Juarez where Joe Bates knocks the whole army of insurrectos dead and then he brings the horses back across the Rio Grande River and the girl gets engaged to a jockey and Joe gives them a horse shower and I suppose they get married and Jess don't care as he has already got a wife in Lawrence, Kan.

Well, gents, I will have to admit that Jess isn't half bad as a movie actor but they ought to have a lecturer up on the stage to tell what's going on towards the tail end of the picture. The subtitles are original, especially when the Mexicans are supposed to be talking as most of the time they talk in French dialect, but all their remarks end up with "si, senor" to give the whole thing a kind of a Spanish touch. This effect is added to by the girl that plays the music as she plays "Sole Mio." During one of the Mexican scenes, only she overlooked a chance to bring in the Russian national hymn while Jess was massacreaing a room full of greasers.

There isn't much news to write about here, gents. Some of the experts has been on the scene so long they are getting cuckoo, you might say, and beginning to pull what is called practical jokes, though the jokees can't see nothing practical about them.

The local papers say that the City Council has just passed a law providing that all crooks must be drove out of Toledo. If this goes into effect before next Friday out-of-town fight fans needn't worry about getting a place to sleep when they come here, as the hotels will be practically empty.

Tiny Maxwell of Philadelphia arrived on the scene today, and paid a visit to my suite. "Have you noticed the signs on the doors of the hotel rooms around here?" he inquired. "They say. Stop! Have you left anything!"

"What of it?" in asked him.

"Well," he said, "the answer after July 4 will be, yes, everything."

Lardner Won on Allies and Picks Willard Now

JULY 4, 1919

Toledo, O—Gents: Well, gents, after taking a look around the lobby of this hotel this evening I came to the conclusion that they's absolutely no chance of us having a sane Fourth in Toledo. In fact, gents, if a stranger come to town that had never heard about this so-called fight and if he looked and listened for a couple minutes he would think that the students from all the nut houses in the middle west had decided to spend their summer vacation here.

But I suppose you gents is all impatient to hear me pick the winner of the fisticuffs like I promised exclusively in these columns yesterday. Well, gents, I like the big fellow, not only because I give him that nickname, but also because I never seen neither of the two matadors fight. Probably some of you will say to yourselves what does this bird know about the manly art of selfdefense? Well, I don't know nothing and don't expect to learn, but I can point with a whole lot of pride to some of my pickings in the past. For instance, I thought all along that the allies would win the war, especially after America got in it. I chose Jack Johnson to lick Jeffries, though I didn't tell nobody for the fear of affecting the betting odds. I picked the White Sox to win the world's series from New York in 1917 and didn't make no bones about it, though some of the New York players did. I picked Hughes to beat Wilson in 1916 and he come pretty close at that. That's my record of picking, gents, and you can do whatever you like about it and if Dempsey should win, why I will pretend I was just joking when I said it will be the big fellow.

Now I don't want you gents to think I have got anything against Dempsey and even if I had I would keep my mouth shut about it. I met him once in a hotel in old Chicago, and far from quarreling with him, he was very friendly. He didn't even hurt my hand when he shook, which is more than I can say for Barney Oldfield, which got into town this morning. No, gents, Dempsey acted fine during the minute we was together, and I bet we could pal around a whole day without having a cross word, on my part, at least. As I told some of my admirers last night, I don't care if he wins or loses. Only I kind of figure that he can't. If the big fellow gets trimmed I won't even feel bad about picking him because if I picked for a living I wouldn't never need to even pick my teeth, you might say.

Well, the two profiteers done what they call their tapering off today and neither of them ate much, while on the other hand, the experts stuck to their regular liquid diet. The announcement was gave out that they wouldn't be no spectators allowed out to Dempsey's camp and two or three of us broke right down and cried. They was another announcement that the rabbit punch wouldn't be barred after all but I don't know if that makes much difference or not as I have never tasted it.

The chief of police of Toledo, which I didn't know they was one, warned the people through the public prints that all horseless carriages that drives over fifteen miles per hour going or coming from the fight will have to spend a night in the local bastile, as I have nicknamed the jail.

Well, gents, from what I have seen of Summit avenue on a common week date, they's only one way a man could drive more than fifteen feet an hour tomorrow and that would be for him to run over to Cleveland or Detroit. Speaking about Detroit, I borrowed Rollie Zeider's demon roadster last Sabbath and drove to the city of straits and flushes, as I have nicknamed it, but what I started to say was that before I left Toledo somebody told me that as soon as I crossed the Michigan line a couple of soldiers would stop me and search the old boat for liquor. Well, sure enough, I hadn't hardly no more than crossed the old line of the old native state when two soldiers held me up and said did I have any liquor in the car and I said no and they said all right and let me go on my way. Some search!

I see in the papers that all the seats in the arena is going to be flooded tonight so as they won't be no danger of them catching on fire tomorrow in the case a man or lady dropped a lighted cigaret or match on them. So if my story of the fight is worse than the fight you will know it was because I been swimming all day in a puddle which pretty nearly always throws me out of my stride. . .

When I Picked Jess to Win I Thought He'd Have Two Eyes to See With

JULY 5, 1919

Toledo, O—Well, gents, here is Ring at the ringside and the battle is all over, and it didn't last long, but at that Willard thought it lasted a week. I don't know what he is going to do tonight, as he can't read on account of his eyes being shut and he couldn't see a show if he went to it and he don't care for music. Maybe he can have a good time thinking about that 100,000 berries, which is more comfort than I can get. But at that, I don't know if I would of took what the big fellow got for any such pin money as that.

I spose you gents will want me to kind of explain how I came to pick Jess to win the fight. Well, gents, it was just a kind of practical joke on my part, and to make it all the stronger I went and bet a little money on him, so pretty near everybody thought I was really in earnest. As a matter of fact, I knew all the while that Jack would knock him for a gool. You can't expect a man 37 years old to lick a man 24 years old. Beside, I kind of felt all the time that Jess wasn't in no shape to put up a fight. He didn't train right, and he ought to of practiced falling down, as he certainly looked awkward when he tried it the first time.

The experts around here told me the big fellow went to the mat seven different times in the first round, but personally it seemed to me like he went down just once and stayed down for the duration of the war. He was still down yet when the gong rang and a lot of people said the bell saved him. I would say the bell ruined him, as it made him go out there for two more of them awful rounds. Well, they was such a noise going on when the gong rung that they couldn't nobody hear it, and who ever was keeping time had to tell Referee Pecord that the round was over. The general public, including Mr. Dempsey, thought the big fellow had been counted out, and one fat gentleman jumped up into the ring and kissed Jack on the cheek, so you can't say the new champion didn't take no punishment.

Well, as soon as Dempsey had recovered from the kiss, he climbed down through the ropes and started home, thinking the afternoon's amusement was over, and Manager Jack Kearns had to chase him and bring him back to finish the job. At this stage, I offered Geo. McManus my bet for 10 cents, but he was deaf on that side.

Now, just a word about the big fellow, gents. When a bird gets knocked for a gool seven times in one round, and comes back and took what Jessica took for two more rounds, you can't exactly call him yellow. After seeing what he went through I would say Fred Fulton was Lucky.[6] During the second and third Jess did not know if he was in Toledo or Lawrence. Kan., but wherever he was he stayed there and tried to enjoy his visit. And another thing you can't say, and that is that the big fellow wasn't in condition. If he hadn't been they would now be naming his honorary pallbearers.

As for Dempsey, I have kind of changed my mind about him. Before I seen him fight I didn't know if he could or could not. Now I kind of think he can and if I was Georges Carpentier I would stay in France till the new champion dies of old age.

The regular experts will probably give you a description of the fight by rounds. Personally my mind works kind of slow and I couldn't keep up with what Dempsey done. The first thing that happened was Jess leading with his left. He didn't come close. Then he led again with his left and landed and Jack must of thought a flea had bit him.

About this time Jack took it into his head to do a little leading, and he landed with all five of his gloves at once. Next thing you know, the big fellow was setting on the carpet looking kind of half witted. His eyes was aiming in my direction, but he didn't seem to recognize me. Mr. Pecord begun counting out loud and Jess sort of woke up and acted startled, and he clumb up on his feet, but he didn't seem to like it so well standing up, so he tried setting on one of the ropes; this wasn't comfortable, so he got up again and stood a minute and then thought he better give the floor another trial. But no matter where he was, on his feet or on the ropes, he seemed uneasy. He finally got the idear in what was left of his head that maybe it wouldn't be so uncomfortable on the south side of the ring. Up to this time he had did all his setting down over near the northeast corner. Well, he started kind of edging around the west ropes and as I was setting three rows back I felt kind of nervous for the fear he would pick out my lap for his next resting place. Well, Dempsey knocked him down twice on the way around, but he didn't hit him as hard as he could and he stayed in the ring.

He dropped him a couple of times more when he got over to the South limits and the second time he went down over there he wanted to stay the rest of July, but as soon as Mr. Pecord made it known that the gong had rang Walter Monaghan and whoever else was his second, made him get up and take a chair. While he set there they throwed water on him and kept rubbing a sponge over his face, but they couldn't wipe off Dempsey's punches. Dempsey never knocked me down seven times in his life, so I don't know how the big fellow felt when they told him it was time to go out and take some more of it. Anyway he pretended like he was willing and maybe he figured Jack had already delivered 12 whole rounds of wallops and wouldn't have no more left. But they hadn't stood up there for more than a second when this hero devil-dog completed the task of shutting the ex-Champion's right eye. Jess only seen half of the rest of that round. A couple of times Jack showed a little mercy, and hit the big guy in the tummy instead of the map. This must have been a big relief. By this time they was corpuscles splashing all over the place. Dempsey was all bloody, but it wasn't his own. As for Willard's face it looked like they ought to of hung a sign on it saying: "Fresh Red Paint."

There wasn't nobody in Mr. Rickard's arena that would of bet a transfer that he could last through the round, but he held on some way mostly by either clinching or turning his back. The spinal punch must of been barred, because Jack never made no effort to smash him while he was looking the other way, but just the minute he kind of began to turn around to see where Dempsey was parked, Jack would take aim and fire at his jowls or the place where his eyes used to be.

Personally, I think it would of been pretty good judgment for the boys in the big fellow's corner to of tossed in the towel a round sooner than they did, and it would of been even better judgment to of throwed it in right after Jess sat down for the first time.

Well, the third round was the second round's twin sister, only Jess didn't lose quite as much blood, as he didn't have as much to lose. They tell me that he found out along about this time that his jaw was broke. I don't know yet if it's true or not, but if he thought that he couldn't chew on a steak for a few days it's no wonder he got kind of discouraged. Anyway he hadn't been setting in his chair more than a few seconds after the third gong when Mr. Monaghan rose up and flang the towel in the general direction of mid-ring.

The towel looked like it might of been raised in the old Pike House at Niles, Mich., but even a dirty towel means defeat.

Well, a bug that had been standing on my back and screaming now thought it was about time to smash my hat, and everybody else seemed to go nuts at once, and for half an hour what I have nicknamed Pandemonium reigned. I am sorry to say that I didn't get a chance to see Maj. Biddle or Tex Rickard after the scrap to find out what their decision was, but I still take it on myself to say Dempsey had the shade.

Now gents, when I said the big fellow should ought to win, I thought he was going to have two eyes to see with. But something happened to one of them about two seconds after the two guys got together. A whole lot of experts had also told me that Jack was too little to reach Jess' features, but as far as I could see they wasn't none of them he missed.

It must of been a great sight for the ladies, as they couldn't of saw more blood if they had of went through the Union Stockyards. Nobody can say that the big fellow didn't have a whole lot red blood in his veins before the battle, mother, as he left enough of it on Dempsey and the floor of the ring to stock a whole family of champions.

Well, when Walter Monoghan tossed the towel in at the end of round three, some bugs behind me that had also bet on him stood upon their hind legs and hollered quitter. Well, gents, if I had took what the big fellow took, why, even I would of quit.

At the hour of going to press maniacs of all kinds is up in the ring cutting off little pieces of rope to take home for souvenirs. Personally, I wouldn't give a nickel for a piece of rope unless it had been used to hang some bird for murder. And then it would have to have a few drops of blood on it before I would value it very high.

DEMPSEY VS. CARPENTIER

Getting to Know Geos.

BELL SYNDICATE, APRIL 11, 1920

To the Editor:

A great many of our readers has probably heard of Geos. Carpentier that busted a bird name Beckett in London, Eng., last fall and win the worlds championship of Europe and now he is over here on U.S. soils to spend his honeymoon and maybe combine a little business with it on the side and I kind of figured that on acct. of him being in the public eyes some of our readers might like to know what he is like personly and who could tell them better than myself on acct. of my command of francais and what other reporter was they that could talk to him in his native tongue sandwich?

So the other day I was down in N.Y. city and dropped into the Biltmore hotel and seen G. L. Rickard, who I immediately nicknamed Tex, and Tex took me up to Geos. suite and the valet opened up a door and begin leading us through different rooms till finely we got to one where he told us to set down and believe me I was ready. If they have any trouble finding a hall to hold the so called fight between Geos. and Dempsey in it, why all as they will half to do is hold it in Geos. suite and if they ½ fill it why, Geos. widow will have enough to keep her in ease and luxurys the rest of her life.

Well I and Tex sat down and in a few minutes a door opened a mile away and we could see Geos. comeing along in the distants in toe of the valet and I ast Tex if we shouldn't ought to arise and sing the Marsellaise, but he told me to shut up and after a wile Geos. finely got to where we was at and we was both introduced to each other and now I guess I better exclaim what he looks like.

Well he has got a lot of hair combed college style and it is about the color of a gin fizz as I recall them. His face is one that I would just as soon trade him mine for if only for the nose witch looks like he might maybe of done some blocking with it. He had on a shirt the color of sponge cake with collar to match and a suit made of gray squirrel skin witch you couldn't match on U.S. soils and even if you could you wouldn't. He wore a couple (2) bedroom slippers, witch I suppose is on acct. of wanting to keep his feet in shape for the big fight though pretty near any one of Dempsey's oppts. could tell him that the condition of the feet don't make much differents vs. that bird as you only use them a minute.

Well the valet also come along and I whispered to Tex why do we half to have the valet as I just got my suit pressed but Tex said the valet was also the interpreter and then the valet says does Monsieur sprecken francais and I said, "Ah, oui; vingt mots. (Oh, yes; twenty words.")

"Well, Monsieur Carpentier," I said in perfect French, "I seen you up to the Frolic last night. Comment aimez vous les poulets. (How did you like the girls?")

"No thank you," said Geos. in perfect anglais.

"Il comprends anglais si vous parlez slow," says the valet.

"Imagine, a Frenchman telling us to talk slow," I says to Tex.

"Avez vous jamais been in France (Have you ever been in France)?" ast Geos.

"Ah, oui, je was there in 1917 (Oh, yes, I was there in 1917)," was my reply. (I didn't tell him that I didn't take no uniform along.)

"Comment did you like Paris (How did you like Paris)?" ast Geos.

"No thank you (No thank you)," I said. "Comment do you like New York (How do you like New York)?"

"Tres bien,'" says Geos.

"Attendez till you see Chi (Wait till you see Chicago)," I said. "And are you going a la Toledo?"

"Not as far as I am conserned," interrupted Tex.

Well by this time my twenty words was all used up and Geos. looked like he wanted to do some more road work around the suite so I and Tex got up and I shook hands with Geos. and the valet and the latter acted kind of surprised at the honor though what was the war for if it wasn't for democracy, but any way when we finally got to the outside door I finely thought of two more French words that I once picked up somewheres but hadn't sprang them yet, namely, "au revoir" so I said them though it is a wonder I didn't say "auf wiedersehen" and then I wouldn't of had to write this letter, but any way when I said "au revoir" Geos. smiled and said it back to me and we left and Tex said to come to his room a minute and he would show me something that was 11 yrs. old and I thought of course it must be a child or I wouldn't of went, but it wasn't a child but it tasted better than one. So Tex said:

"Well what do you think of the Frenchman?"

"Well." I said, "I like him fine. But what a little thing he would be along the side of Dempsey."

"Yes," said Tex, "but if I remember right and I genally always do, Dempsey was a little thing along side of Jess and you bet on Jess and I don't believe you had to pay no excess profits tax on that acct."

So I said, "Did you bring me up here to entertain me or insult me?" and he didn't seem to have nothing to say back so I walked out on him.

Ring Will Bear Up No Matter Who Wins

JUNE 19, 1921

Great Neck, N.Y.—Well friends it is just 2 yrs. ago today when I paid my first visit to the Willard and Dempsey training quarters at Toledo and looked the boys over and give it as my opinion that Jessie would win, and wile I may of loose a few hairs since that time, still my judgment is just as good now as it was then and no wonder they has been a public clamor for me to come out of retirement for a couple wks. and join the corpse of experts that is writeing about the biggest international sporting event which has took place in this country since the heart rendering race for the Lipton cup between the 2 stationery wash tubs. I refer to the coming Dempsey-Carpentier fiasco at Jersey City which one of my friends has aptly termed "the title bout."

In response to the gen. demand which would not take "No" for an answer, I have undertook to write from 12 to 14 articles in regards to the affair includeing visits to training camps of both beneficiarys, reports on the condition of same and interviews with the 2 boys in their native tongue, and finely to set beside the ring side the day of the spat and tell my readers who win, which I have decided this time to wait till they are through fighting before I make up my mind.

As this is my first article and as I will half to write one every day for the next 2 wks. I may as well exclaim to the reader at the start that I some times write in a light vain and make up figures of speech to express my meanings, like for inst. if I should say that it looked like Dempsey would kiss the canvas why that don't mean that I expect him to walk up to some famous painting and give it a honeyed smack on the mush, but it would mean like I expected Carpentier to knock him down on the flr. of the ring which is generally always made of canvas unlest Beckett[7] is 1 of the principles and then they pave his side of it with a feather mattress and charge him by the wk.

In the same way, 1 am libel to not always refer to the 2 fighters by their real names but am libel to give them catchy nicknames like at Toledo I called Willard the Big Fellow and the name stuck to him like Dempsey's glove.

So don't be surprised if I should say "the Champ" meaning Dempsey or refer to Carpentier as "the Frenchman," and the sooner my readers get familiar with these little tricks of verbage, why it will make the articles almost as enjoyable to read them as it is to write them which I can't think of nothing I would rather do except play "Going to Jerusalem."[8]

In this article it might not come amiss to state that the writer is neutral in regards to whom wins as I haven't nothing vs. neither of the boys only that they both like dancing, but a man can't help from admireing a Adonis like the handsome young oo-la-la and as for Dempsey I took a likeing to him the first time I seen him which was in the Morrison Hotel in Chi, and we met in kind of a rm. where they was lot of men standing on 1 ft. looking in a mirror till they finely all begin looking at me so I asked them what did they want and Dempsey was the only one that didn't want nothing.

They's some people that is pulling for Jack so as the title will stay in the U.S. but as far as that is conserned why it says in the record books that the world's fly weight champion is Jimmy Wilde, an Englishman, but even knowing that, I can still go to the theater once in a wile and enjoy the show.

It's just a question of mind control. Like for inst., when Johnson beat Burns they was a lot of birds that squawked and said we must hunt around for a white hope as life was unbearable wile a colored man held the title, but I just set my teeth and said I wouldn't think about it at all and the result was that I spent some of the happiest days of my life dureing the time Johnson was champion. So if Carpentier should win and take the title back to France I will try and loose myself in my kiddies.

Other folks is pulling for Georges on acct. of him being in the war wile Dempsey sent regrets, but you must remember that they pulled it off right in Carpentier's home town and even if he hadn't of enlisted the noise would of probably kept him awake and further and more if Jack had of went over with the Marines, he wouldn't of been takeing as many chances as rideing around San Francisco in a taxicab, and last but not lease, I know some of the boys that has been picking on Dempsey that had to be dragged over there themselfs wile still others stayed right here and kept me company, but on the other hand Georges deserves a whole lot of credit for his record as a aviator and took such a interest in his work that even when they had give him his hon. discharge he run over to England and learned Beckett the nose dive.[9]

Both boys is great specimens of humanity when it comes to strength and physic and both comes of fighting stock. Georges is a full blooded frog while Jack is Scotch and Irish with a strain of Indian which ain't nothing to hold against a man provided he don't try and write love letters.

It will be one of the few heavy weight bouts in ring annuals when the both rivals is such young men though of course Jack was even younger yet when he win the championship but his oppt. in that fight was pretty near 40, even when it started.

In my next article I will have something to say about the men's records and how the both of them compare with the other one and etc. and maybe also a few wds. about myself.

Ring Gives Dry Statistics on
Preparations for Fight

JUNE 21, 1921

Great Neck, N.Y.—Before visiting the training camps of the fighters and writing my reports of what I see, it might be well to exclaim where and when the big event is going to be held and other statistics in regards to same so as my readers will know which fight it is that I am writing about, as up to date they seems to of been a kind of a secret pack amongst the newspapers to treat this affair as they done Stillman case[10] and give it just a bare mention.

Oh well then the date is July 2 and the place is Jersey City. The 2 main principals are Jack Dempsey and Georges Carpentier and they will split $500,000 as a reward for their efforts, which I want to say here no 2 men ever so richly deserved so lucious a plum unlest it was Smith Brothers.

It must be remembered however that more than half of Jack's $300,000 and a similar morsel of the Frenchman's $200,000 will be cheerlessly turned over to their resp. governments in taxes so that Jack won't only get less than $150,000 while Georges will have a little under $100,000 to spend if he lives.

It might be mentioned at this point that while the U.S. treasury will make somewhere around $300,000 to $500,000 out of the fight, still it will be considered kind of low down for the president to attend a event in which 2 strong men are trying to knock each other for a goal, so Mr. Harding will be obliged to send regrets though there are occasions when he presents himself at sessions of our congress which many people thinks is a great deal more brutal.

The original idear of the scrap, from a word pt. of view, was to net a small profit to Tex Rickard the promoter but I am now informed that the most of what is left over after Geo's and Jack is paid off has allready been subscribed to an involuntary fund known as the relief of devastated New Jersey.

The battle will be staged in a specially built arena which the estimated cost of same was $100,000 but the estimated actual cost is said to agree like Mr. and Mrs. Stokes.[11]

Prices of seats range from $50 to $5 and the man that buys a $5 seat may have the laugh on the $50 bird as the latter will have to make the trip to Jersey while the former is libel to be located in New York. The trip to Jersey and back will be some trip and Jack Curley runs past my heavily mortgaged home every morning in a rubber shirt getting in shape for it.

Last but not least it is vs. the Jersey laws for a referee to give a decision in a bout that goes the limit so if this one don't end in a knockout drop, you will halve to depend on the newspapers to tell who win and personally I will try and give an impartial verdict and as for being competent to judge, why I was one of the first to announce that Dempsey had a shade on Willard and within a week after the last election I said in the presence of witnesses that things looked bad for Cox.

I may as well admit here that I turned down a suggestion from one of my children to referee the fight myself, however I will hold the watch and I advise other spectators to do the same. Even some of the ministers in Jersey seems to have glue on their fingers. As for a prediction on the outcome I have promised to not comit myself, but would like to say that within practically all the comical cartoonists in New York picking Dempsey to win, I still figure he has a chance.

It may not be generally known but Carpentier's training quarters isn't only about a mile as the ford flies from what I jokeingly call my home so it won't take me nowhere near as long as other experts to get there, get rebuffed and get back. Newspapermen is au gratin at the Mathews farm across from the Sherry estate and in fact the guy that guards the entrance is said to be so hard boiled that the two neighboring farms has been nicknamed "Sherry and Egg."

Laying that joke and all others to one side, I don't expect to get turned down. Strategy kept me out of war and will get me into the French camp. I had two plans but have past up one which was to not go as reporter at all but leave my mouth sag open and pretend like I was a Long Island Country Gentleman. My other plan which I am going to try I will tell about in my next article if it works.

Ring Uses Strategy to Buzz Frenchman

JUNE 22, 1921

Great Neck, N.Y.—In yesterday's article I hinted at a plan by which I was going to crash the gate at the Carpentier camp. Well, here is the strategy I used which was as follows. I called up Bob Edgren[12] in New York and said for he and his golf tools to get on the 8 o'clock train next morning and I would meet him at the Manhasset station and we would go some wheres and bat the little pill acrost the green sword. Trying to coax Mr. Edgren out on a golf course is like luring a song writer to the piano, but I put it over and he showed up and we was soon gliding merily eastwards along the turnpike.

As we neared the French lines I said why wouldn't it be a good idear to stop and ask Georges if he would like to go along and jouer avec nous. Mr. Edgren says it was ok with him so we turned in at the Mathews farm and was as welcome as letters from France.

I may as well exclaim to the reader at this time that they is a certain man in Paris that is editor of a big sporting paper there and a great pal of Georges and this man once visited the U.S. and became a great pal of Mr. Edgren and before Georges left France this bird told him they was only one honest man in America, meaning Mr. Edgren, and for Georges to not pay no attention to nobody else but do whatever Mr. Edgren said. So when Georges got here he looked up Mr. Edgren and insisted on him being stake holder for the fight.

Well, these facts were all stored away in what I laughingly call my brain and that is how Mr. Edgren come to get invited out to play golf. A great boxer may be exclusive but he ain't going to give the raspberry to the only honest man in a strange land, a specially when that man is going to slip him a paltry $200,000 less than 2 weeks from hence nor any friend of that man. That is the kind of a diplomat I am and they send Harvey to England.

Well, to make it a short story, we shook hands all around and I had met Georges pretty near 2 years ago and he pretended like he remembered it, but any way him and his friend Mr. Mallet and his trainer Mr. Wilson clumb in what I sometimes refer to as my motor and Georges set on the front seat with me but I managed to stay in the road and soon we was on out to the North Hempstead country club where we hadn't no sooner than been recognized when all the boys in Nassau county run up to grab our bags. These attentions touched me to the corps as I ain't use to being drooled over by caddies.

Well, Mr. Edgren plays a round in 80 or better as a rule which is a good score for anybody—let alone the only honest man in America, so any way, him and Georges was partners as Georges hadn't played but once before, whereas Mr. Mallet is a 5 handicap man in France and I am usually give a stroke a hole in the Scandinavian countrys.

Well, we started out and Mr. Wilson was appointed to keep track of Georges' strokes which was ok except that wiles Georges was trying to get out of an apple tree with a brassey Mr. Wilson was busy telling me why he made Georges wear suspenders, namely because a belt is bad for a fighter's viscera when they are training, so Georges was on the edge of the green in 6 and sunk a 9 mile putt for a 7. Mr. Mallet and myself had a pair of sixes and the honest man was down in a 4 which made the hole all even on pts. and give the honest man the honor which you might say was like coals to Newcastle, Pa.

I wanted to ask Mr. Wilson what harm it done a fighter to not wear carnation perfume, but the 2nd hole is a water hole and Georges got in it and I didn't want to interfere with the count but anyway this ain't no golf story and will merely say that we only went 9 holes and I and Mr. Mallet won, which wasn't no fault of the present writer, and Georges had soixante six coups and will be a mighty good golf player if he keeps it up. Also between coups he whistles all the wile and his favorite tune is "whispering."

When we was through playing, Mr. Wilson called Mr. Mallet to one side and confided that Mr. Edgren and myself had played bad on purpose so as to not embarrass our guests, so when Mr. Mallet told me that I freely forgave Mr. Wilson for overlooking a few coups.

Well, the reason why we quit so soon was on account of it being ½ past 11 and Dejuner at the Mathews farm is 12 o'clock sharp so we drove back here and they asked us to eat with them which we did and the chef had wrote out a menu and put it in front of Georges' place and I read it and one of the items was biefstak a la russe which turned out to be hamburger and after Mr. Edgren had got away with 2 hunks of it I made the remark that he was a ideal stake holder but only got 2 laughs out of a possible 10 which besides ourselves was composed of Messrs. Carpentier, Mallet, Descamps, Wilson, Journee, Italian Joe Gans, Georges' dog and a good-looking French kid about 19 years that seems to be a kind of another household pet.

The house reminded me like some of the places we use to go calling Sunday afternoons when I was a kid, where the parlor was always kept ready for the sabath. On the dining room wall they was a picture of the battle of Gettysburg where the fighters didn't get no ½ million for their trouble, and they was also a picture of Mlle. Jacqueline Carpentier, age 6 mos., which I said she was a mighty pretty baby and Georges smiled, but the honest man told him I had 4 boys and that kind of spoiled his lunch.

After lunch we set around on the porch and Messrs. Descamps and Carpentier talked to us in broken English and we replied in ruined French and Georges says that a friend of his had wrote and asked him for 200 ringside passes to the big fight and he had also received a anonimous letter from a man that said he had overheard 2 men plotting to kill Georges just before he entered the ring and if Georges would send him carfare he would come out and tell him who the 2 men was.

Finely, I noticed that our hosts was yawning in both languages so I said we must go and we went, but Mr. Wilson said I was welcome to come back the next p.m. and see Georges work out which I will report same in my next article.

Lots of "Trebles" at Carpentier's Ringside

JUNE 23, 1923

Great Neck, N.Y.—Monday and Thursday is at home days in the Carpentier camp and the theory is that on them 2 days experts can crash the gate and watch the Frenchman go through his stunts. Well, the term experts seems to include such members of the treble sex as has obtained a certain degree of skill in pruning the eye brow. In fact, the last time I graced the chicken yard where Georges ring is pitched, pretty near ½ the spectators were members of New York's exclusive co-respondent colony and it was quite a chore for even a old married man with 4 cunning offsprings to keep his eyes focused on what is generally accepted as the roped arena.

That a good many of the ladies was of the theatrical world did not come as a big surprise, as I have often noticed that when they's going to be a championship fight, the dress rehearsals of the 2 beneficiarys is generally always witnessed by celebritys of the speaking stage as well as stars of the silent drama who I have nicknamed dumb actresses, and you would find all the great ball players there too, if they could get away. On the other hand, theaters and ball yards is always infested by champion pugs. It's an eternal triangle of hero worship and us poor writers can only stand on the outside looking in and wished we had sold our birthright for a mess of cauliflower ears.

Along about 3 o'clock I looked away from one of the blonde heroines of the poetic drama, "Ladies Night," long enough to witness the arrival of Georges and his retinue, of which the most impressive figure to me is always old Joe Jeanette, the man of mystery.

The first number on Georges' program was bag punching in the barn which I had watched it a couple times before and enough is enough. Afterwards he clumb in the ring and boxed with Jeanette, Gans and Journee and I guess they's no need of me describeing same in detail only to say that a female fan about 14 yrs old laughed out loud and got called down by Mgr. Descamps. I set this down as a warning to people who expects to have ringside seats at the big fight, namely, you mustn't laugh out loud, not even when you remember paying $50 for your ticket.

Carpentier didn't cut loose vs his sparring partners and I heard the remark made that he is a whole lot better boxer when they's nobody looking on, which if that is true I don't see why him and Descamps don't insist on fighting Dempsey in private.

The gen. opinion of people standing around me seemed to be that the Frenchman was in the pink and that he looked every inch a fighter except his neck. I couldn't see nothing the matter with his neck only of course that it ain't customary for a fighter to have one.

After the sparring was over Georges indulged in shadow boxing and jumping the rope and even laid down on the floor and practiced writheing and they say he don't leave nothing unrehearsed. However, though I heard many of the other experts praise his rope jumping, it looked to me like he would have to leap a whole lot higher if he wanted to get out of the ring at Jersey City.

In line with his strict attention to details I was talking to a fellow expert that had been trying different times to see him and get an interview, but every time he asked for Georges they told him he was asleep, so this expert said it looked to him like he even practiced 10 second naps.

Jokeing to 1 side, you can't see Carpentier stripped for action and be sorry for him, and if I felt as good as he looks I believe I could almost be persuaded to face the man who one of the experts has so aptly termed the Manassa Mauler, provided of course they was a $200,000 booby prize.

On his way back to the farm house Georges seen me and smiled which is going some for a famous athlete, as it generally takes them 5 to 10 yrs to recognize an expert's face unless the expert has panned them in the public prints.

Blondes and others that the Frenchman had to walk past them encouraged him with such remarks like:

"We are fond of you, Geo., and knock Dempsey dead," and etc. and in fact pretty near everybody in these parts appears to be pulling for the invader. This should ought to make him feel pretty good provided he ain't studied fight fans long enough to know that if Dempsey does happen to slip over an accidental punch and crumple him up, the most of these same fish will crowd around Jack's dressing rm. door in the hopes that when he comes out he will rub against them.

Everything Goes When You Hit Dempsey's Camp

JUNE 24, 1921

Atlantic City N.J.—Well friends, here I am at the town which has modestly nicknamed itself America's Playground and am stopping at a hotel which we call the Traymore and from my window I can look right out at one of the biggest oceans I ever seen and even on a clear day you can't see ⅓ way acrost it. The town was named after the Ocean and they's a suburb named Egg Harbor after Damon Runyon.

I hadn't no sooner got settled down when Tiny Maxwell, the football referee from Philadelphia come to call and asked me had I brought my golf sticks which I said yes so he said he would make inquirys and see if they was a course we could play on so he found out that they would be glad to have us make ourselfs at home on the sea view course and the green fees was $10 a person.

Tiny told them we seldom used the greens, but they said that wouldn't make no differents, so all and all we made up our minds that a week's rest might be the best thing for our game.

I asked the man in the hotel how to get out to Mr. Dempsey's camp and he says to go over on Pacific Avenue and hire a Jitney and sure enough I found several cars that was marked Jitney and I got into one and was whisked out to the camp where I had a little talk with the driver on the subject of how much more significants some people puts in certain words than others. Like for inst. the word Jitney means 15 times as much here as back in Niles, Michigan.

Well, I didn't have no trouble crashing the gate, though it was kind of hard to remember not to talk french after I get in. The Champion's camp ain't nowheres near as pleasant a location as Carpentier's as it is pitched in a spot where theys no trees for a mile around, so after all it looks like the Frenchman has the shade.

Dempsey's quarters consists of the arena where he works out and 2 cottages which he lives in one of them, and his sparring partners lives in the other. The cottages aint what you could call desirable home sites, but as far as Dempsey's sparring partners is concerned, they are tickled to death every time they wake up and find they haven't moved to the morgue.

We set down a while on the Champ's front porch and pretty soon Jack come out and I realized for the first time that they really is something in being champion fighter of the world. It exempts you from shaveing,

Dempsey was asked to set down amongst the scribes wile we had our pictures taken. Bull Montana set near me and there will be one picture where I look handsome.

We all crossed across the lane to the arena where they was 300 or 400 bugs that had paid to get in. Dempsey worked out with 3 or 4 so-called partners including Larry Williams who got knocked cuckoo in less than a round. Like Carpentier, Dempsey always says "I'm sorry," when he hits one of his partners too hard. The difference is that Carpenticr's partners can hear him say it.

I wish to state at this point that wile I don't suppose theys anything the newspapers could say about me that would be libellous, still and all they was a story in one of yesterday's papers that after the Champion had floored Williams, that me and Mayor Bader of Atlantic City was amongst the first to congratulate Jack on the power of his wallop. Well, I can't speak for his honor, but personally I never got the habit of running up and ringing a fighter's hand in appreciation of their Glorious victory over a sparring partner.

During the bouts Jack wears a head guard, but his sparring partners don't for the same reason that you don't hardly ever see a policeman walking his beat in a deserted village.

John Coulon, the old bantamweight champion, was around showing off his stunt which is defying anybody to lift him wile he holds his finger on a certain spot on their neck. When he seen Tiny Maxwell, who crashes the beam at 320 pounds, he says that here was a big strong fellow that ought to lift him if anybody could and wanted Tiny to try it

"No," says Tiny, "but I will make a counter proposition, you try and lift me and I won't only not touch your neck but will keep both my hands in my pockets."

Johnny lost by default.

Tomorrow I will pay another visit to the Champions camp and also expect to make my bow on the Beach in a 1 piece bathing suit that will create a sensation like a home run in the big leagues.

A Surprise Party for Jack

JUNE 25, 1921

Atlantic City, N.J.—This was Mr. Dempsey's 26th birthday and his admirers tore themselves from the boardwalk long enough to pull a surprise party on him. On account of the news of the party not being printed nowhere except in the papers the champ was as much surprised as he was over the announcement that the referee argument had been settled and the fight would be held after all.

Many of the boys remembered Jack with gifts. But personally I went empty handed as I always believe in giving people something useful and couldn't make up my mind between an invalid chair or a bottle of hair restorer.

The brother Elks from Longbranch, who was here with their present a couple days ahead, didn't have no such trouble making a selection. What they brought him was a handsome cup of the kind that goes by the name of loving cup though I never seen one of them that acted or looked more amorous than a mustache cup or even a demi tasse. The cup was daintily bedecked with purple and white ribbons which is said to be the lodges colors and was so big that it took 4 full grown elks to carry it.

The brothers reached Mr. Dempsey's cottage at 1 p.m. and was met the door by Teddy Hayes the champions keeper. They told Teddy what they had come for and he believed them, but Jack was taking a nap and he didn't dast disturb him even for a loving cup which he probably wouldnt use anyway till he woke up, so the brothers spent a pleasant hour and half on Jack's front porch which is prettily furnish with wooden steps which you can either stand or set on, but finaly they got kind of restless and walked around the house and who should they spy in the barn but Mr. Dempsey, who was punching the bag, presumably in his sleep. The brothers advanced and the spokesman made the following presentation speech without referring to his notes:

"On behalf."

"Is that for me?" says Jack, "fine."

And it looked like the incidents was closed, but the brothers had a camera on the hip and give the champ a brand new thrill by snapping his picture both before after taking the cup. The ever, ever loving cup also posed alone and I only wished I could afford to buy copies of its photo to send all my fond readers as I have always believed that the next best thing to having a loving cup in the home is having a picture of one.

The brothers stuck around to see Jack box which his victims on this occasion was only little lightweights who he dont dast paste them as hard as he can. The real target, Larry Williams, was taking a day off which he spent laying down on a couch instead of the floor, wondering to himself how they came to call Atlantic City "America's playground."

Another visitor at the camp was lady named Madame Marino that spoke with a frog dialect and announced that she wanted to bet $100 even on Carpentier to win.

Some of the survivors began question her and it seems like she is a medium and her control, which I have forgot whether it was bright eyes or little black bear, advised her to bet on the Frenchman and she had always played the control tips and hadnt never lost a bet. So she had spoke to her brother about this hunch and he had given her $300 and told her to bet it. As she is only betting $100 it looks like she will be $200 ahead no matter what happens to Carpentier and her brother.

Life continues gay along the boardwalk but nowheres as in the old days though some of the boys claims that the beer gives a 8 per return on their investment. Take it from one who used to be a connoisseur it dont pay no dividends at all. However, the boys that believes in it seems to get a kind of a mental heat and one of them was so affected that he sent his bathing suit to the laundry.

They's a man across the street that has just begun practicing, "I need thee every hour" on a cornet and in closing I only hope he aint talking to his instrument.

Ring Sizes Up Critics from Europe

JUNE 28, 1921

Atlantic City, N.J.—None of us boys realized what an International affair this here affair was till we drifted upon Mr. Dempsey's front porch yesterday and was introduced to 3 gents that had crossed acrost the old pond from sunny Europe just to report it. The 3 foreign additions to the corpse of experts is Benny Bennison of The Daily Telegraph in London, Victor Breyer, editor of the Echo of Sport in Paris, and Jeffrey Farnol, the English book writer.

They look just about like we home brews, only that their trousers ain't cut so decollete, and M. Brewer wears a shirt with a collar that leaves little to the imagination. Mr. Farnol is kind of short whereas I am tall and skinny, but the main differents between him and I is that I have heard of him. Mr. Farnol and Mr. Bennison both speaks broken English, and it is said the last named cables 2000 words a day in regards to the battle. Personly I had no idear they was that many.

M. Breyer is a great pal of Carpentier and has just came down from Manhasset. As he has seen Georges in all his big matches and has now watched Dempsey work, he probably has an opinion as to how the fight is comeing out. That makes one more opinion.

He said that while he was at Carpentier's camp, Georges received a parcel post package containing a block of wood with this inscription on it:

"This is your block which Dempsey is going to knock off."

Georges smiled at the subtle humor. Anonymous comedians like the above always runs amuck on an occasion like this and the other day a bug sent Dempsey a toy gun along with the message:

"If Carpentier don't kill you, please take a gun and blow your brains out."

Jack was puzzled at first, but laughed heartily when he got the force of the unnuendo namely that the guy was an admirer who wished him dead.

The last sabbath before the battle also brought a new flood of native experts to America's Playground, to say nothing about a small flood of rain which is as welcome here on a Sunday as a party that brings their own lunch. I maybe shouldn't ought to mention that it ever rains in Atlantic City on a Sunday as one of my best friends is a hotel man named Dan McLoughlin of the Traymore, who lets me have a room at no more than he would charge a stranger.

One of the new arrivals was Jack Root,[13] who retired from the ring a long wile ago which is just as well for Johnny Wilson.[14] Jack ain't writeing no pieces, but he knows something about fighters so I asked him his opinion in regards to the approaching fiasco.

"Well," he says, "I was just thinking what a differents they is between the money these boys is going to get and the money I use to get."

So when he pulled that remark I sobbed out loud to think of poor old Jack with a home in a slum like Pasadena and him and his Mrs. spending a week at a $20 per day hotel here before they go bumming around Europe,

Another pitiful figure I run into last night was Charley Dooin, the only Irish ball player that can sing Mother Machree without strangling. Charley has a real estate business with a Boardwalk minstrel show on the side and more money than a cartoonist.

"This is the only spot in the world," said Charley. "I love the air."

"Well," said Tiny Maxwell, who always seems to be nearby, "you got that in Philadelphia."

The Eagles, which was in convention here last week, has flew away, leaving the nest to the Cuckoos. Battling Nelson is amongst the latest to show up, but to date he hasn't had no luck interviewing the champ. When Bat went out there today and tried to crash in the gate man says: "I'm sorry but I got my orders and I wouldn't disobey them for the mayor of Egypt."

"Who is mayor there now?" asked Bat.

How to Overcome the Shock of Battle

BELL SYNDICATE, JULY 2, 1921

South Orange, N.J.—On the eve of what has been so aptly termed the battle of the century, though a few critics think that the Marne and Verdun was pretty near its equal in importance, I wish to offer a couple of suggestions to the general public of this country and France, in regards to their conduct on and after July 3. These suggestions is called forth by some remarks made the other day by a French boxing expert that was sent over here to report the fight and here is his remarks:

"France as a nation prays as one that Georges will be returned the victor, his success or failure is a matter of national concern. On the result may hinge the elevation of France. His defeat would be regarded as a national calamity."

Well, friends, if this here scrap means that much to La Belle France why it means that much to La Belle Amerique, and as it looks like a cinch that either Georges or Jacques is going to get knocked for a ghoul, it is also a cinch that either France or America faces a calamity which it may take them years to recover from same, perhaps never. That is unless everybody keeps their head and scools themself to face the worst that can happen,

That is what I want to say a few words in regard to, as I have an idear that maybe if I confide how I acted in different instants like these and made the best of situations even more desperate, why maybe the general public of France and America can profit by my example and conduct themselves so as no matter how the fight comes out, they won't be no collapse of the government at Washington or Paris.

Well, friends you will doubtless remember last year when the Resolute and Shamrock was racing for the Lipton mustache cup and one day the Resolute had stomach trouble and couldn't finish the heat, and that meant that the English boat had win a temporary victory, what did I do I hired a taxicab and told the driver to take me into the open spaces where I got out and set under a leather tree and fought my battle alone in God's great out doors.

"This must not break up my home," I says to myself and kept repeating it over and over till I believed it and in three weeks time no visitor at our house could of told that I had past through a crisis. Or take the day when word came that Mrs. Mallory had lose her tennis match to Mlle. Lenglen, the first impulse was to get ahold of a time table and find out when was the next train for Honolulu, but I pulled myself together and with the little woman always at my side whispering words of encouragement, it wasn't more than a week when I eat 2 eggs. So I say to you loyal citizens of France and America, no matter if Jack socks Georges or vice versa, keep a hold of yourself and remember the wife and kiddies and if possible take up some musical instrument.

As my customers has maybe noticed from the date line on this dispatch, I am spending the eve of battle in the citrus belt of Sunny New Jersey less than a one hour run from the thirty acres of boils. Before retiring I may indulge in a rubber of bridge with mine host and the rival Mrs. but will play in a lighter vain as I always make it a pt. to give my brains a complete rest the night before a big fight.

The fighters carry this custom to even greater extremes and go whole years without subjecting themselves to unnecessary strain. In my dispatch I may be able to give you some idear of who win or at least who I think win. But I am firm to the last in my determination to not pick a winner, suffice it to say that I learned this pm that Carpentier wasn't the only party that was floored at the Manhasset training camp. One day this week a sweet lady reporter come to interview him and says she wanted to ask him a few questions. Allright, says Georges.

"Well says the lady, I want to ask you first, when does that heart of yours beat the fastest, when you are in the ring or when you think of that little kiddie back home. According to eye witnesses, the champion of Europe fell over backwards, hit his bean on the edge of a Long Island cuspidor and took the count of 10.

Ring Is Glad He Wasn't in the Ring

BELL SYNDICATE, JULY 3, 1921

Jersey City, N.J.—The boss told me write what I seen in the order named so I will start with Bert Williams, who had arranged his season so as to be laying off today. Al Jolson had done the same thing and it looks like they was two exceptions to rule that comedians can't think.

I clum in my seat in time to see the second preliminary, which was between Frankie Burns and Packey O'Gatty. Nearby experts sed Burns had a little the best of it, but it looked to me like neither of the boys was mad at the other one.

Attention was attracted off this bout by the arrival of Gov Edwards of New Jersey and the governor of Florida. Much has been written about Mr Edwards and all as I add is an item which may contain heart interest. One of the gents in his party had a soft hat which got knocked off; as they was passing it back to him the governor took it and pretended to use it for what is known in New Jersey as a spittoon. Then he handed it to his friend and said to his friend, "get yourself a straw," which goes to show that even a governor has their lighter moments.

The governor of Florida had his necktie tucked in and wore 3 Owls cigars and a mustache. The third preliminary was between Babe Herman, one of Dempsey's little playmates, and a boy from New Orleans named Joe Mitrango. Joe was polite enough to stay pretty near five rounds, though you could see he was bored.

During the so-called fight between Gene Tunney and Soldier Jones a bunch of pretty Jersey gals passed through the crowd taking up a collection which Rube Goldberg said was for Dempsey and Carpentier. I had already wasted a couple weeks on these two birds and did not feel like I owed them any money. Jones sung the soldier's farewell in the seventh round.

Carpentier was the first to enter the ring, wearing a pretty gray bathrobe. Dempsey had on his old red sweater and a pretty good growth of whiskers, as it was not yet Saturday night.

As soon as the photographers was chased out of the ring everybody but Carpentier himself crowded into Jack's corner to see the champion put on his bandages. Francois Deschamps pretty near set in Dempsey's lap to see better, though personally I know many a better way to spend an afternoon or any part of one.

The champion was presented with a floral horseshoe by the citizens of Jersey City, famous for picking out useful gifts,

When the fighters first entered the ring it was hard to tell which got the biggest ovation and neither really got enough to brag about. But when Joe Humphries introduced them, which I didn't think was necessary, they was no question but that the crowd was with the Frenchman.

As the men stepped to the middle of the ring to get their instructions, which was given in New Jersey english and didn't mean nothing to Georges, my only regret was that Bernard Shaw was not at the ringside to see how his 1-to-50 superman stacked up alongside the delicate little boy from Manassa. Dempsey's weight was given out as 188 pounds, but I would hate to pay a dollar an ounce for all he was over that.

Georges said he weighed 172 and whatever he did weigh, I don't believe his Mrs will ever make him give up potatoes. Most of the people that picked Carpentier was just like Mr Shaw, they hadn't never seen Dempsey fight. I once made a little bet on a horse named John P. Grier in a two-horse race. I hadn't never seen the other horse run. His name was Man o' War.

Now, as to the fight you can read the description of the first three rounds somewhere else. All I will say about them is that in round 1 it looked like Georges wasn't going to leave this country with his Greek nose. They was also a nasty cut under his left eye. The boys in the press coop didn't think it would go beyond another round,

But in the second, Carpentier made it a real fight and proved to everybody that even if he wasn't good enough, still he was a long ways from being hopeless. A right-hand lounge seemed to be his best bet and it landed several times, and Dempsey won't have to read the papers to know it landed. Jack was hurt. Two things became apparent. One was that Georges can knock and the other was that Jack can take it.

I don't suppose Dempsey was ever hit as hard before unless it was by Willard in the second round at Toledo. But when the Frenchman landed with a blow that would of knocked Becket down twice, and all it done was stagger Dempsey and make him frown a little deeper, why it must have been kind of discouraging.

In the third chukker, they was still no reason for the Frenchman's friends to give up. Georges was as game as they come and as long as he had that right hand he had a chance, even if it was a long one.

But I can speak at more length about round 4 because when theys a knock-out in a fight like this all we boys see it different even if we are experts. What I seen was a terrific right that seemed to land somewheres toward the Frenchman's heart. You could hear the crack in the $25 seats.

This was followed immediately by a right hook to the jaw and Georges went down. I couldn't see his face during the first two or three counts. Then he turned so as I could get look at him. He looked kind of surprised, but perfectly sensible. He knew enough to stay down for the full count and when he got up he was careful to keep away from the corner where Jack stood. But now it was just a question of time. One more good sock would have been enough and the only way Georges could of avoided it would of been to jump out of the ring.

He chose to stay and in another instant Dempsey had him cornered again and hit him with everything in the book. I don't know what the boys will say was the real knock-out blow, it looked to me like another right hook to the chin, probably it was just a case of general debility. Carpentier fell and for three or four seconds I thought he was going to get up again. He made one feeble effort and then turned over on his face licked.

Referee Ertie and Dempsey himself picked the battered Frenchman up and took him to his corner. He was conscious and knew it was all over. Dempsey shook his hand and said: "I'm sorry I had to do it to as a good man as you."

Personally I was glad he didn't have to do it to as a good man as me. The ring which usually is infected by bugs on an occasion like this kind, was kept clear of everybody but fighters, their sponges and the Jersey City cops. Carpentier probably didn't feel any too good, but I wish to state that he managed to acknowledge Dempsey's kind words with a more or less pleasant smile.

All and all Georges made a much better showing against this guy than Willard. Willard kissed the canvas seven times to the Frenchman's twice. If I was in there I'd beat both those records. I'd only kiss it once and it wouldn't be for no paltry $200,000 neither.

They's a rumor in the press coop that Carpentier has broken with

Manager Descamps. The last named is accused of getting balled up in the excitement and using his hypnotic on the wrong party.

Well, friends, I don't pretend to be like Bernard Shaw and always know what I am writing about, but now that the big feasco is history I guess it's O.K. to go ahead and make one prediction in regards to the outcome, namely that Dempsey won't get no credit for doing what he done and the fight writers will get even less for telling you in advance that he was going to do it.

When Dempsey knocked Fulton cuckoo it was a frame-up. When he beat Willard, it was a lucky punch and besides, Jess was too old and wasn't in no shape. When Jack socked Brennan, he ought to done it a whole lot quicker, And now they will say, "Well, who was Carpentier anyway." They haven't never been a champ with a record like Dempsey's for quick and decisive wins against all-comers. But the bugs don't like what he done in the war, so they insist he can't fight. Well, I don't like what "Lefty" Williams done in the world series of 1919, but that don't mean I have to go around saying that "Lefty" can't pitch and never could.

The fight writers don't hold no brief for Dempsey as a patriot, but they have got a stealing idea that he is above the medium as a box fighter and they told the public so and made no bones about saying that this match was uneven, but the fans insisted that Georges had a chance. They wanted Dempsey licked and the wish was the daddy of the thought that Georges could do it. The bugs can't accuse the writers of steering them wrong on this business, that is outside of Bernard Shaw and a couple of experts of the opposing sex. The bugs was blind and if you tried to restore their sight they get mad at you.

Speaking about Bernard, his best line was the one about the fight writers boosting Dempsey so as they could clean up on Carpentier. Well, brothers, some of my best friends is fight writers and in the last two weeks I seen and talked with them all and they don't lie to me because I ain't worth the trouble. Well in all the gang they was only one that even suggested laying a bet on the Frenchman, provided he could get to 4 to 1.

"But what is the idear," I asked him. "Well," he said, "It might be a fake."

The result of this bout has learned me that Mrs. Wharton ought to write another "Age of Innocence" and make the time the present. Also that Greek profiles and long eyelashes is O.K. in their place but their place ain't in a 18 feet ring with Dempsey for a roommate.

I suppose my admirers will say if this bird knowed so much why didn't he come out and prophecy. Well, friends; I have found out that a prophet gets nothing but abuse, whether he is right or wrong, and abuse is one of a whole lot of things I don't crave. In conclusion allow me to state that the last 500 words of this story was wrote Friday afternoon at Great Neck, Long Island, but if you won't believe why we won't argue.

DEMPSEY VS. FIRPO

They Ought to Spell It Furpo

BELL SYNDICATE, SEPTEMBER 1, 1923

New York—I have just been asked by a little group of willful men to write a few wds. daily in regards to coming fiasco between Dempsey vs. Firpo who I have nicknamed the Wild Bull of the Pampas.

I may as well state at the outset that I won't make no predictions right now as to the fight only to prophesy that when the 2 principals enters the ring, the fish who has paid to get in will wonder what caused the apparent estrangement between the said principals and a barber.

It may not be the goriest battle of the century but it looks pretty sure like it will be the hairiest. Neither of the boys likes to shave and that is why I wished the both of them could win as I am in sympathy with anybody that don't like to shave, but they can get away with it and I can't on acct. of them not being married.

Now in the 1st. place for the benefit of those that depends on me for there fight dope, will state that the party of the second part hales from the Argentine. That is a joint in S. America which is next to the biggest state down there, the biggest state being Brazil where the nuts comes from and the last named told Firpo he could fight.

The word Argentine comes from the Latin word argentum meaning silver and the country was so called on acct. of the guy that discovered it was dirty with silver, but Firpo never seen no silver till he come to the

United States, which reminds me like one time back in 1849 a uncle of mine heard they was gold in California and he went out looking for it and finely come back to Michigan with nothing but a toothache and a dentist give him a nugget to fill up the cavity and that is all the gold he had when he died.

As far as I am conserned, the feature of this next fight is that it won't be fought at Boyle's 30 acres and I assure you if it was going to be fought there you would have to get along without my expert opinion as I am all through with trying to tell a Jersey City policeman that a working press ticket means anything.[15]

They think it is confederate money and you can't very well talk to them when they are giving you the bum's rush out of the joint with a club and a revolver in there pocket where all you got to fight against them with is a portable typewriter and a dirty look.

Mr. Dempsey is going to get a ½ a million dollars out of this fight and Mr. Firpo will make over a 100 thousand and I don't envy them as somebody is bound to get hurt and I would rather have my $35.00 a wk. and not get hurt which I know I will not get hurt in the Polo Grounds, where policemans is policemans and not Jersey City policemans.

Now in regards to the merits of the 2 fighters. This gives all the advantage to Firpo. I have seen the both of them fight Willard and Dempsey knocked the giant of the Pottawatamies down seven times in one rd. and the alleged giant stuck out 2 more rds.

Well I seen the wild bull knock Willard down once and I know just how he felt on acct. of his legs could not raise him. He did not get up till the referee had counted 11 to make it safe.

This leaves the score 1 to 7 in flavor of Firpo. The odds should therefore be 1 to 7 with Firpo the favorite and my telephone number is Great Neck 103 in the case anybody is looking for a bet. At those odds I will take the short on acct. of the price and not having no idear as to how the fight might come out.

I forgot to say in regards to the first paragraph of this remarkable story that the reason the 2 boys come into the ring with there whiskers on is on acct. of strategy. The point of your body where a person generally always gets knocked out is on there jaw or what not and if you wear enough whiskers nobody can tell if its your jaw or what not so that is why these boys

lets there whiskers grow is to deceive the other fellow. That is smart thinking on the part of each.

They's another thing which I might mention and that is in regards to
the spelling of the challenger's name and the way we spell it here is Firpo
which is the Spanish or Espanola spelling, but the real spelling is Furpo
and if Dempsey kills him they will take what is left of him and make a
coat which will keep you warm for the winter. And they ain't libel to be
any coal for sale north of the Argentine. So all and all, my advice is to bet
on Dempsey and take a insurance policy allowing you Furpo's skin and
you can't loose, win or draw.

In my next story I will probably give you a interview which I will have
at Atlantic City with Furpo without even seeing him. This story will be
in the original Espanola.

Theys No Doubt Wild Bull Can Hit If Jack Lets Him

SEPTEMBER 3, 1923

Atlantic City, N.J.—Have been setting all day in Dan McLaughlin's hotel
waiting for an invitation from Senor Firpo's manager to come out and
see the Wild Bull of the Pampas do his daily dozen, but so far nobody has
called up in Spanish, so will have to depend on hearsay for my first day's
report of the Bull's activities.

Luis is training out to the park where they have the dog races and when
the greyhounds take their workout he follows them around the track in
the hopes that between now and the fourteenth he will learn to run as fast
as they do, in which case he will have Dempsey worn out inside of ten
rounds and can spend the last five trying to fell him.

Luis has overlooked the fact that Dempsey has been following the horses
up at Saratoga some of who can run almost as fast as a greyhound when
I ain't betting on them. Joking to one side, the boys say that Firpo's trainers is making frantic efforts to get him to use his left hand which he ain't
never employed except to lift mashed potatoes.

A great many men shaves the left side of their face with their left hand thus keeping the muscles supple, but Firpo's left lacks even that much training as he is razor shy. The experts says that a man that don't lead with his left won't never make a fighter and that in his alleged fights with McAuliffe, Willard and Weinberg, Luis didn't hit with nothing but his right. As far as results is concerned you might as well say that Babe Ruth don't hit with nothing but his bat, however it is my own personal observation that champion box fighters do depend on their left leads to keep the other guy worried and when they have got him believing that their right arm is paralyzed, they bring it into action and smack him on what I call the chin.

A notable example of this method was Champion Jess Willard and the only trouble with him was that by the time he got the other guy to believing that his right arm was paralyzed he was believing it himself. Jess had a haymaking right, but before he begun to make hay the sun had generally always went down.

This fight ain't going to be no such affair like a fight between Johnny Wilson and Harry Greb, for instance, where either one of them could hit the other with a crowbar and they would think a gnat was biting them. Dempsey and Firpo can both sock and when a couple of sockers is matched the question always rises which of them can take it or leave it. Well, friend I never seen nobody hit Firpo as most of his opponents is always laying on the floor where they can't reach, so am unable to say whether or not he will stand up under the blows that finished Fulton, Willard, Brennan, Miske and the Greek God.

It will be recalled that Brennan, after his little brawl with the Bull made the classic remark that Luis was inhuman to punishment but Brennan may of been over estimating his own ability to inflict same. However, I would judge from the Argentine's gen appearance that he won't topple over from the effects of a slap with the open glove and even if he does get spilled for the full count, he is lible to get up again on account of not knowing the North American word for ten.

In regard to Dempsey I have seen his jaw act as receiving teller for two smacks that anybody could of got along just as well without. One of them was deposited in the second or third round at Toledo by the giant of the Pottawatamies, and for a second Jack looked like it had come as a big surprise. But he stayed vertical and an instant afterwards he was engaged in closing Willard's other eye.

The second and last time I saw him really socked was on a July day in the beautiful and hospitable edifice known as Boyle's Thirty Acres and the socker on this occasion was none other than the Greek god. The last named took a running jump and landed his far-famed right flush on the point of the chin. Some of my brother experts and a host of Carpentier's admirers, many of them of the female gender, remarked afterwards that this punch staggered Jack and almost floored him. Personally, I was setting just as close to the ring as anybody and my testimony is that Dempsey was about as much staggered as you are when you pick up Monday morning's paper and read where a man and two gals in a motor car was met at a grade crossing by a speeding train and neither of them was his wife. The party that got the worst of that punch was the Greek god himself. It kind of discouraged him.

Firpo is big and strong enough to hit a whole lot harder than Carpentier and if Dempsey forgets himself for a minute and reaches in his left pants pocket for his lip stick or something the bull will hand him a wallop that will hurt a good deal more than the Frenchman's did, in which case Jack will probably remain standing, as he is very polite when they's ladies present.

In a spirit of kindliness towards my readers I will make an earnest effort to crash the gate of the bull pen and give you a first-hand, open and above board account of what is going on.

No More Salutes from Firpo to Sid

SEPTEMBER 5, 1923

Atlantic City, N.J.—The Atlantic City progressive boosters was not present at Atlantic park Tuesday p.m. and nobody called Senator Firpo a big bum. However they was a slight epidemic of new newspaper men included amongst which was a scribe from Chicago who had covered the fight between Luis and Homer Smith at Omaha some weeks ago and made the remark in the paper that Firpo was a large gorgonzola cheese. This remark had been translated to Luis and he did not relish same.

"I don't mind being called cheese," he said, "but I hate gorgonzola."

Well, when this scribe, Sid Sutherland showed up at the park today, somebody told Firpo that here was the guy who had called him a gorgonzola. We was all sitting in the stand together and Luis was down in the ring getting ready to shadow box. He pointed up in our general direction and for a minute it looked like he was pointing right at the undersigned and the last named was looking around for the nearest exit, but Firpo finally spotted the right party and the following dialogue, which we was told about afterwards, ensued;

"You are sure that is the man," said Luis.

"Yes," replied his informant.

"Well," said Luis, "if he ever speaks to me again, I will not salute him."

The Chicago scribe's grief over the prospect of never again being saluted by the 'wild bull' was assuaged somewhat by the definite knowledge that the bull was not going to salute with a punch to the chin. Personally I shall be very careful not to call Luis any kind of food I do not know what kinds he likes outside of beef and I would hate to go through life without being saluted.

Speaking in regards to beef, it seems like Luis trains different than other fighters who are supposed to not eat nothing at noon except maybe a bowl of soup and a couple of vegetables. Firpo gets away with a one-half of a cow and won't have nothing to do with vegetables or fruits. In fact it is rumored that the reason why him and Deforest split up was on account of Deforest insisting that he eat stewed rhubarb at every meal. Firpo refused on the ground that he don't like stewed rhubarb. If it wasn't for the question of patriotism I would almost be pulling for him to win the big fight as I can't help from sympathizing with a man that sneers at stewed rhubarb and don't like to be called a gorgonzola cheese.

Amongst the spectators at todays workout was the new middle weight champion Harry Greb and his fellow townsman, Frank Klaus. I did not see Greb personally after the show, but was told that he had predicted that Firpo would not last two rounds with the champion of the world. Mr. Greb is a smart fighter and when smart fighters start predicting they are generally always right as us newspaper boys.

It is said that Klaus received an offer from Firpo's camp to join the little group of sparring partners but when they told him that the fee was $25 a day he laughed at them in all languages. A wage of twenty-five dollars a day is quite a wage as wages go but it aint so good when you stop to think that your widow is the one who will spend it.

Buddy Jackson and Leo Gates are going to be added to the stable Wednesday and Firpo is liable to do more boxing from now on. One of the experts said today that along about next Monday or Tuesday Luis intended to quit pulling his punches and cut loose with all he has got. If the sparring partners are not one-half wild they will find an excuse for leaving Atlantic City Sunday night.

Firpo may be slow in action, but it is to be recalled that two of the guys whom he has fought lately immediately afterwards took long leases on a room in the hospital. That is where some of these sparring partners are going to spend the winter, unless they watch themselves.

That is about all the news of the day except that Fannie Brice landed in town and tomorrow the pageant begins during which the most beautiful gal in America will be picked by competent judges. Fannie has had a certain feature of her face remodeled and is wearing it in a cast. The architect who done the remodeling is one Dr. Henry Schireson of Chicago aud Fannie wanted that I should go to Firpo and tell him that in case Dempsey broke his nose, the Doc would make him a even prettier one. After careful thought I decided not to do this.

Fight fans with the interests of North America at heart is said to of sent a wire to Dempsey adviceing him to not come into the ring this time wearing that old red sweater that adorned him when he entered Boyle thirty acres to encounter the Greek God. You know what a red thing is to a bull, was the sense of the wire.

Lardner Sees the Wild Bull

SEPTEMBER 6, 1923

Atlantic City—We had a date Wednesday a.m. to go out to Firpo's headquarters at 10:30 which is practically the middle of the night in Atlantic City you might say. However, we made it and only to find that Luis was still down on the boardwalk doing his morning exercises which consists of a game of leapfrog. Playing leapfrog on the boardwalk at this time of year is a good deal like trying to stage a double-header ball game at 8 p.m. on the corner of Forty-second street and Broadway. Firpo's training is different than anybody's training I ever see, but I certainly ain't going to try and give no advice to a boy who five years ago was working as a porter in a drug warehouse and now he's got $300,000 in different banks, to say nothing about the $125,000 or some such figures which he is bound to get out of the coming fiasco with the so-called Manassa mauler.

Well, anyway, we landed at Firpo's cottage while mine host was still out, and was greeted by the chef who was about to start to commence the light lunch which forms Firpo's noonday meal, consisting of the other half of the cow which he enjoyed for breakfast and six eggs to wash it down and last, but least, the chickens that laid the eggs.

Included amongst the young visitors was a couple of artists from New York who had come out to draw portraits of the challenger.

The artists was namely: Wm. Deleftwich Dodge and Joe Chase. While we awaited Firpo's return, an Argentine blowed in and told us a little incidence that occured the last time Luis posed for a picture. This incidence come off in Havana while Luis was preparing himself for his scheduled bout with Joe White. Firpo and party was setting in a restaurant enjoying the usual kind of a light lunch that Luis is fond of. The artist come in and introduced himself and said he thought he could make the picture during the meal. When he had it done, he handed it to Firpo who didn't seem to think much of it. The picture was then shown to a Argentine friend of Firpo's and after giving it one glance, the friend got up and dropped the artist with a punch to the chin.

A passing policeman heard the fight and come into the restaurant to enjoy it.

The artist demanded the Argentine's arrest for assault. The Argentine showed the picture to the policeman and the policeman said the Argentine had been perfectly justified in hitting the artist, whereupon the Argentine got up and parked another punch on the artist's jaw which discouraged him. While this story was being related, Messrs. Chase and Dodge listened very carefully and decided to take pains with their work.

Firpo finally blowed in and proudly showed us a kind of a diploma which he had just received from a guy in Rochester, N.Y. The parchment showed a picture of the Firpo coat of arms and words to the effect that the original Firpo's was born in the twelfth century and that any offspring was bound to be intrepid warriors. This seemed to tickle Luis, but he said don't write too much about it, as it might be a fake.

Boys in the camp told us that the bull don't never sleep in a bed but when he goes into the Rm. nights, he takes a pillow off the bed and throws it on the floor and lays on the floor all night. This is probably a part of his training for Dempsey. Willard should ought to of rehearsed this system and maybe he would of been more comfortable during his frequent naps on the canvas.

I was kind of hoping to get invited to lunch as it has been a long time between meals in Atlantic City, but they was such a gang of us that even the ½ cow wouldn't of hardly went around, so we beat it down town to a cafe and the waiter heard us talking about the fight and asked us how we thought it would come out. One of the boys expressed a opinion and then asked the waiter who did he like.

"I don't like none of them," said the waiter and they was no further argument.

Tomorrow they are going to pick the most beautiful gal in America and all day today the different candidates was walking up and down the board walk and the result was that the attendance out at Firpo's daily exhibition was kind of light. Personally I am betting on Miss Albany, but the judges has been in Atlantic City pretty near a week and is libel to be blind by this time.

Firpo Takes the Day Off

SEPTEMBER 7, 1923

Atlantic City, N.J.—Senor Firpo announced this a.m. that he would do no boxing today. This proclamation was greeted by his sparring partners with a howl of protest that could be heard as far as you can hear a pin drop. Jeff Clarke, of ebony hue, wasespecially vociferous in his squawking.

"I dont know how I can stand it," said he, who gets slapped. Firpo explained that he had been working hard for two weeks and thought himself entitled to a day off of rest.

"Listen," he said in Spanish, "I am my own manager and trainer and I think I ought to know how much I need. The newspaper men have been criticising me for not working enough, but they don't know how hard I work. Every morning I am down at the beach working while the newspaper men is still in bed."

This was a slightly inaccurate statement. What he should of said was "I am down on the beach working while the newspaper men ain't in bed yet."

Well anyway, the wild bull of the Pampas as I call him got a fine day's rest. It seems like a whole flock of newspapermen suddenly found out that he was training in Atlantic City and they all blowed into town this a.m. When we landed at the bull's home, they wasn't hardly enough chairs to go around. Senor Firpo himself picked out the hardest and most uncomfortable one in the room and set there for hours bored to death while us boys talked him over in a language he can't understand. If he could of understood he might of been even more so.

Finally one of the experts suggested a game of craps and Luis brightened up, as that is his dish. But when he searched his pockets he could not find no money and had to borrow off his trusty interpreter, Senor Vega. The game lasted about twenty-five minutes and Firpo lost $2. Everybody felt awfully sorry for him. During our visit to the little cottage which has been the big boy's home down here, in come a gent who said he was the greatest trainer of fighters in the world and would Luis give him a job. One of the Argentines asked him who had he ever trained.

"Well," he said, "I have trained Willard and Ketchell." The Argentines did not seem interested, but they did not know how to get him out of the house as they are very polite, so we horned in to help them out and asked him where was Ketchell now, which he could not answer. So I says, "was it you that trained Willard at Toledo?" This got a big laugh from the man who said it, but anyway, it succeeded in getting the gent out of the house and thining down the crowd.

The guy who really suffered the most from Firpo's decision to take a day off was the man who does his cooking. This chef was lent to the camp for the training period by the New York council from Uruguay. He cooks a mean steak and the only time he has a chance to rest is when Luis is out at Atlantic park doing his stuff. With Luis home all day, the chef has to practically live on the kitchen stove. He spent this P.M. preparing a dish called puchero which is a kind of an appetizer which Luis takes between meals. It is composed of chicken, rice, beef, and peppers.

At this junction I will half to bring myself personly. While we was all setting around there I made the remark that the height of all athletes was generally always exaggerated. I said my height was 6 feet 1¼ inches, and that Luis height was supposed to be 6 feet and 2½ inches, but that I have stood up talking to Luis the day before and I could see that he wasn't no taller than me. So the boys made us get up and stand back to back, and we done so and all of a sudden Luis seemed like he growed a whole inch. Anyway, I loose the argument, but I turned it off gracefully and got a big laugh by saying it was Firpo's hair that made the difference. It is certainly wonderful to be able to think quick.

They was such a full house that it was nigh impossible to enjoy any private conversation with the big fellow, but he did manage to confide that after he had win the South American championship by a knockout the president of Chile had give him a gold belt weighing six pounds and pretty near as wide as the board walk.

Well, when Luis was about to fight Willard in Boyle's dirty acres, he got a cable from the Chilean president requesting that he wear this belt in the Jersey City bout. He cabled back that he could not wear the belt as it might break Willard's hands. He did not know that Jess was not going to use them.

As I write these lines the boardwalk is jammed with the spectators of the big parade of the 80 gals from who is going to be chose the prettiest gal in the U.S. So it is kind of hard to write but by this time tomorrow everybody will know who the judges has selected and a person can keep their mind on their work.

Ring Discovers What's Wrong with His Feet

SEPTEMBER 9, 1923

New York—Well friends, I stopped off over night in little old New York on the route from Firpo's to Dempsey's camp and found the big town, as I have nicknamed it, about the same as usual with Mike Hylan still mayor. Personally I kept in seclusion and did not leave the gen. public know I was back in town as they would storm the joint where I was hiding and demand my opinion of the Wild Bull which might affect the betting.

However it become necessary during my brief stay to call in a doctor to treat my feet which was ailing me. The Doc diagnosed the disease as brass rail poisoning and said it was prevalent amongst people that has spent some time in New Jersey. In payment for his advice I was going to tell him how to bet on the approaching event but come to find out he hadn't never heard of Jack or Luis, neither one, and wanted cash.

Mr. Dempsey and his companions in the camp at White Sulphur Springs is probably awaiting my arrival with a eagerness that practically amount to insanity. I probably won't no sooner than heave in sight when the champ will drop whatever he is doing and insist on me telling him what I seen in Atlantic City. The two of us will probably be closeted for a hr. provided theys a window in the closet big enough for one man to jump out of in the case the other man gets mad.

"Champ," I am going to say as him and I is pretty close, "this Firpo is Argentine and the papers has give it out that he can't speak a word of English, but he has learned one English sentence which he sprang on Willard and throwed such a scare into the big fellow that he fell down and couldn't get up without too much of an effort. I will tell you that sentence so as you will not be surprised and scared when he springs it on you. The sentence is, 'I am going to send you to the hospital!'

He rehearses it once a day vs. his sparring partners and has got so as he can say the whole sentence in one three minute round.

"In regards to his fighting ability, he has been practicing up to lead with his left like all sound boxers is supposed to do, but if you manage to hit him once, he will leave his left hand in his corner and tear into you with his right, and if I was you I would kind of keep my head and body covered up or else I would do some road work."

I am putting this in the paper because while Firpo can say one English sentence, he can't read none so theys no danger of him seeing this and following me up to White Sulphur. However, though he can't read our language they ain't a day passes when he don't buy all the papers and when he has found the sporting page, he sets there and stares at it by the hr in hopes that all of a sudden, some day, a great light will break and he will understand.

In the meantime nobody can't help from feeling sorry for a man that ain't able to enjoy what we boys is writing in regards to this fight. . . .

Ring Gives Dempsey Some Advice

SEPTEMBER 10, 1923

Saratoga Springs, N.Y.—Residents of Saratoga must of read in the paper that I was about due to arrive here as they was a big crowd down to see me come in though I had not told nobody what train I was coming on. Tom Mix was on the same train and also got off here. He was wearing a cowboy hat and I guess it is a custom amongst cinema performers to always wear some article of clothing indicating what kind of parts they play and it occurred to me that it would be a good idear if everybody would wear some article of clothing typical of their profershion so as a person looking at them would not half to strain themselves guessing. Like for inst. Dempsey might go around with his hands taped and personly I could appear on the streets with a typewriter ribbon in my hair and a vest made out of newspapers.

This would give everybody a square deal and would do away with such humiliating experiences as I had in the station here, namely Mr. Mix got in a taxi just behind mine and the crowd all looked at him because they did not know who I was.

I asked the taxi man how much would it be to take me out to the lake where Dempsey is training and he says he charged six dollars for a leave out. So I asked him if he thought I looked like a leave out but he made no reply. On the way to the camp we come up behind a bunch of cows that took up the whole road and we had to drive into a ditch to get past them. I suppose when Tom Mix's taxi came along the cows jumped over the fence and give him the right of way.

I was too late to see the champion work out and can't tell you yet how he compares with Firpo, but they seemed to be more of a air of confidence amongst his followers than was evident at the wild bull's joint. I reached Mr. Luther's resort in a downpour of rain and in the midst of a picnic which was being indulged in by the foreman of the General Electric company. It was a damp picnic. The crowd was so big that it was impossible to get service unless you was somebody with a drag so I kind of attached myself to Dempsey's brother Bernard. After a long argument in regards to religion I expressed the desire to see the champion of the world and Bernard led the way to the cottage where Jack sleeps. It is about 400 feet from Luther's and the path winds amongst trees. We went in pitch darkness and I hit all the trees but none of them fell down. They was about fifty visitors in the cottage so the champ did not mind just one more and acted like he was glad to see me. He asked me what I thought of Firpo and I says if I was you I would look out for his right hand.

"I'm awfully glad you warned me," says the champ.

"I thought you ought to know," was my reply.

Jack noticed through my silk hosiery that my ankles was done up in bandages and wanted to know what was the matter, so I told him I got a defection of the feet down in Atlantic City. The doctor told me to not stay on my feet more than five minutes, I says.

"I wish," says Jack, "that he would tell Firpo the same thing."

So we talked back and forth a while and finely he acted sleepy so I got up to go and I says I bet you are anxious to get into the ring where you will be alone with Firpo and the referee and not half to talk to a bunch of eggs like you got hanging around here, myself inclusive.

"That is one place where Firpo has got it on you," I says. "When we talk to him he can't understand what we're saying."

"Well," says Jack, "I dont mind understanding what you are saying as long as I don't half to pay no attention to it."

I bounced back from tree to tree till I got to Mr. Luther's where I found some of Jack's sparring partners engaged in a unfriendly game of cards. I was amazed at first at how wild a game they was playing, but finely realized that people as near death as these boys don't mind a little thing like the loss of a few dollars.

Lardner in Great Shape for Wordy Battle

SEPTEMBER 13, 1923

New York—Thursday marked the end of my hard training for the Dempsey-Firpo fight and I can assure my friends and admires that at no time in my career have I been as confident on the eve of battle and will promise to write at least 600 words Friday night provided I am given a square deal by policemen, ushers and spectators.

Thursday will be devoted to a little light work to keep my fingers supple and expect to put in part of the day oiling my typewriter and supplying same with a new ribbon. On Friday morning I will go over the keyboard a couple of times to develop speed and during the P.M. will indulge in a short nap to insure myself vs. dozing off during the big fight. I will enter the press seats weighing 183 pounds dressed, and will wear a dirty collar and heavy shoulder pads as a protection against the moroons that crowds down to the ringside after a fight is over and rounds out the evening by setting on newspapermen's necks.

Coming down on the train from Saratoga I had a little talk with Farmer Lodge and George Godfrey. Mr. Dempsey had just told me that he would not need them no more and both of them was bearing up well under the news.

"I sure will get good sleep to-night," said Mr. Godfrey.

"My slumbers has been interrupted lately by worry over what the next day would bring forth. But the worst that can happen to me Thursday is to get bumped into by a ten-ton truck which will feel like a flea bite after what I been through."

I made the remark that it seemed a kind of a shame that two as famous boys as these should be making the five-hour trip in a day coach.

"Listen," says Farmer Lodge, "we are tickled to death that we ain't riding in the baggage coach ahead."

I asked them what a sparring partner thinks about when they are in there facing Dempsey.

"You ain't thinking of nothing," said Mr. Godfrey. "He don't give you time."

In contrast to Farmer and George, the champion will roll into New York in a private car which he was doing ten years ago only this time the car will be attached to a passenger train.

The champion of the world is greatly interested in the progress of the case of Harry Wills vs. the boxing commission.[16] The way the case stands now, the judge has promised to hand down a decision on the first of October. If the judge decides that Dempsey must fight Wills before he fights Firpo, why it is going to cause a great deal of confusion among the boys and gals that is going to be at the Polo grounds Friday night. We will all half to pretend like that we wasn't there and didn't see no fight or else we are libel to be held in contempt of court.

Another thing that cause confusion is the fact that Dempsey and Firpo ain't never seen each other and unless they happen to weigh in Friday at the same time, they won't never see each other till they climb into the ring. Dempsey won't know which fighter is Firpo and vice versa until Joe Humphreys introduces them. In fact, if Joe should forget to introduce them Firpo is just as libel as not to swing for his own jaw, thinking he is Dempsey. What makes the situation all the worst is that both men is brown of complexion and black of hair and both will probably be wearing the same size glove and yesterday's set of whiskers. Theys just a chance that Dempsey can identify Firpo by his bath robe, but if the Argentine should happen to stroll into the arena that night with a red sweater instead of a bath robe, heavens knows what would happen.

The betting out in Great Neck remains at even money with Dempsey a slight favorite. In other words, my son has bet a nickel even on Dempsey, his nurse taking the Firpo end. Bill has also bet two cents even on Firpo, his brother Jim being on the Dempsey end.

"I can't lose more than three cents any way it comes out," said Bill.

A Word from Bernard Shaw

SEPTEMBER 14, 1923

New York—On the eve of the 2d battle of the century friends and admires from all sections of the country kept ringing up my training headquarters on Long Island to try and find out my opinion in regards to the outcome of the struggle before placing their bets on same. To each and all of these friends and admires, my handlers give the same reply, namely that I was out. As a matter of fact, I wasn't more out than the promoters of the fight, but I do not like to make no predictions without knowing what I am talking about and in this case I did not want to put myself on record without first consulting Bernard Shaw, who I consider the greatest male boxing expert in the world.

Late last night I succeeded in getting Mr. Shaw's apartment on the long distance and was told by a maid that he had went roller skating but had left word that he thought the fight would go the full limit of 15 rounds and that Firpo would win on points by a wide margin. That is Mr. Shaw's opinion according to his maid and I would advise my friends to make their bets accordingly though personly I think the fight is a toss-up, but ain't saying which corner the tossing will be done from.

Firpo may not last as long as Carpentier did, but the Argentine will enter the ring with one big advantage over the Frenchman, namely no women that I know of has picked him to win. The ladies' vote put a awful crimp in Georges' chances and the fact that most of the fair sex favors the champion vs the wild bull should make the bout a even money proposition with the odds about 2 to 1 against Dempsey.

So much for the betting on the result itself.

Aside from that, a few freak bets have been recorded around the town where I live. One prominent mechanic wagered a pocket comb against a empty beer bottle that Firpo would not come up for the first round. An employe of the local postoffice bet a lockbox against a package of after dinner mints that both men would be off their feet between the first and second rounds. A fat man who refused to tell his weight put up all his superfluous flesh against a second hand tripod that they will be one or more photographers in the ring before the main event starts.

Personly, after watching both men in their daily preparation for the bout, I would not be surprised to see the fight decided by one punch.

Tex Rickard announced tonight that the show would start at eight o'clock irregardless of a cabled request from Argentine fans that he postpone it till they get there. These fans left Brainless Aires on a special excursion boat yesterday morning and even if they miss the fight itself they should ought to reach the Polo Grounds in time for the world serious.

Six ringside seats have been set aside for a little group of wilful bankers from Eaves Trough, Montana, who will try to persuade the winner to come to their city during October and fight Johnny Wilson for this year's deposits in the local banks. Eaves Trough has a population of 235 men and women and won't half to depend on New York, Chicago, San Francisco and etc. for patronage. It is located 12 miles from a railroad so they won't be no danger of the two contestants getting ran over by a train.

Last minute statements was issued by both challenger and champion.

Dempsey said: "I will give him everything I've got except my 37 and ½ per cent of the gross."

Firpo said: "I hope he leaves me some good teeth as a man like I can't live on soup alone."

On Saturday morning I will tell my readers what come off from the view point of a eye witness provided they don't call in no Jersey City policemens to see that newspaper men gets seats outside the grounds.

It Was a FIGHT

SEPTEMBER 15, 1923

New York—I will take back everything I ever said in regards to Jersey City. At that well-known joint, they at least leave you in before they give you the bum's rush out, but up here tonight they had a up and down sliding door on the press gate that acted like a guillotine and the minute you stuck your head under the gate and showed them a working press ticket, they would start the gate downwards in the hopes they would cut a newspaper man's head off.

After the boys had missed me 2 or 3 times, they give up in despair and closed the gates down for one and all, so I went around and walked through a pay entrance where they did not know me. But they's still several working newspapermen standing outside the Polo Grounds waiting to see this fight and the next time they come to one of these here battles of the century they will bring cigar coupons which may entitle them to more respect than a mere working press ticket.

I been hanging around these big events a long wile but never seen one handled like this except once in Niles, Mich., when everybody of school age made up their mind to ring the school bell one Hallowe'en and they was only one policeman to try and stop us.

Jess Willard was right ahead of me in the line that was trying to crawl under the drop curtain and he made it by a fast movement on his hands and knees, but a man has got to be used to that position to get the best results.

Mr. Rickard give me a pass to this fight but in return for which he owes me one (1) new suit of clothes, one (1) new pair shoes and one (1) new disposition.

Entering the arena in my company was Earl Sheely, Harvey McClellan and Pitcher Thurston of the White Sox. They would not make no predictions in regards to the fight, but said they knowed how the loser would feel.

I got to my alleged seat in time to see part of the family quarrel between Bartley Madden and Leo Gates, the last two of the Mohawkans. Messrs. Dempsey and Firpo thought the same of this fight as I did and tried to enter the ring before it was over.

Mr. Madden was said to be the winner.

Mr. Dempsey crossed everybody by entering the ring with a white sweater. Luis wore his checker-board kimono and a full set of Thursday's whiskers. The champ wasn't so clean shaven himself. It was murmured in my ear that Miss Neysa McMein[17] had placed a modest wager on the wild bull. The old thought come to me about how woman's intuition worked in the Carpentier match, so I increased my modest little wager on the champ.

I was parked right behind Firpo's corner and I was kind of scared that I might suddenly set up and find the Bull setting in my lap. But the champion himself was the one that got knocked out of the ring and Grantland Rice was there to receive him.

Firpo done all his falling on the canvas. The experts will tell you how many times he fell. I lost count, but every time he did go down his pal and interpreter, Senor Vega, would shout "Viva, Firpo," or whatever it is in Argentine, and the Bull would rise again, that is, till the final one-two punch put him down for keeps. Then Senor Vega broke right down and cried in all languages and nobody in the vicinity felt like laughing at him.

The experts on this fight was both right and wrong. The most of them figured that Jack would win and win quick, but I didn't hear none of them predict that the challenger would get up off of the floor 4 or 5 times and then knock Jack over the second strand of ropes and make everybody nervous.

They was a big question before the fight as to whether or no the Wild Bull could take it. He took it and took it plenty and come back for more, and got it. They ain't nobody living that could take what he took before he finally took that left and right in succession and became the Tame Cow of the Pampas. Anybody that said he quit ought to be writing jokes for the theater program. In fact, Luis didn't know when the fight was over and was still groggy when he staggered down the steep stairs out of the ring, escorted by some of the same policemens that had tried to keep me from seeing the fight.

And they was another question settled tonight, namely can Dempsey take it. Jack was on the receiving end of four or five of the most murderous blows ever delivered in a prize ring, but he come back after each one and fought all the harder.

Even when he fell into Mr. Rice's lap, he picked himself up without assistance and stepped right back to the place where all the shooting was going on.

Between the first and second round, Messrs. Kearns and Benjamin in champion's corner asked him as a personal favor to not leave himself quite so exposed and, in the second round, it was noticeable that he was making himself a much tougher target to hit. He kept his head low and covered up, but still flayed away with both hands and never lost sight of the main idear that he must get this guy and get him quick. He didn't get him none too quick and if the fight had went a round longer, they would of been wholesale deaths from heart disease with maybe some of the victims in Dempsey's corner. All and all, you wont hear no squawk to the effect that those who paid to get in didn't get their money's worth, even they paid a hundred smacks for a seat. It was a FIGHT. . . .

DEMPSEY VS. TUNNEY

Monosyllables to Jack's Jaw

BELL SYNDICATE, SEPTEMBER 24, 1926

Philadephia—This is only 7 o'clock, almost three hours before the battle, mother, but I am going to start writing now because I have got quite a lot to say, and it has been my experience at events of this kind that whatever writing a person attempts in the 30 minutes immediately following the finish of a big fight is done under a severe handicap. This handicap is in the form of large, unwashed morons, who storm the press section and round out the evening's jollity by bestraddling your neck, stamping approval on the first page of your stuff with one of their feet and trying to operate your portable typewriter with the other.

Down somewhere near the tail end of this article I will give you a hint as to the outcome of the thing we have journeyed here to see. Just now I want to tell you how I happen to be present and to explain what is really a desperate situation. Among my readers there may be some who are four years old and if so they will recall that in the autumn of 1922 my little woman expressed a desire for a fur coat. When I asked her "what fur?" she misunderstood me and said "mink." Well, I couldn't get it out of her head and whatever remark I made to her she had only the one reply— "Mink." So finally I said I would bet on the Yankees in their world's series with the Giants and if the Yankees won she could have her mink. The Yankees lost, and it was a series that only the Yankees could have lost. Anyway, no little mink came to bless our home, and she had to face Jack Frost in a garment fashioned from the epidermis of three little kittens that were so cute, that, well, I must not think of them or I will make a scene.

It happened that fall that I myself had a pretty swell overcoat with a fur lining and every time we would go out, the little woman would say. "Look at me, and then look at you, with a fur lined overcoat." And I would say "Yes, but haven't you a feline overcoat?" This amused her for a time, but not forever.

Well, the catskin coat is now no longer wearable. It has been ravaged by time and by the neighbor's dogs, who snapped at it whenever she appeared on the street. And madam has once more become a woman of one word—"mink."

That is why I am here, friends, I who had intended to stay in Great Neck and see Laurette Taylor's[18] opening. I am receiving a certain amount of money for what some might call this work, and I am betting that amount of money on Mr. Dempsey and giving odds of 2 to 1. If Dempsey wins— mink. If Tunney wins—monk, for we are out of cats.

Aside from my regard for the little woman's comfort, I will be an unbiased spectator of the coming brawl. Both the boys call me by my first name when they can remember it. and I will hate to see either of them dozing off before bedtime.

I have not told Jack that I was betting on him. Such a revelation would shake him even more than his recent mash notes from Jack Kearns, for he is cognizant of my betting record where he is concerned. I lost on him, or rather off him, against Willard. I could not win on him against Carpentier because nobody I happened to meet was drunk at the time. I bet he would knock out Tom Gibbons, and Rube Goldberg and I bet on him against Firpo and never got paid.

The preliminaries have not yet started and I will take this opportunity to thank Mr. Bert Bell for the use of his apartment during our pleasant little sojourn in Philadelphia. Mr. Bell, as you know, used to play quarterback for Pennsylvania and cover patch on the Yellow Jackets. He is now teaching the Penn backfield field how to run. Red Grange had this job last fall. Mr. Bell is no relation to the Liberty Bell, which is said to be cracked.

Mr. Rickard has just announced to we experts that a trainload of Madison Square Garden ushers was imported for the occasion. They came in day coaches, and if it had rained and a postponement had been necessary they would have stopped at the House of Usher.

Something has just happened that kind of upset me. I heard Abe Attell say he had bet $4000 dollars of his own money on Gene. That he is betting his own money is bad enough, but the outlook becomes even worse when I recall that the last time I heard of his betting was at that lovely world's series in Cincinnati when I plunged on the White Sox, and the little woman had to go to church Christmas morning wrapped in a burlap bag.

A gent behind me is explaining the meaning of the sesquicentennial to his companion, who looks something like Willie Stevens.[19] He is told that it is the celebration of the 150th anniversary of the signing of the Declaration of Independence. This document is said to be the only one in history that Dempsey has not signed. Now the same gent is telling Willie that he seen Tunney up at Stroudsburg and the day he was there, Gene was presented with a pair of gold cuff links by the Mauch Chunk Catholic high school. Maybe Dempsey will give him the cuffs.

This thing is getting on my nerves. I don't want to see the champion licked, and I don't want the little woman to catch cold. But on the other hand, I don't look forward with any relish to the slaughter of such a nice boy as Gene. And besides, Gene reads books, and people who read books sometimes buy them. They say that when this fight is over, Jack is also going to buy a set of books, the complete works of Blackstone.

It will be noted that the entire card of preliminaries is made up of heavyweights. This is because the customers in the $16.50 sections are so far away that they would think a battle between welters was a flea circus. The boys and girls in some of these seats have brought along their receiving sets, hoping to hear the fight broadcaster. Back of them are a bunch of clifts who have asked Gene and Jack to send them postcards tomorrow, telling them how it came out.

In the expensive section close behind me I can see Peaches Browning[20] and her keeper. Peaches is standing up for fear somebody will recognize her. No far from her are Mr. and Mrs, Gene Buck,[21] and they must be getting a thrill in addition to that, for the radio contrivance, which seems to be under the ring, is playing stuff from Gene's show. And next to them is Mr. Yawkey, head of the Milwaukee Elks. I remember once writing a poem about him. It ran——"Mr. Yawkey of Milwaukee." It was considered quite comical at the time.

As for my seat, some would think I was to be envied, for it is less than six feet from a corner to be occupied by one of those big he-men and whichever one it is will have to almost brush me aside as he enters the ring. But just the same, it is a hard, uncomfortable seat and as far as space is concerned Tex must have thought the fight was being reported exclusively by midgets' grandchildren. I might even be prevailed upon to trade seats with the gent in the second row of the high priced sections who is right beside Peggy Joyce.[22]

The first preliminary is over. Monte Munn was in it and his victim was a boy from my native state of Michigan who made a mistake coming east. George Godfrey and Bob Lawson, both of whom look as though they had negro blood in their veins, have completed six rounds of a bout that was marred by a lack of race prejudice.

Jack Demave of Hoboken, weighing 186 pounds, has now made a fool out of a big Italian who had a 45-pound advantage in weight and nothing else.

Tommy Loughran has now given Jimmy Delaney a six-round boxing lesson. Tommy has been working out with Dempsey and Delaney's punches felt like prickly heat.

Sergeant Jack Adams took a terrible licking from Harry Pershon, the tattooed countess from Sweden. The sergeant is a good place bet every time he starts. He would have been much better off if the war had never ended.

Now the two big boys are coming on and we will soon know what kind of a winter it is going to be. Mr. Tunney is in my corner. I wish I had his bathrobe. It is my favorite and most becoming shade of blue.

Forty minutes have elapsed since I wrote the last line. There is a new champion of the world and a practically drowned citizen of Great Neck. Poor old Jack got soaked and so did I.

It was only this morning that Dempsey told the papers he would fight like hell. He did. His favorite tune seemed to be. "Oh, How I Miss You Tonight." Maybe he was really a shell, as some of this experts have said. But marines aren't afraid of shells.

Gene may use long words, but he won with monosyllables to the jaw and other features. He has saved Dempsey the trouble of shutting his eyes when he goes to sleep tonight. And it will be a long time before Jack is able to start reading that set of Blackstone

My God, little woman, you will freeze this winter! But maybe we can find something to do at home during the long, cold evenings. Maybe we, like the new champion, can cultivate a taste for books. Anyway, please don't be harsh with me when I return minkless. I am all wet and I wish I had not come.

Best Fight of Tunney's Career
Found Dempsey at His Worst *by Grantland Rice[23]*

NEW YORK HERALD TRIBUNE, SEPTEMBER 25, 1926

As a rule, one answer, if it is correct, is sufficient to solve the ordinary problem. But when it comes to the matter of solving the problem of the recent heavyweight championship battle, wherein Gene Tunney hammered Jack Dempsey's face into a bloody parallelopipedon,[24] there are two answers needed. One answer is that Gene Tunney, with all his conservatism and his lack of flame and flash, is a much better fighter than he has ever received credit for being.

You will find today thousands who knew that Tunney was going to win, and yet about nine-tenths of these were picking Dempsey. Tunney fought the best fight of his career at the most important moments of his ring life.

That is one answer. The other answer is that that no champion ever ret-rograded under fire in such an astonishing manner as Dempsey did.

I have seen Dempsey in all his championship fights, and from being a champion who was at times a great fighter and at other times at least a good fighter, he suddenly dipped into the realm of a third rate, a street corner paluka or mug. Even the elongated Joe Stoessel and the punch drunk Sergeant Adams were willing to make at least some effort to keep their battered features out of the way, where Dempsey, the heavyweight champion of the world, left his features to be hammered, chopped up and smeared without attempting to duck or cover them up.

There is a big difference between being wide open while on the offen-sive and being a stationary target that soaks up every punch thrown in that direction as if in a trance.

Whenever a topheavy favorite in a heavyweight championship match is beaten, there are thousands of people, among them people "in the know," who say that the thing looked "queer." This reporter is not natu-rally suspicious and makes no such allegation, but he does maintain that Dempsey fought a queer fight, for Dempsey.

On a few occasions, very few, he started the bull-like rushes that have wound up in the demolition of his opponents. But on Thursday night, he never once "followed through." He seemed to change his mind sud-denly, to decide to postpone it till later on, though he must have known that later on might be too late. His hesitancy, his uncertainty may have been due to a lack of confidence in his timing, or his ability to go through with what he had started, but this lack of confidence certainly was not visible to the naked eye of experts at Saratoga or Atlantic City.

As one former boxing champion said after the bout, "Why, he only 'threw' fifty punches in the whole ten rounds, and a week ago, in Atlantic City, I saw him 'throw' more than that in two rounds against Tommy Loughran, whom he was not trying to slaughter."

And another thing that Jack must have known (everybody else knew it) was that Tunney had a big lead on points by the end of the seventh round. But was there any grand final rush, any big finish staged in an effort to overcome that lead? Decidedly there was not. In fact, Dempsey was in at least one clinch of his own choosing in the last round of the fight, when there was absolutely no hope for him to win except by landing his haymaker, and you can't land haymakers with both arms entwined around the foe.

Coming back to the matter of his timing, it is very possible—probable, in fact—that a man who was once a wonderfully accurate hitter will lose some of his accuracy by staying a long while out of the game. But can he lose it so completely that he will miss his target by two or three feet, which the former champ did at times Thursday night? There were spells during the argument when his attack actually resembled that of Luis Angel Firpo, than whom there have been few heavyweight contenders who could shoot so wide of the mark.

I saw Dempsey at Saratoga. He wasn't wild then. And there are men whose opinion I respect that have told me he was still a sharpshooter at Atlantic City. It may be that Dempsey suffered a complete nervous collapse, as Stribling evidently did against Paul Berlenbach. Stribling was a clean hitting sharpshooter against Risko, the man who had Berlenbach on the floor. But against Berlenbach he was either a nervous wreck or something approaching the stage.[25]

It may be that our leading boxers are suffering entirely too much from nerves with entirely too much money at stake. They are getting, as a rule, about ten times as much as they deserve. The public and the press together are largely responsible for this. Both are building fake heroes, who are heroes in no sense of the word.

Coming back to the first answer there is no question but that Gene Tunney is a far better fighter than most of the experts have believed him to be. Gene is conservative and Gene is methodical and often plodding. But Gene is also courageous, intelligent and a better boxer and a harder hitter than many know. He isn't a killing hitter, but he is a damaging puncher, a straight, clean jabber, who can hurt and cut.

It might also be noted that Gene can take more than his share of punishment. He is game to the final ounce. The man who knocks Tunney out will have to have him unconscious. He took the few hard punches which Dempsey landed without wavering. And Dempsey landed only a few. He crowded Tunney many times and then suddenly abandoned his offensive at the big moment. Tunney's skill and craft had much to do with this. But also it must be stated that Dempsey's old fire and flame was in the main a smoldering ash that had few sparks.

Don't credit the statement that Dempsey was a hollow shell, a physical wreck. Dempsey, physically, wasn't. He was a young fellow of thirty-one in pretty good condition physically. But in this contest he was certainly a flivver, a bust, a paluka, a mug, a third-rate boxer and a third-rate fighter. He wasn't as good as Johnny Risko on just a fair night. He was far below anything he had ever shown, even taking in those years before he reached the top.

Jack Dempsey took punishment and took a lot of it from a man who wasn't afraid to meet him. And he took a lot of it because he apparently made no effort to keep his features out of the way. He left them in the road when Tunney started either a left jab or a right-hand punch.

For a champion who rose to the heights that Dempsey did at Toledo, he sank to depths that no thirty-one-year-old champion should have known. It would not have been a surprise to see Dempsey outpointed by the cleverer Tunney. But to see him a third-rate flop was another matter.

Part of this flop was due to the fact that Tunney was a vastly improved fighter; and part of it was due to the fact that he had suddenly come back in one night for more than he had ever come back in his training. To see Dempsey beaten was not surprising; to see him a soddy, floundering spectacle, hopelessly incompetent in every angle of boxing and fighting, was something of a jolt.

But the fact remains that Gene Tunney has proved the value of concentration on one thing, coupled with courage and determination and the will to reach a certain goal.

Much had been said before this engagement about Tunney's lack of punching power. Here again the new champion was a surprise. The appearance of Dempsey's face, battered and bruised, was proof enough that Tunney can hit hard. It was the sting of his hooks on Dempsey's jaw that nullified the value of Jack's rushes. Dempsey's strength was weakened with each succeeding smash. While Tunney is not a one-punch crusher, his short, swift blows are relentlessly punishing.

7

The Noble Experiment

It need hardly be said that Prohibition and the hypocrisy surrounding it were made-to-order subjects for Lardner. He included scathing references to it in many of his columns and expounded on the subject at length several times over the years.

In the column "1919" he anticipated some of the effects Prohibition might have on the average man; in "Prohibition Blues" he told of how he happened to write a song that was championed by Nora Bayes, one of the most popular singers of the day; and in several columns he considered the possibilities of how homemade liquor might be used in cooking and medicine.

As for the likelihood of Prohibition being repealed, Lardner noted in "Oh, Shoot!" that there was no need for those opposed to the Eighteenth Amendment to campaign against it because its supporters were so ineffectual that "we should be grateful that they are not enlisted on the side of some more salutary statute such as the one which restricts husband-killers to four kinds of dessert during the week of penal servitude."

1919

CHICAGO TRIBUNE, JULY 13, 1919

> When it's water, water everywhere,
> and not a drop to drink;
> When a guy who's dry can either die
> or patronize the sink,
> How will a wife enjoy a life

of twilight tete-a-tete
With him who used to phone and say:
"I won't be home till late?"

When it's water, water everywhere,
and the grand old Forty club
Gives dinners where the bill of fare is
just a lot of grub,
I wonder if there'll be a stiff with
nerve enough to tell
The story of two Irishmen—say, won't
that bird get h—l!

When it's water, water everywhere
when January first
Wrings many a moan from guys
who've known just one sure cure for thirst,
'Twill be my luck for some rich duck
to croak, with me sole heir,
And nuttin' to drink but water, water
EVERYWHERE!

Prohibition Blues

CHICAGO TRIBUNE, FEBRUARY 18, 1919

New York—Friend Harvey: Well, Harvey, I suppose everybody is wild to hear how I come out with that song[1] that I come down to N.Y. City to sell it. Well, I showed it to a couple of birds and they said it was a Nora Bayes[2] song and she was the only bird that could sing it so the next thing was to meet Nora and that's a cinch like getting invited to the White House for breakfast, but finely we got the mayor and everybody to pull their different wires and I obtained an audience with her for Saturday night after her show was over and the trysting place was back of the stage and honestly when I got up there I was so excited I couldn't do nothing but blush furiously.

Well, Nora was tickled to death to see me like Hindenburg when he got the post card saying Bulgaria had quit their job, but the minute the piano player played the song through she warmed up and how could you help it if you heard the song.

So as soon as she heard it she said, "Mr. Lardner, this song is so good that I would like to rewrite it."

So I said, "Miss Bayes you go ahead."

You see I don't call her Nora except when she is out of earshots.

So then she said, "How about publishing the song? Do you want me to talk to the publishers?"

So I said, "Certainly, yes," because I have already talked to song publishers and I thought it was nice to let her have that sensation once.

So she asked me how much money I wanted out of the publishers and I said fifty-fifty with her, so you see her and I are partners now so that's why I call her Nora when she is out of earshots. Well, Harvey, Nora is going to sing the song, and it will be a scream with her singing it, but I don't know if anybody will buy a copy or not, and if I get any jack out of a song I will be so surprised that I will give it to the Armenians.

But anyway, after we got through talking song she asked me what I thought of the country going dry, so I said I was for it and she said she was not for it, though she didn't care if it went dry or not, but she was afraid that if they began making laws like that they would get the habit and pretty soon they would make a law against divorces and then where would a person go for amusement?

So then she begun to look restless, so I said, "Good-night Miss Bayes," but after I got out of her earshots I said good-night Nora.

So that's what happened about the song, Harvey, and I only wish we could be down here to hear her sing it the first time, but what is our loss is somebody's gain as they say, and besides I am having a grand time and wish you was here. Respy, R. W. L.

Some Recipes with Kicks

BELL SYNDICATE, APRIL 18, 1920

To the Editor:

I don't know how it is where you are at, but where we are at most of the conversation amist the house wifes these days is swapping recipes for things that you don't eat and how much kick there is in this one or that one and how big a per cent of alcohol and etc. Ladys that use to refuse a grape juice high ball because it had the word high ball in it are now wondering what can they put in grape juice to give it a wallop and most of them has quit carrying powder puffs around with them so as to make room in their bag for a cake of yeast.

Before Belgian begun the last war with Europe, the Germans was supposed to be the greatest chemists in the world but if hard study and persistents gets people any place, why pretty near every New Englander of the opposeing sex will soon be wearing a great big registered pharmist badge on their apron.

I can remember back in the old colonial days when women done their own cooking, why they use to be a lot of rivalrys around the different neighborhoods about whether Sallie Adams could bake nicer bread than Amy Madison and etc. And then come a long stretch of yrs when the women couldn't no more understand a cook book than a time table, and when their husbands was hungry, why they stayed down town and eat. But now the prohibition waves has broughten back all the old rivalrys and jealousys only now the argument in old New England is, witch is the best brewer, Sarah Stein or Becky Goldberg?

Well friends since the saloon become the rich man's club I been spending most of my evenings around in different people's houses because they don't seem to be nobody in my own home that has got the brewing instinct. Well I have tried everything that was set in front of me and most of it is what you might call neither here nor there but once in awhile you run acrost a concoction that brings back the old haunting memorys and every time I get a taste at one of these why I kind of call the hostess to one side and get her idears and copy them down and the result is that I have got a hold of a few recipes that's tried and true and I am going to publish them for the benefit of my friends in other parts of the country that still craves stimulant but not at $20 dollars a quart.

Rye Whiskey

Put a pt. of sour milk in a rain bbl. Add the whites of one-half doz. Class C eggs and one order of hashed brown potatoes. Go to Rye Beach and pick up a few beach nuts. Tip the bbl. on its side and roll back and 4th on it like you was drowning. Add the yolk of an olive and a cake of yeast and one raisin. Cook in a slow oven.

Scotch Whiskey

Add the juice of four golf clubs to the yolk of one caddy and pour into a plaid bag. Stand near the bag for several yrs. saying "Hootch mon!" Drop a raisin and a cake of yeast in it. Do the highland fling and blow into the bag with a pair of bagpipes. Put a Harry Lauder record on the phonograph and set it near the bag. Change needles and replace all divots.

Bourbon Whiskey

Add a cake of yeast to one order of corn on the cob and munch it thoroughly.

Beer

Add a cake of yeast to some junior hops. Dip the brush in hot water and moisten the beard thoroughly. Put some shaving cream on the brush and work up a good lather. Pour it into the above. The kick comes from the guys that drink it.

Creme de Menthe

Take the juice of a certain brand of chewing gum and mix it with a cake of yeast. Look for the spear.

Those is the ones friends witch I picked up witch I can guarantee and you can try them or not witch is neutral to me as far as I am concerned, but they have all been tried here in the Yeastern part of the grand old U.S.A. and every one of them is a knockout.

An Ounce of Prevention

BELL SYNDICATE, APRIL 10, 1921

Every once and a wile a military expert comes out and says that if this country had of been prepared for war before we got into it, why the length of the war would of been shortened by a yr. at lease and maybe sooner. Along the same lines students of finance and etc. is always giveing their opinion that we wouldn't of had so many bank failures and loss of money and etc. if people had of had their eyes open and got ready for what was bound to happen after the war.

Well friends I guess they's no question about the value of preparedness whether it's in war or money matters or what not and nobody can doubt the truth of the old sore, "4 warned is 4 armed," and the same thing applys to helth like everything else. So for that reason I am going to run the risk of being wrote down as a kill joy and tell my readers what the experts on helth is saying around here, namely that the coming summer of 1921 will see a record crop of epidemics and sickness in some parts of the U.S. and Canada and the sooner the public wakes up and looks the facts in the face, why it won't be near as bad as if it come like a surprise.

I suppose my readers will laugh at this prophesy and ask have I went crazy and where do I get that stuff and etc. Well friends I am not crazy and I wished I was at liberty to tell you where I got a hold of this information, but sufficient to say that the writer is not one of the kind that make predictions without knowing where they speak of and I would certainly be a fine bum to know what I know and not tell my readers and admires so as they can get ready for the biggest carnival of disease this country has seen since the hoof and mouth escapade.

The last named was a novelty when the cows first sprang it and the comeing epidemic will also introduce 1 or 2 ailments that hasn't never been heard of before which makes them all the harder to fight. Luckily the leading doctors is of the opinion that very few of them will be fatal. But they will take a long time to cure unlest they are tended to in time and for that reason I am going to give a list of a few of them and symptoms of same and the treatmunts which the doctors has worked out.

German Measles

This is a new disease under a old name. The patient breaks out with a thirst in place of a rash. The gen. symptoms is a dry throat and a parch tongue which water don't seem to do no good wile grape juice, birch beer and etc. makes them even sicker. In advance stages the tongue hangs out. Remedy—Aromatic spts. of malt. Dose—1 seidel after every pretzel.

Chronic Drought

Symptoms—The tongue hangs out and they's a sensation of dryness in the throat which water don't seem to do no good. Remedy—Six per cent solution of barley, 1 stein after every pretzel.

Oil of the Liver

Symptoms—The tongue hangs out and the very word water brings on nausea. Remedy—Sweet spts of hops, and eat plenty of liverwurst.

Falling Arches

Symptoms—The tongue hangs out and the patient don't like to dance. Remedy—Sweet spts. of wurzburger to be drunk in a setting posture.

Chronic Hangnail

Symptoms—The tongue and the nail both hang out. Remedy—Sweet spts of pilsener.

Chronic Baldness

Symptoms—The tongue hangs out and the patient can't use a comb. Remedy—Shampoo with the foam and take balance internally.

These is a few of the expected ailments together with remedys for same but patients is advised to get their prescriptions filled at a reliable drug-gist and not try no home made remedys which I know of a case right here on Long Island where an experiment of this kind not only pretty near killed the patient but the rest of the family.

The head of the house had been suffering a long wile with chronic drought and falling arches and beer was prescribed and the Mrs. got a hold of a recipe some place and made a doz. bottles only she has lived all her life on the theory of 2 qts. makes a gallon so she didn't only put in ½ as much water as the recipe called for so one day wile the medicine was parked in the pantry getting seasoned, why we all set down to supper and next thing you know they was a series of terrible explosions and glass flied in every direction and the walls looked like they'd been out all night in a storm and I finely snuck up on the only bottle that hadn't went blooie and opened it up and tasted it and ever since then when I taste quinine I think its ice cream.

So don't try to cure yourself with no home brew because in a little wile the drug stores will be all set to take care of you and I notice that some of them in N.Y. City has all ready changed their names from "Riverside Pharmacy" and etc. to "Jack's Place," and where they use to hang out a big shaveing mug they have stuck up a stein, and most of them has put in swinging doors and curtains and more mirrors and a brass rail in front of the prescription desk and recarpeted the flr. with saw dust, and all of them is advertising for drug clerks named Gus and Eddie.

And I hear that a N.Y. physician named Dr. Dorgan has broke ground right here on Long Island for a Hospital for beer cases only and its right acrost the street from a druggist with a capacity of 10,000 bbls. a day. The Hospital will be named the Palmer House after the best atty. gen. we ever had and the nurses will all wear white aprons and the internes will visit the different wards every midnight and undress all the patients that seems to of been absent minded when they went to bed. A daily suds bath will be part of the treatment.

So much for treatmunt and etc. but they's another old saying that 1 oz. of prevention is worth a pt. of cure so I might say to those of my readers that wants to avoid these diseases, don't take no exercise and don't eat nothing salty. Personly I am beginning to feel kind of sick myself and I am afraid the old trouble is comeing back. Well I always say a man must take the bitter with the sweet in this life and personly I prefer the bitter.

The Benefits of Prohibition

BELL SYNDICATE, JANUARY 20, 1924

To the Editor:

Congressman Volstead of the lowest house yesterday issued a proclamation declaring this Sunday a legal holiday as it is the 4th. or glass wedding anniversary of the date when his act preventing the sale or manufacture of liquor went into such good and lasting effect. Everything will be closed but the saloons.

Some of us is old enough to remember back 4 yrs. ago last New Years eve when the papers all come out and said that the celebration would be the wildest that ever took place in the U.S. as it was in the nature of a farewell to hootch which by next New Years eve, meaning Dec. 31, 1920, would be a thing of the past. The boys that made this prediction was as near right as Bernard Shaw on pugilism. Three weeks ago Monday was New Years eve 1923 and I gather from hearsay that never before in history was they more and better people that had to be poured home.

I can also remember disgusting the prohibition question in the privacy of the household and I made the remark that wile I might not approve of the proposition on principle, still and all I was glad it had went through on one acct. at lease, namely that by the time my boys growed up to college age they wouldn't be no chance for them to run wild as they wouldn't be nothing left to run wild on. This was another great prediction and judging by the increasing numbers of rah rah boys that staggers to classes, why in 6 or 7 yrs. when the first of my kiddies is ready to die for old Rutgers why they won't no football player think of going into a big game without a qt. on the hip.

It seems like about the biggest difference between now and 5 or 6 yrs. ago in big cities at lease is that in them days most cities had a law that you must close your saloon at 11 o'clock or 12 o'clock or 1 o'clock. Now days according to the law, they ain't no saloons so they can and do stay open as long as they feel like. In this connection however I might relate a little incidence that come off near where I live and they was a couple of boys going home from a dance at their golf club and they stopped in at a roadhouse just as the prop. of the same was turning out the lights and the door was locked but they knocked and a waiter left them come in and they said they would like a drink.

"He won't leave me serve you nothin," says the waiter referring to the prop.

Well the 2 boys hadn't never been in there before so they thought it was on acct. of the prop. not knowing them as they begin mentioning a lot of names of people that was regular customers of the place and had recommended it to them,

"Oh that is all right," says the waiter. "You gents looks all right, but he won't leave me serve you because it is 10 minutes after 1 o'clock."

"What has that got to do with it?" says one of the thirsty ones. "Under the Volstead act its just as much vs. the law to sell drinks one time as another time."

"That may all be," says the waiter, "but the boss doesn't know they is a Volstead act. He has been stone deaf for 10 yrs,"

The pastime of raiding is conducted on a whole lot more sensible lines now than in the old days. When the law allowed saloons but said they must close up at some certain time of night, why every little wile you would read in the paper where So and So bad been raided the night before and him and all his help arrested just because they had been surprised at 3 a.m. with their bar open.

Compare this proceedings with the way things is handled under absolute prohibition. Like for inst. I was in a certain town in Jersey a wile ago and was setting in a cafe talking to the mgr. of same and all of a sudden a man come in and come to our table and whispered something to the mgr. and went right out again and then the mgr. called the head bartender and told him to take all the hard stuff upstairs and put it in the rm. under the roof and be sure and have this done by 8 o'clock and leave it there till 8:30.

Well I asked the mgr. what was the idear and he says that the man had broughten him word that the federal officers was on a raiding party and his place was scheduled for 8 o'clock. He says that the man who had just been in and warned him was employed by all the places in the town to do just that thing, and he was now making his rounds telling the mgr. of each place just what time the raiders would call at that particular place.

"We only been caught once," says the mgr. "On that occasion the enforcement boys dropped in on us without sending advance word or nothing and of course they found all kinds of stuff in the bar. It was a raw deal and we certainly told them what we thought of that kind of monkey business and they ain't never tried it since."

All and all it is no wonder that the congressman felt like the holiday should ought to be proclaimed as prohibition has sure been a godsend in a whole lot of ways. It has given lucrative employment to a great many men that did not have nothing before only their courage. It has cemented the friendship between the U.S. and Canada. It has give gals and women a new interest in life and something to talk about besides hair and children. And it has made our govt. appreciate the enormous extent of our coast line and how tough it would be to defend same vs. invasion.

As far as it affecting the present and future consumption of alcohol is concerned, why a person that said that drinking in the U.S. was still in its infancy would be just about hitting the nail on the hammer.

Oh, Shoot!

COLLIER'S, AUGUST 10, 1929

When it was suggested that I write something about prohibition, I snapped at the idea as a starving dog goes after a deck of cards. Here was a subject that had escaped the attention of other members of the writing graft, and you don't have to be so skillful in the handling of a given theme if the theme itself is sufficiently novel.

I thought I could tear off two or three thousand words almost as fast as I could type. I forgot that even a mental contact with the Demon or anything pertaining to same always filled me with an almost overwhelming desire to abstain from work for a period of thirty-four days. So the composition of this article has been a tough job and not a siesta, and I ask my friends to bear that in mind while they are thinking what a tough job it is to read it.

I do not believe I am betraying a confidence when I say that there are, in this country, several organizations whose aim is to effect the modification or repeal of the Eighteenth Amendment.

Nearly every citizen who isn't living under an assumed name has received invitations to join one or more of these tongs. If I have been asked once, I have been asked twice. But I have consistently declined to go into them because I figure it is silly to interfere in any way with the efforts of the Drys to knock their own pet legislation for a nose dive. If they fail, it will be time for outsiders to step in.

But they won't fail. They are experienced Gummers and we should be grateful that they are not enlisted on the side of some more salutary statute such as the one which restricts husband-killers to four kinds of dessert during the week of penal servitude.

The Drys of our land are to a large extent identical with the people who have fought the good fight for purity and decency in books and plays. If their war on rum is conducted only half as shrewdly as the struggle against literary and dramatic dirt, we boy scouts need have no fear. You can hardly name one legitimate show of the past season that could possibly give offense to any 125-year-old paralytic who was unable to attend it, and parents are safe in leaving a volume of Milne or Guest on the living-room table, while the children are away at kindergarten.

With a modicum of the same energy and skill applied to the anti-alcohol campaign, the Pros will soon have it fixed so a person can't buy a drink from a horse. It were folly for an amateur to offer advice to these needle-witted strategists, but it does seem to me that if the idea is to stop tippling by homicide, bigger results could be obtained, and at less expense, through the withdrawal of artillery and snipers from the border and the free and untrammeled admittance of all the stuff the consumer wants.

The price of what is screamingly called liquor would shortly drop to a point where even actors could afford it and the consequent fatalities would outnumber those resulting from the present system by at least a hundred to one.

Moreover, this sort of war of attrition would be carried on at little or no cost to the government; the customers would have to pay for their own demise unless they died before they settled, in which case the laugh would be on the bootlegger where it belongs.

But even if the current scheme is adhered to, I believe it should be carried out with more thoroughness and zeal.

In the first place it should be under the auspices of the War Department instead of the Secretary of the Treasury. Revolvers, shotguns, small-bore rifles and pea-shooters ought to be supplanted by long-range cannon, and bullets that can kill only one man or child at a time, replaced by high explosives, shrapnel and all the latest delicacies in the way of gas.

Electrically charged wire should guard the Canadian border from ocean to ocean and the Mexican border from the Pacific to the Gulf. Scout planes and observation balloons should locate Canada's distilleries and direct our shell fire, and the fields of hay from which the liquor is made could be destroyed by poisoned confetti.

The entire eastern half of the Dominion to the north of us might be inundated by a company of volunteers under Capt. Gertrude Ederle,[3] who would stand at the bottom of Niagara Falls and splash the water back as fast as it came over. Our aces could drop souvenir post cards from George Creel[4] assuring the Canadians that we have no quarrel with them as a nation, that all we want is peace without whisky, and that this is merely a war to make the United States safe for the soda fountains. An armistice would be granted, we'd tell them, as soon as they pledged themselves to eliminate entirely the alcoholic content of the stuff they have been selling to our importers. This would mean a reduction of nearly two per cent.

Some of the war-time regulations should be in effect once more. No meat on Mondays; no heat on Tuesdays; no sweet on Wednesdays; no wheat on Thursdays; no treat on Fridays, and no eat on Saturdays. Censorship of all mail passing between us and Canada and Mexico; four-minute speeches; adoption of Belgian orphans; purling; saving fingernail parings to fill in the shell holes on the Texas and the Minnesota thoroughfares.

I do think, though, that this war should be made much more bearable and entertaining to the stay-at-homes by the adoption of a liberal policy in regard to press dispatches. I never did understand what good was accomplished by the exclusion of the names of people and places from the dull, daily stories from France in 1917 and 1918.

The theory seemed to be that if the Grand Rapids Herald printed the news that Hendrik Van Hooten of Holland, Michigan, was in hospital at Chalons-sur-Marne with anthrax, a German spy employed by the Grand Rapids Furniture Company would call up the Kaiser who would thus suspect that a division containing Michigan regiments was, or had been, somewhere near Chalons. Wilhelm would then confer with Ludendorff on what style of defense to use against Michigan's passing game with Van Hooten on the sidelines.

Let's cut down on caution this time; the danger of disclosing military secrets would be more than offset by the certainty of improving the country's morale with a few human-interest stories such as:

El Paso, Tex. Aug 2—Corporal Charley Judson of Company B, Fourth Regiment of the Eighth (Hawk-eye) Division, American Prohibitionary Force, was being congratulated by his buddies tonight for shooting the left ear off a two-year-old child who was crossing the bridge from Juarez with a peculiar waddling gait. Corporal Judson said he had witnesses to prove that the fellow had been seen drinking out of a bottle; he fired at his ear instead of his heart because he just wanted to frighten him. The bottle was found to contain a little over an ounce of a liquid identified as milk. "Yeh?" said the Corporal, who has a certain dry humor. "Well, milk don't make people walk funny."

Sault St. Marie, Mich., Aug. 2—Miss Muriel Chapin of this place was scattered all over the Northern Peninsula today by a machine-gun squad in charge of Capt. Felix Lord of Houghton. The captain picked up one of the girl's lips and showed it to his colonel, H. R. King of Calumet. The lip was a pale red. "That's what fooled me," said Captain Lord. "It's just some kind of rouge, but I thought it was grenadine."

Niagara Falls, N.Y. Aug. 2—A depth bomb dropped by Lieut. Ed. Frawley of Herkimer demolished a barrel that was seen shooting the Falls late today. Frawley suspected that the barrel was full of liquor, but it developed that the contents had been John E. Gardner and wife and two children, a Buffalo family out for an outing. "This was self-defense if there ever was one!" declared Lieut. Frawley. "I acted only after assuring myself that the barrel was shooting the Falls."

Plattsburg, N.Y., Aug. 2—A bearded man on a bicycle was stopped here today by Clarence Dutton, an M.P. of the A. P. F. Dutton demanded the man's name and the man said he was Eli Kolp, a farmer residing three miles south of Plattsburg.

"Then why are you wearing a beard?" asked Dutton.

"I look funny without one," replied the bicyclist.

"You look funny with one," retorted Dutton. "You look suspicious to me. How do I know what you've got in those tires?"

"I've got nothing but some air. I'll open them and let it out."

"I'll let some into you," said Dutton, shooting him full of holes.

The bicyclist was later identified as Eli Kolp, a farmer residing three miles south of Plattsburg.

8

The America's Cup and Other Sports

In the summer of 1920 the America's Cup yacht races were held in New York Harbor, as Sir Thomas Lipton of Scotland, who created the brand of tea that bears his name, challenged for the fourth time, sending his *Shamrock IV* against the New York Yacht Club's *Resolute*, which was trying to defend its title. After being disabled in the first race and losing the second, *Resolute* swept the final three races to continue the club's perfect record of Cup defenses. Though Lardner said he was bored to death covering the event, and that he despised the early-morning sailings on the boat carrying the press corps, he clearly had a fine time spoofing the arcane terminology of sailing.

From time to time over the years he also aired his feelings about other sports—including polo, hockey, dog racing, and deep sea fishing—and occasionally wrote about bridge and poker, games he often played with his friends. But he didn't cover any other sporting events for the Bell Syndicate, and that is a shame. It is curious, for instance, that Lardner wrote so little about horse racing, which, along with baseball, college football, and boxing, was one of the most popular sports of the day. Grantland Rice and his other friends who wrote sports columns regularly attended big horse races, often at the Jamaica and Belmont race tracks, which were not far from Lardner's Long Island home.

Lardner did occasionally write about his frequent trips to the track, if only so he could joke about his losing bets. A section of *Big Town,* one of his most highly regarded short stories, shows he had a real feel for the sport. But "A Perfect Day at Saratoga" may have been written only because Dempsey was nearby, in training for his fight with Firpo, while an account of the opening of a new race track at Hialeah in 1925 was a product of one of his winter trips to Florida. At the latter, he bet $10 on a horse named Socket in the first race and wrote, "This horse run so much like the train I had just been riding on that I begun feeling around in my pockets for a dime to tip the porter."

Lardner also ignored championship golf, which was coming into its own as a popular spectator sport in the 1920s, when such great players as Bobby Jones, Walter Hagen, Gene Sarazen, Francis Ouimet, and Chick Evans were in their prime. He often wrote about his own game—not to mention such fanciful articles as "Lardner Reviews His Golf Season" and "Learn to Play Lip Golf"—but he never covered the U.S. Open or U.S. Amateur national championships, even when they were played near his home on Long Island or in New England.

The one exception is "Bobby or Bust," which he wrote for Collier's in 1929. Noting Jones's humiliating elimination by the unknown Johnny Goodman in the first round of the U.S. Amateur championship that year, Lardner wrote, "If you're giving a show, don't kill the star in the prologue."

Ring Can't Stand the Excitement of Yacht Racing

BELL SYNDICATE, JULY 16, 1920

New York—The first heat went to the Shamrock, but there's many a slip-ton between the cup and the lipton. I don't know if that gags been used before, but it's my own idea.

As I couldn't stand the excitement of continually watching the 2 cat boats as they sped forwards in the teeth of a 3-mile calm I happened to be down in lieut. Annotyn's room when the Resolute done a willard. Word was rushed in that the rest of the race would be a monologue as the Resolute's sails had flopped and I couldn't help from feeling sorry for her as I went to a evening dress suit dance one night and broke a suspender. I went out on the porch and asked one of the Newspaper Boys how it could of happened and he said she had broke a gaff. You know how a woman feels these days when she breaks a gaff at the present price of gaffs. But anyway

I went and seen Captain Newton of our destroyer that use to play football at the navy in Annapolis, and made all American but treated us fine and he said he didn't think it was a broken gaff but thought it was a broken throat halyard, and maybe she had died of tonsilitis. Well I would of been satisfied with the broken throat diagnosis only Lieut. Comm. Dowes said he thought it was a combination of broken gaff jaw and a busted spinnaker.

Personly I come to the conclusions that imight as well use my own judgments as I once rowed a rowboat out on Lake Michigan. So I borrowed a pair of opera glasses off of a bum cartoonist and took a look at the irresolute and it looked to me like she had croaked from a barnacle on her binnacle, whatever it was. The boys on board of her all but perspired trying not to fix it She was toed to a marine hospital and now they say that the second leg will be run off Saturday if she can stand the gaff.

Maybe some of you boys has never seen an international yacht race so I will try and tell you a few of our experiences. In the first place we had to get up in the middle of the night so as we could be down to the battery in time to catch the press boats which was to leave at 8 a.m. but didn't. On the way down I borrowed a paper off a guy and read about the coming event so as I would know what was going on and it said in the article the race might not maybe very good as both boats needed more time to tune up. You see the race was sprang on them kind of suddenly as they didn't know it was coming off till way back in 1913. It was also said the Resolute would have a time allowance of seven minutes and one second on account of the difference in time between here and Belfast where the Shamrock grows and the river Shannon flows.

Speaking about Shamrocks I always thought they was supposed to be three leaves, but what old Tom had yesterday was a four-leaf clover. Well along about half-past eight we fell into a tug and was dragged out to the middle of the river where two destroyers was waiting for us, though some of the boys looked like they had been destroyed the night before. Out there they separated the goats from the sheep, putting us guys on the destroyer Semmes, wile the sheep, namely, the P.M. newspaper men, was herded onto the Goldberg. On the way to the race track was past J. P. Morgan's dinghy, the Corsair, but he didn't see me.

Somebody asked a lieut. on our destroyer if the Semmes was a steady ship and he says she was the best little rocker in the U.S. Navy. Several of use forced a smile. We reached the paddock along about 10 o'clock and the 2 yawls was already there warming up. The Shamrock was painted green for some reason another. We set there on the porch rocking till noon, which was starting time. By that time the grounds was really too wet to play on, but they started the game anyways, and the 2 scows got away to a pretty even start. They hadn't went very far however when it began to rain, but Klem wouldn't stop the game.

I will let the experts tell you about the technical side of it as all as I found out was that on one occasion the Irish sloop was going at a speed of 7 nuts per nautical mile when the other slop was doing a little better. Personly I wished we was at a 6-day bicycle race where you get about the same thrills only you don't half to set in a rocker. Saturday if the jaws and throat halyards and gaffs is all fixed up, I will go out and see the next leg and that night I will go to the follies and see a whole lot more of them. As for old Tom's victory, I say why not leave him have the cup as he has got tea to pour into it, and what have we got? Nothing.

Yachts Sail Like a Snail with Paralysis

BELL SYNDICATE, JULY 18, 1920

New York—In the evening by the moonlight you could hear those experts wondering who had won. The Resolute was five miles ahead, but that don't mean nothing on acct. of the time allowance. Whatever you see wrote by the experts, don't believe it. A little thing like a five-mile lead combined with a handicap of six minutes and some seconds is no proof that the defender has beat the challenger or vice versa, and personly I don't know which is which.

As me and my destroyer go to press the vote stands 546 electoral votes for Resie and 46 votes for Shimmy. But the complete returns from Ohio and California are still uncomplete. The latest returns was as follows:

California—456 precincts out of 604 gives the Resolute 4,517 and the Shamrock 2,809.

Ohio—516 precincts out of 607 gives Shamrock 4,517 and the
    Resolute 2,809.
Governor Hughes has evidently won Nevada.

At latest reports it looks like each sloop had lost a leg in the race, but
I have seen one-legged men go faster than them two cat boats and don't
think for a minute that Tuesday's race will be slowed up by the loss of a
leg apiece. You couldn't slow these birds up any more than you could slow
up a detective on the Elwell case.[1] They're stopped before they start.

Somebody must of shot a albatross between Thursday and Saturday
noon. Anyway, when it was time for the two fishing smacks to make their
get-away, the sea and wind was both in what they call a dead calm, which
just about agrees with my sentiments in regards to this here race. If they
want the fans to go out there and see them again next Tuesday, they better put on a double header for one admission.

At high noon the wind was blowing a two-inch gale backwards and
neither scow would move, so the starter postponed it till along come a
breathe of fresh air, which was a ¼ to 2. Then away went the 2 slops like
a snail with paralysis.

"It's a long sleepy swell," said the captain of the destroyer on which
we was on.

"'Dont get personal," I said. "If you had to get up at 5 o'clock in the
morning to see race that dont start till 1.45 in the p.m. and when its started
you dont know if its started or hasnt started you would be a long sleepy
swell too, provided you was long and sleepy and a swell."

"Shamrock's got the advantage today," said the captain after a wile,
"'theys 3 legs in the stead of 2 and the first leg is a beat wile the other 2
is reaches and Shamrock is supposed to be good on reaches."

"That's all right," I said, "but I was down to Toledo last 4 of July a year
ago and by the time Dempsey got in the first beat, Willard's reaches didn't
do him no good."

So the captain asked me what happened to Willard down there. "Well,"
I said, "it looked to me like his throat halyard parted at the winch and his
gaff busted all to pieces."

Finally I asked the captain why he did not challenge for the cup as his destroyer could go along at a speed of 35 knots per hour as against nothing per hour for the 2 slopes that was out there supposed to be racing.

"Listen," he said, "you under estimate the speed of my ship. It didnt only take us 2 hours to get out here this morning with 150 nuts to say nothing about cartoonists."

One of the common reporters come along about this time and announced that tea Lipton had 2 belated guests on the board of his yacht the Victoria. The guests was Dewar and Garret both of which is in the same business on the other side.

As far as we are concerned, they may as well of stayed on the other side, though they might have been more friendly if they had of known that we boys throat halyards was parted at the winch.

They was a few squalls on this occasion but they was a whole lot of squawks from the birds that payed 25 seeds each to come out on the steamer Orizaba in the hopes that they would be something to look at besides the race as the rumor has been spread about that old Ori had something on the hip last Thursday. But she had spent the interims in dry dock and was still in the same conditions when she started out for the battle ground today. Good by forever 25 seeds.

The morning papers announce that if the wind was to leewards instead of windwards why one of the legs of the race could be easily observed from the New Jersey coast so that the famous shore was thronged with gents and womens with picnic lunches and etc which shows that theys more kinds of bugs than mosquiters over on the Jersey, Jersey, Jersey, over on the Jersey side.

The Closest Race We've Slept Through Yet

BELL SYNDICATE, JULY 22, 1920

New York—They say that Wednesday's race was the closest that we have slept through yet.

About 4 something o'clock on the starboard tack (daylight saving time) somebody came into Lieutenant Annato's room which I have nick-named my room on this destroyer and said the 2 flat bottom fishing smacks was finishing right close together and it was going to be a pretty finish and didn't I want to see it. So I told the bird to go out and look at it in my behalf and come back and report. So I went back to sleep and pretty soon old faithful come back and said that the Resolute had crossed the line 19 seconds behind the Shamrock, which, in other words, means that the Shamrock lost the race. In races like these the boat that finishes ahead, loses. This is according to the rules under which the international yacht races is sailed. The rules was made up by a cuckoo that fell and lit on his head wile a child.

At the end of the perfect day the Shamrock hoisted a flag with the word "D" on it and I had to ask what that meant and they said it meant they won't be no race Thursday. I don't know what the other 25 letters in the alphabet means in nautical terms but anyway it looks now like the 2 scows would keep on racing every other week. And they will probably be close to a decision by the time the 2 Philadelphia ball clubs meets for the world's series. The only difference between an international yacht race and a world series is that in a world series the team that is behind when the game's over, loses.

The boys from the U.S. Navy give us a treat this time. Instead of making us go down to the Battery to catch a hold of the destroyer, they had us come up to 96th Street, which is a garbage dock. At a quarter to nine the garbage and other newspaper men was loaded on to a tug that took us out to the Semmes, one of Josephus's dryest boats. There was a race for the beds and I got one.

The yacht race was scheduled to start at noon, so they started at 1 o'clock. I had boughten myself a set of binoculars and therefore couldnt see the start of the race and can't tell you which slop got away first. But it don't matter on account of the difference in time between here and London. The first leg of the race was to windwards and both horses pointed high. After they had gone a furlong it was seen that the Shamrock was listing to port, whereas the Resolute seemed to lean toward sherry. At the half mile mark the Resolute took down her club sandwich and substituted a bicuspid. The Shamrock reefed in the throat halyard and set up a free lunch.

Both catfish looked at this time like they was afraid they would get somewheres. At this point Captain Norton of our destroyer said I might as well go back to sleep so, as I said above, the race wound up several hours later with the Shamrock ahead and the Resolute winner. Captain Burton and Captain Adams was about equal in strategy as both of them dropped the definite article off their ships' names during the lunch hour. The race was 30 miles, like they all are, and so I don't want to criticize Sir Thomas or whoever is running the American end of it. But you can get up to Yonkers and back on the subway in 1/8 of the time it takes to sail the same distance in one of these here yachts and it don't make no difference if the wind is blowing or not. The next race will probably be sailed on Friday and us boys can hardly wait.

The Race Is Between a Snail and a Hearse

BELL SYNDICATE, JULY 24, 1920

New York—This would be a very enjoyable event if they would keep the 2 sloops out of it. The way they have got things fixed now a person has to get up every little while and go up on the porch and look at the 2 contenders, which between you and I, can't neither of them go fast enough to get up a perspiration. The only people that is sweating on this assignment is the newspaper boys and speaking about them, I wished you could of seen the bunch that was on board of our destroyer Friday. Of course a person can't say that they was a lot of strange faces, because the reporters themselves has all got that kind, but these was birds that we never seen before and I asked somebody who they was, and they said they was advertising managers from Gimbels and Macys and etc., and I don't know what they was doing out there, but if thats their idear of a perfect day, they are welcome. Personally, I would of had rather stay in the store.

Friday's race was 'nother 3-legged affair, 1 leg vs. the kind which they call a beat and the other 2 retches. The beat was about an even break, but when it come to the 2 retches the Shamrock was a whole lot the most retched.

If Sir Thomas will take suggestion from a bird that knows nothing about yachts and cares a whole lot more, why if I was him I would take down my club jib and put in a gasoline engine which they say you can get pretty reasonable if you go to the right place. In this race whoever was skipping the Shamrock kept changing sails and the more they changed the slower they went. I wouldn't be surprised to find out that the Shamrock had a bet on the Resolute.

Now I don't want to criticize the U.S. Navy, but I can't help from saying that the officers' sleeping quarters is not adequate. For instants, its getting so now that the officers themselves wants to take a nap once in a while and half to lay down on the deck because their own beds is occupied by reporters. Why, Friday, for example, I was having my siesta in Lieut. Annato's room and all of a sudden who should loom up in the doorway but the Lieut. himself and looked kind of drowsy and I felt kind of embarrassed on account of being in his room and his berth where he wanted to be, but if I had of had to get up it would of meant going up on the porch and looking at the 2 catfish that was out there trying not to get anywheres, so I pretended like I was sound asleep and the Lieut. had to go out and find a soft place on the deck as I have nick named the porch.

The officials' story of the race may be told in the following words by one who did not see it: It started at 1 o'clock because starting time was high noon and they got away about even with neither slop making any headway. In fact, they both looked like they was in reverse. I don't know if they have emergency brakes on yachts or no, but if they have they was certainly both using them. In about 2 hours they rounded the first stake and the boats that was watching give a resounding cheer on their sirens.

Speaking about the boats that was watching them, the attendance is getting so good that if they keep on a few more days you will have to have a set of binoculars to find the spectators.

Well, Resolute was ahead at the first stake and the second stake and the last stake and it looks now like the defender had a even chance of winning, but personally I say its a race between a hearse and a snail and may the slowest team win.

Too Slow to Give a Kick

BELL SYNDICATE, JULY 28, 1920

New York—As far as us boys are concerned the Shamrock and the Resolute can have our riparian rights to Sandy Hook and environs.

In the first place if the Shamrock was as good as old Tom claims it is, why and the he—ll don't he ride on it instead of on his steam yacht. It looks fishy to me.

At 11:45 yesterday the Shamrock hoisted the signal "V" which means in the nautical language "that they's too much salt in the water for a race today."The Resolute countered with the signal "M," the significance of which is "that they's too much sugar in Mr. Lipton's tea." But as Grantland Rice says, "Mr. Lipton's last off the tea, last on the green." What could be sweeter?

Speaking of green, nobody knew why Old Tom had his sloop painted green till the race was over. Then it was rumored that the color matched his skipper and speaking of skippers, nobody knew why they called them skippers till everybody found out that it was because they skipped so many days when they might be sailing. Dont leave nobody forget that the Shamrock had a handicap of six minutes and forty seconds on account of her sail acreage or something.

Its just like putting Dempsey into the ring with Carpentier and saying to the last named, "Now look here, Georges, vous must keep both votre hands behind votre back and extend the chin in a prominent place in the foreground," which means in the England language:

"George, keep your hands behind your back and your chin up front where he can get a crack at it."

Well boys the library of the destroyer Semms was exhausted yesterday and if the race had of went one more day we boys wouldn't of knew what to read to go to sleep and probably would of had to take a sedative of some kind. All they left was a Zane Grey novel and Damon Runyon was hanging to that like it was an all day sucker.

Technically, when the race started both scows went on the carpet tack and the consensus at the finish was that the Philadelphia athletics could of beat either for the title, which is an awful thing to say about the two slips. But if you could of seen them for the last two days, you wouldn't say that anything was good enough to say about them.

One of the officers on the board of our destroyer said he wished we had left 2 subs in the German navy so they could rise up and smite both these catboats and put them out of their Missouri. Personally, when the race was over, all too soon, us reporters went to the ship hospital and had our throat halyards taken out. 'They's no use of monkeying with a disease like that.

Lipton made five challenges for the America's Cup and lost them all. Lardner may have been pleased to know the competition was not held in New York harbor for nearly one hundred years.

Learn to Play Lip Golf

BELL SYNDICATE, DECEMBER 5, 1920

To the Editor:

It takes all kind of golf players to make a world in the good old summer time, but along about this time of yr. they's only 2 classes you might say, namely haply marred men and guys that can afford to go south. The 1st. named has got a big advantage in many ways. For inst. they don't half to spend from 1 night to a wk. in one of them new fangle Pullmans witch some people jokeingly calls a sleeping car. I could go on and name a whole lot of other advantages witch a marred man has got if they was any.

On the other hand, the bachelors goes south in the winter and can golf all the yr. around and are right on their game when the season opens up north whereas the men with baggage has got to begin all over again every May, and it generally always takes them till the 1 of Nov. to find out what is the matter with their game. Besides witch the bachelors either don't have no job or at lease they can quit whenever they find out it's interfering with their regular business, wile a haply marred man has got to park his nose vs. the grind organ at all seasons of the yr. and even in the summer time life with him can't be 1 long round of 36 holes. Like for example take the case of myself witch I hate to talk on that subject though many of my admirers is always makeing the crack that they wished they knowed more about me personally and they are sick and tired of haveing me keep my private life and insides to myself like Mary MacLane² or somebody.

Well, anyway, last spring I hadn't no more than mastered the nack of getting off of the 1st. tee in 2 when they was a nation wide clamor for a good reporter to write up the big subjects of the day and I had to spend most of the summer in the rough, namely, the Republican convention in old Chi and the one out in San Francisco where they pulled the joke on Cox, and last and most roughest, the races off Sandy Hook between the 2 stationary wash tubs.

Dureing the last named I broke a gaff and had a halyard removed from my boom and was just comeing out from the ether when they sent me to the world serious and I come down with Brooklyn.

The net results was that I didn't realy start to begin to commence my golf till the central part of Oct. and couldn't make out what ailed my game till 2 wks. ago when one of the boys told me I was sticking out my tongue when I swang and a person couldn't of never fell into a quaint habit like that if they had of played winter and summer both, and it don't seem fair that a man like I that has got a wife and kiddies to support should ought to be asked to compete on even turns with some old roue that don't take his golf shoes off from 1 yrs. end to another except to look for a lost ball in a water hazard.

My brother marred men will say yes, but what are going to do about it? Well, gents, I don't know what you are going to do about it, but personally I have got up a game witch I have named lip golf, and I have tried it out with grand success and wile it don't give a man no physical exercise, why it keeps their mind on golf and don't allow them to forget it dureing the off season and when they start playing again in the spring they have at lease got the language at their tongues and don't half to waste 7 or 8 wks. mastering the verbage all over again and it can be played in the house any time of day or night and in all kinds of weather.

The rules of lip golf is the following rules. No matter what remarks the wife makes, the husband's replys is to be give in golf parlance. That's all they is to the rules and anybody can learn it in one lesson and the best time to try it out is at a meal. For inst. suppose the kiddies has been tucked away for the night in the waste basket and you and the wife has set down to dinner. Your part of the folling conversation would be what you might call par lip golf.

Wife—What train did you come out on?

Husband—I missed the first two but got home on my third.

Wife—This is a fine bouillon cup Carrie give me, both handles broke.

Husband—Use your spoon.

Wife—We caught a mouse this p.m.

Husband—Did he get into a trap?

Wife—No. Carrie killed him with a broom.

Husband—That's a good Carrie.

Wife—I'm going to get rid of her, though. I'll tell her I've decided to do my own work.

Husband—A fine lie!

Wife—Well, then, I'll say we can't afford to pay $80.

Husband—That's the fair way.

Wife—Will you have some more bread?

Husband—I can't get rid of this slice.

Wife—No more potatos or nothing?

Husband—How is the greens?

Wife—All gone. I'm sorry. Did you have much lunch?

Husband—I had a couple of good rolls.

Wife—We must hire a new chauffeur. Gus don't never clean the car.

Husband—Can't drive, neither.

Wife—The garage man says he can get us a good one.

Husband (pretending he has a cold)—Caddy?

Wife—Yes, you better see him.

Husband—I hooked one today.

Wife—Oh, you did! Who?

Husband—Hazzard.

Wife—The Bucks' driver? But I thought they paid him $25 a wk.

Husband—I topped it.

Wife—But we can't afford it.

Husband—Why not?

Wife—You can't always win at poker. By the way, how much does the boys owe you from last night?

Husband—Spalding 50, Victor 75 and the Colonel 31.

Wife—I bet Victor didn't dast tell his wife. She's a terrible loser. You and her would make a good team. You ought to know her.

Husband—Ouimet.

Wife—Oh, that's right. Say. what do you think of them salad forks Ma sent?

Husband—Stirling?

Wife—Certainly. They cost $30 a dozen.

Husband—Evans!

Wife—I suppose if I am going to can Carrie I should ought to give her notice. But I'm afraid she would get mad and quit before I could find somebody else.

Husband—Locker room.

Wife—You must run upstairs and change your close. We only got 15 minutes.

Husband—I'll be down in 7.

This is a sample of par lip golf and if the wife knows the game why so much the better as she can make it a 2 some. If she don't, why she will probly think you have went cuckoo and sew you for a bill of divorce. In that case you are as good as a bachelor. But give it a trial any way, Brother, and if your game is anywheres near like mine why at lease you can't do it no harm.

Ring Reviews His Golf Season

AMERICAN GOLFER, DECEMBER 17, 1921

To the Editor:

Well, the golf season is over as far as I am conserned as I am not one of these here red blooded he-men that revels in God's great outdoors with the wind blowing a mile a minute through your whiskers so anyway I am through till next Spring unless some sucker invites me to their country home in Florida R.R. fare inclusive, and it occurs to me that maybe some of my friends would like to read a kind of a resume of my 1921 golf which I don't claim to of broke no course records but it would make your eyes pop out to look over the list of who I have played with and practically all

of them a celebrity of some kind and yet I am just as common and democratic as if they was so much scumb.

Well, I was going to write down a list of the famous players that was
either my oppt. or partner during the season but it looks to me like we
would save time by naming those that wasn't, namely Lloyd-George,
Ambassador Harvey and Eugene V. Debs. I can't think of nobody else in
the Who's Who book who I didn't either play golf with them or it was
their own fault as I could always be reached by phone.

Of all the games I played they's a few that stands out in memory and
of course the most important from a political standpoint was the time I
and Grantland Rice played vs. President Harding and Secretary Fletcher
and we would of beat them a whole lot worse if I had missed the train,
but neither that game or my match with Geo. Carpentier which was played
entirely in French will live as long in memory's walls as some of the contests which I took part in with luminaries of the world of art and letters
to say nothing about the realms of the drama like for inst. my famous
match with Miss Florence Moore the comical actress and a member of
my home club.

This match come off at Great Neck in the early part of last month and
they wasn't a soul knowed it was coming off 5 minutes before it begin,
but by the time we got to the 5th hole we was followed by a gallery of men
and women of all sexes that cheered themselves hoarse hollering fore.

This match was sprang on me as a big surprise as I was in the caddy
house trying to borrow a midiron as I had broke mine scolding one of the
kiddies and anyways Miss Moore come in to borrow a ball at the same
time and she asked me would I play with another lady and she, and I says,
"Yes," and away we went and I win the 1st hole with a birdie 8 but after
that I kind of held back as it was all in fun.

Well they ain't space to give the full details of the match but sufficient
to say that Miss Moore and the other lady broke double figures twice and
when we come to the 9th hole Miss Moore was 1 up but the other lady
squared the match by sinking a long putt for a 15 and they wasn't no extra
hole played as Miss Moore's show starts at 8:30 P.M. The 9th hole is about
100 yds. and it use to be straight up a hill and you had to play it with a niblick, but us 3 fixed it so as you wouldn't hardly know they had been a hill.

One of the most exciting holes on the round was the 5th where Miss

Moore got on the green for a wile with her 7th and laid her 1st putt 90 yds. from the cup and then got back on the green with a driving iron and laid about ½ a ft. from the cup and her next putt hit the pin and broke it in two. On the 7th she sunk her putt for a 20 which is known as a double eagle. The ladies' total for the round was 116 and 120 respy. and would of been even lower on a clear day but 8 of the 9 holes was played in a divot storm.

I played a couple of times with Irving Cobb and one time the two of us was in a tournament together and finished a tie for the low net prize and they divided the 1st 2 prizes between us and they give Irving 1st choice and one of the prizes was a silver flask so I got a driver that was made for Mrs. Tom Thumb but I suppose a man should ought to be satisfied that can tie anybody's score that takes 1-3 off.

Besides which, Irving is a roving hazard and he points his ball like a hunting dog and the minute he hits it he is right after it and if it's your turn to shoot next you have got to shoot over his head as that's the only place they's room, and he is also a man that takes advantage of every technicality like for inst.:

We was playing on a course where they had winter rules and his 1st drive went off the course and he asked if he could tee up and they told him not in the rough so he took that to mean that you could tee up anywheres but the rough, so after that when he got in a trap he would build a steeple of sand and use a brassey.

The time I played with Geo. Carpentier was the 2d time he ever had a golf stick in his hands but for the 1st few holes it was the toughest match I ever was mixed up in as in the 1st place no matter where you stood the Frenchman thought you was the direction flag and in the 2d place his trainer counted his strokes for him and he had been brought up in the fight game where you stop counting when you get to 10.

I managed to win the match by underbidding and after the 3d or 4th hole when it was his turn to shoot I kept out of danger by standing in the line between his ball and the pin.

Personally my game averaged pretty near 2 strokes better per round than the 1st day I ever played and when people asks me now days what I play in, I say:

"Oh, about 93," because 93 is what I would of got one day if I had of had a par 5 instead of a 8 on the last hole.

As for the ladies and gents I played with I guess they had a pretty good time or at lease I noticed them laughing a good deal and all and all they ain't nobody the worse for me playing with them either financially or physically, though I did manage to hit Geo. Ade in the feed bag with a brassey and also come within a couple of inches of making Calvin Coolidge president of the U.S.

A Perfect Day at Saratoga

BELL SYNDICATE, SEPTEMBER 2, 1923

To the Editor:

I suppose the most of the readers has visited Saratoga, where they have the horse races dureing dog days and maybe that is why so many of the horses acts like dogs but any way last month was the occasion of my first visit to the celebrated spa and for the benefit of those who has never been there I will try and describe my first day at the spa.

In the first place we left N.Y. City on the well known night boat to Albany and arrived at the capital of N.Y. State about 6 A.M. the next morning and we got off the boat and went to a hotel to get breakfast which I ordered a veal chop and some wheat cakes and got the veal chop and when that was gone we clumb in a car and drove up to Saratoga, a distance of about 41 miles and a man took us in a place where the only way you could get a cocktail was go up to the bar and ask for a cocktail.

So after a wile we went out to the races and I had been told to overlook the lay-out and see how beautiful it was as it is suppose to be the prettiest race track in the U.S. but they was just time to plant a bet on the first race and then watch it and I wished now that I had went around admiring the scenic beauties instead of being so anxious to plant a bet on the first race which was a horse named Mirthful that seemed to think the race track was a mass of detours. They was one horse that finished behind her and he came in without no jockey.

Between the first and second races I had time to admire the scenic wonders and the first one to catch my eye was Jack Dempsey's new suit which I asked the ladies on the party what color was it and they agreed on mauve. Had quite a nice talk with the champion and was careful to make it nice as I don't like to make a scene in front of so many strangers;

Later in the p.m. a photographer insist it on takeing a picture of I and Jack and Bud Fisher in a group and when the picture is published, in case they don't put our names under it, why I am the one that is standing next to the other two.

Also seen Jack Kearns and asked him what kind of luck he was haveing and he asked me to shut up.

The second race was a jumping race and my favorite was a horse named Irish Sea and at the end of the first mile and a ½ he was way out in front and the only way he could loose the race was to fall down so he fell down.

After that race my tension was called to how pretty the infield is at this track so I took a look at it and sure enough they have got a little lake out there with a couple of canoes and a ½ dozen swans that looked so nice and clean but no cleaner than I was after the races.

Next we was all asked out to the paddock which ain't like the paddocks at other tracks but at Saratoga they have got a great big forest full of trees and before every race the different horses trainers and jockeys picks out different trees and walks there horses around them so as everybody can see them and some of them certainly looked beautiful but when the ones I bet on finely got out on the track to race they thought they was still walking around trees.

The trees which the different trainers picks out for there horses to walk around ain't picked out by no guest work but if it is a bay horse they make him walk around a bay tree and a chestnut horse walks around a horse chestnut tree and a black horse walks around a blackberry bush and etc.

All but five horses was scratched out of the third race and I placed a modest wager on a lady horse named Last Straw which was where she finished but Brainstorm which was my choice in the fourth race made a whole lot better showing as they was only three horses in the race and only two of them beat him.

But the fifth race was the feature of the day as far as we was conserned as they was a horse in it named Hyperion which Bud Fisher had boughten him and before the race Bud took us out to watch him walk around his tree and the best jockey in the U.S. was going to ride him and the horse walked around the tree in great form and the people watching him says that any horse that walked around a tree like this horse walked around a tree was surely worth a bet so pretty near everybody at the track seemed to be betting on him and finely the buggle blowed and the horses went around to the starting pt. and pretty soon the barrier was sprang and we all looked to see how Hyperion was doing and they seemed to be something missing in the picture and it turned out to be the best jockey in the U.S. who had fell off his horse 6 ft. from the barrier and was setting in the middle of the track rubbing himself.

The track was muddy but the jockey was Sande.[3]

Well Hyperion went all the way around to the finish line but they wasn't nobody to whisper sweet nothings in his ear and the other entries was giveing him the horse laugh so he finished in the special place reserved for horses who this writer bets on.

They was so many horses in the last race that everybody forgot who they was backing and I can't even say who win but I know who did not and all and all when the races was over and we was rideing back to town the entire party joined in the singing of "A Perfect Day."

Tips on Horses

BELL SYNDICATE, NOVEMBER 1, 1925

To the Editor:

Once in every so often the undersigned receives a circular from the Horse Breeders assn. of America or something, along with a request to give same all possible publicity to the end that peoples' interest in horses will be revived and roused up and not allow the genus equine to become extinct in our land from lack of attention. And just as often as one of these literary broadsides hits my happy home just so often I feel it incumbrance on myself to come out flat-footed and open and above the boards and state my attitude towards what is known in exclusive livery stable circles as his highness le Horse.

Children, dogs and horses is regarded in this country as sacred items and it is considered pretty close to a felony to even make a face when any of the 3 is mentioned. Well, I am fond of children, well at least 4 of them and can tolerate a few dogs provided they keep their mouth shut and ain't over a ft. high. But irregardless of less majesty and the deuce with same, I can't help from admitting at this junction that the bear mention of a horse has the same effects on me like red flags to a bull or gingerale to an Elk.

A horse is the most overestimated animal in the world with the possible exception of a police dog. For every incidence where a horse has saved a human life I can dig you up a 100 incidences where they have killed people by falling off them or trampling them down or both. Personly the only horse who I ever set on their back throwed me off on my bosom before I had road him 20 ft. and did the horse wait to see if I was hurt, no.

Devotees of horse flesh is wont to point out that King Richard the 3rd once offered his kingdom for one of them, but in the 1st place he was not the kind of a person who I would pin any faith on his judgment of values and in the 2nd. place the kingdom had been acquired by a couple of mild little murders and it was a case of easy come easy go.

A study of some of the expressions in usage at the present day serve to throw light on the real personality of a horse. Take for example the phrase "eat like a horse." The picture you get from this phrase is the picture of somebody eating without regard to ethics or good manners, the picture of a person who you would as leaf have a horse at the table as they.

Or take "horse laugh." This indicates the coarsest, roughest kind of a laugh and a person of breeding and refinement would pretty near as soon have their friends give them a head cold as the horse laugh. Or "Horse play." How often do you hear theater-goers complain that such and such a comedy has got too much horse play or observe parents order their kiddies to cut out the horse play. The answer is that a horse can't play nice like kittens or oxen or even wolfs but has got to be ribald and rough in their sports as in everything else. And when a man gets very mad at another man and wants to call him just as bad a name as he can think of why 90 times out of 100 he calls him a horse thief as something which you can't get no lower.

Defenders of le horse will no doubt point to the term "good, common horse sense" or the simile "work like a horse" as being proof of the beast's virtues, but if a horse has got such good common sense why do they always half to have a jockey show them the way round a fenced in race track where you couldn't possibly go wrong unless you was dumb and as for working like a horse I never met a horse who worked because he thought it was fun. They work for same reason the rest of us works.

Whenever you are trying to drive somewhere in a hurry and suddenly the traffic comes to pretty near a standstill and makes everybody mad you will generally always find a horse at the head of the blockade and usually tied up to a milk wagon which should be the exclusive business of cows.

I will pass over what different horses has done to me in places like Saratoga, Belmont, Havana and New Orleans. Suffice it to say that none of them ever lived up to what I had been lead to believe. And one day just last month I had to walk across 34th. street in N.Y. city and dodge my way amongst taxicabs, trucks and street cars and was just congratulating myself on making the trip unscathed when a horse reached out and snapped at me, a stranger.

Horses ain't been no good in battle since trench warfare come into its own and besides you never heard of a horse volunteering for an army. And do you think Paul Revere even would of even looked at a horse if all the taxis hadn't been engaged with the theater crowds that night?

Last but not lease, have you ever been bit by a horsefly, which never would of been thought of only for his highness le horse.

Ring Discovers Polo

CHICAGO TRIBUNE, OCTOBER 17, 1916

Friend Harvey: Maybe you have never seen a polo game and if not why that is one place I got it on you because when you told me I would not have to look at Indiana last Saturday I felt like I ought to see something so I got in my former automobile and started out to Lake Forest and we were late getting there because I tried to take a short cut south of the tracks just the other side of Fort Sheridan and pretty near got to Onwentsia that way only I come to a place where the road was under repairs and all the other roads that run in the same direction was under repairs and

I don't doubt they had it coming to them but anyway we had to go back across the tracks and clear round through Lake Forest again and we didn't get to Onwentsia till the fourth chuckle.

I guess you don't understand what I mean by that Harvey. Well a polo game is divided up into eight chuckles and that means eight periods instead of four like in football. The game is like shinny only you ride on wild ponies and wear a funny hat and you hit the ball with the kind of a vacuum cleaner they use on buffet cars.

There is four players on each side and they are numbered one two three and four and number four is the Back and the other three are just plain horse backs. Before the game they find out who is going to play on each side and if some one pretty good is on one side they have to spot the other side two or three points, like as if Detroit come here and Cobb was able to play and that would mean the game would be 10 to 0 in favor of the White Sox before it started.

There is two goal posts at each end of the field and every time a back or a horse back or one of the ponies hits the ball with their vacuum cleaner or their feet between the other side's goal posts it counts a point and then it costs you ½ a point for falling under one of the other team's ponies' feet to strip him up and try and kill the rider. And there is also a safety where you get dizzy and hit the ball between your own goal like in football.

The chuckles is seven minutes and a half apiece and when the gong rings that means the end of a chuckle, but you don't have to stop chuckling till the ball hits one of the side boards and breaks the china ware or goes off one end of the field and then the referee blows his whistle if he has got anything left to blow with and the chuckle is over.

The game we seen was between the local nine and the team from Dayton, Ohio, that won the Central league pennant. The home boys beat them 7 to 5 so if they want to claim the championship of the Central league they are welcome to it.

The fans stand up in the band stand or on the side lines or set in automobiles and those that have friends or relatives in the game look at it every little while, but the most of them keep their backs turned and talk to the boys that just got back from the border. I seen some beautiful ladies but I did not have on a soldier suit and they would not look at me though if

I had known the dope I could of squeezed into the one I bought for my little boy and made myself strong.

Well along in the last chuckle the ball was way off alone somewhere down the field and only one man had a chance to get to it and he started for it and one of his partners yelled at him. "Watch out!" and he yelled back: "What in hell shall I watch out for?" and everybody heard him except one of the ground-keepers who is stone deaf. I did not hear what the other man said back, but it was probably "The goblins will get you if you don't."

Coming back we were in a hurry and I tried to take another short cut off of Sheridan's mountain pass and got into some common clay and a neighbor loaned us a shovel to get out with and by that time it was dark and every four or five feet between Highland Park and Evanston there is a detour but I did not make any of them because I did not see the signs on account of all the lights being out on my car and not even a little spark of love still burning. So while I was wondering how we would ever get as far as Kenilworth we found ourself at Central st. in Evanston so that is the quickest way to get from Highland Park to Evanston at night is to put out all your lights and go over the hurdles.

We stopped at a hotel in Evanston to eat and I asked the telephone girl how the football games had come out.

"I don't believe they came out," she said. "I haven't seen anything of them."

And O yes Harvey it is customary to give a list of the society people you seen at polo matches. So here is the list of those I knew:

John P. Brady

Yours, R.

How to Stork Big Game

BELL SYNDICATE, JANUARY 21, 1923

To the Editor:

You may maybe remember that in the last couple mos. I have turned out 3 or 4 articles in regards to such outdoor sports like fishing and duck shooting and when I wrote same did not have no idear that they would meet with such popular flavor and was greatly surprised when the letters begin to pore in congratulating me on these articles and asking for more along the same lines and I did not have time to count the letters recd. on this subject but would say off hand that they must of been at lease a trio of same.

Of the letters recd. no less than one was a hard felt request that I keep on continuing with those kind of letters of advice to nimble rods, Isaac Newtons and etc. and the writer of the letter reffered to is a man named Jno. Sharp liveing in Richmond, Va. and he wants I should lay off the lest dangerous sports like duck shooting and fishing and give the girls and boys the benefit of my experiences on how to stork big game such as is found in the wilds and jumbles of Africa and some of the larger cities along the Lincoln highway.

Well friends on acct. of so many children and I half to put them to bed night and morning and dress them and give them their meals and take care of them when they are sick and etc., why I have not had time to pay my annual visit to Africa for the past 9 or 10 yrs. but will state that the habits of big game don't change in that length of time and would be willing to wager any amt. within reasons that if I was able to leave today for Africa, India, Canada or any of the other cities where wild beasts has their lare why I would not have no difficulty filling my bag within a hr. after tying my horse and running a schwab through the bbl. of my riffle, a precaution which I have always took since one day when I shot at a grisly without cleaning my weppon and the bullet come out of the mouth of the gun saturated with nicotine.

Most men when they stork big game goes after only the one kind which they have sat their heart on killing and which is suppose to be in abundance in the locality where they have chose for their sport. Personly I have lerned that it is a big mistake when a man goes hunting to not carry the right kind of weppons for all kinds of beasts irregardless of whether some of them has ever been seen in that vicinity or the reverse.

As a example of what is libel to happen to the man who goes hunting unprepared I will sight the folling example. A friend of mine who wants to be called H. M. Beezer had always had his heart sat on killing a sway-backed mammal which is probably the most vicious wild beast on the American continent and no other beast dast venture near them on acct. of how vicious.

These beasts make their habitat in Montgomery, Ala., and Lumbago,

Wis. They are much sought after by the Cree Indians because of their whiskers being just the right higth and weigth to form the handle of a jackstraw.

As I don't probably half to tell some of my readers, the proper weppon with which to bring down this sway-backed mammal is a concrete pop gun. They hate them. So that is the weppon and the only weppon which my friend took with him.

Imagine his supprise when he hadn't no sooner entered the Lumbago city limits when an alto-horned roebuck burst out of a tree and was on him like a collection agency. In vain did Beezer load and re-load his pop gun and shoot in all directions.

They found him dead with the labels of his clothing carefully removed so as they would be no clew as to his identity.

Personly I will hardly ever forget how close I come to the same kind of a ending through carelessness. On this occasion I and a man friend was in Syracuse, N.Y., hunting hare-lipped kwombies.

These gigantic bipeds falls a easy victim to a charge of hare-oil injected intravenously but on this occasion I had just caught sight of my first kwombie and was raising my riffle to let fly when I suddenly realized I had loaded the weppon with gravy instead of the proverbial hare-oil and was as helpless as a ½ lb. of xmas candy.

But lucky my man friend had broughten along his hunting dog which he always takes with him on these kind of ventures and we was able to go home and get the right kind of lubricant with which to put the final quietus on our quarry, the pekingese holding him down with the weigth of his foot wile we made the trip.

Thus it will be seen that it pays to go well heeled when storking big game and ½ the battle is won if a man always carries along the right kind of implements and knows when and how to use them.

If you are going after yams take a fork wile on the other hand a charge of yellow fever germs is about the only thing that will bring down a 4-footed easel and if you miss your first shot they will be after you like a snail.

Elks is plentiful in Atlantic City a specially in the summer and can be brought down with about $8.00 dollars worth of ammunition shot out of a qt. bottle.

Possum hunting has been all the rage in the south this winter and a man friend of mine recently wrote that he had went out at 3 o'clock one morning last mo. and bagged no lest than 40 of these little rascals, useing loaded dice.

Possums make good eating at this time of yr. and is even more tender than the ones which frequent Ireland known as O'Possums.

The yr. ended was a great one for wild bores in N.Y. state and the best weppon to use vs. them was to pertend like you was asleep.

How Winners Quit Winners

BELL SYNDICATE, JULY 8, 1923

Editor, The State Journal:

One of the toughest problems faced by the people that indulges in the so-called games of chance like craps, poker, bridge whist, chemin de fer and kindred ilks is the problem of how to quit when a winner and still give the losers the impression that you wished to he-ll you did not half to quit.

Personally I ain't hardly ever been bothered by this problem but have seen it faced numerable times by parties that is blest with horse shoes which the undersigned certainly is not owing to a all wise providence system of giving one person luck, another beauty, another brains and etc. And the methods employed by the lucky ones to try and create the above named impression is so crude that they would seem funny if they did not occur at a time when they didn't seem funny.

Like for inst. I was amongst the heavy sugar men in a so-called friendly stud game 2 or 3 weeks ago and one of the other boys was also way behind and I was setting almost opp. him and I never seen nobody so wide awake and finely he win 5 pots in succession and was more winner than he had been looser and all of a sudden he was ceased with an attack of sleeping sickness though it could not of been more than 4 o'clock and when he yawned you could of throwed a basket ball down his throat and they had to dash ice water in his face when it was his turn to deal.

So he had to cash in and go to bed and the only wonder was that he could make such a accurate count of his checks while practally unconscious. About a ½ hour later another member of the winning team begin to groan with indigestion and when we ast him did he want to quit he said no but he said it in tones like the death whinnies of a poisoned tweel and the game finely broke up in a wave of sympathy.

Another time honored method that ain't quite so crude is prepared for in advance. This is to have the Mrs. stay home and call you up every so often and sooner or later one of her calls is libel to coincide with the time you are ready to quit and then you go back to the table and tell the rest of the boys that you got to get home right away as the baby has swallowed some sheet music.

The trouble with this system is that a good many wifes won't stay home and if they do stay home they seem to have a kind of a prejudice vs. getting up to telephone between 3 and 4 in the A.M.

So much for the crude methods in gen. usages and now I am going to tell you about a friend of mine that has originated some methods of his own and so far they ain't been nobody suspected him. This is a man named Elva Waffle and during day times he is a tree tickler by trade but makes his heavy dough nights at the gaming board.

Well Elva lives in a suburb which is right near 5 other suburbs and each of the suburbs has got at lease one fire house so they ain't hardly a ½ hr. passes day or night when you can't hear a fire whistle blowing.

So Elva bought himself a badge that says on it the Ever Ready fire dept. and he always wears this badge where you can't help from seeing it.

Well we will say one of the fire whistles blows and if Elva is a big winner he shoves his checks at the banker, says he has got to go to the fire and dashes out of the house willy nilly.

If he is a looser when the siren sounds and one of the other guests asks him why don't he go to the fire, he says, you poor sap don't you know the difference between the Ever Ready whistle and the Qui Vive whistle?

But Elva ain't a sucker enough to always pull the same stuff in the same joint. He has got another scheme which is said to of been thought up by Ed Reulbach when the last named was pitching for the Cubs.

Ed was losing a game vs. Brooklyn and between innings he says to Mgr. Chance I tell you what I will do. I will eat some soap and when I get out there next innings I will have a fit and froth at the mouth and the crowd will go into a panic and swarm down on the field and the umpires will half to forfeit the game to Chicago.

Well Elva always has a tube of shaving cream in his pocket and when he sees it is time for him to quit he secretly takes a swig out of the tube and the next minute he begins frothing at the mouth and making funny noises and as a rule the game breaks up instantum as very few people even loosers cares to play in a game with a man that is conducive to fits.

Another one of Elva's tricks is to go to a poker party with a bag of chocolate creams which he has warmed up over a gas jet before leaving home. When he feels like he has win enough for one evening he pulls out the bag of chocolates and passes them around but they won't nobody take one as they look terrible.

So Elva eats them himself and gets his hands all smeared up and it ain't long before they ain't a deck of cards left in the house that decent people would play with.

Those is only 3 of Elva's little stock of ingenuities and he has ast me to not reveal no more of them but make people do their own thinking and planning like he done and I will say for Elva that he has been so successful with his schemes that he plans to soon give up card playing entirely and devote all his time to tree tickling which acts on him like a drug.

Why It's Called a Dog's Life

BELL SYNDICATE, AUGUST 19, 1923

To the Editor:

Maybe some of your readers would like to know a few details in regards to my recent wk. in New Jersey. In the first place I was asked to go over to Jersey City and write up about the alleged fight between the Pottawattamie giant and the Wild Bull of the Pampas which was held in what is called Boyle's 30 acres on acct. of so many of the spectators being Boyled.

Well, on this occasion they was a hundred thousand spectators setting on each other's lap and the 200 press seats was occupied by 390 gents the most of who could not even read a newspaper let alone write for same.

Well the first so called fight was supposed to start at 8:30 p.m. so I walked down the aisle at 8:15 and showed one of the Jersey City police-mans my ticket which says on it Seat No. 82 Working Press.

"Get the he–11 out of here" was his comment and begun rushing me up another aisle to the nearest exit and I would of been chased right out again into the beautiful scenery of Jersey City only for Wm. A. Brady the theater producer who seen what was going on and told the Wild Bull of the Jersey City police force that I was not as big as I looked.

Anyway I come back and found a seat on Walter Trumbull's ample lap and seen the so called fights even if they wasn't no chance for me to try and write about them.

Well the fights is now history and I may sum them up in the words of Jimmy Daugherty the well known referee, namely that here was 5 bouts between the big fellows which a hundred thousand customers had paid to see them and Benny Leonard could of took all 10 of the contestants one or two at a time and knocked them for a row of $2.00 seats.

Well I was kind of disheartened with my reception at the hands of the Jersey City police so I got the little woman and we clumb into the costly motor and set out for Atlantic City where Mayor Bader is a friend of mine and I figured he would tell his policemans to kindly lay off of me.

Well they wasn't no special incidence on the trip except that I was going along pretty fast in a town called Tuckerton and I thought we was still in the country but a policeman rushed out and held up his hand and I said now we are gone sure but all he said was slow down a little please and that is the kind off policeman I like and I hope they hold the next big fight in Tuckerton where policemans is policemans and not Wild Bulls.

Well we finely hit Atlantic City and of course there was a convention going on and I asked what was it and they said it was a convention of the Containers, but from all I seen of them they didn't contain noting we can't get on Long Island.

I got hold of a rm. at Dan McLaughlin's hotel and they was a bath con-nected with the rm. though they's a big ocean right acrost the sidewalk and I had broughten a bathing suite and went swimming every day only you can't swim in this ocean very good as some of the waves must be a ft. high.

One night we went to see Ethel Barrymore in the 12 Pound Look[4] but it seemed to me she was underestimated a couple of pounds.

The last day down there we was recommended to go out and see the dog races which is supposed to be greyhounds but they are all colors of the rainbow and we got out there and I asked for two tickets and the man said I would only need one as it was ladies day and women was let in free which is the only piece of luck I ever had at a race track.

Well it was the first time I ever seen dog races though I have often bet on horses that turned out to be dogs, but maybe some of the readers has never seen them neither so I will exclaim what they are like.

Well they have got a ¼ mile track and they's a rail around the inside of same and the rail has got a electric current in it and a rod sticks out of the rail and on the end of the rod they's a rabbit only it ain't a real rabbit but is made out of sawdust or something but if you was behind it you would think it was a real rabbit, that is if you was a dog you would think so.

Well the dogs is all brought out and paraded like race horses and after the parade they are locked up in coops which has got windows in them so the dogs can see the track.

Then the electric light is sent around the track once so as all the dogs can get a look at him and the 2d. time the rabbit comes around the coops is opened and the dogs starts after the alleged rabbit but they don't never catch him because just past the finishing line they's a opening in the inside rail which the rabbit disappears into it. The dog that gets to the finishing line first wins the race.

I forgot to say that the dogs is muzzled and when you come to think it all over that here is a ½ dozen muzzled dogs going after a mock rabbit that ain't there when they get to it, why all and all you can see it is a dog's life.

They have got programs with the dog's names and their father and mother's name just like horses and who owns them and who trains them and what are their colors and etc. The prettiest dog I seen was a dog in the first race named Oakland Grit and I kind of hoped it would win but the jockey give him a bad ride.

I forgot to mention that the dogs is all rode by fleas. In the whole six races only two dogs was scratched though they must of all been suffering. Maybe Oakland Grit will win his next start as they say every dog has his day.

Well to make a long story short we started home the next A.M. and got to Great Neck that P.M. and the kiddies was glad to see their mother.

Ring's Sensitive Nature Recoils at Hockey

BELL SYNDICATE, JANUARY 30, 1927

To the Editor:

This is the season of the year when most insane asylums throw open their doors and let out enough patients to take part in the various winter "sports" that have become so popular in Canada and the northern part of the United States. Hockey, which is said to be a variation of the German game, Poison Gas, has come forward rapidly in the recent past and the majority of the refugees from the bug houses, especially those with suicidal mania, earn big salaries on the hockey teams, while they live.

There are big league hockey games in New York almost every night, but I have not yet attended one as I once went through the Union Stockyards in Chicago and got kind of nauseated watching them massacre the pigs, steers and horses.

A hockey game starts with six men on each side, but it is very seldom there is more than eight or nine altogether on the ice at the same time after the first minute of play.

As soon as a player does anything illegal, which is almost impossible, he is allowed to sit out two minutes or four minutes and watch the game if he can still see.

Personally if I was forced into a hockey match, I would break enough rules in the first scrimmage to keep me on the sidelines the balance of the evening. The principal cause of temporary disqualification is unconsciousness, but you can also get penalized for poke checking, scragging, slashing, hooking or murder.

The six positions on a hockey team are goalie, puck, tripper, right dasher, left dasher and face off.

Hockey promoters are already looking to the future with a view to livening up the sport and it is said that at the next meeting of the rules committee, a proposal will be made to permit the spectators to throw boulders and flatirons at the contestants' feet.

Morons who fail to land berths on hockey teams can usually find employment driving in the dog races between Canada and St. Paul. These races are only five hundred miles long and the prize is given to the driver who drives nearest to St Paul.

The main event is the Eskimo dog race, five or six of these plodding felines being hitched to a sludge or mush on which the driver sits because he is frozen there. The Eskimo dogs used to be the only ones used for these races, but lately they have added preliminary events for pekingese, sealyhams, chows, etc., drawing, of course, smaller sludges or mush and driven by backward children.

At Lake Placid this winter there has been introduced a new pastime called bobbing for fish. The contestants leap up in the air, break the ice with their heads, continue on through the water, and bring up whatever fish they can catch in their mouths.

In New York the latest fad is bicycling across the Hudson to New Jersey or vice versa. As the river is very seldom frozen anywhere near even halfway across in this vicinity, the trick is to make the distance without rusting the wheels. So far this has been accomplished by only one man, Nels Stewart of Hoboken. He did it by putting his bicycle on a ferry boat and riding up and down the decks till the boat was safely across the river.

"I bet you I could do that all winter and never rust a wheel," said Mr. Stewart to his wife.

Not receiving any reply, he looked over at her and found she had dozed off.

With Rod and Gun

COLLIER'S, APRIL 7, 1928

One January night a little group of 120-proof, right-thinking Americans sat in the Flamingo lobby at Miami Beach discussing literature and the question rose as to why the reading public buys almost twice as many of Zane Grey's books as mine, and somebody was kind enough to remark that it could not be on account of the respective merits of the books, and possibly it was because Mr. Grey had received more publicity and was better known.

"But," I objected, "I am pretty well known myself. Just the other day a reporter in Charleston, S.C., asked me when I was going to write another 'Houseboat on the Styx'!"[5]

Up spoke Jess Andrew, boniface of the King Cole Hotel and the Indiana State Penitentiary:

"Mr. Grey's personal appeal gets them. They admire him as a disciple of God's great out of doors."

"I hope you don't think I'm a house cat," I said. "Why, last year alone, I played over a hundred holes of golf, saw the Army–Notre Dame and Harvard-Yale football games and walked twice from Times Square to the Long Island Station."

"People don't hear about those things," said Mr. Andrew. "What you ought to do is go deep-sea fishing and then write it up. Deep-sea fishing made Zane Grey what he is today."

"And what is that?" inquired George Ade, but was called to the telephone before anybody could guess.

Well, I thought it over, and the result was that two or three mornings later a crowd of our friends consisting of Charlie Krom wished us good luck as we chugged away from the Flamingo dock in charge of Captain Fagan. In the party were Grant Rice, Steve Hannagan of Indianapolis, my own self and a Mr. Medos Gravelle, who went along in compliance with Clause 1 of the Florida Constitution, which provides against any person over three weeks old leaving the bedroom unless accompanied by a photographer.

Another law, the one which prevents a fishing guide from getting the tackle ready until he is well out to sea and realizes that you haven't engaged him to rehearse a glee club, kept us idle the first half hour, and we wasted the next at what Mr. Gravelle called thralling for sailfish.

Then Captain Fagan said he didn't think the sailfish were in a mood to be thralled, and would we like to get some amberjack, and I said I had never drunk any and he told me it was a fish and we would have to go back close to shore and catch some grunts for bait.

I declined to take part in this pastime as being unworthy a rival of Zane Grey, and Mr. Rice passed it up for fear we would nickname him Grunt. But Steve and the captain and Mr. Gravelle soon had a dozen of the little fellows, and we moved out to where the amberjacks live.

Grant and I had simultaneous strikes, and then began the treat of reeling them in.

In the autumn of 1901 I held a high-salaried position in the M. C. R.R. freight house at Niles, Michigan, and I would be at a loss now to tell you which is the most fun, unloading a car of four-inch iron pipe or landing a forty-five-pound amberjack that has another appointment. After some twenty-seven minutes of banter I had him alongside the boat ready for the gaff when Mr. Gravelle announced that our position was not right for a picture. I moved where I was told to, but just as I thought we were set, the fish, a girl, decided to go home and powder her nose before being photographed. The hour I spent convincing her that she looked all right is as a string of blisters to me.

I then willingly yielded my pole to Mr. Hannagan and that lucky stiff immediately caught a grouper, which put up fight like something like Sharkey and Heeney.

We had wearied of still fishing and were again thralling for sailfish when Captain Fagan spied a school of herring hog.

"You better wake Mr. Rice," he said.

"Grunt," said Mr. Hannagan, "there's a school of herring hog."

"Who coaches them?" said Mr. Rice drowsily.

But he got a thrill out of the next episode, which was the harpooning of a 400-pound hog by the captain. The latter brought his quarry to the stern of the boat and tethered him.

"He's a kind of porpoise," we were informed. "Every twenty-four hours, he eats forty times his own weight in fish."

I remarked that it must be a real nuisance to have to keep getting weighed all day so you would know whether you were behind your schedule.

"It would be a nuisance if he didn't have his own scales," said Mr. Rice.

The ocean in our neighborhood was now red with the herring hog's blood and the boat was surrounded by sharks. A shark's eyes, we learned, are so placed that he can see only the cross-town traffic and he has to be guided to his food by a pilot fish. He will follow, said Captain Fagan, wherever the pilot leads.

"We might as well catch a few sharks," said the captain. "The big one right down there will weigh close to six hundred pounds and you'll find him a lot tougher to land than your amberjack."

"My idea," I said, "would be to hook the pilot fish and make the shark follow him right into the boat."

"I don't want a live shark in my boat," said the captain. "There might be only Mr. Gravelle left to tell the story."

"Why Mr. Gravelle?"

"Because sharks won't eat photographers."

Mr. Hannagan was about to make some comment, but didn't.

Well, Captain Fagan got the big shark on his hook, and Mr. Hannagan was elected to bring him in. He worked an hour and turned the job over to me. I worked a minute and turned the shark over to the ocean along with a hundred and fifty feet of line and a good part of the captain's best rod. I had loosed the brake when I shouldn't have, or something, and the captain did not join in the general merriment.

He tossed another line overboard, and at once another big shark was hooked. Mr. Gravelle was assigned to this one, and the gallery appeared to be pulling for the shark.

Finally Captain Fagan relieved Mr. Gravelle, and the next thing I knew the fish, a 300-pounder, was on top of the water and the captain was firing a revolver right past my ear. Thirteen bullets in the neck and bosom just made the shark laugh. The captain then pointed the gun down his throat and shot out both his tonsils, and still he seemed amused. But a bullet between the eyes gave him a headache, and the humane Mr. Rice suggested offering him some aspirin.

Three more shots, or nineteen all told, took all the fight out of him and Captain Fagan gaffed him onto the deck and pounded him senseless with a club, after which we christened him Rasputin and finished him off with bichloride of mercury.

Well, we caught a few smaller sharks and thralled a while longer for the elusive sailfish, then chugged back to the Flamingo dock and telephoned the womenfolks to come down and have a look at our day's haul. They were mad at us for interrupting a game of Russian bank.

My next book will appear in the fall.

9

Family Life

Lardner's family was an ongoing subject in his columns over the course of his career. He wrote about the births of his four sons, often in verse, and their words and deeds were cited many times. This began a few years after John, the eldest, was born in 1912, with his versions of fairy tales supposedly dictated to his father, as in this excerpt from "Jack and the Beanstalk":

So his mother said they would have to sell the cow, so she told him he would have to sell the cow, you know, and the man gave him some beans. When his mother saw the beans, she was pity angry at him, you know; pity angry; She didn't give him any supper, though. She jes threw the beans out in the back-a-yard and the next morning he saw the beanstalk grew and grew and grew and grew and grew.

Lardner adopted the same technique in one of his most acclaimed series of short stories, *The Young Immigrunts,* which was allegedly told by Ring Jr. One of the conversations between father and son in that book resulted in what has become Lardner's signature line: "Shut up he explained."

Most of Lardner's poetry about his sons had to do with ordinary childhood events—getting the chicken pox, learning to talk—and some of it is very touching in the manner of Robert Louis Stevenson's *A Child's Garden of Verses*. The poems were popular with *Tribune* readers, perhaps because they were a change of pace from Lardner's usual work. In 1915 some of them were collected in the book *Bib Ballads*.

But perhaps his most profound feelings about his sons were expressed in prose near the end of a column bearing the headline "Confused with

Thunder Shower by Radio Fans." Lardner's description of how he felt when David, his youngest son, first refused a good-night kiss is among the most tender passages he ever wrote.

It may be no surprise that all of Lardner's sons became writers, but the fact they were all such good ones is quite remarkable. John became one of the finest sportswriters of his generation—his work has appeared in many anthologies—and Ring Jr. won two Oscars for best screenplay. (He was also one of the key figures in the Hollywood blacklist, which resulted in his spending nearly a year in prison.)

In 1921, when Lardner attended the international disarmament conference in Washington, he wrote of the "little male quartette in my home, which in 20 yrs. from now they will all be draft age at once and it ain't on the cards that the whole four of them will be lucky like their dear old dad and have falling arches." James and David would not be that lucky.

While covering the Spanish Civil War for the international edition of the *Herald Tribune* in 1938, James joined the Abraham Lincoln Brigade and was killed on one of the last days of fighting. He was twenty-four. David died six years later while covering World War II for the *New Yorker*, when the jeep he was riding in ran into a pile of mines in Aachen, Germany. He was twenty-five.

Lardner's references in his columns to his wife, Ellis, tended to be more indirect. She was a regular presence who played the role of wise counterbalance and voice of reason to his enthusiasms. If she was occasionally depicted as wanting something—that famous fur coat, for instance—the request would be described in such exaggerated terms that two things were clear: the reader was not to believe a word of it, and she probably deserved whatever it was, and more. Nor did Lardner address any poetry to her publicly.

There is no doubt of Lardner's feelings toward Ellis, however. He courted her for four years before their marriage—a period during which they were seldom together—and he wrote hundreds of long impassioned letters that contained a great deal of poetry and helped convince her to marry him. The closest he ever came to declaring his love publicly came in a column (see page 226) as he and Ellis prepared to travel to Washington for the Harding inaugural:

"it might be a good idear to warn my admirers amongst the opp. sex that expects to be there that I expect to be accompanied by she who come so close to being the first lady of the land, and I thought she was or I wouldn't of married her."

Lardner's home in Great Neck, and Long Island society in general, were other regular column subjects, and he got some mileage out of his attempts to come to terms with owning a radio. A decade later, his skepticism would abate as the radio provided him both enjoyment and a regular source of material for magazine pieces during his periods of convalescence from tuberculosis.

FAMILY POEMS

To the Absent One Again

CHICAGO TRIBUNE, MAY 25, 1914

I wonder what you'll have to say
And what you'll think and do, sir,
When I, a week from this fair day,
Show your new toy to you, sir.

I wonder if you'll like it, son,
Or turn away disgusted
From one that's new to play with one
That's cheap and old and busted.

I wonder if you'll laugh or cry
And run in fright to mother,
Or just act bored to death, when I
Show you your brand new brother.

To the New One

CHICAGO TRIBUNE, JUNE 1, 1914

Some people think it is a shame
That Barbara is not your name.
Well, let them worry if they will;
Between us two, I'm glad you're Phil.

If you were Barbara, I know
You'd cost your dad a lot more dough,
And when you maried, it would be
Like last night's second round—on me.

And who'd expect a girl to fix
The furnace, or get up at six
And, in the well known early dawn,
Hoe garden or massage the lawn?

I guess it's tough on you, old head
For some day you must earn your bread.
You'll have to work, you'll have to save,
And, worst of all, you'll have to shave.

You'll have to take some licking, too,
For Brother John will pick on you.
But p'rhaps you'll grow to look like dad,
So cheer up, kid, life's not so bad.

To the Latest

CHICAGO TRIBUNE, AUGUST 23, 1915

I love you, New Arrival;
I love you, No. 3.
That's why I won't allow them
To name you after me.

Make you the butt of wheezes
Such as I'm subjected to;
No, kid, I won't allow them
To wish my name on you.

Help Wanted

CHICAGO TRIBUNE, AUGUST 30, 1915

I have no objection to washing your face
And putting your playthings back in their place,
And fixing your fruit and potatoes and bread
And reading you stories when you are in bed.

It's not a bad job, being nursemaid to you
And most of my duties I cheerfully do,
But I'll certainly welcome relief from the task
Of answering all of the questions you ask.

The Eternal Question

CHICAGO TRIBUNE, SEPTEMBER 6, 1915

If I grow old before my day,
If, in a night, my hair turns gray,
'Twill be from answering when you say
"What for?"

If I have softening of the brain,
If I'm adjudged unsound, insane,
'Twill be from trying to explain
"What for?"

So, youngster, if 'tis your desire
To have a loony, senile sire,

Simply continue to inquire:
"What for?"

Exit Madge

CHICAGO TRIBUNE, SEPTEMBER 20, 1915

Madge has moved back to the city,
With her year and a half of good cheer.
The neighborhood sighs, the neighborhood cries;
The neighborhood's dismal and drear.

Madge has moved back to the city,
And left a young lover behind,
Who, mourning her loss, is excessively cross,
And very unwilling to mind.

Madge has moved baok to the city,
With her smile and her curls and her fun.
And to make matters worse, she has taken her nurse,
Who took such good care of our son.

A Mysterious Antipathy

CHICAGO TRIBUNE, SEPTEMBER 27, 1915

He's a dear little thing, is No. 3,
Dear to his mother and dear to me,
While his older brother's idea of bliss
Is to give him a gentle hug and kiss.
But the one ambition of Brother Jim
Appears to be to demolish him.

All that he does is eat and cry;
He wouldn't and couldn't harm a fly.

There's nothing about him that might inspire
A brother's aversion, a brother's ire.
Nevertheless, his Brother Jim
Would give one eye for a slap at him.

He lacks attainments; he's shy on looks,
Compared with his brothers, he has no books.
He has no games, and he has no toys
To make him the envy of other boys.
But the fact remains that his Brother Jim
Is looking for chances to wallop him.

Parting

CHICAGO TRIBUNE, OCTOBER 4, 1915

I've got to leave my little ones
And journey through far eastern lands.
I've got to leave my three small sons
And trust their care to other hands.

Boys, will you miss me when I go?
Will you be wretched while your dear
Papa is absent from you? No.
You'll get along all right, I fear.

Exalted Above His Fellows

CHICAGO TRIBUNE, JANUARY 9, 1917

Amelia Galli-Curci, I presume, is justly proud
Of the voice that wins the plaudits of Chicago's opera crowd;
The kaiser, very likely, is as chesty as can be
When he thinks of those courageous Teuts who fight for Germany;
Chick glows at his successes in the ancient Scottish game;

The relatives of Willard thrill at the mention of his name;
Frazee swells up to think that he now owns the Boston Sox;
But John's the proudest thing on earth since he got the chicken pox.

Successes in the market have no doubt made Lawson glad;
Ohio State is tickled pink about the year it had;
The friends of Col. Lowden must be overcome with joy
To realize that he is now the Gov. of Illinois;
It makes Chief Henley happy that he kept the lid down tight;
It cheers the Lake Shore drive to think it wasn't robbed last night;
But no one's joy can be as great by many city blocks
As my son John's since he acquired a case of chicken pox.

Daddy's beneath all notice, for no doctor calls on him;
A fig for Bill who isn't ill! A sneer for healthy Jim!
Who's read to when he's asked to be? Who's promptly waited on?
Who's salved and pitied when he cries? No one but my son John.
If it would please me half as much to scratch and scratch and scratch,
I'd buy myself a germing net and see what I could catch.
If I could get one-third his fun from medicine and docs
I would not be a day without a case of chicken pox.

Declaration of Independence

CHICAGO TRIBUNE, SEPTEMBER 21, 1914

"MYSELF!" It means that you don't care
To have me lift you in your chair;
That if I do, you'll rage and tear.

"MYSELF!" It means you don't require
Assistance from your willing sire
In eating; 'twill but rouse your ire.

"MYSELF! "It meant when you are through
That you don't want your daddy to
Unseat you, as he used to do.

Time was, and not so long ago,
When you were carried to and fro
And waited on, but now! No! No!
You'd rather fall and break your head,
Or fill your lap with cream and bread
Than be helped up or down, or fed.

Well, kid, I hope you'll stay that way
And that there'll never come a day
When you're without the strength to say,
"MYSELF!"

Welcome to Spring

CHICAGO TRIBUNE, MARCH 22, 1915

Spring, you are welcome, for you are the friend of
Fathers of all little girlies and chaps.
Spring, you are welcome, for you mean the end of
Bundling them up in their cold-weather wraps.

Breathes there a parent of masculine gender,
One whose young hopeful is seven or less
Who never has cursed the designer and vender
Of juvenile out-of-doors-winter-time dress?

Leggings and overcoat, rubbers that squeeze on,
Mittens and sweater a trifle too small;
Not in the lot is one thing you can ease on,
One that's affixed with no trouble at all.

Spring, you are welcome, thrice welcome to father;
Not for your flowers and birds, I'm afraid,
As much as your promised relief from the bother
Of bundling the kid for the daily parade.

The Youngest One Breaks In

CHICAGO TRIBUNE, APRIL 19, 1915

Sound triumphal music!
Give three rousing cheers!
Shout the joyful tidings
In everybody's ears!
Write it on the fences
In white and purple chalk!
Sing it from the housetop;
Brother Jim can talk!

Sentences? Of course not.
Don't be so absurd.
So far he has uttered
Just a single word.
And the word? It's "Daddy."
Foxy boy is Jim;
If 'twere not, would daddy
Give this space to him.

I, when first I heard it,
Numskull that I am,
Thought that it was "Przemysl";
Either that or "Damn."
But of course it's "Daddy,"
For it's spoken when
Daddy's here or going
Or coming back again.

Let the warring nations
War, if war they must;
Let the market weaken;
Let the banks go bust;
Let the cars quit running;
Let the people walk.

What care we for trifles?
Brother Jim can talk!

Moving to the East

BELL SYNDICATE, NOVEMBER 2, 1919

To the Editor:

No doubt your subscribers is wondering what has become of me and the last time I was in your city the genial editor of this paper whom this letter is addressed made the remark that it was too bad that a man like I whose friends was legions (according to the editor) did not keep in touch with their old friends in the different cities and correspond with their friends in all the different citys. So I says maybe some people has enough spare time to write to all their friends but personally time means money to a man like myself and if I was to even take time to drop a card once in a while to all my old pals why they would not be time for me to do nothing else, while the wife and kiddies went out in the forest and gathered herbs and wild hurtleberries for the evening meal.

The editor laughed heartily at the way I put it, but after he had recovered made the remark that this paper reached all my old friends as well as people that takes a interest in a man like I and feel like they know me though we have never met and if I cared to keep my old friends posted on my movements and etc. why he would feel highly honored would I write in a letter once in a while that he could publish it in this paper containing news of my family and I as well as itms of interest occurring in the big world which I have the privilege of comeing in contact with them more so than you dear people of this old town beautifull though it is.

I have excepted the kindly editor's genial offer and while I do not claim merits as a literary man the editor says that does not matter and if I will just write in my own breezy style (the way I talk as he expressed it) he and his readers will be more than satisfied. I will do my best which as I often say is as much as any man can do and I will have to crave your indulgents if a word or two of up to date slang drops into these cols. once in a while as I am only trying to be natural which is where a man is at their best after all.

Many friends all ready knows that I am going to move east from dear old Chi where I been located on and off for the past ten years but perhaps a few of you is curious as to how I come to make this decision. Well they was a show name Chu Chin Chow that come to Chi last winter and the bird that owned it was name Mr. Gest and one night we become acquainted and he asked me why didn't I write him a play. So I says I haven't never wrote one and don't know if I can or no, and while I was making the experiment the wife and kiddies would half to live on memorys so when he got through laughing at the quaint way I put it he says yes but suppose I was to give you enough jack to keep them in fruit and cereal wile you are writening the play so I says O .K. and he set down and wrote out a check and come out it was good.

Well I told about it at home, and I says we must not leave this wild bird get out of our clutches but we have got to move somewheres within touching distants of him so she says what do we half to move for, as when the jack is all spent you can go down to his hotel and tell him you will write him two plays in the stead of one. So I says just because his name is Gest that is no sign he always stays in a hotel and she laughed out loud.

Well I found out that he makes his home in N.Y. so I says we would move down there, but she said she wouldn't live there as she heard they couldn't nobody sleep on acct. of the Brooklyn baseball fans acrost the river so I said we would find a quiet place somewheres close so I asked a friend of mine from N.Y. where he would recommend us to and he said Greenwich, Conn. So I asked him where was that and he says on Long Island Sound. So I says how could that be a quiet place and be so near the sound, but he said he had heard that one before or read it in a book.

Well the next thing was getting rid of our lease in Chi and they wasn't no trouble about it as people is so hard up for homes that some of them has even sold their gold fish and moved into the bowl, but when we went to Greenwich to get a hold of a place to live we found they wasn't nothing at liesure till the middle of fall. So there we was without no roof to cover our head so she says she had been wanting for a long wile to visit her family at Wawasee Lake, Ind., and I said yes and I have been anxious for a long time to visit my folks in Niles, Mich. So we packed up and went to Wawasee Lake and when her family seen us comeing they forced a smile.

Well the time past quick down there as it is the biggest lake in Ind. and over your head in some places and every day I went fishing up to the time I finely caught the fish and after that I played golf as they have a 9 hole course that a old man and a horse takes care of it and the horse also acts as a roving hazard when he isn't busy mowing the fair way with his teeth and they say you can tell how old a horse is by looking at his teeth but this old codger never cracks a smile so all you can do is guess, but judging by the fair way I would say he was about 2 wks. of age.

One day, they was a bird from Ft. Wayne playing the course and he was sore because you half to play all your brassey shots with a niblick and he was on the 3d. hole which runs along the B. and O. from Gary to Fostoria and it looked like he would get on what they call the green with his 12th, and maybe sink his putt for a eagle 13 and just then the old man and Rover popped up from nowheres and he asked them if you played winter golf on this course. Well the horse didn't pay no tension but the old man said he guest not as it gets pretty cold down here.

Well, I been staying at my aunt in law in Goshen since the world serious and they keep a chicken and believe me I am never late for breakfast though I sometimes set up till 8:30 playing halma[1] but now I guess I better cut this letter short as if the genial editor prints this letter in toto to use the Latin, I am afraid he won't have no rm. left for the dead people and gags so I will save the rest of the news for the next time.

Why Not a Husbands' Union?

BELL SYNDICATE, NOVEMBER 16, 1919

To the Editor:

Well we finely arrived safe and sound on the Sound and been getting settled and the big bulk of my kids goes to school every day so the house is pretty quite mornings and a person has a chance to set down and read the papers and while the sporting pages is shy of baseball news these days why a man can turn to Page 1 any a.m. and read about 3 strikes and it begins to look like strikeing was our national pastime and a man that is not takeing part in some strike feels like a kind of a social leopard you might say what with the miners and the steel workers and the printers and the short and long shore men and everybody else doing it and apparently haveing the time of their life. So I made the remark the other day that I wished I was in on some sort of a strike and the madam said well why don't you get into one and I said how can I strike when I haven't got no job answer me that which for once she couldn't.

Well afterwards I got to thinking it over and finely I seen a way to get in the game and that was by organizeing a husbands union and demanding a fair deal for the married men and I talked it over with a couple other husbands who I am on friendly turns with them and the idear was a riot with them and we set down and figured out a set of demands which will 1st. be gave to other husbands for their O.K. and then presented to the wifes in the shape of a ultimatum which if each and every demand is not granted the married men will walk out on them the day before xmas and leave them to explain to the kids why Santa didn't show up.

The demands as mapped out is as follows:

1. A 20-Hour Day and a 6-Day Week

Under the present system a husband is on the job the whole 24 hrs of the whole 7 days and even while he is asleep he can't dream nothing that don't remind him of it. The husbands wants the hours between 8 and 12 every night for rest and recreation and Sundays to themself for meditation and prayer somewheres away from home.

2. The Closed Mouth

The way it is now you don't no sooner get in the house when the owner wants to know where was you. The husband wants the right to not answer.

3. A Increase of at Least 60 Per Cent in Pocket Money

The owners is getting a bigger allowance than ever before, but the husbands is still supposed to go along on the old scale though it costs 4 and

5 times as much to mingle around and where a person use to be able to get paralyzed on $10 it now takes $25 or $30 to even feel like you wanted to hear the Rosary.

4. Collective Marketing

In rare cases the owner consults the husband as to what would he like for dinner, but they generally always wait till just after breakfast, when the bare mention of food stuffs rubs the fur the wrong way and even when a husband can remember 1 of his favorite dishes at that hour in the morning and mentions it out loud why he has his trouble for his pains you might say as the matter will either be forgotten and hushed up before night fall or else they tried to get it but the man at the store advised them to pass it up as it was libel to be a little rancid at this time of yr. or something.

In regards to Demand No. 4 wile I don't like to drag in personaltys however I feel strained to say that I have now been a husband for better or worse than 8 yrs. and have never kept it a secret from the owner that my 2 favorite viands was oyster-cream stew and doughnuts and yet dureing the entire Eight Years War the No. of messes of doughnuts in our home has hardily ran into double figures wile the oysters that has droped in on us could be counted on the fingers of 1 thumb. In the case of the doughnuts it is generally always broughten up that lard is to expensive for lardners or doughnuts don't set good on the kids or the owner don't know if Iola can make them or not and they don't seem to be no way of finding out and it you get them from the bakery you don't know what is in them, though personly I don't give a d—m as long as they taste greasy and fill you up.

As far as oysters is conserned they's a verse in the psalms that says don't eat them only in months which is spelt with a r and though it goes vs. the grain for a man to speak of their wifes short comeings suffices to say that they's many a nice girl that was born a bad speller and just as many that can't bare the looks of a calendar around the house so for all as they know oysters may be at their zenith in July instead of vice versa.

5. Abolition of the Birthday

The normal husband has as many birthdays per annum as the owner, but where as the husband is expected to remember the 10 of April or whatever it is and spend the equal of half a yrs. golf dues where as on the other hand the owner if they don't forget the 6 of March entirely why they buy you a book that until they have read it through you can set around evenings and pare your finger nails.

That is the demands as they will be presented to the owners as soon as the husbands can get organized and I hope dear editor that you are in sympathy with this movement and will urge all the husbands on your staff as well as those amongst your subscribers to at once join the Amalgamated Married Men of America and put a end to the humiliations to which a member of the servile sect becomes a party to the minute they are drug up to the harmenial alter and if a walk out is nessary on the date chose which is xmas eve, why I hope the owners will see the light and bow to the inevitable and not try and continue in business with a gang of scabs.

It's a Good Thing Birthdays Don't Come Oftener

BELL SYNDICATE, APRIL 17, 1921

To the Editor:

Letters has been recd. from hundreds of readers asking how did I celebrate my birthday and why wasn't they something about it in the society col. Well friends so many folks has been getting their name in the society page that didn't belong there that the papers made up their mind to draw the line somewheres so they past a rule to not print nobody's name that is still liveing with his first wife.

But on acct. of the nation wide interest in the subject and to repay in a measure the kindness of my family and friends maybe it would not be out of place for me to publish a report of the occasion which will long be remembered as one of the biggest fiascos in the annuals of N.Y. society.

But first let me take this occasion to publicly thank my family and friends for remembering me and what they done towards giveing me a grand good time as well as the many valuable gifts which I am afraid they could ill afford though perhaps they are better off than a person would think to look at them.

Well in the first place they was a celebration at the home and it was a Sunday and I got up late and come down to breakfast and they was a chair covered with presents from my kiddies who couldn't hardly wait for me to open up so as they could see what they was. Well they was a can of tobacco and a box of stationery both charged at the drug store and they was a book that I forgot the name of it, but it's a mystery story and the mystery is how it got printed. They was also a sweater from the Mrs. and I may as well explain that we only been married 10 yrs. so she probably ain't hardly had time yet to find out that I all ready got 3 of them.

Well instead of the regular Sunday dinner of chicken and ice cream and cake we also had a few candles which they made the kiddies blow out as soon as they was lit because you got to be careful of your candles when you live in a place where the electric lights goes out every time the paper says cloudy tomorrow.

But the big party come off at night in N.Y. city. This was give in my honor at some friends of mine and when we entered the apt. all the merry makers was there and the lounge was a litter of presents and the first one I opened up was a tie from my boss which didn't have no card to tell who it was from, but I have seen him wear it too many times not to know.

G. Rice and R. Goldberg presented me with some handsome golf accessorys and one of the ones Rube give me was what they call a parachute golf ball which is a regular golf ball with a parachute tied to it and the directions says its "for practicing driving and all other strokes in a limited area." The parachute prevents the ball from traveling very far." Which I suppose the theory is O.K. but I can get the same results without no parachute.

Mr. Rice give me a split midiron and a golf bag that you can put clubs of any length in it because they's no bottom, and he also give me a dozen golf balls that I washed them up the next day with soap and water and 2 of them turned pretty near white.

Mine hostess give me a kind of a patent lighter that you fill it with kerosene and use it to start a fire in the fire place instead of kindling wood. Most of these here patents is no good and I ain't tried this one yet, but if it don't work it certainly won't be from lack of experience.

Another of the fair ladies give me a electric flash light to use when they was tire trouble at night or something. And a artist name Preston give me a original drawing that was worth real money which he waited till later in the evening before he took it with a couple of full houses.

Other gifts was a cigarette holder pretty near like new and a copy of the golf rules for 1916 which is just as good as any as far as I'm conserned, and all and all when I seen what my friends had spent on me I couldn't hardly help from yawning and felt like I shouldn't ought to take all these gifts a specially the ones from ladies that wasn't my wife, and I got to feeling so miserable over it that I throwed some of them out the flivver window on the way home,

But the costly gifts was just a drop in the bucket along side the 5-course birthday supper which we eat off our laps on acct. of the host and hostess never dreaming when they bought their dining rm. furniture that they would ever live anywheres bigger than Nashville.

The piece of most resistance was a Virginia ham that friends had sent them and the hostess said she had showed it to her butcher and he said it was worth $22, but he was stocked up with ham so we had it and it made 4 courses and the 5th course was individual birthday cakes which I eat one of them but the other guests just tasted theirs and said they would save the rest till their birthday.

After supper they was a choice of minoru² or deuces wild and they made me play in the deuces wild because they seen me win once at minoru and they kept the jazz turned on and if a person wasn't interested in their hand they could get up and dance and the only hand I got all evening was 4 deuces and a ace and it come when I and my brother was the only ones not dancing.

Well, the Mrs. finely come up and says it was time to go home, and I knew without counting my chip that I was $15 loser as she is a stickler for the conventions one of which is that when your husband's a $15 loser its time to go home. So everybody says many happy returns and we started home and was all most there when a tire blowed out and the Mrs. says here is a chance to use your new flash light so I got out and pointed it at the tire, but it looked even flatter than without no flash light.

That is how I spent my birthday and I won't have no more of them for pretty near a yr. But I suppose its like makeing a hole in 2 or being a honorary pall bearer and if it happened oftener a person wouldn't enjoy it ½ as much.

Got a Radio in Your Home?

BELL SYNDICATE, MAY 14, 1922

To the Editor:

I don't suppose by this time that they's more than a few families left in the world that ain't got a little radio in their home though personally we are still without one as you half to pay cash for same and any way they ain't nobody in my family that can tell a wave length from a lightning rod and if anything was to get out of order on our machine we would half to hire a piano tuner from Schenectady or somewheres.

But Great Neck has got its share of the machines and I been lucky enough to be invited to a couple homes where they had them and will admit they are a great institution and libel to go a long ways towards keeping the men and boys in nights though in a good many cases I would rather have them out if I was mother.

The places I have been to hear them, why they was connected with sending stations in Newark, Schenectady and Pittsburgh and if you didn't like the program that was going on one place why you could change plugs and switch to another which sounds like a grand scheme but the trouble with it is that you pretty near always seem to go from bad to worse.

Well we started out one night with Schenectady and heard a voice say that the program would open up with the base ball scores for that p.m. and he says St. Louis or somebody had beat N.Y. in the American League by a score of 6 to 4 and just as he said it the instrument let out a terrific blatt and I thought maybe it was Huggins squawking to one of the umpires but our host said it was static.

Whatever it was we did not hear no more baseball scores but personly I figure that a person that has got any kind of self control can wait for the morning papers to tell how the ball games come out a specialy in May.

Well the next number was a bed time story but it wasn't much more than 7 o'clock and wile that may be bedtime in Schenectady why most of we Great Neck folks don't hardly ever turn in till 8 and sometimes ½ past so we switched off of Schenectady and cut in on WYZ which is code for Newark.

Well a gal started to sing I love you truly and I made the remark that no wonder there was so many murders in New Jersey and another of the boys said he didn't think there had been quite enough.

The next piece was a cornet solo which was mostly what they call triple tongue work and it would of drove me right to Pittsburgh if I had had my say but our host was a bug on cornet playing and set there beating time with his tongue till the last squawk.

When we finely got to Pittsburgh a man was just commencing a speech about a new expedition to the Pole but the next thing you know he was making a political speech about what a big mistake it would be to cut down the personal of our navy just at this time and here in his speech verbatim as near as I can remember.

"With the far eastern question still unsettled in spite of the foreward strides taken by the disarmament conference in Washington, now is surely not the time to reduce our static squawk blah ma-a-a-a-a.

"The present personal of the U.S. navy amounts to blatt, where as the least possible number of men who could man it properly would be a-a-a-a-a, buzz-z-z-z-z-squawk.

"When asked the other day what he thought about the reduction in naval personal Asst. Secretary Roosevelt said ah-h-h-h-h-h, bizz, buzz-z.

"No country on the great green footstool desires peace more earnestly than the U.S. but blah, bizz-z-z-z ., dot, dash, two dots, dash, ma-a-a-a-a."

The host informed us that these last few noises was a police station cutting in, but I don't know if they got the guy or not.

This speech was followed up by a guy talking on the business outlook and he give quotations from the people that owns the steel Co. and owners of different big factories and dept. stores and they all seemed to think between blatts that the business outlook was pretty bright. This come as a big surprise because you take most capitalists and when you ask them for publication what they think about the business outlook they generally always break right down and cry.

The closeing number of the program from Pittsburgh or where ever we was switched to by that time was a reading from Shakespeare by one of these here gal elocutionists and this seemed to be the real bed time story of the evening or at least I noticed pretty near everybody in our party acting kind of sleepy before she ½ way through with it.

Well they tell me around here that the theater managers and opera managers and etc. is kind of leery that the radio folks will sign up some of the star song birds and comedians and etc. and the next thing you know these people would be singing or springing their gags to a audience of 2 or 3 million people a night without the audience paying a nickel to hear them and in the case of most of the divas and tenors only you could enjoy them a whole lot more if you didn't half to look at them while they was singing. This is what makes grand opera phonograph records so popular.

Well the time may come when they will have entire radio programs that will keep you thrilled all evening, but I ain't heard one yet that a person wouldn't run a few wave lengths to miss the most of it and a majority of the performers seems to be cornet players and readers and speech makers that wouldn't dast do their stuff if they was where you could get at them.

Two years later, Lardner broke down and bought a radio.

Ring Loves His New Radio

BELL SYNDICATE, MARCH 16, 1924

To the Editor:

Well friends we finely got one of these here radios put in the house and all my friends is giving me the hoarse laugh because when radios first come in style I says not for me because I never had no trouble spending a evening without help from Newark and Toronto and further and more it is a standing joke in our cozy little home that whatever we buy is either always out of order when we buy it or goes wrong the next day and ain't never the same since.

Like for inst. we bought a grandfathers clock which they said was a 8 day clock and would guarantee perfect time if you wounded it once every 8 days whereas in realty you got to wind it every day and keep kissing it and petting it to make it run at all and when it does run, why when you want to know what time it is all as you half to do is call up central.

And we bought a piano that got a whole octave out of tune the 1st. wk. to say nothing about all the ivories coming off of the white keys as fast as you touched them so that when our guests insisted on playing a piece we would half to ask them to play it in 8 or 9 sharps or else promise to replace all divots.

And we bought one of these attachments to the phonograph which you put on a wax record and sing or talk into it and it reproduces what you said or sung, so we would show it to our friends and tell them about it and they would speak a piece or sing a song into the patent attachment and after they was all through we would turn on the reproducing needle and wait for the result which was genally always absolute silence.

But any way my friends kept pestering me and pestering me about this here radio and if you don't want it for yourself think of the kiddies heaven bless their little hearts so I invested in one and instead of being a complete flop like we expected, why on a still day when they ain't no interference, we can all but hear stations in N.Y. city a distance of over 14 miles.

Some of our neighbors that is also infected with radios are always telling us that last night they listened to a fine concert from PWX Havana or WFAA Dallas but I figure that these is the same kind of people says their baby don't never wake up nights or that they can get 12 miles out of a gallon. However leave them rave and personly I am satisfied as long as I can tune in on the Happiness Boys at Newark or maybe catch a few stray sentences from WPAB on Life Amongst the Women Students at State College Pennsylvania.

What amazes me the most in regards to the radio ain't the scientific angle which I don't make no pretense of how do they do it, but the genius displayed by the boys and gals that gets up the programs for knowing just exactly what the public wants and providing same, in fact it is getting so bad that a right minded man don't feel like he can afford to leave the house for even 5 minutes a day for the fear they will put over something which he would not of missed it for the world.

Like for example I had to be away from home a few hours the other night in connections with a Get Together Meeting of the Seven Card Peek League and when I got back the Mrs. had compelled a list of the following features that had took place in my absents:

The Importance of Funding the Inter-Allied Debts.
England's Political Situation from the Viewpoint of a Defeated
    Candidate.
Handy Flashlight Battery Entertainers.
The Happiness Boys.
Elks Banquet Broadcast from the Copley Plaza Hotel, Boston.
Closing Reports of the New York State Department of Farms and
    Markets.
Reading of the Scout Oath.
Vanderbilt Coffee Orchestra.
Cutting Out Cross Talk and Spark Interference.
Housing Conditions in the United States.
Mouth Organ Selections by Charles Holland.

"Now," says the Mrs. "I guess that will learn you to not leave me home alone evenings."

"You said a mouthful," I says. "But still and all a man has got to practice self-denial. Besides which I am glad I did not hear the mouth organ selections as mouth organ selections over a radio always upsets me."

"What is they about mouth organ selections over the radio upsets you?" asked the Mrs.

"Just the thought," I says, "that nobody can get at the guy that is playing them."

In conclusions would like to state that I have just one criticism to offer namely that the afternoon programs should ought to be devoted more to stuff the kiddies likes and evening programs appeal more to grown ups instead vice versa. The gents in charge seems to think that anywheres from 9 p.m. is O.K. for bedtime stories whereas I will say that any bedtime stories listed after 6 p.m. means a upheaval in this family at lease.

And the other day in the middle of the afternoon they was a number put on over in Newark by a chorus of beauties from the Music Box revue and nobody to hear them except the wife and kiddies who don't appreciate beauties from the Music Box or any other revue a specially when they half to look at them through a loud speaker.

Ring's Long Island Estate Opens to Visitors

BELL SYNDICATE, JULY 14, 1923

To the Editor:

People that don't live on Long Island if any may not have heard that for the last 4 or 5 wks. the show places of same has been open to the public for a couple of hrs. every Saturday and everybody that wanted to get a eyeful of same has paid a ½ of $1.00 and the receipts of same is going to be turned over to a school for gals.

Well for some reason another the committee did not put our joint on the list and the public is said to be making a terrible squawk on acct. of same so we have decided en famille to keep open house between 2 and 3 a.m. every holiday during August and have cut the price to $.25 for adults and $12.00 for children and the proceeds will be turned over in person to the Long Island Chapter of Blind Caddies.

Though what is boisterously referred to as our estate may not be no bigger than Sam Harris'[3] bath mat, still and all we feel like it will provide a interesting hr. for people interested in rare old furniture and vegetables, in fact hardily a day passes but what finds a collector of one kind another at the front or back door of the joint which I might state that the reason it is called a joint is because they's a mortgage Co. over in Mineola that claims to be a joint owner.

If you enter the estate by motor the 1st thing that attracts your tension is the driveway which we rent out in the spring as a practice grounds for steeple jacks. This driveway is aptly nicknamed Death mountain on acct. of how many engines has been killed trying to get up it.

Once up the driveway, which is hardily ever the 1st time, you come to the parking space which is also used as a outdoor sleeping porch for the kiddies' bicycles. Having stepped out of your costly motor onto the bicycles, the client next limps to the 3 family garage where adjoining stalls is shared by a unpaid for touring car, the first D–e sedan and a cow with a Jersey license.

Students of dead languages will be interested in the mysterious signs infesting the walls such as Pleese no smoke and Bill Lardner is a d–f–l.

Hard by the garage lays the tennis court now nearing completion. The man that begun work on this court quit when he was awarded the contract for the Brooklyn bridge. Since then many different experts has took a hand in the construction retiring on a pension when old age claimed its own. Great Neckers who likes to boast of their long residents in this wonder city is frequently heard exclaiming why I remember when the Lardners started their tennis court.

All and all it is said that enough clay has been put on the court and took off again to make full length statues of over ½ the former Follies girls that has married Yale men.

Inside the house the customer is first escorted down in the basement where he may see a ¼ ton of real coal and a empty pt. bottle that says Schlitz on it. A couple minutes glance at these gruesome objects is genally always enough and the visitor is glad to mount again to the ground floor where he enters the dining rm. where they's a spot on the rug which has been identified as part of the gravy served the day Garfield was assassinated.

In one corner of the living rm. is seen a grandfather's clock which students has told me that it could not of been built since 1914 and was maybe built a whole yr. before that which would make it 10 yrs. old, an age when hardily anybody is even thinking of becoming a grandfather unlest you include insect life.

Opening the door of the clock one observes a doughnut fried by the next to the last Jap that left us and is now used as one of the weights for the clock.

The light bulbs in the living rm. is another point which can't fail to evoke squawks of delight from lovers of the antique.

But the prize relic of the lot is found on a table in the hall and is a first edition of the N.Y. city telephone directory bound in brownish yellow and sent us by the company themselves 3 or 4 yrs ago.

Friends have told us that a couple new editions of this rare work has been broughten out since but the new ones don't contain nowheres near as many names of dead peoples and if a person wants a alphabetical list of the men who founded New York, or New Amsterdam as it was called then, this book is where to look for same.

On the 2d. floor is the dormitories and most of the curios is assembled in the master's bed rm. Amongst these is the pr. of white trousers that was made for the master to play golf in them with President Harding and come from the tailor kind of soiled so they had to be sent to the cleaners and when we appeared in them at Washington the present administration was embarrassed for the first time.

This rm. also boasts the only one way screen on Long Island which the mosquitoes don't seem to have no trouble in getting through it on a empty stomach but the meshes is too small for them to get out after a heavy meal.

Other relics to be found in the closet and the dresser drawers is keys from practically every hotel in the two big leagues, two or three checks drawed to our order on banks which don't recall ever having met the boys that signed them and a season pass for 1914 to the Federal league ball pk. in Buffalo.

These is only a few of the attractions and could go on all day numerating same and visitors is guaranteed their money's worth of same but is warned to not go too near the children or put their hands inside the cages.

Ring's Water Bill Is $1,643—and Nobody Drinks It

BELL SYNDICATE, JANUARY 6, 1924

Well its kind of quiet around our town as New Yrs. eve was lest than a wk. ago and they's still a good deal of sickness. The next big celebration will take place on the 20th, which will be the 4th. anniversary of the day when Prohibition went into effect and everybody stopped drinking.

Supplies is all ready being laid in for this occasion and the popular taste seems to run to straight scotch as it is said to act quicker and the price is a whole lot lower than a yr. ago. For inst. you can get Dawson for $50.00 a case and Buchanan for $65.00.

The both of them comes from the same powder works and is made of the same explosives but the Buchanan label costs more on acct. of printing it in 3 different colors.

I been busy ducking the constable that comes around every couple days trying to serve a subpoena for me to show up as a witness of something I never seen.

It seems like last summer some time, why the boy that was driving what

I laughingly call my car had a collision with another guy and I did not have a very good view of the accident as it occurred on Long Island and I was in Atlantic City at the time getting acquainted with Luis Firpo, but any way my insurance Co. says they would pay for the repairs to the other guy's car, but he says no, he must also have $10.00 per day for every day he was without a car, and the insurance Co. squawked and that is what they are having the quarrel about it.

Personly if I charged $10.00 per day for every day of my life that I been without a car, why somebody would owe me $109,500.00 in round numbers. But what they want me for a witness is a misery to me unlest they think I will spring a few of my gags and keep the court rm. in a uproar.

Well the kiddies kept insisting on a radio so we had to come acrost with one for xmas and now from 3 p.m. till there bed time why a person that wants to get any work done has to wear ear muffs indoors.

The little ones thought at first that you could broad cast into the machine as well as hear through it, so they spent the most of one day making up a song to sing for the benefit of there cousins that is scattered around in different parts of the country. The song is as follows.

Yes, we have no pajamas, we have pajamas tonight.
We've got some night dresses,
We've got some mattresses
And sheets that are snowy white;
And there's a blanket so yellow
For each little fellow,
But yes, we have no pajamas, we have no pajamas tonight.

The above is supposed to be a comic all song, but after you have heard it 6 and 7 times per day for a couple wks. it begins to Paul.

Well one of the few other incidence which my readers may be in a fever to hear about is in regards to our last water bill. Now we don't have much company and hardly any of them drinks water and as far as the family is conserned why the younger members genally always quenchs there thirst with milk and they ain't none of them got the habit of dashing up to a faucet every little wile and washing there hands.

Well any way the water Co. sends there bill around once every 6 mos.

so last mo. the bill come in for the water used between May and November. The amt. of the bill was. $164.30.

"My goodness, we must be clean," says the Mrs.

"We will be if you pay that bill," I says.

Everybody that heard the remark laughed. Well any way we called up the water Co. and make a squawk and they sent a man over to look at the meter so the man looked at the meter and took it all apart and put it together again and went back to the Co. and the Co. called up and says we can't find nothing the matter with your meter, but the man that read the meter made a mistake,

"I thought so," says the Mrs.

"Yes," says the water Co., "the right amt. of the bill should ought to of been $1643.00."

Well that is all they is to the story only that we still owe them for 66 mos. water bill and are libel to keep on owing them and I suppose they will come along some of these days and shut off the water but we can get along for a wile by using Canadian ale for the bath and to wash dishes, and for beverage purposes they's always coffee, tea and milk.

And if the worse comes to worse, why Manhasset Bay is right across the st. and makes fine drinking water after you have picked out the salt.

The Latest Dope from Great Neck

BELL SYNDICATE, JUNE 15, 1924

To the Editor:

This is the time when most people has either went away from the summer or getting ready for same but when you live in a ideal summer resort like we do why it ain't nessary to go nowheres and in fact the population of Great Neck increases 25 per cent in the good old summer time instead of vice versa. So I will half to leave it to others to write back to the paper in regards to their experiences in northern Michigan and Lake Louise and the 1000 and no hundreds islands wile I confine my reports to our own little community.

Well I told you a few weeks ago how we get a hold of a milch cow that was jet black and we left it to the kiddies to give her a name and after they had only thought a part of one day they all of a sudden hit on Blackie just like they was inspired. Well we give our little boy Jimmie a parrot for his birthday and the bird could not of been in the house more than 2 hrs. and a ½ when all 4 kiddies was calling her Polly. The parrot was one of those kind that they guarantee them to talk but I figured she would be just like everything else we buy for our kiddies namely it don't work.

But this bird must of been hatched out in a telephone booth and keeps saying hello but don't never get her number. However, she is like the deceased radio which we give them last Xmas and don't never tune in till after the kids has went to bed and to sleep. Besides hello she has been heard by 3 witnesses saying Polly wants a cracker and once or twice I been called in to hear her say Jimmie but it sounds more to me like um.

Well most of the different sections of the town has been corporating themselfs into separate villages so as not to get too clubby and finely our section decided to corporate and what name to give us was the next question. Well I had read in the papers where a man in Youngstown had win $20,000.00 and got his family's picture in the paper by giving the name Liberty to that new weekly magazine so I thought maybe the neighbors had not heard about it so I says why not call ourself Liberty. But nobody offered me no $20,000.00 or nothing else and the name was anonymously voted down by the husbands on the grounds of not being apt. So then I thought that on acct. of pretty near all of us either having parrots or fords or babies or cows or dogs or guests over the week end, why maybe Zone of Quiet would hit the nail on the hammer but this was another flop so I give up.

Speaking about Quiet they's a family out here who the husband stays out late 4 or 5 nights a wk. and one day at a bridge party the ladies was saying how nice he was and how handsome and at the same time such a quiet dresser and his wife says yes but you ought to hear him undress.

Well the day it didn't rain in May, why the kids from our school went over acrost the island to Lawrence and played a ball game with the Lawrence school kids and it was our school's 1st. game and when they come home I asked Jimmie what was the score and he says they beat us 45 to 2 but we only played 5 innings. I asked him what he done and he says he didn't do nothing but Bill spoke up and said I got a base on balls. So Jimmie spoke up and said no you didn't, you struck out but the ball went way past the catcher. So Bill says Oh if I had known that I would not of gone to first.

In the school exercises a couple weeks ago Bill was in a play and played the part of a toad probably because he looks like he would squash if you stepped on him.

They ain't much news around the yard except that they are making a rock garden which consists of going somewheres and getting all the big rocks you can find and planting them between the flowers. In all the other estates I ever lived on we used to hire men to pick up all the rocks out of our garden and throw them over in the neighbors yard.

As for items in other sections of Great Neck, why it seems that what is laughingly referred to as the prohibition enforcement officers raided a house the other night and didn't find nothing. That certainly is picking the longshots.

Gene Buck has had a house full of composers fixing up tunes for the new Follies. When Gene's boys gets a couple years older he won't need no outside help.

The F. Scott Fitzgerald estate has been least for the summer to Mr. and Mrs. Gordon Sarre. Mrs. Sarre is known on the stage as Ruth Shepley. Mr. Sarre is known on the golf course as Gordon.

Ring Confused with Thunder Shower by Radio Fans

BELL SYNDICATE, SEPTEMBER 6, 1925

To the Editor:

Many weeks has lapsed since the writer give you the news of this neighborhood and some of it may sound kind of stale on that acct. Like for example a item in regards to the Harry Payne Whitneys taking the Cornelius Vanderbilt Whitneys and the Oliver Iselins to Newport on their yacht to tend the wedding of Muriel Vanderbilt vs. Mr. Church. The Ring Worm Lardners spent the day at home en famille.

The last named recently had the pleasure of receiving a call from the

Quinn Martins, he being the motion picture critic of the N.Y. World and one of nature's noblemen. They brought along a German police puppy age 3 months and a grandson of Rin Tin Tin. The pup was give to Quinn by Jackie Coogan and has been christened Jackie after the donor (the party that give it to him). Speaking about Jackie Coogan they has been a lot of talk about he having outlived his usefulness as a scream actor on acct. of getting so old but Quinn says he (Quinn) understands that he (Jackie Coogan) is going to have his face lifted.

Not never having had a police dog before Quinn was at a lost at first in regards to what to feed him, but he (Jackie the dog) soon manifested a preference for Mrs. Martin's shoes, or Katherine as I call her.

Long's Island in gen. and Great Neck in a special was all a grog several nights ago when the radio programs announced that the undersigned would sing bass to some of Sig Spaeeth's barber shop ballads in a quartet at station WGBS. This event was scheduled for 8 P.M. and you can imagine the situation in many homes when the fateful hour was struck and immediately they was such a crashing and booming in the air that women shreeked and fainted on all sides and some of them had to be taken to the hospital, others to the morgue. It was not until the next day that the truth come out, namely that it was not me but a violent electric storm and that all programs for the evening had to be called off. "Thank God for the storm" was the way Miss Blyth Daly an Elm Point blonde put it.

Residents of a certain section of our main street has been clamoring for the removal of the all night lunch wagon on acct. of so many stews of the kind that ain't edible frequenting same at all hours of the night and raising what my little kiddies would call the deuce. Mr. Schutzman the prop. of the wagon says is it his fault if drunks eats once in a wile and besides he don't serve no liquid refreshments himself only coffee, milk and gravy and if some of his clients acts corned it is because of stuff they had before they got on the wagon. The neighbors complains that one of the principal pastimes of Mr. Schutzman's customers is boombarding each other with dishes to which Mr. Schutzman replies that the said customer's families owes him a vote of thanks because if it wasn't his dishes that was being broke it would be theirs and if he didn't furnish a play ground for the boys to throw dishes at each other they would be home throwing them at the wife and kiddies.

The other Sunday a mother and father and their 9 kiddies stopped their Ford in front of our estate (The Mange) and decided to go claming as it was low tide. All went well until the mother, who had been slow in extricating herself from the car, joined the others in the clam pasture. The mother I might state was built along the lines of a former expresident of the U.S. and now chief justice of the supreme court in 4 letters and she hadn't no sooner touched ft. to mud when she begin to sink like she was torpedoed and it took the Ford and 2 other high power cars and 3 tow ropes to hall her out. She was ear deep before the rescuers got to her and the clams has been working like mad ever since to replace the divot.

Now friends the paragraph I am now writing is supposed to bring tears from the reader a specially those amongst you who is the male parents of male offspring. It ain't no secret by this time that I am the father of 4 boys and have made it a rule that as soon as each of them got to be 7 yrs. old I would cease from kissing him goodnight as boys of such advanced age don't relish being kissed by parents of their own sex. Well 3 of them has been over the age limit for some time and I only had one left on who to vent my osculatory affection, namely David who was 6 yrs. old in May. Lately I noticed that he did not return my caress with any warmth and one night he held out his hand to shake like the other boys and then run upstairs and told his brothers gloatingly that he had escaped daddy's good-night kiss. Naturally this remark was repeated to me and naturally it meant the end as far as I am conserned being a man of great pride and I suppose in time the wound will heal but meanwile hardly a evening passes when I don't kind of wish down in my heart that one of them had been a daughter.

Mr. MacDonald Smith our professional at the Lakeville golf club has been criticised for saying that it was the crowd's antics that kept him from winning the British open. Mac might learn me a whole lot about golf and on the other hand I might learn him something about crowds, at lease they never bothered me in a golf match.

The Grantland Rices of Fifth Ave., N.Y. City, was the guest of the Lardners in Great Neck for 6 days during August. Anyway they said that's all it was.

Carpenter's Concert Mars Ring's Speech

BELL SYNDICATE, MAY 30, 1926

To the Editor:

So far I ain't never heard of nobody ever offering to take the negative side of the proposition that girls will be girls and no wonder when you come to think of it. For instants we had callers the other week for some reason another and one of the ladies hadn't never been inside of our little love nest before and she asked to be showed all around and her verdict was what a pretty home you have got and it is arranged so lovely too.

So after the Co. had gone the madam asked me did I have any money and I said not much but was expecting a check from the man who I had sold them 2 loads of gravel to that I had shook out of my shoes when we had come home from Princeton that time with the Hammonds.

"Well," she says, "I have got to have some extra money as I want to make a lot of alterations on the house."

"Alterations!" I explained. "Why that woman tonight said she thought it was a lovely house and also arranged lovely."

"Yes," said the madam, "but she might come again and if she seen it the next time just like it is now they wouldn't be nothing she could say."

So anyway we are in the throws of alterations and the main idear of same seems to be to provide a kind of a private ward for the master which I don't never half to poke my head out of the same even for meals and I can be kept a absolute secret from both friends and morbid curiosity seekers and will be living under practically the same conditions like Mrs. Haversham or the guy's wife in Jane Eyre.

The only time I been consulted in regards to the affair was one day when I happened to collide with the interior decorator in the hall and she said her and the madam had been disgusting it between themselves but just to satisfy her own curiosity she would ask me what would I like my new room done in. So I told her I would like it done in a hurry.

As luck would have it I was brought up on morning newspapers and have never been able to get over the habit of doing my best sleeping between 8 a.m. and noon and it seems that those is the same hours when carpenters does their loudest work and while our house ain't no police booth, still and all neither is it big enough so as you can be rooming in any one corner of it and not know that they's 17 carpenters giving a concert elsewheres on the premises. So that is why I been kind of anxious that they would hurry and get through so as I could get some sleep and I made a remark to that effect to the madam yesterday.

"It won't be much longer," she says. "They are going at it hammer and tongs."

"Well," I says, "I wished they would get to the tongs solo."

Was it not for my training with my kiddies it would of certainly been impossible for me to tour the house lately without serious accident. Children, or at least my children, uses chairs for only one purpose, to stand on the rungs of same to see if they will break. When they want to read or play some sedentary game, they lay or set on the floor.

So I have just naturally acquired the habit of watching my step in roaming from room to room so as not to scrunch no bodies and only for that practice why in the last few wks. they's no telling how many brave union men I would of trampled under ft. while patrolling my baronial halls which a former Marine told me reminded him of Belleau Wood in late July, 1918, as far as human hazards was concerned. Because no matter if the contract is to build a new fire escape or a skylight or a bookcase, a carpenter's place is evidently on the floor, or as the French have it, aux fleurs.

It may be only fair to the madam to confess that plans for my new cell resulted from complaints on my part that they was certain features of the old one which made the creation of immortal literature a difficult proposition. It was on the ground floor and the only logical site for desk and writer was at a window plainly visible from the street and vice versa. I will quote a few incidence where this situation come near being fatal.

One day Pola Negri was riding by at the wheel of a high powered Corona and happened to look up at my window and recognized who I was and one of our Kings Point motorcycle policemens catched her 3-quarters of a mile further up the road going 55. On another occasion I was working about a quarter to 4 in the morning and the milkman come by asleep but his horse was not asleep and pulled the milk wagon up to the window and stared in the window and begin making suggestive grimaces and the only way I could get him to leave was by going out and waking up the driver with aspirin and by this time my train of thought was blooie.

They was still another occasion when I forget what did happen, but all and all it was impossible to do my best work down there and no wonder with crowds of admirers always standing in the street staring in the window and especially women and they would get mad and quit reading your stuff if you didn't just quit work entirely and give them smile for smile.

But when this job is done I will be heard and not seen and I hope and pray that the deprivation to the eye will be more than offset by the added pleasure and benefit acrewing to the intellect if any.

10

On Journalism

One reason Lardner never abandoned his journalism career may be that he never got over his youthful infatuation with newspapers and the people who wrote for them. He often put the names of his colleagues in his columns, both those he worked with in Chicago—Harvey Woodruff, Hugh Fullerton, James Cruisenberry, I. E. Sanborn, Walter Eckersall—and those from other cities he met while out on the beat—Grantland Rice, Damon Runyon, Irvin S. Cobb, Heywood Broun, George Ade, and more.

He also had an affection for newspapers cartoonists and the names of Bud Fisher, who created "Mutt and Jeff," Rube Goldberg, whose cartoons of complex gadgets left his name to posterity, and Tad Dorgan also appeared in what he wrote.

Lardner commented regularly on the problems he encountered on the job—a policeman who wouldn't let him get to his seat at a championship fight, a mob of fans that overran the press area, the freezing temperatures in the press box, and other indignities. He inserted joking comments about the newspaper business and his own writing in columns on other topics, such as the following from the *Chicago Tribune* on August 24, 1917, which he sent from France:

In a moment of unprecedented generosity your correspondent loaned his portable typewriter to Floyd Gibbons, who was off for the British front today, Mr. Gibbons' own portable typewriter being used by a fish somewhere at the bottom of the Atlantic, so he says. Well, we asked a female journalist from somewhere in Texas if we might occasionally borrow her machine during Mr. Gibbons' absence.

"Sure," she said, smiling sweetly, "but I don't believe you will get on very well with it. The 'u' doesn't work."

"Oh," we replied, extemporaneously, "there will be no difficulty so long as the capital 'I' is available."

When he returned home to cover the World Series that year, the lead on his column after the first game was:

The large majority of correspondents try to get a punch into the opening paragraph of their story, believing that the reader will think "Good Gracious! This goop certainly starts off well. He must be a great writer. I must read the rest of it." As good a system, I opine, is to make the first paragraph as dull and uninteresting as possible, so that he who reads will say to himself, "I must find out why the devil the paper ever hired this bird." That is my system, and I'm sticking to it.

Lardner also devoted a number of columns to comic portrayals of life in the city room. In "Office Secrets," a three-part series he wrote for the *Tribune* in 1916, the reader encounters the city editor: "A giant in stature, his fierce black eyebrows and untrained mustache making his appearance the more forbidding, he stands, whip in hand, in the very center of the room, ready to spring in any direction at the slightest hint of mutiny. Attached to his ears, nose, throat and lights are telephone receivers."

In columns and occasional poems he complained about working conditions, about where his next idea would come from, and about the constant pressure to come up with something fresh. He even wrote a column about the poor reader who had to bear with him and suggested a cure that seemed more designed for alcoholics. When the *Tribune* wanted him to write every day, even if it was just a short item, he replied, "I now say that if it is necessary that the undersigned's name be never out of the paper, why not print merely the undersigned's name on Monday mornings, adding perhaps some phrase such as 'who did not work yesterday.'"

Lardner was his usual satirical self in nearly all of these columns, but there were times when he was perfectly serious in his attempt to let readers know just how newspapers worked. No sportswriter today can read "A Plea for Mercy," which appeared in the *Tribune* more than one hundred years ago, without realizing how little some things have changed: the writer, he says, "congratulates himself on getting the score right, on having his lineup within three or four names of correct, and on being quick enough to beat the deadline for copy."

Perhaps the final piece of evidence indicating the hold newspapers had on Lardner came in late in 1928, eighteen months after he had stopped writing for the Bell Syndicate when he was diagnosed with tuberculosis. A huge salary offer of fifty thousand dollars lured him back to the *New York Morning Telegraph,* which was devoted primarily to the news of horse racing but employed some well-known writers who chose any subject they liked. Among them were Westbrook Pegler, Ben Hecht, and Walter Winchell, who wrote under the pseudonym "Beau Broadway," which Lardner couldn't resist parodying.

The paper folded soon after he joined it, however, and two years elapsed without Lardner's work appearing regularly in any American newspaper. Then, in February of 1931, he was offered $750 a week to write a series of "night letters," which were to consist of one hundred words a day. He wrote these for two months and that was it. With his health failing, he finally had to say good-bye to newspapers for good. Though he continued writing stories and articles for magazines in the two years he had left, most of them for the *Saturday Evening Post* and the *New Yorker,* the keystone of his career had fallen.

JOURNALISM POEMS

Monday

CHICAGO TRIBUNE, JUNE 13, 1913

A friend of mine, who reads the Wake (a friend he sure must be)
Had me to dine a week ago last Sunday,
And after we had dined awhile, the friend inquired of me:
"Why is the Wake so very short on Monday?"

I told him, and I'll tell you, too—'twas thus my boss did speak:
"Each week, to rest your brain, we'll give you one day.

We really can't expect a man to keep a Wake all week,
So just send in a verse or two for Monday."

And, yielding to the boss, which is the proper thing to do,
I set aside each Sunday as a fun day.
And Tuesday, Wednesday, Thursday, Friday—all the whole week
    through—
I wonder wotinel to write for Monday.

Come On, You Roseate Day

CHICAGO TRIBUNE, FEBRUARY 27, 1914

When you've penned an especially bright bit of verse,
It's good for one day in the year;
When you've made a neat hit or an epigram terse,
In only one sheet 'twill appear.
No matter how bright be the stuff that you write
About organized ball and its quarrels,
Don't stop, trip, or shirk, but keep up the good work,
For you never can rest on your laurels.

When strenuous rhyming bedews your pale brow,
And you've gained an effect really snappy,
Don't think, "That'll hold 'em a while, and so now
I'll rest up a bit and be happy."

For when you do well, you have to excel
Your own lyrics and sonnets and chorals;
So keep on with the dance, O you Anatole France,
For you never can rest on your laurels.

Keep the engine a-going, the furnace keep hot,
With plenty of pepper and spice.
For you see that's the kind of a job you have got—
Oh, I say. this is beaucoup advice!

But don't get too good, or really you would
Revolutionize all baseball morals.
Ah, well, you should fret, for some day, you bet,
Some roseate day in the far, far away,
[Funereal? No, for I don't mean it so],
You'll take a long rest on your laurels.

Lardner had been writing the Chicago Tribune's "In the Wake of the News" column for a year when, on June 6, 1914, his byline was changed from R.W. Lardner to Ring W. Lardner. His poem in that day's column spoke of his self-doubts.

West Town Storm

CHICAGO TRIBUNE, JUNE 6, 1914

I wonder if there's anything
That I, tonight, can rhyme about.
It's 'most too late to write of spring
And—Wait a bit; the lights are out.

Now naught to do but watch the flash
Of lightning, listen to the rain.
And tremble at the thunder's crash
And—Wait a bit; they're on again.

Where was I headed at the time
The darkness came? O, yes, I know;
I sought a subject for a rhyme.
Well—Wait a minute; there they go.
I wonder if my meter keeps
Right on when current's on the bum.
Or if it, through the darkness, sleeps
And—Wait a minute; here they come.

Why didn't you stay out all night,

False lights? For now ideas have fled.
I'll wager, though, you'll burn all right.
Yea, steadily, when I'm in bed.

This Afternoon

CHICAGO TRIBUNE, NOVEMBER 21, 1914

O shivering creatures
Down there in the bleachers,
And fans in the cold concrete stand,
You've willfully chosen
To come and get frozen,
While I must be here or get canned.

You leave when you care to,
While I must prepare to
Remain to the end, I suppose.
I'll perish. I fear me,
But one thought will cheer me:
That I didn't pay to be froze.

To the Man Higher Up

CHICAGO TRIBUNE, AUGUST 5, 1915

Sometimes I write my stuff at home
And bring it down with me.
When that's the case, the stuff is good
As stuff of mine could be.

At other times I have to come
Before it's off my mind,
And try to do it at the desk

To which I've been assigned.

And when, before the stuff is writ,
Downtown I have to come,
The stuff as maybe you have guessed,
Is very, very bum.

O Mr. Boss, you'd rather have
The good stuff, I presume.
If that is so, I pray you, sir,
Give me a Private Room.

First Aid

CHICAGO TRIBUNE, FEBRUARY 9, 1916

A rhyming dictionary is
A handy little thing.
My uncle, though, got tired of his
And passed it on to Ring.
So now, when hard up for a rhyme
And when I need one quick,
I save a lot of precious time
By looking up the Dic.

When I must rhyme with some tough word—
We'll say, for instance, "twelve"—
'Tis then I grab my Dicky bird
And find "delve," "helve," and "shelve."
Or if, as often is the case,
I want to rhyme with "babe,"
By looking in the proper place,
I run on "astrolabe."

It happens every week or so
That I must rhyme with "doge."

My book advises me to go
And utlize "gamboge."
And when I seek a running mate,
A word to pair with "gulch,"
I do not have to hesitate;
I'm tipped right off to "mulch."

Or when it's necessary to
Wind up a line with "shalt,"
I find what p'rhaps is known to you,
There's such a thing as "alt."
Or when I cannot think offhand
Of playmates for "cartouch,"
I look into my booklet and
Am introduced to "smooch."

My rhyming Dic's a hit with me;
It really is a gem,
Containing all the words there be
And all the rhymes for them.
But what my book neglects to tell,
The thing my book leaves out,
Is whattheell and whotheell
To write my rhymes about.

Valentines

CHICAGO TRIBUNE, FEBRUARY 14, 1918

To a Rewrite Man:

Reporters furnish you with plot,
With facts, with dates, with names, and if you
Turn out good stuff sometimes—Why not?
You lucky stiff, you!

To a Dramatic Critic:

You write stuff once a week or so,
And when it's punk, why, you should worry.
One alibi will always go:
"I had to write it in a hurry."

To a Bold Editorial Writer:

They read him and they cry: He's not afraid,
This supergink, to call a spade a spade!
He says Jess Willard's just a great big bluff!
Yea, brothers, but he doesn't sign his stuff.

To a Lineman:[1]

When the pile of A1 contributions is low,
And Babette is especially cunning,
He phones to the office, "Because of the snow,
The Northwestern trains aren't running."

To a Society Editor:

Says, girls, don't you think it must be just immense?
Can you imagine a job that's as pleasant
As witnessing all the big nuptial events
Without being stung for a present?

To a Reel Critic:

She pays no attention to riffraff like me.
She thinks she is awfully smart,
'Cause she once got a letter from Francis X. B.
And an autographed picture from Hart.

To a Sporting Editor:

Wherefore that broad, contented smile, adorning
The visage of the editor of spo't?
He doesn't have to wait until the morning
To see the Gumps and read what L——r wrote.

A Plea for Mercy

CHICAGO TRIBUNE, NOVEMBER 17, 1914

No human being is more generally panned of a Sunday morning than the football reporter. The losing team's coach reads his story and says: "Fine stuff! Not a word about the rotten deal we got from the officials. I wonder whether this bird was at the game or out joy riding."

The winning team's coach says: "What do you know about that! No mention of that triple delayed pass that put us in position to score. Nothing about that defense of mine that made their open attack look like a joke.'

The guard who played a wonderful game says: "The only place my name appears is in the lineup, and it's spelled wrong there."

The sub half back says: "Look! They give that touchdown of mine to Smith. Those reporters are a fine lot of stiffs."

The fan says: "A column of the real kind of stuff and two columns of dry detail that nobody wants to read."

And so on.

As for the reporter, he congratulates himself on getting the score right, on having his lineup within three or four names of correct, and on being quick enough to beat the deadline for copy. He knows what he is up against if outsiders don't. A statement of some of the facts may soften said outsiders' hearts and make their comment less caustic.

Important football games are played on Saturday. Early editions of Sunday papers go to press at 6 o'clock Saturday night. The story of the game must be in the office before 6 o'clock. To allow for delay in transmission, wire trouble, etc., the reporter tries to have his story all written and turned over to the operator by 5:30, or about an hour after the close of the game.

The reporter, as well as the sporting editor and the fan, knows that detail is dry as bone to the average reader. But detail is about the only copy that can be sent in as the game is in progress. It is dictated by the reporter to his telegraph operator as the plays are made. It is sent in and printed because it is early copy and because it will tell the reader some important facts that the reporter may forget in the hurried writing of his "lead." Nobody dislikes dry detail more than does the reporter, but he realizes that it is a necessary evil.

As soon as the game is over the reporter sends in his nearly correct lineup and summary. He has credited the touchdowns to the men who he thinks made them. He has written in the substitutions as he guessed them. If the players were numbered, he is more likely than not to be right. If the players were not numbered, he is probably wrong in some particulars.

The lineup off his mind, the reporter turns to the notes he has made during the game's progress, notes on which to base his "lead." The notes were made during the rather confining labor of dictating the detail and keeping his lineup and summary written up, to say nothing of responding politely to the more or less useless remarks of bystanders and bysitters.

He begins writing or dictating his lead. The difficulty here is usually increased by the fact that the reporter is half frozen and can think of little else. Nevertheless, the story is supposed to have a punch in it and to cover the important features of the game; and it must be in the office in an hour. There is no time to consult with a coach, or an official, or a player as to who did this or that, who made the second touchdown, and what a certain penalty was for.

His "lead" finished, the reporter makes a run for his train. On his way to it he thinks of the really good story that he could have written, and remembers all the important things he left out

On the train or on his way to it he meets one of the coaches, or one of the players, or one of the officials, and finds out that he was wrong in a number of particulars. He wires a correction to his paper, but the correction is almost sure to ball things up worse than they were before. He finds out that a star on this team or that broke a leg early in the first quarter and remained in the battle on sheer nerve. He sends a short story covering this but the reader thinks something should have been said about it in the regular story, which was written in blissful ignorance of the star's mishap.

The winning team's adherents get mad at the reporter if he offers any alibis for the loser, and the losers get mad if he doesn't. By years of experience he has found out that the better policy is to gloat with the winners rather than sympathize with the vanquished. The latter are already sore, so they might as well be a little more so. The winners are happy, and it is foolish as well as dangerous to have "ifs" at them.

The reporter has no idea, unless one of the players tells him, that a certain guard played a wonderful game. If he watches a guard or a pair of guards all through the combat, he is not going to be able to watch the man with the ball.

As for the official's bad decision, that, too, is unknown to ye scribe. If the plays could be seen more clearly from the press box than the field, wouldn't the officials sit up there and announce their rulings through a megaphone?

Another Plea for Mercy

CHICAGO TRIBUNE, NOVEMBER 25, 1914

Chicago—Frend Harvey. I supose now that the football season is over your expecting me to eat up a little more space evry day because they wont be no news but just a hole lot of bunk but you musent forget that when they is not no news in the paper it a hole lot harder for me to find some thing I can write a bout then when theys a hole lot of live stuff & how can a man write his head off when theys not no idears in the paper for him & I cant get no idears out of the paper when all it says is that may be 15 or 16 big leage stars has sined with the federal & bresnanhan says he will not allow no body to enter fear with him manageing the cubs & the Un. of Chi basket ball team will may be be good and may be be rotten & Lee Magees best frend says Lees going to manage the brooklyn federal & thats a rotten thing for a man to say & then call him self your frend, & some fire man down to Urbana has had a baby & named him after the coach man & north westerns sined up willie Mcgill for nurse of the foot ball team next yr. & chief Johnson got the jumping habit so bad last summer that hes jumped his famly & Joe brickleys went & had his apendisitus cut out so as he can get his name in the paper like Chas. & its all frammed up for White & welsh to fight out on the coast & welsh is going to get an other awful beating like up to Milwaukee & over to Buffalo.

They aint nothing in all that stuff not even the bowling scores that I can get any idears out of it & yet at the same time I know Harvey that youll be looking for me to fill up more space now that theys nothing more in the paper a bout foot ball accept whos going to be capt. here & whos going to be capt. there next yr. & if you want me to I will even tell you who is going to be some of the capts. so as you can get the head lines wrote in add vance.

I cant give you there names right out because that wouldnt be fare but I can give them so as you can under stand them & the public cant & the Chicago capt. is going to be R———l and the Ill. capt. is going to be W———n probably but may be P———e & the Harvard capt. is going to be M———n & thats some of them & I could give you a few more but that aint got nothing to do with what I started out to talk a bout & what I started out to talk a bout was how am I going to fill up all this here extra space with nothing to write a bout & a wile a go they was a girl give me a good story & I was going to write it all out & it would of been a peach when I got threw with it only I thot may be I better call up the people the story was a bout before I printed any thing & when I ast them did they care if I printed it they got up in the air & jumped on to me like as if it was my falt they was such a story & dident give me creddit for calling them up and asking there permishon to print it & I feel like as if I should ought to get back at them by going a head & printing it only Im not that mean.

But heres what Im getting at as long as theys nothing to write a bout that will fill up enough space why not let me run some pitchers in my colun & I could run a large pitcher of my self for 3 or 4 days and give the public a treat & then I could run pitchers of all my famly & then when I got threw with all my famly I could run pitchers of diffrunt frends I got and may be some day I would run your pitcher & I think I could get hold of all the pitchers with out no edishnel expense because most of the people would furnish me with the pitchers free gratus because no matter what they say most people likes to see there pitchers in print accept the homly ones & I havent got no homly frends or famly. If this idear sounds O K to you let me know & I will rumige a round in the basemunt where the famly has put my pitcher a way so as to keep it safe & I will have a cut made of it & briten up the sporting page dureing these dull times.

Respy. R. W. L.

Part 1

There is nothing quite as fascinating as a great newspaper office unless it be a four round exhibition between a third rate fighter and his brother. But few of the outside world, or demi-monde as it is often called, ever have the opportunity of even peeping into the mystic temple, let alone of studying the remarkable life of sanctum sanctissium. The purpose of these articles is to give the public an inkling of what goes on and what is to be seen behind those mystery walls and to get five days' work done at once.

Situate kittycorner from the Grant is the Tribune building, which houses la Boheme who daily and Sunday, in picture and story, lighten with their art the world's great burden of pain. Exteriorly the building impresses only with its hugeness and beauty of architecture; it fails even to hint at the weirdness and strangeness of the contents of its third, fourth, and fifth floors and whatever floor the Sunday department has leased for the winter. It is when one disembarks from the elevator at three please, that one first senses that here is no common workshop, no mere tabernacle of the great god Gain.

Accompany me if you will through this wonder palace. At the third floor we are met by the liveried Prefect de 1'Adore (master of doors). We show him our credentials, state our wishes and are turned over to one of the ten female ushers.

"Dese Weg' bitte (This way please)," she says crisply, and in a trice an automatic panel slides back to admit us into a soft-carpeted corridor lined on both sides with the studies of the famous.

"Wo petzt?" queries our guide,

"Ueber Alles (All over)," we respond in her native tongue with horse-radish.

The door of the first studio opens at her touch. It is the local room. The first Bohemian to meet the eye is the city editor. A giant in stature, his fierce black eyebrows and untrained mustache making his appearance the more forbidding, he stands, whip in hand, in the very center of the room, ready to spring in any direction at the slightest hint of mutiny. Attached to his ears, nose, throat and lights are telephone receivers, and to his shoes——'s rubber heels.

At his side we find the assistant city editor, feeding his chief gruel with a syringe. Immediately in front of them is the local copy desk, where an army of readers in evening clothes peruse what the reporters have written, pop-eyed with excitement. One of them speaks in a whisper to his neighbor.

"How much did you win?"

"Eight or nine bucks," is the low-voiced reply. "Whatever it was, it's gone."

Along two walls of the studio are the reporters' shelves where the Bohemian news gatherers with rapid fountain pens jot down the items of the day. They are made to write standing up, to keep them awake. Each transcribes his items from a portfolio bound in real leather. There are four or five distinct groups of these workers, one consisting of the graduates of Harvard School of Journalism, another of the University of Illinois College of Journalism, and so on. A great deal of college spirit is manifest.

Above the reporters and copy readers is an overhead system of wires, equipped with baskets in which the copy kids, or copy cats, ride to and fro. These boys are learning the "game" as it is vulgarly termed, and when they are not doing that, they are exchanging playful wallops on the jaw.

(To be continued)

Part 2

CHICAGO TRIBUNE, FEBRUARY 16, 1916

The studio next to the local room is occupied by the sporting editor and his corps of humorists. Bronze images of Jess Willard, Ty Cobb, Tod Sloan, Walter Camp, and other heroes of this or a past era of sport adorn every desk, and each writer pays homage to his especial god before attempting to indite his piece for the paper. For example, the football writer, with bared head, prepares for his work by implanting a reverent kiss on the bronze bean of Walter Camp.

The decorative scheme of every desk also testifies to the line of sport in which its owner is expert. The baseball writer's desk is inlaid with bone and diamonds; the golf writer's desk has eighteen pigeon holes; the football writer's desk has the general appearance of a rough scrimmage; the basketball editor's desk is surrounded by waste baskets; the fight writer's desk is of bone, smeared with blood; the bowling editor's desk is littered with pins and is next to the alley, etc.

The sporting editor is a small but wiry bundle of nerves, quick tempered and of the driving type. His desk is a veritable gymnasium, equipped with every imaginable kind of athletic paraphernalia. When there is a moment's pause in the day's labor he is out of his chair in an instant, swinging heavy Indian clubs, exercising with the pulley weights or boxing with one of his men. Since leaving the University of Chicago he has moved rapidly up and is now as far as North Evanston.

The next den in the corridor is shared by the whist, chess, poker, and shooting experts. There is always a game of some sort in progress here, the writers keeping in touch with their subjects constantly. The shooting specialist fires when there is too long a delay between chess moves, when a pokerist offers to make deuces wild, and when one of the auctioneers remarks that his hand would be grand for nullos.[2]

The automobile editor's suite adjoins. The editor himself is seldom in, for at intervals of half or three-quarters of an hour he must take a spin from Rensselaer to Lansing or from Gary to Little Rock so that he may gain first hand information as to which is the best route the very day an inquirer wants to know. But his assistant is found at a table, on which are set up two, four, six, eight and twelve cylinder engines for testing purposes, and which is equipped with tire wrenches, pumps, pliers, jacks, queens, etc. This suite boasts its own office boy, who runs errands in a ford.

The next studio is the Rodents' room.

(To be continued)

Part 3

CHICAGO TRIBUNE, FEBRUARY 17, 1916

Between the Rodents' department and the society studio there is a line of trenches. To be admitted to the presence of the society editors one must wear a shave and carry a deck of calling cards. It is customary, but not compulsory, for visitors to bring flowers, or candy, or both, but if only one be brought, let's have candy.

Before half past 3 in the afternoon, at which hour the society editor and his assistants reach the studio, their invitations for that night are brought in on two trucks. They are then arranged in a neat stack, and when the editor is ready the whist or the poker editor comes in and shuffles the cards. The society editor takes a first cut, and the invitation he cuts is the one he accepts. The assistants then cut in the order of their dancing ability. Hard feelings are often displayed, and occasionally two or three of the assistants come to blows over the result of the draw, but it is against the rules to trade.

The next studio, an enormous one, is occupied by the Sunday and Moving Picture departments. This is a scene of great activity on Saturday nights, when the artists and writers are at work on their assignments for the Sunday paper. A moving picture operator is constantly turning his crank, photographing the employes at their various tasks. He uses a dollar kodak and takes time exposures.

The social life in this suite is at its height in the afternoon. About 2 o'clock Frank Bushman, Molly Pickford, Chas. Chaplin and other peaches drop in and take tea. The staff pours, assisted by Madame X., Madame Y., and Madame Z. After tea they all go to the theater on State street.

In this suite are also the beauty and love doctors. Many people suppose that their answers to queries are based on guesswork. Nothing could be further from the truth. If a girl writes in and wants to know how to turn her light hair dark the beauty doctor experiments until she has discovered a lotion that will accomplish the purpose on herself. She answers accordingly. Or if a girl wants to know how to make a man love her, well, the love doctor simply goes and finds out.

In one corner of the suite is the Sunday moving picture department's desk, sometimes called the mint, because so many words are coined there.

The health adviser's studio is conducted with the same attention to detail and accuracy as is the rule with the love and beauty doctors. If a lady wants to know why Joseph isn't gaining, the health adviser calls up the baby and asks him point blank.

Next in order we come to the Line studio. The editor lies in a hammock all afternoon reading The Little Review and sipping cordials. Every thirty-six minutes the latest mail is brought up with a crane. The skilled laborers immediately get busy with it. One man opens it, another pastes it on sheets of copy paper, a third reads it, a fourth writes captions on it, a fifth pastes all the sheets together, and a sixth hangs it the wall to be perused by the editor at his leisure. Occasionally he is seen to cease reading for a moment and to write a bit of poetry on his cuff. At 6 o'clock his help leaves, and at 7 he has thought of a last line and is through for the day.

In the We Will studio we find the editor interviewing a statistician or a murderer, taking notes, and heartily wishing that he could see a boxing match tonight.

Conquering a Bad Habit

CHICAGO TRIBUNE, MARCH 16, 1916

"You're not the only one that rested," writes an ardent admirer, who, possibly because he cannot spell his name, signs initials only. "While you were gone, over 300,000 readers of the W.G.N. enjoyed a good rest, too. Why din't you stay longer?"

Reading this department is a habit which, if continued indefinitely, is certain to effect a general physical breakdown. First the eyes are weakened; then the digestion, and finally the heart and the rest of the giblets. The victim becomes morbid, loses interest in his work, avoids society, contracts insomnia, cannot sleep, and has spells of dizziness. In extreme cases, there is total paralysis.

If the author of the letter quoted above has not been misled, if there are actually 300,000 odd persons who daily read the Wake it is time for country-wide reform. The department of health should take steps. Meanwhile, in the interests of the future race, individuals should make a sincere effort to conquer the habit.

But as in the case of alcohol or nicotine, there is danger in quitting too suddenly. One should cut down gradually, indulging semi-weekly for a time, then only on Fridays, and, when the system has tossed off most of the poison and functions properly without it, not at all.

That a complete cure is possible where the will is strong, is proven by the testimony of a man in Flossmoor, which, in the interests of humanity, we reprint:

"I got to the stage where I awoke in the morning with a hacking cough, which would sometimes continue until the middle of the forenoon. When I rose from a sitting posture, I would frequently stagger and invariably feel faint. Nausea would seize me whenever I rode on the train or the surface lines. I began to limp badly and black specks were continually before my eyes. My clothes wouldn't stay pressed. I couldn't keep a cigar afire. I was morose and lost my temper on no provocation.

"I consulted a famous specialist at Hegewisch and was told what I already knew, that the habit must be conquered if I expected to live.

"I went about the task systematically. I hired a maid who could not read English. I taught her to identify the column from a glance at the heading. I bought her a pair of sharp scissors. I instructed her to be on the porch every morning when the paper arrived, to cut out the objectionable feature, and to lay the denatured journal on the breakfast table; then to paste the segment face downward on the pantry shelf.

"In less than three weeks, I found that I didn't miss it at all, and in two months my system had resumed its normal healthfulness. I honestly believe that I could now be trusted to look the stuff right in the eye and not read it, but I am going to wait a few more weeks before making that test.

"Will power was, of course, the biggest single factor in my successful fight. But many other things aided me. I chewed gum and ate candy. I took plenty of outdoor exercise. I slept in a room that was well ventilated. I bathed twice a day in ice cold water. I drank a pint of buttermilk every noon. I quit wearing suspenders. I studied Spanish and played horse tennis.

"It was a hard pull, but the result is worth all the suffering. And anybody can do it who really and sincerely wants to."

Thus the man in Flossmoor. And Mr. Initials and the other 300,000 odd can be just as successful as he. Try it.

As for the query, why didn't we stay longer? the subject is too painful to discuss.

Ring Wants a Day Off

CHICAGO TRIBUNE, MAY 17, 1917

Chicago—[Sporting Editor The Tribune.]—It is a known fact that one day off per week is allowed everybody on this floor except the comical cartoonists, who have five to six, and the undersigned, who has none. The first two principles of journalism are honesty and a day off in every seven. The latter has been carried to extremes by some persons I could name and would name, but for their families, who may be all right at heart, though gullible. And what did Moses say about it?

The undersigned is differentiated against, as some might say, in that he alone of all the true workers on this floor, works every day in the week. It was the original understanding that he was to have something in the paper every morning but one. Then came your honorable request that the seventh morning, Monday, also show some product of his creative genius. "Not a great deal," you said, "but perhaps a little verse or two in order that your name may be never out of the paper."

I now say that if it is necessary that the undersigned's name be never out of the paper, why not print merely the undersigned's name on Monday mornings, adding perhaps some phrase such as "who did not work yesterday."

"A little verse or two" sounded very reasonable to the undersigned at the time you mentioned it, and he agreed, as he usually does to everything, being at heart a prince of agreers. But for some months past the little verse or two has palled; it has become a drain on the nervous system not only of the writer but also of many of the circulation, several of whom have had the kindness to write in and tell me about it, usually winding up their letters, "Get wise to yourself! Who the hell cares about your family!" or something.

It is from no lack of ideas that the request is made. The subjects of the little verses have been most generous about furnishing same. But they have now progressed so far beyond average males of five years and under, that certain readers find their present pranks and conversations impossible of belief. And one hates to be regarded as a malicious falsifier when one has always regarded truth as one of the two great essentials, the other being one day off a week.

In conclusion let me say that inadvertently the little verse or two, as well as the undersigned's name, stayed out of the paper last Monday morning, in spite of the fact, Max tells me, many papers were sold and several were even read.

A personal reply would be appreciated.

Voice of the People

CHICAGO TRIBUNE, JULY 17, 1917

Chicago—[Editor of the Wake.]—I have been a subscriber of your-paper for twenty-years and it was with deep-regret that I noticed in your paper the other morning in the Beg-Your-Pardon column, which I don't know who writes it, where Mr. Carey-orr, the man who draws the Tiny-Tribune, was criticised for misspelling the name of Bill-Sikes, one of the leading men in Oliver-Twist, by Charles-Dickens.

Things have come to a pretty-pass when a comical cartoonist is criticised for miss-pelling a name or a word.

In my years of experience I have found it to be a fact that there is nothing to it. When a comical cartoonist applies for a position on a news-paper, the first question the door-man asks him is "Are you a good-speller?" If he says "Yes," they kick him down-stairs and take-on the next applicant. If says "No," they examine him o-rally. Suppose his name is Sidney Smith. The examiner says, "How do you spell your name?" If the applicant replies "S-y-d-n-e-e S-m-y-t-h-e" he is immediately hired at a co-lossal salary. The miss-pelling is part of the comicality of the cartoon.

Further-more, what makes the editor of your Beg-Your-Pardon column so sure that Sikes, not Sykes, is correct? My recollection is that Mr. Sykes was a rough-neck and probably did not know how to spell his own name. We have Mr. Dickens'-s word for it that the correct spelling is Sikes, but where did Mr. Dickens get his information? Personally, I don't believe there was ever such a person as Mr. Sikes. I believe he was a character of Mr. Dickens'-s imagination. If this be true, what is the difference how you spell his name, and who knows where Mr. Dickens got his authority for the spelling?

Not only-that, but I will gamble there is no one in your office who knew Mr. Dickens personally, whereas there are several of you who know Mr. Orr, and those of you who do, know also that he is trust-worthy and that when he says this-or-that, he has grounds for his state-ment.

Look here, I have stood for a lot of raw stuff that you have been printing in your paper, which I have subscribed to it for twenty years, in kind, but when you begin taking sides with a person you never knew against one of your own employes, with whom you are well-acquainted and who has never given you cause to suspect him of being anything but on-the-square, and what is the difference if he does make a mistake in spelling, we all make mistakes, and when a person is doing the best he can, who can do any better than that. I would say it was time to call-a-halt.

In June 1919 Lardner left the *Chicago Tribune*, where he had spent the previous six years and had become a national figure. The following is his farewell column.

Mister Toastmaster and Gentlemen

CHICAGO TRIBUNE, JUNE 20, 1919

It is with mingled feelings of pain and astonishment that I stand before you tonight on the occasion of the sixth annual dinner of this organization. Arduous as the duties of this office have been at times, I have enjoyed the work as much as a person of my social position can enjoy work of any kind and have more than enjoyed the association with you gentlemen which my incumbency has afforded. In retiring from this office I wish to express my profound thanks to each and every one of you who have been of assistance to me in my carrying on of this great work.

That reminds me of a story I just read in a book called "Toasts and After-Dinner Stories": "A man who had just lost his wife said to a friend, who happened to be fresh from a reminder at home that he was very much married: 'I tell you, old man, it is hard to lose a wife.' 'Hard!' said the henpecked husband. 'Why, man, it's impossible!'" The book does not state whether the two men were named Pat and Mike or what.

I have been asked by the committee to say a few words to you in regard to my successor to this high office. This man, gentlemen, is a man who scarcely needs an introduction. In fact, I have seen him speak to people whom he had never met. This man, gentlemen, is a man whose name is known from the short-ribbed shores of Maine to the grape juice highballs of California.

This man's name is usually pronounced as spelled, but in France, whence this man's ancestors came, the final t would be silent. The name, translated from the French, means Milk, which reminds me of another story which I will copy out of the book:

"A small boy who had been very naughty was first reprimanded, then told that he must take a whipping. He flew upstairs and hid in the far corner under a bed. Just then his father came home. The mother told him what had occurred. He went upstairs and proceeded to crawl under the bed toward the youngster, who whispered excitedly, 'Hello, pop; is she after you, too?'"

The person holding this high office from which I am retiring is supposed to know something of sport. I can say for my successor that he possesses a far greater knowledge of the manly art of poker than I myself do and proved this several times as far back as 1908, when the both of us was single and employed on Market St. In those days, gentlemen, this man to whom I refer got a salary of $35 per week besides mine.

Gentlemen, I know there are a great many of you who live in the suburbs and who must catch your trains home, so I will not take up any more of your time. Gentlemen, it is my pleasure to present to you, Mr. Jacquin Lait,[3] the new president of the Wake of the News.

I thank you.

On the Scarcity of Paper for Newspapers

BELL SYNDICATE, DECEMBER 7, 1919

To the Editor:

From everywhere comes the cry save white paper and in my letter last wk. I all ready mentioned about the props. of all the big newspapers in the country held a meeting in N.Y. City and disgust the shortage and promised they wouldn't use no more of it then was nesary but from all as I can see the papers is still comeing out daily and Sun. as big as life and all the paper they been saveing wouldn't make a night gown for a cigarette and a outsider might think they had give their promise as a practical joke and with no intentions of carrying them out. But a friend of mine that knows some of the big editors personly claims they would be tickled to death to live up to the agreement only they haven't no idear in regards to how to go at it in other words they don't know what they could leave out of the papers without the subscribers getting sore.

Maybe the genial editor of this paper is in the same pretty pass and would welcome a few suggestions from a person like I who has given the matter a good deal of thought and have got my finger on the public pulse at all times you might say.

In the 1st. place gents I would cut out the news from foreign countries. They's a paper lying here along side of me which has got a ½ a col. on Page 1 about Egypt being give a constitution and another ½ a col. about 115 million gals. of whiskey being released from bondige and throwed on the market in England. Well if the item about Egypt had of been left out the most of us would have thought that Egypt always did have a constitution but even the few that knowed better could of stood it a few more months to go on thinking Egypt didn't have no constitution at lease till the white paper shortage is over. As for the other item it is like rubbing salt in a raw wound and if the papers wants to spend a ½ col. lacerating their readers on a exposed nerve why they can holler their heads off about the paper famine and not get no sympathy from thinking men.

I don't know of no case where printing the news from acrost from the old pond ever done any good where as they's plenty of times it has caused a lot of trouble like back in 1914 for inst. when the papers all came out 1 day and said the Belgiums had started a big war and all the big Europe countries was messed up in it and they kept printing about it till finely we go into it ourselfs where as if the news had of been suppressed in the 1st. place we wouldn't of knew they was a war or where to go to get into it. And if we hadn't of got into it I could of kept it a secret of haveing 4 vertical children and 2 flat feet.

2. You can pick up the paper every day and find where President Wilson is mentioned in it about a average of 10 times. Well it looks to me like most of your subscribers knows by this time that the President's last name is Wilson and they's no sense following up the word President with the word Wilson every time you got to mention him and as they's suppose to be 1,200 words in a col. why every paper could save a col. in 120 days by just saying President done so and so or President said this and that and the other thing instead of President Wilson said it or done it etc.

3. Cut out the death notices. When a man dies their family usually finds out about it without looking in no paper and as for his friends why I don't know of nobody that reads the death notices every day to find out if any of their friends has died on them, but if they got a friend that they think they's any chance of him dying on short notice why they will give his house a ring a couple of times a day and say is so and so still alive or dead or neutral. People that dies suddenly with or without help usually eats up a couple of paragraphs in the news section so all and all the mortician col. could be cut bodily and everybody have just as good a time.

4. Pretty near every paper now days has got a page or 2 of comical pictures that they call them strips which is suppose to make their peal to the readers risibles and cheer them up. The strips the way they have got them now is divided up in panels usually 4 or 5 of them in 1 strip. But as far as I can see all the cackles is crammed into the last panel so why not cut out the other 3 or 4 and just leave the comical one where Pat beans Abie with a crow bar and says Bam.

5. Finely gents I would cut the advertising cols. You can't never make me believe that a person don't know they need something without waiting till they see it in the ads. Or you can't make me believe that when I need a certain thing the ads is going to make me buy something else. For inst. what do I do when I need a hair cut why I go to a barber shop and

make my wants known either by word or token to the nearest vacant barber and they won't no amt. of advertising make me go in a animal store
and buy a pet wolf for my children instead of go in a barber shop and buy
a hair cut for myself. Or take when a female subscriber needs a new shoe
why her toes knows without her seeing the word mentioned in the advertising cols. and if she is a stranger in the city why she can find out by
walking up to a policeman and saying where can I get a new shoe. Or if
it's a pt. of gin she wants instead of a shoe why she can substitute the word
pt. of gin for the word shoe and say where can I get a pt. of gin.

The advertising cols. crowds out more live news such as "Jack Dempsey
took a foot bath last night" than any 1 feature in a newspaper and personly
I have penned many a comical line that never seen print because it had to
make way for a eulogy of somebody's embalming fluid that nobody will
ever know if all they claim for it is true or not.

Cut out the ads gents and all so the other items which I have mentioned
and 1st. thing you know people will be throwing white paper around like
it was 200 proof Scotch.

A New System for Running Newspapers

BELL SYNDICATE, JUNE 21, 1925

To the Editor:

Not long ago I seen a acct. of a debate between 2 college debate teams
and the subject disgust was whether or not the newspapers should ought
to publish crime news and whether the publication of same was libel to
increase crime or decrease same and the acct. did not state what arguments was used on one side or the other side but the side that spoke vs.
publication win the debate and what they must of argued was that the
romance and heroics connected with a bold burglary or hold-up or murder inspires young readers to follow the example to say nothing of the
financial gains enjoyed by the criminals till they get caught.

However the undersigned ain't never felt no crave towards law breaking by reading about it and if anything just the opp. and a specially when

I follow the story up and see the finish of the boys that went wrong. The glory and excitement and currency which comes as a reward of grand larceny and etc. ain't never going to make up for spending a summer without golf at Joliet, Ossining or Atlanta or wearing a piece of braided hemp for a neck tie.

They may of been quite a thrill to be got out of the story of Joe Diamond's[4] iron nerve as he set in the chair waiting for them to turn on the current but when the story was printed Joe was where newspaper deliveries is very uncertain. And while a good many of us was no doubt envious at all them love letters the gals was writing to Gerald Chapman[5] still and all I personly would rather have the postman hand me a dozen gas bills through my own front door than a 1000 mash notes between the iron bars of a Connecticut death cell.

No I don't believe crime news makes others go and do like wise but I do think they should ought to be a censorship for newspapers which bar out news that certainly does incite people to not only crimes of all kinds, but to divorce, revolution, sedition, wife desertion, anarchy and all around nashing of teeth, the news I refer to being the hundreds of items and stories which appears in the papers every day and which the sole purpose of same seems to be to make everybody wished they was somebody else.

A sample of the kind of item I mean was a recent dispatch from Munich only about 50 words long but it spoiled for me the entire month of May. The item said that the government and diet of Bavaria had adjourned for a whole day so as the members could make a thorough test of the new bock beer. In the face of such a item as that how is a person going to appreciate the beauties of a Long Island spring time or the fresh sweet milk supplied by she who we have aply named Bossie.

Or the story that was printed in regards to the arrival of Mr. and Mrs. Jack Dempsey in N.Y. city and they was a bran new spick and span $16000.00 automobile at the depot to meet them with a livered chauffeur and Mrs. Dempsey asked Jack if it belonged to some friend and he says no sweetheart it is just a little trinket I bought for you. Well gents after that do you imagine that she who I sometimes call my Mrs. is libel to get excited over the 60 cents worth of candy which I carefully selected at the station news stand as I dashed by to catch the 5.55?

Or the story about Gloria getting rid of a Swede name like Swanson and becoming the Marquise de la Falaise de la Coudray at one fell swoop and when they have read that kind of news how is our women folks going to be satisfied with husbands named Jones and Brown and without no title to go with it except maybe licensed garbage inspector or even worthy kleagle?

Or a story like the one about the dame that come home from the other side a few weeks ago and had to pay a duty of $5000.00 on the new gowns and etc. she bought in gay Paris and when our gals reads stuff along those lines what a fat chance we have got to argue with them about blowing as much $85.00 on a complete new summer wardrobe.

Or a story like the one about the doctor that took out his own appendix without no antiseptic or nothing and smiled and chatted during the operation. Suppose your wife reads that, do you think she is going to give you any sympathy when you moan and groan because you blistered a finger playing golf?

If I was running a newspaper I would put the quietus on all stories such as the above and also all passenger lists of steamers sailing for Europe, all news and pictures about Palm Beach or Pasadena in the winter time or Bar Harbor or northern Michigan in the summer, all reference to the latest styles of women's dress in Paris, all mention of anybody's private yacht, all mention of any automobile costing more than $500.00 and all reference to real beer or to weddings where one of the contracting parties was worth more than $62.50 cash.

So much for the news columns, And as for the advertising, I would limit it to the 5 and 10 cent stores and then not let them mention more than 30 cents worth of their merchandise in any one ad.

Going Back to Work

MORNING TELEGRAPH, DECEMBER 4, 1928

Convinced that New York is in a coma over the announcement that I am going to work, the head man has asked me to explain the phenomenon in a few well-rounded gutturals.

Well, it seems that one day last month a big story broke; a man went into a restaurant and ordered a pot of tea and the waiter said do you want lemon or cream and the man said neither, I just want the tea, and the waiter brought him the tea. The paper got a tip on this story and the head man told the city editor to send a reporter to verify it and perhaps pick up some interesting sidelights: Was the waiter married? How did he happen to be a waiter? Had he ever been gassed?

"I'se mahty sorry boss," said the city editor, "but this paper, she's got no reporters. All she's got am feature writers and experts.'

"Hire a reporter, then!" ordered his superior. "After all, a newspaper should have some news. Hire an old-fashioned go-getter, the kind that ain't too blase to register a scoop,* the kind that takes pride in scoring a beat.** Tell him money is no object."

"He may have his own ideas about that," said the city editor.

Nevertheless, I was approached and a proposition made, and, as is my custom in such cases, I consulted she whom God hath joined us together more years than I cares to admit.

"Can you do it at home, like your other work?" she inquired.

"I'm afraid not," I replied.

"Take it!" she said, and the thing was done.

Now then, if other papers have two or three dozen reporters, press associations, etc., to gather their news, and still don't seem to get even half of it, you can see it will be something of a strain on one man to cover the whole field himself; few would undertake it. Neither would this fellow, but for a clause in the contract which gives him three days off per week instead of the regular reporter's allotment of one. The results of my talent and notorious hustling proclivities will appear in the issues of Tuesday, Wednesday, Thursday and Sunday. I have arranged to spend the other three days with the chiropodist.

It is obvious that space limitations will compel me to be a little choosey about the items printed. But readers may be sure that whatever they find here is either true or a forgery and that it happened very recently or hardly ever.

There are certain innovations I have in mind, notably in the way of pictures. I have always contended that people tire of seeing the same faces in the paper day after day, even if they belong to Norma Shearer or Nicky Arnstein, who, so far as I know, was never a leading candidate for Miss America or Queen of Comus.[6] Personally I can vouch for the fact that it doesn't help my breakfast to be confronted by Bugs Baer's lineaments every morning of my life.

If it becomes necessary to run frequent stories about Babe Ruth or Queen Mary I will attempt to furbish them at least a little bit with likenesses of Gertie Lawrence or Paulino Uzcudan.

Other novel ideas in news treatment and illustrations will be inserted and developed here from time to time and in closing this foreword I heartily urge my sweet public to send me any suggestions they may have or any hot tips that may come to their ears. Just call or dial the operator and say "I want an ambulance."

* A large ladle for dipping liquids; a utensil for bailing boats.
** A biennial plant producing a root much used for food, and also for making sugar.

11

People, Places, and Pieces of Ring's Mind

Some of Lardner's most essential nonfiction defies easy categorization. In "Have a Spelling Bee of Your Own," for instance, he put forth his views on the vagaries of the English language: "Nobody but a nut could spell our language right—that is according to the dictionary. In fact the dictionary way of spelling wds. is so hard that after every wd. they half to write down some other wd. that means the same thing so as people can tell what the 1st wd. meant."

Similarly, "If You Ain't in the Monday Opera Club, You Don't Belong" gives an unfiltered view of his feelings about snobbery, a recurring theme in his short stories, while "Marry a Man or Caddy For Him" is a scathing rebuttal to the concept of speak no ill of the dead. Obtuse congressmen, the advertising business, mail-order writing courses, actresses denying press accounts of love affairs, celebrity beauty tips, and more provided objects of opportunity and he made the most of them.

Lardner traveled often for pleasure—he and Ellis, along with Grantland Rice and his wife, took long annual vacations to Florida and the Caribbean—and these trips provided fertile ground for column material ("Pretty near everybody at Palm Beach has there secretary with them wile most of the visitors to Miami can read and write.") as well as a place to relax.

A trip out west left him unimpressed with the Grand Canyon ("I never seen such a divot and further and more they don't heat it very good and maybe should put in a oil burner"). But he had a memorable stay in Hollywood, where he brushed a number of famous elbows and was so impressed by Charlie Chaplin's hospitality that he uncharacteristically gushed over him in print. His encounter with Pola Negri was another matter.

Also included here are "Fifteen Cents Worth," which anticipates "Haircut," in format though not in subject matter, a recounting of his reaction to learning he owed the city of Chicago fifty dollars, a story and a poem about his encounters with New York traffic, and more.

Fifteen Cents Worth

CHICAGO TRIBUNE, JANUARY 6, 1916

Victim—Just a shave.

Barber—Yes, sir. Funny weather for this time o' year. Unhealthy weather. 'Least everybody seems to be ailin'. Grip or influenza or whatever you want to call it. Reg'lar contagion. You had it yet?

V. (through a towel, darkly)—Burrh.

B—You're lucky if you ain't had it. But you better knock wood. I had it bad Christmas week. Great time to be sick! Felt rotten. Just my luck to have it come Christmas week. Did you have a good Christmas?

V. (chewing lather)—Tuh.

B.—Christmas is all right in a way, but they's too much useless givin'. Man gets ten things he can't use for every one he wants. Was you in town for Christmas?

V. (through another towel)—Caw.

B.—Well, we're better off than them poor fellas over in the trenches. They must of had a fine Christmas! And most o' them don't even know what they're fightin' about. Nobody knows except the kaiser and the king and the fella that started it, and they don't know themselves. All as I hope is that we don't get mixed up in it. But I guess they's no danger o' that with Wilson at the hellum. We'd been mixed up long ago if Rusefelt was president. We're pretty lucky to have a man like Wilson at the hellum just at this time. Razor hurt? But still and all Wilson lets them make a monkey out of him. Look at the Lusitaynia! He made Germany promise they wouldn't sink no more boats without givin' warnin' and they go right ahead in a week or two and sink a couple more. A nice massage would fresh you up. And every time they sink a boat and kill a few hundred people he writes them another note and they say it was a mistake and they was aimin' at a fish or somethin' and promise they won't do it no more and next thing you know you pick up a paper and they's been another boat sank and Wilson stands for it. You wouldn't never see them monkeyin' with ol' Teddy that way. First time they done somethin' he didn't like he'd say: "Here!" he'd say. "You fellas cut that out or you'll have the stars and stripes on your neck," he'd tell them. And they'd cut it out, too, because they'd know he was talkin' business. That's the kind o' guy we should ought to have at the hellum. They make a monkey o' Wilson. You must shave yourself most o' the time; you got it all uneven up here. What do you think o' Henry Ford.[1] That was a fine flivver! I wonder what he thought he was goin' to pull. Guess he thought they'd all jump out o' the trenches when they seen him comin'. Wanted some free advertisin', I guess. Well, he got it, but I'd hate to make a monkey o' myself for advertisin'. Still, I guess his intentions was all right. You know they laughed at Columbus. But he showed them. Ford's all right and a whole lot better than the people that's been laughin' at him. A nice massage'd clear that skin all up. Well, the Feds is all through. They'd ought to knew better than buck organized ball. They was too much money against them. And they didn't have no real stars neither. Maybe one or two, but take them all through and they was no class to them. I guess Ward and them's sore they ever went into it. Weeghman'll come out all right, but it'll cost him some money. They certainly made organized ball quit at that. I'd hate to of lose all the dough that's been dropped in baseball these last two years. But next year'd ought to be good, and they'll be better ball played. Last year they wasn't enough good ball players to go round. The Cubs'd ought to be good this year if Weeghman combines the two teams. I think he's a sucker, though, to play on the north side. It'll get a lot o' people sore that's been goin' to games on the west side for twenty years. But, o' course, the park's new out north and I guess they'll draw all right with a good club. They won't hurt the Sox none though. Old Commy's got the crowd with him; Commy and the hitless wonders. What do you think o' Thompson closin' up Sundays? They must of been some reason or he wouldn't done it. It made a lot o' people sore. I think a man'd ought to be able to get a drink Sunday if he wants it. Still I guess they's enough time durin' the week to get all that's good for you. I don't touch it myself. You got a couple o' blackheads there. Nice massage'd clean that all up. All right, you know best. Wet or dry?

(Victim leaves chair, puts on collar, coat, and hat, takes check to cashier, pays it, and walks out.)

Barber (to himself)—The cheap stiff!

Starring in the Movies with Billie Burke

CHICAGO TRIBUNE, MARCH 11, 1916

It isn't often I go to the movies. I never saw a single one of Kathlyn's Adventures[2] and I don't know to this day the solution of the Million Dollar Mystery.[3] But I purpose to be a regular when the still unchristened Billie Burke[4] serial is under way.

The company was down in this swell Florida place—I forget its name—and of course our crowd was there, too. And Jimmie Sheldon wanted a lot of extras to stage a tea party in the cocoanut grove, so he named me as one of his recruiting officers. I was on speaking terms with one other person at the place, so I engaged the two of us to be in on the party.

We all donned the best-looking day clothes we had and were ushered to various tables and told to wait. Much as I dread publicity, I was forced to take a seat at the table nearest the camera.

What this portion of the plot was I don't know. But pretty soon they began turning the crank and Miss Burke walked into the grove and sat at the table right next to our'n.

Then the director says: "Now, Miss Burke, you pretend you recognize somebody at the next table—just anybody—and go up and speak to him."

Well, sir, believe it or not, I was the just anybody. But my back was turned to her and I didn't know when she was coming, and when she came and held out her hand, instead of registering polite surprise and pleasure, I showed a faceful of petrified embarrassment. I didn't even rise; I couldn't make my knees behave.

"We'll take that again," says the director. "I'd rather have you go to his table before you sit down at your own."

You can wager that this time I knew when she was coming and had the correct expression all set before she arrived. I didn't want that picture spoiled.

So while I was standing up shaking hands with her, she says:

"We're supposed to say something to each other."

"Are we?" I says.

"Wa-wa-wa-wa-wa," says Miss Burke. And I couldn't answer to save my soul.

"Wa-wa-wa-wa-wa," she says again. "Just say anything you think of."

And I couldn't think of a thing.

So after she'd wa-wad once more and held my hand for a few feet, she went back to her own table and I fell into my chair unconscious.

The others gave me the laugh and boasted about how garrulous they'd have been under the circumstances. But I noticed they were dumb all the time she was there and there was nothing in the directions to keep them still.

When it was all over, I thought of any number of things, many of them mirth-provoking, which I might have said to her.

Later I asked Jimmie Sheldon if extras didn't get $5 for speaking parts.

"Yes, they do, for speaking parts," he says. and begged a cigaret.

Marry a Man or Caddy for Him

BELL SYNDICATE, OCTOBER 31, 1920

To the Editor:

They seems to be a kind of a unwritten law that when a man dies, why him dying makes him one of the best guys in the world no matter how much of a bum he was wile still amongst us yet, and they's a old saying witch says:

"Don't never speak no ill about the dead," and it don't make no differents what you know about the corps delicti before he become such, why you are suppose to keep the facts to yourself and when ever the recent decease is mentioned you got to say, "He was one grand character," and what a crime it is that he had to be took when so many crooks and etc. is let live.

Personly I can't see no sense to the above rules as in the 1st. place statistics shows that when the majority of men dies they do it against their will and try not to and don't deserve no credit for same, and the only gents who a credit mark is comeing to them for passing out is the ones that does it on purpose. But these birds is few and far between and you take even a soldier that gets bumped off in the war and his friends and relatives make the remark that he made the supreme sacrifice hit and died for his country, but if you could get at the details of the case you would probably find out that when this bird dashed into the thickest of the fray he kind of hoped that the enemy would be the one that would miss him instead of his friends and relatives.

In the 2d. place it looks to me like the best time to pan a guy is when the last sad rights has been wished on him and he don't give a d-m no more what you think, where as on the other hand it don't do him no good at this stage of the game to say what a humdinger he was before the angels signed him up, though the kind words may furnish a hearty laugh to the people that use to live with him, his Mrs. incluseive. Many a bereft widow has to dash in the other rm. to choke back a smile when her callers begins to rave about what a super man it was that has walked out on her.

In the 3d. place what kind of a effect does it have on you and I that is still alive to hear the boys drool over the decease? Why, we say to ourself what is the use of being a right liver and haveing one, and etc. if they shower words of praise and economys on a bird like that the minute he is parked in the wood kimona?

For inst. a wile ago they was a friend of mine that croaked and I had been friends with both himself and wife and knew the both of them pretty well and how they felt towards the other and etc. and when he was gone I kept away from the house so as to not half to tell her things about him that she all ready knowed, and knew they wasn't so and knew I knowed it, and when this bird died they was a piece in the home town paper that says it didn't see how the world was going to shimmy along without this bird and everybody that had knew him loved him on acct. of him being kind and frank and ernest and had such a sweet disposition and so generous and etc. and also admired him for his intelligents and what a whiz he had been in college and etc.

Well, I don't know if his relic seen this write up or not, but if she did I hope her lips wasn't cracked because she must of knew him a whole lot better than I did—and I knowed him on the golf course.

This baby was nuts over the ancient scotch vice and you may as well talk about a square gambler or a baby that dont never wake up in the night as to say a man is a honest golfer. This bird was honest and above the boards about once in 2 wks. when he shot a hole in par. When he was on his game and clicking off 7s and 8s and a occasional eagle 10 spot, why you'd be surprised. When he would get on the green in 6 and you ast him how many he lied, he would think a minute and then say:

"Let's see. Caddy, how many shots have I had?"

Well, when a man asks their caddy how many shots have they had, keep your hand on your watch. And if the caddy says, "Six," instead of five or or four they'll be another caddy holding the bag next time out. As for him being ernest and generous, well I have seen this party hook into a few acres of alfalfa and hold the game up sine die wile we all of us helped hunt for the ball and every 2 or 3 minutes he would say:

"I will drop another ball," expecting us to say:

"Oh, no, let's look for this a wile longer," but we didn't never say it because we knowed he didn't have no intentions of dropping another ball and when we would get home a hr. and ½ late for dinner and tell our Mrs. that it was this guy's fault as he kept us looking for his ball all P.M. why she would probably say:

"Well, you didn't half to wait for him, did you?" The he—ll you didn't.

The sweet flavor of the dispoish lasted as long as he got his brassys up in the air, but leave him top a couple of them and it would all of a sudden turn sour and the caddy would be a dirty, low life, no good bum with ancesters that wasn't human.

As for the meddles that this bird win at college they couldn't of none of them been for mathematics as he hadn't never learned to count over 9 even with us all trying to help him, and further and more a man that makes a name for himself as a student has got to have a pretty fair memory where as this guy was the champion forgetter in our club.

Yes. gents, the write-up this guy got when he croaked give me a good laugh but it also made me wonder why should I go to church every Xmas and pay my debts and etc. because when I croak they can't spread no more salve about me than they handed this baby, witch I knowed all of it was wrong even if I didn't know him nowheres only on the golf coarse, where as his wife knowed him a whole lot better, though if you can't marry a man, the best way to learn him is to watch him golf. If you want the truth about a guy, ask his wife or his caddy.

So when my time comes I am going to give the boys cart Blanch to say whatever they want to about me that will get through the mails because their compliments won't make me feel any the less deader and they wont fool nobody especially the bereaved family and only make the latter smile at a time when they are doing their best not to.

Keep the Reform Fires Burning

BELL SYNDICATE, JANUARY 30, 1921

To the Editor:

Several people has wrote to me lately complaining that they hasn't been no new reforms suggested in the land of the free in the last couple of wks. and it begins to look like the boys that takes care of our morals was loafing on the job and why didn't I step in and give them some new idears to work on.

Well, I can name a whole lot of things that could stand a trip to the cleaners only you can't expect to reform everything at once, and you half to pick out one to start in on so why not begin with the advertiseing business which some of my best friends is mixed up in it, but when the public wellfare is conserned a man shouldn't let personal feelings interfere. They's plenty of room for a moral uplift amongst the boys and gals that writes our ads and a man don't realize how much till you make a study of it like I done.

The way I come to get interested in it was last fall when I was talking to a friend of mine that writes ads and I was telling him how hard it is to make both ends meet the other and he asked me why didn't I try and write ads too which he says they was good money in it.

So I told him I couldn't never be a ad writer because I haven't got no imagination, so he says that is the last thing a man needs to write ads because when you write them now days for a first class consern they won't let you tell nothing but the truth about their goods and further and more if you don't tell the truth, the high class magazines won't print the ads.

So I says do you mean to say that all the ads you read in the magazines is nothing but facts, and he says you bet they are and I will give you a dollar for every miss statement you find in them so I asked him what he considered was the high class magazines and he named a few of them and I bought them and when I didn't have nothing else to do I looked through them at the ads. Well friends, if I had of tooken this bird up on his offer he could of paid his sir tax with the change from a ruble.

One of the first ads I run acrost was a ad of a cold cream and the people that makes it is A. No. 1 and O.K. but here is how the ad started out.

"Most of us can remember when our mothers or grand mothers on retiring used to take with them to their rooms a saucer of fresh cream."

Well personly I didn't remember no such a thing but I wanted to make it a fair test so I chose 10 people at random and says to them one at a time:

"Can you remember when your mother or grand mother on retiring used to take with them to their room a saucer of fresh cream?"

Six out of the 10 replied with the short and ugly word "no!" Three of them give me a dirty look and the other says:

"I have heard that one!"

I come to a ad of a winter top for cars that for all as I know it may be a good winter top, but the ad says:

"Bad weather is the time you need your car most."

So I asked 4 guys when they needed their car most and 3 of them says in summer when its the golf season and the other one says whenever it's laid up in the garage. And wile we are talking about automobile accessorys, they was another ad that said:

"Every owner wants his gold initials on side door of his automobile."

I made inquirys about this from 3 birds that owns cars and couldn't get a civil answer out of none of them.

Then they was a ad that said:

"No gift from a father to a son could be more sensible than a . . . razor."

I didn't half to make no inquirys about that as I have got 4 sons of my own and its just a question in my mind whether it would be more sensible to give them a razor or lock them up in a room with a mad dog.

And speaking about razors they was a shaving cream that they claimed made shaving a pleasure, but I will bet that even when the men that makes it and gets it for nothing, I bet when they are through their work and out for a good time they don't run home and shave themselfs all the evening or they don't never think of spending their vacation removing their wiskers with this here cream.

Another ad sung the praises of a certain mince meat and it said down at the bottom "Thursday is pie day and as such is observed nationally."

Well friends how many of you gets every Thursday off or tends special church services once a wk. in honor of mince meat and how many of you goes around all day Thursday saying, "Merry Pie Day," to your friends?

"Cleanliness brings happiness and good cheer," is another bold statement which it looks like it was open to question.

For inst. I got 4 people right here in the house that ain't happy if they ain't dirty, and just the idear of getting cleaned up is enough to send them into tantrums.

Then I come acrost 2 ads of musical instruments one of which I happen to know about personly myself. It says:

"You can double your income, your pleasure and your popularity with a saxaphone." Well one of them things was give to me 2 yrs. ago and so far my income ain't nowheres near double, and in the second place I can enjoy a good show or a fight just as much or even more so if I leave my saxaphone home, and as far as popularity is conserned I kind of feel like maybe we would have more callers if we traded this elegant instrument for a couple bottles of Scotch.

The other ad said:

"If you can play quaint dreamy Hawaiian music or latest songs on the ukelele you will be wanted everywhere."

Well, I know a bird that can do that little thing and I can name a 100 places he ain't wanted, to none where he is wanted, and if the mail man didn't have nothing to do but deliver this guy's invitations they would lock him up as a vagrant.

And another one was the washing machine ad. It says:

"For a mother, young or old, no gift could be better proof of thoughtful affection."

I know mothers both young and old that if you handed them any kind of a washing machine they would show their appreciation of your thoughtful affection with a wallop in the jaw.

Those is only a few samples but they are enough to convince me that the advertiseing game is far from pure and I don't see why the lords day alliance or somebody don't get busy and not only make these guys tell the truth about their goods but make them tell the whole truth.

For inst. if they are advertiseing say the Perfect Cord Tire, why let their ad read:

"The Perfect Cord sells for $70 and it's pretty near as good as a $75 tire. It is a non-skid tire when the car is standing still on a dry road and it don't hardly ever get a puncture unless you run over a nail or something. The Perfect Tire is guaranteed for 6000 miles which means that if one of them blows out when you haven't only drove it 1000 miles, why take it to one of our agents and try to get new one."

Or if they was advertiseing a car itself:

"The price of the Echo Six complete is $1685 F.O.B. Albany, meaning that if you live way off somewheres like Utica the chassis won't only cost you $1750 and then all as you half to buy is a body and a steering wheel and a couple spare tires. The 7 passenger model has room for 3 grown ups and a weasel. The Echo don't use hardly any gas as she is laid up most of the time. The Echo don't need no patent safety locking device. Her looks is her protection."

That is the way to make them advertise, gents, and when you get a system like that working, they won't be no more pitifull cases like the poor sap I spoke of, that went and learned how to play quaint dreamy Hawaiian music on a ukelele and there's only one place he is ever asked to go.

Automatic Writing

BELL SYNDICATE, FEBRUARY 6, 1921

To the Editor:

Pretty near all the papers and magazines you pick up now days is devoteing considerable space to the question of whether they's spirits or whether they ain't spirits which I guess they's no question about life after death for those kind as old John Barleycorn was suppose to die a yr. ago last month but you can still go to a banquet or a card party and find 50 per cent of the guests pretty well haunted. What I refer to is the spirits that they claim is in the human body and keeps on liveing long after the Knights of Pythias has seen you properly sunk.

Most of the wise crackers laughs and calls it all bunk but they's a few bright minds that has fell for it even in countrys where they still got the kind of liquor that you can get plastered without going cuckoo. Take for inst. Conan Doyle over in England who I don't mean that he drinks, but if he did he could get good stuff, but any way you got to pay some tension to his opinion in these matters in regards to life after death as he spilled Sherlock Holmes into the royal Geo. or somewheres in one book and then brought him back to solve 80 thousand wds. of more mysterys.

But wile I use to eat up Sherlock and always put Conan amongst my favorite authors, still and all his psychic articles didn't never prove nothing to me only that you can go to sleep a whole lot easier reading them than his detective storys. And I ain't even got no desire to believe the stuff that was in that last one I read where it said that some kind of dope flowed out of a medium and formed itself into the shapes of people that had departed and one of the shapes looked like President Wilson with a mustache. If I had 3 wishes the 4th. one would be to die and then trickle out of some medium and get in such shape that I looked like President Wilson with a mustache.

They's no doubt but that Conan is a bright mind and has made a study of the subject and is a expert on it and he believes in it, but that don't mean nothing. Look at the baseball wisenheimers that hadn't did nothing all their life but watch the game or play it and yet they didn't taste nothing sour in a team like Cincinnati knocking a pitcher like Lefty Wms. for 3 gools in a row.

No matter how smart or honest a person is they are libel to go wrong and as far as this baby is conserned I have quit takeing hearsay evidents for anything. For inst. plenty of guys that has apparently got a good mind and they wouldn't lie to me when it didn't get them nothing, well plenty of these guys has told me about different photo plays that they said was good, but until I see one that is good I won't believe they is such a thing.

And the same way about spriits. I wouldn't of never believed in them from reading Conan or Mr. Lodge. It took personal experience to win me over and I will tell you about it, not with no idear of makeing converts but because I guess pretty near everybody is interested in the subject just at this time.

Well the other night I was talking to a friend of mine and we got talking about spirits and etc., and she said a friends of hers had told her about a friend of the gal I was talking to's friend, and this guy had a piece of property that he wanted to get rid of it and he got a offer for the property and he set down to write a letter accepting the offer, but when he got all ready to write the pen begin writeing for him and here is what it wrote:

"Don't sell now but wait till the 4 of Jan. and you will get a offer that is $1200 more." And the pen signed his old man's name that had died in the real estate business. So the guy waited till the 4 of Jan. and sure enough he got the offer with the $1200 raise and took it.

So my friend that was telling me about this says:

"That is what they call automatic writeing. It hasn't never happened to me personly but you can bet that if it does I will follow the advice they give me, because I heard of another man that was a Yale man and just before the Yale-Princeton game last fall he got a wire from a friend of his out west asking him did he want to bet on Yale and he did, so he went to the telegraph office to wire and take the bet, and just as he was going to write the telegram the pencil begin moving in his hand and wrote down:

"Don't bet on Yale."

"But the man was a unbeliever so he made the pen write what he wanted it to and took the bet and lose $500."

Well, I said the spirits seemed to have the right dope in both them instants though a whole lot of people that wasn't dead yet had told me to not bet on Yale, but I said it was silly to disregard tips like that when you got them because if they was such a thing as spirits they probably knowed more about things that is going on than we do.

But I says I didn't suppose a experience such as those would ever come to me as I don't hardly ever use a pen only to sign mortgages. So my friend said she supposed it could happen with a typewriter just as good as a pen or pencil so I come home and didn't think no more about it till the next morning when I set down in front of the typewriter to work.

For over an hr. I set there with my fingers in position to write but not a word come. Then all of a sudden my fingers begin to move and before they stopped they was a sentence wrote on the paper but so dim I couldn't hardly make it out. Here is what it said:

"Now is the time for all good men to come to the aid of the party and get a new ribbon."

That was what was wrote on the paper and I set there maybe a couple hrs. more but not another word showed up and finely I remembered what happened to the man that took the advice, and what happened to the man that didn't, so I jumped on a train and went to N.Y. city and bought myself a new ribbon and set up most of that night getting it fixed O.K. in the typewriter.

The next day I set down at the desk again and waited and this time it was 2 hrs. before my fingers begin to move. The words was a whole lot plainer than the other time and was as follows:

"Don't work today don't work today don't work today."

Three straight days I set there the same length of time and three straight days I got the same advice and followed it to the letter and this is the 4th. day and I have been working but just now my fingers begun to run wild again and this is what they wrote:

"Don't work no more you are all wore out."

So I guess you won't blame me if I obey and you won't blame me neither for changeing my mind about spirits though as I say I don't expect to convert no skeptics with my testimony. My own family for inst. She asked me just last night why I hadn't did no work lately and I told her because the spirit had advised me not to and she says whose spirit and I said I didn't know.

So she says, "I know. It's your own spirit."

So I says, "Don't be silly because when it's automatic writeing the spirit that dictates has got to be the spirit of somebody that is dead."

"Well," she says.

Some Cigars Would Cure Any Smoker

BELL SYNDICATE, AUGUST 21, 1921

To the Editor:

I don't expect no coupons from the United cigar stores for writeing this here letter but a man has got to write about something and if such famous men as Irving Cobb and Samuel Blythe sees fit to bare their soul in confidential articles like how I got skinny and how I quit cocktails and etc. why I guess it is O.K. for a man like I to tell the story of how I conquered my lady Nicotine a specially as it seems to me like this subject must be of greater gen. int. than the other 2 as I believe they's more people wants to quit smokeing than wants to get thin or dry. But in writeing this article I will half to raise the veil of secrecy in regards to some of my most intimate details which I ask the readers indulgents in advance for same.

Well friends I did not begin smokeing till I was 9 yrs. old and kind of went at it slow even then as I had been warned that smokeing would stunt a person's growth and I might say here that if that is true, why if I had not of smoked at all I would now be holding a lucrative position with Ringling's circus.

Most men of 9 yrs old that is raised in small towns begins their career of crime with a pipe load of corn silk, but I started right in at the top with my father's cigars which on acct. of him haveing a whole box of them I did not think he would miss a couple a day but he found it out some way another and him and I had a meeting and I give in on a couple minor points amongst which was that I would quit smokeing if he would quit acting that way. So I lived pretty clean for 3 yrs. and then begin again but this time it was cubebs and finely cigarettes which I rolled my own with a brand of tobacco that is now out of print which it was named Duke's Cameo and it looked like it had been swept off the barber shop floor and probably tasted the same.

Well it ain't my intentions to bore the reader with a history of the different articles I smoked but sufficient to say that by the time I was 21 I was takeing 2 or 3 pills before breakfast wile dureing the rest of the day I didn't play no favorites but indulged in home mades and ready mades and pipes and cigars in whatever order they come handy and nobody had to rack their brains to try and think up what to give me for xmas.

Well 5 or 6 yrs. later I went to a Dr. and asked him what was it and he says it was whooping cough which it was on acct. of my palate being too long and kept tickling me, so he snipped off ½ of it and for all as I know he has still got his 50 per cent and I will furnish his name and address to bona fide collectors.

Well as a person grows older they learn that the secret of happiness in this life is makeing the best of what you have got and it wasn't long till I found out that I could cough just as good with only ½ a palate and I enjoyed myself that way for 6 or 7 yrs. more and then seen a throat specialist and he says it was the tonsils so I give them to him but kept the cough. A few days after this operation which I won't go into the details of it the bird that had ministered the ether come to see me and asked how many cigarettes did I smoke a day and I told him 50 and he says it ain't none of my business but if I was you I would quit before I got the habit.

So at this time we had a Dr. writeing health articles for the paper and he didn't charge nothing for advice to fellow employs so I asked him if they was anything that would help a person quit smokeing and he says to go to a drug store and buy some gentian root and whenever I felt like smokeing, to just chew a little of that instead. Well friends maybe some of you has tasted gentian root but if you haven't I would advice you to try it. It won't cure you from the tobacco habit but it will fix you so that your Mrs. can serve quinine for dessert and you will wonder if she has bought a bee.

Well things went along till about a yr. ago when a friend of mine that had also whooped it up for several yrs. said he had found a kind of tobacco that you could smoke as many cigarettes as you wanted and not cough your head off so I give it a trial and it was just like he said. Only they was a slight draw back namely that the ashes on these kind of cigarettes don't half to be knocked off but they fall off themselfs and they never light nowheres but on your pants leg and when they light they stay lit and by the time you have smoked these cigarettes a wk. your clothes is as full of holes as an ocarena.

Well friends I would rather cough my way through life than go around looking so porous so I went back to the ready mades and stuck with them till this last June when I got the big idear which was to not try and quit smokeing entirely but to cut out the cigarettes and smoke nothing but cigars on the grounds that you wouldn't smoke near so much.

Like for inst. you wouldn't be libel to light one before breakfast or in the middle of the night or dureing meals or go out between acts at the theatre and smoke one, and in fact you wouldn't have time to smoke more than 8 or 9 of them per day. Whereas 2 to 4 pills before breakfast ain't nothing you might say and between then and bed time you can easy get away with 40 or 50 and when you go to bed you don't no sooner get to sleep than you wake up and they won't nothing put you back to sleep but another pill, till it gets so as the night is divided into 24 shifts of 20 minutes each, which you sleep one shift and smoke one shift and vice versa.

So friends and readers I cut out the cigarettes and have took up the cigars and that is all they is to the story of how I win my battle with the lady Nicotine only I might add that the first 2 days under the new regime I didn't hardly cough at all but now I am hitting again on all 4 cylinders, and I don't wake up no more in the night because in order to do that it is first necessary to go to sleep.

Have a Spelling Bee of Your Own

BELL SYNDICATE, JANUARY 8, 1922

To the Editor:

I see by the papers where they are putting on a old fashion spell down in Detroit and giveing away prizes to the kids that can spell the best and etc. and a event like this kind always stirs up a lot of int. in a town and is a good thing for a town though it does seem kind of funny to hold a spelling contest in a place where they put a z in Cousins.[5]

But any way they's no subject which I am more interested in it than the subject of spelling and this may come as a surprise to some of my readers as the impression seems to of got around that I am not a A. No. 1 speller though nothing could be further than the truth. They may be a good many wds. which I don't spell them in the same way like they are spelled in the dictionary but that is no sign that my way ain't just as good and maybe a little better and I always say that if people can understand easy what a man means, why that means he is a good speller and I will bet you can't find no wds. in any of my writeings that is ½ as hard to understand as wds. you will find in the dictionary.

In fact the dictionary way of spelling wds. is so hard that after every wd. they half to write down some other wd. that means the same thing so as people can tell what the 1st wd. meant.

Speaking about the dictionary it has got a couple of chapters in it which you can read without going to sleep and one of them tells where several different men of learning has tried to fix up our language so as every letter would have only one sound and as soon as you seen a wd. spelled out you would know the right way to pronounce it, and one of these men said the only way that could be done would be by adding 14 more letters to the alphabet. This idear was throwed in the ash can on the motion of the people that makes alphabet soup.

In another chapter it tells where a man named Ellis was trying experiments with the letters we have all ready got and he found out that you can spell the wd. scissors 6,000 different ways. It didn't tell what he done with himself the rest of the morning. And it didn't tell why we half to go on spelling it scissors when sizzers would cut your nails just as pretty.

H. L. Mencken has wrote a book on the American Language, which he brings out in it how different we spell than the English though we are supposed to both be useing the same tongue.

Well, they will be more and more differents as the yrs. go by, so what I say is that it don't do no harm for me to spell a wd. different from the way some old English dictionary writer spelled it, provided I make the spelling easier, which is what Americans generally always do. Like for inst. an Englishman would say:

"I have the honour to enclose a cheque."

Whereas we would say:

"I have the honor to enclose a check," which is two less letters which don't amt. to much in one sentence but would be a big saving in a long book. Take Wells's history book for example, and if he had used American spelling I bet he could of wrote it in at least a 1/2 hr. less time.

Wile we are on the subject of spelling, though I don't want to discourage none of the Detroit boys and gals that's trying to improve themselfs along those lines, yet it seems nessary to say at this pt. that spelling is something which you can't master no more than singing alto. Either you are a born good speller or a born bum speller and if you are a good speller you won't half to spend no time in school studying how to spell this wd. or that.

On the other hand if you are a rotten speller you will keep on being a rotten speller though if you have got a good memory you can get high marks.

Like for inst., I know a gal that when she was in school she always got a 100 in spelling because she studied all the wds. that was in the book and memorized how to spell them. But for the 1st. 2 yrs. after we was married we lived on Prairie Ave. in Chicago and every time she wanted to write and tell one of her friends her address, she would half to go out first and look at the street sign. But a woman don't half to be a good speller to be a good wife and in fact some of the best wifes I know has their bad spells.

But they's another wd. of cheer which I might breath to folks that has trouble with their spelling and that is that some of the most famous people in history was rotten spellers and men like Shakespeare and Chaucer and etc. was so bad that if you read their stuff you will sometimes find the same wd. spelled 4 and 5 different ways on the same page. Geo. Washington, Babe Ruth and John L. Sullivan is others who might be mentioned as guys that clumb to the pinnacle but if you asked any of them to spell pinnacle they would probably bust you in the jaw.

As for good spelling being nessary for financial success it would almost seem like the facts of the case was just opp. The richest people in the world is the boys that draws the comical cartoons. These guys makes more money than a boot legger, but when they get their cartoons all drawed they half to send out for a copy of yesterday's paper before they can sign their name.

If those ain't enough alibis to tell teacher, why you might mention that nobody but a nut could spell our language right—that is according to the dictionary—with all the paradoxs and inconsistents and etc. which we have got in it. We may think the Russians and frogs has got a hard lingo to master, but suppose you was a foreigner going to school in this country and you thought you was getting wise to the system of spelling when all of a sudden you would run across 5 wds. like lough, bough, dough, rough and cough. There is 5 wds. spelled the same way only for the 1st letter. Try and make them rhyme.

Try Love Letters on Your Creditors

BELL SYNDICATE, APRIL 9, 1922

To the Editor:

They was 2 stories that occupied a good deal of space in the papers lately in the both of which one of the leading rolls was played by actresses, one of them a screen actress and the other one a regular actress on the stage and in one case it come out that they was a certain guy that carried the actress's picture in his watch and he also had another picture of her which said on it to my sweetheart or some such words and in the other case the papers got a hold of a bunch of letters which the actress had wrote to a gent and pretty near every other word in them was honey or sugar lamb and down at the bottom a row of xs which is suppose to represent kisses but personally I always thought they was a very poor substitute.

Well any way the first actress owned up that she had give the guy her picture and had wrote to my sweetheart on it, but said that as a matter of fact him and her wasn't nothing more than good friends and the relations between them was more like brother and sister than anything else.

The 2d. actress admitted that she had wrote these here letters but as for her being stuck on the guy she had wrote them to, why that was a joke. Her family and his family had always knew each other and of course she was acquainted with him but only in a business way you might say.

Well friends after reading all that has been printed in regards to these 2 cases I have came to the conclusion that the most of us is a way behind the times in our attitude not only towards our friends and acquaintances but also towards folks who we have business dealings with them and it looks to me like it was high time we come out of our shell and warmed up and they's no time like the present and personly I have got 2 important letters to write today which I will now copy down the way I am going to write them so as my readers can get the new idear and follow it up in their own correspondence if they see fit, and I will exclaim that the 1st. letter is addressed to the man that has got a mortgage on what I often laughingly refer to as my home, a payment on which was due the 1 of April.

To the Man with the Mortage.

Sweetheart:—

Just a few lines to let you know I have not forgotten you but have been thinking of you a whole lot and also the payment on my home which become due the 1 of April.

Listen dearie I done a good deal of traveling this last winter and it cost me a whole lot of money and a specially down in Cuba where they have got a race track which horses runs on it and you bet on which one you think will win and I was out to the track 5 different days and bet on 31 different horses and 3 of them win.

Well honey I would of give anything in the world if more of them could win just as much for your sake as my sake because then I would of been in a position to make the payment on the mortgage which become due the 1 of April. They never was a minute dureing them races, not even the most exciteing parts, when I wasn't thinking of you dear. You believe that don't you honey?

I seen a good many nice looking men out to the race track but nobody as handsome as my mortgagee.

And another thing, my pretty one, on the 15 of March I had to send a check to the collector of internal revenue over in Brooklyn and it took all the money I had in the bank and then some, but don't get the idear in your funny old head that I like the man in Brooklyn better than I like you. I don't even know him so you ain't jealous is you sweetie?

Maybe by the 1 of May or June I will be able to make the payment which become due on the 1 of April and in the mean wile I am sending you a picture of myself and you will notice that I have wrote on it "Yours" and I mean every word of it but I would not of meant it near as much had I made the payment which was due the 1 of April.

My other letter is going to a piano Co. who I bought a piano from and here is what I am going to write and you will notice that I have put some poetry in it like actresses generally always do when they are writeing a business letter:

The ——— Piano Co:

New York City,

Sweet Patootie:—

About a yr. and ½ ago I bought a piano from your ever loving concern and paid a good price for same and wish to inform you that same has been tuned 6 times but don't stay in tune a wk. and not only that honey but the keys keep sticking and the ivory has also came off 2 of the keys and makes it look bad.

Now babe I am no Paderewski at best and all the more so when so many of the notes on the piano is rancid so if you want to keep a hold of my affections you will send out somebody that knows something about pianos and find out what ales this piano.

Send out one of your experts,
One you will understand.
Send out one of your experts
To look at your baby grand.

It certainly was great to get them 3 letters from you last month and in reply to same will say that I would not of got so far behind in the installments only I visited Cuba this winter and bet on 31 horses and only 3 of them win. You know what that means dearie but still and all I don't think you have got any holler comeing if I ain't always right up to date paying for a piano that don't stay in tune a wk. Burn this letter.

Ring Observes the Miami Mermaids

BELL SYNDICATE, MARCH 4, 1923

To the Editor:

In response to demands from numerable readers will devote my article this wk. to a few more of my ventures in sunny Florida. We left Belleair at 11:42 A.M. bound for sunny Miami via way of sunny Jacksonville.

They's a shorter way of going from Belleair to Miami by cutting acrost the state but you half to change trains 3 or 4 times and wile a person might think that every time you change trains in sunny Florida it could not help from being a improvement, still and all the shoe might be on the other ft.

They was no incident worth recording en route to Jacksonville except when we past through a city name Newbury and seen a store which it says on the outside "John G. White Jeweler, Shoes, hats, notions, furniture and coffins."

I says to the Mrs. that it looked to me like Mr. White was making a mistake to not branch out and get a couple side lines like musical instruments and false teeth because the town did not look like it was big enough for a man to specialize.

I said this in a joking way and sure enough she laughed heartily.

We arrived at Jacksonville at 7 P.M. and asked the man what time was they a train for Miami and he says they was a train leaving at 9:40 and another train leaving at 10:00 o'clock so I says which was the best train and he says "Well the 9:40 is faster but the other stays 20 minutes behind it all the way down."

I thought this was kind of wonderful at the time but all the more so after we had spent the night on the 9:40 and realized what a trick it must of been for the 10:00 o'clock train to not gain no ground.

While we was getting on the board of the 9:40 at Jacksonville a man come up and spoke to me and who was it but Joe Moeller that use to be a motorcycle cop in old Chi and 1 night he arrested me for speeding on the west side boulevards.

He got on the 9:40 with us but had no occasion to take the engineer's number.

Officer Moeller said that shortly after arresting me they had promoted him to the detective corpse and 1 night they sent him out after some gun men and he found them O.K. and they shot him 4 times, 2 of which was still inside him and he had been sent down to Florida in the hopes that the 2 bullets would want to come out and enjoy the climate.

Though on his vacation, he had been asked by a detective agency to try and find a man that had stole another man's wife and automobile. The bereaved husband was anxious to get the car back. Officer Moeller had a picture of it and of the wife but said the thief had probably took the precautions to have them both repainted.

We arrived in Miami at 10:45 A.M. and was whisked by automobile to the Flamingo for the nominal sum of $4.00 dollars.

Amongst the 1st people we met was John Golden the play producer and he asked how I was and I says I was O.K. only that my dogs hurt referring to my ft. So he says maybe your kennels is to small, referring to my shoes. I laughed heartily.

This was our 1st visit to Miami and I suppose my admirers is wild to know did I like it better than other points in Florida. Will state that Miami Beach is 1 of the prettiest spots I have ran acrost and the beach itself is a 100 per cent beach and as far as the costumes and etc. is concerned why the bathing suits wore by the gals at Miami Beach makes the Palm Beach gals look like eskimos.

If the Miami gals wore sox and shoes you would think they was preliminary fighters and speaking about fighters, why the 1st man I seen out to the beach was Walter Monaghan who the last time I seen him, he was throwing a used towel in to the middle of a boxing ring at Toledo, O.

Walter is running a physical culture school at the beach which is more money than acting as Willard's sparring partner but he has still got faith in old Jess and he says he could of kept on fighting that famous 4 of July only he could not get his eyes open after the 1st rd.

What made Jess so sleepy was lying on his back and looking up at the bright sun.

In regards to the social life at Miami Beach and Palm Beach, why about the only differents is that the high monkey monks at Miami don't seem to carry so many servants along with them. Pretty near everybody at Palm Beach has there secretary with them while most of the visitors to Miami can read and write.

People changes there close 4 times a day at Miami vs. 6 at Palm Beach but I seen 1 costume at Miami Beach that made Palm Beach look like a sucker namely a man in a white linen suit and a black derby.

Palm Beach is probably a whole lot more exclusive and personaly we wasn't flooded with invitations the yr. we was at Palm Beach wile in Miami they was never a day when the mail box did not yield cards from chiropodists and etc.

The day after we reached Miami they was a atmosphere of gloom in the air which it seems the reason for same was a item of news in the Miami papers in regards to the weather in California. It seems the thermometer at San Bernardino the day before had fell to 31 above zero and it looked like the southern California almond crop would be spoiled. The Miami papers tried to suppress this item by putting it on top of the front page but a whole lot of Miami people seen it and they was not a dry eye in the town.

Ring Discloses His Beauty Secrets

BELL SYNDICATE, AUGUST 10, 1924

To the Editor:

In a recent issue of the Liberty weekly, which somebody from Youngstown, Ohio, win a prize of $20,000 for picking out such a remarkable name for a magazine, well any way in this issue why Miss Gertrude Lawrence, one of the lady stars in the Chariot English revue which the other lady is Miss Beatrice Lillie and they come over here last December expecting to stay a couple months but are still hanging around, well anyway this Miss Lawrence who is undoubtedly one of the prettiest ladies that ever just happened give a interview to a gal named Miss Josephine Day, which the title of it was a woman's duty to be beautiful plus.

What Miss Lawrence seems to of meant by plus was that you should ought to be smart as well as beautiful, in other words if a gal is just beautiful without no brains why after a wile you get tired of setting there and just looking at her because you think to yourself I could get a copy of the sistine Madonna and set there and look at that and between looks I could read the paper and find out where Firpo was going to train. But if it is a live gal setting there why it seems kind of rude to read the papers and the gal should ought to be able to say something besides I, yes or no when you talk to her.

Well Miss Lawrence in this article tells not only how she keeps beautiful, but how she also keeps snappy and I will quote her following words:

"A woman should give over a few minutes every day to reading something good. Memorize two lines of poetry a day, a paragraph or two of good prose. Add a few words daily to your vocabulary. Do this for no other reason than to keep mentally active, enthusiastic and consequently young."

So much for keeping the brains alert. Now in regards to how to keep beautiful, Miss Lawrence says:

"Take a warm bath, then lie flat on the back, draw the knees up so that the base of the spine may feel the soothing caress of the mattress. Lie thus for fifteen minutes with every nerve and fiber relaxed."

Now then gals, Miss Lawrence has certainly showed you how to be beautiful and bright, and also she adds a little hint in regards to how to keep the pores of the skin closed—"First you cleanse the face thoroughly, then with a tiny brush or a piece of clean cloth apply the unbeaten white of an egg to the skin. Let the albumen dry on the skin. And etc."

But that don't tell the male sex how to be pretty and clever at one and the same time and at least one person has wrote in and requested me to tell them how I do it.

Well gents when I go to bed nights if ever I always do one knee up in a plaster cast to be sure it won't go nowheres. Then I always lay down on the left side and memorize a couple of paragraphs of the official football guide. Like for inst.

"The service is a fault as provided for by Rule 9, or if the ball served touches the Server's partner or anything which he wears or carries."

"In case a player is hindered in making a stroke by anything not within his control, except a permanent fixture of the court, the point shall be replayed."

By this time I am generaly always so exhausted that I have to call in a chiropractor, but only for a few hours. After that I uncast my knee and set up in bed and read the first few pages of the Syracuse telephone directory. Then I lay back again and scream a few moments to keep my throat clear. The next step is to call up a general practitioner and try and find out what is the matter. His name is usually Dr. Patterson, but you can't depend on that. Before finally retiring for the night I see that all the pores is closed and all the doors locked. Then I dust my face off with a whisk broom.

When dawn comes, I always get up and, like Miss Lawrence, try and add a few words to my vocabulary. Like for inst. yesterday morning I put on the following nouns:

Wham.

Kurtell.

Grafe.

The first two mean that a caravan is just starting out and the noun grafe means that you ain't paid your insurance.

That is about all of my system gents and as for comparisons, why look at my picture and then look at Miss Lawrence's and judge for yourself.

If You Ain't in the Monday Opera
Club, You Don't Belong

BELL SYNDICATE, JANUARY 18, 1925

To the Editor:

For the benefit of visiting firemen I would better exclaim what this is all about as near as I am able to judge from hear say and reading the newspapers.

Well it seems that a big bunch of the riff and raff has been horning their way into N.Y. society the last yr. or 2 and things has came to such a pass that the elite was libel to find themselfs time after time attending parties which people that work for a living was also guests at same with the result that the high mucky mucks would half to rush home early and disinfect themselfs. Some hostesses has forgot their social standing to such a extent that they have included Indiana and Wisconsin born folk in their invitations. It has got so that a person of breeding and refinement don't hardily dast go out of the house for the fear of being spoke to in public by some scum that they had met the night before by mistake and it certainly is a terrible thing to be crouped up at home without nobody but your own wife or husband to talk to.

Well a little wile ago, along some time last summer a select group of our best women including the queen Kleagle of the Colonial Dames of America got together and decide it that it was time for a gen. shake up which they would get rid of the vermin once and for all and make society look something like it used to 40 yrs. ago when the 400 come into being. At that time a prominent butcher's grand daughter in law or something give a party and left the inviting to a gentleman friend that had the family history of everybody in America at both ends of his tongue. He issued just a even 400 invitations and made the remark that anybody not included in his list might consider themselfs permanently barred from organized baseball. The 400 and their assigns carried along the burden until just a short time back, when as I say some brother Elks and Mooses begun to horn their way in and spoil the party.

Last summer the committee of chosen people consisting almost entirely of women of the opp. sex made up their mind to raise the limit from 400 to 500 so as to let in a few families that had sold out their meat markets and livery barns and turned square since the last shuffle. The queen Kleagle was sent to Paris to meet some royalties and invite them over here to get acquainted with the reconstructed elite. The first royalty to who a invitation was extended was the grand duchess Cyril of Russia whose husband will be czar of Russia as soon as they decide to have czars again. This event is expected to take place the same fall that Utica wins the pennant in the Cotton States League. They say that the Kleagle had to slip the duchess tres beaucoup francs for steamer fare and tips. When the good ship Paris reached N.Y. some months later the duchess disembarked by way of the steerage gang plank and most folks said how clever she was to outwit the newspaper boys and etc. but some of the deeper thinkers suspects that the reason she disembarked via the steerage gang plank was, well, on acct. of it being right there.

Now the committee had this scheme worked out, namely they was to announce in the papers that a party would be give at the Monday Opera Club in honor of the duchess and who ever got a invitation to this party would know that they was numbered amongst God's chillun wile them that didn't get no invitation was quarantined from now on. Personly—but any way I had tickets that night for "What Price Glory."

Well, they say the czarina was a terrific hit with everybody except the bell hops and other employs of the hotel where she was stopping and the hit was made in spite of the fact that they ain't no danger of her highness running Gloria Swanson out of the picture game.

But the main pt. is that now society in N.Y. has been re-established on a solid basis. If you are in the Monday Opera 500 club, you belong. If you ain't you don't. On the nights when they don't have royalties or dances, they probably play 500, but any way the scheme has done what the committee expected it to do, namely, to use their own words, "to preserve dignity and good breeding, otherwise there will be a social revolution here like the French revolution." Us boys and gals should certainly ought to feel grateful and personly its a big load off my mind.

During Cyril's stay over here she was accompanied every place she has went by Detective Sergeants Brown, Kelly and Herman of the bomb squad. These boys was going along for the nominal purpose of protecting her vs. attacks from rabid reds, some of the women folks was catty enough to say however that she wasn't afraid of no reds but having a male escort all the wile appealed to her on acct. of the novelty.

The future czarina ain't the only notoriety that is that is going to be a guest of the club. All ready they have booked Queen Marie of Roumania, the Duchess de Vendome, head of the Bourbons who still hopes to regain the throne of France though it is pretty near impossible to get Bourbon over here any more, and the grand duchess Xenia of Russia who is a sister of the last czar, and the last czar's cousin Michael, and the Dowager Marchioness of Milford Haven, grand daughter of Queen Victoria.

When this list has ran out we can look forward to visits from the Kaiser, the Crown Prince, Count Salm of Austria, Max Oser of the royal Swiss Yodelers, and Prince Hari Singh, the Robinson gal's little boy friend, and if we coax hard enough maybe we can enjoy another call from Luis Angel Firpo and lady.

Ring Denies He Owes Chicago $50

BELL SYNDICATE, DECEMBER 6, 1925

To the Editor:

Judging by letters recd. in the last few wks. pretty near every man, woman and child in the U.S. must of read that item that come out in the papers in regards to the undersigned getting pinched for speeding in Chicago one time and fined $50 for same and how I run out on the fine and now they have got a capias vs. me and the minute I sit ft. on the soil of what I use to fondly call my home town I will be surrounded by a pussy of great big whopping policemens and assigned to a room without bath in a certain Clark St. hotel where they have got a clerk named Sergeant.

According to the item this here fine was assessed on the 17 of June, 1919, and the record of same has just been dug up by a record inspector named Mr. Clyde Dyckman, who seems to lose his temper over a little boost I wrote for the Hotel Sherman which I said in it that I always tried

to get a room where I could look acrost Randolph St. at the county bldg.
and see how the other half lived without working.

With the kind indulgents of my admires I will waste this space today
in copying down a letter which I am going to send to Mr. Dyckman as
soon as the madam remembers to bring home a stamp, and I am in the
hopes you won't get bored by a recital of some of my ancient history which
I been led to believe you are all interested in same or you would not of so
thoughtfully wrote and kidded me about this here blemish on my past.

"Dear Mr. Dyckman: Well Mr. Dyckman I and you has never met as
you was probably too busy, but we have got a street here in New York called
Dyckman St. which may of been named after you in a spirit of levity. Dyckman St. is way up in the 2 hundreds and you can get a board of a ferry
there for Englewood, N.J., though I don't know no reason why you should.

"Now listen Mr. Dyckman I know you must be rushed to death what
with spending hours and hours delving into 6 yr. old records and one
thing and another, but if you do happen to get through a little early some
day I wished you would take a run down to Toledo, O., and they's a good
train for there leaving Chi at 5:25 p.m. if they ain't changed it between
now and 1919 and you might maybe meet some South Bend or Goshen
people on that train and just mention my name and they will tell you who
I married and when so you won't half to look that up and who I use to go
with prior to my nuptials, but any way when you get to Toledo climb into
a barouche and have yourself drove to the Hotel Secor and ask the clerk
with the funny mustache to show you the register for June, 1919, and you
will find me stopping there on the 17 of June and before and after same
and I can't remember the room number but it was a kind of a small room
where a person couldn't hardly turn around a specially when it was clut-
tered up with Hype Igoe, Rube Goldberg, bottles of charged water, Damon
Runyon, Tad and Harry Witwer, but any way that is where I and the rest
of the boys was at the time stated and we was there covering the alleged
training activities of Dempsey and Jessie Willard and may as well state at
this junction that I bet $600 dollars on Willard so you can judge for your-
self Mr. Dyckman whether we was enjoying ourselfs and I am sure you
would like Toledo, too, provide it that some day you get through pouring
over the vital statistics of 1874 in time to catch the 5:25.

"Those was the days Mr. Dyckman when they use to have fights for the heavyweight championship and the Toledo fight was a great spectacle for those that could still see and those who did not have no $600 bet on the Kansas Zephyr who set down in the resin to rest after the so called contest had been going on fully a quarter of a minute and then and there I offered to sell my bet to Geo. McManus for $.10 cash but Geo. was on the wagon so afterwards I paid off the $600 verbatim and I ask you Mr. Dyckman if that sounds like the kind of a man who would run out on a $50 fine.

"Well Mr. Dyckman I went back to Chi and stayed there till October and I wasn't no recluse that summer neither but mixed around just like always and didn't even wear no wig or mast or false whiskers or nothing and Chicago was just as full of eagle eye policemens then as now and when I would see one of them what did I do, did I walk around the block to get out of their way? No Mr. Dyckman I went right close to them and sometimes positively nudged them and never heard a wd. in regards to a unpaid fine for speeding.

"Further and more we wasn't living in a tent that summer but had a home and a st. number and a telephone with our name in the book in just as big letters as Harold McCormick or Wm. Wrigley, and my Mrs. is like all women namely they think a telephone has got to be answered though they know or should know by experience that it means trouble 99 times out of a 100, but honest Mr. Dyckman all that summer long they wasn't no call from no court about no fine and whatever judge it was that assessed it, he can keep a secret so good that I would almost be willing to show him some of my mash notes. All and all Mr. Dyckman I wouldn't of never heard of this fine only for you and I won't never forget you.

"Came October and I went down to Cincinnati for the world's serious and bet another $600 on the dear old White Sox or a total of $1200 I lose in 4 mos. and me with a wife and 4 kiddies and now you come along and make it a more memorable yr. by adding on this $50 plaster that it is now too late to deduct off the income tax. Which is it you ain't got Mr. Dyckman, no family or no heart?

"Now listen Clyde I have 2 wonderful sister-in-laws in and around Chicago as well as a host of girl friends and admires that is always clamoring I should come out there and brighten their life but $50 is $50 not to mention fare and berth both ways on the 20th Century Limited which I call it the Century on acct. of the round trip coming so close to a $100 and which I always half to ride on because I love speeding, but you take this $100, or rather $90 and then slap the $50 on top of that which you say I owe some judge that probably ain't got no children at all or one or 2 at the outside, and—well Clyde those poor girls ain't going to feel none too kindly disposed towards you and you needn't never expect to open up one of them big windows of yours and see Randolph St. gummed up by a parade of maids and matrons shouting thank God for Dyckman, he kept Ring out of Chi."

A Cordial Greeting from Pola

BELL SYNDICATE, APRIL 18, 1926

To the Editor:

Armed with letters of introduction from what I have dubbed the Big Town, we swept down on Hollywood one March morning and was recd. by most of the screen celebrities with well concealed enthusiasm. At the Famous Players studio we run acrost old acquaintances in the person of Alan Dwan. Charlie Furthmann and Marshall Neilan. The pictures in the making were "The Rainmaker," "Beau Geste," "Naughty Cinderella," and Rex Beach's "Padlocked." This was my first visit to a big studio during the filming of heart-gripping romance.

I had read and heard that these giants of the film world could not even begin to start to act unless a orchestra was playing "Humoresque" or "Barcarolle," but always thought it was just a gag till I seen it with my own eyes. I asked one budding star if the music really did have any effect on her and she said she couldn't do anything without it. Afterwards I watched her in a scene with full orchestral accompaniment and it seemed to me like she must be almost stone deaf.

The thing that impressed me the most in this and the other big studios was that everybody that is getting more than a beginner's salary, say $6000 per wk., has their own chair to set in with their name painted on it and though the chairs is all exactly alike, no real artists can feel they's a load off his ft. unlest he is setting in his own chair. As picture actors does more setting than anybody except ball players it is no more than natural that they should want and have chairs, but it come to me like a bolt from the blue that a chair with your name on it would be any more settable than a anonymous chair.

My first act when I get back home will be to have my name in full on the chair I generally always set in and if I catch one of the kiddies setting in that chair I will have one of the hired help give him a kind of a hint that he is de trop. I gleaned that this is proper procedure from a episode that took place while we was watching Buster Collier and Georgia Hale do a love scene in "The Rainmaker." The young lady with me was setting in a chair inscribed with the name of Ernest Torrence, who was also playing in the picture but not in that scene. A polite attendant come over and asked her would she mind changing chairs and he give her Buster Collier's chair so Mr. Torrence wouldn't half to spend his recess in a strange environment.

Buster Collier come to Hollywood three yrs. ago to stay 8 wks. and ain't never been home since though his home is only 3 miles from Great Neck. He is a likable boy and didn't make no squawk when he seen that the young lady with me was setting in his chair. We disgust his old man Willie and we talked about this in that and I happened to mention that Grantland Rice was in our party and he said, "Oh, another of my admirers," which I will modestly half to exclaim that what he meant to say was "Oh, I read his stuff, too."

There was no music at Charlie Chaplin's studio, but the promising young comic made up for it by treating us like our visit had rendered it a perfect day. We set in nameless chairs and watched him make several scenes in his new picture, "The Circus," which comes out next fall and will be a wow from what we seen of it. Wile the different lights and etc. was being got in readiness, Charlie entertained us with imitations of various nuts and finely overwhelmed us with a invitation to dine at his house on the following Saturday night.

So we dined there en famille with Mr. and Mrs. Charlie and the mother-in-law and Harry Crocker, a genial friend of Charlie's who doubles as his secretary and also gives him advice which he don't take. Charlie has got his own screen and projecting machine and after dinner he said he had 3 new pictures which we could take our choice. The 3 was "Tumbleweeds" and "The Devil's Circus" and something else and we chose "The Devil's Circus." This was our mistake.

Another feature of the Chaplin home is a big pipe organ which Charlie played on it for us. His taste runs to soft, foreign sounding tunes and improvisations and he plays everything in the key of F. All and all this was as nice an evening as we spent in the West and from now on I will be a Chaplin booster. You remember how I used to pan him.

We dropped in for a few minutes at a midnight party given by Mr. and Mrs. Conway Tearle, she being the former Adele Rowland and one of my favorite musical comedy gals. We met Buster Keaton and Trixie Friganza[6] and renewed a old acquaintance with Nora Bayes and seen 4 or 5 of the Talmadge girls and etc., but by this time we was so immune to brushing shoulders with different notorieties that I swear I can't remember a fraction of those we was introduced to.

And our last day in Hollywood we was taken in toe by Teddy Hayes who used to train Jack Dempsey. Teddy can get in more places than Houdini can get out of and is welcome everywhere he goes. His chief enjoyment in life seems to come from doing things for people and the only time he gets mean is when you try to pay a check. Well, anyway he introduced us to Valentino and Vilma Banky[7] and Syd Chaplin and "Chuck" Reisner, who is directing Syd in "The Better 'Ole," and finely, in the Famous Players studio, he asked me if I wanted to meet Pola Negri[8] and I said yes and Miss Negri was resting between scenes of "Naughty Cinderella," which they are going to call "Good and Naughty" for no reason, and she was reading a magazine and I will hardly forget the self-control she exhibited when the introduction was made.

"Miss Negri," said Teddy, "this is Mr. Lardner, the writer."

"Oh," said Miss Negri, and never raised her eyes from the magazine.

At the Universal City we had our photograph taken with Norman Kerry who was busy with a picture called "The Love Thief." I asked him what the story was about and he said he didn't know as he had only been working on it 2 months. Wile he was there a lady come up and asked for his autograph and he wrote it for her. It is no novelty for screen stars to be asked for their autograph by mail, but the practice of movie fans coming right up to you and asking for it in person is libel to cause a upheaval in the lives of Hollywood's artistes, many of who will half to take a course in penmanship and spelling.

Swimming the Transit Channels

MORNING TELEGRAPH, DECEMBER 19, 1928

With turkey a dollar a gobble, gin $1.25 a peep, music shows $9.90 on the hoof and three starving children homeward bound for the "Holidays," ye impecunious parent has taken a sudden fancy to the subway and munic-ipal bus lines as a means of locomotion to and from work. The round trip costs only 20 cents and is seldom devoid of interesting experiences, either going or coining.

(Oh, tell us some of your interesting experiences on the subway or municipal bus lines, either going or coming.)

Well, when the day's druggery is over I generally grovel to Broadway and Fiftieth street and grab a local to Eighty-sixth, where I dismount, ascend the stairs to God's great al fresco, and board a crosstown bus that conveys me through the park and virtually to the door of the bin in which ich bin spending the Winter.

But gestern Nachtmittag I had to walk from the office to Forty-second street to buy hoecake for the chameleon, and afterwards I went into the Times Square subway station to catch an uptown train. An express appeared first and I got on it, deciding that if I saw a local on the way to, or at, Seventy-second street, I would get off at the latter station and take it; otherwise I'd go on to Ninety-sixth and walk home from there.

A local was standing at Seventy-second as we pulled in and lots of people on our train wanted to give it a ride, but with the unfailing spirit of raillery that makes the I.R.T. so much clean fun, the local's doors started to shut as the express's started to open. A few of us whippets dashed across the platform in time to squeeze through the rapidly diminishing crevice, but one Amsterdam avenue dowager had just managed to insinuate a flac-cid forearm when the door closed on it and the local began to move.

From the lady's buxom fingers dangled a package that might have con-tained stogies or asparagus. Anyway, I didn't want it and, mustering the full strength of a man who had been in strict training for sixty-seven days and four hours, I managed to fling the door wide enough to admit the entire dowager, who by this time was giving vent to various college cries. I was about to fondle her throat when my attention was called to the approach of a guard who might have been all-American if he could have controlled his temper and kept up in his studies.

"What's the matter with you?" he demanded, though not forty minutes previously an acquaintance had told me I was looking fine.

"Can't you read that sign?" he continued, and pointed to an inscription inviting me and other excursionists to keep our hands off the door.

I was faced with a problem that must be solved quickly or very seldom. Should I say no and brand myself an illiterate before a crowded carload of the Upper West Side's demi-monde, or remain silent and try to outglare him? I did neither, but with a propitiating smile and in a dialect that had them all wondering what borough I hailed from, l replied quietly, "I no spik ze English," and the holocaust had been averted or at least postponed.

The Subway Sun has occasionally sought suggestions for the good of the service. Mine is that the sliding doors be equipped with a razor edge that will sever the part of the body which gets in from that which stays out, so there will be no danger of dragging the ostracized portion along the rails from station to station, and perhaps electrocuting the better part of a good customer.

And to the municipal bus lines I suggest that they either pass an ordinance against standees or buy a bus that wasn't specially built for Miller Huggins.

Christmas Card

MORNING TELEGRAPH, DECEMBER 23, 1928

To George M. Cohan, Harold Lloyd,
Walter Huston, Willie Heston,
St. John Irvine, Sigmund Freud,
Fielding Yost, May Wilson Preston,
Miller Huggins, John McGraw,
Eugene Buck and Marion Hollins,
Texas Guinan, Harry Thaw,
Eddie Cantor, Eddie Collins,
Wild Bill Rogers and the Stones,

Groucho Marx and all his brothers,
Grover Whalen, Bobby Jones,
Margie Baer and many others:

I've been sending, recent Yules,
Cards of my own composition,
Funny as the football rules
Or a veteran mortician.
Written out by my own hand
With a maximum of labor,
Personally blotted and
Mailed to every friend and neighbor.
In some precincts here and there,
They were hailed with loud hosannas;
Cries of "Goody!" rent the air,
Staid old stiffs forgot their manners,
And this writer must confess
That the said appreciation
Thrilled his bosom hardly less
Than a Whiteman orchestration.

But in other ports and climes,
Spots too numerous to mention,
Those to whom I sent my rhymes
Paid them not the least attention.
Countless thousands, East and West,
Answered neither with a card nor
Ten-word telegram addressed
To a lonely lad named Lardner.
Was this whole-souled negligence
Grateful to me? No, it wasn't.
Does the praise make recompense
For the pain? I fear it doesn't.
And this Christmas I'll not spend
Precious time or novel notion
On each relative and friend
In Los Angeles or Goshen.

Being snubbed is what I hate;
I just can not bear a slighting,
So for 1928
This is all the card I'm writing.

Folks who feel they simply must
Get my greetings in some shape or
Count the holidays a bust—
Well, they'll have to buy this paper.

From a Bottle Found in the Ocean

MORNING TELEGRAPH, JANUARY 30, 1929

On board S.S. Pan America (found in an empty bottle by The Morning
Telegraph's empty bottle department)—If this is picked up, please publish it under the title Immune

This rather ancient mariner
Is now abaft Cape Hatteras.
The fog has gone, the skies are clear
But biggish billows batter us.
And many of les voyageurs
Are just a wee bit seasick.
But it takes more than mal de mer
To make a man like me sick.

The waves can be as rough and tough
And punishing as Greb was,
As loath to quit and cry, "Enough!"
As R. E. Lee, the Reb, was;
Can pound until the hardened crew
Its voice in anguish lifteth;
But I have toured Eighth Avenue
From Forty-first to Fiftieth.

I've crossed from California's shore
To Santa Catalina;
From France to England, which is more
Chopped up and therefore meaner.
As wartime scribe I jolted through
French roads with shell holes reeking.
These routes were billiard tables to
The "street" of which I'm speaking.

To dodge the frequent barricades
As thick as well-kept privets,
You either climb up Pike's Peak grades
Or plumb Gland Canyon divots.
One moment you're St. Peter's pal
Then chumming with the devil;
Your course is always vertical
And never on the level.

Roll on, roll on, O stately ship!
Roll on till you roll over!
Give us ten times as rough a trip
As from Calais to Dover!
Let every swell be big as hell.
Each wind-pushed wave a staggerer,
Till people yell: "We might as well
Ride surf-boards down Niagara!"

Roll on or pitch! I don't care which
This is a rug contrasted
With that half mountain range, half ditch,
That most completely blasted
Of thoroughfares in history.
You have a nerve now, now haven't you,
To think the sea could sicken me
Who've taxied on Eighth Avenue.

With Rope and Gum

COLLIER'S, FEBRUARY 2, 1929

Another of those penetrating, intimate biographies giving you vivid pictures of great men and the things that made them great. Dr. Lardner this week turns his attention to Will Rogers. And who is better qualified to dissect the prominent rope-spinner than this painstaking biographer and scientist who devoted seven years of his learned life—seven lonely years in his attic laboratory—to the study of the Rogers fauna and flora?

Editor, Collier's Weekly,

NEW YORK, N.Y.

Gents:—

Amongst those who took a good sock in the jaw at the recent election was none other than Will Rogers, who attributes his defeat to a lack of notoriety. As Mr. Rogers expects to run again in 1932 and I take a great interest in his career having been like a mother to him since infancy, I will attempt in this space to present a few facts to the public designed to familiarize them with this diffident genius and show them what a sucker they were to overlook him so unanimously when they done their balloting.

Mr. Rogers undoubtedly could have had the Democratic nomination for the Presidency in 1924 only for the fact that he was not yet the required age, 35, when the convention opened. Before it was over, he was 28, but by that time he had gone home.

Will was born on the Dixie Highway in Georgia and talks with a decided Southern drool. He is half Indian, half American, one third vermouth and the other two thirds wire-haired fox terrier. But he lost his own hair during a siege of rabies and the thick hirsute adornment you now observe on his skull is not a cleverly wrought coupé.

During Will's youth the highway and all other automobile roads through the state of Georgia had a terrific undertow which no make of car was able to resist. The motorist would get just so far when he would feel his vehicle sinking beneath him and himself sinking with it and no hope of rescue even though the sinking spell occurred within the sight and hearing of persons standing on either shore. Hundreds of machines and their occupants burrowed all the way to China, which the latter liked so well that they became Chinese citizens and joined the Chinese Davis Cup team. As a result, our own population was falling off to such an extent that President Buchanan ordered the Georgia legislature to devise some way, any way, by which to check the wholesale egress of Americans via the Georgia bogs.

The legislature went into session for the first time in its life and at the end of a two years' bender appointed a committee consisting of Bobby Jones to work out a solution. At this time Georgia was famous for two things—the Hollis Girls and the manufacture of stout lynching rope. Mr. Jones decided to concentrate on the rope and in a few months' time had organized and trained a roping association, the members of which were assigned to positions at brief intervals along the dry land bordering the roads and at the first sign of a car going under, they were supposed to lasso the occupant or occupants and jerk them ashore. Medals and trophies were awarded the men making the most rescues and for a while the majority of these were won by Bill Roper, now a fairly successful football coach at Villa Nova or Rutgers.

But Mr. Roper was soon obliged to play second fiddle to a youngster named Will Rogers, whose speed and accuracy eventually earned him the title of poet lariat of Georgia.

"I guess I must have saved twenty thousand people and, from what I have heard of them since, I done China a big favor." He said this the other evening to his wife, who was asleep, as luck would have it.

One cannot live forever on medals and words of praise and young Rogers, wishing to commercialize his prowess with the rope, at length made up his mind to go to New York, which he had heard of through a mutual friend. His fame had preceded him and he had no difficulty obtaining a position as a rope-holder to keep the crowds back at parades in honor of such returning heroes as General Pershing, Admiral Dewey, Colonel E. M. House and Dr. Cook. Next he got engagements doing rope tricks in the lesser vaudeville houses, and several scouts and agents recommended him to the revue producers as capable of putting on an interesting specialty. The producers, however, could not see how a common, Wild West lassoing act would amuse an audience which had paid $6.60 for an eyeful of Anastasia Reilly[9] and it was not until Gene Buck discovered Mr. Rogers could talk (the others must have been stone deaf) that he was engaged for a stunt in the Ziegfeld Follies at a salary of $175.00 per week.

This sounds like the sort of story dreams and success articles are made of—a young man beginning an unpromising stage career at $175.00 and gradually, over a space of fifteen years, working himself up to his present high standing and an income (including appearances on the stage and in motion pictures, lecture tours, syndicated newspaper writings and magazine stories) said to be in excess of $11,000 per annum. In other words, an increase in weekly stipend of almost $38!

But Mr. Rogers has not permitted his triumphs to go to his head. He is the same old Will—simple, self-effacing, diffident and so crowd-shy that when in New York he stops at the Hotel Astor.

The title of the musical in which he is now substituting for his friend Fred Stone was originally Three Beers, so christened by Will himself as a compliment to the amount of refreshment he allows himself every five minutes after each evening performance. He is almost a total abstainer from the hard stuff and only the other night he and a fellow named W. C. Fields invited me to sup with them at a jernt where, they said, real draught beer was readily obtainable. It was an Italian place and after I had taken a sip of the beer I began to specialize in Martinis and became quite amusing to everyone but the fellow Fields, who was paying the cheek.

Mr. Rogers has a remarkable hold on his public, especially in the small towns where they don't know what he's talking about. I was in St. Petersburg, Fla., one night when he was giving his lecture. He was on the stage alone, just talking and chewing gum and fooling with his rope, for an hour and forty-five minutes at a stretch, and nobody walked out. This either beats or ties my own record. I collaborated on a play which ran two hours a performance and there were several performances where hardly anybody walked in.

When Will went into the movies he built himself a palatial house in Hollywood, about the size of the Fairbanks' shower bath, and was soon elected mayor of the town. Following the excellent example of up-to-date mayors, he proceeded to leave home and stay away for months at a time, but few residents of the famous motion picture colony will ever forget the wild parties he threw during the few nights he was in Beverly Hills. Mr.

and Mrs. Rogers, as I may not have told you, have fourteen children, all named Pat, and this number, with the parents, makes four tables of contract bridge. But neither Mr. nor Mrs. Rogers nor any of the kiddies cares for cards, so on party nights thirteen members of the family would sit around the room and listen to the fourteenth member talk and any of them caught asleep or laughing at the wrong time or not laughing at all was penalized by being made to sit up an extra hour, listening.

The house is at the apex of such a steep hill that fragile folk like Miss Garbo, Miss Negri and Miss Gish cannot climb it and have to send their doubles to the elaborate siestas which Will and the Mrs. are accustomed to give every eclipse.

To add to his value as a stage performer Mr. Rogers has recently taken up what he refers to as singing. His voice has something of the quality of that of a water spaniel with nightmare, but resembles more closely the mellow resonance of an Eighty-fifth Street car making the turn on to Madison Avenue.

Will's favorite sport is polo. He is rated a minus 12 goal man in the national rankings and is said to have barely missed two free shots in a match against the Hollywood Girl Scouts. He golfs, but gave it up because the sand made his eyes so sore that he couldn't read the daily papers. He once suggested to Mr. Grantland Rice a game to be called polo-golf wherein a polo mallet and ball would be used and the player would go around the course on horseback, making all his shots from the saddle. Mr. Rice, a good-natured fellow, changed the subject.

Mr. Rogers is a member of the Knife and Fork Club of South Bend, the Nut and Toothpick Club of Des Moines, the American Association of Ferris Wheel Pullman Conductors, the University Club, the Harvard Club, the League of American Pen Women, the Knickerbocker Club, the Junior League, the Susie Sunshines, the A. and P., the A.T. & S.F., the Union Pacific, and the Seaboard Air Line.

The theatrical folk he pals around with in New York are W. C. Fields, Ann Pennington, the Albertina Rasch Girls, Andy Tombes, Wallace Eddinger and Mrs. Fiske.

He bears the distinction of having given the only performance not painful to Sir John Irving since the latter was imported from England to review American plays.

Every day he sends a gag by telegraph to two or three hundred newspapers throughout the country and you are always hearing people ask one another, "Did you read what Will Rogers had to say this morning?" When they ask me that, I keep myself well in hand and reply: "No, I didn't read it, but I probably wrote it."

(The next one might be about Babe Ruth, and again it might not.)

12

Parodies and Reviews

Lardner wrote many parodies over the years—fractured fairy tales, spoofs of operas and popular songs, and other flights of fancy. Several of the early parodies he wrote for the *Chicago Tribune*, such as "Cubist Baseball" and "The Spoon," were simply inspired. Others, such as the occasional "bed-time stories" first written as fairy tales supposedly told by his young son, John, provided a template for what was to come.

The parodies he wrote for the Bell Syndicate were longer, more complex, and, at their best, wildly funny. The exchange between Cinderella and her fairy godmother as the latter transforms her for the ball is priceless, and his description of how the poisoned apple was removed from Snow White's throat may be as good a gag as he ever delivered. His takeoffs on operas such as *Rigoletto* and *Madam Butterfly* came with a promise: "of coarse I wouldent go there on the bargun night when the Hoys and Polloys and riffle raffles gos there."

"Mary MacLane and Her Passionate Male Quartette" is a deft parody of the author of one of the first confessional autobiographies, which scandalized polite society with her discussion of bisexuality, feminism, self-love, and her desire to marry the Devil.

In 1932, the last full year of his life, Lardner began writing a column of radio criticism for the *New Yorker* called "Over the Waves." This made him one of the country's first national media critics, and he told of his affection for such comedians as Gracie Allen, Ed Wynn, Fred Allen, and Fanny Brice, while in the case of "Heavy Da-Dee-Dough Boys," he complained about what he saw as the coarsening of popular music.

He also began a strange campaign, one he admitted he had no hope of winning, against what he considered to be dirty song lyrics. The objects of his ire were such songs as "Paradise," which he called "unmistakably off-color," and "As You Desire Me," which he said was "flagrantly immoral." "I say these things at the risk of being considered queasy and a prude," he wrote. "At the risk and in the hope."

This was completely out of character for Lardner who had always been against censorship and, in railing against Prohibition only three years earlier, had said, "The Drys of our land are to a large extent identical with the people who have fought the good fight for purity and decency in books and plays. If their war on rum is conducted only half as shrewdly as the struggle against literary and dramatic dirt, we boy scouts need have no fear."

Anyone searching these articles for a complicit wink or any sign of irony did so in vain. Lardner's displeasure was real and he displayed it in a number of columns. This did not go unnoticed among his contemporaries when he died the following year. F. Scott Fitzgerald referred to Lardner's "odd little crusade," while Ernest Hemingway, whose childhood infatuation with Lardner had turned to disdain, recalled "those pitiful dying radio censorship pieces."

It is possible to attribute these out-of-character rants to the stress of Lardner's increasingly dire physical condition. He was suffering from tuberculosis, which led to the heart attack that would soon take his life, and he wrote some of the pieces from his hospital bed, which he labeled "No Visitors, N.Y." and "Do Not Disturb, N.Y." There was also the fact that Lardner was a lyricist himself—he wrote the words to many songs and collaborated with George S. Kaufman on a musical, *June Moon*, which was a success on Broadway—and was offended by what he saw as pandering by his fellow songwriters.

Whatever the case, Lardner redeemed himself a few months before he died when the campaign led him to a parody of "Night and Day" that contains some rhymes Cole Porter might have envied. It is the master parodist at his best, and an excellent antidote to "Lyricists Strike Pay Dirt."

Cubist Baseball

CHICAGO TRIBUNE, JUNE 9, 1914

A Seldom.

A White Sox base hit, a base hit with a man on third base is a seldom. Is strange to. Is a curiosity. Is sincerely fainting to fans. Why not once in awhile? Or why? The time to make a base hit a White Sox base hit is too late or later. The whole thing is unconscious.

The Pittsburgh.

A Dutchman and first place first place in April May. No sooner. A series a series with New York was abominable. A little speed is a necesity altogether but not a necessity because it did not. Now where are they at? The system of pitching curving hurling no good where speeding base running and weakening at bat is absence. Hopelessly now maybe and maybe hopeful and worrying because knocking.

The Spitball.

The spitball is nastiness and not talk about is polite. It breaks it breaks red it breaks red it breaks white it splashes. Batting hitting and fielding throwing erring red erring is spitball fault. Suppose a miss and running stealing. Catching throwing wilding and center field. Scoring and is spitball fault. Suppose disease germ and contagion making everybody sicking and doctor bill. Abolition is leading.

A Annunciator.

Might as well say enthusiastically hull house hot house grapes Lou Houseman Frank John Henry Van Dyke dog house summer house house of correction. Might as well say anything nothing unintelligent unintelligible. Buy a program a program five cents.

The Federal.

Butt in butt in butt in. Spend filthy and make everybody else spending I should worry. Expenses up flagpole high tree high sky high and receivings down low down well down hell down. Welcome. The Federal. How long. Cause a whole thing joke.

A Disastrous.

Umpire is disaster. Rotten. Awful rotten. Get rid of them all is favorable. All wrong system is all wrong. Decide plays should be by fans by fans in the stands by fans in the bleaching.

Fungos.

Nothing flat nothing quite flat and more and more round rounder. Not smaller nothing smaller and more small than regular bat longer and narrower and fuller and thicker and thinner. White Sox can hit fungos.

Charlie Murphy.[1]

He was president is he president? Out or in? Say sell out maybe sell out maybe not sell out. If not sell out ought to have solding. If not solding out maybe running million back into shoestring and maybe lose shoestring too. Contemplation miserable. Weeping writing arithmetic.

A Sweater

A sweater is a sweet and a sweeter a hat and a hitter. An undercoat and an overcoat and a banquet. A sweater is more comfort comfortabler than a collar in winter snowing and not in summer shining. A world's champion an Athletic a Philadelphia sweater is ugliness, homeliness like whole world's champion uniforming. Why not Athletics buy new suits new uniforming new sweating sweaters? Poverty.

A Georgia.

Crack a rib crack a pennant hopes. Ty Gers is Ty Cobb. Ty down grandstand or Ty steal it. Detroit first place crack a rib third place heal a crack rib second place going up. Suppose he dying buried. Where is Detroit then? In Michigan.

The West Side Parking.

All the seats are needing renewing. A white dress is ridiculous. A peanut a peanut a popcorn a pop a cigar a tobacco chocolates and bon bons. Aisles narrow corns. Pillars, invisible. Beautiful, beautiful, beautiful, beautiful. $800,000.

A One Hit.

Nothing a one hit is nothing minus. A White Sox pitching monotonous. Everybody's doing it. There is no gratitude in similar. Scant glory and a sore souper. Aching arm and vacuum of victories. Benz a bear Scott a skillful scamp and Cicotte a cyclone. Succotash. One hit and no hit simply unexcitement and mildly without consequence. More victories.

Rollie Zeider.

A hook a hook a hook a Hoosier hook a prominent proboscis a promontory a preeminence a peninsula. But a good guy a funny fella a perfect poker player a bear base runner and a hook slider. A hook.

The Spoon

CHICAGO TRIBUNE, JULY 7, 1917

The spoon has more loft than the knife, but less carry. It is seldom used for meat or potato shots, but is valuable when it comes to cereals, puddings, soup, and ice cream. Some players even prefer it for peas. It is also used for short coffee shots, but only by the most experienced players, as the club has a tendency to tip and wabble and a novice is likely to discolor shirt or vest, as well as to suffer physical discomfort if the coffee be too hot or too wet.

The table spoon has more carry than the regulation spoon and is sometimes resorted to in cereal shots when the player is particularly hungry.

The soup spoon was formerly little used, soup players as a rule preferring to use a piece of bread as a sponge or to tip up the plate itself. Recently the club has come into favor, especially in cafés, though it is mighty dangerous in the hands of a beginner, particularly one who is dressed up. The soup spoon should always be used sidewise to avoid the peril of getting it caught in the mouth. The player should be careful not to get the spoon too far under the soup. Short, snappy soup shots will pay better in the long run, even though you be in a hurry.

The regulation spoon is frequently utilized by doctors when a throat infection is suspected, the average leech preferring not to take a chance of having his fingers bitten off.

A recent invention is the glass spoon, played almost exclusively in high ball and rickey shots. In the former as a stirrer and in the latter to overcome lime seed hazards. Other spoons are the iced tea spoon and the demitasse, played only by professionals. The spoon should never be used for chocolate shots and only most sparingly for gravy.

Rigoletto

CHICAGO TRIBUNE, JANUARY 13, 1918

Friend Harvey:

Well Harvey I don't know if you get the papers down there so maybe I better tell you what's come off. Outside of my sensational testimony in the Healey[2] trial, they's been only the 1 big story and that was the brawl between Campanini, the orchestra leader over to the Auditorium, and Amelia Galli-Curci, that sings the air.

It seems like Cleo had dated her up to sing some songs in Boston and N.Y. when she got through here and all of a sudden she says she was too tired. So he says:

"But my Gali, you promised!"
"But I tell you I'm tired out," she says.
So he says:

A few more shows won't hurci,
Amelia Gali-Curci
And she says:
You tell that stuff to Swini,
Conductor Campanini.

And that give her the last word, but she wasn't satisfied. So she begun telling how little she got for singing. Tuesday morning it was $300 a night, and Tuesday afternoon she raised it to $332. We all just stayed except a reporter that was blear-eyed and had misread his hand. So he made it $500 and she tilted it to a thousand and everybody else dropped out. But can you imagine anybody kicking because they only get $300 or $1,000 a night and they're all through by eleven o'clock? Why, I've sang whole nights at my own expense and got nothing but h—for it.

Well, instead of her going on as the manicure in the Barber of Seville next Thursday night like it was scheduled, she winds up this P.M. as Minnie in The Bohunk. I can't be there because it's my afternoon with the dog, so I'll have to stand pat on seeing her only the once this season and that was in Rigoletto. I'll say she earned whatever they give her that night. They done so much to her in the last act that they had to wrap up the details so's her old man could get her all home in one load.

Her part in the show is Gilda and her father plays the title roll. He used to travel out of South Bend for an Italiano wholesale grocerino house and his dialect stories about Pat and Mike kept the Pullman washrooms in an uproar and helped him to sell many a spray of garlic in Lawton and Paw Paw. But one morning a local freight overtook the Accommodation that was wrenching him from the Bend to Plymouth and when they got enough of a hold on one eyelid to pull him of the holycaust, he was just a pretzel of his former self. So his drumming days were over, Jessie dear, and he and Gilda moved to Chi and took a small house in the exclusive Lower Wentworth Avenue district, in the hopes that he could land as a comedian at Colosimo's and maybe she could get in there as hat checker. But Abie said nothing doing, so Rigoletto begun to hang around saloons and tell his stories to the cash customers and then nudge them for a piece of change. He was getting plenty of red ink to drink and a couple of lires a day to buy ravioli for Gilda, when a guy named Duke moved into the neighborhood and started messing things up.

Within a month pretty near all the females in the precinct was calling themself Duchess. The killer purchased a saloon, naming it Bar le Duke, and every night the back room was jammed with Mariutches and Lucias.

Well, Rig hung out here and had the fine taste to start kidding the other habituals about their family affairs.

One old bird named Macaroni, whose only child was in Duchy, actually resented it when Rig says to him:

O, well, you've only leased one daughter.
I'll take a little hydrant water.

And old Mac called him everything he could think of and give him the official curse of the Parents' Protective association, which scared Rig stiff on account of Gilda, so he staggered home to be sure she was still there. Outside of his house he run into Frank Sparafucile, who begun to whine about dull trade.

Since Christmas (he says) I have killed only one man.
This war is sure hell on a poor honest gunman.
My funds are so low it's beginning to scare me.
Have you a few lires on your clothing to spare me?
And Rig tells him:
I have a few lires on my clothing, but really
I haven't so much I could Sparafucile.

So then Rig goes on into the yard and there's Gilda waiting for him. He kisses her and she sways a little and expresses the wish that he'd prepare for his homecoming with sen sen or cloves or something. So he says "That's either here nor there. What I want to know is, Have you got any guys on your staff?" "Cut it out, pa; my lips are cracked," she says.

But she's holding out on him. She's stuck on Duke and vice versa. But they don't neither of them know who each other are.

In the meantime the gang has decided to get back at Rig for kidding them, and one of them says Rig's got a lady friend and they'll kidnap her, so they all put whitewash on their nose so's they won't be recognized and they go to Rig's house. He asks them what's the idear and they tell him they're going to kidnap a lady that Duke's got a case on. So he wants to go along and they tell him he'll have to be blindfolded and then they walk him over to Archer and Twenty-first and back so he won't know where he's at and then they make him hold the ladder right up to his own second story window while they abduct his own daughter, and when they've took her away and he tears off his gas mask and finds out what he's done, he lays down in the front yard and indulges in a weeping jag.

The next day, he's in Bar le Duke bright and early and the rest of the gang's there and they're riding him something fierce when Gilda eases in through the family entrance and hears her father's voice and comes out front.

She says: "Good morning, daddy. Have you had your finnan haddie?" And he says: "You needn't bother. Food has no appeal for father."

That's the first time the gang knew she was his daughter and not his lady friend, so they're sorry and they leave the pair together and go to the next saloon. Rig says he'll have the Mann act on Duke, but it comes out that he hasn't taken her across the State Street line. So then he says, "All right. I'll inveigle him out to Burnham and have him served with a lead sandwich."

So then comes the last act, and it's out to the roadhouse, and Duke and the head waitress is spooning in a private dining room. Rig and Gilda stand outside and listen to them. You could of heard them clear to Hammond because their soft nothings was all screamed at the top of their voice instead of swapped back and forth in the conventional whisper. Duke and his new gal and Gilda and Rig finally put on the quartet number that you buy with your first victrola and then Rig tells Gilda to beat it and he wig wags to one of the gang and offers him $1.75 to croak Duke. It's a bargain. But when Duke goes upstairs the head waitress asks Dago Frank to lay off'n him for her sake and Frank says, "Yes, but I already got my $1.75 for the job." And she says, "Yes, but he don't care who you kill as long as you kill somebody." "Well, then," he says, "you rustle up a substitute." Well, Gilda's disobeyed her father and heard the whole thing and she's a great practical joker, so she gets Frank to croak her in place of the Duke, so's to have the laugh on her old man and besides the opera can't wind up till the soprano's massacred and it's pretty near 11 o'clock and what do you want for $300@$1,000 a night?

When Rig comes back for the corpus delicti Frank gives him a sack full of it, but just as he starts to tote it over to Lake George he hears the Duke upstairs gargling with listerine, and he opens up the sack and pulls out a piece of Gilda, and you ought to of seen his jaw drop.

"Well," he says, "I guess I'm holding the bag."

That's about all the news they is Harvey and I will close for this time. R. W. L.

Lilac Time

CHICAGO TRIBUNE, JANUARY 27, 1918

Friend Harvey:

Yours received and you say you been invited to see the show over to the Grand and what clothes should you wear. Well, Harvey, if you are going in the evening you might get by O .K. with a mackintosh and rubber boots, but if it's a matinée you're a sucker if you don't go in a bathing suit, because when all them women gets lachrymosical they make Niagara Falls look like a eye-dropper.

If the flood all come at once at the end of the show a man might rush home and get into something dry, but there's a deluge in Act 2 and a couple more in the last act, which they ought to call the cataract, and unless you got waterproof garments you'll catch your death.

Personally I seen a matinée and the only thing that saved me was setting between two girls that had been there before and come prepared. The lieut. that Jane Cowl[3] and him have a case on each other gets order to go to Berlin and pull the Kaiser's nose. This lieut. and some other British officers is billeted in a French farm house which Jane's mother is the farmer's wife that owns it. So of course these officers all pay for their board and lodging and Jane don't want the Lieut. to go away because it will mean one less customer so he says, "Oh, don't worry about that. I will keep my room and send my billet dues."

So then they clinch and say goodbye and all the girls in the theater begins to snuffle because it looks like he'll be a cadaver when he gets back, and at first everybody's kind of ashamed and does their sniveling quietly, but when they see everybody else doing it they open their tear ducks wide open and the ushers gets ready to bale out.

Well, the two girls that surrounded me reached into their old kit bags and pulled out a dozen new sponges, and as fast as they filled one they'd stick it back in the bag and start on a fresh one. So I asked one of them, I said, "Why don't you throw the used sponges away, and why do you save them?" "So she says, "O, you know salt has gone up like everything else, and I got a patent separator at home, and I separate the salt from the rest of the lachrymose fluid and sell it to the trade." So I said, "Oh you little salt seller," and that made everybody that was in earshot quit crying and burst out laughing, and I got a scowl from Miss Cowl.

But the real débâcle occurs in Act 3 when Jane hears that the Lieut. is O.K. and coming back, but the Colonel comes in and says the Lieut. got bit in the arm by the Kaiser and died of hydrophobia. Then's when you want to tie on the old life belt, Harvey, and stand near your boat, because they don't no sooner get through blubbering because he's dead than they start again because he walks in and says he ain't. His arm's in a sling, but it was a cootie bit him. Then the curtain falls and you trudge on upstream to Clark street.

I bet there's more than one engagement broke off between fiancées that goes to Lilac Time together. A man may think he's got a peach till she cries, and then they don't none of them look very good except Miss Cowl, and if girls cried all the time before they got married like they do afterward there wouldn't be no afterwards.

Well, Harvey, good luck to you, and be sure and not set right under the balcony rail or you'll think you're caught in the equinox.

R. W. L.

Mary MacLane and Her
Passionate Male Quartette

CHICAGO TRIBUNE, FEBRUARY 12, 1918

Yesterday.

It's a Tuesday morning and I'd amazingly love to eat a Cold Boiled Prune.

I shall never be able to tell one-tenth of my quaintly-vulgar Tuesday morning fondness for a Cold Boiled Prune.

But now I must work, work, work, work, work. So I write me this stuff of me.

I find Me in this Chicago-Illinois, in a sweetly madison street picture-show. I am fascinatingly late. The things I see are garbledly-tangled into an indescribable heap in my abdomen. I can write of them only vaguely-jumbley.

The picture is You, Mary MacLane, and your Passionate Male Sextet.

I see your white flannel-trouseredly naughty boy.

And I see your portfolioly pen-pushing black-black-black bow-tied writer-man.

And your too easily ossified son-of-a-baronet.

And your napkin-in-his-necked box fighter.

And your anti-alcoholic bucolic bank clerk.

And your married devil-in-his own-hometown.

I see all six of the Men Who Have Made Love to You (and by the way, Mary, I'll say you weren't entirely on the defensive).

And I hear them and others subtitley addressing you with such remarks as "Say listen" and "I should worry" and "You're some jane" and "For God's sake, lay off him." And I see you standing for it.

And I must admit that even if you do play with a doll and drink cocktails and don a kimono at 7:50 P.M., I'm off'n you, Mary MacLane, and never again will I believe that a girl is damnably different because of what she says in a book.

You're a broken idol with I, Ring Lardner, and in spite of my futile way-of-life and my rotting destroying half acquiescence in it I have a furious positive Murder in me.

I do not know why I don't do the Murder. It is not from fear of consequences—not in this Chicago-Illinois.

It would be simpler and finer for me to do this Murder than to keep it in me.

It would be a simpler and finer thing to do any Murder than to feel even once, the strangling damnedness rising, rising at my throat.

I wish I'd been born a Wild Boar.

Madam Butterfly Was Some Insect

BELL SYNDICATE, FEBRUARY 15,1920

To the Editor:

A wile ago I read in the N.Y. papers a write up of a show they put on down to the opera house name Zaza that was so warm that Geraldine Farrar[4] took off her coat and vest and everything in the 1st. act and she was going to do it again Thursday so I give up $7.70 per each for some tickets but when we got there they announced that a tenor name Creamy that had been on the stage when she done it the 1st. time was still in bed yet with a high fever and they wasn't no other tenor in the Co. that would stand around in such a exposure so they was going to put on Madam Butterfly instead with Geraldine playing the insect. Well when you've brought a couple of gals you don't feel like saying let's get our money back and go home, a specially when you have just road in 28 miles on the N.Y. N.H. and H. and had to set up all the way. So we stuck for Madam Butterfly and maybe some of you hasn't seen the show so I will explain it.

Well for about a hr. after we got in all that happened was the orchestra makeing different squeaks till finely a bird stepped up in front of them that everybody clapped, so I ast the gals who he was and they said it was Roberto Moranzoni the conductor.

"Oh yes," I said. "I use to know him when he was a brakeman and his name was Bob Moran."

Pretty soon the curtains floped open and we begin to get the plot. It seems like married life in Japan, where this show comes off, is a good deal like amongst the movie actors over here. You can call it off by giveing 2 wks. notice. Well they was a detective name B. F. Pinkerton that was in the U.S. navy intelligence burro and they had sent him to Japan to try and find out who give Sims them orders and wile he was there he seen Geraldine. So he ast her if she would make 1 of them Hollywood marriages and she said yes, or they wouldn't of been no show.

Well Pink has rented a honeymoon cottage way up on top of a hill and when the play opens him and his friends the American consul is up there waiting for Butterfly to show up for the ceremony. The consul was played by a bird name Scotti but his name in the show was Sharpless so they had to write all his songs on the white keys.

Wile they are waiting Pink sings "Would you like a highball" and Scotti answers yes and when they drink it the orchestra plays part of the star Spangle banner, deuce knows why.

Well finely Geraldine come in and she hit a couple of cracked tones in her first song and Pink says to her "Are you trying to make us believe what the libretto says about you being 15 yrs. old and pretending like your voice is changeing." So she says back "Who and the h—ll wouldn't sing a couple of sour notes after climbing a hill like that?" So Pink said "If you was a real Butterfly you'd of flew up the hill." "Yes" she says "but I was a caterpillar when I started."

She had broughten a lot of other bugs with her that she said was relatives and a justice of the peace and they put on a wedding that was a worlds record tor speed probably because Pink's initials was B. F. so Butterfly didn't half to change hers. They was a good alto singer from Chicago name Frances Ingram visiting the bride and if I had of been Pink I would of hesitated a long wile before I picked Gerry instead of she.

Well Act 2 is 3 yrs. later and its broughten out that a little wile after the wedding, Pink had found out that his wife smoked a pipe so he had snuck back to the U.S. and secretly married a cigaret feind. Meanwhile Madam Butterfly has a little son witch she has named him Larva Pinkerton and they are waiting for his dad to come back and see him. Finely Mr. Sharpless shows up and trys to tell the Madam in naturals that he has had a letter from Pink and Pink is married again and for her to forget him, but she won't listen and she brings in Larva and tells Mr. S. to write back to Pink and tell him he's got a kid. After Sharpless goes, Frances, who seems to be makeing quite a visit, looks out on the bay and sees a U.S. war ship and its the same ship that brought Pink the last time, and they figure he must be on it, so they set up all night thinking he will come and call, but he don't come. In the morning Frances says to Gerry, you better go upstairs and take a nap. "No" says the Madam. "I'm a Pinkerton. I never sleep."

But Frances makes her go up and during her absents, sure enough in comes Sharpless and Pink and the new Mrs. Pink. It seems like Pink was on the ship after all and he has seen Sharpless and Sharpless told him about Larva and he has come to claim him. So they ask Frances to ask Madam Butterfly to give Larva up and she says she will and Pinkerton remembers that he has left some of his disguises in a unlocked suit case down at the Tokio House, so he blows and then Madam comes downstairs and Mr. Sharpless introduces the new Mrs. Pink and tells Madam that Pink is in town and wants his kid, so Madam says he can have him if he will come alone and get him himself.

But just before he comes, Madam says to herself "So he has got a harem has he" so she commits harem scarum with a Japanese pie knife and when Pink gets there all he has got left is 1 wife and Larva.

Well when the show was over the ladys with me was weeping though I was the bird that had spent the $23.10. So I says "What do you go to a show for, to sniffle?" So 1 of them said "What do you go for?" So I said I go to learn something. They ast me what had I learnt and I says I had learnt that the way for a Jap that didn't understand English and an American that didn't understand Jap to carry on a conversation was for both of them to sing to each other in Italiano.

Cinderella

HEARST'S INTERNATIONAL, AUGUST 1923

Once upon a time they was a prominent clubman that killed his wife after a party where she doubled a bid of four diamonds and the other side made four odd, giving them game and a $26.00 rubber. Well, she left him a daughter who was beginning to run absolutely hog wild and he couldn't do nothing with her, so he married again, this time drawing a widow with two gals of her own, Patricia and Micaela.

These two gals was terrible. Pat had a wen, besides which they couldn't nobody tell where her chin started and her neck left off. The other one, Mike, got into a brawl the night she come out and several of her teeth had came out with her. These two gals was impossible.

Well, the guy's own daughter was a pip, so both her stepmother and the two stepsisters hated her and made her sleep in the ashcan. Her name was Zelda, but they called her Cinderella on account of how the ashes and clinkers clang to her when she got up noons.

Well, they was a young fella in the town that to see him throw his money around, you would of thought he was the Red Sox infield trying to make a double play. So everybody called him a Prince. Finally he sent out invitations to a dance for just people that had dress suits. Pat and Mike was invited, but not Cinderella, as her best clothes looked like they worked in a garage. The other two gals made her help them doll up and they kidded her about not going, but she got partly even by garnisheeing their hair with eau de garlic.

Well, Pat and Mike started for Webster Hall in a bonded taxi and they hadn't much sooner than went when a little bit of an old dame stepped out of the kitchen sink and stood in front of Cinderella and says she was her fairy godmother.

"Listen," says Cinderella: "don't mention mother to me! I've tried two different kinds and they've both been a flop!"

"Yes, but listen yourself," says the godmother: "wouldn't you like to go to this here dance?"

"Who and the h—l wouldn't!" says Cinderella.

"Well, then," says the godmother, "go out in the garden and pick me a pumpkin."

"You're pie-eyed," was Cinderella's criticism, but anyway she went out and got a pumpkin and give it to the old dame and the last named touched it with her wand and it turned into a big, black touring car like murderers rides in.

Then the old lady made Cinderella go to the mouse-trap and fetch her six mice and she prodded them with her wand and they each became a cylinder. Next she had her bring a rat from the rat trap and she turned him into a big city chauffeur, which wasn't hardly any trouble.

"Now," says the godmother, "fetch me a couple lizards."

So Cinderella says, "What do you think this is, the zoo?" But she went in the living-room and choose a couple lizards off the lounge and the old lady turned them into footmen.

The next thing the old godmother done was tag Cinderella herself with the wand and all of a sudden the gal's rags had become a silk evening gown and her feet was wrapped up in a pair of plate-glass slippers.

"How do you like them slippers?" asked the old dame.

"Great!" says Cinderella. "I wished you had of made the rest of my garments of the same material."

"Now, listen," says the godmother: "don't stay no later than midnight because just as soon as the clock strikes twelve, your dress will fall off and your chauffeur and so forth will change back into vermin."

Well, Cinderella clumb in the car and they was about to start when the chauffeur got out and went around back of the tonneau.

"What's the matter?" says Cinderella.

"I wanted to be sure my tail-light was on," says the rat.

Finally they come to Webster Hall and when Cinderella entered the ballroom everybody stopped dancing and looked at her pop-eyed. The Prince went nuts and wouldn't dance with nobody else and when it come time for supper he got her two helpings of stewed rhubarb and liver and he also had her laughing herself sick at the different wows he pulled. Like for instance they was one occasion when he looked at her feet and asked her what was her shoes made of.

"Plate glass," says Cinderella.

"Don't you feel no pane?" asked the Prince.

Other guests heard this one and the laughter was general.

But finally it got to be pretty near twelve o'clock and Cinderella went home in her car and pretty soon Pat and Mike blowed in and found her in the ashcan and told her about the ball and how the strange gal had come and stole the show.

"We may see her again to-morrow night," says Pat.

"Oh," says Cinderella, "is they going to be another ball?"

"Why, no, you poor sap!" says Mike. "It's a Marathon."

"I wished I could go," says Cinderella. "I could if you would leave me take your yellow dress."

The two stepsisters both razzed her, little wreaking that it was all as she could do to help from laughing outright.

Anyway they both went back to the dance the next night and Cinderella followed them again, but this time the gin made her drowsy and before she realized it, the clock was striking twelve. So in her hurry to get out she threw a shoe and everybody scrambled for it, but the Prince got it. Meanw'ile on account of it being after midnight, the touring car had disappeared and Cindy had to walk home and her former chauffeur kept nibbling at her exposed foot and annoying her in many other ways.

Well, the Prince run a display ad the next morning that he would marry the gal who could wear the shoe and he sent a trumpeter and a shoe clerk to make a house to house canvass of Greater New York and try the shoe on all the dames they could find and finally they come to the clubman's house and the trumpeter woke up the two stepsisters for a fitting. Well, Pat took one look at the shoe and seen they was no use. Mike was game and tried her best to squeeze into it, but flopped, as her dogs was also mastiffs. She got sore and asked the trumpeter why hadn't he broughten a shoe horn instead of that bugle. He just laughed.

All of a sudden him and the shoe clerk catched a glimpse of Cinderella and seen that she had small feet and sure enough, the slipper fitted her and they run back to the Prince's apartment to tell him the news.

"Listen, Scott," they says, for that was the Prince's name: "we have found the gal!"

So Cinderella and the Prince got married and Cinderella forgive her two stepsisters for how they had treated her and she paid a high-price dentist to fix Mike up with a removable bridge and staked Pat to a surgeon that advertised a new, safe method of exterminating wens.

That is all of the story, but it strikes me like the plot—with the poor, ragged little gal finally getting all the best of it—could be changed around and fixed up so as it would make a good idear for a play.

Ring Tells the Story of Snow White

BELL SYNDICATE, OCTOBER 28, 1923

To the Editor:

Some of the boys in the radio company has been pestering me to death to come to the broadcasting station and tell a couple bedtime stories as they recd. numerable requests from mothers all over the country asking for something that would put their children to sleep and the rumor had got out some way another that whenever I tell a story, why who ever is within hearing distance dozes right off.

Well friends I aint got the voice nessary to carry over the radio but will write out a fairy story like I told it to my own kiddies the other night and it acted like chlorform and parents is welcome to read it out loud to their children if they wish and the story is Little Snow-White and I can't remember how it goes in the book so am obliged to tell it in my own wds.

Well once at a time they was a Queen and she cut herself shaving and 3 drops of blood fell in the snow and it looked so pretty that the Queen wished she could have a red and white kid and pretty soon she gave birth to a little girl that soon learned to fix herself up in the above color scheme and her mother nicknamed her Snow-White and that winter the mother died of home made gin and the King without needless delay married a chorus gal as he loved beautiful baritone voices.

The new bride had once been elected Miss America at Atlantic City and if you seen her at certain times in the day she was not ½ bad though the King gave her a mirror for a wedding present and told her to get some of that stuff out of her eyelashes.

Well the new Queen was a woman at heart and could not help from talking even when alone and one day she stood up in front of the mirror and said:

"Mirror, mirror on the wall,
  Who is the dame for whom you'd fall?"
  And the mirror replied:
"I'll half to hand it to you O Queen,
  You are the best I ever seen."

Well this kept up till little Snow-White was a 7 yr. old flapper and one day the Queen says to the mirror:

"Mirror, mirror on my dresser,
Do I still lead? No sir or yes sir?"
And the mirror replied:
"You use to top the list O Queen,
Now Snow-White has got you beat old bean."

Well this made no hit with the Queen as she could not stomach the position of runner up so she said a wd. that is always spelt with a capital letter and took a smash at the mirror and then give a boy from the east side $15.00 to take Snow-White out to the park and bump her off and he was to bring back some of the little gal's giblets to show he had not missed.

But the gun man was noble at heart and could not bear to kill Snow-White and turned her loose near the zoo and then spent a very small portion of the $15.00 on some chicken livers en brochette which he took back to the Queen as evidence.

Well Snow-White was scared at being left alone and she run till she could not run no more on acct. of how her dogs fret her so she finely set down on the steps of a apt. bldg. along about midnight and pretty soon the 6 Green Brothers who had a musical act come home to this bldg. in which they had a apt. and they took Snow-White in and made her their house keeper.

She told them her story and they warned her to never let nobody in the apt. unlest she knew who it was as the Queen would find out sooner or later that she was still alive and would try and get her.

Mean wile the Queen eat the chicken livers and then visited the mirror and says:

"Mirror, mirror upside down.
Who is the prettiest gal in town?"
And the mirror replied in a cracked voice:
"You still run second, O you Queen,
To Snow-White who is working for the Brothers Green."

Well to make it a short story the Queen tried 3 different times to get rid of Snow-White and the first time she made up like a corset salesman and Snow-White was sucker enough to let her in and the Queen sold her a corset that was too small and the poor gal was choking to death when the Green boys come home and released her. On another occasion the Queen sold the gal a poison comb which she stuck in her hair and the Green boys got there just in time to prevent total baldness.

On the last occasion the Queen posed as a fruit pedlar and Snow-White ast her did she have any apples and the Queen says Yes I have some apples today but Snow-White said she was scared to eat one as it might be poisoned so the Queen says that to prove they was no danger, she would eat the corpse of the apple herself wile Snow-White eat the outside.

Well the outside was the part that was poisoned and when Snow-White eat it she fell dead.

Now the way the Queen found out that the corset gag and the poisoned comb had flopped was by consulting with her mirror, like for inst. after the poisoned comb episode she says to the mirror:

"Mirror, mirror, gift of the King,
Who leads the Looks League now, old thing?"
And the mirror was obliged to answer:
"You use to be fairer than all the others,
But Snow-White is still rooming with the Six Green Brothers."

But after the apple episode the mirror said in reply to a query:

"You lead the league once more old head,
For Snow-White seems to be practally dead."

However when the Green Brothers arrived home and found Snow-White laying on the floor with her neck kind of bulging out like it was a cyst or something they called in a X-ray expert and he soon located the apple in her throat and a man from the garage got it out with a applejack, where on Snow-White jumped up as good as new.

To celebrate the occasion the Greens took her along that night to the Supper Club where they was employed and there she met a wealthy bond thief who like them young, and merrily rang the bells. So the same day they was married, the Queen put the usual query to her mirror and the last named replied:

"I'd like to say you, but I've got to hand it
To Snow-White, the wife of a well to do bandit."

This made the Queen so sore that she drunk a qt. of $55.00 Scotch which she had been saving for company and the next day her widower married the gal who had been sent to Atlantic City that year as Miss Seattle.

A Dog's Tale

BELL SYNDICATE, NOVEMBER 18, 1923

To the Editor:

Well children, here is the story of little Red Riding Hood like I tell it to my little ones when they wake up in the morning with a headache after a tough night.

Well, one or two times they was a little gal that lived in the suburbs who they called her little Red Riding Hood because she always wore a red riding hood in the hopes that sometimes a fresh guy in a high power road-ster would pick her up and take her riding. But the rumor had spread the neighborhood that she was a perfectly nice gal, so she had to walk.

Red had a grandmother that lived over near the golf course and got in on most of the parties and one noon she got up and found that they wasn't no gin in the house for her breakfast so she called up her daughter and told her to send Red over with a bottle of gin as she was dying.

So Red starts out with a quart under her arm but had not went far when she met a police dog. A good many people has police dogs, and brags about them and how nice they are for children and etc. but personally I would just as leaf have my kids spend their week-end swimming in the State Shark Hatchery.

Well, this special police dog was like the most of them and hated everybody. When he seen Red he spoke to her and she answered him. Even a dog was better than nothing. She told him where she was going and he pertended like he wasn't paying no tension but no sooner had not she left him when he beat it up a alley and got to her grandmother's joint ahead of her.

Well, the old lady heard him knock at the door and told him to come in, as she thought he must either be Red or a bootlegger. So he went in and the old lady was in bed with this hang over and the dog eat her alive. Then he put on some pajamas and laid down in the bed and pertended like he was her, so pretty soon Red came along and knocked at the door and the dog told her to come in and she went up to the bed to hand him the quart. She thought of course it would be her grandmother laying in the bed and even when she seen the dog she still figured it was her grandmother and something she had drunk the night before must of disagreed with her and made her look different.

"Well, grandmother," she says, "you must of hit the old hair tonic last night. Your arms looks like Luis Firpo."

"I will Firpo you in a minute," says the dog.

"But listen, grandmother," says Red, "don't you think you ought to have your ears bobbed?"

"I will ear you in a minute," says the dog.

"But listen, grandmother," says Red, "you are cock-eyed."

"Listen," says the dog, "if you had of had ½ of what I had last night you would of been stone blind."

"But listen, grandmother," says Red, "where did you get the new store teeth?"

"I heard you was a tough egg," says the dog, "so I bought them to eat you with."

So then the dog jumped out of bed and went after Red and she screamed.

In the mean wile Red's father had been playing golf for a quarter a hole with a couple of guys that conceded themselfs all putts under 12 ft. and he was $.75 looser coming to the 10th tee.

The 10th hole is kind of tough, as your drive has to have a carry of 50 yards or it will fall in a garbage incinerating plant. You can either lift out with a penalty of two strokes or else play it with a penalty of suffocation. Red's old man topped his drive and the ball rolled into the garbage. He elected to play it and made what looked like a beautiful shot, but when they got up on the green they found that he had hit a white radish instead of a golf ball.

A long argument followed, during which the gallery went home to get his supper. The hole was finely conceded.

The 11th hole on the course is probably the sportiest hole in golfdom. The tee and green are synonymous and the first shot is a putt, but the rules signify that the putt must be played off a high tee with a driver. Red's father was on in two and off in three more and finely sunk his approach for a birdie eight, squaring the match.

Thus the match was all square coming to the home hole which is right close to grandmother's cottage. Red's father hooked his drive through an open window in his mother-in-law's house and forced his caddy to lend him a niblick. He entered the cottage just as the dog was beginning to eat Red.

"What hole are you playing father?" asked Red.

"The eighteenth," says her father, "and it is a dog's leg."

Where at he hit the police dog in the leg with his niblick and the dog was so surprised that he even give up the grandmother.

"I win, one up," says Red's father and he went out to tell the news to his two opponents. But they had quit and went home to dress for the Kiwanis Club dance.

Fifteen Rounds with Shakespeare and Tunney

MORNING TELEGRAPH, JANUARY 15, 1929

New York—Dame Rumor hath it that the master minds of Hollywood intend to star Gene Tunney in Shakespearean lisping pictures. The retired champ has not given his consent or denied the accusation and his friends think there may be some disagreement over terms. It seems hardly possible that financial bargaining is going on; money means nothing to either side. My guess is that Gene considers the Bard's stuff too plain, simple and blunt; also that he differs with some of his opinions. He will sign if the lines are rewritten in less abrupt and ungrammatical language and if certain of William's ideas are altered to fit the Tunney code.

Well, this writer is as phlegmatic about dough as Gene or Adolph or

Carl: moreover I am in a fever to have the deal go through. So I will gladly donate my services as play doctor and herewith submit a few samples by which the parties may judge my talent:

Macbeth

"Remain recumbent, Mr. Macduff, and may condemnation proceedings be instituted against him who is first to vociferate 'Surcease, a plethora!'"

"I convey a talismanic entity." (I bear a charmed life).

Hamlet

"Something is putrescent in the suzerainty of Denmark."

"To have being, or to become non-existent: that is the interrogation:

"Whether 'tis more pietistic in the pericranium to suffer

"The ballistae and javelins of demonical opulence.

"Or to join the Marines against a catastrophic Meditteranean.

"And by adopting a course of oppugnancy, conduct same to an omega."

Julius Caesar

"Be admonished regarding the Ides of a military progress!"

"This was the most malevolentest incision of the ensemble."

"If you have tears, make arrangements to extravasate them instantaneously."

"Distant Cassius is possessed of an attenuated and rapacious aspect:

"He cognitates inordinately: such individuals are fraught with precariousness."

Romeo and Juliet

"What are the contents of a cognomen? That which we designate a Rosenbaum

"By any other appellation would exhale as saccharine a redolence."

"He perpetuates jokes regarding stomachache whom Dempsey never punched in the torso."

King Henry IV

"Jehovah preserve the purchaser of ringside seat!"
(God save the mark)

King John

"Zounds! I was never so bethumped with polysyllables
Since I first denominated my brother's progenitor pater."

As You Like It

"Down on your knees, and thank Heaven, gasping, for a Chicago
     referee's Love."
"For in my youth I never did apply
Combustible and contumacious liqueurs in my blood."

The Merchant of Venice

"I am Sir Oracle, and when I one my lips let no sealyham ululate."

Much Ado About Nothing

"Similitudes are mephitic."

Measure for Measure

"Oh, it is excellent to have a giant's strength; but it is imbecilic to
     use it gratuitously."

The Tempest

"Billy Gibson[5] acquaints a man with strange sparring partners."

Your Broadway, Beau, and You Can Have It

MORNING TELEGRAPH, JANUARY 22, 1929

New York—Guiseppe Verdi (Joe Green, as a Frank Adams contrib tagged him) seems to have penned another smash in "Aida," George Gershwin is Sullivan-Gilberting with his own brother, Ira.

Mrs. Palmer is anticipating a quadruply blessed event (the Marx Brothers) . . . Cal Coolidge is sealed to Grace Goodhue, a Burlington brunette.

A. Lincoln and Gen. McClellan are on the verge . . . Jimmy Madison and Dolly Payne Todd are THAT WAY. (Ed: This is the absolute Choynskie.)

Aleck Hamilton and Aaron Burr have phfft . . . The Geo. Washingtons (she was Martha Lorber of the Follies) have moved into their Valley Forge snuggery for the Old Man Shiver Days.

Naps Bonaparte has suggested Renovation to his femme, Josie . . . They say Jerry Kern was forced by the Society of Composers and Authors to auction his li-ber-ary, the other boys fearing it would smirch the industry's good name to have a song-writer own a book.

What writer on what paper is taking whose golf clubs to what Bahamas? . . . Arthur Brisbane has signed up to do a daily colyum for William ("Randolph") Hearst.

An Exchange Place investment firm is recommending stock in a company that will convert hootch from liquid to solid form and thus be able to peddle it legally, perhaps as sandwiches . . . You can order me a Scotch on rye.

Recommended to diversion seekers: The Florida East Coast R.R. timetable . . . The Lynn Fontannes. . . . Iodine as a nose gargle to pfffend off the phffflu . . . A Madison Square Garden phfffight decision . . . A motor trip on Eighth Ave.

F. P. F. has quit the evemaily and is running a swell colyum on the World . . . Heywood Broun and that last-named rag have phfft . . . The subway is going to install automat turnstiles which you can go through by dropping Anne Nichols[6] in the slot.

Danny Deever is halter bound . . . What subscriber to the N.Y. telephone directory has got a cold?

Heavy Da-Dee-Dough Boys

NEW YORKER, JUNE 25, 1932

No Visitors, N. Y.

My nurse, Miss Graham, who seems to know more about radio than most of the people financially interested in same (and when I say this I am not handing the young lady a Phi Beta Kappa key), is a chum of a chum of a cousin of one Bing Crosby, and several weeks ago she (Miss Graham) told me a story about Mr. Crosby which came from the chum-cousin via the chum.

Bing was a featured singer at a night club or something in California. A scout for one of the big broadcasting companies heard him sing and thought he was good. This sounds like a knock at Bing, but isn't intended that way; the big broadcasting companies have had a few good pickers in their employ, hired, perhaps, through some misunderstanding. (And that reminds me that in the recent retrenchment exercises, Reinald Werren-rath, who certainly was no sap about arranging worth-while musical programs or recommending good new talent, received his notice of unconditional release, or was permitted to resign, from the N.B.C., and as soon as this news reached the ears of New York University, the latter made him a Doctor of Music.)

Well, anyway, Bing was engaged, brought east and given a good spot in the WABC schedule. His style and his programs were extremely popular, particularly with the ladies GBT (God Bless Them), and when it was an announced not long ago that he was going to quit and do some pictures in Hollywood, hundreds of thousands of fair radio addicts simply swooned.

Bing's departure from the California night club left the club's proprietors and clients in a tearful mood and they remained so until Russ Columbo was engaged to replace him and instructed (according to Bing's cousin's report) to copy as closely as possible the Crosby method and style of singing.

So long as Russ remained in the night club, Bing had no objection to being imitated, but when Russ carried the alleged imitation to the point of coming east and getting himself a radio job, Mr. Crosby (Cousin to

Chum to Nurse to Me) squawked. The squawk wasn't a loud one; merely an outspoken expression of opinion that Mr. Colombo's whole method and style of singing were based on his own.

Now this got me kind of interested and I, a neophyte in radio criticism, but (he said shyly) a person who knows music, even the quaint sort that usually is miked onto the defenseless air, decided I would eavesdrop on both of the boys over a period of weeks and find out for myself and my own invisible audience whether Mr. Crosby's plaint was justified.

Well, the first time I listened, it occurred to me that if I had originated the Capone system of depopulating Chicago and Brooklyn, I wouldn't brag of it and hint at plagiarism on the part of Scarface Al. (And I wouldn't be calling him Scarface if he weren't summering in Georgia behind reliable bars.) It also occurred to me that at least one thing could be said in favor of both Bing and Russ: When you hear either of them, you don't think, "Why, that's Connie Boswell!"

Analyzing their similarities and differences that first time and many other times, expertly and with great care, I have reached the following conclusions, which will be incorporated in my charge to the invisible jury.

Both are extremely proficient in the art of not hitting a tone on the nose. They sneak up on it or slide down to it or miss it entirely.

Another thing they have in common is a talent, amounting to genius, for being left at the post by the orchestra or other accompaniment. They usually start from two to six or seven beats behind and as a rule frighten those who have bet on them by seeming hopelessly out of the race until they are right at the wire.

For the benefit of the untutored I must explain that in the days before the Musical Depression, a singer ordinarily ended a song on the keynote, or tonic. If a song is in the key of F, F is the tonic. The "third" is A natural and the "fifth" is C. (Am I educated!) In those days it was the exception when a number was wound up on a third, and even more so when the vocalist fifthed at the finish. Bing and Russ use the fifth nine times out of ten, or at least, they nibble all around it. It must be part of the Crosby system, but I hope Bing doesn't claim it as original. If he does, he should accuse not only Russ, but also Ruthie Etting, Artie Jarrett, Streetie Singer, Katie Smith, and countless others of stealing his stuff, and among the countless others is the late Giacomo Puccini, who put it in the script of an important tenor aria in "La Bohème," which was composed before the invention of static. At any rate, the "trick" has become more or less familiar and I have been tempted to write to both of the boys and say, "Take a tonic." ("Oh, dear!" as Harry Richman remarks after his gags on the Chase & Sanborn Oh Dear hour, taking the words out of the indestructible audience's mouth.)

It is just about a toss-up between the lads in the matter of putting lyrics across. My favorite melody of the current supply is "Dancing on the Ceiling," Dick Rodgers' best piece since "My Heart Stood Still"—a better piece than the last-named if you're asking me. I presumed that the lyric was by Mr. Rodgers' regular collaborator, Lorenz Hart, and wondered what it was about. Mr. Columbo sang it one evening. I am still wondering what it's about. Russ can outsyllable Bing over a distance; for example, Russ, without apparent effort, sings, "Na-hight shall be fa-fa-filled with mee-hew-hew-sic, Na-hight shall be fa-fa-filled with luh-uh-uh-uhv," or whatever it is. Bing, however, is unbeatable in a sprint, such as the word "you," which he nurses along till you would swear it was spelled yoohoo-hoohoohoohoo-oo. When Russ repeats a refrain whose lyric bores him, he usually substitutes dee-dee-dee-dum, whereas, in like circumstances, Bing uses da-dee-dee-do. Occasionally Bing even improves the song a lot by whistling eight or twelve or sixteen bars.

So far as I know, Russ is innocent of song-writing. Bing is a part author or part composer of at least two numbers, one of them his own theme song, "Tit-Willow," done in collaboration with John Gilbert and Mike (Twin) Sullivan. No, no. I must be getting confused. The song I mean starts:

"Where the blue of the night meets the gold of the day,
Someone waits for me."

Probably the someone is the orchestra leader. I haven't heard the latest Crosby product, but it is boosted in Rudy Vallée's "Tuneful Topics," which he writes for *Radio Digest*, one of the publications subscribed for by Nurse. The title of the number is "My Woman" and Rudy says "I am sure you will like it." "Its minor vein makes one think of 'Deep Night,'" and "The first syllable of the word 'Woman' gives Bing on the record an excellent chance to utilize his exaggerated glissando." When Rudy plugs a song, it is praise from Caesar, and very high praise in this case because Rudy himself co-authored "Deep Night," of which the minor vein of "My Woman" makes one think. Recent blood tests in my own minor veins didn't show any glissando and I had to call for a dictionary. Well, it's a gliding effect, as the playing of a run on the pianoforte by sliding the fingers over the keys. O.K! Funk & Wagnalls! You may call it gliding, but I calls it da-dee-dee-do-dee-dee-da-dee-dee-do-dee-dee-Dumb.

The mention of Caesar reminds me of another Shakespearean creation, Romeo. Mr. Colombo's sub-title, as you doubtless know, is "The Romeo of Song." Miss Graham doesn't think Bing has an intriguing alias, and though she shares her sex's devotion to Mr. Crosby and grief at his projected desertion of the air, she admits that Russ is the more beautiful of this exciting da-dee-dee-dee-do-dum duo and wants to wager that he could give conclusive evidence to support the truth of the old saw, "There's Always Juliet."

Jury, the case is in your hands. You have read the testimony and my clarifying analysis of same. It is my honest and expert opinion that the boys are pretty evenly matched, that any decision save a draw would be unfair to one or the other. But don't let me influence youhoohoohoohoohoo-oo.

Lyricists Strike Pay Dirt

NEW YORKER, NOVEMBER 19, 1932

No Visitors, N.Y.

You can count on the fingers of one thumb the present-day writers of song who could wear becomingly the mantle of W. S. Gilbert, or even the squirrel neckpiece of Ira Gershwin. Some of them should be fitted out with rompers, the costume for which their birth, bringing-up, and education qualify them; some with sturdy boys' suits appropriate for children belonging in the third, fourth, and fifth grades. Some ought to be garbed in nightgowns, pajamas, and lounging robes provided for rest cases at Bellevue. And a few, I am afraid, would feel at home only in strait-jackets.

This department has been laughed at for prudishness, but has not been laughed out of it. This department has reached a stage where it almost doesn't mind a song whose only faults are inanity, terrible rhyming, and glaring infractions of simple grammatical rules. Unfortunately, the "lyricists," the singers, and the whimperers are not satisfied with that comparatively harmless kind. They are polluting the once-pure air of Golly's great out-of-doors with a gas barrage of the most suggestive songs ever conceived, published, and plugged on one year.

Weeks ago in these fascinating columns, I wrote to the effect that it seemed silly for radio to bar words like God, Hell, and damn and to permit the "comedians" to get by with gags running the gamut from vulgar to vile, and the singers to use unmistakably off-color "Paradise" and the flagrantly immoral "As You Desire Me." In that piece, I charged Ray Perkins with unnecessary roughness, and a more or less amicable correspondence between us left him unconvinced and me pretty sad. N.B.C. asked Allie Wrubel,[7] author of "As You Desire Me,"[8] to rewrite his refrain, cleaning it up. The rewritten version means absolutely nothing, but surely we can't complain of that. Mr. Wrubel charged me good-naturedly with responsibility for the N.B.C. edict. I hope I was guilty. But the boys in the Columbia studios didn't read my stuff that week and their singers (notably Charles Carlile, who ought to know better) still stick to the original mess. The melody, also by Mr. Wrubel, is pretty enough to deserve what it is getting: a much longer life than is usually in order in the radio regime.

Perhaps you wonder why I revive this tedious subject when there is so little chance of a queasy crusader making headway. There are several reasons, and one is that Mr. Wrubel and the authors of "Paradise" ought not to be the only boys criticized when scores of their fellow-geniuses are trying their worst (and with ever-increasing signs of ultimate success) to outsmut them. Another reason is that, queer as it may seem, I don't like indecency in song or story, and sex appeal employed for financial gain in this manner makes me madder than anything except fruit salad. Reason 3: A large percentage of the invisible audience is composed of old people who retain the faculty of being shocked and of children between the ages of nine and sixteen who are not morally damaged by the words Hell, damn, and God, but can't help wondering what the heck when they hear songs that glorify defiance of the seventh amendment to Moses' constitution. Reason 4: A curiosity as to whether there is such a thing as radio censorship, and if so, whether those in charge if it are morons themselves or simply don't know what is what and what is not; and whether they will take the hint lying down when their attention is called to this squawk, as it shall be. Reason 5: A curiosity as to whether the sponsors and their advertising agencies are just plain dumb or as broad as the ocean and as lewd as the sky. Reason 6: Something happened on a very recent Sunday night which rekindled the smoldering ashes of offended prudery and forced me to mention the six-letter surname of a New Testament character with such volume that even the nurse woke up.

The stations I usually play are WEAF, WOR, WJZ, and WABC. Tuning in first on WABC, I found myself listening to a risqué song. Tuning in on WJZ, I heard another one. Similar thrills were waiting on WOR and WEAF, and it was then that I lost control of my tongue and frightened poor Miss Graham out of her nap and her cap. An apology and an explanation were in order.

"Well," she said, "it's Sunday. They probably thought of that and now they're celebrating the Fourth Commandment which begins [she whisked out the midget Bible that she carries in her hypo case]: 'Remember that thou keep holy the Sabbath Day' and ends: 'Wherefore the Lord blessed the Sabbath Day and hallowed it.'"

Now I won't put your credulity to a test by averring that there was nothing except risqué songs on the four stations that night, but between speeches and risqué jokes, the boys and girls managed to crowd in a flock of numbers that were "questionable" in title, or in one or more lines, or in toto. I took down a few titles and print them here so that when you go Christmas shopping, you can visit your favorite music store and buy something educational to read aloud or sing to the baby. Some of them may be classified as bedtime stories, as you will see when you get them. Ready?

"I'll Never Have to Dream Again," "You're Telling Me," "Good Night, My Lady Love," "Pu-leeze! Mister Hemingway!" (a swell tune and a good idea, marred by two or three words), "You Little So-and-So," "Forbidden Love," "Let's Put Out the Lights and Go to Sleep" (just on the border. They say that in the original lyric, the last word was not "sleep"), "Love Me Tonight," "I'm Yours for Tonight," "Horses Carry Tales" (sung by what I thought was a new Negro quartet which could make "Rock of Ages" sound nasty), "Bring 'Em Back Alive," "And So to Bed" (an ingenious finishing touch), "Please," "Take Me in Your Arms," "Here Lies Love," and "What Did I Get in Return?"

Others you might buy, if the kid is bored by those I have named, are "Ain'tcha Kinda Sorry Now?" and "Thrill Me!" The latter I have not yet heard on the air, but I expect to, for it probably touches a new low for the year. A copy of this number ought to be in every right-thinking, kiddy-loving American home. Why, the refrain goes: "Thrill me with a kiss that's vicious with love delicious . . ." No, I won't spoil a sale. And I'll try hard not to feel so comstocky next time.

We're All Sisters Under the Hide of Me

NEW YORKER, MAY 6, 1933

Do Not Disturb, N. Y.

Nearly a year ago this department was expressing its admiration for the line "Let come what may" in the refrain of Allie Wrubel's nursery rhyme "As You Desire Me." It struck me as perfect when it first came over the air, but in order to make sure of its perfection, I tried to improve it and asked my four spawn to do the same. Our efforts, including "Leave come what may," "Let may what come," "How come leave may," etc., were cast aside as inferior to the original, and the latter was ranked high gun (a high-gun expression) in our love nest until we heard an anthem entitled "It's Just a Little Street," or "Where Old Friends Meet," or both.

As in Mr. Wrubel's number, the stand-out line of this one occurred in the midst of the proceedings. It was, as I recall it, "Although I'm rich or poor, I feel sure I'm welcome as the flow'rs in May." Once more I summoned the whippersnappers and conferred with them on a possible substitute for "Although," which could convey a similar meaning and add to the sublimity of the lyric. My own candidate, "What ho," was voted down as too risqué, but before that defect was discovered by a prowling helpmeet, the boys thought old daddy had again come through in a pinch, and John, the eldest, was about to lead the famous victory yell—"Old Daddy! Old Daddy!" (All respire.)

Consideration was given to "Except" suggested by James (Jake the Barber) Lardner, and to "Suppose," which David (Winnie-the-Pooh)

Lardner submitted. Both were discarded for not being in modern usage as conjunctions. Bill (Jake the Barber) Lardner was in one of his ribald moods and would offer nothing but "Hotcha," which didn't even scan. John (Winnie-the-Pooh) Lardner finally hit on a couple of likely ones— "Unless" and "Until"—and now, when the five of us get together for a sing, we frequently employ one or the other, preferably the other, as a replacement for "Although." Thus: "Unless I'm rich or poor, I still feel sure," and so on. But we do this merely for variety, not because we think we have improved on "Although."

"The Little Street" enjoyed a long radio life, a fact that ought to silence those pessimists who argue that a song can't last unless it's got something. However, it is seldom heard now, and the foregoing discussion was just a prelude to some stuff about the song "Night and Day," which continues to thrive on its own merits and because Freddie Astaire refused to believe the obituary notices of "Gay Divorce," the show in which it is featured.

You must know that Mr. Cole Porter, lyricist of "Night and Day," shares the mantle of W. S. Gilbert with Ira Gershwin, Lorenz Hart, Irving Caesar, Irving Berlin, Joseph V. McKee, Howard Dietz, Bert Kalmar, George M. Cohan, Gus Kahn, Primo Carnera, and George Herman (Columbia Lou) Gehrig. Well, it seems to me that in this number, Mr. Porter not only makes a monkey of his contemporaries but shows up Gilbert himself as a seventh-rate Gertrude Stein, and he does it all with one couplet, held back till late in the refrain and then delivered as a final, convincing sock in the ear, an ear already flopping from the sheer magnificence of the lines that have preceded. I reprint the couplet:

Night and Day under the hide of me
There's an Oh, such a hungry yearning,
burning inside of me.

So what? Well, I have heard the song only by radio, and those whom I have heard repeat the refrain have sung that immortal couplet the same both times. Fortunate friends who have seen "Gay Divorce" report that the number is generously encored and reprised, and as a matter of course, most of the encores are pedal, not vocal. When they are vocal, the words are not changed.

Again, so what? Well, just as the apparently perfect lines in the Wrubel song and the "Little Street" courted an attempt at improvement, so did this superb couplet of Mr. Porter's, and though the attempt is as much of a failure as the others, the fact that the song is still being sung on stage and air encourages me to publish a few modifications to which Freddie and the radio artists are welcome if they ever tire of the original.

This time my own kiddies were left out of the conference, most of them being away at school, taking a course in cuts. A little niece of mine, Miss Ann (Jake the Barber) Tobin of Niles, Mich., was the only party consulted. We agreed that there must be no needless trifling with the impeccable five words—"There's an Oh, such a"—which begin the second line; they should stand as written except where our rhythm made changes imperative.

Well, then, here is the first variant from Little Anne's pen, with spelling corrected by uncle:

Night and day under the rind of me
There's an Oh, such a zeal for spooning,
ru'ning the mind of me.

And another, wherein she lapses into the patois:

Night and day under the peel o' me
There's a hert that will dree if ye think
aucht but a' weel o' me.

And now a few by uncle himself:

1. Night and day under the fleece of me
   there's an Oh, such a flaming furneth
   burneth the grease of me.
2. Night and day under the bark of me
   There's an Oh, such a mob of microbes
   making a park of me.
3. Night and day under my dermis, dear,
   There's a spot just as hot as coffee
   kept in a thermos, dear.

4. Night and day under my cuticle
   There's a love all for you so true it
   Never would do to kill.
5. Night and day under my tegument
   There's a voice telling me I'm he, the
   good little egg you meant.

As usual, the space is nearly all gone before I have said anything. There may be enough to admit that Jack Benny was recently very funny in a Jekyll and Hyde sketch; to express the opinion that Joe Cook, in two trial heats, has convinced me that he is as valuable a radio comic as any sponsor is likely to find; and to report that Mr. John Underwood of Buffalo listened in on the Washington baseball opening and heard Ted Husing speak of Maxie Bishop, Joey Kuhel, and Lukey Sewell, and is indignant because he didn't state that Pressey Roosevelt had thrown out the first ballie.

13

Buried Treasure and Night Letters

Perceptive readers of Lardner's work for the *Chicago Tribune* and the Bell Syndicate did not turn the page away from his columns simply because they were not interested in his topic of the day or because he did not seem particularly inspired. Somewhere in each column, they quickly learned, he might make a joke, coin a phrase, or invent a malaprop so delicious that it would have been a shame to miss it. A few of these buried treasures appear on the following pages.

The same was true of the short columns titled "Night Letters," which the Bell Syndicate and Chicago Tribune News Syndicate asked Lardner to write in 1931, perhaps thinking he could come up with some lively comments on a daily basis without having to write entire columns. Overall they do not measure up to his best work, but there were still flashes of the old spark, as in his comments on the events that led to the "Bonus March" in 1931, the holiday for George Washington's birthday, and a few other observations.

Some of the "Night Letters" were written from Florida, some from his home on Long Island, and some from a sanatorium in Tucson, Arizona, where doctors had sent him for his health. While in Tucson he "discovered" a naïve young pitcher named Willis Clough, a direct descendent of Jack Keefe, whose exploits were recorded under the heading "Ring Lardner hears from Willis Clough."

The "Night Letters" concept was not as successful as Lardner had hoped, as many of the newspapers that once ran the Bell Syndicate columns opted out and the idea was abandoned after only a few months. The entry for April 25 is the last thing Lardner ever wrote for a newspaper.

Buried Treasure

CHICAGO TRIBUNE, SEPTEMBER 19, 1915

Bill writes a letter to Steve in which he says he won't let his wife Gussie learn how to drive because ". . . she would want me to leave (their car) home all day for her to drive it and I would half to walk to the ball pk. or crall on my hands and niece."

CHICAGO TRIBUNE, DECEMBER 7, 1915

After seeing seeing "Carmen" in Chicago, Lardner writes, "The bills says the opera would beggin at 8 bells so a bout ½ past 8 the drum major showed up and the band beggin playing a tune they couldent no body dance to so we all set around there like bums on a log and finely the lights was all turned out and the curtain went up and the chorus was on the stage and they looked like they might be the ants of the chorus that's in the follys."

The next night, he describes seeing another opera:

"The show this time was Amours Dei Tre Re and it means the love of three kings and Ive often felt that kind of love my self till the other guy showed three aces."

CHICAGO TRIBUNE, JANUARY 9, 1916

In "The Diary of a Siren," an occasional series in which Lardner records the adventures of an extremely unpleasant young woman, he writes, "I was going to take a nap and read a little after dinner but while we was eating Lottie says something about she and Harry going skating and would I help her with the dishes so as she could get a early start. Hows that for nerve and if I done it once it would set a president and she would be asking me to do it all the time like I was a servant so I said "who was your dish washer last year."

"In response to Gen. Demand, the Wake is, in a couple of weeks, going on its last summer's vacation, Where it's going is neither here nor there, though near both places."

After taking his seat at Republican Convention, Lardner writes, "Bryan came in right after me and the band played Rock of Ages. He bowed his acknowledgement. Then the band played a malady of Scotch airs and when they came to Old Lang Sign the southern degradation cheered thinking it was Dixie."

In Springfield, Ill., to write about soldiers at training camp for the war against Mexico, Lardner is told not to bother. "They ain't nothing doing today, because they are just mustarding the troops."

After Woodrow Wilson's Thanksgiving Day proclamation, Lardner writes, "Or leave us quote again from Pres. Wilson's article where he says "our harvests have been plentiful and of our abundance we have been able to render succor to less favored nations." Well that about the harvests is all the more welcome as it comes like a big surprise and even if it don't do you no good why you can give thanks in behalf of whoever has been rendering our abundance to the succors in the less favored nations.

At the Republican convention, Lardner writes, "Acrost the street, at the Auditorium was the delegates for Mr. Johnson and Mr. Hoover. Most of them was delegates at large, but others had brought their wives along."

In a column about diet and exercise, Lardner writes, "Like for inst. you wouldn't go to Babe Ruth for beauty hints no more than you would ask Lillian Gish which cheek to park your tobacco in vs. a left hander."

Describing a World Series game, Lardner writes, "That is about all I know of to write except a little experience I had with a couple of tickets. I drove in from Great Neck with Tad, the cartoonist, and I told him I had a couple of extra tickets for the game and he says why not give them to a couple of poor little kiddies. Tad has a big heart, especially when the tickets is mine. So anyway we picked out two kids about 10 years old outside the Polo grounds and I gave them the tickets and they acted tickled to death. So when I finally got in the press coop, I looked up to the seats which my tickets called for. The kids was 35 years older than the last time I saw them.

Night Letters

Miami, Fla.—My dear public: If I come out and see my shadow tomorrow noon you will probably get a message from me every day for the next six weeks or more and if I don't come out and see my shadow the same thing will happen. I will leave the government in the capable hands of Will Rogers and confine myself to things with which I am more familiar, such as what is going on in society and different hospitals. I trust Mr. Rogers will not think I am intruding. After all we are both Indians only he ain't been scalped.

Miami Beach, Fla—Sweet people: The economical thing to do in a place like this is rent a drive-it-yourself car by the week unless you want to stay in your room all the time and play blind man's bluff with the chambermaid. I had the good fortune to rent the first sedan ever made in America. It has no glass in the windows and no lights anywhere and the emergency brake won't work and the foot brake won't do anything else. It won't start unless it is facing downhill and it won't stop except when straddling a street car track. Boys, remember me kindly and take care of your mother and don't smoke till you are twenty-one.

FEBRUARY 19, 1931

East Hampton, L.I.—Back in 1917 and 1918 a bunch of young whippersnappers from this country went to France on a joy ride and forced dotards like myself to leave our pleasant firesides nights and go out dancing and carousing with debutantes who had not yet learned the facts of strong drink. Now congress is arguing the propriety of giving these truants and refugees a bonus. Don't give 'em nothing, is my slogan. Fine 'em a year's salary, even if they ain't getting it.

FEBRUARY 23, 1931

New York, Feb. 22—This is the day set aside for the commemoration of George Washington's birth and another holiday for the unemployed. It is said of George that he threw a dollar across the Rappahannock river, but Mr. Coolidge examined the opposite shore carefully and couldn't find it. It is also said that George never told a lie, but that was long before they had an income tax.

APRIL 8, 1931

Tucson, Ariz—Willis Clough, Pittsburgh's recruit pitcher from Tucson, keeps on writing:

"San Francisco is not as big as Los Angeles but bigger than Paso Robles or Tucson. It is a funny town as so many of the streets runs pretty near straight uphill, but Paul Waner says they built them that way on purpose so as to offset the streets that runs straight down.

"The other day I asked George Grantham why they call Capt. Traynor

"Pie," and he says it was on account of him training on pie, but last night Manager Ens balled me out in the dining room when he seen me eating pie a la mode with ice cream on top for desert.

"I reminded him about Traynor and he says it was all right for him to get fat because he would not always be taking up room on the bench.

"He says Brooklyn would have win the pennant last year only their manager William Robinson was so big that the players had to stand up between innings and was all worn out by the middle of September."

APRIL 14, 1931

Tucson, Ariz.—Willis Clough, Pittsburgh's rookie pitcher, has been so overwhelmed by his first glimpse of a big league town that he is no longer content to relate his experiences by mail, but is now using that new invention, the telegraph, to keep his friends informed as to what is going on. Here is the important wire received from him tonight from Chicago: "Am so excited that I can't hardly hold the pencil still on account of being so excited on account of opening the regular season tomorrow against the Cubs and maybe I will get into the opening game as I asked Manager Ens this afternoon who was libel to pitch and he says it was between Kremer or Wood or French or Heine or Spencer or Swetonic so I says any chance of me getting in and he says yes if the game runs over till Wednesday. It looks like manager Hornsby would pitch either Root or Blake or Smith or Bush or May or Sweetland. We had a morning practice at the Cubs park this morning. There has been a lot of worry about whether Paul Waner would be able to play on account of his leg. He is O.K. and I found out why they call him 'Poison' and it is because he was bit by a fish in the leg and 'poison' is the French word for fish."

APRIL 25, 1931

Pittsburgh, Pa.—Ring Lardner hears from Willis Clough:

Dear Friend I have not yet picked out no place to live as we are only here such a short time this time and leave Saturday night for a series in St. Louis. So I been staying at the Schenley hotel which is almost right across the street from the ball park and George Grantham said it was too bad they could not move the ball park into the hotel as that would save me the trouble of taking any exercise day or night both, he is a great kidder. I made the remark how silly it was to only play 4 games here when the fans has been waiting all these weeks to welcome the club home and you would think they would leave us stay here long enough for the fans to get use to the new faces and Bill Hinchman. There was no way of judging how long that would take because, for instance, he has seen me every day for 6 weeks and roomed with me pretty near a week and he don't believe he will ever get use to my face especially when he wakes up in the morning. I said any way I wished we would make an eastern trip before we go to St. Louis as I am always wanted to see the big eastern cities but Paul Waner said you better be glad we are going to St. Louis because if Manager Ens should happen to get the idea that you was homesick for Arizona it would be a lot better for your feet if he got the idea in St. Louis than Boston.

Acknowledgments

Several years ago I came across an article James Lardner had written for the *New York Times* in 1985, on the occasion of the Ring Lardner centennial celebration at Olivet College in Olivet, Michigan. In that piece James casually mentioned that most of his grandfather's journalism had never been collected. Of such casual mentions are anthologies born. James and his cousin Susan Lardner offered their encouragement and support from the moment I suggested this book to them. Susan, who is the Lardner family's literary executor, granted me the rights to reprint the contents of this book, and James agreed to write the foreword. I am grateful to them both.

A third person whose help was invaluable is Richard Layman, who is the Ring Lardner of Ring Lardner scholars. The vice president of Bruccoli Clark Layman, Inc., which publishes the *Dictionary of Literary Biography* and other reference works, Layman graciously sent me *Ring W. Lardner: A Descriptive Bibliography,* a book he and Matthew J. Bruccoli published in 1976, which has an entry for every piece of fiction and journalism Lardner ever wrote. It is a heroic work of scholarship that proved indispensable in assembling this book. Layman read the manuscript and made a number of valuable suggestions. He is not responsible for any mistakes I may have made in the introductory material or notes and, of course, the opinions expressed in them are mine alone.

Dan O'Brien, journalist, sportswriter, and archivist extraordinaire, was extremely helpful in providing readable copies of Lardner's "Pullman Pastimes" pieces in *The Sporting News* and the columns he wrote for the Bell Syndicate. O'Brien supplied me with many of these pieces and directed me to a website where I was able to find the rest. I'm most grateful to him, and to Pete Cava, who wrote a fine article on Lardner for the *Dictionary of Literary Biography,* for pointing me in his direction.

Lardner is the subject of two excellent biographies that provided some of the background information in this book: *Ring Lardner* by Donald Elder, which was published in 1956; and *Ring: A Biography of Ring Lardner* by Jonathan Yardley, published in 1977. Elder's book, which is out of print but very much worth seeking out, benefits from interviews with Lardner's wife and children as well as a number of his friends. It provides a fascinating look at his early years in Niles, Michigan, and describes the influence of his remarkable mother. It also paints a fine portrait of Lardner's later years as, with his health failing, he roamed the streets of New York.

Yardley, a Pulitzer Prize–winning critic, approaches Lardner from a greater distance, which allows him to step back and assess the work in detail. His portrait of the state of professional baseball when Lardner covered it, and how the game shaped his views and his writing, is particularly interesting. Both books offer generous samples of his work and the critical assessments of their authors.

Biographical information of another sort can be found in *The Lardners: My Family Remembered*, a clear-eyed yet sweetly evocative memoir by Ring Lardner Jr., which tells what it was like to grow up as part of the remarkable Lardner family. We are fortunate that when it came to storytelling skill and an ability to see things straight, "Bill" was every bit his father's son. More recently, the third Lardner generation has produced another first-rate memoir that carries the family story into the twenty-first century. *Shut Up, He Explained* was written by Kate Lardner, whose father was David, the youngest of Ring's sons, but who was raised by her mother and Ring Jr., who married after David's death.

The most current and thorough anthology of Lardner's fiction is *Ring Lardner: Stories and Other Writings*, which is part of the Library of America series that reprints the work of the country's greatest writers. The book also includes samples of Lardner's plays, song lyrics, letters, and sketches.

In seeking out Lardner's work I visited a number of libraries around the country, both in person and on line. Fortunately, the entire run of the *Chicago Tribune* is available through the Chicago Public Library's website, while microfilm copies of the *Chicago Inter-Ocean* and *Chicago Examiner* are at the Harold Washington Library Center. I found microfilm of the *Boston American* at the Boston Public Library and located other articles Lardner wrote for newspapers and magazines at the New York Public Library, the Los Angeles Public Library, and the Santa Monica Public Library.

I am grateful to Kevin Wadzinski at the St. Joseph County Public Library in South Bend, Indiana, for locating some of Lardner's work at the *South Bend Times,* and to Gary Johnson, the president of the Chicago History Museum, and Ellen Keith, the museum's director of research and access, for their assistance. Thanks also to Tim Wiles and Bill Francis at the Baseball Hall of Fame, Sreenath Sreenivasan at the Columbia University Graduate School of Journalism, and Alex Belth, David Israel, and Robert Kimball.

Many thanks as well to my friend John Schulian, who has collected John Lardner's work in *The John Lardner Reader,* for lending a patient ear during the time I was putting this book together. And more thanks than I can properly express here go to Barbara Isenberg for her many valuable suggestions and ideas and her constant support.

Thanks to my agent, Claire Gerus, for her wise counsel and efforts on this book's behalf, and, at the University of Nebraska Press, thanks to sports acquisitions editor Rob Taylor, manager for editorial, design, and production Ann Baker, and associate acquisitions editor Courtney Ochsner. Nebraska has published two collections of John Lardner's work and one of Ring's brother Rex in recent years and when James Lardner learned that it would publish this book as well, he said, "I guess that officially makes the Lardners Cornhuskers, doesn't it?"

Notes

1. Lardner apparently cannot bring himself to say Indiana won 12–0.
2. Lardner is being disingenuous here. Fullerton was impressed by his baseball knowledge and became a mentor who recommended him for several jobs.
3. Years later, in a piece for the *Saturday Evening Post,* Lardner embellished the story of his hiring, quoting Duke as asking, "Have you figured how you're going to live in Chicago on eighteen-fifty?" "I can get on the wagon." "You can get on the wagon," said Duke, "but nobody can work for us and stay there."
4. Hall of Famer Ed Walsh, who pitched thirteen years with the White Sox, won 40 games in 1908 and completed 42. His brother, Marty, never made it out of the minors.
5. Lardner directly transferred the fact that Floyd Kroh "called with four kings"—an unforgivably conservative play in poker—to *You Know Me Al.* He altered the facts a bit, perhaps thinking that nobody would believe any poker player would stand pat with such a good hand. In the story, Jack Keefe stands on four sevens and wins fifty cents.
6. The mention of Orval Overall should not pass without notice. He was the winning pitcher in the game that clinched the 1908 World Series. More than a century later he remained the last Cubs pitcher to claim that distinction.
7. Short for "Peerless Leader," a nickname Charles Dryden, then the highest-paid sportswriter in the country, gave to Frank Chance. Lardner, a devoted fan of Dryden's, trailed around after him so much that the players called him "Charlie's Hat."
8. "Merkle's generous act" refers to perhaps the greatest mistake ever made in a World Series game: the failure of rookie Giants runner Fred Merkle to touch second base on a play that would have won the game and sent his team to the 1908 World Series. Amid great controversy, the game was replayed; the Cubs won and went on to win the Series.
9. From 1891 to 1911 the official spelling of the city's name was changed to

Pittsburg. After pressure from a U.S. senator from Pennsylvania who sat on the United States Geographic Board, the final "h" was restored to the name.

10. Third baseman for the Cubs and Pirates, respectively.

11. A nickname George Gibson earned the first time he walked into the Pirates' dressing room, causing Honus Wagner to shout, "Here comes Hackenschmidt," referring to George Hackenschmidt, a famous wrestler of the time. Gibson was just under six feet tall and weighed 190 pounds, about average for a major leaguer today, which indicates how much professional athletes have grown.

12. In seasons when the Cubs or White Sox didn't play in the World Series, the teams would meet in a postseason series in Chicago. The games were very popular and sometimes drew larger crowds than the World Series.

13. A scrub or backup player.

14. Second baseman Bill Collins.

15. William Hepburn Russell, owner of the Rustlers.

16. Lardner had noted the players' shaved heads a day earlier, under the heading "Society Notes."

2. BASEBALL

1. It's hard to know what Lardner meant to say here. "Skun" is a variation of "scum," but "got him skun" leaves us wondering.

2. A vicious racist, Cobb was involved in a number of incidents with black people. This one, which occurred in 1907—Lardner got the year wrong—concerned Cobb's attack on a groundskeeper in Augusta, Georgia; the man had committed the unpardonable sin of trying to shake Cobb's hand. When the man's wife tried to intervene, Cobb began to choke her. The assault ended when Schmidt pulled him off the woman and punched him in the face.

3. Cobb and others have told the story about his battle with Morgan several ways. Cobb's version is that after Morgan had beaned him, he "shook my finger at him as much to say he would get his when the first opportunity arose." Cobb made it to second and Morgan threw a wild pitch. Though he was only a few steps beyond third base as Morgan received the ball at the plate, Cobb kept running and "made a long and vicious slide straight at him." Morgan stepped out of the way and Cobb scored.

4. An example of the casual racism of the times. African Dodger, also called Hit the Coon, was a popular carnival game in the early twentieth century in which an African American man would stick his head through a canvas curtain and attempt to dodge balls thrown at him by customers.

5. Telegram delivery boy.

6. Lightweight boxer from Wales who had won the world championship a month earlier.

7. Though Walsh was dominant for seven seasons his career was shortened by injuries, possibly because of overwork

8. Red Sox manager Jake Stahl.

9. Lardner's story on the final game of the 1912 World Series appears on page 80.

10. Phillies owner Bill Shettsline.

11. The best second baseman in the National League in the 1910s, Doyle famously said it was "good to be young and a Giant."

12. A popular stage and film actress who achieved notoriety as the spurned mistress of Florenz Ziegfeld.

13. Regular features in other sections of the *Tribune*.

14. A reference to the original hitless wonders, the 1906 Chicago White Sox, who had the lowest team batting average in the American League but upset the more powerful Cubs in the World Series.

15. The best second baseman of his era, Collins led the Philadelphia Athletics to three World Series championships then was sold to the White Sox for $50,000 in 1914, the highest price ever paid for a player.

16. President of the Chicago Cubs from 1919 to 1933 and the father of Bill Veeck, the maverick owner of the Cleveland Indians and White Sox.

17. Pirates pitcher Deacon Phillippe.

18. The error, one of the most memorable in World Series history, continued to follow Giants' center fielder Fred Snodgrass wherever he went. "Hardly a day in my life," he said in 1940, "hardly an hour, that in some manner or other the dropping of that fly doesn't come up, even after thirty years. On the street, in my store, at my home . . . it's all the same. They might choke up before they ask me and they hesitate—but they always ask."

19. The *Tribune*'s I. E. (Sy) Sanborn was one of the top baseball writers of the era.

20. President of the National League.

21. President of the National Baseball Commission.

22. President of the American League.

23. The Zimmerman Telegram was a secret proposal sent by Germany in 1917 asking Mexico to join it if the United States entered the war. Intercepted by British intelligence, it inflamed U.S. public opinion and generated support for America's entry into the war.

24. Wagner had played for the Red Sox earlier in the season.

25. Some sixty Army Air Force planes appeared over Comiskey Park as part of the opening ceremonies, becoming the first flyover at a sporting event. With the United States at war, the regular season was shortened and the

series was played in September. These were also the first games to feature a performance of "The Star Spangled Banner," though it was played during the seventh-inning stretch.

26. Alexa Stirling, a childhood friend and golfing companion of Bobby Jones, won three straight U.S. Women's Amateur championships, including the 1920 Open at Mayfield.

27. After winning seven games without a loss in the final two months of the regular season, Mails pitched 6⅔ scoreless innings in relief in Game 1 of the Series and a 1–0 shutout in Game 6.

28. The watches were to celebrate Wambsganss's unassisted triple play and Smith's grand slam home run, both World Series firsts.

29. With the help of a ghostwriter, Ruth was reporting on the World Series for a syndicate run by Christy Walsh, who was baseball's first agent for players.

30. Giants pitcher Phil Douglas. The following year he was banned from baseball after an argument with Giants manager John McGraw led him to write a letter to a former teammate indicating he would be willing to do anything, even intentionally lose a game, to keep the Giants from winning the pennant in 1922.

31. Yankees second baseman Aaron Ward.

32. Both former major leaguers, Altrock and Schacht performed comedy routines before games and, with Lardner's help, took their act to vaudeville. Two days later Lardner wrote that "Altrock denies sending me that seventy-six-word telegram the other night and he and I have about made up our minds that it was the work of some man or men who had found a place to get a drink in New York in spite of the Volstead Law."

33. A British racehorse, Papyrus won the 1923 Epsom Deby and was sent to the United States for a match race with Kentucky Derby winner Zev on October 20. In front of seventy thousand people at Belmont Park, Zev won by five lengths.

34. Jack Dempsey's knockout of Luis Firpo had taken place three months earlier.

35. Lardner was writing so little about the games at this point that he all but ignored one of the most famous home runs in World Series history: Casey Stengel's inside-the-park homer in the ninth inning. With one of his shoes falling apart, Stengel limped erratically around the bases and it was left to Lardner's friend, Damon Runyon, to write the most celebrated description of the event: "This is the way old 'Casey' Stengel ran yesterday afternoon, running his home run home."

36. For the rest of his life Rice would be questioned about whether or not he had caught the ball. His usual answer was, "The umpire said I caught it."

He left a sealed letter at the Baseball Hall of Fame to be opened after his death. It said, "At no time did I lose possession of the ball."

37. Bluege, the Senators' third baseman, had been hit in the head by one of Aldridge's pitches two days earlier.

38. When he lost his shirt during the 1925 World Series, Lardner wrote, "Lost, a gray shirt with pin stripe and collar attached. Size 16 neck, 35 sleeves and a long nose. Looks like it had been in a world series in Pittsburgh. Owner will give finder a cuff."

39. A pill to relieve motion sickness that was popular at the time.

3. RING GOES TO WAR

1. Secretary of War Newton Baker.

2. The *Tribune*'s chief political correspondent. Thirty years later he wrote the story that led to the paper's infamous headline "Dewey Defeats Truman."

3. A story written six months earlier by *Tribune* war correspondent Floyd Gibbons, who was a passenger on the *Laconia*, a Cunard liner converted into an armed merchant ship that was torpedoed by a German submarine, causing twelve deaths. After spending six hours in a lifeboat, Gibbons was taken to Liverpool, where he telegraphed his story home within thirty minutes of being rescued. Gibbons makes a cameo appearance in another story in this section.

4. Major-league pitcher who, at 6'5", was the tallest player of his era.

5. *Chicago Tribune* theater critic.

6. Coldcuts.

7. "The Gumps," a popular comic strip about a middle-class family created by Sidney Smith in 1917. It ran until 1959.

4. FOOTBALL

1. Harvard fullback and place-kicker Charles Brickley, a two-time All American, who set records for most field goals in a season and in a career. In the 1913 Harvard-Yale game, Brickley's five field goals scored all of Harvard's points in the 15–5 victory.

5. POLITICS

1. Chicago Cubs first baseman Vic Saier.

2. Theodore Roosevelt invited African American leader Booker T. Washington to the White House on October 16, 1901, a gesture that led to vicious oratory from Southern politicians. Senator James K. Vardaman of Mississippi said the White House was "so saturated with the odor of nigger that the rats had taken refuge in the stable."

3. Pioneer auto racer in the first two decades of the twentieth century.

4. Woodrow Wilson's nomination in Baltimore in 1912 came on the forty-sixth ballot.

5. Bryan resigned as secretary of state in 1915 because of his pacifist position on World War I.

6. The first American to win the world heavyweight free-style championship and often credited with popularizing professional wrestling in the United States.

7. French general Joseph Jacques Césaire Joffre, whose strategy led to a German defeat at the first Battle of the Marne in 1914.

8. Jean Raphaël Adrien René Viviani, French prime minister during the first year of World War I.

9. As head of the U.S. Food Administration during Woodrow Wilson's presidency, Hoover encouraged voluntary meat rationing to support the war effort. Other commodities such as gasoline and sugar were also rationed.

10. Craps.

11. Founder of the Anti-Cigarette League of America, which advocated the abolition of cigarettes.

12. A pepper mostly grown in Java and Sumatra and used as a substitute for cigarettes.

13. Five-time socialist candidate for president. In 1920 Debs ran from a prison cell where he was serving a ten-year sentence for violating the Espionage Act of 1917.

14. The Oakland Long Wharf or SP Mole, a huge railway pier that marked the end of the transcontinental railroad. From there passengers took ferries to San Francisco.

15. U.S. senator from California who unsuccessfully challenged Warren G. Harding for the 1920 Republican presidential nomination.

16. An avid White Sox fan, Pass lost $3,000 betting on them in the 1919 World Series. When William Fallon, the lawyer for Series fixer Abe Attell, returned the money, Pass testified that he had never met Attell or made any bets with him.

17. A banker who would later become vice president under Calvin Coolidge, Charles Dawes was in charge of procurement for American forces in World War I. At U.S. Senate hearings on overcharges by military suppliers after the war, Dawes said, "Hell and Maria, we weren't trying to keep a set of books over there, we were trying to win a war." Afterward he became known as "Hell and Maria Dawes."

18. George B. Christian, Harding's personal secretary.

19. Suzanne Lenglen of France, the queen of women's tennis, created a

sensation when she defaulted during her match against U.S. champion Molla Mallory in the 1921 U.S. Open, claiming she was ill. Roundly criticized by the press and subjected to an investigation, Lenglen avenged the loss at Wimbledon the following year, beating Mallory 6–2, 6–0 in twenty-six minutes, the shortest grand slam final ever played.

20. Sample lyric: "Teddy, you are a bear / Teddy, we want you where / Our one best bet should be. / Teddy, pack up your grip. / Get ready to take a trip / To Washington, D.C."

21. Boss of the Democratic political machine in Brooklyn.

22. Herbert Hoover's presidential secretary and chairman of the Republican National Committee.

6. BOXING

1. French general Ferdinand Foch, who was named commander in chief of the allied armies in World War I at the age of sixty-six.

2. Thomas Aloysius Dorgan, a newspaper cartoonist who signed his drawings Tad. Like Lardner, Dorgan used the vernacular in his work and is credited with creating or popularizing such words and phrases as "dumbbell," "for crying out loud," "cat's meow," "hard-boiled," and "drugstore cowboy." Lardner, who occasionally used friends' names in his short stories, titled one of them "The Courtship of T. Dorgan."

3. A flashy dresser and incorrigible braggart, Benny Kauff was a promising young baseball player who never lived up to expectations. His career ended suddenly in 1921 when he was indicted on charges of auto theft. Though Kauff was acquitted, baseball commissioner Kenesaw Mountain Landis banished him from the game for life.

4. Three days later Lardner wrote, "Gents: I got word yesterday that some of you gents wished I would write more about the fighters and not so much about the different costumes the newspaper experts is wearing."

5. The movie was *The Challenge of Chance*, a silent western in which Willard played the starring role.

6. Dempsey knocked Fulton out in 18.6 seconds of the first round on July 27, 1918.

7. British heavyweight Joe Beckett, whom Carpentier knocked out twice.

8. Musical Chairs.

9. The following day Lardner again noted the fighters' war records, "which I make a motion that we lay off from now on as it is old stuff and I haven't no sympathy with the member of congress that brought it up the other day and said that even Carpentier was slow about getting into it. Suppose he was, he had nothing on congress."

10. A flamboyant court case in which James Alexander Stillman filed for divorce saying that his wife's youngest child was the daughter of an Indian guide from Quebec. His wife denied the charges and accused him of fathering two illegitimate children with a chorus girl. The case dragged on for five years, ending only after Stillman gave his wife a $500,000 necklace. The couple remained married.

11. Isaac Newton Phelps Stokes, a highly regarded New York architect, and his wife, Edith Minturn, who ran a sewing school for indigent women, were renowned for their work with the poor. When they were married in 1895 a friend had John Singer Sargent paint their portrait as a wedding gift. The painting hangs in the New York Metropolitan Museum of Art.

12. Sports editor of the *New York Evening World* and cartoonist whose *Sketches from Death* drawings of atrocities he saw during the Spanish-American War shocked readers. Edgren's integrity was such that in the era when the law did not permit judges to decide fights, his decisions were accepted by all sides.

13. Winner of the light-heavyweight championship in 1903, who claimed to be the first title holder in the new division.

14. The world middleweight champion.

15. Lardner often wrote about his problems getting into boxing matches. He describes his encounter with the Jersey City police in greater detail in "Why It's Called a Dog's Life," which appears on page 374.

16. Wills, who held the World Colored Heavyweight Championship three times, is considered by boxing experts to be the best black boxer denied a chance at the heavyweight title. He spent six years trying to get a fight with Dempsey, without success.

17. Popular artist and, like Lardner, a member of the Algonquin Round Table.

18. Considered to be one of the greatest stage actresses of the twentieth century.

19. A key witness in the Hall-Mills murder case in which an Episcopal priest and a member of his choir with whom he was having an affair were killed. The suspected killers, the priest's wife and her brothers, were acquitted. The newspaper coverage of the killings and the trial set a new standard for sensationalism that would not be surpassed until the Lindbergh kidnapping a decade later.

20. An actress best known for her marriage at the age of sixteen to New York real estate magnate Edward West "Daddy" Browning, who was thirty-five years older. Her failed attempt to obtain a divorce drew frenzied coverage from the New York tabloids.

21. Lyricist, sheet-music illustrator, and president of ASCAP, he was one of Lardner's Great Neck neighbors.

22. Actress, model, and dancer whose six marriages to weathy men, divorces, affairs, and opulent lifestyle were another staple of the tabloids.

23. Written by Lardner under Rice's name.

24. A prism whose bases are parallelograms. The appearance of this word, one Rice would not have used, might have been a tipoff he had a ghost.

25. The match between light-heavyweight champion Berlenbach and challenger Stribling was held at Yankee Stadium three months earlier. Berlenbach won a unanimous decision.

7. THE NOBLE EXPERIMENT

1. The song was "Prohibition Blues," which Lardner wrote for a musical farce called *Ladies First*. In part, it went:

> I've had news that's bad news about my best pal
> His name is Old Man Alcohol but I call him Al
> The doctors say he's dyin' as sure as can be
> And if that's so then oh oh oh
> The difference to me
> There won't be no sunshine no stars no moon
> No laughter no music 'cept this one sad tune
> Goodbye forever to my old friend "Booze"
> Doggone I've got the Prohibition Blues.

2. Bayes's popularity was such that George M. Cohan asked her to be the first to record "Over There" in 1917, which became an internaational hit.

3. First woman to swim the English Channel.

4. Head of U.S. Committee on Public Information, a World War I propaganda organization.

8. THE AMERICA'S CUP AND OTHER SPORTS

1. A notorious lothario who kept a card file on more than fifty women he had seduced, John Elwell was shot dead on June 11, 1920. To someone who asked, "Who would want to kill Joe Elwell?" the answer was, "Who wouldn't?" The case, which created a frenzy in the press, was never solved.

2. A controversial Canada-born American writer whose frank memoirs helped usher in the confessional style of autobiographical writing. Lardner's parody of her appears on page 502.

3. Earl Sande, a Hall of Fame jockey.

4. A play by J. M. Barrie that was later turned into a silent movie.

5. A novel by John Kendrick Bangs, published in 1895, in which everyone who has ever lived has gone to Styx, the river that circles the underworld.

9. FAMILY LIFE

1. A board game in which players try to move their pieces to their opponents' bases.
2. A parlor game popular between the world wars that featured metal horses painted in different colors. It was named after a race horse owned by King Edward VII, which had won the Epsom Derby.
3. Broadway producer and theater owner who produced eighteen musicals with George M. Cohan.

10. ON JOURNALISM

1. A dig at Bert Leston Taylor, who edited the popular *Tribune* feature, "A Line o' Type or Two."
2. In whist, a bid to take no tricks.
3. Jack Lait left the *Tribune* six months later. He held many other newspaper jobs and, with Lee Mortimer, wrote the popular books *New York Confidential, Chicago Confidential,* and *Washington Confidential.* Many other columnists have since written "In the Wake of the News," which to this day appears in the *Tribune*'s sports section.
4. One of three men convicted in April 1925 for the murder of two bank messengers during a robbery. He claimed to be the victim of perjured testimony and protested his innocence even while sitting in the electric chair.
5. Leader of a criminal gang who was the first man to be named Public Enemy Number One by the press. After killing an informant against him and his wife, he was hung in April 1926.
6. Mardi Gras Queen.

11. PEOPLE, PLACES, AND PIECES OF RING'S MIND

1. An early opponent of World War I, Ford sent a "Peace Ship" to Europe in 1915, where he and others met with peace activists. The idea was widely ridiculed and Ford left the ship soon after its arrival.
2. A movie serial starring actress Kathlyn Williams.
3. A twenty-three-episode movie serial that followed the success of *The Adventures of Kathlyn.*
4. A popular actress best remembered for her role as Glinda the Good Witch in *The Wizard of Oz.*
5. A reference to James J. Couzens, U.S. senator from Michigan, mayor of

Detroit, industrialist, and philanthropist. Asked how to pronounce his name, he said, "Pronounced exactly as cousins."

6. Musical comedy and vaudeville star who later played comic roles in films. At the height of her popularity she promoted such social and political issues as self-love and women's suffrage.

7. Hungarian-born silent film star who appeared in two films with Rudolph Valentino.

8. A Polish stage and film actress, she was the first European film star to come to the United States, where her dramatic roles made her world famous and the richest woman in Hollywood. She had well-publicized love affairs with Chaplin and Valentino.

9. A star of the Ziegfeld Follies of 1921, her face was famous throughout the country by the time she was seventeen.

12. PARODIES AND REVIEWS

1. Despite owning the Chicago Cubs when they won their only two World Series titles, Murphy became widely disliked and eventually sold the team.

2. Chicago police chief Charles C. Healey, who was charged with malfeasance and a plot to nullify the city's anti-gambling laws. He was defended by Clarence Darrow and acquitted.

3. Popular actress who often played in tearjerkers. She co-wrote "Lilac Time," which was turned into a silent film starring Gary Cooper. Lardner was amused when he and Cowl were introduced and she asked him what he did for a living. She was not amused when, after saying he was a writer, he asked, "And what business are you in?"

4. Popular opera singer and film star noted for her beauty and acting ability.

5. The promoter of Tunney's fights.

6. Author of several Broadway plays, including, most famously, *Abie's Irish Rose*.

7. Hollywood songwriter who shared an Oscar in 1947 for the lyrics to "Zip-A-Dee-Do-Dah."

8. Sample lyric: "As you desire me, / So shall I come to you. / Howe'er you want me, / So shall I be!" It has been recorded by such singers as Frank Sinatra, Sarah Vaughan, Ella Fitzgerald, and Peggy Lee.

Selected Bibliography

Berg, A. Scott. *Max Perkins: Editor of Genius*. New York: Penguin, 1978.

Bruccoli, Matthew, and Richard Layman. *Ring W. Lardner: A Descriptive Bibliography*. Pittsburgh: University of Pittsburgh Press, 1976.

———. *Some Champions: Sketches and Fiction by Ring Lardner*. New York: Scribner's, 1976.

Carruthers, Clifford M. *Letters of Ring Lardner*. Washington DC: Orchises, 1995.

Elder, Donald. *Ring Lardner*. Garden City NY: Doubleday, 1956.

Lardner, Kate. *Shut Up, He Explained: The Memoirs of a Blacklisted Kid*. New York: Ballantine, 2004.

Lardner, Ring. *Ring Lardner: Stories and Other Writings*. New York: Library of America, 2013.

Lardner, Ring, Jr. *The Lardners: My Family Remembered*. New York: Harper & Row, 1976.

Yardley, Jonathan. *Ring: A Biography of Ring Lardner*. Lanham MD: Rowman & Littlefield, 1977.